Butterworths New Law Guide
Guide to the Legal Services Act 2007

General Editors

Iain Miller
Bevan Brittan LLP

James Thorne
Farrer & Co LLP

Members of the LexisNexis Group worldwide

United Kingdom	LexisNexis, a Division of Reed Elsevier (UK) Ltd, Halsbury House, 35 Chancery Lane, London, WC2A 1EL, and RSH, 1–3 Baxter's Place, Leith Walk Edinburgh EH1 3AF
Argentina	LexisNexis Argentina, Buenos Aires
Australia	LexisNexis Butterworths, Chatswood, New South Wales
Austria	LexisNexis Verlag ARD Orac GmbH & Co KG, Vienna
Benelux	LexisNexis Benelux, Amsterdam
Canada	LexisNexis Canada, Markham, Ontario
Chile	LexisNexis Chile Ltda, Santiago
China	LexisNexis China, Beijing and Shanghai
France	LexisNexis SA, Paris
Germany	LexisNexis Deutschland GmbH, Munster
Hong Kong	LexisNexis Hong Kong, Hong Kong
India	LexisNexis India, New Delhi
Italy	Giuffrè Editore, Milan
Japan	LexisNexis Japan, Tokyo
Malaysia	Malayan Law Journal Sdn Bhd, Kuala Lumpur
Mexico	LexisNexis Mexico, Mexico
New Zealand	LexisNexis NZ Ltd, Wellington

Published by LexisNexis

A CIP Catalogue record for this book is available from the British Library.

ISBN: 9781405744539

ISBN 978-1-4057-4453-9

9 781405 744539

Typeset by Letterpart Ltd, Reigate, Surrey

Printed in the UK by CPI William Clowes Beccles NR34 7TL

Visit LexisNexis at www.lexisnexis.co.uk

Foreword

David Edmonds, Chairman, Legal Services Board

We are on the brink of an unprecedented period of change. Parliament, in passing the Legal Services Act 2007, has given us a vision for a future legal services market that will deliver not just personal benefits to individual consumers, but collective benefits to society as a whole. A market where lawyers will no longer face historic constraints on the way they choose to practice, but where their rightly respected tradition of the highest standards of professional ethics, still remains.

In opening up the market to new forms of business practice, we can legitimately expect consumers and providers alike to take advantage of new opportunities and benefits. We can anticipate innovation and creativity in service provision as new entrants seek to join the market and existing providers at last have the chance to access new sources of capital. Non-lawyers, who for many years have played a central role in developing legal businesses, can at last have a seat at the boardroom table and their contribution properly recognised. Consumers can start to influence service delivery by identifying and negotiating for the business models that may best suit their needs.

Such change is not without risk and we know that we must exercise caution and judgement if we are to get it right and to mitigate those risks to a minimum. Such an approach calls for dialogue and consultation; it must be a genuinely collaborative undertaking between all who have in an interest in the provision of widely accessible, affordable, quality legal services.

Central to this will be the securing of robust, proportionate, independent regulation focused on promoting the public interest. Such traits are the hallmarks of a publicly credible regulatory system. The Act respects the long-standing role played by the professions in their own regulation but is unequivocal about prohibiting regulation by lawyers for lawyers. Approved Regulators with dual representative and regulatory functions made commendable pre-emptive steps in anticipating the Act's requirements. It is likely that they will need to move further down that road. This is not to exclude the legitimate voice of the profession in regulatory debate — far from it; regulation needs to carry the confidence of those who must observe compliance. Lawyers must see these new arrangements as underpinning their integrity, not undermining it.

At the same time, lawyers must seize the nettle and be proactive in managing their own reputation. It is sadly inevitable that, on occasion, things will go wrong, no matter how high standards generally are. For too long, the public has had a poor perception of legal complaints' handling. And whilst this may be based on historic failings, perhaps no longer justified, a new model is rapidly approaching. The Office for Legal Complaints will offer swift, effective and informal dispute resolution — but the ideal must be for as many complaints as possible to be resolved at source. The current high standards of client care offered by some must become the usual standards offered by the many. This will benefit the reputation of the profession and increase consumer satisfaction.

I have no doubt that change on such a scale is challenging and for some it may even be threatening. But what I am certain of is that change is going to come. The Legal Services Board and the Approved Regulators must work together to ensure a shared and robust confidence in the justice system, and in particular, in the individuals and organisations charged with protecting our rights and freedoms.

In contributing to this evaluation of the new regulatory framework, the authors of this book have made a stimulating and well-balanced contribution to the debate around the opportunities and challenges that lie ahead. Those who read it will find themselves well placed to embrace the change ahead.

David Edmonds
Chairman, Legal Services Board

April 2009

Preface

The Legal Services Act 2007 will have a profound effect on the provision of legal services in this country. This Guide attempts to explain what the Act says and where its impact will be felt.

The Act is a blockbuster of regulatory law. It runs to 214 sections covering 120 pages even before its 24 schedules are taken into account. The Act and the principal schedules are set out as an appendix to this Guide. The Act is not an easy read. Its length and language are a long way from the elegance and comparative brevity of the Partnership Act 1890, its distant antecedent. It is also notable that it is the first gender neutral Act of Parliament.

Part 1 of this Guide describes what the Act says. Lawyers and the legal press have focused on the prospect of non-lawyers owning some or all of a business providing legal services through alternative business structures but the Act covers much more than this which we we discuss in Part 1.

In order to enable alternative business structures to fit into an overall statutory scheme the architecture of legal services regulation has been changed in a way that will affect every legal practitioner. In addition, the opportunity has been taken to add to the existing structures and where appropriate increase regulatory power. The Act was clearly conceived in an age of 'light touch' regulation but will now need to be implemented in a very different context. Preparation of this part of the book has not been assisted by what seemed like the daily arrival of new draft rules and consultations. There are still many gaps to be filled.

Part 2 speculates on the impact of the Act on providers of legal services. We start by looking at the substantial changes there have been to the legal profession in the last 20 years. We then consider what lawyers can do in anticipation of the full implementation of the Act, which is expected to be in 2011. We next turn to the prospect of greater merger activities amongst law firms, and how the nature of mergers might change, before considering the prospect of outside investment in law firms, either through listings or the injection of private equity. Outside ownership of legal practices in the form of consolidators and by the threat of so-called 'Tesco Law' are the next examples of ownership structures that we examine.

The possible impact of the Act on the Bar is then reviewed. Later the effect on the provision of legal services in the public sector and in-house are covered. The way in which complaints are dealt with going forward, and how the training of lawyers might change, both of which are relevant to the way in which law practices are run, regardless of their structure, are considered. Finally, tax aspects of the anticipated changes in the structure of law firms are dealt with.

These future developments cover a great deal of ground and we hope show the wide-ranging impact of the Act. Of course, its impact cannot be considered in a void and it is undoubtedly true that the recession triggered by the credit crunch will impact more harshly and more deeply on high street practices in particular than it would have done otherwise. The Act was conceived in more benign economic circumstances than now apply; of course, the world might have changed back to better times by 2011 but there must be a concern that things will not improve so that the Act and the recession combine to produce a double-whammy for many practitioners. Whether the recession will help or hinder in meeting the aims of the progenitors of the Act remains to be seen.

Preparation of this Guide has been surprisingly enjoyable, at least for us as its editors. Our task has been made a great deal easier by the responsiveness of our contributors and the quality of their contributions. We have been cheerfully encouraged along our way by Cara Annett, our commissioning editor at Butterworths, and our secretaries Jo Page and Jackie Goodwin who did a lot of the hard graft. We are delighted that David Edmonds CBE, the Chairman of the Legal Services Board, has contributed a preface to this Guide, at a time when he is working hard on the full implementation of the Act. Our thanks go to all of them, and of course to our wives Helen and Maria who not only gave us much appreciated support but also demonstrated a great deal of tolerance when 'that book' was our excuse for ducking out of domestic and familial duties.

The law is stated as at 31 March 2009.

James Thorne and Iain Miller
March 2009

Authors

About the General Editors

Iain Miller
Iain Miller is a partner in Bevan Brittan's Commercial Dispute Resolution department and Head of the London office. He has acted for the Law Society since 1994 and has acted for both the SRA and LCS since their inception. He has been instructed in relation to several leading cases on solicitor regulation. Iain appears regularly as a solicitor advocate both before the Solicitors Disciplinary Tribunal and on appeals from the SDT to the Divisional Court. He is an editor of Cordery on Solicitors.

James Thorne
James Thorne is a Partner at Farrer & Co LLP where he has been since joining as an assistant in 1981. Having served on its Management Board for six years until May 2008, he is Head of the firm's Partnership Group and advises partnerships and LLPs on governance issues, as well as individual partners and members. His earlier career focused on corporate matters and he was a Contributing Editor to Butterworths Corporate Law Service for 15 years, writing on sales acquisitions and mergers, and General Editor of the third and fourth editions of Butterworths Corporate Law Guide.

About the Contributors

Marianne Butler
Marianne Butler is a barrister at Fountain Court Chambers. Called in 2003, she has a broad commercial and civil practice in line with Fountain Court's profile. In addition to the more traditional aspects of a commercial practice, Marianne has particular interest in, and experience of, professional discipline, regulation and negligence. She regularly advises and acts for the Law Society/SRA in a wide range of matters, from hearings in the Solicitors Disciplinary Tribunal and appeals to the Master of the Rolls under the Solicitors Act, to issues of construction under the Solicitors Indemnity Insurance Rules. She is equally at home advising the regulated as the regulator.

Timothy Dutton QC
Timothy Dutton QC was called to the Bar in 1979, was appointed QC in 1998, and is a Bencher of Middle Temple. He is currently Head of Fountain Court Chambers. He was the Chairman of the Bar Council in 2008, having served as its Vice Chairman in 2007. He was appointed a Recorder in 2000 and between 2004 and 2006 was the Leader of the South Eastern Circuit. Timothy's practice encompasses general commercial, public, regulatory & administrative law and professional (professional negligence and disciplinary including sports). Timothy has for many years conducted a substantial specialist practice in professional regulation and discipline, and the related professional negligence and public law matters which arise in large regulatory and disciplinary cases.

Bethan Evans
Bethan Evans is a partner in Commercial Department of Bevan Brittan. She has over 18 years experience in local government. As a lawyer in local government she worked for four councils in different roles, including Deputy County Solicitor for a County Council and was Director of Corporate Services for a large unitary authority for four years. Bethan has practised in many areas of local government and public sector law, but particularly in relation to corporate governance, democratic decision making, judicial review and probity. She advises on partnership arrangements, externalisation of services, local authority companies and joint ventures and standards/conduct issues.

Jonathan Haley
Jonathan Haley is a solicitor with Farrer & Co specialising in partnership and Limited Liability Partnership law. He advises a broad range of partners and partnerships including solicitors, surveyors and architects. He has particular experience of LLP conversions for professional services firms and the use of LLPs as tax-efficient vehicles for non-resident clients. He is a member of the Association of Partnership Practitioners and is recognised by Chambers & Partners as an expert on partnership and LLP law.

Melissa Hardee
Melissa Hardee is a consultant with international consultancy firm, Hardee Consulting, specialising in legal education and training, knowledge management, and professional regulation. Melissa has extensive experience in the practice, education and regulatory sides of legal training, having been Training Partner at CMS Cameron McKenna before taking up the post of director of the 'Excellent' graded Legal Practice Course at City University's Inns of Court School of Law. Melissa has also chaired the Legal Education and Training Group, the City of London Law Society Training Sub-Committee, and the Association of LPC Providers. Melissa has been a member of both the Law Society and SRA Education and Training Committees.

Andrew Hopper QC
Andrew Hopper QC was admitted a solicitor in 1972 and was appointed Queen's Counsel in 2001, the fifth solicitor to be appointed Silk. He has specialised in the field of professional regulation and discipline since 1979. He now concentrates almost exclusively on advising and representing solicitors in professional matters, but also acts for the Solicitors Disciplinary Tribunal in judicial review and other litigation. He is described in Chambers as 'the oracle of all things relating to solicitors' disciplinary proceedings'. He has been an editor of Cordery on Solicitors since 1995 and is co-author of the Solicitor's Handbook 2008 (and of the 2009 edition shortly to be published).

Colin Ives
Colin Ives is head of professional services tax at BDO Stoy Hayward LLP. He has nearly 30 years experience in advising professional practices in relation to their tax affairs and commercial matters. He is a recognised expert on the tax issues involved in mergers and incorporation and regularly advises on partnership dispute situations. Colin is a recognised authority on partnership matters and is co-author of several books. He is a Committee Member of the Association of Partnership Practitioners and has served on their working

parties dealing with Limited Liability Partnerships, Multi-Disciplinary Partnerships and the Law Commission Review of Partnership Law. He also advised the Law Commission on the taxation and accounting issues of their proposals to reform UK partnership and limited partnership law.

Ian Jones
Ian Jones is the Head of the Real Estate Legal team at BT plc, a post he has held since April 2004. He is a solicitor. He read Law at Kingston Polytechnic and has a broad legal experience including property, corporate/commercial and insolvency. In 2001, he led the in-house BT Legal Team which completed the BT/Telereal sale and leaseback financing deal. He has recently been involved in an innovative process of legal services procurement for BT. When not working, he paints watercolours and is a keen cricketer, both of which represent a triumph of enthusiasm over ability.

Michael McLaren QC
Michael McLaren QC was called to the Bar in 1981 and was appointed QC silk in 2002. He has a wide practice at Fountain Court Chambers focused on commercial disputes, with an emphasis on aviation, regulatory and administrative law and professional issues (including professional negligence and regulation / disciplinary matters). He has acted on behalf of the Law Society and the SRA in a variety of cases, as well as on behalf of solicitors in regulatory matters. He also has substantial experience of disciplinary cases involving accountants, including various appearances before the Joint Disciplinary Tribunal.

Nicholas Peacock QC
Nicholas Peacock QC is a member of Maitland Chambers. Since his call in 1989 he has developed a broad commercial Chancery practice with a particular emphasis on financial services and solicitors' regulation. Over the course of the last 15 years he has acted for and against the Law Society and the SRA on disputes concerning interventions, regulatory sanctions and disciplinary matters.

Patricia Robertson QC
Patricia Robertson QC is a barrister at Fountain Court whose practice includes a broad range of regulatory and disciplinary work, in particular in the field of legal services and financial services regulation. She has advised both the Law Society and the Bar Standards Board on aspects of the Legal Services Act 2007 and was a speaker on that topic at the 2009 Clementi Debate. Patricia has appeared in a number of cases concerned with the powers of the Law Society, including *Re Ahmed*, a test case relating to the Law Society's powers as statutory trustee. She is currently a member of a Bar Standards Board working group on ABSs. She took silk in 2006.

Rebecca Stubbs
Rebecca Stubbs is a member of Maitland Chambers and was called to the Bar in 1994. She has a commercial Chancery practice with particular emphasis on insolvency issues, and has advised and acted for and against both the Law Society and the Financial Services Authority in regulatory and disciplinary matters. She is a member of the Bar Standards Board working group on ABSs.

Katherine Watt
Katherine Watt was called to the Bar in 2002 and practises at Fountain Court. She has a broad commercial law practice encompassing professional negligence and discipline, insurance and reinsurance, banking and finance, financial services, and general commercial litigation. Katherine specialises in particular in claims against professionals, including solicitors, barristers, trustees, accountants, auditors, financial advisers, surveyors and valuers. Her expertise in this field is well complemented by her experience of disciplinary and regulatory matters, which includes advising and acting for the Law Society and Financial Services Authority, and her experience of professional indemnity and wider insurance disputes.

Tony Williams
Tony Williams is the principal of Jomati Consultants LLP, a law firm consultancy that advises a wide range of primarily UK and US-based law firms on strategic issues that include potential mergers and reorganisations. Prior to establishing Jomati Consultants, he had almost 20 years' experience at Clifford Chance as a corporate lawyer, his last role as Worldwide Managing Partner. He left in 2000 to become Worldwide Managing Partner of Andersen Legal prior to the collapse of the Andersen organisation in 2002 in the wake of Enron. He established Jomati Consultants in October 2002.

Contents

Chapter 3: The LSB's Role in the Regulatory Framework

Chapter 4: Alternative Business Structures and Legal Disciplinary Practices

Chapter 5: The Office for Legal Complaints

Chapter 6: Other Significant Regulatory Changes brought about by the LSA 2007

Chapter 7: Market View

Chapter 8: Preparation and the Partnership Deed

Table of Statutes

Paragraph references printed in **bold** type indicate where the Statute is set out in part or in full.

Table of Statutory Instruments

Paragraph references printed in **bold** type indicate where the Statutory Instrument is set out in part or in full.

Table of Cases

A

PARA

B

G

H

L

R

Table of Abbreviations

ABS – Alternative Business Structure

BSB – Bar Standard Board

CLC – Council of Licensed Conveyancers

FSA – Financial Services Authority

ILEX – Institute of Legal Executives

LCS – Legal Complaints Service

LDP – Legal Disciplinary Practice

LSB – Legal Services Board

LSCC – Legal Services Complaints Commissioner

LSO – Legal Services Ombudsman

OLC –Office for Legal Complaints

SRA – Solicitors Regulation Authority

restrictive, and that may have negative implications for consumers. The press release announcing the publication of the report said as follows[9]:

> 'Competition brings consumers lower prices, more choices and new services. The law to combat restrictions on competition should apply as widely as possible and the scope to exclude professional rules from competition law should be removed. There remain numerous restrictions on competition in the professions. Apart from those shown to be necessary for economic efficiency and consumer benefits, restrictions on competition should go.'

These were not challenges that could simply be ignored by the Government given, in particular, the high value of the legal services market[10]: in real terms the growth in the turnover of legal activities rose by almost 60% between 1995 and 2003, when turnover reached £19 billion. In 2003, UK legal services exports totalled £31.9 billion, three times that of 1995.

The Government's response to the OFT report was a consultation paper, 'In the Public Interest?'[11], published by the Lord Chancellor's Department (subsequently the Department of Constitutional Affairs (DCA) and now the Ministry of Justice), which highlighted a number of its concerns about the regulatory framework and proposed the setting up of a review. The report which followed[12] confirmed the view that, 'the current framework is outdated, inflexible, over-complex and insufficiently accountable or transparent', set out various proposals as to the Government's position for reform, and concluded that:

> 'Government has therefore decided that a thorough and independent investigation without reservation is needed. The terms of reference are: to consider what regulatory framework would best promote competition, innovation and the public and consumer interest in an efficient, effective and independent legal sector; and to recommend a framework which will be independent in representing the public and consumer interest, comprehensive, accountable, consistent, flexible, transparent, and no more restrictive or burdensome than is clearly justified.'

Sir David Clementi (the former Deputy Governor of the Bank of England) was appointed on 24 July 2003 to conduct the review and in October of that year he announced that its focus would be on issues relating to:

- the current institutional structures and what the Department of Constitutional Affairs report referred to as 'the regulatory maze';
- the level of self-regulation and professionalism within the legal services industry;
- the handling of complaints against lawyers and disciplinary matters;
- unregulated providers of legal services and 'regulatory gaps'; and
- new business structures, including employed lawyers, legal disciplinary practices and multi-disciplinary practices.

As part of his review, Clementi published his own consultation paper in March 2004 and the resultant report was delivered in December of the same year (the Clementi Report). The consultation paper asked respondents key questions, which included: what were the appropriate objectives of a regulatory system for legal services; whether a regulatory system should see a clear distinction between the regulatory and the representative role of a professional body; whether the mechanism for handling consumer complaints is better organised within the professional bodies, or outside, reporting directly to an independent regulator; and what demand and what advantages and disadvantages exist in respect of alternative business structures. In publishing the paper Clementi stated that he hoped for 'the widest possible level of debate and response, both from providers and consumers of legal services.'[13] Clementi received 265 written responses from a wide range of individuals and bodies, and including all the likely interested parties, such as the Law Society and Bar Council.

The Clementi Report can be neatly divided into three key issues arising from the review: concerns and recommendations about the current regulatory framework; concerns and recommendations about the current complaints system; and concerns and recommendations about the restrictive nature of the current business structures.

1 'The Future of Legal Services: Putting Consumers First', White Paper (October 2005), p10.
2 'The Future of Legal Services: Putting Consumers First', White Paper (October 2005), p13.
3 National Consumer Council, Solicitors Complaints Bureau: A Consumer View (December 1994).
4 Annual Report of the Legal Services Ombudsman 2000–2001, p7.
5 Annual Report of the Legal Services Ombudsman for England and Wales 2003–2004, p7.
6 Annual Report of the Legal Services Ombudsman for England and Wales 2003–2004, p10.
7 See the Which? press release, 'Which? Wants law regulation' (21 March 2005).
8 Office of Fair Trading,'Competition in the Professions – A report by the Director General of Fair Trading' (2001).
9 Office of Fair Trading press release 10/01, 'Reform for competition needed in professions' (7 March 2001).
10 Department of Constitutional Affairs, 'The Future of Legal Services: Putting Consumers First' (October 2005).
11 July 2002.
12 'Competition and Regulation in the Legal Services Market' (July 2003).
13 See the Department of Constitutional Affairs' press release, 'Review of the Regulatory Framework for Legal Services in England and Wales' (8 March 2001).

THE OLD REGULATORY FRAMEWORK

1.3 Echoing the views of the Government and others, Clementi's concern about the current regulatory framework for legal services was that it was complex, inconsistent and had insufficient regard for the consumer's interest.

At the time of his review, seven forms of legal service were subject to statutory regulatory control, namely: the right to conduct litigation; the right of audience in the courts; the provision of immigration services; certain probate services; conveyancing; notarial services; and acting as a commissioner for oaths. These services had, historically, been regulated by a variety of front-line professional bodies such as the Law Society and Bar Council which, in turn, were overseen (to varying degrees) by higher level regulators. Among the front-line practitioner bodies, five of them (including the Law Society and Bar Council) combined regulatory and representative functions.

As explained above, it was this fusing of functions that had exacerbated consumer dissatisfaction with the legal services sector. Clementi adopted four criteria: that the regulatory arrangement chosen should promote the public and consumer interest; that it should promote competition; that it should promote innovation; and that the regulatory arrangement should be transparent.

The conclusion that Clementi came to was that where the same body acted as representor and regulator, there was an inherent conflict of interest: in a regulatory body, the public interest should have primacy and, in a representative body, the interests of the membership should have primacy. He found that this potential conflict of interest was most clear in the context of fee negotiation for lawyers, as to which the Law Society and Bar Council had historically played a key role. Clementi thought it particularly difficult for professional bodies to combine their representative and regulatory roles as regards competition: regulatory bodies should be expected to encourage open competition, subject to maintaining quality standards; whilst representative bodies have a legitimate right to fight their corner, warning that the public may suffer if the market is opened too widely. Clementi was specifically critical of the record of the Law Society and Bar Council on the issue of innovation (citing, for example, the Bar Council's past resistance to the extension of higher court rights to solicitors) and the role of the Inns of Court in sharing with the Bar Council regulatory responsibility for barristers in turn fell foul of the transparency test.

A further concern for Clementi was the governance structures for the main front-line professional bodies, which he considered to be inappropriate for the regulatory tasks that they faced. The points of particular note were the low level of lay involvement and the practice of changing the chairman on annual basis. The effect of this was that individuals would be 'in office long enough for the incumbent to want to ensure that no damage is sustained "during his watch" but not long enough to see through difficult change.'[1]

The Clementi Report drew attention to the (indisputably) complex system of oversight regulatory arrangements currently in place: the Law Society was being overseen in many of its functions by the Master of the Rolls; much of the Bar Council's work and that of the Council for Licensed Conveyancers and the Institute of Legal Executives was regulated by the Department for Constitutional Affairs; the Office of the Immigration Services Commissioner was being overseen by the Home Office; the Chartered Institute of Patent Agents by the Department of Trade and Industry; and the Faculty Office by the Archbishop of Canterbury. Other bodies acting in a regulatory capacity included the higher judiciary, the Legal Services Ombudsman, the Legal Services Complaints Commissioner, the Home Secretary, the Office of Fair Trading and the Financial Services Authority.

Clementi reported that there was an absence of clear objectives and principles underlying the system, which he was of the view had insufficient regard to the needs of consumers. He pointed to the piecemeal nature of reform as having often added to the list of inconsistencies.

To address a situation that observers tended to liken (not unsurprisingly) to a 'maze', Clementi recommended the establishment of a new regulatory framework, the lynchpin of which would be a Legal Services Board (the LSB) to act as a new overarching legal regulator and provide consistent oversight of the front-line bodies. The LSB would have statutory objectives, which should include the promotion of the public and consumer interest, and would have the power to devolve regulatory functions to front-line bodies, subject to their competence and governance arrangements. In order to avoid the conflict between the regulatory and representative functions of the front-line bodies, they would themselves be required to make governance arrangements to separate out these functions.

In his consultation paper, Clementi had proposed two distinct models for regulation and complaints handling: the first (Model A) would remove all regulatory functions from the professional bodies and place them in the hands of a new unified regulator; the second (Model B) would allow the professional bodies to retain their regulatory responsibilities, but with oversight from a new overarching regulator. The two models were polarised constructs and it was recognised that there could be a number of variants. Arguments in favour of Model A included complete independence of the regulator from the regulated and a reduction in the number of regulators leading, it could be suggested, to a simpler, more accountable and coherent system. The main concern with Model A was that the removal of regulatory functions from the profession could reduce a feeling of responsibility amongst lawyers and lead to a huge increase in overall cost and bureaucracy. Model B, by contrast, kept regulation close to those who provided the services, which would undoubtedly be cheaper and could encourage a greater feeling of responsibility amongst the profession. The proposals endorsed by Clementi amounted to a recommendation for a system based on Model B.

[1] Clementi Report, p37.

THE OLD COMPLAINTS SYSTEM

1.4 Historically, if consumers wished to complain about a legal service received in respect of a single case they needed a certain amount of perseverance. In the first instance, they had to take the complaint up with the person they were complaining about. If that complaint was not satisfactorily resolved at an in-house level, the consumer would then need to make a complaint to the regulatory body responsible for regulating the person providing the service (the front-line regulator – be it the Law Society, the Bar Council or any of the other relevant bodies). Each of the approved regulators operated their own complaints handling and disciplinary arrangements.

If that complaint still did not produce a satisfactory result, the complainant would then turn to the Legal Services Ombudsman (LSO) who would look into the manner in which the complaint had, to date, been handled. If the Ombudsman believed that the investigation had been inadequate, he or she could require the front-line regulator to look at the matter again. Whilst the

LSO technically had the power to investigate individual complaints, that power was exercised in a miniscule percentage of cases.

On complaints, Clementi's view was that[1]:

> 'There is considerable concern about how consumer complaints are dealt with. The concern arises at a number of levels: at an operating level, there is an issue about the efficiency with which the systems are run; at an oversight level, there is a concern about the overlapping powers of the oversight bodies; and at a level of principle, there is an issue about whether systems for complaints against lawyers, run by lawyers themselves can achieve consumer confidence. A large number of the responses to the Consultation Paper expressed dissatisfaction with the current arrangements.'

His concerns at the operating level focused on the record of complaints handling by the front-line bodies, as to which he specifically highlighted the issues of substantial delay in the handling of complaints and the questionable quality in terms of outcome. At the oversight level, the report focused on the inconsistency and lack of clarity about the avenues for redress in the mind of the consumer (most noticeably where a complaint is made about both a solicitor and a barrister or where there is uncertainty in the mind of the consumer as to whether a fault actually lies) and the overlaps and fragmented oversight arrangements outlined above. Clementi also referred to the number of responses to his consultation paper regarding the lack of independence of the complaints handling systems operated by the front-line regulatory bodies, which was contributing to a lack of public confidence in the legal professions.

Clementi's recommendation was for the establishment of a new Office of Legal Complaints (the OLC), a single independent body to handle consumer complaints in respect of all members of front-line bodies subject to oversight by the LSB. His view was that this should provide a complaints system which is easy to access and independent in dealing with consumer complaints.

1 Clementi Report, p2.

THE RESTRICTIVE NATURE OF THE OLD BUSINESS STRUCTURES

1.5 Prior to the passing of the LSA 2007, there existed a wide range of restrictions on the type of business structures through which legal services could be provided, and the business structures though which legal services were delivered to the public had changed little over a considerable period. The OFT's response to the consultation paper (which is quoted in the Clementi Report) identified the most significant restrictions affecting the types of alternative business structures able to offer legal services as being contained within the rules of the main professional bodies and as constituting:

- rules that prohibit partnership between barristers and between barristers and other professionals (both lawyers and non-lawyers); employed barristers may work for firms of solicitors, but may not without requalification become partners;
- rules that prohibit solicitors from entering partnership with members of other professions (both lawyers and non-lawyers); and

– rules that prevent, with a small number of exceptions, solicitors in the employment of businesses or organisations not owned by solicitors (eg banks or insurance companies) from providing services to third parties.

In addition, regulators had not, historically, had the power that they would need in order to regulate business structures that fell outside the traditional models.

Clementi's view was that many of the restrictive practices as to the structures under which lawyers could work could no longer be justified as being in the public interest. He pointed to the most easily recognisable structure being that of the high street solicitor, practising either on his own or in partnership with other solicitors[1]:

> 'But business practices have changed. In particular the skills necessary to run a modern legal practice have developed; but whilst those with finance or IT skills may sit on the management committee of a legal firm, they are not permitted to be principals in the business. There is concern also about whether the restrictive practices of the main legal professional bodies can still be justified, in particular those which prevent different types of lawyers working together on an equal footing. There is pressure for change from those who represent consumer interests, but also from many in the legal profession, particularly the Law Society who have made a strong case for liberalisation of law practices.'

Clementi's proposal was for the establishment of alternative business structures (ABSs), which would bring together lawyers from different professional bodies and permit non-lawyers to be involved in management and ownership.

Clementi agreed with the widespread view expressed to him that it would be a good start to get lawyers to work together in legal disciplinary practices (LDPs), and to assess the regulatory consequences of that, before proceeding with full blooded multi-disciplinary practices (MDPs)[2]. Adopting a 'learn to walk before you run' approach, he concluded:

> 'The proposal of this Review is that attention should focus on the setting up of a new regulatory system for lawyers with the LSB at its centre, and the authorisation of LDPs. This would represent a major step towards MDPs, if at some subsequent juncture the regulatory authorities considered that sufficient safeguards could be put in place.'[3]

So Clementi's proposal cautiously opened the way for the establishment in due course of alternative business structures (ABSs) that would bring together lawyers from different professional bodies and permit non-lawyers to be involved in management and ownership.

His view was that such practices should encourage new capital and new ideas in promoting cost-effective consumer-friendly legal services. The Government's 2003 report had already expressed its support for the principle of enabling legal services to be provided through alternative business structures, the benefits of which (as subsequently spelt out in its White Paper[4]) would be extensive, as follows:

- More choice: consumers will have greater flexibility in deciding from where to obtain legal and some non-legal services.
- Reduced prices: consumers should be able to purchase some legal services more cheaply. This should arise where ABS firms realise savings through economies of scale and reduce transaction costs where different types of legal professionals are part of the same firm.
- Better access to justice: ABS firms might find it easier to provide services in rural areas or to less mobile customers.
- Improved consumer service: consumers may benefit from a better service where ABS firms are able to access external finance and specialist non-legal expertise.
- Greater convenience: ABS firms can provide one-stop shopping for related services, for example car insurance and legal services for accident claims.
- Increased consumer confidence: higher consumer protection levels and an increase in the quality of legal services could flow from ABS firms which have a good reputation in providing non-legal services. These firms will have a strong incentive to keep that reputation when providing legal services.

Potential benefits for legal service providers would be:

- Increased access to finance: at present, providers can face constraints on the amount of equity – mainly debt equity – they can raise. Allowing alternative business structures will facilitate expansion by firms (including into international markets) and investment in large-scale capital projects that increase efficiency.
- Better spread of risk: a firm could spread its risk more effectively among shareholders. This will lower the required rate of return on any investment, facilitate investment and could deliver lower prices.
- Increased flexibility: non-legal firms such as insurance companies, banks and estate agents will have the freedom to realise synergies with legal firms by forming ABS firms and offering integrated legal and associated services.
- Easier to hire and retain high-quality non-legal staff: ABS firms will be able to reward non-legal staff in the same way as lawyers.
- More choice for new legal professionals: ABS firms could contribute to greater diversity by offering those who are currently under-represented more opportunities to enter and remain within the profession.

1 Clementi Report, p2.
2 Clementi Report, para 98.
3 Clementi Report, para 104.
4 Department of Constitutional Affairs, 'The Future of Legal Services: Putting Consumers First' (October 2005), p40.

THE PASSAGE THROUGH PARLIAMENT

1.6 Following the Clementi Report, on 17 October 2005 the Government published its White Paper, 'The Future of Legal Services: Putting Consumers First', which set out proposals for the future of legal services in England and

Wales. Announcing the publication of the White Paper, Lord Falconer confirmed that the purpose of the changes was to put the consumer first. The Government stated that it had accepted Clementi's recommendations and set out its proposals[1]:

- That the objectives of the regulatory framework and principles of the legal profession would be set out in legislation: 'Consumers will be clear about the system, and will be able to hold all partners in the framework to account for delivering these commitments. Front-line regulators will be required to separate their regulatory and representative functions. These steps will increase confidence in the regulatory system and in legal professionals.'
- The creation of a new Legal Services Board to act as the oversight regulator: the board would authorise front-line regulators to carry out day-to-day regulation provided they meet its regulatory standards, including a requirement for the separation of their regulatory and representative functions.
- The development of alternative business structures: these would enable legal and certain other services to be provided to high standards and in ways that suit different consumers. The arrangements would ensure competition and innovation can continue to flourish.
- That consumers would be protected by quickly putting into place safeguards where new gaps in protection open up.
- The creation of a new Office for Legal Complaints which would deal with all consumer complaints about legal service providers who are members of bodies or organisations regulated by the LSB. The OLC would be independent from government and from providers of legal services. It would be accountable to the LSB and would be funded by the sector.

Legislation would be needed to effect most of these changes and, in consequence, the draft Legal Services Bill was published on 24 May 2006 together with explanatory notes and a regulatory impact assessment. It started life at a 'mere' 159 clauses and 15 Schedules. By the time it emerged from Parliament over a year later, it had swollen to 214 sections and 24 Schedules, having been subject to extensive scrutiny and debate, much of which focused on the areas in which the draft Bill was perceived as having departed from the recommendations made by Clementi.

In general terms, consumer organisations welcomed the proposals to reform complaints handling. There was a mixed reception from the principal front-line regulators. Whilst welcoming the recommendations of Clementi – in advance of the draft Bill, for example, both the Law Society and Bar Council had put into action his recommendation of splitting the profession's regulatory function from its representative roles, with the creation of the Solicitors Regulation Authority in January 2005 and the establishment of the Bar Standards Board a year later – there was concern about other features of the proposed Act which resulted in extensive lobbying and (ultimately) amendment:

- An ongoing issue throughout the Bill's passage through Parliament was the extent to which the independence of the legal profession could be ensured by the independence of the LSB from government. Central to this issue has been the role of the judiciary in the appointment of the LSB and the level of interference from the LSB in the work of the front-line regulators. The Bill gave the Lord Chancellor the power to make appointments to the LSB without consultation. In addition, the LSB had wide powers to intervene in the work of the front-line regulators. The concern of the legal professions was that such involvement and intervention could threaten the public's confidence in the impartiality of lawyers and, additionally, undermine the reputation of the profession in the overseas market. Following revision, the Act provides that the Lord Chancellor may only make such appointments after consultation with the Lord Chief Justice (Sch 1, para 1(3)). In addition, the Act makes it clear that responsibility for regulation rests primarily with the front-line regulators and that the LSB will only interfere where their actions are unreasonable (section 49(4)). Notably, section 1(1)(f) provides that 'encouraging an independent, strong, diverse and effective legal profession' is one of the Act's regulatory objectives.

- In the area of complaints handling the main point of contention was over who should be required to pay the costs of the OLC where a charge against a lawyer was not upheld. The Government initially envisaged a complaints system whose running costs would be borne entirely by those against whom the complaints were made, irrespective of whether or not the complaints were upheld. This was perceived by the legal bodies as being profoundly unfair and onerous. In its final days of passage, it was at last conceded that lawyers do not have to pay where a complaint has not been upheld provided that the firm is able to show that it took all reasonable steps to deal with the matter in-house (section 136(2)).
- Another significant battleground was the impact that the ABSs would have on the public's access to justice. The concern was that new entrants to the market would cherry-pick and, in time, dominate the more profitable areas of work thereby squeezing out of business existing firms, who would find themselves forced to focus on the less profitable (though nonetheless socially valuable) areas of work. Rather than increasing services to the public, this would have the opposite effect. This concern should be mitigated by the inclusion of section 83(5)(b) in the Act, which provides that a licensing authority must, in its licensing rules, provide for the ways in which it should, when considering an application for an ABS licence, take account of the regulatory objective of improving access to justice.

The most significant area of contention where the Bill was not revised, was with regards to who should pick up the bill for the costs of establishing and running the LSB and the OLC. Despite intensive lobbying from the legal bodies, the unwavering position of the Government was that the costs of these new bodies (and the associated transitional costs) would be met by the legal profession. Accordingly, the LSB is required to impose a levy on the front-line regulators to cover the full cost of establishing and running the new system.

1 Department of Constitutional Affairs, 'The Future of Legal Services: Putting Consumers First' (October 2005), p8.

THE LSA 2007: LOOKING AHEAD

1.7 Much of the LSA 2007 has yet to be brought into force: for example, it appears likely that the provisions relating to ABSs may not come into effect until 2011 and there will then be a lead time before the first ABSs complete the process of obtaining licences. The LSA 2007 itself creates no more than a framework: the detailed scheme of regulation, within that framework, will be contained in the rules and policies to be laid down by the LSB and the front-line regulators, respectively. As yet, therefore, much remains to be defined. However, the LSB has made clear that it intends to force the pace of change[1].

The new regulatory framework introduced by the LSA 2007 is described, in overview, in Chapter 2. The remainder of Part 1 of this book then deals in turn with the different elements in that framework: the LSB and its powers; the new business structures (LDPs and ABSs); the new system for dealing with complaints (the OLC); and the changes that are being made to the existing regulatory and disciplinary regimes of the front-line regulators. Part 2 looks ahead to future developments once the new regime is fully in force.

1 LSB 2009/10, Draft Business Plan (29 January 2009).

Chapter 2

THE REGULATORY FRAMEWORK

Patricia Robertson QC and Katherine Watt

AN OVERVIEW OF THE REGULATORY FRAMEWORK: WHAT IS NEW ABOUT IT?

The Legal Services Board

2.1 The LSA 2007 establishes a new oversight regulator, the Legal Services Board (the LSB), whose primary role is to regulate the 'approved regulators'[1]. The approved regulators are, in turn, responsible for front-line regulation. The LSB's powers over the approved regulators include the ability to impose sanctions, approve new regulators or revoke the approval of existing ones. The LSB also acts as a front-line regulator of last resort in certain limited circumstances[2].

1 See para 2.2 below.
2 See Chapter 3 below.

Approved regulators

2.2 The eight existing regulators of the various branches of the legal profession (including the Law Society and the General Council of the Bar) are approved regulators[1]. However, the LSA 2007 opens the way for new entrants to the ranks of approved regulators and/or (potentially) for competition between approved regulators to be the regulator of choice. Approved regulators will be subject to various new obligations under the LSA 2007, including an obligation to keep their representative and regulatory functions independent of one another[2].

1 See para 2.11 below and Sch 4, Pt 1, para 1.
2 See para 2.11 ff below.

The Office for Legal Complaints

2.3 The LSA 2007 removes jurisdiction over complaints from the approved regulators and vests this function in a single body, the new Office for Legal Complaints (the OLC), which is responsible for dealing with all complaints across all of the different branches of the legal profession. Disciplinary action remains a matter for the approved regulators[1].

1 See Chapter 6 below.

Regulatory objectives

2.4 All of the regulators, including the LSB itself, are obliged to act compatibly with the regulatory objectives in the LSA 2007, s 1 and best regulatory principles (or, in the case of the OLC, best practice amongst those who administer ombudsman schemes) [1].

1 See paras 2.10–2.13 below.

Defined regulatory field

2.5 A new umbrella concept of 'reserved legal activities' defines the field of activity which is subject to this scheme of regulation[1]. Carrying on reserved legal activities without authorisation is an offence.

1 See para 2.15 below.

Entity-based regulation

2.6 Regulation will no longer apply solely to individuals who are members of the relevant professions but will also extend to regulation of entities (including unincorporated entities) through which reserved legal activities are carried on. Both the entities and the individuals working as lawyers within them will need to be authorised persons in order to carry on reserved legal activities. The approved regulator responsible for the entity will take the lead[1].

1 See para 2.22 below.

Alternative business structures

2.7 A new and distinct regulatory regime will be created for alternative business structures (ABSs), ie entities that are part-owned and/or managed by non-lawyers. These will have to be licensed by an approved regulator which has been designated by the LSB as a 'licensing body' (or by the LSB itself, acting as such) and will be subject to additional requirements and controls over and above those that apply to other types of authorised person[1].

1 See Chapter 4 below.

Extended regulatory reach

2.8 Regulation will not be confined to lawyers but will be extended to non-lawyer managers, employees and (in the case of ABSs) owners of regulated entities[1].

1 See para 2.16 below.

THE REGULATORS

The LSB: composition and governance

2.9 The LSB is established as a body corporate under the LSA 2007, s 2 and its constitution is set out in Sch 1.

The LSB consists of a chairman appointed by the Lord Chancellor and between seven and ten ordinary members appointed by the Lord Chancellor in consultation with the Lord Chief Justice, together with a chief executive appointed by the LSB itself[1]. The chairman and a majority of the ordinary members must be lay persons. In appointing ordinary members the Lord Chancellor is to have regard to the desirability of securing expertise on the LSB across a wide range of matters: the provision of legal services; legal education and legal training; consumer affairs; civil or criminal proceedings and the working of the courts; competition matters; the maintenance of the professional standards of persons who provide legal services; the maintenance of standards in professions other than the legal profession; the handling of complaints; commercial affairs; non-commercial legal services; the differing needs of consumers; and the provision of claims management services[2]. Members are appointed for a maximum of five years and can be reappointed no more than once[3].

In managing its affairs, the LSB must have regard to such generally accepted principles of good corporate governance as it is reasonable to regard as applicable to it[4]. The LSB has a wide discretion to adopt such internal arrangements and procedures as it considers effective and appropriate for the performance of its functions: for example, the LSB has power to appoint staff or engage external advisers; to establish committees and sub-committees (subject to the requirement these must have a lay majority); to regulate its own procedures (subject to a quorum of three); and to delegate its functions (other than specified rule-making functions) to any LSB member, LSB committee or sub-committee or member of staff[5].

The LSB has no power to borrow money, unless authorised by the Lord Chancellor[6]. Its members are disqualified from membership of the House of Commons[7]. The LSB is not an agent of the Crown and does not have Crown immunity; however, the LSB, its members and those to whom it delegates its functions are not to be liable in damages unless found to have acted in bad faith or in breach of the Human Rights Act 1998[8].

1 Schedule 1, paras 1–2.
2 Schedule 1, para 3.

3 Schedule 1 para 5.
4 Section 5.
5 Schedule 1, paras 13–23.
6 Schedule 1, para 24.
7 Schedule 1, para 30.
8 Schedule 1, paras 26–33.

The LSB: overview of functions, powers and obligations

2.10 The general functions, powers and obligations of the LSB are defined in Pts 2 and 6 of the LSA 2007. Powers relating to its oversight of approved regulators are set out in Pt 4, whilst Pt 5 contains those powers that are specific to the new licensing regime for ABSs.

In discharging its functions, the LSB has a general duty under LSA 2007, s 3:

1 to act compatibly with the regulatory objectives (in s 1)[1] and in a way which it considers most appropriate for meeting those objectives;
2 to have regard to:
  - the principles under which regulatory activities should be transparent, accountable, proportionate, consistent and targeted only at cases in which action is needed; and
  - any other principle appearing to it to represent the best regulatory practice.

At the time of writing, the LSB is consulting on its draft business plan, which sets out its proposed agenda and how it sees this as relating to the regulatory objectives and principles of best regulatory practice[2].

The LSB's principal role is the oversight of approved regulators (including those approved regulators who take on the status of licensing bodies). It has an array of draconian powers over approved regulators, if needed, and can be asked to make directions as to how any regulatory conflicts between the regimes of different approved regulators are to be resolved. The LSB is also responsible for exercising control over the funding of the regulatory system (raising its own levy and policing the practising fees charged by approved regulators) and it has various specific functions in relation to the operation of the regulatory framework generally: for example, setting standards; providing guidance; overseeing the OLC and being empowered to recommend to the Lord Chancellor changes to the scope of reserved legal services or to the functions of approved regulators. The LSB does not have any direct control over authorised persons, save insofar as it may be required itself to act as an approved regulator in certain very limited circumstances.

The LSB's functions, and the powers it may exercise in carrying out those roles, are described in more detail in Chapter 3 below. The LSB must report annually to the Lord Chancellor (who in turn reports to Parliament) as to the discharge of its functions, the extent to which it has met the regulatory objectives, how the activities of licensing authorities and licensed bodies have affected the regulatory objectives, and any other matters as directed by the

Lord Chancellor[3]. It also has supplementary powers to do anything calculated to facilitate, or incidental or conducive to, the carrying out of any of its functions[4].

1 See para 1.6 above and para 2.14 below.
2 The draft 2009/10 Business Plan, dated 29 January 2009, is available on the LSB's website, at http://www.legalservicesboard.org.uk/.
3 Sections 6 and 110.
4 Section 7.

Approved regulators: overview of functions, powers and obligations

2.11 Approved regulators are the gatekeepers, and gamekeepers, of the territory designated as 'reserved legal services'. With few exceptions, anyone (whether an individual or an entity) wishing to enter the controlled territory, ie carry on reserved legal activities, has to be authorised by an approved regulator and the approved regulator is responsible for ejecting those who transgress the rules[1]. Only if the approved regulator is falling down on the job should the LSB step in[2].

Approved regulators are either bodies which existed prior to the introduction of the new regime created by the Act and are designated as approved regulators by the Act itself, or such bodies as may, following implementation of the relevant provisions of the Act, apply to the LSB under Sch 4 for a recommendation to become, and obtain designation by the Lord Chancellor as, an approved regulator[3].

The bodies designated as approved regulators pursuant to the Act itself (in relation to specified reserved legal activities) are: The Law Society, The General Council of the Bar, The Master of the Faculties, The Institute of Legal Executives, The Council for Licensed Conveyancers, The Chartered Institute of Patent Attorneys, The Institute of Trade Mark Attorneys, and The Association of Law Costs Draftsmen[4]. The existing statutory powers and functions of these bodies are, in some cases, modified in certain respects by the LSA 2007.

In particular, Sch 16 introduces a number of important modifications to the powers of the Law Society under the Solicitors Act 1974, AJA 1985 and Courts and Legal Services Act 1990. These include a power for the Law Society to authorise a form of ABS (subject to limits on the nature and extent of non-lawyer involvement) in advance of the full ABS regime coming into effect[5]. The Law Society's powers over non-solicitors are also extended[6]. For a description of such changes, the reader should refer to Chapter 6 below.

Approved regulators retain the right to set their own rules, subject to the obligation to draft them with due regard to their duties under the LSA 2007 and to get approval for them where the LSA 2007 so requires.

The regulatory arrangements of approved regulators must be approved by the Lord Chancellor on the recommendation of the LSB[7], as part and parcel of the process of initially obtaining approval, whilst any subsequent modification to those arrangements must generally be approved by the LSB[8]. The term 'regulatory arrangements' is given a wide meaning, and includes arrangements for authorising persons, conduct and practice rules, disciplinary arrangements, qualification regulations, and indemnification or compensation arrangements, amongst other things[9]. The regulatory arrangements of those bodies expressly designated as approved regulators by the Act itself, are treated as having been approved by the LSB for the purposes of the Act[10]. However, if any of these bodies wish to act as a regulator of ABSs and become a licensing authority, they will need to apply separately for that designation, giving details of their proposed licensing rules[11].

Where an approved regulator plays a dual role, exercising both 'regulatory functions'[12] and 'representative functions'[13] in relation to authorised persons subject to their oversight, the approved regulator is obliged to comply with corporate governance rules to be made by the LSB for the purpose of ensuring:

- that the exercise of an approved regulator's regulatory functions are not prejudiced by its representative functions; and
- that decisions relating to the exercise of an approved regulator's regulatory functions are so far as reasonably practicable taken independently from decisions relating to its representative functions[14].

Developing appropriate rules for this purpose is one of the LSB's key short-term priorities: by the end of 2009/10, the LSB intends (among other matters) to have agreed rules requiring all approved regulators to establish and maintain a clear and demonstrable separation between their regulatory and representative functions, and to have designed mechanisms that will test the degree to which regulatory independence has been achieved, enabling approved regulators to demonstrate, and the board to test, such effectiveness[15].

When discharging their functions, approved regulators have a general duty, defined in the same terms as that which applies to the LSB itself: namely, to act, so far as is reasonably practicable, in a way which is compatible with the regulatory objectives (and which they consider most appropriate for the purpose of meeting those objectives) and to have regard to the principles under which regulatory activities should be transparent, accountable, proportionate, consistent and targeted only at cases in which action is needed, (and any other principle appearing to the approved regulator to represent the best regulatory practice)[16].

Approved regulators also have obligations to seek to prevent regulatory conflicts with the rules of other regulators, whether other approved regulators or external regulators. As to this, see para 2.21 below.

The LSA 2007 imposes duties on the part of those who are subject to a given approved regulator's jurisdiction to comply with that regulator's regulatory arrangements, including its conduct rules: see para 2.19 below. Those conduct rules must maintain and promote the professional principles.

Given that the LSA 2007 is not yet fully in effect, and the parts relating to ABSs will not come into effect for some time yet, a number of the approved regulators are currently engaged in consultations as to how to change their regulatory arrangements to cater for these provisions coming fully into force and it is to be expected that this process will continue for a number of years. The first chair of the LSB, David Edmonds, has indicated a determination to drive ahead with ABSs as soon as possible[17]. The LSB's first business plan, published in draft in January 2009, makes clear this is regarded as a priority[18]. Approved regulators who are seen as dragging their feet or who continue to maintain regulatory provisions which are an unjustified obstacle to the new forms of collaboration the Act was designed to permit (between lawyers of different sorts or between lawyers and non-lawyers) risk finding themselves on the wrong side of the LSB's extensive powers of sanction. For a detailed description of the LSB's powers over approved regulators see Chapter 3 below.

1 See paras 2.16–2.20 below.
2 See Chapter 3 below.
3 See generally Chapter 3 below.
4 Pursuant to Sch 4, Pt 1, para 1.
5 See, further, para 2.18 and Chapter 4 below.
6 See Chapter 6.
7 Schedule 4, Pt 2, para (2)(b).
8 Schedule 4, Pt 3, para 19(2).
9 Section 21(1).
10 Schedule 4, Pt 1, para 2.
11 Schedule 10, Pt 1, para 1(4)(b) and see para 2.12 below.
12 Defined as 'any functions the approved regulator has (a) under or in relation to its regulatory arrangements, or (b) in connection with the making or alteration of those arrangements' (s 27(1)).
13 Defined as 'any functions the approved regulator has in connection with the representation, or promotion, of the interests of persons regulated by it' (s 27(2)).
14 Section 30.
15 LSB's draft business plan (see para 2.10, note 20 above).
16 Section 28; and see para 2.10 above.
17 Speech at the Law Society Breakfast, 25 September 2008 (available on the LSB's website at http://www.legalservicesboard.org.uk/).
18 2009/2010 Business Plan, available on the LSB's website at http://www.legalservicesboard.org.uk/.

Licensing authorities: overview of functions, powers and obligations

2.12 The purpose of the LSA 2007, Pt V is to create a distinct regulatory regime under which it will be possible to permit non-lawyers to participate as investors or managers in businesses which provide legal services falling within the scope of reserved legal activities. When the provisions of Pt V are brought into effect, those approved regulators who, on the recommendation of the LSB under Sch 10, are so designated by the Lord Chancellor, may act as a licensing authority[1] for licensable bodies[2] (otherwise known as ABSs), namely those entities which include non-authorised persons amongst their managers or those with an interest, defined as shares or control over voting rights. Such a regulator can then act as a body authorised to grant licences to and regulate such licensable bodies and exercise powers over those who are their managers, employees or owners.

Licensing authorities have additional functions, powers and obligations by virtue of that status, over and above those which apply to approved regulators generally. In particular:

- Licensing authorities must put in place licensing rules covering the matters specified in s 83(5) and Sch 11 (which include qualification regulations for the grant of licences to licensable bodies, and conduct and discipline rules relating both to the licensed body and its managers and employees). Licensing authorities have to provide in their rules for how they will take into account the objective of improving access to justice when determining licence applications[3]. They must not grant a licence unless satisfied the applicant will comply with its licensing rules[4].
- They must (with the approval of the LSB) issue and publish a statement of policy as to how they will exercise their functions[5].
- They must keep a register of all bodies who hold or have held a licence from them, which is open to inspection without charge[6].
- They have an array of statutory powers, including powers to grant a licence subject to conditions[7]; to alter the terms of a licence[8]; or suspend or revoke it[9]; to require information from the licensed body, or a manager employee or person with an interest in it[10]; to impose financial penalties[11]; to refer a manager or employee of a licensed body to their own professional regulator[12]; to disqualify a person from being a manager or employee of a licensed body or acting as Head of Legal Practice or Head of Finance and Administration of such a body[13]; to apply to the High Court for divestiture of a non-authorised person's interest in a licensed body, subject to the conditions and procedure laid down in Sch 13[14]; and to exercise various intervention powers in respect of a licensed body (broadly analogous to the Law Society's intervention powers under the Solicitors Act 1974), subject to the conditions and procedure laid down in Sch 14[15].

The LSB itself is also a licensing authority[16] and must prepare licensing rules so that it can act as a licensing authority of last resort for any licensable body who comes within the provisions of Sch 12 (broadly, where there is no other appropriate licensing authority)[17].

See para 2.17 below for the meaning of 'licensable body'. The regulatory regime for licensable bodies is discussed in detail in Chapter 4 below.

1 Section 73.
2 Licensable bodies are defined in s 72.
3 Section 83(5)(b).
4 Section 84(3).
5 Section 82.
6 Section 87.
7 Section 85.
8 Section 86.
9 Section 101.
10 Section 93.
11 Section 95.
12 Section 98.
13 Section 99
14 Section 89 and Sch 13, Pt 5.

The professional principles fall into three groups. The first group relates to the conduct of those who are authorised persons, generally; the second relates specifically to the conduct of those authorised persons who are advocates or litigators; and the third is directed to protecting client confidentiality, without being tied to the conduct of authorised persons. The professional principles are not, however, themselves made directly applicable to regulated persons[2]. Rather, they express core values that those with regulatory functions must ensure are promoted and maintained by the rules of conduct and disciplinary procedures they put in place for those whom they regulate.

The professional principles, in summary, are that:

- authorised persons should act with independence and integrity; maintain proper standards of work; and act in the best interests of their clients;
- persons who exercise a right of audience or conduct litigation by virtue of being authorised persons should comply with their duty to the court and act with independence in the interests of justice; and
- the affairs of clients should be kept confidential.

1 The Explanatory Notes to the LSA 2007 (para 28) disavow any suggestion that the order in which these objectives appear in s 1 should be taken as ranking their priority.

2 The LSA 2007 does, however, directly impose certain duties on regulated persons under ss 176 and 188: see para 2.19 below.

The scope of regulation

Reserved legal activities

2.15 LSA 2007, s 12 defines reserved legal activities as: the exercise of a right of audience; the conduct of litigation; reserved instrument activities; probate activities; notarial activities; and the administration of oaths. Each of these is further defined in Sch 2.

Reserved instrument activities means the preparation of any instrument or charge for the purposes of the Land Registration Act 2002, making an application or lodging a document for registration under that Act and preparing any other instrument relating to real or personal estate for the purposes of the law of England and Wales or instrument relating to court proceedings in England and Wales. This includes contracts for sale or disposition of land (other than for a short lease), but excludes other types of contracts unless intended to be by deed, wills, powers of attorney or transfers of stock containing no trust or limitation of the transfer[1].

The other categories of reserved legal activity are largely self-explanatory and (other than in the case of notarial activities, which are statutorily defined for the first time) their definitions are, broadly, carried over from previous legislation[2]. The key point to note is that where, before the LSA 2007, there was no restriction on the persons entitled to exercise rights of audience, or to conduct litigation, or to carry on reserved instrument activities, the Act then does not treat those as reserved legal activities and therefore does not restrict them[3]. For example, an individual who is a party to litigation does not require authorisation to exercise a right of audience on his own behalf, after the LSA 2007, anymore than before. At present, therefore, the extent of the territory which is regulated is the same as before, but the Lord Chancellor has power to extend or contract the scope of 'reserved legal activities' by order[4].

It is an offence under s 14 to carry on reserved legal activities without being entitled[5], subject to a defence where the accused shows that the accused did not know and could not reasonably have known the offence was being committed[6]. Where the offence relates to conducting litigation or exercising a right of audience without being entitled, it is also a contempt of court[7]. There is an obvious parallel between this new provision and the general prohibition under the Financial Services and Markets Act 2000 (FSMA 2000), s 19 on carrying on activities regulated under that Act without being either authorised or exempt (and indeed that is not the only point of resemblance – in a number of other respects the LSA 2007 borrows from the FSMA 2000 regulatory framework). It is also an offence, under s 17, for a person wilfully to pretend to be entitled to carry on a reserved legal activity.

The question of entitlement to carry on reserved legal activities is dealt with in more detail at para 2.16 ff below, but in essence, unless exempt under s 19, a person (defined as including a body of persons, corporate or unincorporated)[8] must be authorised to carry on reserved legal activities by an approved regulator, who is designated as such in relation to the relevant type of reserved legal activity, or in the case of a licensable body, must hold a licence from a licensing authority covering the activity in question[9].

'Legal activities' are defined in wider terms. They include those activities that are reserved legal activities, and in addition any activities consisting in:

- providing legal advice or assistance in connection with the application of the law or any form of resolution of legal disputes; and/or
- providing representation in connection with any matter concerning the application of the law or any form of resolution of legal disputes.

On the recommendation of the LSB, the Lord Chancellor can extend the scope of reserved legal activities, making a given legal activity a reserved legal activity[10], or can remove an activity from the scope of reserved legal activities[11]. Where a request is made to the LSB in this regard, the LSB has to follow the procedure laid down in Sch 6 before making such a recommendation (or deciding not to make one).

1 The definition of 'reserved instrument activities' is essentially the same as the definition in the Solicitors Act 1974 of instruments that could be prepared (for or in expectation of reward) only by qualified persons (ie solicitors) or other specified persons (see the Solicitors Act 1974, ss 22(1), (3)), save that the Act refers to 'instrument[s] relating to court proceedings in England and Wales' (as opposed to 'instrument[s]... relating to any legal proceeding'.

2 The definitions of 'rights of audience', 'conduct of litigation' and 'probate activities' have essentially the same meanings as under the Courts and Legal Service Act 1990, s 119(1), save that the definition of 'probate activities' does not include 'drawing' of probate papers (in addition to 'preparing') and does not include the administration of the estate of a deceased person. The definition of 'notarial activities' essentially adopts customary practice immediately before the date on which the relevant provisions of the Act come into force.

(The functions of notaries were not previously defined by statute, but were a matter of practice.) The definition of 'administration of oaths' is essentially the same as under the Courts and Legal Services Act 1990, s 113(3).

3 Similarly, the Courts and Legal Services Act 1990, ss 27(7) and 28(4) provided that where, before the commencement of that Act, no restriction was placed on the persons entitled to exercise any right of audience or right to conduct litigation in relation to a particular court or in relation to particular proceedings, nothing in the Act was intended to place any such restriction on any person.

4 LSA 2007, ss 24 and 26.

5 Section 14(1).

6 Section 14(2).

7 Section 14(4).

8 Section 207.

9 See LSA 2007, ss 13–21 generally and ss 13(2) and 18(1) in particular. The current approved regulators are not all designated as such in relation to all forms of reserved legal activity. For example, the Institute of Legal Executives designation is limited to the exercise of rights of audience and the administration of oaths, whereas the Bar Council and the Law Society are designated in respect of everything but notarial activities. See Sch 4, Pt 1, para 1.

10 By order made under s 24 and Sch 6.

11 By order made under s 26 and Sch 6.

Authorised persons

2.16 Only those who are authorised persons or exempt persons are entitled to carry on reserved legal activities[1]. Authorised persons fall into two distinct categories: persons (a term which includes corporations and unincorporated bodies) who have been authorised by one of the approved regulators; and licensable bodies licensed under the new regime for ABSs in Pt 5[2]. As to the latter, see para 2.17 ff below.

The exemptions are detailed in Sch 3. In particular, there are exemptions for certain office holders (such as the Attorney General)[3]; parties to proceedings or individuals who have a right of audience or to conduct litigation independently of the LSA 2007 (for example an individual to whom the court has granted a right of audience in the given case)[4]; European lawyers who are entitled to carry on an activity which is a reserved legal activity under mutual recognition provisions[5]; and (subject to some exceptions) employers who carry on reserved legal activities through managers or employees who are themselves exempt[6]; as well as a variety of other exemptions.

As regards rights of audience, there is an exemption for hearings in chambers or the county court which (in effect) permits these to be dealt with by paralegals or other unqualified litigation assistants who are acting on instructions from a person who is authorised to conduct litigation[7]. There is, however, no equivalent exemption for persons conducting litigation under the supervision of a person who is authorised to do so, and the implications of this omission will have to be worked out. In relation to reserved instrument activities, there is also an exemption for persons employed merely to engross the instrument or application, and in relation to reserved instrument activities and probate activities, an exemption for persons who are employees carrying on the relevant activity at the direction and under the supervision of another individual provided that, at the time the employee does so, (i) the other individual is the employee's employer or fellow employee, or a manager or employee of a body which is an authorised person in relation to the activity and of which the employee is also a manager or employee; and (ii) the other individual is entitled to carry on the activity for or in expectation of any fee, gain or reward[8]. In addition, for a transitional period, Sch 5, paras 13 and 18 exempt the employer of a public notary or costs draftsman from the requirement to be authorised, as long as the employee through whom they are carrying on the relevant reserved activity is authorised.

Subject to these exemptions, the LSA 2007 requires both the individuals who carry on reserved legal activities, and the entity through which they provide them, to be authorised. This is the effect of ss 15 and 16, taken in combination with the offence created by s 14.

Section 15 deals with the position of employers and employees. It treats employees who are carrying on reserved legal activities on behalf of their employer (or managers providing such services on behalf of the entity they manage)[9] as themselves persons carrying on such services, and therefore requiring authorisation in their own right even if their employer (or the entity) is already authorised[10]. This, however, only applies where it is part of the employer's (or entity's) business to provide to the public, or a section of the public, services which include reserved legal activities[11]. It follows that where an in-house lawyer is supplying services which are reserved legal activities solely to their employer, and the latter's business does not involve supplying such services to the public, the lawyer must be an authorised person but the employer will not need to be. There is a carve out for trade unions, deeming their membership not to be a section of the public, which enables them to provide their members with legal advice in connection with their work or membership of the union without the trade union having to become an authorised person[12].

Section 16 makes it an offence for an employer to carry on reserved legal activities through an employee who is unauthorised (and who is committing an offence under s 14 by carrying on those activities), even if the employer itself is authorised[13]. Again, this also applies to an entity carrying on reserved legal activities through a manager, who is carrying on the activity in that capacity[14].

Note that the definition of a manager is a director of a body corporate (or member, where the body corporate is governed by its members), a partner in a partnership, or a member of the governing body of an unincorporated body other than a partnership. The Lord Chancellor has power to extend this definition by order[15].

The net effect of all this is that, regardless of how a business providing legal services to the public is structured (ie whether as a corporate body, partnership or other unincorporated body), both the business entity, and those of its employees or managers (ie directors, partners or members of governing body) who are themselves engaged in providing reserved legal services, need to be authorised to do so, save insofar as those employees or managers are exempt persons in relation to the relevant legal activity under Sch 3. Equally, although managers and employees who are not themselves engaged in carrying on reserved legal activities will not need authorisation, they will be regulated persons and therefore non-lawyers in these roles will now become subject to regulatory control[16].

Once again there are parallels here with the regulatory regime under FSMA 2000, where businesses engaged in providing regulated services must be authorised and the individuals performing controlled functions within those businesses are also subject to regulation as approved persons[17]. The fact that the regulatory regime for legal services is now to apply both to entities and to individuals has some important consequences, discussed at para 2.22 below.

1 Section 13.
2 Section 18(1).
3 Schedule 3, para 1(4) and (5), 3(2), 5(3).
4 Schedule 3, para 1(2), (3), (6) and 2(2), (3) and (4)8).
5 Schedule 3, para 7.
6 Schedule 3, para 8.
7 Schedule 3, para 1(7), (8). This exemption also applies to individuals assisting in the conduct of litigation on the instructions of a person within the scope of s 193 (which preserves the rights of the Treasury Solicitor and other solicitors to public departments or the City of London to carry on reserved legal activities without holding a practising certificate).
8 Schedule 3, paras 3 and 5.
9 Section 15(11).
10 Section 15(2).
11 Section 15(4).
12 Section 15(6) to (12).
13 Section 16(1), (2).
14 Section 16(3).
15 Definition of manager in s 207 and subsection (5) of that section.
16 Section 21(3), (4).
17 Financial Services and Markets Act 2000, ss 31 and 59(1).

Licensable bodies

2.17 Licensable bodies, to which the provisions for ABSs in Pt V apply, are defined in s 72 as a body in which a non-authorised person is a manager or has an interest.

The term 'body' is not itself defined in s 207 (the interpretation section), but has a very broad natural meaning and there can be little doubt the term was chosen with a view to ensuring that any entity in which non-lawyers might participate as owners or persons with an interest would come within the definition, regardless of its legal form or (if a partnership or other unincorporated body) lack of separate legal personality.

Acting as a manager includes being a director, partner or member of the governing body (see para 2.12 above). An interest, for these purposes, means holding shares in the body or being entitled to exercise or control the exercise of voting rights[1].

It follows that, for example, a non-lawyer with voting rights in the affairs of an unincorporated body has an 'interest' and that body is then a licensable body. This would appear to bring within the definition of 'licensable body' a chambers of self-employed barristers which chose to give its clerk or other non-legally qualified manager voting rights under the terms of its chambers constitution[2]. If a chambers (which is otherwise an unincorporated body) were to choose to do this, which they might do with a view to being able to attract a better calibre of business manager by giving them a say in the governance of chambers, they would then have to seek a licence. The same would be true if, for example, a partnership of solicitors made a non-lawyer a partner because they could bring to bear managerial skills that were regarded as valuable to the business.

As to shares, these are defined as allotted shares within the meaning of the Companies Acts; or rights to share in the capital of a body without shares; or interests conferring a right to share in profits or obligation to contribute to the debts of a body without capital[3].

Section 72 also caters for licensable bodies at one remove: where another body (A) has an interest in or is a manager of a body (B) and non-authorised persons control at least 10% of the voting rights in A, then B is a licensable body[4].

Sections 15 and 16 apply to licensed bodies in the same way as they apply to other entities: thus, where a licensed body carries on reserved legal activities through employees or managers who are providing those services in their capacity as such, the employees or managers must themselves also be authorised persons, in addition to the body being licensed. As to the position of non-lawyers who are employees or managers in a licensed body see para 2.19 below.

See Chapter 4 below for a detailed discussion of the new regime for regulating alternative business structures.

1 Section 72(3).
2 See also the definition of 'manager' in s 207 as this applies to an unincorporated body, namely someone who is a member of its governing body.
3 Section 72(6).
4 Section 72(2).

Legal disciplinary practices

2.18 As noted above, the Law Society already has power to authorise a limited form of ABS. This power is conferred by extending the definition of a 'recognised body' under the Administration of Justice Act 1985 (AJA 1985), to entities (whether corporate or unincorporate) that are owned and managed by a combination of different types of lawyer and up to 25% non-lawyers[1]. Under the transitional regime in Sch 16, the Law Society cannot authorise such a body unless (i) at least one manager is a solicitor or (broadly) another person subject to regulation by the SRA[2] and (ii) the proportion of non-lawyer owners/managers does not exceed 25% and any non-lawyer owners are also managers. The SRA refers to these as legal disciplinary practices (LDPs) [3]. Once the full ABS regime comes into effect, those LDPs which include non-lawyers will require to be licensed as ABSs under that regime.

LDPs involving only different sorts of lawyers, without any non-lawyers involved, are outside the definition of 'licensable body' and therefore the approved regulators do not need to wait for the ABS regime to come into effect, or become a licensing authority, to permit such arrangements. That said, however, whether other approved regulators are currently able to regulate LDPs will depend on the scope of their existing powers. There is, for example, no equivalent provision within the LSA 2007 conferring powers on the Bar Council to regulate LDPs (whether with or without the involvement of any non-lawyers) as Sch 16 does in the case of the Law Society. Whether it has power to do so therefore depends on an analysis of the Bar Council's constitution, disciplinary proceedings and code of conduct, as they currently stand. These do not, as presently drafted, extend to LDPs, as entities, or to solicitors, other lawyers, or non-lawyers involved in LDPs, but are limited to individuals who have been called to the Bar[4].

1 LSA 2007, Sch 16, paras 81 and 82, amending AJA 1985, s 9 and introducing a new s 9A. A draft statutory instrument making further amendments to s 9A is currently before Parliament.

2 AJA 1985, s 9A(4).

3 This is somewhat confusing, since the term 'legal disciplinary practice' does not appear in the LSA 2007 or the AJA 1985. It is in fact the terminology used in the Clementi Report for combinations involving lawyers only, in contradistinction to the term 'alternative business structure', which he used for combinations which include non-lawyers. Under the transitional regime, the Law Society can authorise LDPs which include up to 25% non-lawyers as managers and owners. However, this blurring of the boundaries between LDPs and ABSs is only temporary and will end once the full ABS regime comes into effect, when any LDPs that include non-lawyer owners and managers will have to be licensed as ABSs.

4 The statutory framework for the Bar Council to act as approved regulator for wider classes of person is already there, in LSA 2007, ss 20(6) and 176, which permit it to act as approved regulator for any person carrying on any of the activities it regulates and impose a duty on any such person to comply with its rules. However, to implement a regulatory regime for non-barristers under these powers would require changes to the Bar Council's constitution, rules of conduct and disciplinary procedures. Whether the Bar Council can and should seek to extend its powers, and in what respects, is likely to be controversial. See paras 2.21–2.23 below.

Duties of regulated persons

2.19 LSA 2007, s 176(1) imposes a duty on a regulated person to comply with the regulatory arrangements of an approved regulator as they apply to that person. This is not restricted to those involved with ABSs but is of general application. A person is a regulated person in relation to a given approved regulator if either authorised by that regulator to carry on a reserved legal activity or (although not so authorised) a manager or employee of a person who is authorised by that regulator[1].

It follows that the duty under s 176(1) encompasses:

1 a duty on the part of authorised persons to comply with the regulatory arrangements laid down by the approved regulator who has authorised them (which, in the case of individuals, means the regulator from whom they hold their practising certificate and, in the case of entities, the regulator who authorises the entity)[2]; and
2 a duty on the part of managers and employees of an entity that is an authorised person to comply with the regulatory arrangements of the entity's approved regulator, even if they themselves are not authorised by that particular approved regulator (or indeed at all)[3].

Within Pt 5 are a number of provisions imposing additional duties on those involved with ABSs. Sch 13 imposes various notification requirements on those who have or wish to acquire an interest in an ABS which exceeds certain specified thresholds[4]. Section 90 imposes a duty on a non-authorised person who is an employee or manager of or has an interest in a licensed body, not to do anything which causes of materially contributes to a breach by the licensed body, or an authorised person within it, of duties applicable to them under s 176. Section 91 requires the Head of Legal Practice of a licensed body to take all reasonable steps to ensure that the licensed body itself, authorised persons who are its managers and employees, and non-authorised persons who are subject to a s 90 duty in respect of it, each comply with the rules applicable to them. The Head of Legal Practice is under a duty to report any non-compliance to the licensing authority. Responsibility for compliance with those licensing rules that relate to accounts is placed on the Head of Finance, under s 92.

Two things follow from all this:

1 An individual who is an authorised person holding a practising certificate from one approved regulator, but who is working as an employee or manager in an entity which is authorised by a different approved regulator, will be under a duty to comply with the regulatory arrangements of both of those approved regulators. However, there are provisions for resolving any regulatory conflicts; see para 2.21 below.
2 Secondly, non-lawyers are subject to the regulatory arrangements of the approved regulator who authorises an entity they manage or work for, including any parts of the code of conduct and disciplinary procedures that are applicable to them. The regulatory reach of approved regulators therefore now extends to non-lawyers when they work in the specified capacity within the regulated field. There are provisions dealing with a situation where the non-lawyer is subject to the rules of another professional regulator outside the field of legal services; see para 2.21 below.

Section 176 gives statutory underpinning to the rules of approved regulators, creating a duty to comply with them which is free-standing and, as against managers and employees of entities, operates independently of whether or not an individual is a member of the relevant professional organisation. For example, a barrister will be able (once the necessary changes to the Bar's Code of Conduct are introduced)[5] to act as a manager or employee in a partnership authorised and regulated by the SRA[6], whilst continuing to hold a practising certificate from the Bar Standards Board. The barrister will be obliged to comply with the conduct rules of the SRA so far as they apply to managers of such entities and will likewise be subject to the SRA's disciplinary jurisdiction in relation to his conduct in that capacity, even though he does not hold a practising certificate from the SRA and is not a member of the Law Society[7]. The fact that approved regulators will be regulating individuals who are not their members and who have no stake or interest in the representative side of their operation makes it all the more critical that a rigorous separation is maintained between their regulatory and representative functions[8].

There is an elliptically worded provision in s 176(3) which adds that 'this section applies in relation to the Board in its capacity as a licensing authority and its licensing rules, as it applies in relation to an approved regulator and its regulatory arrangements.' This is presumably intended to impose a like duty on the part of licensed bodies and their managers and employees to comply with the LSB's licensing rules, but one would have thought this could have been more clearly expressed (and extended to other licensing authorities).

Section 188 applies to all advocates and litigators, when exercising rights of audience or to conduct litigation in their capacity as authorised persons, and imposes on them a duty to the court to act with independence in the interests of justice. That duty, together with their duty to comply with relevant conduct rules under s 176 (which, by virtue of subsections (4) and (5), for these purposes means the conduct rules of the approved regulator from whom they hold their rights of audience) overrides any other obligations they may have, other than under the criminal law, so far as inconsistent with them.

It would appear that the effect of s 188(4), (5) is that, for example, a barrister who continues to hold a practising certificate from the Bar Council will, when exercising right of audience as a manager or employee of an SRA regulated entity, remain subject to the Bar Code of Conduct as far as concerns the duties of a person exercising a right of audience, rather than any equivalent provisions in the SRA's Code of Conduct (and vice versa, should a solicitor-advocate become a manager or employee in a Bar Standards Board regulated entity)[9].

This could matter, because there are currently some significant differences between the SRA's rules for solicitor-advocates and the rules applicable to the Bar. For example, a barrister in a criminal case is currently prohibited from attending a suspect at a police station without a solicitor being present or, save in narrowly defined circumstances, from taking a proof[10]; whereas solicitor-advocates are expressly permitted to do both[11]. Another obvious distinction, currently, is the cab rank rule (para 602 of the Bar Code of Conduct) but it appears likely, following consultation[12], that this will in future apply only to the self-employed Bar and not to those working as managers or employees in regulated entities. Barristers working in the latter context would remain subject to an obligation not to discriminate (under para 601 of the Bar Code of Conduct) in comparable terms to that which applies to solicitors (under Principle 11.04). The Bar Standards Board is currently considering what other amendments to the Code of Conduct should be proposed and the SRA has already consulted on a variety of amendments. See, further, Chapters 4 and 12 below.

1 Section 176(2). See also s 21(3), (4), which define the meaning of 'regulated person', for the purpose of the regulatory arrangements of approved regulators, as including persons not authorised by the regulator in question but who are employees or managers of a person who is so authorised.
2 Section 176(1).
3 Section 176(2). As drafted, the section applies to such individuals even if they are not authorised persons at all. It is not clear this was intended. It may be that only s 90 was intended to apply to non-authorised persons acting as managers and employees (and then only when they are involved with ABSs). The wording of s 91(3), (4), where s 176 is treated as applying to authorised persons and s 90 to non-authorised persons, would tend to suggest this. However, the wording of ss 176(2) and 21(3) seem to point the other way.
4 See Chapter 4 for further details.
5 LDPs and Partnerships of Barristers are currently the subject of the Bar Standard's Board's Second Consultation Paper dated December 2008.
6 The partnership will need to include at least one solicitor before the SRA can regulate it. See further, Chapter 4.
7 The process is underway of revising the SRA's Code of Conduct so as to cater for the obligations of non-solicitor managers and employees of bodies recognised by the SRA under AJA 1985, ss 9 and 9A. For example, where the Code of Conduct refers to 'principals' of 'firms', this is being reworded to refer to 'managers' of 'recognised bodies'. Copies of the relevant consultation papers and drafts are available from the SRA's website at http://www.sra.org.uk/sra/legal-services-act/.
8 See para 2.11 above.
9 There is an oddity here; because s 52 would otherwise give overriding effect to the conduct rules of the SRA in the event they conflict with those of the Bar. It is not clear how the two are supposed to be reconciled in this situation.
10 Bar Code of Conduct, paras 401(b)(iii), (iv) and (v) and para 707.
11 Guidance to Principle 11 of the Solicitors Code of Conduct, at paras 18 and 27.
12 Bar Standards Board First Consultation Paper, dated February 2008, on the Legal Services Act 2007: 'Implications for the Regulation of the Bar in England and Wales', questions 2, 3, 4 and 5. The responses will no doubt in due course be published on the BSB's website at http://www.barstandardsboard.org.uk/consultations/.

Powers over non-authorised persons

2.20 As noted, one effect of LSA 2007, ss 90 and 176 is that an approved regulator will acquire a regulatory hold over any non-lawyers who become involved as managers or employees in an entity regulated by that approved regulator: such persons will have a duty under the LSA 2007 to comply with applicable rules of the entity regulator. Defining the obligations to be imposed on non-lawyer managers and employees, and enforcing those obligations by disciplinary proceedings against non-lawyers is, however, likely to require changes to the entity regulator's existing regulatory arrangements as few (if any) of the approved regulators currently purport to exercise any direct jurisdiction over non-lawyers[1]. Such changes will, in turn, require approval under the LSA 2007. For the licensing authority's powers in relation to those who hold an interest in an ABS see Chapter 4 below.

1 For example, to date, the Law Society's jurisdiction over non-solicitors has been limited to an essentially indirect form of jurisdiction. Under the Solicitor's Act 1974, s 43, if a non-solicitor has misconducted him or herself whilst employed or remunerated by a firm, the Law Society can prevent solicitors from involving that individual in a solicitor's practice in future. LSA 2007, Sch 16 extends the s 43 jurisdiction to cover misconduct by

managers and those with an interest in recognised bodies in connection with any recognised body and bolsters that indirect form of jurisdiction by adding the Solicitor's Act 1974, ss 34A–34B, which entitle the SRA to make those who are employees of solicitors directly subject to the Solicitors' Code of Conduct and Solicitors' Accounts Rules. Sch 16 also confers on the SRA and SDT disciplinary powers over employees, by the addition of ss 44D and 47(2E) to the Solicitors Act 1974.

Regulatory conflicts

2.21 As noted at para 2.19 above, where an individual lawyer authorised by one approved regulator works as a manager or employee within an entity engaged in providing reserved legal services and authorised by a different approved regulator, that lawyer will be subject to two sets of regulatory arrangements, including the rules of conduct and disciplinary arrangements of both approved regulators. The same will be true where a non-lawyer who is a member of another profession, and subject to regulation by that profession's regulator, acts as a manager or employee of an entity which is an authorised person under the LSA 2007.

The LSA 2007 therefore includes a number of provisions for resolving regulatory conflicts:

- Under s 52(1), approved regulators are obliged to make such provision as is reasonably practicable to prevent regulatory conflicts. This will no doubt include negotiating with one another over changes to their respective rules to remove such clashes.
- Under s 52(2) the rules of the entity regulator prevail in the event of a conflict between those rules and a requirement imposed on a manager or employee of an entity by their own, individual, approved regulator.
- An approved regulator who considers that another approved regulator has failed to make appropriate provision to prevent regulatory conflict can apply under s 53 for the LSB to make a direction ordering the offending approved regulator to modify its arrangements so as to remove the conflict. Affected persons can apply to approved regulators to get them to reconsider their own provisions for avoiding conflicts or to get them to institute proceedings under s 53 against another approved regulator.
- Approved regulators also have a duty under s 54 to make such provision as reasonably practicable to prevent regulatory conflicts with external regulators, or resolve any such conflicts as do arise, and to prevent unnecessary duplication. This may include providing for the LSB to intervene in some way with a view to resolving such conflicts.

It remains to be seen how the term 'regulatory conflict' will be interpreted. Clearly there will be a conflict where the code of conduct of an individual's professional regulator prohibits something which the entity regulator permits managers or employees to do, or vice versa. However, it is less clear whether there is a 'conflict' when the code of conduct of an individual's professional regulator imposes, for example, additional requirements or a more stringent standard than would apply if the matter were governed by the entity regulator's rules alone. No doubt much will depend on the specifics of any given case. Too broad an interpretation of s 52 might result in a dumbing-down of professional standards to the lowest common denominator.

Entity-based regulation

2.22 Clementi proposed that, as a consequence of permitting alternative business structures, regulation of legal services would have to shift towards entities:

> 'It will be evident that the proposals in this Chapter [ie the Chapter of the Clementi Report dealing with ABSs] shift the balance of regulation significantly towards regulation of the economic unit, beyond regulation of the individual practitioner. The proposed regulatory system focuses principally on who runs the practice and how. This is not intended to lessen the responsibility of each individual lawyer to meet the high standards to be expected of his profession. But it recognises the business reality that, in a practice of any size, the Regulator would be particularly interested in the competence of the senior Managers who ran the firm and the management systems they employed ... It follows that the prime focus of each recognised body, authorised to act as the front-line regulator of LDPs, would be upon the practice itself; and that it would be best if each lawyer Manager, irrespective of the branch of the legal profession he came from, were subject to the same recognised body as his lead Regulator ..."[1]

Under the LSA 2007, the entity will become the unit for regulation, in the sense that the entity itself must be authorised and (as a result of s 52)[2] the entity regulator's rules, including conduct rules for managers and employees, will predominate in any case where there is inconsistency with the rules of any other approved regulator from whom those individuals hold a practising certificate. Approved regulators will have to introduce new requirements applying specifically to those entities they regulate, as entities, as well as regulating the individuals who act as managers and employees within those entities in relation to their conduct as such. It is to be expected that these new rules will include provisions that are designed to minimise the risk of breaches by individuals operating within the entity (for example, obligations as regards systems and controls, allocation of responsibility, training, employment of unsuitable individuals, etc). There will therefore be a new, additional, element of regulation specifically applicable to the entity.

Note, however, that Clementi says 'beyond' regulation of the individual, not 'instead of', and that is significant. The LSA 2007 introduces entity regulation in parallel with, and not as a replacement for, regulation of individual lawyers. Once you permit lawyers who hold their practising certificates from different regulators to come together to work within a given entity, and all the more so once you permit them to join forces with non-lawyers, it is necessary (a) to regulate the entity and (b) to have a means of resolving any regulatory clashes between the regime applicable to the entity and other applicable regulatory regimes (including those of external regulators, such as the accountancy profession, whose members might become involved in such arrangements). Otherwise, the likelihood of unintended regulatory gaps or conflicts, and the lack of clarity as to who was responsible for regulating what, would create significant risks to the public and be a huge obstacle to realising Clementi's vision of liberalising the structures through which legal services can be delivered.

Entity-based regulation is therefore fundamental to the new forms of collaboration permitted by the LSA 2007, even though one nowhere finds that phrase used in the Act. It is brought about by the combination of ss 13–16 (the effect of which is that the entity as well as the lawyers within it must be authorised) and s 52 (which prioritises the regulatory arrangements of the entity regulator over any conflicting arrangements).

It does not, by any means, follow from any of this that when an individual employee or manager in an entity is in breach of a professional obligation in a code of conduct applicable to that individual, or causes the entity to be in breach of an obligation applicable to it, the default course of action should be to discipline the entity alone. We can certainly expect to see disciplinary proceedings brought against entities for breaches of obligations that specifically apply to the entity (and both the rules of conduct and the disciplinary procedures will need to be overhauled to permit this)[3] but, if the regulatory regime is to be effective, this approach needs to be carefully balanced against the need to maintain standards by taking action against individuals in appropriate cases. Individuals acting as managers and employees within regulated entities are subject to the entity regulator's code of conduct and disciplinary procedures (as well as those of their own individual regulator, if they are themselves authorised persons) and the fact this is so is a crucial bulwark of the professional principles in LSA 2007, s 1[4].

It is worth noting that, in the financial services sphere, the FSA (which operates a broadly analogous regime of regulating both businesses and individuals within them, with the entity as the primary unit of regulation)[5] has recently been emphasising its preparedness to take disciplinary action against individuals on the basis that research has shown this to be a more effective form of deterrence[6]. If the entity regulators under the LSA 2007 get the balance wrong and focus their disciplinary processes too much on entities, there will be a risk of phoenix firms flouting the regulatory process by the expedient of creating a new entity in order to escape the poor regulatory record of a predecessor (and the sanctions imposed on that predecessor). In circumstances where the entities themselves had no separate legal personality and there were no disciplinary findings against the individuals involved in them such practices might be difficult if not impossible to control.

Entity-based regulation is not without other inherent problems. Not all of the approved regulators currently have powers which enable them to regulate entities, as opposed to individuals. For example, the Bar Council's powers are rooted in the fact that an individual has been called to the Bar and is a member of an Inn of Court, and the Bar's code of conduct and disciplinary processes are currently limited to such individuals. Indeed, the only avenue of appeal from the Disciplinary Tribunal is to the Visitors of the Inns. In order to regulate entities (or individuals other than those called to the Bar), the Bar

Council would need to amend its constitution, rules of conduct and disciplinary procedures, and might need to seek additional powers under the provisions permitting the Lord Chancellor to modify the functions of approved regulators[7].

By way of contrast to the position in relation to the Bar Council, the Act provides for extensive changes to the Solicitors Act 1974 and the AJA 1985, which paved the way for the SRA to undertake entity regulation[8] and to regulate managers and employees of SRA-regulated entities who are not solicitors[9]. These include introducing a requirement that a solicitor who wishes to practise as a sole practitioner will have to obtain from the Law Society both a practising certificate and an endorsement of that certificate authorising him to practise as a sole solicitor, thus taking entity regulation down to the level of such individuals[10].

Moreover, the LSA 2007 requires entity regulators to regulate as entities types of association (partnerships and unincorporated associations) to which the general law does not ascribe separate legal personality. In recognition of this, the LSA 2007 does make specific provision for how such bodies are to be prosecuted in criminal proceedings, but in a civil context (including disciplinary proceedings) their lack of separate legal personality could potentially create problems.

Section 197 makes provision for dealing with any offences under the LSA 2007 that are committed by bodies corporate or unincorporated bodies. Where an offence is committed with the consent or connivance of, or is attributable to any neglect on the part of, an individual in a management position (ie an officer of a body corporate; member of a company governed by its members; partner; officer or member of the governing body in the case of an unincorporated body) that individual as well as the entity is liable for the offence. The section expressly provides that proceedings against unincorporated bodies are to be brought in the name of the body, served as if it were a corporation, and that the Criminal Justice Act 1933, s 33 and the Magistrates Courts Act 1980, Sch 3 are to apply. Any fine imposed on in unincorporated body on conviction of an offence is to be paid out of the funds of that body.

There is, however, no similar provision altering the position under the general law as to the civil liability of unincorporated bodies or attribution of knowledge to such bodies or how disciplinary proceedings against such bodies are to be served. No doubt approved regulators may seek to provide for these matters in their rules for entities they authorise, but if, for example, an unincorporated body refused to pay a fine imposed upon it, any proceedings to enforce that penalty would have to be brought in accordance with existing rules of court, as they apply to partnerships or unincorporated associations.

Finally, it is questionable whether there is a value in entity regulation in the case of an entity without its own legal personality and made up entirely of lawyers who are all individually subject to the rules of one and the same approved regulator.

Chapter 3

THE LSB'S ROLE IN THE REGULATORY FRAMEWORK

Patricia Robertson QC and Katherine Watt

OVERSIGHT OF APPROVED REGULATORS

3.1 The LSB's principal role under the LSA 2007 is the oversight of approved regulators[1] – that is, to 'regulate the regulators' by setting out (following consultation) rules and requirements with which approved regulators must comply[2], providing guidance, overseeing the functioning of individual approved regulators and the system of approved regulators as a whole, and, if necessary, taking enforcement action in respect of any approved regulator who falls short of the requirements and standards expected. Particular aspects of the LSB's role in this regard are described below.

1 This is expressly stated in s 49(3).
2 Note that save in relation to rules made by the LSB for the purposes of Sch 1, para 21, in its capacity as an approved regulator or a licensing authority, or under ss 37(4), 95(3) or 173, if the LSB proposes to make or modify any rules, it must publish a draft of the proposed rules or modified rules, allow an opportunity to interested persons to make representations, and have regard to any representations duly made. If the rules differ materially from the draft, the LSB must publish details of the differences. The LSB must also publish the rules actually made; see s 205.

Designation and modification of functions of approved regulators

3.2 The designation of bodies as approved regulators, and modification of or making of provisions as to the functions of approved regulators, are matters which can be effected only by order of the Lord Chancellor[1]. However, the Lord Chancellor may only make such orders on recommendation by the LSB[2]. The LSB thus plays a central role in the process by which would-be and/or existing approved regulators may obtain or lose designation as such or make other changes to their functions. It may exercise this role both at the instigation of (or with the agreement of) the body in respect of whom the order is recommended[3], and by way of enforcement action against an approved regulator[4].

So far as concerns designation of an approved regulator or changes to functions of an approved regulator, the LSB may make a recommendation to the Lord Chancellor to that effect only if the order is with a view to enabling the relevant body:

- to become designated as an approved regulator in relation to one or more reserved legal activities;
- to authorise persons to carry on reserved legal activities in relation to which it is an approved regulator, or to make regulatory arrangements;
- to carry out its role as an approved regulator more effectively or efficiently;
- to become a qualifying regulator in relation to the provision of immigration advice or services[5]; and/or
- if it is a designated qualifying regulator under the Immigration and Asylum Act 1999, s 86A, to authorise persons to provide any additional advice or services amounting to immigration advice or services[6].

The LSB must first publish its draft proposed recommendation and order, allow an opportunity for interested persons to make representations, and consider any representations made. The LSB must also publish any changes made to the draft proposed order and reasons for the changes before making the recommendation[7].

The LSB's role in relation to designation of bodies as approved regulators is set out in detail in Sch 4 of the Act. A body wishing to become an approved regulator in relation to one or more legal activities first applies to the LSB for the LSB to recommend to the Lord Chancellor the body's designation as such and to approve what the body proposes as its regulatory arrangements if such an order is made[8]. Before determining the application, the LSB takes advice from the OFT, the Consumer Panel, the Lord Chief Justice and such other persons as it considers reasonable to consult, which advice is provided to the applicant, and the LSB considers any representations the applicant may wish to make following receipt of that advice[9]. The LSB also publishes the advice and representations received[10]. The LSB is responsible for determining the application process to be followed by would-be approved regulators, and the procedures and criteria that it will itself apply when determining whether to refuse to consider, refuse to continue its consideration of, or grant, an application, subject to the requirement that its rules cover certain matters specified in the Act[11]. In particular, the LSB's rules must provide that it may grant an application in relation to a reserved legal activity only if it is satisfied that if the Lord Chancellor were to order designation of the applicant as an approved regulator in relation to that activity:

- the applicant would have appropriate internal governance rules in place at the time the order takes effect[12];
- the application would be competent, and have sufficient resources, to perform the role of approved regulator in relation to the reserved legal activity at that time[13];
- the applicant's proposed regulatory arrangements are appropriate to avoid regulatory conflict[14], require authorised persons to establish and maintain appropriate complaints procedures and to provide all reasonable assistance in relation to complaints under the ombudsman scheme[15], and make appropriate provision generally, including for separation of representative and regulatory functions[16].

The LSB must publish its recommendation or, if the application is not granted, a notice to that effect and the reasons for its decision.

So far as cancellation of a body's designation as an approved regulator is concerned, the LSB must recommend cancellation of an approved regulator's designation as such if the approved regulator applies for such recommendation (and publishes details of the application) in accordance with rules made by the LSB[17], and the LSB also has a discretionary power to recommend cancellation by way of enforcement action[18] (as discussed in para 3.13 below). In either case, the LSB may also recommend transfer arrangements for putting in place replacement regulatory arrangements for persons authorised by the former regulator and dealing with practising fees[19]. The LSB also has power to apply to the Court for a search order and to take possession of the former regulator's records[20].

1 Sections 45(1) and 69(1).
2 Sections 45(2) and 69(2).
3 Under Sch 4, paras 3 and 19.
4 Under Sch 8, para 1.
5 As to which, see Sch 18.
6 Section 69(3). Recommendations for a modification of functions under s 69 can only be made with the consent of the approved regulator: s 70(1).
7 Section 70.
8 Schedule 4, Pt 2, para 3.
9 Schedule 4, Pt 2, paras 5–9, 11.
10 Schedule 4, Pt 2, para 12.
11 Schedule 4, Pt 2, paras 3–4, 7, 14. The LSB has a period of 12 months from the date on which the application is made, subject to extensions if necessary of up to a total further four months, in which to decide whether to grant an application.
12 Schedule 4, para 13(2)(a). See para 3.3 below.
13 Schedule 4, para 13(2)(b).
14 That is, comply with the requirements imposed by ss 52 and 54: Sch 4, para 13(2)(d).
15 That is, comply with the requirements imposed by ss 112 and 145: Sch 4, para 13(2)(e).
16 Schedule 4, Pt 2, paras 13(2)(c) and 13(3).
17 Section 45(3).
18 Section 45(5).
19 Sections 46 and 47.
20 Section 48.

Overseeing the regulatory functions of approved regulators and ensuring the independence and effectiveness of those functions

3.3 An important theme in the LSA 2007 is the separation between the regulation of authorised persons on the one hand and their representation within the regulatory framework on the other. The LSB is responsible both for overseeing the exercise by approved regulators of their regulatory functions, and also for ensuring that the separation of those functions from representative functions is maintained effectively. In contrast, the LSB is excluded from interfering with the exercise by approved regulators of representative functions, save insofar as necessary for the purposes of ensuring effective separation of regulatory and representative functions[1].

To this end, the LSB is responsible for developing internal governance rules setting out requirements to be met by approved regulators for the purpose of ensuring two key principles: first, that the exercise of an approved regulator's regulatory functions is not prejudiced by its representative functions, and second, that decisions relating to the exercise of an approved regulator's regulatory functions are so far as reasonably practicable taken independently from those relating to exercise of its representative functions (together 'the regulatory independence principles'). The internal governance rules must require approved regulators to have in place arrangements which:

- ensure that the persons involved in the exercise of its regulatory functions are in that capacity able to make representations to, be consulted by and communicate with the LSB, the Consumer Panel, the OLC and other approved regulators;
- ensure that the exercise by those persons of those powers is not prejudiced by the approved regulator's representative functions and is, so far as reasonably practicable, independent from the exercise of those functions;
- ensure that the approved regulator provides such resources as are reasonably required for or in connection with the exercise of its regulatory functions; and
- enable persons involved in the exercise of the approved regulator's regulatory functions to be able to notify the LSB where they consider that their independence or effectiveness is being prejudiced[2].

The LSB may also specify requirements with which the regulatory arrangements of approved regulators must comply as regards a number of specified matters:

- Requiring authorised persons regulated by the relevant approved regulator to establish and maintain procedures for the resolution of relevant complaints (or be subject to such procedures established and maintained by another person), and for enforcement of the latter requirement by the relevant approved regulator[3];
- Providing for the relevant approved regulator to disclose particular information to the OLC, an ombudsman or a member of the OLC's staff[4];
- Requiring authorised persons regulated by the relevant approved regulator to give ombudsmen all such assistance requested by them[5].

More generally, the LSB has control over the regulatory arrangements made by approved regulators because they may not, except in certain specified circumstances, alter their regulatory arrangements without its approval[6]. The procedure to be followed where an approved regulator wishes to obtain such approval and the constraints on the LSB's power to refuse any such application, are set out in Sch 4, Pt 3, paras 20–27. An approved regulator whose arrangements are found to contravene the regulatory objectives will be liable to disciplinary sanctions (see below).

So far as the LSB's wider oversight role is concerned, the Act makes express provision for the LSB to provide assistance in maintaining and developing professional and regulatory standards in relation to reserved legal activities and persons authorised to carry on those activities. In particular, the LSB has a duty to assist in maintaining and developing standards in relation to the regulation by approved regulators of persons authorised by them to carry on reserved legal activities ('authorised persons'), and the education and training of such persons[7]. The LSB may also give guidance on any matters about which it appears desirable to the LSB to give guidance[8]. In particular, the LSB may give guidance about the operation of the Act and any order made under it; about the operation of any rules made by the LSB under the Act, about any matter relating to the LSB's functions; for the purpose of meeting the regulatory objectives; or about the content of licensing rules[9]. The guidance may consist of such information and advice as the LSB considers appropriate[10]. The LSB may publish its guidance, and may charge for its guidance[11]. It may give financial or other assistance to other persons providing information or advice of a kind the LSB could itself give under these provisions[12]. When exercising its functions, the LSB may have regard to the extent to which an approved regulator has complied with any applicable guidance issued[13].

In addition to giving general guidance, the LSB may enter into arrangements with any person under which the LSB will provide assistance for improving standards of service and promoting best practice in connection with the carrying on of any legal activity, including as to best regulatory practice or the contents of codes of practice or other voluntary arrangements, on such terms as the LSB wishes. However, the LSB must publish a statement giving details of the arrangements and explaining what they are intended to achieve[14].

A key element of the LSB's oversight role is its responsibility for ensuring that approved regulators do not act (or fail to act) in a way that would or might have an adverse impact on the regulatory objectives, that they comply with the requirements imposed on them by or under the Act or any other enactment, and that they meet the two regulatory independence objectives. The powers available to the LSB for the purpose of carrying out this function are described in paras 3.8–3.15 below. The LSB must issue a statement of policy with respect to the exercise of those powers[15], to which it must have regard when exercising its functions[16]. In preparing the policy, the LSB must have regard to:

- the principle that its principal role is the oversight of approved regulators;
- the principle that the LSB should not exercise any of the functions to which it relates by reason of the act or omission of an approved regulator unless the act or omission was unreasonable;
- the desirability of resolving informally matters which arise between the LSB and an approved regulator, and

must also specify how, in exercising the functions to which it relates, the LSB will comply with its duty to have regard to the principles under which regulatory activities should be transparent, accountable, proportionate, consistent and targeted only at cases in which action is needed[17].

Before issuing any policy statement (or alteration or replacement thereof), the LSB must first publish a draft of the proposed statement, allow interested persons an opportunity to make representations, and consider any representations made[18]. If the statement differs materially from the published draft, the LSB must publish details of the differences[19].

The LSB may also issue a statement of policy in respect of any other matter[20]. Again, the LSB must permit and consider representations, and must have regard to the principle that its principal role is the oversight of approved regulators[21].

1 Section 29.
2 Section 30.
3 Section 112.
4 Section 144(2), (3).
5 Section 145(2).
6 Schedule 4, Pt 3, para 19.
7 Section 4.
8 Section 162(1).
9 Section 162(1).
10 Section 162(2).
11 Section 162(4).
12 Section 162(3).
13 Section 162(5).
14 Section 163.
15 Section 49(1) requires this statement of policy to cover the LSB's exercise of its functions under s 31 (performance targets and monitoring), s 32 (directions), s 35 (public censure), s 37 (financial penalties), s 41 (intervention directions), s 45 (cancellation of designation as approved regulator), and s 76 (cancellation of designation as licensing authority by order), as to which see, further, paras 3.8–3.15 below.
16 Section 49(8).
17 Section 49(3)–(4).
18 Section 50.
19 Section 50(4).
20 Section 49(2).
21 Sections 49(2)–(3) and 50.

Conflict between approved regulators

3.4 The LSB plays an important role in managing and resolving actual or perceived regulatory conflict. An approved regulator ('the applicant regulator') which considers that the regulatory arrangements of another approved regulator ('the conflicting regulator') do not make appropriate provision to prevent a regulatory conflict with the applicant regulator, may apply to the LSB for it to exercise its powers under s 32 to direct the conflicting regulator to take steps to modify its existing provisions or, if it does not have any provisions to prevent regulatory conflict, to make such provisions as the LSB may specify. The LSB will consider representations by both regulators and may consult any other persons it considers appropriate; it will then decide whether or not to give a warning notice in response to the application with a view to exercising its powers to give directions under s 32[1]. The LSB is also required to consider requests and/or applications arising out of regulatory conflict between an approved regulator and the LSB itself, acting in its capacity as an approved regulator[2]. In addition to exercising its powers in response to an application under s 53, the LSB can take action of its own motion if it considers that an approved regulator has failed to comply with its obligation, under s 52, to make such provision as is reasonably practicable to prevent regulatory conflicts[3]. The LSB may also exercise such functions in connection with the resolution of conflicts between approved regulators and external regulators as may be specified, with the LSB's consent, in the regulatory arrangements of an approved regulator[4].

[1] Section 53. The LSB must make its decision within six months of receipt of the application. The LSB's powers under s 32 are discussed in para 3.10 below.
[2] Section 68.
[3] Sections 52 and 32(b).
[4] Section 54(4).

Competition issues arising from regulatory arrangements

3.5 Although primary responsibility for investigating competition issues in relation to approved regulators lies with the OFT[1], the LSB also has a role to play in this regard. The LSB is required to consider any report made by the OFT to the effect that the regulatory arrangements of an approved regulator prevent, restrict or distort competition with the market for reserved legal services to any significant extent (or are likely to do so). The LSB will allow the approved regulator at least 28 days to make representations to the LSB about the report, and may receive advice from the Consumer Panel; it will then notify the OFT of the action (if any) it proposes to take in response to the report[2]. If the OFT considers that the LSB has failed to give full and proper consideration to a report, the OFT may, on notice to the LSB, send the report to the Lord Chancellor, who will seek advice from the Competition Commission and may then direct the LSB to take such action as the Lord Chancellor considers appropriate[3].

[1] Under s 57.
[2] Section 58.
[3] Sections 59–61.

Control over approved regulators acting as licensing authorities

3.6 The LSB exercises similar functions, subject to similar requirements and constraints, in relation to the designation of approved regulators as licensing authorities and cancellation of their designation as such. The detailed provisions are set out in ss 73–79 and Sch 10.

The LSB exercises final control over statements of policy issued by licensing authorities as to how, in exercising their functions as such, they will comply with their obligation to promote the regulatory objectives and have regard to the regulatory principles[1]. It must also make rules (subject to the Lord Chancellor's approval) prescribing the maximum amount of financial penalty that a licensing authority may impose on licensed bodies (or their managers or employees) under the licensing authority's own rules[2]. Further, the LSB is required to keep lists of persons who are disqualified by a licensed authority from acting as Head of Legal Practice, acting as Head of Finance and Administration, being a manager, or being employed, of or by any licensed body[3], of non-authorised persons in respect of whom a licensing authority has objected to or imposed conditions on the person's holding of a restricted interest in a licensable body, and of non-authorised persons in respect of whom a licensing authority provides notification to the LSB of that person's acquisition of a degree of control over a licensed body which exceeds what is permitted under the Act[4].

[1] Such statements can only be issued with the approval of the LSB: s 82(2).
[2] Section 95.
[3] Section 100.
[4] Schedule 13, Pt 5, paras 47(1), 49(2) and 51.

ENFORCEMENT BY THE LSB

3.7 The LSB has extensive and draconian powers to force approved regulators and licensing authorities to comply with their obligations under the LSA 2007, where necessary.

Powers in relation to the regulatory objectives

3.8 If the LSB is satisfied that an act or omission by an approved regulator (or series of the same) has had or is likely to have an adverse impact on one or more of the regulatory objectives, it can exercise a wide range of remedial, preventative and punitive powers over the approved regulator, provided in each case that it is satisfied that the action it intends to take under that power is appropriate in all the circumstances (including in particular the impact that taking the proposed action will have on the other regulatory objectives).

Performance targets: s 31

3.9 In such a case, the LSB may set performance targets relating to the performance by the approved regulator of its regulatory functions, or direct the approved regulator itself to set performance targets and specify conditions with which those targets must conform, and take such steps as it thinks fit to monitor compliance by the approved regulator.

Before setting performance targets, the LSB must give notice to the approved regulator of the proposed action and reasons for it, allow the approved regulator an opportunity to make representations, and consider those representations[1]. The LSB must publish any target set or direction given[2].

[1] Section 31(4).
[2] Section 31(9).

Directions: s 32

3.10 The LSB may direct the approved regulator to take such steps as the LSB considers will respectively counter, remedy, mitigate or prevent the occurrence or recurrence of the act or omission adversely affecting the regulatory objectives[1]. The LSB may take such steps as it thinks fit to monitor compliance by the approved regulator[2]. In giving a direction, the LSB may require an approved regulator to take steps with a view to modifying any part of its regulatory arrangements, or to refrain from taking a particular course of action, but may not give a direction requiring an approved regulator to take steps in respect of a specific disciplinary case or specific regulatory proceedings (as opposed to all, or a specified class of, such cases or proceedings).

Before giving directions, the LSB must give a warning notice together with the proposed direction to the approved regulator and allow the approved regulator an opportunity to make representations. The LSB must then take advice from the OFT, the Consumer Panel, the Lord Chief Justice and such other persons as it considers reasonable to consult, which advice is provided to the applicant, and must consider any further representations the applicant may wish to make following receipt of that advice. The LSB must publish its decision whether to give the approved regulator the proposed direction[3].

If at any time the LSB considers that an approved regulator has failed to comply with a direction given under s 32, the LSB may apply to the High Court under s 34, and the High Court may order the approved regulator to take such steps as the High Court directs for securing that the direction is complied with. The LSB may also impose financial penalties (discussed in para 3.15 below).

If the LSB revokes a direction made, it must give notice to the approved regulator and publish the notice[4].

1 Section 32(1) and (2).
2 Section 32(8).
3 The procedure that the LSB must follow is set out in detail in Sch 7, Pt 1 (s 33).
4 Section 32(9).

Censure: s 35

3.11 The LSB may, when satisfied it is appropriate, publish a statement censuring the approved regulator for an act or omission (or series of the same) which have had or are likely to have an adverse impact on any of the regulatory objectives.

The LSB must first give notice of the terms of and reasons for the proposed statement to the approved regulator, allow the approved regulator an opportunity to make representations, and consider any representations made[1]. The LSB must also give notice of and allow and consider representations in relation to any variation of a proposed statement[2].

1 Section 36(1), (2).
2 Section 36(3), (4).

Intervention: s 41

3.12 The LSB may, under s 41, give the approved regulator an intervention direction in relation to any of the approved regulator's regulatory functions – that is, a direction that the relevant regulatory function is to be exercised by the LSB or a person nominated by it[1], and that the approved regulator must comply with any instructions of the LSB or its nominee in relation to the exercise of the function. However, before doing so, the LSB must be satisfied that the matter cannot be adequately addressed by exercising its powers under ss 31–40.

Before giving an intervention direction, the LSB must follow a similar notice and consultation procedure as that required in relation to the giving of directions under s 32[2].

Where an intervention direction has effect in respect of a function of an approved regulator, the LSB is entitled to receive all reasonable assistance from the approved regulator in exercising the relevant function[3], and also has two further powers available to it with a view to exercising the relevant function effectively.

First, the LSB or person nominated by it in the intervention direction, or a person acting on behalf of the same, may apply to the High Court, a Circuit judge or justice of the peace for a warrant to enter and search the premises of the approved regulator and take possession of any written or electronic records found, and, if granted, may (for the purpose of exercising the relevant function) copy any written or electronic records found[4]. However, the judge or justice of the peace may only issue a warrant if satisfied that its issue is necessary or desirable for exercise by the LSB or its nominee of the relevant function, and may only do so in accordance with any other regulations as to the further requirements or factors material to the issue of a warrant, and terms upon which powers conferred by a warrant may be exercised, as may be made by the Lord Chancellor on the recommendation of or in consultation with the LSB[5].

Second, if the LSB considers that an approved regulator has failed to comply with an obligation imposed on it by or by virtue of an intervention direction or with the regulator's obligation to provide the LSB or its nominee with all reasonable assistance in exercising the relevant function, the LSB may apply to the High Court. The High Court may order the approved regulator to take such steps as the High Court directs for securing that the obligation is complied with[6].

An intervention direction has effect until it is revoked by the LSB[7]. When considering any application by an approved regulator for revocation of an intervention direction, the LSB must take advice and allow the approved regulator an opportunity to make representations before making its decision[8].

1 The LSB must make rules as to the persons it may nominate for the purposes of an intervention direction (s 41(5)).
2 The procedure that the LSB must follow is set out in detail in Sch 8. The procedure in relation to directions under s 32 is summarised in para 3.10 above.
3 Section 42(2).
4 Section 42(3), (4).
5 Section 42(5), (6).
6 Section 43.
7 Section 44.
8 The procedure that the LSB must follow is set out in detail in Sch 8, Pt 2.

Cancellation of designation as an approved regulator and/or licensing authority: ss 45 and 76

3.13 As a last resort, the LSB may recommend to the Lord Chancellor that he cancel a body's designation as an approved regulator (under s 45) and/or as a licensing authority (under s 76) in relation to one or more reserved legal activities[1]. Before doing so, the LSB must be satisfied that the matter cannot be adequately addressed by exercising its powers under ss 31–40 and ss 31–43 respectively, and must follow a similar notice and consultation procedure to that required in relation to the giving of directions or an intervention direction[2].

If the Lord Chancellor decides not to make a cancellation order as recommended by the LSB, the Lord Chancellor must give the LSB notice of the decision and reasons for it and must publish the notice[3].

The LSB may also make recommendations to the Lord Chancellor as to the terms of an order making transitional or consequential provisions and/or transfer arrangements, pursuant to which authorised persons regulated by the relevant body are by consent treated as being authorised by another approved regulator who consents to the transfer arrangements, or by the LSB acting in its capacity as a relevant approved regulator by virtue of an order made under s 62[4]. There is a power in the same terms in relation to licensing bodies whose designation has been cancelled[5]. Transfer arrangements must make provision for the relevant authorised persons to be subject to the regulatory arrangements of the new regulator, subject to any appropriate transitional provisions, and may also provide for amounts paid to the former regulator by way of practising fees to be paid to the new regulator. The LSB must first publish its proposed draft recommendations and draft order, allow an opportunity for interested persons to make representations, and consider any representations made. In the event of material changes to the proposed draft order, the LSB must also publish the revised draft order with a statement detailing the changes made and reasons for them[6].

Where a body has its designation as an approved regulator in relation to one or more reserved legal activities cancelled, the LSB may request the former regulator to provide assistance to the new regulator and the LSB for the purpose of continuing regulation[7]. The LSB may also appoint a person to act on its behalf in applying for a warrant to enter and search the premises of the former regulator and take possession of any written or electronic records found, subject to similar restrictions as are set out in para 3.12 above[8]. Again, there are like provisions where designation as a licensing authority is cancelled[9].

1 The procedure that the LSB must follow in relation to cancellation of designation as an approved regulator is set out in Sch 9 and, in relation to cancellation of designation as a licensing authority, in Sch 10, Pt 2. Note that cancellation of designation as a licensing authority follows automatically in the event of cancellation of designation as an approved regulator (s 75). However, the LSB may not exercise its discretionary power to recommend a cancellation order in respect of an approved regulator during a transitional period under Sch 5, Pt 2 (s 45(10)).

2 Sch 9; Sch 10, Pt 2. The procedure in relation to directions and intervention directions is discussed in paras 3.10 and 3.12 above.
3 Sections 45(8)–(9) and 77(8)–(9).
4 Sections 46–47. As to s 62, see para 3.24 below.
5 Sections 76–77.
6 Sections 47 and 77.
7 Section 48(2).
8 Section 48(3).
9 Section 79.

Powers in respect of failure to comply with other rules and requirements

Directions: s 32

3.14 The LSB may also exercise its power to give directions under s 32 if it is satisfied that an approved regulator has failed to comply with any requirement imposed on it by or under the LSA 2007 or any other enactment[1], or that an approved regulator has failed to ensure the two regulatory independence requirements[2].

1 Section 32(b).
2 Section 32(c).

Financial penalties: s 37

3.15 Further, if the LSB is satisfied that an approved regulator has failed to comply with any requirement imposed by rules under s 30 (internal governance rules), or by a direction given (for whatever reason) under s 32, or by or as a result of rules under s 51 (control of practising fees charged by approved regulators), the LSB may impose financial penalties on the approved regulator. The penalty must not exceed the maximum amount prescribed under rules made by the LSB with the consent of the Lord Chancellor[1].

Before imposing a financial penalty (or varying a proposed financial penalty), the LSB must give notice to the approved regulator of the proposed penalty and reasons for it, allow the approved regulator an opportunity to make representations, and consider any representations made[2]. As soon as practicable after imposing a penalty, the LSB must give notice to the approved regulator of the penalty, its amount, the reasons for the penalty, and the time by which it is to be paid[3]. The LSB must publish any notice given under s 38[4].

The approved regulator is entitled to challenge the time for payment of a penalty by way of application to the LSB, and the imposition, amount or time for payment of a penalty by way of appeal to the High Court[5]. The approved regulator is not required to pay the penalty pending the determination or withdrawal of any such application or appeal[6].

Penalties carry interest at the judgments rate[7] specified from time to time in the Judgments Act 1938, s 17, and are recoverable by the LSB from the approved regulator as a debt[8].

1 Section 37(3)–(5).

2 Section 38(1)–(4).
3 Section 38(5).
4 Section 38(8).
5 Sections 38(6) and 39.
6 Sections 38(6) and 40(2).
7 Ie the rate specified from time to time in the Judgments Act 1938, s 17.
8 Section 40.

Powers to obtain or disclose information

Obtaining information or documents: s 55

3.16 The LSB may, by notice, require an approved regulator (or a body which was, but is no longer, an approved regulator) to provide any information or documents (or information or documents of a description) in a manner and form, and within a period of time, to the LSB or a given person, as specified in the notice. The LSB may also require a person representing the approved regulator to attend at a time and place specified in the notice to provide an explanation of any information provided or document produced[1].

If an approved regulator is unable to comply with the notice, it must give the LSB a notice to that effect stating why it cannot comply. If an approved regulator, or person required to attend, refuses or fails to comply with a s 55 notice, the LSB may apply to the High Court for an order requiring the approved regulator to do so[2].

1 Section 55. The LSB may pay to any person reasonable costs incurred by that person in complying with the provision of, or attendance to explain, information or documents.
2 Section 56.

Disclosing information

3.17 The LSB's powers to disclose information obtained by it in the exercise of its functions (whether under s 55 or otherwise) are circumscribed by the provisions of s 167; in particular, the LSB may disclose such information only if it is in the form of a summary or collection of information so framed as not to enable information relating to any particular person to be ascertained by it, information which is already available to the public from other sources, and information obtained more than 70 years before the date of the disclosure, or if it is to specified persons or for the specified purposes set out in ss 168 and 169 (which, broadly, relate to disclosures to or by others with regulatory responsibilities).

ALTERATIONS TO THE SCOPE OF REGULATION

3.18 The LSB's role includes considering, if appropriate, the merits of any amendment to the scope of the regulatory regime.

The LSB is responsible for holding investigations into whether a given legal activity should be made a reserved legal activity and, conversely, whether a particular reserved legal activity should cease to be such[1]. The LSB must consider whether to hold such an investigation if requested to do so by the Lord Chancellor, OFT, Consumer Panel or Lord Chief Justice, and may do so if requested by any other person or if it considers it appropriate to do so[2]. Before deciding whether to hold an investigation, the LSB may seek advice from the OFT, Consumer Panel and/or Lord Chief Justice, and may only refuse a request it is required to consider if it has taken such advice and the Lord Chancellor consents to that decision (unless the request was made by the Lord Chancellor)[3]. If the LSB decides to investigate, it must produce a provisional report, allow an opportunity for and consider written and oral representations by affected practitioners and any other parties permitted under rules made by the LSB, and produce a final report setting out its decision on whether to make the relevant recommendation and reasons for that decision[4].

The LSB is also responsible for making recommendations to the Lord Chancellor as to orders adding to, amending or removing the categories of exempt persons specified in Sch 3[5].

1 Sections 24, 26; Sch 6.
2 Schedule 6, paras 3–4.
3 Schedule 6, paras 5, 6 and 8.
4 Schedule 6, paras 9–17.
5 Schedule 3, para 9.

FUNDING OF THE REGULATORY FRAMEWORK

3.19 The LSB plays an important role in relation to the funding of the regulatory system, both in relation to the levy imposed on approved regulators by the LSB and practising fees imposed by approved regulators on authorised persons, and in terms of overseeing the costs of the regulatory system more generally.

First, under s 173, the LSB is responsible for making rules (subject to the consent of the Lord Chancellor) providing for the imposition of a levy on approved regulators, the regulator in relation to claims management services[1] or any other person prescribed by the Lord Chancellor by order. The purpose of the levy is to fund the expenditure of the LSB, the OLC and the Lord Chancellor, save insofar as that expenditure is already covered by sums received by the LSB and OLC for specific purposes and paid into the Consolidated Fund (such as application fees and financial penalties) [2]. The LSB must be satisfied that the apportionment of the levy as between the different bodies by whom it is payable will be in accordance with fair principles[3]. The LSB is also responsible for collecting payment of the levy, which is payable to the LSB[4] and recoverable as a debt due to the LSB[5].

Second, the LSB exercises final control over the levying and use of practising fees payable by authorised persons to approved regulators.

Practising fees are only payable by authorised persons under the regulatory arrangements of an approved regulator if the LSB has approved the level of the fee[6]. The LSB is responsible for establishing the requirements and application process that approved regulators must follow in order to obtain approval of their practising fees, and the procedures and criteria by which the LSB will determine applications for approval[7]. The LSB's role in this regard includes ensuring that the amount of fees is not set without adequate prior consultation, particularly in relation to the impact on non-commercial legal services. In particular, the LSB must make rules as to the persons with whom approved regulators must consult before applying for approval[8], and must itself consult with such persons as it considers appropriate about the impact of the proposed fee on persons providing non-commercial legal services before determining any application for approval[9].

The LSB is also responsible for making rules specifying the purposes for which amounts raised by practising fees may be applied by an approved regulator[10]. The permitted purposes must include six matters in particular, namely:

- the regulation, accreditation, education and training of relevant authorised persons and those wishing to become such persons, including the maintaining and raising of their professional standards and the giving of practical support and advice about practice management;
- the payment of a levy imposed on the approved regulator under s 173;
- the participation by the approved regulator in law reform and the legislative process;
- the provision by relevant authorised persons and those wishing to become such persons of reserved legal services, immigration advice or immigration services to the public free of charge;
- the promotion of the protection by law of human rights and fundamental freedoms; and
- the promotion of relations between the approved regulator and relevant national and international bodies, governments or the legal professions of other jurisdictions[11].

Finally, the LSB exercises ultimate control over the funding of the OLC and Solicitors Disciplinary Tribunal (SDT): it is responsible for approving the annual budgets of both bodies[12]; and for authorising any borrowing by the OLC (subject to the consent of the Lord Chancellor)[13].

1 Under the Compensation Act 2006, s 5(1).
2 Sections 173(6)–(10) and 175. Note that the Lord Chancellor may pay to the LSB and/or the OLC such sums as he considers appropriate (s 172).
3 Section 173(3).
4 Section 173(2).
5 Section 174(5).
6 Section 51(5).
7 Section 51(6)–(7).
8 Section 51(6)(b).
9 Section 51(7)(a).
10 Section 51(3).
11 Section 51(2)–(4).
12 Schedule 15, para 23; Sch 16, Pt 1, para 48.
13 Schedule 15, para 25.

FUNCTIONING OF THE REGULATORY FRAMEWORK

3.20 The LSB has four further responsibilities in relation to the functioning of the regulatory system as a whole: to establish and maintain the Consumer

Panel (see para 3.21 below); to establish and oversee the OLC and provide input in relation to the system for the resolution of complaints about legal services (see para 3.22 below); to exercise control over the rules and functions of certain tribunals (see para 3.23 below); and to act itself as an approved regulator and/or licensing authority, if necessary, in certain limited circumstances (see para 3.24 below).

Establishing and maintaining the Consumer Panel

3.21 The LSB's role includes establishing and maintaining a Consumer Panel to represent the interests of consumers[1]. Specifically, the LSB is responsible for appointing consumers, or persons to represent the interests of consumers, to the Consumer Panel, subject to the approval of the Lord Chancellor, and for then appointing one of the members of the Consumer Panel to be its chairman[2]. In appointing the Panel, the LSB must secure that its membership is such as to give a fair degree of representation both to those who use or may use the services of authorised persons in connection with businesses carried on by them, and those who do or may do so otherwise than in such capacity[3]. The LSB determines the terms and conditions upon which appointments to the Panel are held by its members, but may not remove a member of the Panel in accordance with those terms and conditions except with the approval of the Lord Chancellor. The LSB also determines and is responsible for the remuneration of both members of the Consumer Panel and members of any committees established by the Panel (who are not also members of the Panel itself) [4]. However, the LSB's role does not extend to determining how the Consumer Panel actually operates internally; that is a matter for the Consumer Panel itself to decide[5].

The LSB must consider any representations made by it to the Consumer Panel and, if the LSB disagrees with any views or proposals made in such representations, it must give the Consumer Panel a notice explaining the LSB's reasons for disagreeing[6]. The LSB must publish the notice if the Consumer Panel published information about the representations to which the notice relates[7]. If the LSB requests the Consumer Panel to carry out any research for or give advice to the LSB, the LSB must consider the research results or advice given[8].

1 Section 8.
2 Section 8(2)–(3). In making appointments, the LSB cannot appoint anyone who is a member or employee of the LSB, the Office for Legal Complaints, an ombudsman appointed by the OLC or an approved regulator, an authorised person, or an advocate or solicitor in Scotland or Northern Ireland (s 8(5)).
3 Section 8(4).
4 Sections 8(6)–(7) and 9(6).
5 Section 9.
6 Section 10.
7 Section 10(4).
8 Section 11.

Complaints about legal services

3.22 The LSB is responsible for appointing the chairman of the OLC (subject to approval by the Lord Chancellor) and between six and eight other persons to be members of the OLC (after consultation with the chairman of the OLC) [1]. The LSB must ensure that the chairman and a majority of the members of the OLC are lay persons, and are not ombudsmen[2], and in appointing members of the OLC, the LSB must have regard to the desirability of securing that the OLC includes members who (between them) have experience in or knowledge of the handling of complaints, the provision of legal services, legal education and legal training, consumer affairs, civil or criminal proceedings and the working of the courts, the maintenance of the professional standards of persons who provide legal services, non-commercial legal services, the differing needs of consumers, and the provision of claims management services[3]. The LSB has power to remove members of the OLC (in the case of the chairman, subject to the consent of the Lord Chancellor) if satisfied that the member has failed without reasonable excuse to discharge the functions of the office for a continuous period of six months, has been convicted of an offence, is an undischarged bankrupt, or is otherwise unfit to hold the office or unable to discharge its functions[4]. The LSB is responsible for remuneration of the members of the OLC, but its role does not extend to determining how the OLC actually operates internally or remuneration of staff appointed by the OLC; those are matters for the OLC itself[5]. The LSB is entitled to receive a copy of the OLC's annual report and financial statements[6].

Although the development and implementation of processes for dealing with complaints about legal services are essentially the responsibility of the OLC, the LSB is responsible for overseeing the OLC's performance of those functions. Thus the LSB has a final say over any scheme rules made by the OLC (save in respect of charges payable by respondents, in respect of which the Lord Chancellor's consent is required)[7], and may also direct the OLC to modify scheme rules, provided that the LSB must first give the OLC notice of the proposed direction and allow an opportunity for representations by interested parties[8]. Further, the LSB may require the OLC to prepare a report in respect of any specific matter relating to the OLC's functions[9], and is empowered to set (or direct the OLC to set) and monitor performance targets relating to any of the OLC's functions, provided that any targets set or directions given in this regard must be published[10].

Finally, the LSB has a non-exclusive role (together with the Consumer Panel and OLC itself) in relation to changes to the parameters of schemes for dealing with complaints about legal services. First, the LSB may be requested by the Lord Chancellor to consider whether it is appropriate to recommend that the Lord Chancellor specify certain kinds of legal services complaints in relation to which the OLC may make rules establishing a voluntary scheme for their resolution. If the LSB is so requested, the LSB must act on the Lord Chancellor's request and, before making any recommendation, must publish its draft proposed recommendation, invite representations regarding it, and consider any representations made[11]. Second, the LSB may recommend to the Lord Chancellor alteration of the maximum amount of compensation that can be ordered by the OLC, which under s 138(1) is set at £30,000[12].

1 Schedule 15, para 1.
2 Schedule 15, paras 2–3.
3 Schedule 15, para 4.
4 Schedule 15, para 8.

5 Schedule 15, paras 10–22.
6 Section 118; Sch 15, para 26.
7 Section 155.
8 Section 156.
9 Section 120.
10 Section 121.
11 Sections 164–165.
12 Section 139.

Control over the Solicitors Disciplinary Tribunal and other tribunals

3.23 The LSB has a limited oversight role in relation to the operation of the SDT. First, the SDT may not alter its rules of procedure and practice unless the alteration is approved by the LSB, is exempted from the requirement to obtain approval by the LSB, or is made at the direction of the LSB[1]. Second, if the SDT fails to perform any of its functions to an adequate standard (or at all), the LSB may give it directions under s 32 (as to which see para 3.10 above)[2]. Third, the LSB may recommend that the Lord Chancellor modify the functions of the SDT, provided that such recommendation may only be made with a view to an order being made which enables the SDT to carry out its role more effectively or efficiently[3].

The LSB has an additional role in relation to tribunals so far as the licensing regime is concerned. Specifically, the LSB may recommend to the Lord Chancellor that he establish a body to hear and determine appeals from decisions of licensing authorities, or that he modify for the same purpose the functions of the SDT or the Discipline and Appeals Committee established by the Council of Licensed Conveyancers[4]. However, the LSB may not make such recommendation without first allowing an opportunity for representations by interested parties and without the consent of the body in respect of whom it is made[5].

1 Section 178. The procedure to be followed is that set out in relation to approved regulators in Sch 4, Pt 3, paras 20–27, save that the Law Society is also entitled to make representations.
2 Section 179.
3 Section 180.
4 Section 80.
5 Section 81.

Approved regulator/licensing authority of last resort

3.24 Finally, although as a general rule the LSB has no direct involvement in the regulation of authorised persons or licensing of alternative business structures, leaving front-line regulation to the approved regulators, the LSB must itself act as an approved regulator or licensing authority in certain circumstances.

In the event that an approved regulator's designation as such in relation to a reserved legal activity is cancelled under s 45, or an activity becomes a reserved legal activity by virtue of an order under s 24, the LSB may recommend to the Lord Chancellor that the LSB itself be designated as an approved regulator in relation to the reserved legal activity, together with any modifications to the LSB's functions with a view to enabling the LSB to discharge its functions as an approved regulator effectively and efficiently (for example by making practice rules, conduct rules or disciplinary rules) [1]. The LSB may subsequently recommend to the Lord Chancellor that he cancel the LSB's designation as an approved regulator in relation to a reserved legal activity, and make appropriate transfer arrangements in connection with the cancellation under ss 46 and 47[2].

The LSB is itself designated as a licensing authority under s 73(1) of the Act. However, it will only consider applications by licensable bodies for a licence in very limited circumstances, namely where:

- there is no approved regulator competent or potentially competent to act as a licensing authority in relation to the relevant reserved legal activity;
- each competent or potentially competent licensing authority has determined that it does not have or will not have suitable regulatory arrangements; or
- in relation to not for profit bodies, community interest companies and independent trade unions only[3], no licensing authority with suitable regulatory arrangements is prepared to grant a licence on terms appropriate to the licensable body[4].

In the event that the LSB (acting otherwise than in its capacity as a licensing authority or approved regulator) decides (on application by a licensable body) that one of these grounds is met and that the licensable body is therefore entitled to make an application to the LSB (acting in its capacity as a licensing authority) for a licence, the LSB must make suitable licensing rules (that is, licensing rules which constitute suitable regulatory arrangements in respect of licensable bodies entitled by virtue of the decision to make an application to the LSB for a licence)[5]. The LSB may make or modify its licensing rules only with the approval of the LSB (acting otherwise than in its capacity as a licensing authority or as an approved regulator)[6].

When acting as an approved regulator or licensing authority, the LSB must take such steps as are necessary to ensure an appropriate financial and organisational separation between its activities as approved regulator and its other activities[7], and when acting as an approved regulator may only make or change its regulatory arrangements with the approval of itself acting otherwise than in its capacity as approved regulator or licensing authority[8]. The LSB must have regard to its own guidance when exercising its functions as an approved regulator or licensing authority[9]. The provisions of the Act relating to regulatory conflict apply to the LSB in its capacity as a licensing authority, and its licensing rules as they apply in relation to an approved regulator and its regulatory arrangements and in relation to the LSB in its capacity as an approved regulator and its regulatory arrangements respectively[10].

1 Sections 62–64 and 66.
2 Sections 62 and 65–66. See para 3.13 above in relation to transfer arrangements.
3 Or such other bodies as may be prescribed: Sch 12, para 1(6)(d).
4 Schedule 12, para 1(3)–(6).

[5] The obligation to make licensing rules arises under s 83 if and when the LSB first decides that a licensable body is entitled to apply to it under Sch 12. The rules must be made within 12 months of that decision.

[6] Section 83(1)(b). In dealing with the application and any licence granted, the LSB must comply with the provisions generally applicable to licensing authorities (see especially ss 84–87).

[7] Sections 62(4) and 73(3)(b).

[8] Section 63(4). Note that the LSB may not exercise its powers under ss 31–51 and 55 when acting in its capacity as an approved regulator, and ss 53 and 57–61 do not apply to the LSB in its capacity as an approved regulator (s 67).

[9] Section 162.

[10] Section 103.

Chapter 4

ALTERNATIVE BUSINESS STRUCTURES AND LEGAL DISCIPLINARY PRACTICES

Iain Miller, Andrew Hopper QC, Rebecca Stubbs

INTRODUCTION

4.1 Prior to the LSA 2007, barristers or solicitors could only provide legal services to members of the public through an organisation owned or controlled entirely by their own profession[1]. Solicitors and barristers who were employed by non-lawyers could only provide legal services to their employer (subject to limited exceptions). It was not possible for different legal professions to practise as principals together in one entity, or for a solicitor or barrister employed by non-lawyers to provide legal services to the public (other than in the same limited circumstances). It is also a feature of the regulatory arrangements that regulation is directed at the individual professional rather than the entities for whom they work.

As we have seen from previous chapters, the regulatory landscape is changed by the LSA 2007. For the first time the legal profession is regulated as one profession which provides 'reserved legal activities'. Also the LSA 2007 shifts emphasis away from the regulation of the individual practitioner to the entity that provides reserved legal activities. All of these reforms are essential to creating a cohesive regulatory structure that enables members of the individual legal professions to practise together as principals and for non-lawyers (non-authorised persons, as defined by the LSA 2007) to own law firms. This latter entity is referred to in the LSA 2007 as an alternative business structure (ABS). In future, it is the regulator of the entity that will be the prime regulator. The regulator of the individual lawyer (which may not necessarily be the same regulator) will take a subsidiary role[2].

The regulation of ABSs cannot begin until the LSB is fully operational and has approved licensing rules proposed by a licensing authority. Whilst the LSB has described ABSs as 'a very high priority'[3], the practical reality is that a significant amount of work needs to be done by both the LSB and any aspiring licensing authority to develop detailed rules and consult upon them. Full implementation is not expected before 2011. However, in the meantime, the LSA 2007 permits interim arrangements by the Solicitors Regulation Authority (SRA), known as legal disciplinary partnerships (LDPs), and these are also described in this chapter. The Council for Licensed Conveyancers (CLC) can also regulate LDPs, and has in practice been able to for some years as there is no restriction on the outside ownership of a licensed conveyancing practice; only controls related to its management.

1 It was possible for a barrister to be employed by a solicitor but not to be in partnership with the solicitor.
2 This is apparent for LSA 2007, s 52(4), which provides that the rules of the entity regulator take precedence over the rules of the individual regulator.
3 Draft LSB Business Plan 2009/10, para 66.

WHAT IS AN ABS?

4.2 The provisions relating to ABSs are contained in LSA 2007, Part 5 and the Schedules referred to therein (being 10–14). Whilst the headings in the LSA 2007 refer to ABSs, the term used in the body of the LSA 2007 is 'licensable body'. This is a body that carries on (or wishes to carry on) reserved legal activities and a non-authorised person[1] is a manager[2] of the body or has an interest[3] in it. The consequence of this is that when the ABS regime is fully in force bodies that are regulated as LDPs with non-lawyer participation in management will have to be licensed as ABSs. Alternatively, a body is a licensable body if another body is a manager of the body or has an interest in it and non-authorised persons are entitled to exercise, or control the exercise of, at least 10% of the voting rights in the body[4]. Accordingly, if a holding or parent company of a firm providing reserved legal activities is owned by a non-authorised person but who hold less than 10% of its voting rights then the firm would not need to be regulated as an ABS, but would still need to be regulated by an approved regulator in the provision of reserved legal activities.

1 The term 'person' includes a body of persons corporate or unincorporated (LSA 2007, s 207). 'Non-authorised' is not defined in the LSA 2007 but clearly refers to a person who is not authorised to provide reserved legal activities under s 18.
2 The term 'manager' is defined in s 207. In summary, a manager will be a member of a limited liability partnership or similar organisation, director of a company, partner in a partnership or the member of a governing body of an unincorporated association.
3 'Interest' is defined in s 72(4) as either holding shares or being entitled to exercise, or control the exercise of, voting rights in the body.
4 Section 72(2).

LDPS: THE FIRST WAVE

4.3 In enacting the LSA 2007 the Government recognised that there was a type of ABS that could be implemented prior to the coming into force of the full ABS regulatory regime. These types of ABSs are referred to as legal disciplinary partnerships (LDPs). They are not statutorily defined, but the term has become a well recognised shorthand to describe a firm in which lawyers of different disciplines may be principals. The statutory mechanism by which this has been achieved for firms regulated by the SRA is by redefining a 'legal services body', through amendment of the Administration of Justice Act 1985[1] by the LSA 2007, and by permitting a legal services body to be regulated by the SRA for the supply of reserved legal activities. Reference should be made to the Administration of Justice Act 1985, sections 9 and 9A to identify all the various permutations that are possible, including the extent to which another incorporated or unincorporated body may be a manager of a legal services body, but in essence LDPs may be owned and managed by any combination of individual lawyers who are authorised persons for the purposes of LSA 2007 (solicitors, barristers, notaries, licensed conveyancers, patent and trade mark agents, legal executives and law costs draftsman), Registered European Lawyers (RELs), Registered Foreign Lawyers (RFLs), and exempt European lawyers[2], provided at least one manager is a solicitor, REL or 'qualifying body' (meaning a body in which at least one manager is a solicitor or REL and one which satisfies other conditions[3]).

Non-lawyers may also participate in LDPs provided that qualified lawyers comprise at least 75% of the managers of the firm and hold at least 75% of the shares[4] and exercise or control the exercise of at least 75% of the voting rights and all those who are not legally qualified who have an interest in the firm are managers, and are approved by the SRA as suitable to be managers[5]. It follows that participation by non-lawyers in LDPs cannot be through the equivalent of shareholding only. Outside investment in law firms in the fullest sense will only be permitted with the advent of the ABS regime described below. Non-lawyers with an interest in LDPs must be managers of the firm.

For regulatory purposes LDPs are simply a form of recognised body (such as an LLP) regulated by the SRA and the provisions as to recognition, and the other regulations applicable to recognised bodies apply equally. They are no different from any other recognised body if the principals, the managers, are all legally qualified and regulated for the purposes of LSA 2007 by one or other of the approved regulators.

Additional rules apply if there is a need to approve managers who are non-lawyers or who are otherwise outside the definition of 'legally qualified' for the purposes of AJA 1985, s 9A. There are three possible categories: non-lawyers in the normal sense that this would be understood; members of a foreign legal profession whose members are not eligible to become RFLs; and non-practising barristers and non-practising members of other legal professions who are prevented by professional rules or training regulations from changing status so as to be able to seek approval as practising lawyers). Any such individual must be approved by the SRA in order to be a manager or owner of a LDP or a manager of a body corporate which is a manager of a LDP[6].

The character and suitability of the individual will be assessed against standards comparable to those which are applied for the admission of solicitors: that there is confidence that the individuals are honest and trustworthy, willing to comply with regulatory requirements, and able responsibly to manage financial affairs for themselves and clients; and that there is no reasonable risk that the approval of the individual as a non-lawyer manager will diminish the public's confidence in the profession or be harmful to members of the public, the profession or him or herself. The approval process will involve a Criminal Records Bureau check.

The application for approval must be made by the LDP or prospective LDP concerned and may be made when applying for initial recognition or at any time after recognition has been granted. It is for the applicant body to demonstrate that the individual concerned meets the criteria for approval. The applicant body must co-operate, and secure the co-operation of the individual concerned, to assist the SRA to obtain all information and documentation the SRA requires in order to determine the application; must obtain all other information and documentation in relation to that individual which the prescribed form[7] requires the body to obtain; and keep all information and documentation for a period of not less than six years after the individual concerned has ceased to be a manager of the body. The individual concerned must confirm in writing on the face of the application that the information supplied about him is correct and complete[8].

Approval takes effect from the date of the decision unless otherwise stated. The SRA's decision to approve or refuse approval must be notified in writing to the applicant body and, separately, to the individual concerned. The LDP must not allow the individual to become a manager until it has received written notice that the individual has been approved. Approval continues until it is withdrawn, or until two years have elapsed during which the individual has not been a manager of a LDP[9]. The SRA may at any time require the production of information or documentation from an approved individual, a LDP in which an approved individual is a manager or the body which originally obtained approval for that individual and which holds the information and documentation required to be retained[10], in order to satisfy the SRA that the individual met the criteria for approval or continues to meet the criteria for approval[11].

The SRA may decide to withdraw approval if it is not satisfied that an approved individual met the criteria for approval or continues to meet the criteria for approval or if information or documentation is not promptly supplied in response to a request. Withdrawal of approval takes effect on expiry of the notice (usually 28 days[12]) or on such later date as may be stated in the notice but if an appeal is made before the withdrawal of approval takes effect, the withdrawal of approval is suspended pending determination or discontinuance of the appeal, unless in the opinion of the SRA the proceedings on that appeal have been unduly protracted by the appellant or are unlikely to be successful[13]. Where withdrawal of approval relates to a director of a company, the SRA may set separate dates for that individual ceasing to be a director and disposing of his shares[14].

Applications for recognition of LDPs are likely to require the provision of more information about the business than has previously been the case. It is anticipated that information comparable to that required by professional indemnity insurers will need to be provided to the SRA as part of the recognition process; that is information as to turnover, the number of non-solicitor fee-earners, a breakdown of the types of work undertaken as a percentage of turnover, and a record of any negligence claims.

The SRA may impose one or more conditions on a LDPs recognition: when granting initial recognition; when granting renewal of recognition; when granting approval of a non-lawyer manager; when deciding to withdraw approval of a non-lawyer manager; or at any other time[15].

The SRA may impose a condition if:

- the condition would limit, restrict, halt or prevent an activity or activities on the part of the body, or of a manager or employee of the body, which is putting or is likely to put at risk the interests of clients, third parties or the public, and it is in the public interest to impose the condition;
- the condition would limit the activities of a manager or employee of the body who is considered unsuitable to undertake a particular activity, either at all or save as specified in the condition, and it is in the public interest to impose the condition;
- the condition would limit, halt or prevent a risk to clients, third parties or the public arising from a business agreement or association which the body has or is likely to enter into, or a business practice which the body has or is likely to adopt, and it is in the public interest to impose the condition;
- a relevant insolvency event[16] has occurred in relation to a recognised body, and the event has not triggered expiry of recognition[17], and the SRA considers that it is in the public interest to impose the condition;
- the condition will, in the public interest, facilitate closer monitoring by the SRA of compliance with rules and regulations on the part of the body;
- the condition will, in the public interest, require the body concerned to take specified steps conducive to the carrying on of efficient practice by that body;
- in any other case concerning a body which is currently recognised, that it would be in the public interest to impose the condition[18].

A condition imposed under this regulation takes effect from the date on which the condition is imposed unless a later date is specified in the condition[19].

The SRA must give 28 days' written notice with reasons to the recognised body concerned, when the SRA decides to impose a condition on the body's recognition, or revoke the body's recognition. The SRA may shorten or dispense with the 28-day period in imposing a condition if it is satisfied on reasonable grounds that it is in the public interest to do so[20].

The SRA must give 28 days' written notice, with reasons, to the recognised body concerned, when the SRA decides to revoke the body's recognition[21]. The SRA may revoke a body's recognition, if:

- recognition was granted as a result of error or fraud;
- the body would not be eligible to be recognised if it were at that time applying for initial recognition;
- the renewal date has passed and the SRA has not received an application for renewal of recognition and all required fees, information and documentation;

- the body has a temporary emergency recognition but has not within the initial 28-day period or any extension of that period commenced a substantive application for recognition;
- the body has ceased to practise;
- an approved regulator other than the SRA has authorised the body;
- the SRA has decided not to renew the body's recognition; or
- a relevant insolvency event[22] has occurred in relation to the recognised body which has not triggered expiry of recognition[23];

and (in any and all cases) if the SRA is satisfied that revocation would not present a risk to clients, to the protection of client money or to any investigative process[24].

Revocation takes effect on expiry of the notice period or on such later date as may be stated in the notice, but if an appeal is made before the revocation takes effect, the revocation is suspended pending determination or discontinuance of the appeal, unless in the opinion of the SRA the proceedings on that appeal have been unduly protracted by the appellant or are unlikely to be successful[25].

Appeals should[26] first be pursued within the SRA's own appeals procedure, but thereafter appeal lies to the High Court. Appeals within the SRA's appeals procedure must be commenced within 28 days of notification of the relevant decision, and appeals to the High Court within 28 days of notification of the relevant decision or of notification of the refusal of the internal appeal[27]. Applications for recognition of a body and for approval of a non-lawyer manager are deemed to have been refused if by the end of the 90th day the SRA has not notified a decision to the applicant body and the individual concerned, and notice of the decision is deemed to have been given on that day[28].

In contrast to solicitors, and as already mentioned, licensed conveyancers have always been permitted to practise in a recognised body that has external ownership, provided that not less than 50% of directors are qualified as licensed conveyancers[29]. Amendments to the Solicitors' Code of Conduct 2007 now permit solicitors to practise as solicitors in such a recognised body regulated by the Council for Licensed Conveyancers[30].

Neither the Act nor the SRA draft rules would prevent barristers from becoming managers of LDPs. However, para 205 of the Bar's Code of Conduct (which lays down the requirements for practice as a barrister and standards of conduct relevant to such practice: see para 104) forbids a practising barrister to supply legal services to the public through or on behalf of any other person (including a partnership, company, or other corporate body) except (pertinently, for present purposes) as the employee of a solicitor or firm of solicitors. The paragraph would preclude the provision of legal services by a barrister acting as the manager or employee of an LDP.

Moreover, para 401(b) prohibits self-employed barristers from undertaking certain activities and para 403.1 prohibits self-employed barristers (with some minor exceptions) from sharing the administration of their practice with anyone other than a barrister. See also para 502.

A further potential complication is presented by the Bar's cab-rank rule (para 602 of the Code)[31], which requires self-employed barristers[32] to accept work which they have the time to undertake, which is within their expertise, and for which an appropriate fee is offered, irrespective of the strength of the client's case or their view of the character, beliefs of behaviour of the client. The rule prohibits self-employed barristers from refusing cases on the grounds of the perceived weakness of the case, or on the grounds of the litigant's character or conduct. The BSB does not consider that it would be possible to require the cab-rank rule to apply to barristers practising in ABS firms or LDPs:

> 'The acceptance or refusal of instructions will be a matter for the firm as a business entity, not for an individual taking part in it. As regards both ABS firms and LDPs the effect of applying the rule would be that a firm could be "conflicted out" of litigation by instructing a relatively junior member of the firm to undertake a minor piece of work. The Board considers that such firms or partnerships would be placed under such a disadvantage by this rule that it would be a considerable disincentive to them to form those structures, contrary to the legislative purpose.[33]'

The BSB is currently consulting on the implications of the Act for the regulation of the Bar. The first consultation paper (BSB: 'The Legal Services Act 2007, Implications for the regulation of the Bar in England and Wales', referred to herein as 'FCP') was published in February 2008 and sought views on the following main issues:

- In what types of business entity should barristers be permitted to supply legal services to the public, and subject to what, if any, conditions?
- Which of these types of entity should the board regulate?
- If barristers are permitted to supply legal services through new business structures, to what extent is it feasible and desirable to maintain the 'cab-rank' rule in its existing form?

The BSB's second consultation paper ('SCP'), which seeks responses by the end of March 2008, consults on LDPs and barrister-only partnerships.

In the FCP, the BSB expressed the view (para 69) that the rules should be relaxed to permit barristers to provide legal services as *managers or as employees of ABS firms*; to prevent barristers to do so: 'would be open to objection both as frustrating the will of Parliament in enacting the Act and as unreasonably restrictive of competition in the provision of legal services'; and the continued restriction 'could be justified only if there were strong arguments of public interest for maintaining the restrictions.'

As to the question of barristers acting as a *manager or owner of an LDP*, and *whether barristers should be allowed to participate in other forms of partnership*: the BSB's initial conclusions (FCP, paras 81–82) was that unless strong arguments to the contrary based on public interest could be advanced, barristers should be permitted to practise while acting as managers of ABSs, and that if barristers are permitted to practise in ABS firms, then participation in LDPs should similarly be allowed, because it is difficult to see any justification for permitting barristers to co-manage firms with solicitors and non-lawyers in an ABS firm, but not with solicitors alone, or solicitors and non-lawyers, in an LDP. In short, the BSB concluded, 'that it is likely to be in the public interest for the prohibition on barristers practising in such partnerships to be abolished'.

The BSB's view, expressed in para 10 of the SCP, is that the Code of Conduct should be amended to permit *barristers employed by LDPs* regulated by the SRA to supply legal services to the public, just as they can practise as employees of firms of solicitors. The questions set out in the SCP for consideration centre around whether the Code of Conduct should further be modified so as to permit barristers to become managers of LDPs.

The BSB considers that barristers should be able to practise as managers of LDPs, 'to enhance opportunities to access the Bar and to facilitate increased value for the consumer through greater competition to the delivery of legal expertise offered by the Bar'[34]. However, the view taken seems to be that, even in the longer term, the substantial majority of any barristers who became managers of LDPs would join LDPs regulated by the SRA (SCP, para 9).

1 Sections 9 and 9A as amended by LSA 2007, Sch 16, Pt 2.
2 Exempt European lawyers are those who are not lawyers of England and Wales but who are entitled to practise as a member of an Establishment Directive profession (Directive 98/5/EC of the European Parliament and the Council) by being registered as the equivalent of an REL with another regulator such as the Bar Standards Board or who are based entirely outside England and Wales.
3 AJA 1985, s 9A(4), (5) and (6).
4 Shares for this purpose are defined by LSA 2007 and include allotted shares in a company, rights to share in the capital of a company, if the body has capital but no share capital, and if the body has no capital, interests conferring the right to share in profits or liability to contribute to losses, or an obligation to contribute to debts and expenses in the event of a winding up; see LSA 2007, s 79.
5 AJA 1985, s 9A(2).
6 SRA Recognised Bodies Regulations 2009, reg 3(1).
7 The SRA form is called an NL1.
8 SRA Recognised Bodies Regulations 2009, reg 3.4.
9 SRA Recognised Bodies Regulations 2009, reg 3.5.
10 SRA Recognised Bodies Regulations 2009, reg 3.4(c).
11 SRA Recognised Bodies Regulations 2009, reg 3.6.
12 SRA Recognised Bodies Regulations 2009, reg 6.2.
13 SRA Recognised Bodies Regulations 2009, reg 3.7.
14 SRA Recognised Bodies Regulations 2009, reg 3.8.
15 SRA Recognised Bodies Regulations 2009, reg 4.1.
16 Within the meaning of AJA 1985, Sch 2, para 32(1A).
17 Under SRA Recognised Bodies Regulations 2009, reg 10, which occurs automatically if the body is wound up or for any other reason ceases to exist.
18 SRA Recognised Bodies Regulations 2009, reg 4.2.
19 SRA Recognised Bodies Regulations 2009, reg 4.3.
20 SRA Recognised Bodies Regulations 2009, regs 6.2 and 6.3.
21 SRA Recognised Bodies Regulations 2009, reg 6.2.
22 Within the meaning of AJA 1985, Sch 2, para 32(1A); see Appendix.
23 Under SRA Recognised Bodies Regulations 2009, reg 10, which occurs automatically if the body is wound up or for any other reason ceases to exist.
24 SRA Recognised Bodies Regulations 2009, reg 9.1.
25 SRA Recognised Bodies Regulations 2009, reg 9.2.

[26] When appeal lay to the Master of the Rolls he always encouraged appellants first to exhaust any internal appeal process and the High Court can be expected to take the same view. Some appeals must first employ the SRA's internal procedure; against a decision to revoke recognition of a body, against a refusal to approve a non-lawyer manager, and against the withdrawal of approval of a non-lawyer manager; see SRA Recognised Bodies Regulations 2009 Regs 7.2 and 7.3.

[27] SRA Recognised Bodies Regulations 2009, reg 7.5; SRA Practising Regulations 2009, reg 7.6.

[28] SRA Recognised Bodies Regulations 2009, reg 7.4.

[29] See CLC Recognised Body Rules 2000 and LLP Rules 2008. New rules reflecting the shift to entity-based regulation came into force on 31 March 2009.

[30] Solicitors' Conduct of Conduct 2007, r 10.04.

[31] Which, it is argued, promotes access to justice, and protects a barrister's independence because, by virtue of the rule, the barrister represents the client because it is a professional duty to do so, not because he endorses the client's story or approves of the client's behaviour.

[32] The rule does not apply to solicitors or to barristers employed in solicitors' offices (although para 601 forbids all barristers who supply advocacy services to withhold such services on the grounds that the nature of the client's case is objectionable, or that the client's conduct or opinions are unacceptable; or on any ground relating to the source of any financial support that may be given to the client).

[33] BSB's First Consultation Paper, para 59.

[34] BSB Chair, Ruth Evans: Press Release dated 11 December 2008 relating to the BSB's second consultation on the implications of the Legal Services Act.

THE FULL REGULATORY STRUCTURE FOR ABSS

4.4 Once the LSA 2007 is fully implemented there will be a distinct regulatory structure for ABSs which is in contrast to the regulation of firms or individuals who undertake reserved legal activities but who do not have non-lawyer participation. The former are regulated by an approved regulator, whilst an ABS has to be regulated by a licensing authority. The Act makes provision for the LSB to be a licensing authority[1] but this is likely to occur only if there are gaps in the regulatory framework because no organisation has applied to become a licensing body of ABSs for particular types of reserved legal activity. It is more likely that one or more of the approved regulators such as the SRA, BSB or CLC will apply to become a licensing authority. In order to become a licensing authority an approved regulator needs to be designated as such by the LSB[2]. LSA 2007, Sch 10 deals with applications by an approved regulator to become a licensing authority, and the removal of such authorisation. This is also dealt with in LSA 2007, sections 75–79. Whilst one or more approved regulators may be approved as licensing authorities in due course, their designation may be limited to particular types of reserved legal activity[3].

LSA 2007, s 83(5) and Sch 11 set out the framework of the licensing rules to be approved by the LSB. These include provision for qualification as a licensed body, arrangements for regulation, appropriate indemnification arrangements and appropriate compensation arrangements[4]. Accordingly, a licensing authority is likely to have detailed provisions for the minimum terms of cover for professional indemnity insurance and will need to establish (or adapt) a compensation fund.

[1] Section 73.

[2] Section 74.

3 Section 74 and Sch 10, para 12(2).
4 Indemnification relates to professional indemnity insurance. Compensation arrangements relate to compensating clients where the insurance is not available such as where insurers avoid cover because of the dishonesty of the ABS.

REGULATION OF THE OWNERSHIP OF ABSS

4.5 Not surprisingly, the LSA 2007 carefully regulates ownership of an ABS by a non-authorised person. This applies where a non-authorised person controls a material interest in an ABS. Broadly, a material interest is where the non-authorised person holds at least 10% of the ABS or at least 10% of the shares of the parent of the ABS, or is able to exercise significant influence in the management of the ABS or its parent by virtue of the shareholding[1]. The licensing authority needs to be satisfied that the non-authorised person holding a material interest in the ABS does not compromise the regulatory objectives set out in LSA 2007, s 1 (see para 2.12 above). In addition it must also not compromise the duty of a regulated person employed by the ABS to fulfil their duties to the regulator. In any event the person must be fit and proper to hold the interest[2]. In determining whether the licensing authority is satisfied as to the above matters, it must have regard to the non-authorised person's probity and financial position, whether they are disqualified under LSA 2007, s 100(1) or included on the LSB's list of persons subject to objections and conditions, and the person's associates[3]. It follows from the foregoing that where the ABS is owned by one or more non-authorised persons who have a less than 10% interest in the ABS, these persons will not be subject to the same controls.

As noted above, the SRA has in its rules for LDPs adopted a test in relation to non-lawyers that is akin to that for admission to the solicitors' profession. It is entirely logical that the character and suitability requirement on non-lawyers having a material interest in a regulated business should be identical to those applied to the lawyers, and this approach is likely to be followed when more detailed licensing rules are developed. Indeed the test may be more onerous as the LSA 2007 clearly contemplates consideration of the associates of the non-authorised owners and managers as part of the assessment process. These are widely defined to include family and other businesses related directly or indirectly to the non-authorised person[4]. There is no equivalent process for admission to one of the legal professions. One issue that will need to be resolved in due course is the extent to which the recognition of a non-authorised person in another regulatory context as being fit and proper will be sufficient to satisfy the licensing rules for ABSs.

The LSA 2007 also incorporates a number of controls to ensure the regulation of ownership. By way of example, there is a requirement to identify any non-authorised persons in the application for a licence[5]. The licensing authority may impose conditions on the approval of the non-authorised person[6]. There is also an obligation to inform the licensing authority when a non-authorised person acquires a material interest in an ABS[7]. The licensing authority may apply to the High Court for an order that a non-authorised person is divested of their interest in an ABS in certain circumstances[8]. In addition, non-authorised persons holding an interest in or employed by an ABS have a positive obligation to comply with the regulatory obligations of the ABS and of the authorised persons working within it[9]. Failure so to comply can lead to disqualification under LSA 2007, s 99.

LSA 2007, Sch 13, para 38 provides that the licensing rules may make provision for the limitation of the level of the shareholding, control or voting rights of a non-authorised person. However, there is no restriction set out within the LSA 2007 as to the number of ABSs a non-authorised person can participate in.

1 Schedule 6, para 3.
2 Schedule 6, para 6(1), (2).
3 Schedule 6, para 6(3).
4 Schedule 13, para 5.
5 Schedule 13, paras 10–13.
6 Schedule 13, paras 17–18.
7 Schedule 13, paras 21.
8 Schedule 13, paras 41–45.
9 Section 90.

APPLYING TO BECOME AN ABS

4.6 The licensing rules submitted by a licensing authority to the LSB for approval must make provision for the form and manner of applications and the fee[1]. A licensing authority must determine an application for a licence to be an ABS within six months of an application although it is possible to extend that period to a maximum period of nine months provided such extension (or extensions) is notified to the applicant before the time when any decision period would expire and reasons are given for the extension[2]. If the licensing authority decides to refuse an application it must notify the applicant of the reasons for the refusal. The licensing rules must make provision for review of a decision to refuse an application for a licence and if a licence is granted the terms of the licence[3]. LSA 2007, s 84(6) provides that the licensing authority may impose conditions as to the non-reserved activities which the ABS may or may not carry on.

The licensing rules may make provision for limiting the period a licence remains in force. The rules would may also provide the form and manner of any renewal and the fee payable. The rules must provide that a licence issued to a licensed body by a licensing authority ceases to have effect if the licensed body is issued with a licence by another licensing authority[4]. Licensing rules may make provision for the continuity of a licence where the membership of a licensed body changes or another body succeeds to the whole or substantially the whole of its business[5]. The licensing rules must make provision about the form and manner of applications to modify the terms of a licence. The rules may also provide that the licensing authority can modify a licence without an application under LSA 2007, s 86[6].

It seems inevitable that an application for a licence to practise as an ABS will be a significant undertaking. The licensing authority will require extensive information as to the ownership of the proposed ABS, its financial position and it management and compliance structures. As indicated above, this is already the case in relation to applicants to the SRA for recognition as an LDP.

1 LSA 2007, Sch 11, para 1.
2 Schedule 11, para 2(3)–(6).
3 Schedule 11, para 3.
4 Schedule 11, para 4.
5 Schedule 11, para 5.
6 Schedule 11, para 6.

THE STRUCTURE OF ABSS

4.7 The LSA 2007 imposes a number of structural limitations on an ABS. At least one of the ABS's managers must be a person who is an authorised person in relation to the ABS's licensed activity[1]. A manager is, in the case of a LLP, a member, in the case of a company, a director, in the case of a partnership a partner and in the case of an unincorporated association a member of its governing body[2].

In addition, an ABS must have at all times an individual who is designated as the Head of Legal Practice and whose designation is approved by the licensing authority[3]. The Head of Legal Practice must be an authorised person in relation to one or more of the licensed activities of the ABS. The Head of Legal Practice is also responsible for ensuring that the authorised persons within the ABS comply with their obligations imposed by LSA 2007, s 176 and that the non-authorised persons comply with their obligations under LSA 2007, s 90; essentially, in both respects, to comply with the regulatory requirements imposed by the relevant approved regulator. He has the obligation to ensure compliance with the ABS's licence, and to report any non-compliance to the licensing authority[4].

A person will only be approved as the Head of Legal Practice if the licensing authority is satisfied that the person is a fit and proper person to carry out the duties imposed upon him. Given the central role of the Head of Legal Practice in ensuring regulatory compliance it is clearly important that the licensing authority is satisfied as to their suitability. As the Head of Legal Practice will be an authorised person their character and suitability will have already been assessed when they were admitted to one of the legal professions. It seems implicit that the LSA 2007 contemplates a higher test for suitability to be a Head of Legal Practice. This is likely to involve additional qualifications[5].

In addition to a Head of Legal Practice, an ABS must also have an individual who is designated as Head of Finance and Administration. This individual is responsible for ensuring compliance with rules made in relation to the keeping of accounts and reporting any breaches of those rules to the licensing authority[6]. The Head of Finance and Administration must also be approved as a fit and proper person by the licensing authority. There are no requirements in the LSA 2007 as to the qualification of the Head of Finance and Administration and there is no requirement that they need to be an authorised person.

The ABS must only carry on a licensed activity through a person who is entitled to carry on the activity. In essence therefore, the delivery of legal services must be supervised by those authorised to provide such services[7]. The ABS must also have suitable arrangements in place to ensure regulatory compliance, and the ABS may not employ disqualified persons[8].

1 Schedule 11, para 9.
2 Section 207.
3 Schedule 11, para 11.
4 Section 91.
5 Rule 5.02 of the Solicitors' Code of Conduct and the Guidance Notes thereto provide that a solicitor can only supervise a practice if they are 'qualified to supervise', which is defined as undertaking 12 hours of management skills training.
6 Section 92.
7 Schedule 11, para 16.
8 Schedule 11, paras 17–18.

'LOW RISK' ABSS

4.8 The LSA 2007 recognises that certain ABSs may require less extensive regulatory safeguards. These are: independent trade unions[1]; not-for-profit bodies[2], community interest companies and a low-risk bodies[3].

Section 106 provides that a licensing authority may make an order that certain of its licensing rules do not apply in relation to such a body, in particular, the rules that impose restrictions on ownership. In any event, independent trade unions are not subject to the ownership restrictions in Sch 13[4].

It is likely that the ABS structure may enable certain public sector organisations to share legal services more effectively and may assist in reducing the regulatory burden on such organisations which present very little regulatory risk. For example, local authorities will be able to share legal services through a separate entity[5].

1 This is defined as having the same meaning as the Trade Union and Labour Relations (Consolidation) Act 1992, s 5; see LSA 2007, s 207.
2 This is defined as a body which, by virtue of its constitution or any enactment: (a) is required (after payment of outgoings) to apply the whole of its income, and any capital which it expends, for charitable or public purposes, and (b) is prohibited from directly or indirectly distributing amongst its members any part of its assets (otherwise than for charitable or public purposes). See LSA 2007, s 207.
3 This is defined by LSA 2007, s 108, but is essentially where the number of managers and/or the interests of owners who are non-authorised persons is less than 10%.
4 Section 105.
5 This is dealt with in more detail in Chapter 13 below.

REGULATION, DISCIPLINE AND ENFORCEMENT

4.9 As previously observed, before the LSA 2007, the powers of approved regulators were primarily directed at individual practitioners. In the case of solicitors, an order could be made against an employee of a solicitor who was guilty of misconduct that he could not be employed by any solicitor without permission of the Law Society[1], but that was the extent of the control upon persons outside the membership of the profession notwithstanding that they worked within the legal profession.

The LSA 2007 contemplates that all who work within organisations providing regulated legal services will be subject to direct regulation and disciplinary sanction even if they are a non-authorised person[2]. Accordingly, a person may be disqualified from being a Head of Legal Practice, Head of Finance and Administration, manager or employee of any licensed body pursuant to LSA 2007, s 99. Section 95 provides that a licensing authority may fine an ABS, or one or more of its managers or employees. The licence of an ABS can be suspended or revoked under s 101 but only in one or more of the seven sets of circumstances set out in Sch 11, para 24.[3] In addition, the licensing authority may intervene into an ABS pursuant to the powers contained in Sch 14. These are in identical terms to the powers vested in the SRA pursuant to the Solicitors Act 1974, Sch 1. This is a draconian step that would enable the licensing authority to shut down an ABS without notice where for example it suspected dishonesty.

1 Solicitors Act 1974, s 43.
2 Many of these provisions in relation to existing legal services organisations came into force on 31 March 2009 by means of rules or amendments to rules made by the SRA or CLC.
3 These include the body ceasing to be a licensable body, failure to comply with licensing rules, and failure by employees to comply with their duties under ss 90 and 176.

APPEALS

4.10 LSA 2007, s 80 makes provision for the Lord Chancellor to designate a body to hear appeals from decisions made by a licensing authority. Section 80(1)(b) and (2) contemplates that two such bodies may be the Solicitors Disciplinary Tribunal (SDT) and the Discipline and Appeals Committee of the Council of Licensed Conveyancers.

Examples of decisions which would be subject to such an appeal mechanism are the imposition of a financial penalty under s 96, and the conditional approval of a notifiable interest in an ABS under Sch 13, para 38. There are no express appeal provisions in relation to a decision to disqualify a person pursuant to s 99, nor is there any provision for an appeal against a refusal to issue a licence under s 84 and Sch 11. However, s 80(1) does contemplate that the licensing rules of a licensing authority may make provision for such appeals.

In contrast to the current disciplinary arrangements in relation to, for example, solicitors, the statutory scheme for ABSs contemplates that the imposition of fines and decisions to disqualify will be taken by the licensing authority, at least in the first instance. Such decisions are likely to engage Article 6 of the ECHR and care will need to be taken to ensure that the decision making arrangements are compliant with the ECHR.

In addition, practical difficulties may arise in relation to disciplinary overlap. If a solicitor who is employed by an ABS is guilty of serious misconduct, then it is likely that the licensing authority would make an order for disqualification of him as an employee of an ABS under s 99. However, the SRA would also need to apply to the SDT to have him struck off as a solicitor based on the same facts. Such arrangements are more cumbersome that the current arrangements, particularly if the licensing authority is the SRA and there is a right of appeal from its disqualification decision to the SDT. It is also entirely possible under the current state of the law that the disqualification application is determined on the civil standard and the application to the SDT determined on a test akin to the criminal standard.

Certain powers under the provisions relating to ABSs are reviewable or exercisable by the High Court. In particular, the power to order a non-authorised person to divest his interest in an ABS under Sch 13, paras 41–45 and the power to enforce conditions imposed on a restricted interest in an ABS under Sch 13, para 46. The intervention powers under Sch 14 are also subject to an application to the High Court. There have been a number of challenges to similar provisions contained in the Solicitors Act 1974, Sch 1 and these authorities are likely to be of direct relevance to determining such challenges[1].

1 See, for example, *Sheikh v The Law Society* [2006] EWCA Civ 1577.

THE FUTURE

4.11 Whilst the LSA 2007 sets out the framework for ABSs, there are clearly a substantial number of outstanding issues that will need to be clarified in licensing rules. It is also not clear which approved regulators will seek to become a licensing authority and for what types of reserved legal activities.

The widening of the ownership of law firms will also create new regulatory issues that did not arise under the previous arrangements, particularly as to the relationship between lawyers and their clients. Prior to the introduction of the LSA 2007, it was rare for a legal professional to have an interest in more than one firm. In addition, it was not usual for lawyers to run businesses that were separate from their practice as lawyers. Indeed, their ability to do so is regulated[1]. Once ABSs are fully implemented it may be possible for an investor to have an interest in more than one legal practice. In addition, an organisation may form an ABS to enable the provision of reserved legal activities as a part of an overall business in, for example, legal expenses insurance or banking. However, every relationship between a solicitor and his client is a fiduciary relationship based on trust. Difficulties will arise if two firms acting against each other in litigation are partly owned by the same investor. Other issues will arise if the wider commercial interests of the ABS are not the same as those of its clients. Similar issues have arisen in the context of regulating solicitors in relation to the payment of referral fees to introducers of work. These are some of the regulatory challenges that are likely to be faced in the next few years.

1 Solicitors' Code of Conduct 2007, r 21.

Chapter 5

THE OFFICE FOR LEGAL COMPLAINTS

Nicholas Peacock QC

SOLICITORS ACT 1974

Introduction

5.1 The concept of inadequate professional services – namely the provision by solicitors of poor quality services falling short of negligence or professional misconduct – was first introduced by the Administration of Justice Act 1985. The sanctions that could be imposed by the Law Society or the Solicitors Disciplinary Tribunal (SDT) for such inadequate services were disciplinary and involved the imposition on the solicitor of a penal sanction.

These provisions were replaced by the Solicitors Act 1974, Sch 1A (headed 'Inadequate Professional Services' and referred to as 'IPS'), which was inserted into the Act by the Courts and Legal Services Act 1990 and came into force on 1 April 1991. These new provisions removed the penal element of the previous regime and instead substituted a regime under which the solicitor might be required to take certain specified steps (such as, for example, to limit his costs or to pay compensation to the client) in order to remedy the deficiency in the service provided.

One of the key intended purposes of the IPS jurisdiction was to improve standards within the profession. In *R (Thompson) v The Law Society*[1] Clarke LJ recorded that the Law Society regarded the IPS jurisdiction as being of considerable value and importance not only in order to compensate clients but also in order to encourage higher standards among solicitors. Clarke LJ stated that he considered the Law Society's view to be correct. Thus, the IPS jurisdiction seeks to serve two purposes: first, to compensate clients for poor service; and, secondly, to encourage solicitors to provide better service to their clients in the first place. This latter purpose is essentially sought to be achieved by publicising failures to educate and perhaps also 'pour encourager les autres'.

It appears to have been the experience of the Law Society that a substantial proportion of complaints made by clients that fall within the ambit of the IPS jurisdiction have resulted from poor communication between the solicitor and his client (for example, at the outset concerning fees and fee estimates). Moreover, the experience of the Law Society appears to have been that the operation (in a constructive and sympathetic manner) by a solicitor of a properly formulated complaints handling process (as is now required by r 2.05 of the Code of Conduct) is the best means by which complaints to the Society can be reduced.

This aim – reduction of complaints made to the Law Society – was one of the key factors driving the Society's operation of the IPS jurisdiction. Thus, in 2004 the Society received 11,974 new service complaints and there were 1,768 first instance decisions relating to IPS, which involved total compensation being awarded of over £500,000 (an average of just over £787 per award). Yet, despite the efforts of the Law Society, on page 10 of her annual report 2004/2005 the Legal Services Ombudsman prominently displayed the tagline 'It's not right that complaints about lawyers are dealt with by other lawyers'. As we will see, under the regime introduced by the LSA 2007 this implicit complaint of lawyers 'looking after their own' (or at least there being an appearance of that) has been accepted as the basis for change.

1 [2004] 2 All ER 113.

Operation of the statutory scheme

5.2 By the Solicitors Act 1974, Sch 1A, para 1(1) the Council of the Law Society may take any of the steps specified in para 2, 'where it appears to them' that the professional services provided by the solicitor in connection with any matter in which he or his firm have been instructed by a client, 'have, in any respect, not been of the quality which it is reasonable to expect of him as a solicitor.'

In fact, the decisions in question are not made by the Council but, rather, are made by the Legal Complaints Service under power delegated by the Council. Those decisions are reached through the operation by the Legal Complaints Service of a process that might have up to six stages.

First stage

5.3 At the first stage, a caseworker will carry out an investigation, obtaining evidence and information from both the solicitor and the client. The caseworker will inform the solicitor of the complaint that has been made, will ask for the solicitor's full answer to the complaint and will notify the solicitor that his reply will be disclosed to the complainant. The caseworker will try to broker a settlement between the solicitor and the client but, in default of settlement, will prepare a detailed formal report, termed an Agenda Note (to which relevant documentation is attached) in which will appear the caseworker's conclusions and recommendations based upon the evidence and information acquired during the investigation. The Agenda Note is then sent to both the solicitor and the client for them to make (usually within 21 days) whatever comments on it they wish, in order that (at the next stage) the Adjudicator might take those comments into account when considering the Agenda Note.

Second stage

5.4 At the second stage, the Adjudicator will carry out a quasi-judicial role, making a decision based on the Agenda Note and the parties' observations. This is a first instance decision against which the parties have a right of appeal exercisable within 28 days of being notified of the decision.

Third stage

5.5 At the third stage, an appeal from the decision of the Adjudicator will be heard by the Adjudication Panel, which also has a quasi-judicial role. The Panel considers only the original Agenda Note (together with its annexed documents), the comments of the parties on that note, the first instance decision, the grounds of appeal and the comments on those grounds of appeal.

Fourth stage

5.6 At the fourth stage, in the event that a finding of IPS is made and a direction is made against the solicitor, a complaint may be made to the SDT in the event of the solicitor failing to comply with that direction.

Fifth stage

5.7 At the fifth stage, in the event that the Adjudication Panel on appeal does not find the complaint to be made out, the complainant client may make application to the Legal Services Ombudsman for a review of the decision. In the event of such a review, the Ombudsman may direct the Law Society to reconsider the complaint (or part of the complaint) pursuant to the Courts and Legal Services Act 1990, s 23(2)(a). Any reconsideration directed by the Ombudsman will be effected by the Panel with the benefit of any further submissions from the parties as they think fit to make but otherwise will be based on the material that was before the Panel on its first hearing. It should be noted that there is no requirement that membership of the Panel be the same on each occasion and, indeed, it would in fact be most unusual to have the matter reconsidered by the same Panel members (simply by reason of logistics).

Sixth stage

5.8 At the sixth stage, in the event that the Adjudication Panel (whether on appeal or on a reconsideration) find the complaint to be made out or not made out, the solicitor or the client (as may be the case) may make application for judicial review of that decision.

Points to note concerning the statutory scheme

5.9

1. A solicitor faced with a complaint must act with restraint and must not be aggressive or antagonistic. As Lightman J put it in a case involving a challenge to an IPS finding:

   '... it is part of the professional duty of a solicitor, however much provoked and however ineffective ... any gesture on his part may be to allay the animosity of his client, to behave with restraint. The Adjudicator and the Appeals Committee are the judges of the professional standards which solicitors must maintain.'[1]

   But more than that, a solicitor faced with a complaint must listen to and consider the complaint and then take care to see that the client, who may be confused or ignorant, understands what the solicitor intends to do about the complaint or, if the solicitor intends to do nothing, why that is the case and to whom else (if this is appropriate) the complaint should be directed. (The solicitor is entitled to be rather more robust in his dealings with the Complaints Service concerning the complaint than he is in his dealings with his client concerning the complaint[2].)
2. The trigger for any direction to the solicitor as the result of the complaint of a client is the appearance to the Legal Complaints Service of the solicitor having provided services not, in any respect, of the quality which it is reasonable to expect. It is clear, therefore, that, the discretion is vested in the Legal Complaints Service, to be exercised in its role as regulator of the profession when it appears to the Legal Complaints Service that the professional services provided by the solicitor have been not of a reasonable quality. Through the experience of its Adjudicators and of its Adjudication Panel (which includes both members of the profession and also lay representatives), the Complaints Service is pre-eminently best placed to come to a view on whether or not a solicitor's services have not been of the quality which is reasonable to expect. As with many other of the Law Society's various disciplinary and regulatory jurisdictions in relation to solicitors, the court will always have regard as a relevant evidential factor to the view taken by the Complaints Service as the professional body charged with this aspect of regulation of solicitors' practices – the court's judgment may be significantly, though not conclusively, affected by the Complaints Service's own view of the facts: see *Giles v Law Society (1995)*[3]. Another way of putting this point may be to say – as did Carnwath LJ in *Holder v Law Society*[4] – that the Complaints Service has a margin of appreciation or discretion, or an area of judgment, in relation to the exercise of its discretion under the Act. (The existence of such a margin of appreciation is all the more sensible when one bears in mind the particular difficulties facing the profession in dealing with complaints, referred to above.)
3. The discretion arises to be exercised whenever it appears to the Complaints Service that the professional services provided by the solicitor have *in any respect* been inadequate. Accordingly, the Complaints Service is not required to carry out some sort of overall balance

of assessment of the benefit or detriment to a client from services provided by the solicitor, but can act whenever those services have in any one or more particular respects been inadequate.

4. A finding of inadequate professional service is not dependent upon there being proof of damage or prejudice to the client: *R v Solicitors Complaints Bureau, ex p Singh and Choudry (a firm)*[5]. In other words the compensation awarded to a client (which is presently limited to £15,000) may, in fact, not be compensatory at all, in the sense that it might not be intended to make good any monetary loss that the client has suffered. Nonetheless, in deciding whether it is appropriate to take any of the specified steps the Complaints Service may have regard to the existence of any remedy which it is reasonable to expect to be available to the client in civil proceedings and whether it is reasonable to expect the client to begin such proceedings.
5. Although the matter that is placed before the Adjudicator is the complaint made by the client concerning the solicitor, the Adjudicator is not limited to seeking to resolve that complaint by means of the various specified steps provided for in Sch 1A, para 2. More particularly, the Adjudicator has power to refer a complaint to the SDT, has power to express regret or disapproval of the solicitor's actions, has power to reprimand or severely reprimand the solicitor, and has power to 'vest a discretion' to impose conditions on the solicitor's next practising certificate. It is often these additional matters that are hotly disputed by solicitors, although it should be noted that a decision to refer a complaint to the SDT (being, effectively, a decision to bring a prosecution) is not itself amenable to challenge.
6. Despite the potential serious consequences to the solicitor of findings by the Adjudicator, the solicitor has no right to an oral hearing before, or to make oral representations to, the Adjudicator: see *R (Thompson) v The Law Society*[6]. The statutory regime is operated in a manner that permits both the client and solicitor to comment upon the views of the other (and on the views of the Complaints Service) but will not, usually, encompass an oral hearing. Such a hearing can be requested by either party, and the Complaints Service has a discretion to decide whether or not there should be such a hearing, which discretion must be exercised in accordance with the common law requirement to act fairly. However, there is no right to an oral hearing.
7. There being no right to an oral hearing is not in any manner contrary to the European Convention for the Protection of Human Rights and Fundamental Freedoms 1950, Article 6(1) (as set out in the Human Rights Act 1998, Sch 1). That is because no decision made by the Adjudicator will amount to a determination of the civil rights and obligations of the solicitor unless they were directly decisive of those rights, such as being directly decisive of the right to continue in professional practice. For example: while the effect of a reprimand might well be to increase the cost of a solicitor's professional indemnity insurance, that could not fairly be said to put his right to continue to practise his profession as a solicitor at stake; and the discretion conferred on the Law Society to impose conditions on a solicitor's practising certificate did not determine any of the solicitor's legal rights

and if the Law Society were subsequently to impose a condition, the claimant had a right of appeal, with provision for a public hearing.

8. A direction to a solicitor to take any step (whether to pay compensation or take some other action at his own expense) is not in itself enforceable by the Complaints Service or by the Law Society. It is only if a complaint is made to the SDT (pursuant to Sch 1A, para 5(1)) that a solicitor has failed to comply with such a direction, and only then if the SDT (which has full powers to review the direction both as to the law and as to the facts) decides that the direction is to be enforced, that the direction has any legal effect and can be enforced[7].
9. When considering a possible challenge by way of judicial review to a decision of an Adjudication Panel, a solicitor should consider carefully whether or not a challenge will in fact make matters worse for his reputation: see, for example, *R (on the application of Chong) v Law Society*[8], where a severe reprimand was upheld on review, with the court expressing the view that the solicitor had behaved deceitfully.

1 *White v Office for Supervision of Solicitors* [2001] EWHC Admin 1149, at 27.
2 *R (on the application of Bramall) v Law Society* [2005] EWHC 1570 (Admin), [2005] All ER (D) 291 (Jul).
3 8 Admin LR 105 per Sedley LJ, pp118–119.
4 [2003] 1 WLR 1059 at paras 30–33.
5 [1995] 7 Admin LR 249.
6 [2004] 2 All ER 113.
7 See *Thompson* per Clarke LJ at paras 94–99.
8 [2007] EWHC 641 (Admin), [2007] All ER (D) 91 (Mar).

THE NEED FOR A NEW STATUTORY REGIME

5.10 In the end, it appears that the weight of criticism of the Law Society's operation of the IPS jurisdiction – most notably and consistently made by the Legal Services Ombudsman –brought the present statutory scheme to its knees, at least reputationally. The death knell for the Solicitors Act 1974 scheme can now be seen to have been the final Clementi Report (December 2004). The report quoted a submission made by the Ombudsman to the effect that professional bodies handling complaints against their own members was an idea that 'has lost any legitimacy – consumer culture has moved on' and concluded (with the thinnest of reasoning) that a single independent complaints organisation (the Office for Legal Complaints (OLC)) should be formed covering all front-line legal regulatory bodies.

It was proposed that the OLC should provide quick and fair redress to consumers in whatever form may be appropriate, and 'without undue reference' to the classification of the complaint into one of IPS, one of misconduct or one of negligence. The complaint would be determined by reference to what, in the OLC's opinion, was fair and reasonable in the circumstances of the case, and there should be power to award redress to the consumer, including power to require an apology, order a reduction in fees, require work to be redone, and make an order for redress up to a prescribed limit.

If, when considering the complaint, the OLC was of the view that there had been some element of professional misconduct by the practitioner, it should refer that aspect to the relevant front-line regulator to be considered and dealt with, but redress to the consumer should not be delayed pending the outcome of any disciplinary hearing.

The report expressed no view as to what (if any) procedure there should be for appeals from a decision of the OLC but expressed a hope that a fair process of appeal could be achieved without the introduction of elaborate appeal mechanisms, which would prolong the uncertainty of outcome for the parties and run contrary to the objective of providing quick and appropriate redress with the minimum of formality.

LSA 2007

Introduction

5.11 In the light of the terms of the final Clementi report, one approaches the scheme for dealing with legal complaints set out in the Legal Services Act 2007, Pt 6 in the expectation that it will be a specifically tailored scheme, designed to meet the requirements set out in the report. And the new statutory scheme, at first sight, appears to be that.

It should be noted, however, that the scheme set out in Pt 6 is in fact in terms that are very similar to those which govern the Financial Ombudsman Service as provided for in the Financial Services and Markets Act 2000 (FSMA 2000), Pt XVI. This has, it seems, four potential consequences. First, the Pt 6 scheme is in fact not a scheme that has been tailored to meet the requirements of the final Clementi report or (more importantly) to meet the particular requirements of the legal services market but is, rather, pretty much a generic 'consumer culture' scheme that has been imposed on the legal professions with a 'one size fits all' mentality. Secondly, any court decisions concerning the FSMA 2000 scheme are likely to be extremely persuasive when a court has to consider what is essentially the same scheme under Pt 6. Thirdly, the Financial Ombudsman Service complaints scheme is confidential so the names of complainants and those complained against are not published, thus removing one of the key underpinning reasons behind the IPS jurisdiction. Fourthly, anyone who has been involved in the determination of a complaint under the Financial Ombudsman Service scheme will know that some disputes are not resolved quickly[1] and it would not, therefore, be a surprise if the same were the case under the Legal Services Act 2007 scheme.

1 For example in 2008, 42% of disputes were resolved within three months, 70% within six months, 81% within nine months, and 86% within 12 months.

The OLC and the ombudsmen

5.12 The new scheme[1] maintains the existing requirement that each provider of legal services (termed a 'relevant authorised person') must establish and maintain their own procedures for the resolution of relevant complaints[2]. Thus, it is the original provider of the legal service who is to remain the front-line handler of consumer complaints. The previous second-line handlers of complaints – the Legal Services Complaints Commissioner and the Legal Services Ombudsman – are, however, abolished[3].

In their stead, a new range of complaints handling systems are created under a scheme administered by a new body corporate, the OLC. The OLC must, so far as is reasonably practicable, act in a way which is compatible with the regulatory objectives under the Act, and must have regard to any principles appearing to it to represent the best practice of those who administer ombudsman schemes[4]. The OLC must prepare an annual report for each financial year dealing with the discharge of the functions of the OLC and the extent to which the OLC has met the regulatory objectives[5]. The OLC may be set performance targets or be directed to set its own performance targets (and in either case those targets must be published) relating to the performance of any of its functions[6].

The OLC must appoint a Chief Ombudsman (who must be a lay person[7]) and Assistant Ombudsmen (who may not during their appointment carry on any activity which is a reserved legal activity in expectation of any fee)[8]. The Chief Ombudsman must prepare a report for each financial year on the discharge of the functions of the ombudsmen.

1 What follows is a consideration of the 'compulsory scheme' rather than the 'voluntary scheme' that is provided for in LSA 2007, ss 164–166.
2 LSA 2007, s 112.
3 Section 159(1).
4 Section 116(2), (3).
5 Section 118.
6 Section 121.
7 Schedule 15.
8 Section 122.

Complaints, not conduct

5.13 It is important to note that the Act provides for a division of responsibility between redress for complaints (which is to be the responsibility of the OLC) and sanction for misconduct (which is to be the responsibility of the approved regulator[1]). Thus, under the scheme, redress may be given to the complainant, but no disciplinary action may be taken against the respondent[2] and the Act requires that the regulatory arrangements of an approved regulator must not include any provision relating to redress in respect of acts or omissions of authorised persons[3]. Conversely, the scheme rules may not make provision excluding a complaint from the jurisdiction of the ombudsman scheme on the ground that it relates to a matter which has been or could be dealt with under the disciplinary arrangements of the respondent's relevant authorising body[4].

1 By LSA 2007, s 143 an ombudsman who is of the opinion that the conduct of the respondent is such that a relevant authorising body should consider whether to take action against that person must (even if the complaint is withdrawn or abandoned) give the relevant authorising body a report which states that opinion and gives details of the conduct.
2 Section 113(2).

[3] Section 157. This restriction does not prevent an approved regulator from making provision requiring a relevant authorised person to investigate whether there are any persons who may have a claim against them, to provide a report on that investigation, to notify such persons that they may have a claim and to provide such persons with information about the authorised person's own complaints scheme and also the OLC scheme (s 158).

[4] Section 127(2).

Scheme jurisdiction

5.14 There are tests to be satisfied before a complaint can fall within the jurisdiction of the ombudsman scheme[1].

First, the complainant must fall within LSA 2007, s 128 and also wish to have the complaint dealt with under the scheme. Section 128(2) provides two conditions which a complainant must meet, namely (i) that the complainant is an individual (or a person other than an individual of a prescribed description)[2] and (ii) the services to which the complaint relates were provided by the respondent to the complainant, or by the respondent to an authorised person who procured them on the complainant's behalf[3], or by the respondent in his capacity as a personal representative or trustee or to a person acting as personal representative or trustee, and the complainant is a beneficiary of the estate or trust in question[4]. In addition to satisfying these two conditions, the complainant must not be excluded under s 128(5), namely must not be an authorised person in relation to an activity which was a reserved legal activity and the services to which the complaint relates were procured by the complainant on behalf of another person[5], the complainant was a public body or was acting on behalf of such a body, or the complainant was a person who is prescribed as excluded.

Secondly, the respondent must fall within s 128. That will be the case if, at the relevant time, the respondent was an authorised person in relation to an activity which was a reserved legal activity, whether or not the act or omission relates to a reserved legal activity[6].

Thirdly, the complaint must not be excluded from the jurisdiction of the scheme by s 126 or by scheme rules made under s 127. Section 126(1) excludes a complaint from the scheme if the complainant has not first used the respondent's complaints procedures in relation to the complaint, but this exclusion may be disapplied in specified circumstances as provided for in the scheme rules[7]. Section 127 provides that scheme rules may make provision excluding complaints of a specified description. At the time of writing no scheme rules (or draft scheme rules) have been made public.

It should be noticed that the right of a person to make a complaint under the ombudsman scheme, and the jurisdiction of the ombudsman to investigate and determine a complaint, cannot be limited or excluded by any contract term or by notice[8]. It is far from clear whether or not a term of a settlement agreement which provided for a potential complainant not to make a complaint under the scheme (in consideration of, for example, a payment of compensation) would fall foul of this restriction.

1 Section 125(1).
2 Section 128(3).
3 Thus a client can make a complaint against a barrister instructed by his solicitor.
4 Section 128(4).
5 Thus a solicitor cannot make a complaint about a barrister who provided services that the solicitor procured for his client.
6 Section 128(1). By s 161, Pt 6 is extended to claims management services and, for the purposes of the part, the Claims Management Services Regulator is to be treated as an approved regulator and a relevant authorising body, and a person authorised by that regulator to provide regulated claims management services is to be treated as a relevant authorised person.
7 Section 126(3). The final Clementi report (paras 62–63) expressed the view that a complaint might be to the OLC made prior to the conclusion of an in-house procedure, if an initial acknowledgement was not received within a short period of the complaint being made, or if it was not possible to resolve the complaint within a reasonable time, or if there was evidence of a difficult and possibly acrimonious relationship between a consumer and a lawyer over an extended period.
8 Section 125(3).

Responsibility for acts of others

5.15 LSA 2007, sections 131 and 132 deal with the issue of who is to be responsible for acts or omissions. Section 131(1) provides that for the purposes of the scheme, any act or omission by a person in the course of the person's employment is to be treated as also an act or omission by the person's employer[1], whether or not it was done with the employer's knowledge or approval. Similarly, any act or omission of a partner in a partnership in the course of carrying on, in the usual way, business of the kind carried on by the partnership is to be treated also as an act or omission of the partnership, unless the partner had no authority to act for the partnership and the complainant knew, at the time, that the partner had no such authority[2].

The ability to make a complaint is not affected by any change in the membership of a partnership or other unincorporated body[3] nor (under the scheme rules) is a complaint to be affected by the death or inability to act of the complainant[4]. Furthermore, the scheme rules must make provision determining the circumstances in which a complaint about any act or omission of a 'person [who] ceases to exist and another person succeeds to the whole or substantially the whole of the business' is to be treated as an act or omission of the successor[5].

1 It may be a matter for debate as to whether or not an act by a barrister's clerk – who is usually not an employee of that barrister – is to be treated as also the act of the barrister.
2 Section 131(2), (3).
3 Section 132(1).
4 Section 132(4).
5 Section 132(2). This will be an issue (particularly bearing in mind that compensation under the scheme can now be up to £30,000) that any proposed acquirer of a solicitors' practice will have to consider very carefully.

Determination of complaints

5.16 A complaint is to be determined under the scheme by reference to what is, in the opinion of the ombudsman making the determination, fair and reasonable in all the circumstances of the case[1]. This is an apparently simple and unobjectionable approach but there is a very important point to note. The ombudsman's role is not to determine a complaint about an act or omission on the part of a solicitor by reference to some objective standard of adequacy (IPS), propriety (conduct) or competence (negligence) and to carry out that determination in a fair and reasonable manner. Rather, the ombudsman's role is to assess the act or omission *by reference to* the concepts of fairness and reasonableness[2]. Now, it may well be unremarkable that an act that is considered to have been unfair or unreasonable can found a successful complaint, but there will inevitably be cases where, even though the act cannot be determined to have been unfair or unreasonable, the complaint is nonetheless upheld because it cannot be determined that the act *was* fair and reasonable. In other words, there appears to be an implicit evidential burden on the solicitor to establish that the act was fair and reasonable.

A determination may contain a direction that the respondent make an apology[3]; a direction that the respondent's fees be limited (or fees already paid be refunded, together with interest[4]); a direction that the respondent pay compensation in respect of any loss which has been suffered by, or any inconvenience or distress[5] which has been caused to, the complainant as a result of any matter connected with the complaint; a direction that the respondent secure (at its own expense) the rectification of an error; or a direction that the respondent take (at its own expense) such other action in the interests of the complainant as may be specified. The limit of the total value of the directions that may be made in respect of a complaint is £30,000[6], ignoring any interest that might be payable[7].

The ombudsman who has determined a complaint must prepare a written statement of the determination giving reasons for the determination[8], which is to be copied to the complainant, the respondent and any relevant authorising body of the respondent[9]. The statement must require the complainant to notify the ombudsman, before a specified time, whether the complainant accepts or rejects the determination[10]. If the complainant notifies the ombudsman that the determination is accepted, then it is binding on the respondent and is final[11]. If nothing is heard from the complainant within the specified time then the complainant is treated as having rejected the determination[12], but that deemed rejection may be treated as if it had never happened in certain circumstances if the complainant notified the ombudsman of the acceptance of the determination after the specified time[13].

There are two important points to note concerning determination of complaints. First, the respondent to a complaint has no right of appeal against the determination of the ombudsman. Thus, the only proactive route of challenge available to the respondent will be by way of judicial review. Secondly, a binding and final determination bars any legal proceedings (whether by the complainant or the respondent) in respect of any matter which was the subject of a complaint[14]. Therefore, there would appear to be no point in a complainant making a complaint if the loss he has suffered may be in excess of £30,000.

A final and binding determination made by an ombudsman which includes one or more directions under s 137(2) for the repayment of fees or the payment of compensation is enforceable by order of the High Court or county court, as if it the amount directed to be paid were payable under an order of that court[15]. Similarly, when a direction has been made requiring an act on the part of the respondent other than the payment of money the court may order the respondent to take such steps as it directs for securing compliance with the direction[16]. If one adopts the reasoning of Lewison J in *Bunney v Burns Anderson plc*[17] concerning the similar provisions in FSMA 2000, then it will be open to the solicitor, upon the making of an application for a court order, to oppose the making of the order on the grounds that the ombudsman's determination was made without jurisdiction or is otherwise invalid (rather than wrong on the merits)[18].

Any order made by the court under s 141 must be notified to the OLC by the court[19] and the OLC must (in the case of an order made against a person who is an authorised person in relation to any activity which is a reserved legal activity) make arrangements to ensure that the ombudsman gives a report to each relevant authorising body in relation to that person, which report may require the authorising body to report to the ombudsman what action is taken in response to the report and the reasons for that action being taken[20]. Any serious failure (in the view of the ombudsman) on the part of the authorising body to discharge its regulatory functions may be reported to the board[21].

1 LSA 2007, s 137(1).
2 Section 133(3)(f).
3 Section 137(2). Quite what good a forced apology does for the complainant or the respondent is nowhere explained.
4 Section 137(4).
5 It is likely that the OLC will have to draw up guidelines concerning compensation for distress and inconvenience similar to those promulgated by the Financial Ombudsman Service – see http://www.financial-ombudsman.org.uk/publications/technical_notes/distress-and-inconvenience.htm.
6 This limit may be amended by order made by the Lord Chancellor: s 139.
7 Section 138.
8 Section 140(1), (2)(a).
9 Section 140(3).
10 Section 140(2)(c).
11 Section 140(4).
12 Section 140(5).
13 Section 140(6).
14 Section 140(11).
15 Section 141(2).
16 Section 141(4).
17 [2007] 4 All ER 246.
18 It is to be noted that in such circumstances the matter before the Court will ordinarily be (because an application can be made by the ombudsman: s 141(5)) between the complainant and the respondent and the complainant will therefore be personally at risk as to costs.
19 Section 142(1).
20 Section 142(2), (3).
21 Section 142(4).

Operation of the scheme

5.17 The procedure and time limits for making a complaint under the ombudsman scheme are to be set out in the scheme rules[1] and, in the absence of any draft rules, cannot be known at present. LSA 2007, s 133(3), however, provides some guidance as to the topics that the rules will cover.

First, the rules may make provision for the whole or part of a complaint to be dismissed without consideration of its merits in specified circumstances including[2] where the ombudsman considers the complaint to be frivolous, vexatious or totally without merit; where the ombudsman considers the complaint would be better dealt with under another ombudsman scheme, by arbitration or by other legal proceedings; where the ombudsman considers there has been undue delay in the making of the complaint or in the provision of evidence to support it; where the ombudsman is satisfied that the matter which is the subject of the complaint has previously been dealt with under another ombudsman scheme, by arbitration or by other legal proceedings[3]; or where the ombudsman considers there are other compelling reasons why it is in appropriate for the complaint to be dealt with under the scheme.

Secondly, the rules may make provision about the evidence which may be required or admitted and the extent to which it should be oral or written; for requiring parties to the complaint to attend to give oral evidence and produce documents and for the administration of oaths by ombudsmen[4]. Scheme rules cannot, however, require any person to provide any information or give any evidence which he could not be compelled to provide or give in civil proceedings before the High Court. Furthermore, an ombudsman may by notice require a party to a complaint to produce documents or to provide information (necessary for the determination of the complaint) within such reasonable period and in such manner or form as may be specified[5]. If an authorised person fails to comply with such a requirement then the ombudsman must give each relevant authorising body a report to that effect[6]. The ombudsman may also certify the defaulter's failure to comply to the court, in which event the court may enquire into the case and, if satisfied that there has been a failure, may deal with the defaulter (and, in the case of a body, with any manager of the body) as if that person were in contempt[7].

Thirdly, scheme rules may make provision about the matters to be taken into account in determining whether an act or omission was fair and reasonable. We have considered above the import of the 'fair and reasonable' test[8]. It is likely that the OLC will adopt rules similar to those used under the Financial Ombudsman Service which require the ombudsman to take into account relevant law[9] and regulations; regulators' rules, guidance and standards; codes of practice; and (where appropriate) what he considers to have been good industry practice at the relevant time.

Fourthly, scheme rules may make provision for the ombudsman to award expenses to a person in connection with attendance at a hearing; for an ombudsman to award costs against a respondent in favour of the complainant (but not vice versa); for an ombudsman to award costs against a complainant in favour of the OLC if the person has acted so unreasonably in relation to the complaint that it is appropriate to do so; and for the purpose of facilitating settlement of a complaint[10].

Fifthly, scheme rules must require respondents, in relation to complaints under the scheme, to pay to the OLC such charges as may be specified but the rules must provide for those charges to be waived (or wholly refunded) where the complaint is determined or otherwise resolved in favour of the respondent and the ombudsman is satisfied that the respondent took all reasonable steps to try to resolve the complaint under its own complaints procedures[11].

1 LSA 2007, s 133(1), (2).
2 Section 133(4).
3 Although note that this does not include the matter having already been dealt with in disciplinary proceedings: s 127(2).
4 Seemingly taking the scheme into areas of resolution of factual dispute that the existing IPS jurisdiction (as operated by the Law Society) has in general avoided.
5 Section 147.
6 Section 148.
7 Section 149.
8 See para 5.16 above.
9 But, note, that the ombudsman does not have to apply the law. He could, for example, override a limitation defence to which the court would have to give effect if he considers it unfair to rely on limitation: cf *Bunney v Burns Anderson* (see para 5.16 above).
10 In each of these three cases of costs/expenses recovery, the amount due under an award is recoverable as a debt due: s 133(7).
11 Section 136.

Publicity

5.18 The OLC may, if it considers it appropriate to do so in any particular case, publish a report of the investigation, consideration and determination of a complaint made under the ombudsman scheme, but such a report must not (unless the complainant consents) mention the name of the complainant or include any particulars which, in the opinion of the OLC, are likely to identify the complainant[1]. For the purposes of the law of defamation, proceedings in relation to any complaint under the scheme are to be treated as if they were proceedings before a court and the publication of any matter by the OLC is absolutely privileged[2].

1 Section 150.
2 Section 154.

Chapter 6

OTHER SIGNIFICANT REGULATORY CHANGES BROUGHT ABOUT BY THE LSA 2007

Iain Miller and Rebecca Stubbs

INTRODUCTION

6.1 Much of the focus on the provisions of the LSA 2007 has been in relation to the new regulatory arrangements and the introduction of alternative business structures (ABSs). However, these matters have also resulted in consequential changes to the existing regulatory regimes for some of the legal professionals who are not contemplating becoming either a legal disciplinary practice (LDP) or an ABS. In addition, the opportunity has been taken to introduce new wide ranging regulatory and disciplinary powers where appropriate. The purpose of this chapter is to summarise those changes.

SOLICITORS

6.2 The regulatory and disciplinary changes affecting solicitors are made primarily by amendment to the Solicitors Act 1974[1]. It is unfortunate that it has not been considered appropriate to pass a new Solicitors Act consolidating the relevant changes. As such, amendments (and amendments made by previous Acts) have to be accommodated within the existing numbering of the 1974 Act. We therefore now have ss 13ZA, 13ZB, 44, 44B, 44BA, 44BB, 44BC, 44C, 44D and 44E. Within this chapter reference to 'the Act' is to the Solicitors Act 1974 as amended by the LSA 2007. In common with the other provisions in the Act the statutory powers are vested in the Law Society rather than the Solicitors Regulation Authority (SRA). However, in practice, the powers described below will be exercised by the SRA.

In addition to the substantive changes described below, the LSA 2007 also changes some of the terminology in the Act. Assessment now replaces taxation in relation to costs, to bring the wording in line with the Civil Procedure Rules. Solicitors are no longer Solicitors of the Supreme Court but are Solicitors of the Senior Court to reflect changes to the court system[2]. Partners in firms are no longer required to personally sign bills, but can now authorise others to do so on their behalf[3].

1 The Administration of Justice Act 1985 (AJA 1985) is amended to extend the power described in this chapter to recognised bodies. We have already seen that amendments to the AJA 1985 also facilitate the creation of LDPs. The Courts and Legal Services Act 1990 is consequentially amended to deal with registered foreign lawyers (RFLs).
2 See, amongst others, amendments to the Solicitors Act 1974, s 6.
3 Section 69(2A).

Entity-based regulation – sole solicitor certification

6.3 As seen in earlier chapters, one of the important themes of the LSA 2007 is the introduction of entity regulation, by which the primary regulation of a legal firm is of the entity. It logically follows that such regulation must extend to sole practitioners. Accordingly, s 1B of the Act states that the rules of professional practice must provide that solicitors cannot practice as a sole solicitor unless they have a certificate authorising him to practise as a sole practitioner. This is in addition to the existing requirement to have a practising certificate. There are consequential provisions at ss 13ZA and 13ZB which deal with applications for sole practitioner certificates and the fee. In addition, ss 17A and 17B deal with suspensions of sole practitioner certificates. These arrangements seem an unnecessary additional administrative burden on sole practitioners (who by definition are likely to have limited resources) simply to ensure universal application of entity regulation. However, whilst the vast majority of sole practitioners are hard working practitioners, there is little doubt that as a group they represent the greatest area of regulatory risk, and the SRA's new powers may assist in ensuring more effective regulation of this group. There can be little doubt that these additional regulatory burdens will in due course cause a reduction of the number of sole practitioners.

SRA Practising Regulations effective from 1 July 2009 bring into force this provision. Existing sole practitioners will be passported into the new regime. The process for recognition for sole practitioners is briefly as follows. An applicant must be or be intending to practise from an office in England and Wales, must not be subject, or about to be subject, to a practising certificate condition preventing practice as a sole practitioner, must comply with the supervision requirements of r 5.02 of the Code, and must adopt a suitable name under which to be recognised[1]. The SRA may refuse an application if it is not satisfied that the applicant is suitable to run and manage the business or if for any other reason the SRA reasonably considers that it would be against the public interest to grant recognition[2]. When reaching a decision, the SRA may take into account: any event listed in reg 3.1 of the SRA Practising Regulations applying to the applicant; any other conduct on the part of the applicant which calls into question his honesty, integrity or respect for law; failure or refusal to disclose, or an attempt to conceal, any such matter in relation to the application; or that the SRA is not satisfied that the applicant has sufficient skills or knowledge in relation to the running and management of a business which provides regulated legal services[3]. When granting an application the SRA may impose a condition on the applicant's practising certificate[4].

Authorisation as a recognised sole practitioner ceases on the expiry or revocation of the solicitor's practising certificate or the imposition of a condition on the solicitor's practising certificate which prohibits practice as a sole practitioner[5]. The SRA may revoke a practising certificate at any time, if the SRA is satisfied that the practising certificate was granted as a result of error or fraud; if the replacement or renewal date has passed and the SRA has not received an application for replacement of the practising certificate which complies with the Regulations; or if the SRA refuses to replace a practising certificate on annual renewal[6].

The SRA may revoke authorisation as a recognised sole practitioner at any time if: the authorisation as a recognised sole practitioner was granted as a result of error or fraud; the solicitor is not practising from an office in England and Wales; the SRA is not satisfied that the recognised sole practitioner continues to meet the criteria for authorisation as a recognised sole practitioner; the recognised sole practitioner has a temporary emergency recognition but has not within the initial 28-day period or any extension of that period commenced a substantive application for recognition; or the SRA has decided not to renew authorisation as a recognised sole practitioner[7].

The SRA may also revoke a practising certificate or authorisation as a recognised sole practitioner on the application of the person concerned, but there is no discretion to refund any part of the fee paid for that practising year and the SRA may refuse the application if there is an outstanding complaint against the applicant or for any other reason relating to the public interest[8].

When the SRA decides to revoke a practising certificate or authorisation as a recognised sole practitioner it must give the person concerned 28 days' notice, with reasons. The notice may be given together with notification of refusal of an application to replace a practising certificate or renew an authorisation[9]. Revocation takes effect on expiry of the notice or on such later date as may be stated in the notice, except that if an appeal is made during the period of notice the revocation does not take effect until determination or discontinuance of any appeal[10].

1 SRA Practising Regulations 2009, reg 4.2(a).
2 Regulation 4.2(b).
3 Regulation 4.2(c).
4 Regulation 4.2(d).
5 Regulation 9.1(d).
6 Regulation 9.2(a).
7 Regulation 9.2(b).
8 Regulation 9.2(c).
9 Regulation 9.3(a).
10 Regulation 9.3(b).

Wider regulator and disciplinary powers

6.4 As we have previously seen, one of the regulatory reforms introduced by the LSA 2007 is to bring all those working in firms providing reserved legal activities within the regulatory control and disciplinary sanctions of the approved regulator. This applies to all existing law firms as well as any future ABSs.

Section 34A of the Act now provides that employees of solicitors can be made subject to the Code of Conduct or accounts rules, and failure to comply can be the subject of a complaint to the Solicitors Disciplinary Tribunal (SDT). Prior to the LSA 2007, the only jurisdiction the Law Society had in relation to employees arose under s 43, which enabled the Society or the SDT to make an order in certain circumstances that a person could only be employed by a solicitor with the permission of the Society. It should be added that s 43 has not escaped the attention of those drafting the LSA 2007. Its terms have been widened to cover any person 'involved in a legal practice', which is defined in s 43(1A). This is in contrast to the more narrow terms of new s 34A which limits the disciplinary jurisdiction to 'employees'.

The Law Society acquires new investigatory powers under ss 44B, 44BA, 44BB, 44BC and 44C. Section 44B replaces the old s 44B, which enabled the Law Society to obtain a file (and other documents) from a solicitor. The new provisions enable the Law Society to give notice requiring[1] the provision of information, or information of a description specified in the notice. However, such an notice can only be given if the Law Society considers that it is necessary to do so for the purposes of an investigation within the terms of s 44B(3) of the Act.

Section 44BA provides that where a person has been given notice under s 44B they may be required to attend at an appointed time and place to give an explanation of any information provided or document produced under the s 44B notice. Failure to so comply is a summary offence under Sch 1, para 9(3) to the Act[2]. This section is a rather stark illustration of the onerous burden of being a solicitor (and indeed an employee of a solicitor). A solicitor cannot claim privilege against self-incrimination[3] and therefore is compelled to answer any questions posed. However, as the SRA's usual practice is not to administer a caution in the course of their investigations, it is unlikely that information obtained at such interviews will be admissible in criminal proceedings[4].

Section 44BB enables the Law Society to seek an order from the High Court in respect of any person to whom s 44B does not apply to provide information and produce documents. The High Court may only make an order if, amongst other things, it has reasonable cause to believe that the information or documents are likely to be of material significance to an investigation. Section 44 BC has the rather Orwellian title of 'Information Offences'. It provides that taking steps to avoid compliance with ss 44B, 44BA and 44BA such as falsifying or concealing documents or knowingly or recklessly providing false information in a material particular is an offence.

1 Notice can be given to a solicitor, an employee of a solicitor, a recognised body, or a manager or person having an interest in a recognised body; see s 44B(2).

2 Paragraph 9(3) is rather confusingly adapted by this section; in relation to this section it therefore reads:

> 'Except in the case where an application has been made to the High Court under sub-paragraph (4), if any person refuses, neglects,or otherwise fails to comply with a requirement under Section 44BA(1) he shall be guilty of an offence and liable on summary conviction to a fine not exceeding level 3 on the standard scale.'

3 *Holder v The Law Society* [2005] EWHC 2023 (Admin).
4 *R v Barnett*, Field J, Southwark Crown Court, 7 May 2004.

Disciplinary powers of the Law Society

6.5 Until the LSA 2007 the Law Society did not have any statutory disciplinary powers. The only statutory powers were vested in the SDT. However, a practice had evolved over a number of years for the Law Society to impose a reprimand upon solicitors where it disapproved of a solicitor's conduct but did not consider that the matter was so serious that it justified a referral to the SDT. Such reprimands have been the subject of a number of challenges by way of judicial review[1]. In particular, in *R (on the Application of Thompson) v The Law Society*[2], it was held that the imposition of a reprimand did not engage Article 6 of the ECHR because it did not directly interfere with a solicitor's right to practice.

The new s 44D empowers the Law Society to rebuke and/or fine[3] a solicitor or an employee of a solicitor for failure to comply with a requirement imposed or by virtue of the Act or any rules made under it by the Law Society. In addition, the Law Society may fine a solicitor where he is guilty of professional misconduct[4]. By amendment to the AJA 1985 this power is also extended to recognised bodies[5]. The Law Society also has a discretion to publish details of any fine or rebuke. The Law Society is required to make rules prescribing the circumstances in which it exercises its powers under s 44D and the procedure to be followed[6]. This was the subject of the SRA's Consultation Paper 14 published on 1 December 2008. The new rules are expected to come into force on 1 July 2009.

Section 44E provides for an appeal from a decision by the Law Society under s 44D to the SDT. The payment of any fine or the publication of the decision by the Law Society is suspended pending such appeal[7]. By this mechanism the rights of the solicitor under Article 6 of the ECHR are preserved.

1 See *Thompson* (below); *R (on the application of Chong) v Law Society* [2007] EWHC 641 (Admin), [2007] All ER (D) 91 (Mar).
2 [2004] 1 WLR 2522.
3 The maximum fine is £2000; see s 44D(2)(b).
4 This is an interesting preservation of what used to be known as 'common law' misconduct which is in essence conduct unbefitting a solicitor but not necessarily conduct that is specifically dealt with in any rule. In contrast, the jurisdiction over employees only arises where they breach a specific rule.
5 AJA 1985, s 14B.
6 Section 44D(7), (8).
7 Section 44D(5), (6).

Intervention

6.6 Amendments to Sch 1 of the Act significantly extend the jurisdiction of the Law Society to intervene into a practice conducted by a solicitor. The pre-existing provisions of Sch 1(1)(a) empowered the Law Society to intervene in the practice of a solicitor where it had reason to suspect dishonesty on the part of a solicitor, an employee of a solicitor or a personal representative of a deceased solicitor in connection with that solicitor's practice. To this has been added an additional ground, Sch 1(1)(aa), which empowers the Law Society to intervene where it has reason to suspect dishonesty on the part of a solicitor in connection with the business of any person of whom the solicitor is or was an employee, or any body of which he was a manager or any business which is or was carried out by the solicitor as a sole trader. This would allow the Law Society to intervene in a business that is not a solicitor's practice but employs a solicitor who is suspected of dishonesty. This would appear to include a business that is not otherwise regulated by the SRA. This overcomes some practical difficulties that have arisen where a solicitor has relied upon his status as a solicitor but is not practising within a solicitors' practice[1].

There is now an additional ground for intervention, Sch 1(1)(m), which is more wide ranging than any other ground. The Law Society can intervene where it is satisfied that it is necessary to do so to protect the interests of clients.

1 *Share v The Law Society* [2008] EWHC 2425 (Ch).

Rules, rules, rules

6.7 In common with the trend in parliamentary drafting, many of the statutory provisions of the Solicitors Act 1974 have been replaced with a power to make rules. Sections 12 and 12A in relation to practising certificates are repealed and s 28(3B) makes more extensive provisions for practising certificate rules and other rules such as admissions and the keeping of the roll. Section 31 is amended to provide that the Law Society may make rules dealing with 'fitness to practise'. This additional phrase allows the Law Society to make rules dealing with health as well as conduct. Section 36, which relates to the Law Society's Compensation Fund, is entirely replaced and enables the Law Society to make rules concerning the grant of compensation. Schedule 2, which dealt with the powers of the Compensation Fund, is repealed. The method by which the Law Society deals with practice money vested in it pursuant to the exercise of the intervention power will now be dealt with by rules under Sch 1, para 6B of the Act.

Changes to the SDT and arrangements for appeals from decisions of the Law Society

6.8 The LSA 2007 removes the Master of the Rolls from any appellate function in relation to solicitors (or any other legal professionals such as Registered Foreign Lawyers) by making decisions previously subject to his jurisdiction subject to appeal to the High Court. It also enhances the role of the SDT.

Until the Solicitors Act 1888, the disciplinary jurisdiction over solicitors was exercised exclusively by the courts. By virtue of that Act, applications against solicitors were made to a Committee of the Incorporated Law Society, whose members were appointed by the Master of the Rolls. The Committee made findings which were embodied in a report to the court, but the court continued to exercise the disciplinary jurisdiction.

The Solicitors Act 1919 granted the powers of the court, to strike solicitors from the roll and to impose other penalties, to the Disciplinary Committee of the Law Society, but preserved the court's inherent jurisdiction. The Disciplinary Committee was not a committee of the Council of the Law Society, but a separate statutory body whose members continued to be appointed by the Master of the Rolls. This regime continued through successive Solicitors Acts up to and including that of 1957. The Disciplinary Committee was replaced by the SDT in 1975 under the Solicitors Act 1974. However, the Solicitors Act 1974 did not make any provision for the funding of the SDT save for the payment to lay members introduced by the 1974 Act[1]. By default, the SDT continued to be funded by the Law Society and its employees and clerks were, technically, employees of the Law Society. Its solicitor members could not be remunerated at all. The LSA 2007 introduces amendments to s 46 of the Act which enable all members of the SDT to be paid. It also removes the restriction that the SDT's quorum is three members.

The LSA also introduces s 46A, which puts on a statutory footing the SDT's funding. It will continue to be funded by the Law Society, but this funding will now be overseen by the Legal Services Board (LSB). LSA 2007, ss 177–180 give the LSB powers to oversee the operation of the SDT. In particular the SDT's rules in future will normally be approved by the LSB[2]. The LSB can also give directions to the SDT and modify its functions[3].

Under the LSA 2007 the SDT increases its jurisdiction. It now deals with disciplinary proceedings against employees of solicitors under s 34A of the Act. It also has an appellate jurisdiction to deal with decisions of the Law Society to fine and/or rebuke solicitors, employees of solicitors, and recognised bodies under s 44D of the Act and AJA 1985, s 14A. It is likely that it will in future have an appellate jurisdiction in relation to decisions by the SRA acting as a licensing authority in relation to ABSs[4]. Indeed, there is nothing in the terms of the LSA which would prevent the SDT having an appellate jurisdiction in relation to other licensing authorities if approved by the Lord Chancellor.

Amendments to the Solicitors Act 1974 substitute the jurisdiction of the Master of the Rolls with that of the High Court, which in practice will mean the Administrative Court. However, s 49A of the Act provides that the Law Society may make rules which provide for appeal to the SDT instead of the High Court. This can only be done with the approval of the SDT. These changes would relate to:

- a decision to re-enter a solicitor onto the roll under s 8(2);
- the decision to impose conditions on an existing practising certificate under s 13A(1);
- the refusal to terminate the suspension of a practising certificate under s 16(3);

- decisions under regulations relating to admissions, keeping of the roll, practising certificates, sole solicitor endorsements and the keeping of the register made pursuant to s 28(1); and
- provisions relating to the Registered Foreign Lawyers under the Courts and Legal Services Act 1990.

Taken together, the above changes to the operation and jurisdiction of the SDT represent a radical departure from its previous role. Previously, it had dealt almost exclusively with the discipline of solicitors without any real oversight. In future, it is able to deal with almost all the disciplinary and regulatory decisions of the SRA overseen by the LSB. If the potential under the LSA is fulfilled it will have a much more influential role in the regulatory framework.

As previously observed, the High Court has inherited an appellate jurisdiction in relation to a substantial number of regulatory decisions previously dealt with by the Master of the Rolls. Whilst these may in due course be dealt with by the SDT, it appears that these matters will at least initially be dealt with by the High Court. Certain other appeals can apparently only be made to the High Court under the amendments to the Solicitors Act 1974 and cannot be dealt with by the SDT even if appropriate rules were enacted. These include:

- appeals against decisions to refuse to issue a practising certificate or to impose conditions on a practising certificate under s 13(1) of the Act;
- refusal to issue a sole solicitor endorsement, or to issue it subject to conditions under s 13ZA of the Act.

1 Section 46(5).
2 LSA 2007, s 178.
3 LSA 2007, ss 179–180.
4 See LSA 2007, s 80.

THE BAR

6.9 Historically the regulation of the Bar has been quite different to that of solicitors. Given that most barristers do not deal directly with lay clients, and do not, therefore, have to be concerned about the terms of engagement letters, and that no barrister is permitted to hold client funds, the regulation of the Bar has historically been, and remains, lighter than that of solicitors.

Before the enactment of the Courts and Legal Services Act 1990, it was for the judges of each court acting collectively – as a 'collegiate body' – to decide, as an incident of their inherent power to regulate their own practices, whether or not to modify established practices (including the question of to whom to grant rights of audience), and to promulgate any changes to established general practice by practice directions[1].

The General Council of the Bar (or 'Bar Council') is the governing body of the Bar: it represents the Bar in its relations with others, and has principal responsibility for the formulation of policy. The Bar Council Constitution, which sets out the authority, powers and duties of the Bar Council, is contained in Pt II of a combined document, 'Introduction and Constitutions of the General Council of the Bar and of the Council of the Inns of Court and of the Inns of Court and the Bar Educational Trust'.

The Bar Standards Board (BSB) is (and has since 1 January 2006 been) responsible for the regulatory functions of the Bar Council. The Consolidated Regulations of the Inns of Court and the General Council of the Bar (2007) govern the manner in which a person may be admitted to one of the Inns of Court and qualify as a barrister. The BSB and the Inns' Council may, in consultation with each another, amend the regulations[2].

1 *Abse v Smith* [1986] QB 536.
2 Regulation 59.

COURTS AND LEGAL SERVICES ACT 1990

6.10 The statutory objective of the Courts and Legal Services Act 1990 (CLSA 1990), Pt II is:

> 'the development of legal services in England and Wales (and in particular the development of advocacy, litigation, conveyancing and probate services) by making provision for new or better ways of providing such services and a wider choice of persons providing them, while maintaining the proper and efficient administration of justice.'[1]

1 Section 17(1), (2).

Rights of audience

6.11

1. 'Right of audience' means the right to appear before and address a court, including the right to call and examine witnesses[1].
2. Under the CLSA 1990, whether a person should be granted a right of audience or to conduct litigation in relation to any court or proceedings is determined only by reference to:
   (a) whether he is qualified in accordance with the education and training requirements appropriate to the court or proceedings;
   (b) whether he is a member of a professional or other body which:
      (i) has rules of conduct governing the conduct of its members;
      (ii) has an effective mechanism for enforcing the rules of conduct; and
      (iii) is likely to enforce it;
   (c) whether, in the case of a body whose members are or are to be providing advocacy services, the rules of conduct make satisfactory provision in relation to the court or proceedings in question requiring any such member not to withhold those services:
      (i) on the ground that the nature of the case is objectionable to him or to any section of the public;

(ii) on the ground that the conduct, opinions or beliefs of the prospective client are unacceptable to him or to any section of the public;

(iii) on the ground relating to the source of any financial support which might properly be given to the prospective client for the proceedings in question;

(d) whether the rules of conduct are, in relation to the court or proceedings, appropriate in the interests of the proper and efficient administration of justice[2].

3. Section 27 provides that the question of whether a person has a right of audience before a court, or in relation to any proceedings, should be determined solely in accordance with the provisions of CLSA 1990, Pt II. Section 27(2) makes provision for the circumstances in which a person should have a right of audience, which circumstances include (in sub-paragraph (a)), where a person has a right of audience in relation to those proceedings granted by the appropriate authorised body and that body's qualification regulations and rules of conduct have been approved for the purposes of s 27 in relation to that right.

4. The Bar Council is an authorised body for the purposes of the CLSA 1990[3].

5. Every barrister who has been called to the Bar by an Inn of Court and who has not been disbarred or suspended from practice is deemed to have been granted by the General Council of the Bar a right of audience before every court in relation to all proceedings[4].

6. The right of audience are exercisable in accordance with the qualification regulations and rules of conduct of the General Council of the Bar approved for the purposes of s 27 in relation to the right. The relevant qualification regulations and rules of conduct are contained in the Code of Conduct of the Bar of England and Wales (eighth edition, 2004) and the Consolidated Regulations of the Inns of Court and the General Council of the Bar (2007).

7. The court's power to refuse to hear a person (for reasons which apply to him as an individual) who would otherwise have a right of audience before the court in relation to the proceedings was expressly preserved by s 27(4); s 27(5) required a court which refuses to hear a person to give reasons for refusing.

8. CLSA 1990, s 18:

(a) imposes a duty on the General Council of the Bar a duty to exercise functions with respect to the granting of rights of audience, 'as soon as reasonably practicable and consistent with the provisions' of Pt II; and

(b) requires the General Council of the Bar in exercising such functions:

(i) to act in accordance with the general principle;

(ii) so far as it is possible to do so, in furtherance of the statutory objective; and

(iii) not to act in any way which would be incompatible with the statutory objective.

1 CLSA 1990, s 119(1).

2 Section 17(3), (4).

3 Section 27(9).
4 Section 31 (1), (3).

Duty to the court

6.12

1. There is imposed, on every person who exercised before any court a right of audience granted by an authorised body:
   (a) a duty to the court to act with independence in the interests of justice; and
   (b) a duty to comply with rules of conduct of the body relating to the right and approved for the purposes of this section,

   which duties override any obligation which the person may have (otherwise than under the criminal law) if inconsistent with them[1].

1 Section 27(2A); see also the Code of Conduct, para 302, which provides that a practising barrister has an overriding duty to the court to act with independence in the interests of justice, which appears to be the source of the duty which is given statutory force in the CLSA 1990 in relation to every person who exercises before any court a right of audience granted by an authorised body.

Administration of oaths

6.13

1. Every barrister has the power conferred by statute on a Commissioner for Oaths[1] and the right to use the title 'Commissioner for Oaths'[2].

1 CLSA 1990 s 113(3).
2 Section 113(10)(b).

Admittance; maintenance of standards

6.14

1. The Consolidated Regulations of the Inns of Court and the General Council of the Bar (2007) govern the manner in which a person may be admitted to one of the Inns of Court and qualify as a barrister. The BSB and the Inns' Council in consultation with one another may, from time to time, amend the regulations[1]. Such amendments do not have effect unless approved by the Secretary of State[2].
2. The Legal Services Consultative Panel's duties include assisting in the maintenance and development of standards in the education, training and conduct of persons offering legal services[3].

1 Regulation 59.
2 CLSA 1990, s 29; Sch 4, para 8.
3 CLSA 1990, s 18A.

LEGAL SERVICES ACT 2007

Reserved legal activities

6.15

1. The provisions of the CLSA 1990 pertaining to rights of audience are prospectively repeated by the LSA 2007, Sch 21, paras 83, 84(d), (g) and Sch 23 as from a day to be appointed.
2. The exercise of a right of audience is a 'reserved legal activity' within the meaning of the LSA 2008, s 12(1)(a) and Sch 2 para 3. The other reserved authorities are:
   (a) the conduct of litigation;
   (b) reserved instrument activities;
   (c) probate activities, notorial activities; and
   (d) the administration of oaths.
   The Lord Chancellor may, by order, amend provisions of the LSA 2007 so as to add any legal activity to the activities which are reserved legal activities[1] (see para 2.15 above).
3. Whether a person is entitled to carry on an activity which is a reserved legal activity is to be determined solely in accordance with the LSA[2].
4. A person is entitled to carry on a reserved legal activity where the person is either:
   (a) an authorised person; or
   (b) an exempt person;
   in relation to the relevant activity[3].
5. References to a person carrying on an activity which is a reserved legal activity include an employee who carries on a reserved legal activity in his capacity as an employee. It is irrelevant whether his employer is entitled to carry on the activity. The employer does not carry on the activity by virtue of the employee carrying it on in his capacity as an employee, unless the provision of the relevant services to the public is part of the employer's business.
6. It is an offence for a person to carry on a reserved legal activity unless he is entitled to do so[4].
7. It is an offence for a person to carry on a reserved legal activity, despite being entitled so to do, if:
   (a) the accused carries on that activity by virtue of an employee or manager carrying it on in the employee or manager's capacity as such; and
   (b) in carrying on that activity, the employee or manager commits an offence under s 14[5].
8. It is, however, a defence for the accused to show that he took all reasonable precautions and exercised all due diligence to avoid committing the offence[6].
9. It is an offence for a person:
   (a) wilfully to pretend to be entitled to carry on a reserved legal activity when not so entitled; or
   (b) with the intention of implying falsely that he is so entitled, to take or use any name, title or description[7].
10. An authorised person is:

(a) a person who is authorised to carry on the relevant activity by a relevant approved regulator in relation to the relevant authority; or

(b) a licensable body which, by virtue of such a licence, is authorised to carry on the relevant activity by a licensing authority in relation to the reserved legal activity.

11. The General Council of the Bar is named[8] as an approved regulator with respect to the following reserved legal activities:
    (a) the exercise of a right of audience;
    (b) the conduct of litigation;
    (c) reserved instrument activities;
    (d) probate activities; and
    (e) the administration of oaths.

12. However, the body responsible for the regulation of barristers is the BSB and it is, thus, the BSB that is the Bar's regulator for the purposes of the LSA[9].

13. An approved regulator may authorise persons to carry on any activity which is a reserved legal activity in respect of which it is a relevant approved regulator[10].

14. Approved regulators are subject to regulation in accordance with the provisions of LSA 2007, Pt 4.

15. An approved regulator:
    (a) is required, so far as is reasonably practicable, to act in a way which is compatible with the regulatory objectives and which the approved regulatory considers most appropriate for the purpose of meeting those objectives; and
    (b) is required to have regard to the principles under which regulatory activities should be transparent, accountable, proportionate, consistent and targeted only at cases in which action is needed, and any other principle appearing to it to represent the best regulatory practice.

16. An approved regulator will also be:
    (a) required:
        (i) to comply with the internal governance rules which the Board is mandated by s 30 to make;
        (ii) to meet performance targets set by the Board pursuant to s 31(1)(a) or to set performance targets if directed so to do by the Board pursuant to s 31(1)(b); and
        (iii) to comply with directions given by the board in the circumstances of s 32;
    (b) susceptible to:
        (i) public censure by the Board in the circumstances outlined in s 35; and
        (ii) the imposition of a financial penalty in the circumstances outlined in s 37;
        (iii) the giving of an intervention direction in relation to any of its regulatory functions in the circumstances outlined in s 41;
    (c) subject to control by the Board in respect of the practising fees charged by the approved regulator, as set out in s 51;

(d) required to make such provision as is reasonably practicable to prevent regulatory conflicts (s 52). Moreover, an approved regulator is:

(i) subject to the Board's power, on the application of another approved regulator, to direct a conflicting regulator to take steps to modify the provision made by its regulatory arrangements to prevent a regulatory conflict with the applicant regulator, or, if its regulatory arrangements do not make any such provision, to make such provision to prevent such a conflict (section 53); and

(ii) required to consider any request made by a person authorised by the approved regulator to carry on a reserved legal activity, or an employee or manager of such a person, for the approved regulator to reconsider the provision made by its regulatory arrangements to prevent a regulatory conflict with another approved regulator, or for the approved regulator to make an application under s 53;

(e) required to make such provision as is reasonably practicable and, in all the circumstances, appropriate, to prevent external regulatory conflicts, to provide for the resolution of any external regulatory conflicts which arise and to prevent unnecessary duplication of regulatory provisions made by an external regulatory body (being a person other than an approved regulator who exercises regulatory functions in relation to a particular description of persons with a view to ensuring compliance with rules by those persons);

(f) required to comply with any notice given by the Board to provide information or documentation pursuant to s 55;

(g) required to make provision, in its regulatory arrangements, requiring each person in relation to whom the approved regulator is a relevant approved regulator to establish and maintain procedures for the resolution of relevant complaints or to participate in, or make arrangements to be subject to, such procedures established and maintained by another person, and provision of the enforcement of that requirement, satisfying such requirements as the Board may from time to time specify;

(h) is subject to the rules which the Board is required, by s 173, to make providing for the imposition of a levy on, inter alia, approved regulators for the purpose of raising an amount equal to the aggregate of the leviable Board expenditure, the leviable OLC expendtiture and the leviable Lord Chancellor expenditure (as defined in s 173(6), (7)–(8) and (9)–(10) respectively, and thus liable to pay the levy at such rate and at such times as may be specified in those rules[11]).

17. Authorised persons (including barristers):

(a) will be subject to the scheme provided for in LSA 2007, Pt 6 to be administered by the OLC in accordance with Pt 6 and with scheme rules made by the OLC under Pt 6; and

(b) will have a duty to comply with the regulatory arrangements of the approved regulator as they apply to that person[12].

1 LSA 2007, s 24(1).
2 Section 13.
3 Section 13(2). Nothing in the LSA 2007 affects the power of any court in any proceedings to refuse to hear a person (for reasons which apply to that person as an individual) who would otherwise have a right of audience before the court in relation to those provisions: see the savings provision in s 192.
4 Section 14.
5 Section 16(1), (2).
6 Section 16(4).
7 Section 17(1).
8 Section 20 and Sch 4, Pt 1.
9 Section 20 and Sch 4, para 1.
10 Section 20(6).
11 Section 174(2).
12 Section 176(1).

Duty to the court

6.16

1. CLSA 1990, s 27(2A)(a) is prospectively repealed by LSA 2007, ss 208(1) and 210; Sch 21, paras 83 and 84(d); Sch 23, but effectively restated in s 188, which imposes on each authorised person who exercises before any court a right of audience (or conducts litigation in relation to proceedings in any court) by virtue of being an authorised person in relation to the activity in question a duty to the court in question to act with independence in the interests of justice, which duty, together with the duty to comply with relevant conduct rules imposed by s 176(1), override any obligations which the person may have (otherwise than under the criminal law) if they are inconsistent with them)[1].

1 Section 188(2).

Transitional provisions

6.17

1. The Lord Chancellor will, by order, and on the recommendation of the LSB, appoint a period (specifying the start and end dates of the same) during which every barrister with a current practising certificate will be deemed to be authorised by the BSB to carry on the following activities, namely:
   (a) the exercise of a right of audience before every court in relation to all proceedings;
   (b) reserved instrument activities;
   (c) probate activities; and
   (d) the administration of oaths[1];

   in accordance with the Board's regulatory arrangements[2].

1 Schedule 5, para 4(1), (2)(b)–(d).
2 Section 22; Sch 5, para 4.

Admittance; maintenance of standards

6.18

1. CLSA 1990, s 29 and Sch 4, para 8, which provide that amendments proposed to the Consolidated Regulations by the BSB and the Inns' Council do not have effect unless approved by the Secretary of State, is prospectively repealed by LSA 2007, ss 208(1), 210; Sch 21, paras 83, 100(a); Sch 23.
2. CLSA 1990, s 18A is prospectively repealed by the LSA 2007, s 208, s 210; Sch 21, paras 83, 84(c); Sch 23. As from a day to be appointed the functions formerly performance by The Legal Services Consultative Panel will be performed by the LSB[1].

1 Sections 2–11; Sch 1.

Offence: pretending to be a barrister

6.19

1. Once the provision is brought into force, it will be an offence for an unqualified person to pretend to be a barrister.

1 Section 181.

The authority of approved regulators other than the BSB

6.20

1. The introduction of entity-based regulation has this important consequence: a barrister who (following the requisite amendment to the Code of Conduct (as to which see para 4.3 above) works as an employee or manager in an entity which is authorised by a different approved regulator will be under a duty to comply with the regulatory arrangements of both of those approved regulators (subject to the provisions dealing with resolution of conflicts).

LICENSED CONVEYANCERS

6.21 The primary Act for the regulation of licensed conveyancers is the AJA 1985. The LSA 2007 makes a number of changes to the regulatory arrangements relating to licensed conveyancers and the operation of the Council for Licensed Conveyancers (CLC); these are contained in LSA 2007, Sch 17.

Some of these changes echo the changes made to the solicitors' regulatory regime. So, for example, the Investigating Committee of the CLC assumes the power to fine up to a maximum of £1,000 in relation to matters that are not so serious that they should be referred to the Discipline and Appeals Committee[1]. This is similar to the new Solicitors Act 1974, s 44D. AJA 1985, Sch 5, which sets out the power to intervene in the practice of a licensed conveyancer, is amended to include the same provisions set out in relation to solicitors and described in para 6.6 above.

The opportunity has also been taken to make changes to other aspects of the regulatory regime. Both the Investigations Committee and the Disciplinary and Appeals Committee now have the discretion to make cost awards[2]. The CLC also acquires wider and more flexible powers relating to the issue of licenses and the imposing of conditions in licenses. In line with one of the themes of the LSA 2007, employees of licensed conveyancers are also now subject to disciplinary sanction[3].

Potentially of greatest long-term significance is the amendment to CLSA 1990, s 53, which allows the CLC to apply to become an approved regulator of other reserved legal activities such as the conduct of litigation, probate activities and the exercise of rights of audience. Self-evidently, this enables the CLC to compete with the SRA and other approved regulators.

1 See new AJA 1985, s 24A.
2 See, for example, new AJA 1985, s 26(2A).
3 See, for example, new AJA 1985, Sch 6(3)(aa).

OTHER REGULATORS

6.22 LSA 2007, s 185 transfers the functions in relation to the registers of patent attorneys and of trade mark attorneys to the Chartered Institute of Patent Attorneys and the Institute of Trade Mark Attorneys respectively from the government. The section also provides for the expansion of powers of both bodies that subject to the LSB's oversight.

LSA 2007, s 186 and Sch 18 make provision for the regulation of immigration services. Prior to the LSA 2007, immigration services could be provided by persons registered with the Immigration Services Commissioner and persons authorised by a designated professional body. A designated professional body was overseen by the Immigration Services Commissioner. The LSA 2007 creates a new regulatory category being a person authorised by a designated qualifying regulator. The Law Society, Bar Council and the Institute of Legal Executives are all made delegated qualifying regulators by Sch 18. A designated qualifying regulator is overseen by the LSB rather than the Immigration Services Commissioner.

Finally, LSA 2007, s 19 provides for the LSB to take on oversight functions in relation to the Claims Management Regulator from the Secretary of State.

Chapter 7

MARKET VIEW

Tony Williams

INTRODUCTION

7.1 LSA 2007 permits the biggest ever change in the structure and ownership of the English legal profession. This chapter considers how the legal profession has developed over the last 30 or so years into a legal industry and how it is likely to develop in the wake of the full impact of the LSA 2007. Many of the trends in the profession that have applied over the last generation will continue to apply, but change will be accelerated by four factors: the LSA 2007; the current economic downturn; changing demographics and aspirations in law firms; and the changing needs and demands of the client. In this context, the LSA 2007 is only one, but a major, accelerant of change.

It is often suggested that the law is a conservative profession that has seen very little change in the past generation. In some respects this is true, but in others it is wholly inaccurate. This chapter will review what has and has not changed and the likely changes that lie ahead.

THE CHANGING LAW FIRM

7.2 Until the 1970s law firms were generally small, clubby, male-dominated institutions (the limit to 20 partners for professional firms was only abolished in the Companies Act 1967) often dominated by the members of one or two families. From the mid-1970s a number of factors started to change the traditional firm. First, the post-war baby boomer generation started to aspire for partnership. This was generally a less conservative, more aggressive and less deferential group than the existing partnership. They were prepared to work hard but also wanted a fair share of the fruit of their toils. Once in the partnership they were not prepared to accept the old paternalistic approach to profit distribution and management. Although their progress through the partnership hierarchy was slow and steady, it was to have a profound effect on their firms.

It should also be appreciated how relatively small even the leading firms were in the 1970s. In late 2008, David Morley, the senior partner of Allen & Overy, recalled at a seminar that he recently attended a retirement party for a partner who had joined the firm as a trainee (then an articled clerk) in 1970. At that time Allen & Overy had 18 partners, an annual fee income of £1.2 million and profit per equity partner of £23,000. In the year to 30 April 2008, Allen & Overy had 362 equity partners, fee income of £1,016million and profit per equity partner of £1,122,000.

A second trend in the 1970s was the UK's accession to the European Economic Community (now European Union) in January 1973. This caused many in business to start to look at Europe rather than the Commonwealth as our major market. Some English firms already had small historic offices in Paris or elsewhere in continental Europe, but these were the exception. From the mid-1970s firms started their first tentative steps abroad and this trend increased dramatically in the 1980s, not just in Europe but to Asia (especially Hong Kong and Singapore) and in the early 1990s to Russia and Central and Eastern Europe following the collapse of the Iron Curtain. The growth of British firms internationally has often been contrasted by the reluctance (until relatively recently) of the major US firms to stray away from home. Unfortunately it is probably inappropriate to put this internationalisation down to great foresight by the British firms, although there clearly were some visionaries in them. It is more down to the fact that the UK was and is a relatively small economy. If firms wanted to expand – and with the baby boomers pushing for partnership they had to – they needed to follow their clients (and in some cases anticipate their clients) as they spread their activities outside the UK. Given the size of the US economy, the US firms, then, faced no such pressure.

Two further major changes occurred with the election of Margaret Thatcher's government in 1979. First, the UK abolished exchange control. Before then investments abroad needed Bank of England approval. This was one of the foundation stones of London's emergence 25 years later as the world's dominant international financial centre. Second, were the successive reductions in income tax rates from a top rate of 83% in 1979, first to 60% and then to 40%. Partners now had an incentive to develop their business and to generate more income. The UK has until now maintained a 20-year political consensus that the top rate of income tax should not exceed 40%. This consensus may be broken by the need to fund the effects of the credit crunch.

These events resulted in firms growing significantly through the second half of the 1970s and the 1980s. International offices were opened and expanded, practice groups were established, management structures were developed and time recording was introduced. All of this was achieved organically until, in 1987, Coward Chance and Clifford Turner merged to create Clifford Chance. This was followed later by other mergers such as Durrant Piesse and Lovell White and King. Even at this stage it was not clear that a genuine Magic Circle had arrived. This did not really become apparent until after the recession in the early 1990s when the five current Magic Circle firms – Allen & Overy, Clifford Chance, Freshfields, Linklaters and Slaughter & May – emerged as significantly stronger in terms of depth and breadth in the key practices of corporate and finance. This dominance was enhanced by a series of German mergers in the late 1990s and into 2000: Linklaters with Oppenhoff; Freshfields first with Deringer and then with Bruckhaus; and Clifford Chance with Punder. Since then, these firms have established major operations in the business and financial capitals of the world. The one market where the firms have only had limited impact is the US. Generally, the firms have been limited to relatively small operations in New York and Washington DC. Clifford Chance tried a merger with Rogers & Wells in 2000 with, at best, mixed results and compounded its woes with a disastrous move into California. Whether the current downturn will present opportunities for these firms to expand in the US by lateral hiring or merger remains to be seen.

It is quite staggering to realise how the larger London-based law firms have changed in one working generation. They now have dedicated management, top-level professional support (who, under the LSA 2007, can now be granted partnership status), strong IT infrastructure, effective marketing and business development teams (in the 1970s such marketing would have been considered unprofessional conduct and a breach of the relevant professional conduct rules). But, as firms have changed so to has the role and status of the individual partners.

THE CHANGING PARTNERSHIP

7.3 Partnership in the early 1970s resembled a gentlemen's club (and it was almost solely men). For those who accepted it, in some cases due to a family connection, partnership pretty much guaranteed a job for life. It was unheard of for a partner to leave, and to leave to join another firm was totally impossible. Indeed, until the 1990s there was a 'gentlemen's agreement' in place between the larger UK firms not to try to poach each other's partners and staff. By the late 1980s there were isolated cases of partners being asked to leave law firms, but this situation changed quite dramatically in the early 1990s' recession. This bit particularly deeply in the legal sector and forced many firms to address a range of partner issues that they had been ignoring in the good times. This fundamentally changed the nature of the individual's relationship with the firm. In reality, the partnership for life was gone and replaced by a partnership at will, on both sides. The firm kept the partner if he was developing and managing a good and profitable business, behaved acceptably in relation to other partners and staff, and met the performance criteria that firms increasingly began to deploy. The partner stayed with the firm if he liked the work he was doing, enjoyed the clients, had the support he needed, got on with partners and others, felt fairly rewarded and was content with the direction of his practice group, office and the firm. It was no longer beyond the pale for a partner to leave to join another law firm. Indeed, although partner moves are now far less common than one might assume from reading the legal press, for a partner to move once or twice as a partner in his career is not surprising, although more than two such moves will at least raise an eyebrow.

We have also seen increasing numbers of women become partners in law firms. Given that for over 20 years at least 50% of new trainees have been women, we are still not seeing the appropriate share achieve partnership. In many major firms still less than 20% of their equity partners are women. This situation is improving but at a glacial rate. The increasing role that women have played in law firm partnerships has inevitably helped to break down the male-dominated club culture (although frustratingly few women have senior management roles in leading law firms). It has also encouraged firms to consider more flexible working arrangements for partners and other staff including part-time working, working from home, job sharing and sabbaticals.

Partners are increasingly assessed as to their time-recording, billing, developing of associates, winning new clients and developing existing ones, contributing to know-how and performing leadership roles. Feedback is sought from clients, partners, associates and other staff. After a faltering start in the 1990s, systems of appraisal and goal setting are now much more established and accepted.

As firms have grown, partners have become less involved in the day-to-day management of the business. In many firms the key strategic direction of the firm may be approved by a partnership vote and decisions on equity partner admission, and mergers require a vote, but most other matters will be the responsibility of the leadership group. This has been a difficult transition for some partners, who often lament that they are not partners but highly paid employees. However, the financial rewards have been significant with, in the year to 30 April 2008, many hundreds of partners earning over £1 million a year and thousands over £500,000 a year.

We are now approaching another transition point for the individual partners. Many of the baby boomers that did so much to develop their firms are looking to retire. Many will have held major roles in their firms either with client relationships, practice group management or the firm's leadership over the last 20 years. The transition to the next generation in some firms will be challenging. Some smaller firms may not have a range of younger partners to take over these roles and will face a leadership vacuum. For the baby boomer partner looking to retire there are also challenges. He will have become used to a certain level of income and lifestyle. Given the combination of poor equity market returns over the last ten years, Gordon Brown's raid on the tax exempt nature of pension funds, longer life expectancy and lower interest rates, it is likely that many partners, in the absence of a firm-funded pension, will face a significant drop in their living standards after retirement. This may cause the baby boomer transition to be less smooth than is desirable. Partners who ten years ago may have planned to retire in their mid-50s may now look to stay longer and be prepared to play the age discrimination card to protect their position. Indeed the LSA 2007 makes this even more likely if partners perceive the possibility of a windfall gain arising on the sale or flotation of their firm following the full implementation of the Act.

Over the last 15 years the option of joining a US firm has also arisen, primarily in London. The US firms, from tentative beginnings in London, are now a significant presence in the market and are likely to grow further over the next few years. The working pressures in those firms may be significant, but the remuneration system generally has a strong merit-based element and US firms are much more comfortable with partners staying well into their 60s provided that they can still perform. This has therefore added an extra option to a partner considering his career choices.

THE CHANGING LAWYER

7.4 Over the years much has been written on the attributes or otherwise of Generation X and Generation Y. Much of the commentary is far too simplistic and general to be usefully applied to the legal environment. From my discussions in recent years with trainees a few issues have become apparent. Those entering the profession are now far more diverse in terms of ethnic, educational and social background – perhaps still not diverse enough, but progress is being made, albeit gradually. Those entering the profession have a greater range of commitment to and expectation of the law. Some see it as a well paid job which will enable them to pay off their student debts quickly but not as a long-term career. Others are as determined, hungry and focused as any lawyer in previous generations and are determined to get equity partnership in a well regarded and profitable firm. If their current firm will not offer partnership, or they think they can do better, they will move firms. What is clear is that we have a more diverse workforce with a range of different motivations for joining and staying in the legal profession. It is also apparent that lawyers are increasingly looking at their career path over certain finite periods rather than looking to stay with one firm their entire career. Whether these periods are three, five or ten years, lawyers will commit to their role for that period and then may wish to pursue other interests such as business management, private equity, in-house roles, charities or take a career break to travel, raise a family or care for older family members. These lawyers will be prepared to work differently at certain stages of their careers. Firms will need to accommodate these changes if they want to recruit, keep, motivate and even re-employ the best talent in the market.

The fact that significant numbers of lawyers, and not only women lawyers, look at their current firms and do not aspire to be equity partners in those firms should give considerable food for thought for those firms. Partnership was the goal that many young lawyers were prepared to work hard to attain. It will still attract many, but if others see the path as too long and arduous and the goal, even if reached, too demanding, despite the perceived financial rewards, then firms will be spending large amounts on recruiting and training young lawyers who will not stay with the firm. If partnership is no longer the ultimate career goal for young lawyers the LSA 2007 could have important implications for this group. Employers that offer long-term bonus or share incentive plans, which vest over a three- or five-year period, may find themselves attractive for at least one stage of a lawyer's career, especially if that bonus or incentive is sufficient to pay off the student debt or provide a deposit for a flat. Flexible working hours, home working and first rate training and IT systems may tempt back into the profession those that do not wish to work in a traditional law firm.

7.4 *Market View*

In a period of downturn it may be tempting to downplay recruitment and retention issues. But the most successful organisations are not judged by the number of professionals they contain but by their quality and aptitude. If they can be attracted to new business models the likelihood of these models being successful is greatly enhanced in a conservative profession. It can be surprising how open to new ideas young lawyers can be. In 2000, I joined Andersen Legal, the legal services arm of Arthur Andersen, as its worldwide managing partner. In 2001 it was in the top ten global law firms in terms of fee income. I was surprised and impressed by the calibre of law graduates that we were able to attract. They were excited by something new and wanted to give it a try. Many had offers from major UK firms, including the Magic Circle, but chose to join us. When, in the wake of the Enron debacle, Arthur Andersen collapsed, Garretts, the English law firm, was dissolved and we had to place all of our trainee pipeline elsewhere. The vast majority were employed by major London or national firms. Indeed a Magic Circle partner said that the trainee he took from Garretts was the best trainee he had ever worked with. It would be dangerous for existing law firms to assume that no new entrant can generate that level of excitement and attraction in the recruitment market.

THE CHANGING CLIENT

7.5 It is tempting to think that all of the changes within law firms have taken place naturally without any outside influence. This would be entirely wrong. Law firms have had to anticipate and respond to the needs of their clients in order to stay in business. This is as true in the high street as in the major city firms.

At a retail level, we live in a consumer society. We are used to being able to shop around, to compare products, have clear pricing and recourse to effective customer service teams to deal with any problems that arise. The LSA 2007 is built on the principle of putting the consumer first. It follows a vigorous campaign by the Consumers' Association, which has on many occasions produced surveys showing the lamentable performance by law firms and their regulators on such issues as communication, price transparency, competence and complaints handling. This was followed by a Competition Commission report in 2001 which held that many of the then existing restrictions on the practice of law were anti-competitive and acted against the interest of the consumer.

Accordingly, as buyers of legal services, we want our suppliers to be approachable, responsive, intelligible and to apply predictable and transparent pricing. More consumers now routinely use the internet and email and expect their lawyers to do so.

Case study

In 2007 I sold my house in Hampshire. I usually keep my private matters and my client work separate, so I asked my estate agent to recommend some good lawyers in the area. He gave me three names. I also had the details of the local firm that had acted for me eleven years before on the purchase of the property.

I prepared an email (note: not a letter or phone call) to the firms giving details of my proposed sale and purchase, asked them about the service they could provide and what it would cost. My PA could not find the website of the firm that acted for me on the purchase, so rang them for details of a property partner to email. She was told 'we don't do that, send it to enquiries@... and we will deal with it.' Quite simply, I do not send confidential information to enquiries@anywhere so they were taken off the list. The email went out to the other three firms. One responded in 40 minutes with a detailed review of their service, a full breakdown of costs and disbursements, a schedule of what they would do for free if the matter aborted, a guide to the conveyancing process and a screenshot of an extranet page in case I wanted to deal with them online. Another firm replied about an hour later with a basic quote that was cheaper than the first firm. The third firm responded the next day with a curt letter that it was impossible to give an indication of the price of their services.

Hardly surprisingly, I instructed the first firm to reply and asked if I could drop off my papers one Friday on my way back from London as I was travelling a lot over the forthcoming weeks. The immediate reply was, 'that's fine but as you are very busy and I only live about 20 miles away from you, I can meet at your home on Saturday if that helps.' He did an excellent job, has since bought a London flat and a Hampshire house for me, his firm has prepared my will and he has bought a house for a colleague of mine.

I may not be a representative client, but I do believe that clients are capable of applying the price-versus-quality of service equation to legal services just as they do when buying groceries or the family car. Firms that can position themselves appropriately and maintain their positioning as client expectations change will still do well. However, this is a far change from the deferential meeting in a lawyer's book-lined office 30 years ago when subsequently chasing a lawyer for the promised action or challenging a bill would elicit a response familiar in a Bateman cartoon.

In the corporate world the change in the client has been even more dramatic. Until the 1980s client relationships were pretty static. Clients used one major firm for most of their 'head office' work. There was no direct competition between firms, and advertising and marketing were considered unprofessional. Indeed, at the time one senior partner of a major city firm commented to a young lawyer: 'remember two things; lawyers are professionals so will never compete against each other and clients will never buy on the basis of price.' In the banking world some relationships went back generations: Coward Chance (now Clifford Chance) had acted for Midland Bank (now part of HSBC) since its incorporation in the 1800s, Durrant Piesse (now Lovells) acted for Barclays, Cameron Markby (now CMS Cameron McKenna) acted for Lloyds (now Lloyds TSB) and Wilde Sapte (now Denton Wilde Sapte) acted for National Westminster (now RBS).

The General Counsel (often then known as the Group Solicitor, Head of Legal or Company Secretary) in many corporates was often a relatively relaxed individual who may have formerly been a partner at the main relationship law firm. He (and it usually was a he) saw no need dramatically to change the relationship with the outside law firm. The external legal spend also tended to be relatively small so it did not gain much attention within the organisation.

Three things changed. First, there was a wave of consolidation across a range of industries starting in the mid-1980s and still continuing. Part of this was accelerated by regulatory changes including the abolition of exchange control, privatisation of the utilities industries and Big Bang in 1986, which reformed the stockbroking industry. These much bigger and more diverse businesses owed little to their historical roots and were prepared to look at all of their professional advisors afresh. Second, the rush to globalisation started. British firms actively developed businesses abroad (and particularly as a result of US acquisitions and US litigation discovered the role of the US General Counsel). In addition, foreign organisations established in the UK, often basing their European headquarters in or around London. Of particular note, the major US investment banks rapidly developed their operations internationally and, in the absence of the US law firms, quickly turned to the major UK firms in London, Continental Europe, Asia and, when it opened up, Central and Eastern Europe. It remains to be seen what impact the credit crunch of 2008 will have long term on these global commercial and investment banks and indeed on the globalisation of business generally. Third, we have seen a change in the nature of the general counsel. Increasingly the general counsel has spent most of his career in-house, possibly with a number of different organisations. They see themselves as an integral part of the executive team with good relationships with the Chairman, Chief Executive and Chief Financial Officer. They owe no allegiance to any particular law firm. These much more focused individuals currently face three main pressures in their organisations: to reduce internal legal headcount; to reduce the external legal spend and make it more predictable; and to ensure that the organisation's legal and reputational risk is managed more effectively. If they do not perform these three roles effectively their position will be in jeopardy. As a result, these General Counsel are demanding better service, an investment by the law firm in the relationship, assistance to avoid problems rather than to solve them when they arise and transparency and certainty on pricing. In November 2008 Andrew Garard, the General Counsel of ITV, announced the completion of a panel review process. All of the firms on the panel would be required to quote fixed fees for specific projects with no work done on an hourly rate. Although the demise of the hourly rate has been predicted for many years, this sort of arrangement could have a profound effect on the economics and structure of a law firm.

THE CHANGING MARKET

7.6 For most of the 25 years until 2008 the legal profession had enjoyed a great bull market with double digit compound growth in revenue and profits for 20 of these years. The exceptions were the years 1992 to 1994 immediately following the general economic recession (law is usually a lagging indicator so suffers a downturn 12 to 18 months after the main economy as the early stages of a downturn produce work for lawyers) and immediately following the dot-com collapse in 2001 and 2002 where profits stagnated or dipped.

This is a fantastic record by any standards, but it may not be realistic to expect such a dramatic growth picture in the future.

Writing this in either the early phase of what could be the greatest slump since the 1930s or in the late phase of a short, sharp blip makes any measured projection difficult. However, there appear to be a number of matters emerging that will start, fundamentally, to change the legal landscape even before the LSA 2007 is fully implemented.

First, at a retail level, many small firms (or larger conveyancing or remortgaging 'factories') will fail to survive. Many such firms are reliant on domestic conveyancing and conveyancing of secondary or tertiary commercial and industrial property. Transactions have virtually ground to a halt, and with funding not available transactions are expected to remain subdued for some time. This will result in many hundreds and possibly thousands of small firms disappearing. Some will merge with others, some sole practitioners will retire, there will be interventions by the SRA and some firms will become insolvent. Many banks already have hundreds of such firms in 'special measures'. It is a sad fact that many partners in these firms will end their careers facing insolvency.

Second, there will be a wave of law firm consolidation. It is already starting at the very-small-firm level but will increasingly occur through the size chain. Firms are beginning to recognise that size is relevant to fund investment in premises, IT, marketing and training. Size provides higher profile for recruitment and client development. This issue is being considered across the market. Firms of £1 million turnover want to be £2 million, those of £2 million want to be £5 million, those of £5 million want to be £10 million and so on up to firms of £250 million that want to be £500 million. Accordingly, firms may undertake multiple mergers as they grow through the size bands. Given the unconsolidated nature of the market and the number of opportunities that will arise, some firms will be tempted to turn to private equity and other outside investment as a means of enabling them to grow rapidly in the hope of achieving higher and more sustainable profits.

Third, in the short term at least, the internationalisation of the legal market will continue. The US firms are now in London in force (with about 150 claiming to have an office in London) and are looking to expand in the UK, continental Europe and Asia. Much of this growth will be achieved by merger as it is quicker and cheaper than organic growth, if the right merger partner is chosen. These US firms will look to merge with many of the top 100 UK firms. It remains to be seen if the weakness of sterling and the recession will dampen this ardour, but currently some firms clearly see this phase as a bargain opportunity.

UK firms with an international footprint will continue to develop it, primarily organically. The main exceptions are the US where, if suitable merger partners would talk, some transformational deals could be done and, India, where, if the market opens up, it could change quite rapidly. UK firms without an international footprint may be reluctant to incur the cost of establishing one now so are likely to operate through best friends or alliance structures possibly with a view to eventual merger.

Fourth, profits in the firms that survive are likely to fall significantly in 2009/10 and 2010/11. Law is a lagging indicator. Lawyers make money whether the market is going up or down provided that there is activity. The shortage of credit and general business uncertainty is likely to reduce deal flow significantly. General Counsel are likely to drive a hard bargain for the work that they give out. This will have a profound effect on law firm profitably. If a firm with revenue of £10 million and partner profits of £2.5 million loses £1 million of revenue it is unlikely to be able to reduce its costs quickly enough so its partner profits may decline 40%. A 10% drop in revenue is quite conservative so some dramatic cost-cutting and profit reductions can be expected. This environment will place a sharp focus on the quality of a law firm's leadership, the effectiveness of its management infrastructure and its cohesiveness and strategic direction. Not only will profits fall, but more cash will be tied up in the business so partner distributions will be deferred or capital calls made. This will place some partners under real personal pressure. This may present great opportunities for well run firms to pick up good quality individuals and teams on competitive terms.

Fifth, the downturn will damage the career prospects of many bright and able lawyers. They will not make equity partnership and may be eased out of their existing firms. Many of these will be able and motivated and anxious to prove their worth. If captured by dynamic firms or by new entrants they are capable of having a significant beneficial impact on their new organisations.

THE CHANGING BUSINESS MODEL

7.7 The legal profession has changed profoundly in one generation but more change is necessary before it can properly be described as the legal industry or legal business.

Much of the success of the legal profession over the last 25 years has been brought about by significantly growing firms' headcount with bright and motivated lawyers. Equity partner numbers have increased dramatically, a class of non-equity partners has been added to improve gearing and equity partner earnings, more associates have been introduced to move the partner to lawyer ratio from less than 1:1 to nearer 1:4 and support staff ratios per lawyer have fallen to under 1:1. In addition all lawyers have tended to work harder, record more chargeable time and bill and collect somewhat more efficiently. These changes have had a profoundly positive effect on firms' revenue, equity partner remuneration and lawyers earnings generally in the top 100 or so firms.

IT has been introduced into the practice so that many firms now have effective practice management, document production, document assembly, digital dictation and training and know-how systems.

However, many clients would perceive little change in the way in which the lawyer performs the service. Yes, the lawyer may be more responsive, and may use email, but has the lawyer really changed the way he works? Much of the use of technology can be described as automating the quill pen, ie doing existing things quicker and more efficiently rather than questioning whether that action needs to be performed at all and if so by whom.

This is the next way in which the legal business model may be transformed. If law starts to apply the process management and process re-engineering techniques used for many years by our commercial clients these could not only revolutionise the legal market but present great opportunities for new entrants to the market who are unburdened by historical precedents on the way work has always been done, but can instead look at how it could and should be done in a manner which provides a more responsive, certain and cost-effective service to the client.

Such process re-engineering will examine each aspect of a matter and determine how each part should be performed and by whom. IT will play a major role in managing such workflows and ensuring that quality and cost effectiveness is maintained. This process may lead to increasing parts of a legal project being outsourced or off-shored. The legal off-shoring industry, primarily based in India but also involving South Africa, the Philippines and New Zealand has made great progress on legal process re-engineering US litigation disclosure and is rapidly gaining credibility not only for its cost effectiveness but also for its quality of service.

This re-engineering is likely, fundamentally, to change the structure of law firms. Just as the bulk mortgage conveyancing and personal injury firms adopted different models to meet the needs of their clients and the price point they demanded, then other parts of the legal sector will need to examine the financials of their operations and their real and sustainable profitability. This will impact the number of equity partners, non-equity partners, associates and trainees needed in law firms.

If clients generally and General Counsel in particular push for fixed-price billing this will place further pressure on law firms. Hourly rates are effectively a cost-plus billing mechanism which rewards inefficiency. When cost-plus arrangements were replaced by fixed-price tendering in the construction and defence industries in the 1980s there was a wave of consolidation as players tried to grab market share to compensate for lower margins. Fixed pricing will force firms to look for greater efficiency, as if they fail to do so their profits will erode even faster if fixed prices are driven down further. Many clients may still prefer hourly rates but are likely to be more demanding as to the rates charged, the lawyers allocated to the matter and the tasks that they undertake.

THE CHANGING OWNERSHIP OF LAW FIRMS

7.8 As has been shown, the legal profession is going through a period of profound change as it grapples to come to terms with the new and changing demands of its various clients. The current downturn will, in many ways, accelerate the change only to be followed by the full implementation of the LSA 2007 which may not only transform the ownership and management of existing law firms but, more importantly, introduce new and dynamic competitors into the market. Accordingly the legal business could be said to be entering a perfect storm. It will destroy some, damage others and leave others leaner, more focused and more dynamic to take advantage of the eventual economic recovery.

Given the innate conservatism of the profession, many investors will be tempted to create completely new businesses rather than, initially at least, to take over existing firms. This is particularly the case given that in most areas of legal practice no law firms have strong brands, which would justify paying a premium to control.

When investors do invest in existing businesses they will want a quality leadership team, a credible growth strategy and rigorous operational management. From the firm's perspective, the growth should be sufficient to fund the investor's return as otherwise the partners are merely selling their future incomes with all the intergenerational and motivational issues that entails. In addition to outside investment, law firms have the possibility of floating on the stock market. Slater and Gorden in Australia is the first example of a listed law firm but it will clearly not be the last.

What is clear is that there will be a variety of legal service models that work and are sustainable and profitable and a range that will fail. There is no-one-size-fits-all approach to the firms that will succeed. The key is that they identify and understand their client base and are able to deliver the range of services that the client wants, in the way the client wants them delivered, at a price that the client is prepared to pay and which provides a reasonable return to the supplier. The LSA 2007 permits an almost limitless combination of models with LDPs involving any of solicitors, barristers, licensed conveyancers, patent agents and notaries and multidisciplinary practices (MDPs) (known as ABSs under the LSA 2007) involving accountants, estate agents, financial advisers, surveyors, investment bankers and others. The fact that corporate brands can then be used will accelerate the change either by the creation of new legal brands (similar to Direct Line when it was initially focused on insurance broking) or the use of consumer brands to cover legal services such as Virgin Legal, Consumer's Association, AA and Co-op. Given the existing relative absence of branding in the legal space this could have a dramatic effect especially at the retail end of the market.

In one working generation British law firms have moved from annual turnovers of £1.2 million to over £1 billion, and the largest firms are some of the leading firms in the world. An underrated British success story. But the pace of change is accelerating and the LSA 2007 will clearly be an accelerant to that change. What will the trainee who took up her post in September 2009 reflect at her retirement party in 2049? Will the organisation she leaves even be called a legal services business? Will she be part of a £100 billion revenue business? If so, the growth in her professional lifetime will be less in percentage terms than that of the Allen & Overy partner who retired in 2008!

Chapter 8

PREPARATION AND THE PARTNERSHIP DEED

Jonathan Haley

INTRODUCTION

8.1 With full implementation of the LSA 2007 not due until 2011 at the earliest, firms will be contemplating what action they can take in preparation. The Act will bring about radical changes to the regulation and ownership of law firms and the likely effect on the legal market should not be underestimated. This chapter considers action which firms might take prior to the full implementation of the Act to take advantage of opportunities afforded by the ABS regime or, at least, to protect against the risks facing the profession going forward.

CONSIDERING THE OPTIONS AND DEVELOPING A STRATEGY

8.2 The attitude that each firm takes towards the future will depend on its position in the market, its current needs and its strategic objectives. Certain firms, conscious of a requirement for capital investment, will see the Act as an opportunity to attract finance from sources not previously available. Consider, for example, a mid-tier firm with a solid client base and highly commoditised workload which could benefit from investment in IT resources. In such a case, to give away a proportion of equity in exchange for an immediate capital injection could significantly boost the long-term prospects of the firm and quickly reposition the business in the market above its competitors.

Other firms may seek capital investment for purely defensive reasons. Some firms will see a need for external investment in order to establish a 'war chest' earmarked for defensive strategies that might be needed, for example, in the event of a hostile team move approach.

Conversely, some firms will determine at an early stage that they have no need for additional capital. Prior to the passing of the Act (and indeed since) many commentators noted that large firms with good management and healthy balance sheets have not had difficulties raising finance. It remains to be seen if the 'credit crunch' will change this. In general, though, such firms will have limited need for large-scale capital raising and, even in today's tougher economic climate, in the event that finance is needed it is more likely to be obtained by an overdraft extension than an equity sell-off.

Whatever attitude the firm chooses to take, once the options have been considered and the way ahead determined, business managers will need to prepare properly to steer the firm down the desired path. Those firms which have identified a need for capital investment or structural change will wish to get their house in order to ensure that they are an attractive prospect for potential investors. Those which have resolved not to make any significant changes will still need to be aware of the avenues being pursued by their competitors and to ensure that adequate defences are in place. Whichever path is the favoured one, an unambiguous strategy, a firm commitment to that strategy and a clear view of its implications will be required.

A detailed SWOT (strengths, weaknesses, opportunities and threats) analysis will help firms develop their strategy. Such an analysis will identify not only potential advantages for the firm, but also the key risks. These might include, for example, the likelihood and impact of losing key individuals or teams to competitor firms. Business continuity analyses do not always extend to loss of key staff and yet this is likely to be one of the most significant risks faced by firms under the new regime. Previously, star performers and their business units may not have been susceptible to approaches from competitor firms. But those same approaches coupled with the promise of golden handshakes or staff equity rewards (which may become commonplace under the ABS regime) will be more readily received.

A further part of developing a post-implementation strategy will be internal testing of partner attitudes towards possible change. Law firm partnerships are usually collectives of strong-willed and ambitious individuals, rarely with one partner in control of key business decisions. Early discussion of the issues between partners will have a two-fold effect of encouraging buy-in and support whilst flagging potential objectors. Other straightforward defensive actions that firms can adopt to reduce risk (at little cost) include keeping abreast of market developments and competitor moves, updating the partnership deed to ensure it is robust and workable, and ensuring internal business systems are up to date.

PRE-ABS STRUCTURES – EXISTING POSSIBILITIES FOR THIRD-PARTY INVOLVEMENT

8.3 In developing a strategy, firms should give some thought as to whether, or to what extent, they may already be able to take desired steps within the existing regulatory framework. Perhaps contrary to general perception, it is already possible, in certain circumstances, for non-lawyers to own legal businesses and for solicitors both to share fees with third parties and to enter into referral arrangements.

Non-reserved activities

8.4 Let us consider first which activities are defined as 'reserved legal activities' within the Act, as it is only these which are specifically the preserve of legal professionals. These are the exercise of rights of audience, the conduct of litigation, reserved instrument activities (ie certain conveyancing matters), probate activities, notarial activities and the administration of oaths[1].

Although in some cases regulated under other regimes, activities other than those listed do not fall within the Act's remit and currently can be carried out by non-solicitors. Indeed, recent years have witnessed the emergence of a raft of businesses other than law firms offering services such as conveyancing, will drafting, claims handling and transactional due diligence. These operations have typically invested heavily in IT to produce high-volume, low-margin but profitable concerns. It is quite possible for law firms, under the existing regime, to establish subsidiary businesses consisting wholly of these non-restricted activities and, if required, to invite external investment into such businesses. For example, in 2000 the volume conveyancing division of Addleshaw Booth was rebranded as Enact. The division was equipped with advanced IT and case management technology and was sold off in 2003, by way of a management buyout. It has since been acquired by First American Corporation, a US financial services group. Recent times have, however, placed significant pressures on some such businesses. January 2009 saw HammondsDirect, a similar volume conveyancing off-shoot (established by Hammond Suddards and sold off as a non-reserved activities company, although it has since become SRA-regulated) entering into pre-packaged administration following the sharp downturn in the residential property and remortgage markets.

1 LSA 2007, s 12(1). Prior to full implementation these activities are reserved to certain legal professionals under previously enacted legislation including the Solicitors Act 1974 and/or the CLSA 1990. Under the LSA 2007 these services are re-designated as 'reserved legal activities' and reserved to authorised persons; the activities are defined in detail in Sch 2.

Outsourcing

8.5 One particular trend which has been seen in recent years is the outsourcing of operations to countries with cheaper labour markets such as India and Africa. For example, at the beginning of 2009, Lovells outsourced all of its real estate document production to Exigent, a Cape Town-based company. Outsourced operations cover not only business resources such as IT and document production, but also paralegal operations such as due diligence, claims handling and conveyancing. Furthermore, the establishment of a captive outsourced operation is possible within current professional rules and, indeed, has been actively pursued by several larger firms. Clifford Chance, for example, has established a significant outsourcing facility in India, which provides much of the work previously carried out by London-based trainees and paralegals. The firm reportedly believes that the arrangements will result in a saving in excess of £30 million over a four-year period.

Referral fees and fee-sharing

8.6 Examination of the rules which currently prevent fee-sharing (SRA Code of Conduct, r 8) and referral fees (r 9) also shows that neither of these activities is absolutely prohibited and there are sub-rules within each which afford firms the opportunity to receive third-party fees in certain circumstances. For example, r 8 permits fee-sharing where the sole purpose of it is to facilitate the introduction of capital and/or the provision of services to the firm[1]. The guidance notes accompanying the Code state that the aim of this, 'is to give practitioners greater freedom of choice as to methods available to fund their firms ...' and that the relevant sub-rule, 'allows you to enter into agreements with third-party non-lawyers which provide that, in return for the third party making available capital and/or a service to you, you make payment to the third party by reference to a percentage of your fees.'[2] The rule remains subject to many caveats designed to protect the public interest and is certainly not a carte blanche to enter into fee-sharing or partnership arrangements with non-lawyers. It may, however, provide firms with a way to secure capital funding by sharing fees with a quasi-equity formula. Examples of arrangements which might be so permitted (as set out in the guidance notes) include the provision of bank loans, IT equipment and services or web-based will writing products, in each case in return for a sum calculated as a percentage of the firm's gross fees[3].

Rule 9, dealing with referral fees, provides a similar carve-out provided that firms 'do nothing which would compromise your independence or your ability to act and advise in the best interests of your clients.'[4] Strict disclosure rules apply requiring, broadly, that clients are aware of the nature and extent of the referral arrangement. Subject to these various restrictions, it is quite possible for firms to enter into referral arrangements with third parties for the provision of legal services.

The lifting of the blanket ban on referral fees in 2004 was controversial and has remained so. Considering the issue in 2007, the SRA concluded that 'public confidence in solicitors has been damaged by a number of recent cases in which solicitors have placed their own advantage above their clients' interests'[5] and the recent high-profile strikings-off of principals at Beresfords Solicitors for, inter alia, breach of the referral rules will have done little to improve that view. However, in 2008 the SRA rejected reverting to a complete prohibition of referral fees and it remains the case that legitimate and ethical referral arrangements have the endorsement of the regulator. Examples of such arrangements include Irwin Mitchell's alliances with both the AA and RAC. In each case the household-name retailer is provided with a quality legal service (usually self-branded but making the necessary disclosure that restricted activities are, in fact, provided by the law firm) whilst a high volume of commoditised work is generated for the law firm. After implementation of the ABS regime it would be a small step for the retailer in such a relationship to directly invest in, or even to purchase outright, the law firm.

1 Solicitors' Code of Conduct 2007 (SCC), r 8.02(1)(a).
2 SCC Guide to Rule 8, para 6.
3 SCC Guide to Rule 8, para 12.

4 SCC, r 9.01(1)
5 SRA Referrals Warning Guidance 2008.

Litigation funding

8.7 Also relevant here is the field of litigation funding. Third-party funding (TPF) is the process by which third-party investors fund litigation on behalf of others who lack the resources to litigate themselves. In return, the third-party funder receives a proportion of the claim monies should the litigation be successful.

Given the expense of litigation in the UK, TPF can be an attractive option for prospective litigants. Over recent years there has been considerable growth in TPF in the UK, and investors have looked to capitalise on the perception of the UK court system as being expensive and difficult to access. In October 2008 Addleshaw Goddard secured a £10 million package combining conditional fee arrangements, after the event insurance and TPF for a group of claimants in their action against a London law firm. The package was provided by Allianz ProzessFinanz, QBE and BritInsurance.

TPF, however, does remain a nascent market and the recent high profile withdrawal of the Australian litigation funder, IMF, from the UK market has perhaps dented enthusiasm for it[1]. Yet, despite this, TPF remains an active area with opportunities for some investors. It certainly provides yet further scope for investors to be closely involved with law firms prior to full implementation of the Act.

These various examples demonstrate that, even without the Act, there is scope for certain legal businesses to be owned to some extent by non-lawyers and for a variety of relationships between non-lawyers and law firms to be formed. Thus, firms may already be in a position to develop businesses in which investors can hold a stake or to develop close relationships with retailers. This done, it would be all the more straightforward to integrate fully the two businesses on an ABS basis when the Act allows.

1 An Ipsos Mori poll conducted in June 2008 and commissioned by Addleshaw Goddard showed reluctance amongst senior personnel of FTSE 350 companies for TPF. 64% of those interviewed said that they were unlikely to use litigation funding in the future and only 2% had experienced TPF.

UPDATING YOUR PARTNERSHIP DEED

8.8 In this section we consider how firms should consider updating their partnership deed in preparation for full implementation of the Act and, in particular, the LDP and ABS regimes.

There are important differences between LLPs and partnerships and between their respective governing documents. Most importantly, the LLP is a body corporate, a separate legal entity with its own rights and obligations separate from those of its members. We do not intend to make particular distinctions between partnerships and LLPs in this section since the majority of clauses considered will be present in both partnership deeds and in members' agreements. Unless specific reference is made to the distinction, the term 'deed' should be taken to include both forms of governing document, 'firm' applies to both an LLP and unlimited partnership and 'partner' should be read as including 'member'.

Of course, it is not possible for a firm's deed to cover, in detail, every eventuality under the Act. In the event that, for example, a firm were to consider a flotation or other significant structural change, very material amendments would be required and significant legal process would accompany such a move. The aim of the reviewer must then be to ensure that the firm's deed and internal management processes are robust enough to manage the firm to the point where the decision to pursue a particular avenue under the Act can be made. This will require ensuring that the deed recognises the possibility of the firm going down that particular route as well as providing suitable protections such that any such process is not hindered by cumbersome voting procedures, troublesome individuals or outgoing partners.

Reviewers should be conscious of the fact that the Act will eventually bring about the possibility of firms acquiring a significant and realisable capital value. The prospect of such value being created and realised perhaps enhances the possibility of partnership deeds being litigated, making it all the more important that the firm's constitution is well drafted and up to date.

There follows a list of principal clauses in law firm deeds and a discussion as to how each might be amended. We focus on particular clauses which may be problematic and the list is not intended to be exhaustive.

Nature of the business

8.9 Neither partnerships nor LLPs have limited capacity and there is no requirement per se to be granted capacity by the deed. Most firms will, however, set out the nature of their business within the deed. The core nature of the firm's business is unlikely to change as a result of the Act, but the scope of the business may widen and firms should consider whether their current definition might be too limited. For example, is the business restricted to practising 'as solicitors'? If so, perhaps a wider definition, such as 'the provision of legal services and associated activities' would be more appropriate.

New partners

8.10 The appointment of new partners is, by default, a matter which requires the unanimous consent of the existing partners[1]. In larger firms this is neither practical nor common. However, the requirement for unanimity can still be found in the deeds of smaller firms. Serious consideration should be given as to what is the proper voting threshold for the appointment of new partners.

Further, in respect of such appointments, any eligibility restrictions should be reviewed to ensure they do not unnecessarily restrict the promotion of non-solicitors who would otherwise be eligible for partnership in an LDP or ABS.

1 Partnership Act 1890, s 24(7) and Limited Liability Partnerships Regulations 2001 (SI 2001/1090), Pt VI, para 7(5). In both cases the default provision can be varied by agreement between the partners.

Assignment or charging of partners' share

8.11 It will be necessary to ensure that prohibitions against charging, assignment and otherwise encumbering partnership shares are sufficient.

The Partnership Act 1890 (PA 1890) and the Limited Liability Partnerships Act 2000 (LLPA 2000) include implicit reference to the ability of partners to assign their shares[1] (although the LLPA 2000, by default, excludes the right to do so)[2].

It is likely that most deeds contain such a prohibition against charging, but it may be sensible to tighten up the relevant clauses, for example, to prevent partners from conditionally agreeing the sale or charge of the share to a third party following full implementation of the Act[3].

1 Limited Liability Partnerships Regulations 2001 (LLPR 2001), reg 7; PA 1890, s 31.
2 LLPR 2001, Pt VI, reg 7(5).
3 The SRA has explicitly warned against entering into any agreement prior to implementation which might compromise a firm's independence or 'set up a premature ABS in disregard of the extensive safeguards constructed by Parliament in the LSA' (SRA Guidance, 'Legal Services Act: New forms of practice and regulation', January 2009).

Categories of partnership

8.12 Firms may wish to consider inclusion of one or more additional categories of partnership for non-lawyers and/or legal professionals. The structural flexibility that the PA 1890 and the LLPA 2000 afford to partnerships and LLPs respectively means that there is no restriction on the creation of different classes of partnership with different rights and obligations.

It may be, for example, that a firm will wish to appoint non-solicitors to the partnership but to restrict those individuals from attending certain meetings or being involved in certain decision-making processes (in much the same way as fixed-share or salaried partners frequently are now). In the event that the firm's thinking on the matter is advanced enough to clearly define those rights and obligations, it would be sensible to include provision for this new category of partner in the deed. This assumes, of course, that firms will wish to distinguish the non-lawyers or non-solicitors within the deed. Whilst there may be practical reasons for doing so, careful thought will need to be given to the impact that such a division might have on the partnership ethos and on the individuals concerned. In many cases, the motive for such promotions will be a fostering of the partnership culture and securing buy-in from those individuals. Clearly, such a purpose could be damaged if the position is seen as a second-class one.

Duty of good faith

8.13 Neither the PA 1890 nor the LLPA 2000 provides an explicit statutory duty of good faith[1]. The duty of good faith is of course a fundamental obligation of partnership, but the lack of an explicit statement as to its application is perhaps some explanation for the common practice of inserting the duty into the partnership deed. As far as general partnerships are concerned, the duty is implied as between all of the partners. As far as LLPs are concerned, there is by default no general duty of good faith as between the partners themselves. It is the fiduciary nature of the relationship between the members and the LLP which infers a duty of good faith as between each member and LLP and not between members.

Detailing the exact nature of the duty of good faith is a significant academic exercise in itself. However, for the purposes of this chapter, it should suffice to say that the duty bestows upon the relevant parties an obligation of mutual honesty and integrity at all times. It should be noted that the duty (in whatever form it exists) will extend to the making of any decisions which relate to the Act such as the sale or flotation of the firm. Any decision motivated by personal, isolated gain rather than that of the partnership as a whole may be a breach of the duty. It has been suggested that the specific inclusion of a duty of good faith in partnerships deeds 'adds little from a legal point of view but may serve to remind the partners of their mutual obligations of good faith'[2]. For that reason, reviewers may wish to take the opportunity to insert such a provision and, in the case of an LLP deed, clarify exactly to whom the duty is owed.

1 PA 1890, ss 28–30 include certain specific duties but not an explicit duty of good faith. Such an explicit statutory duty was considered in a draft Partnerships Bill proposed as part of the Law Commission's 2003 review of Partnership Law (Law Com 283, November 2003), but this review has now been shelved in respect of general partnerships.

2 Lord Lindley quoted in *Lindley & Banks on Partnership*, 17th edition, para 10–74.

Special consent issues

8.14 Most partnerships deeds will contain matters of special consent, that is, matters of such significance that they require a higher voting threshold in order to be approved. The Act brings about the possibility of choices which were previously unavailable, including the introduction of non-lawyer partners, the sale of whole or part of the firm to outside investors, and flotation. Firms will need to consider whether their deed and the special consent matters within it make adequate allowance for these possibilities. Without an appropriate mechanism for these issues to be determined they are each likely to represent such a fundamental change to the terms of the partnership that they would require unanimity to be effected. This effectively confers the power of veto on any one partner and is almost certainly undesirable.

It is also worth ensuring that the mechanics of special consent provisions are tight enough to ensure that any transaction is not held up by a difficult minority or, conversely, a provision that would allow any matter not covered by special consent to be passed by a simple majority. This could raise the disquieting prospect of the firm being sold off by no more than 51% of partners.

Power of expulsion by notice

8.15 Both the PA 1890 and the LLPA 2000 specifically exclude the right for a majority to expel an individual from the partnership without an express agreement between the partners to the contrary[1]. Therefore, if such a power is thought desirable – and it invariably makes sense to have it – then it must be included in the deed.

In the event that a firm were to consider not including the power, very careful thought needs to be given to management decision-making and the other matters discussed in this chapter to ensure that a firm considering its options under the Act cannot be held up by a single troublesome partner (whether or not the matter under consideration is a special consent matter).

1 LLPR 2001, Pt VI, reg 8; PA 1890, s 25.

Power of summary expulsion

8.16 Most deeds will (and should) contain provisions permitting the summary expulsion of partners in certain circumstances such as bankruptcy or serious breach of the deed. Firms considering the appointment of non-lawyers under the LDP or ABS regimes should ensure that those provisions include the ability to exclude non-lawyers who cease, for any reason, to meet the 'fit and proper person' test[1] if such an event would lead to default by the firm under the regulatory regime.

1 LSA 2007, Sch 13(1) as regards approval of a non-authorised person holding a restricted interest in a licensable body. As regards LDPs, the requirement is set out in AJA 1985, s 9A(2)(e) (inserted by LSA 2007, Sch 16, para 82). Detailed suitability criteria for LDPs are set out in the SRA Recognised Bodies Regulations 2009.

Outgoing partners: rights

8.17 A very important area for firms under the new regime will be that of how to treat retiring partners. At present, a partner's capital contribution made upon admission to the partnership is likely simply to be returned at the time of exit or soon after. Under the new regime, where partnership shares potentially have realisable capital value and age discrimination regulations make retirement of partners a thorny issue, it is not hard to envisage older partners holding on to their position in the hope of realising that capital value in the near future.

The Act undoubtedly has the potential to bring about a period of generational tension. Inevitably, there will be a spell of overlap where, on the one hand, the older generation feels that it risks losing out to the new guard if its interests are not safeguarded and, on the other hand, the younger generation fears a sell-off of the family silver that it hopes to inherit.

The risks associated with a bottleneck of older partners are obvious and, in order to mitigate these risks, firms may wish to consider implementing some form of anti-embarrassment mechanism. Typically, this would provide a sliding scale over at least three years after a partner leaves whereby, in the event of any sell-off or capital gain, the exiting partner receives a reducing percentage of any sum to which he would have been entitled had he remained at the firm.

Outgoing partners: obligations

8.18 It is unusual for modern law firm deeds not to contain restrictive covenants on exiting partners. In the case of LLPs it is the corporate entity which is entitled to enforce the covenants whereas, in a traditional partnership, it is the other partners who are the beneficiaries of the covenant.

Typically, a firm's exit provisions will provide both for a period of garden leave whereby the partner's access to the office and business is limited during his notice period and a time-limited period of restriction when the partner is prevented from competing with the business post-exit. These can be operated separately. In broad principle, restrictive covenants are enforceable provided they are reasonable and necessary for the protection of the business. They will be strictly interpreted against those seeking to enforce them and, in the event that a provision is found to be unreasonable, the covenant as a whole risks being struck out. Even though strict enforcement of restrictive covenants is relatively unusual, they can be a valuable bargaining chip in the exit negotiation process.

It is likely that, in a world where large capital payments become possible or even commonplace, partner mobility, particularly between large firms, will increase, even beyond the level seen in recent years. The new capital available to some firms coupled with aggressive expansion policies is likely to lead to the more frequent recruitment not only of star performers but of their entire teams, risking very significant damage to the firm from which they depart. For that reason, firms will want to ensure that their restrictive covenants are both effective and enforceable. In addition to the reasonableness requirement, firms will need to ensure that the wording of the covenants covers all possible competitors that a leaving partner may wish to work for, ie not only other law firms but other businesses which may offer legal services and all staff who may be the subject of a team move approach.

Goodwill

8.19 Firms will shortly be in a position where goodwill is a marketable asset. Firms should consider by whom the goodwill is owned, who is entitled to any increase in its value and how it will be apportioned upon a dissolution or sale. In the case of LLPs the goodwill is likely to be held by the LLP with gains being apportioned to partners by reference to the division of capital profits. For partnerships, goodwill will be held by the partners directly. If any outgoing partner is to receive a payment in respect of his interest in the goodwill of the business it will be necessary to develop an internal valuation mechanism for that.

As well as the legal position, firms may wish to consider any moral obligations regarding ownership of goodwill. At the time of any capitalisation of goodwill the encumbant equity partners are likely to have inherited many years of accumulated goodwill (taking my own firm as an example, over 300 years) from their predecessors effectively at nil cost. Is it right, therefore, that those individuals who happen to be in situ at the time of the Act's implementation should be the sole beneficiaries? Any provisions dictating payouts to non-equity parties in the event of a capitalisation of goodwill would require some fairly evolved thinking from the partners and it may be unrealistic to expect many firms to insert such provisions into their deed in anticipation. However, raising the issue and canvassing partner views at an early stage could prove a worthwhile exercise in itself.

Dissolution and winding up

8.20 Whilst it is not particularly palatable to consider the prospect, the Act and the consolidation and investment that it will bring to the legal market will put considerable pressure on many firms. It has been estimated that 3,000 law firms will disappear before 2012 as a result of the Act[1]. Whilst this number includes consolidations as well as dissolutions there can be little doubt that some firms will misjudge the opportunities, miss the boat or simply be squeezed out of the new, streamlined market.

Firms should ensure that dissolution and winding-up clauses are tightly drafted, making the rights and obligations of the parties upon a dissolution quite clear. LLPs should of course take advantage of the limited liability afforded to members and ensure that the deed provides that members are not obliged to contribute to the assets of the LLP upon a winding up[2].

1 Mayson, S, 'Legal Services Reforms: Catalyst, Cataclysm or Catastrophe', Legal Services Policy Institute (21 March 2007).

2 LLPA 2000, s 1(4) with Insolvency Act 1986, s 74 provides that the liability of members on a winding up is generally limited to what each member has agreed with the other members or the LLP to contribute. Thus, an explicit statement to the effect that this sum is zero is desirable.

UPDATING YOUR SYSTEMS

8.21 In addition to an update of the partnership deed, firms should consider reviewing their internal management systems. We discuss here certain systems and processes that will be of particular relevance.

Retirement and expulsion procedures

8.22 It was suggested earlier in this chapter that firms may wish to consider the inclusion of anti-embarrassment provisions with a view to preventing a bottleneck or 'bed blocking' by older partners hoping to benefit from the potential capital value brought about by the Act. Yet there is little point in reviewing the deed and introducing such provisions if the firm's retirement and removal procedures are not also up to scratch. If the introduction of the age discrimination regulations[1] was not, in itself, enough to encourage firms to do this, the Act certainly should be.

The age discrimination regulations have been the topic of much discussion elsewhere and it is not intended to consider them here in any detail, but, broadly, it can be said that retirement processes should be non-discriminatory or objectively justifiable if they are to withstand any challenge.

Once appropriate processes are in place, they need to be adhered to and good procedures should be supported by complete and accurate paper trails. This may sound like obvious advice, yet all too frequently firms ignore their problem partners in the hope that they will shortly retire in any event. The Act is likely to reinforce the desire of partners to remain with the business, and firms should consider what else might be done with a view to minimising the disruption cause by exiting or retiring partners. For example, the introduction and application of fair but robust performance reviews, applied consistently firm-wide, will assist in identifying and weeding out any coasting individuals.

1 Employment Equality (Age) Regulations 2006 (SI 2006/1031).

Soft policy provisions

8.23 We have discussed at para 8.18 above the 'hard' provisions of expulsion and restrictive covenants contained in the partnership deed. Another way that a firm can easily and inexpensively increase its chances of defending against aggressive competitor recruitment strategies is ensure that its 'soft' policies are up to date and present sufficient incentives to partners and employees.

Examples of soft policies might include:

- enhanced maternity/paternity/adoption benefits;
- a reasonable sabbatical policy;
- generous flexible working arrangements; and
- corporate social responsibility (CSR) volunteering allowances.

The capacity of such policies to engender allegiance to the firm at little or no cost should not be underestimated. Having sensible, well publicised policies that apply across the firm will increase staff and partner loyalty and may avoid the need to make ad hoc offers of such arrangements to individuals as they walk out of the door.

Annuities

8.24 Should a firm be considering seeking external investment or a buy-out, it will seek to make the firm attractive to investors. Such investors are unlikely to find cumbersome and expensive annuity arrangements appealing and so firms may wish to consider an offer to capitalise annuities, thereby removing annuitants from the equation. This is, of course, likely to be a costly exercise and, particularly to a firm which has identified a need for capital, may be unaffordable. In such circumstances a capitalisation at the time of an external investment may be a better alternative.

Non-lawyer partners

8.25 Many firms will have already considered the appointment of non-solicitors to the partnership, whether as part of an LDP or an ABS. For larger firms, the most likely appointment is perhaps the Chief Executive Officer or Chief Operating Officer. Other firms may have experienced legal executives or paralegals who could not previously be appointed but who will shortly become eligible for partnership.

A firm will need to take clear policy decisions in relation to the appointment of such individuals as partners. Such individuals may, of course, need to meet the relevant 'fit and proper person' test discussed at para 8.16 above. Assuming that they qualify for regulatory purposes and firms wish to appoint such individuals as partners, the firm should consider whether the individual has a proper understanding of the concept of partnership. Amongst solicitors, the partnership ethos is generally strong and yet there remain frequent difficulties when seeking to integrate lateral hires so similar issues can certainly be expected with non-lawyers. Proper explanations and expectation management for non-lawyers will be appropriate. On a further, practical level a firm inviting non-lawyers to sign the partnership deed may wish to offer independent legal advice to ensure a proper understanding of its terms.

OTHER CONSIDERATIONS

Delaying LLP conversion

8.26 Since the creation of LLPs constant streams of law firms have incorporated to take advantage of the limited liability structure. For a variety of reasons (some reasonable, some less so), not all firms have converted and there remains a significant number, particularly amongst smaller firms, that are still considering the possibility.

The Act does not, of course, create any new form of legal entity. ABSs and LDPs will still take the form of existing business entities – the limited company, LLP or (unlimited) partnership – but the wealth of opportunities under the Act prompts the question: if the traditional partnership is seriously considering changing its corporate status, should it delay an LLP conversion?

Postponing a conversion may be a temptation but, in reality, there is unlikely to be any good reason to do so. First, as full implementation of the Act is not due for several years, there remains a significant period during which the firm would remain with unlimited liability. During the interim years, the firm would remain exposed to all of the potential risks that will have been identified when resolving to convert to LLP status. In a market facing a significant increase in competition and perhaps, in these more straitened times, a more litigious clientele, this is hardly an appealing prospect. Secondly, the tax neutrality on a conversion afforded by the LLPA 2000, s 12(1) is only available when converting from the traditional partnership model to the LLP; from a tax perspective there is little to be gained in waiting and converting directly to a company.

There is, of course, the question of costs, and some firms may validly conclude that to postpone a conversion will mean a costs saving. The magnitude of such a saving will depend on the size of the firm but with LLP conversion now considered a well-trodden path, costs associated with it should be relatively modest in relation to the size of the firm's income and, more importantly, exposure.

Whilst firms will each have their own additional considerations, it seems that there are few arguments, or at least few based solely on the commencement of the Act, to support delaying a conversion and remaining as an unlimited partnership.

Losing sight of the wood for the trees

8.27 One final note of caution: the temptation to explore all avenues that will become available under the Act may be great. For struggling firms or those with poor succession management there may be a belief that Act can provide a panacea. Securing capital finance, infrastructure investment or a merger partner may indeed be high on the list of priorities for such firms. But to be distracted by such possibilities at the expense of the firm's day-to-day business would of course be imprudent and any firm which has taken its eye off the ball is unlikely to be an attractive investment.

CONCLUSION

8.28 Little has been proposed in this chapter which is not good business practice, regardless of the impact of the Act. A firm's deed and business practices should always be 'fit for purpose' and regular reviews are prudent. Only the foolhardy will believe that the Act will not impact significantly on their own business. At the very least, every firm will be competing with other businesses who have embraced the Act and the new opportunities it offers. So, the advice to all businesses must be to prepare properly. A firm whose house is in order is far more likely to be considered a good prospect, whether by an investor, a prospective merger partner or simply its own partners and staff, whom it wishes to retain.

Chapter 9

MERGERS

James Thorne

INTRODUCTION

9.1 Law firms have merged in the past and, with or without the LSA 2007, will do so in the future. Will the Act accelerate the trend? Will the merger process be changed as a result of the Act's implementation?

Before we can consider what changes the Act is likely to bring, we need to know why mergers have happened to date and how they have been implemented.

PAST MERGERS

9.2 Mergers amongst law firms are nothing new. My own firm, Farrer & Co, merged with the practice of Frederic Ouvry in 1855 for reasons that resonate over the years: the lack of succession, the concerns of a significant client, and the need to develop what we (but not they) would call 'critical mass'. The firm became Farrer & Ouvry and prospered[1].

Mergers such as these were typical: small in scale and informally put together. They have not altogether disappeared now; the senior partner of a decent out-of-town firm recently described a merger with another local practice which pretty well matched the experience of this firm more than 150 years ago, with (so far) similar results.

Changes followed the lifting of the limitation on the size of solicitors' firms[2] and the seizing of the opportunities by law firms are described in Chapter 7. The first blockbuster merger was that of Clifford-Turner and Coward Chance in 1987, which took the legal world by surprise and was met by near-universal scepticism, but which on any measure has been transformational for itself, English law firms and for firms around the world.

Look at its merger history:

1987	Clifford-Turner–Coward Chance merger	
	Combined number of partners:	169
	Combined number of assistants:	461
	Combined turnover (estimated):	£200 million
	(Source: *20 years of The Lawyer*, 1987)	
1999	Pünder, Volhand, Weber & Anster (Frankfurt) Rogers & Wells (New York) merger	
2002	Established in California with 50 lawyers from Brobeck, Phleger & Harrison	
2007	Closed in California	
2008	Partners:	613
	Fee earners:	3,204
	Revenue:	£1,329 million
	28 offices in 22 jurisdictions	
	(Source: Clifford Chance Annual Review for the year to 30 April 2008)	
2009	Announced redundancies of 80 professional staff in London	

So, not all has gone right for it, but it has been a stupendously successful merger over all.

The merger story can be repeated for other firms too, not all with the first mover advantage that Clifford Chance had, but successful nevertheless, both here in the UK[3] and now abroad.

Clearly mergers have helped a number of firms at all levels get to a different sale of size and profitability. Of course, even if a firm has successfully merged, it may not feel like a success to many individual partners within it, especially to those who have been de-equitised at the time or as a consequence of the merger, or left the firm altogether, voluntarily or with encouragement. A firm's figures pre- and post-merger tell something of what the firm has done, but cannot tell the whole story.

And what do we mean by 'merger'? As with public company mergers, here the term covers both a joining together of roughly equal bodies as well as acquisition where the larger firm swallows up the smaller one. Examples of the former are actually pretty few and far between – the most obvious examples are Clifford-Turner and Coward Chance; Addleshaw Sons & Latham with Booth & Co to create Addleshaw Booth in 1997; and Berwin Leighton with Paisner & Co to create Berwin Leighton & Paisner in 2001 – but there have not been not too many more significant ones. But even if the latter is the far more prevalent model for mergers, the term is used to describe something more than an out-and-out acquisition. Characteristics of a merger might include a change of name of the merged firm; the creation of a new body to take the businesses of both firms forward; the involvement of both firms' senior management in management going forward; partners from each firm retaining their status as partners and their potential level of remuneration post-merger; significant changes to the larger firm's partnership agreement to accommodate the requirements of its merging firm, and the lack of a cash payment to the merging firm's partners for their goodwill. Not all of these will be present in a merger, but the lack of any of them will suggest a straightforward acquisition rather than a merger in any meaningful sense, beyond the smaller firm's marketing to its clients and staff.

So, what has made a successful merger in the past and will the same apply in the future?

1 Frederic Ouvry attracted such luminaries as Charles Dickens as clients. Mr Ouvry became President of the Law Society. The firm reverted to the name Farrer & Co upon Frederic Ouvry's death in 1881.
2 Companies Act 1967, s 121.
3 What is now Eversheds provides a striking example:

Eversheds & Tomkinson (Birmingham), merged with Alexander Tatham (Manchester), Broomheads (Sheffield), Daynes Hill & Perks (Norwich) 1988
Wells & Hind (Nottingham), Philips & Buck (Cardiff) 1989
Hepworth & Chadwick (Leeds) 1990
Turner Martin & Symes 1991, Holt Philips (Bristol) 1994
Jacques & Lewis (London and Brussels) 1995
Waltons & Morse (London) 1996
Wilkinson Maughan (Newcastle) 1997
Frere Cholmeley Bischoff (London, Paris, Sofia and Moscow) 1998
Sandal Lunoe (Copenhagen) 1998
Palmer Wheeldon (Cambridge) 1998
Linsley & Mortimer (Newcastle) 2000
followed by numerous associations with firms in Europe, Middle East and Far East.
(Source: Eversheds website)

WHY MERGE?

9.3 The effect of a merger is to get bigger, but that is not the reason for it. As Giles Rubens puts it[1]:

> 'Many [mergers] can be considered, most fairly, neither successes or failures; they have resulted in larger firms being created but not obviously better or more competitive ones.'

It is not hard to think of a number of firms which have merged but not thrived; a larger size is clearly not a worthwhile end in itself.

The reason for any merger should be to make a better firm in some way. It might be to deal with a particular issue, say:

- to fix a lack of succession within a partnership – Farrer & Co's merger with Frederic Ouvry referred to in para 9.2 above is an (old) example of this. This is more likely to affect smaller firms;
- to extend the firm's regional and international coverage – Eversheds' many national and international mergers was driven by this[2];
- to reinforce the firm's leading position for a particular type of work;
- to establish a London presence – Addleshaw Booth's merger with Theodore Goddard is just one example of the route to establishing a credible London presence taken by a number of regional firms to make

themselves 'national' and by a number of US firms to establish themselves with a credible presence here – Jones Day with Gouldens, for example;
- to rebuild presence in a field where partners have defected (eg Withers with Crossman Block back in 1987)[3];
- to spread the cost of infrastructure developments over more than one firm – this is more likely to be relevant at the commoditised end of the market.

Whatever the reason – and there will be a mixture – the merger must result from the firm's strategy and not a knee-jerk response to an immediate problem. A danger of the implementation of the Act is that a number of firms, in particular high street ones, will respond to it by seeing a merger as their salvation but without thinking through what the consequences might be. A minus multiplied by a minus might defy mathematical laws and not make a plus.

Two lots of property; two lots of underemployed assistants or, of course, partners; two lots of clients dissatisfied with the service they are getting and its cost; two lots of underperforming management, or any of these will not make for a happy or successful merger. And even with larger firms it should not be assumed that overhead costs or management will be reduced; law firms are complex bodies and a merged firm will often require more rather than less management.

So, a merger should be the outcome of a strategic decision, with the strategy of the merged firm being realistic and deliverable. The merging firm, particularly its senior management, must be committed to that strategy and, once the decision to merge has been made, to delivering the merger.

1 Law Firm Mergers, Taking a Strategic Approach by Giles Rubens and Hildebrandt International, provides a useful introduction to the subject.
2 See para 9.2, note 3.
3 Followed by a de-merger in 1989 because of a 'culture clash'; source: *20 years of The Lawyer* (1987). Withers has of course gone on to merge successfully with a number of firms in the UK, New York and in Europe.

WAYS TO ACHIEVE A SUCCESSFUL MERGER

9.4 There is no fixed template for achieving a successful merger, but a list of the key factors follows:

1. Communication: with partners, staff and key clients

Partners should know that a merger is a way of achieving the firm's strategy and that it is being taken forward by central management. Regular updates on progress should be given, even if the actual target is not identified until a late stage for reasons of confidentiality. The early disclosure of the merger partner, whether intentional or not, can be the death to the chances of the merger happening at all.

Part of the communication exercise will be to prepare the partners for the impact of the merger: for any change in working habits, financial disciplines, seating arrangements, mode of business development and the like which might be expected of them. There may also be particular ad hominem issues to deal with, where one partner has a particular concern about another in the merging firm, but this should not be allowed to derail a merger that otherwise makes sense.

The same need for communication applies to professional and support staff, although inevitably they will be brought into the picture at a later stage in the proceedings, perhaps only at the moment of its completion.

Speaking to key clients, too, is crucial, partly to clear commercial as much as legal conflicts of interest, but also to hear their views and to take them along in the process. They will be key to the success of the merger after it happens. A great deal of wisdom and experience is vested in clients and we ignore it at our peril: the benefit of asking them for their views will give them some pleasure and strengthen the firm's relationship with them.

2. **Culture**

Is culture the glue that binds a firm or an inchoate concept blamed if things go wrong? It certainly has a lot of time devoted to it. Giles Rubens[1] thinks it may be an overused, even abused, term and that it is useful only to apply it in describing how a firm deals with particular issues, such as the role of partners, the style of working, the role of management, the values and standards of behaviour promoted and tolerated by the firm, and the role of support teams. Others can be added, such as a willingness to commit to the merger and an equal willingness to do things differently once it has occurred.

Certainly it is useful to apply the concept of culture to these specific areas and right not to regard 'culture' as a sort of Band-Aid that will make the merger work or not. However, there is still something intangible to be considered in the merger – 'fit' is a possible description – which is a feeling, based on empiricism, that the firms will work together post-merger.

3. **Tackle issues in advance**

We have said earlier that mergers are not a panacea; they will not make problems within a firm simply disappear. And the merger will have a much greater chance of success if it deals with issues in advance. The greatest of these may well be underperforming partners; they should not form part of the legacy of either of the merging firms.

4. **Carry out due diligence**

Mergers have not to date taken the form of private company acquisitions, with extensive due diligence and full warranties covering every aspect of the target's assets and undertaking. Due diligence has generally been limited, covering areas which are likely to give rise to a liability, if not necessarily for the merged firm (as liabilities arising before completion of the merger will generally stick with the merging LLP or, if still unlimited, its partners). Due diligence has been concentrated on issues that may make the merger more difficult or more expensive to implement. Effective due diligence is to this end, of identifying issues and working to resolve them, rather than giving a claim for damages if things go wrong post-merger.

Particular issues for due diligence are:

(a) Tax and accounting. The basis on which firms are taxed has become much more uniform and the problem of one firm being taxed on a cash-received basis and having to switch to an earnings basis has all but disappeared. There will, however, be differences in tax treatments and approaches between the firms, and these need reviewing. The same applies to accounting issues and a firm of accountants is often retained to review both.

(b) The merging firms will wish to check out key information about the other, in particular:

  (i) partnership structure. This will involve reviewing:
  –the full partnership agreement;
  –the current partnership (including areas of expertise for each equity partner), the means by which assistants progress to partnership and how partners progress once admitted to partnership;
  –partner remuneration criteria.

  (ii) finance and accounting:
  –accounts and management accounts;
  –accounting policies;
  –cash flow forecasts;
  –charge-out rates and charging policies; clients are unlikely to be happy if they face a higher (or merely different) basis of charging from the merged firm;
  –hours targets (chargeable and non-chargeable).

  (iii) commercial:
  –professional indemnity cover;
  –claims record (past and present notifications and complaints);
  –details of premises;
  –pension arrangements.

The due diligence process should identify any deal breakers. These could emerge from anywhere, including:

- client conflicts, whether legal or, more likely, commercial ones. If a key client will not countenance instructing the merged firm then it is clearly an issue;
- the position of partners of the junior merger partner in the merged firm. This covers not only whether or not such partners are to retain their status as equity, fixed-share or salaried partners, but also where they fit within the particular band. This is particularly an issue for more junior partners and indeed senior assistants – they are the future of the firm and in normal times might well walk if they are not happy with their position and prospects;
- the availability of leadership and management roles in the merged firm. If the junior firm ends up with none of its partners having a significant role then the merger will look more like a takeover and correspondingly less attractive;
- future funding requirements, including in relation to the costs of integrating the merging firm;

– 'fit', by which we mean culture, management style and the like. Only in the most defensive of mergers, where the reason to do it is above all else to avoid a large problem, can the importance of fit be overlooked.

5. **Business case**

   We are back to where we started; the merger must made strategic sense and be supported by a business case for it. Being bigger for size's sake, or adopting a suck-it-and-see attitude will not make for a successful merger. The business case will show that the strategic reasons for the merger are supported by the evidence gathered from due diligence; that there is a cultural fit; that there are plans in place to implement the merger.

6. **Implementation**

   With many transactions, getting the deal done is the easier part. Getting to completion often seems the overwhelming objective to those involved in the transaction, but it is not an end in itself. As much time should be devoted to planning and then implementing the merger to ensure that the work and expense of getting there was worthwhile. What the planning should cover will of course vary from case to case, depending in part on what has emerged in due diligence, but will include:

   (a) communicating with partners, staff, clients, banks and others about the merger. Many will have already been brought into the loop but none should be taken for granted;
   (b) the physical integration of the two firms. Having each firm sitting in its pre-merger offices for any time will hinder the merger's chances of success.
   (c) integrating IT systems. This is not necessarily easy or cheap, but is critical to success. Each part of the firm must be working off integrated accounting, document management, know-how and marketing systems as soon as is practicable, and trained to do so;
   (d) management integration. Leaving one part of the merged firm out in the cold in management terms will not help the merger succeed (unless the merging firm has suffered from management failures from which the merger is a means of escape);
   (e) taking hard decisions quickly. If cost savings are part of the business case for the merger, they will not be made easier if they are delayed, and quick and decisive actions involving redundancies are likely to reassure those who stay. The merger will not benefit from fudge in this area.

A great deal of this may be regarded as counsel of perfection; no merger will neatly fit the theoretical template, but being conscious of the issues and acting on them will improve the merger's chances of success.

[1] See para 9.3, note 1.

IMPLEMENTATION OF MERGERS

9.5 Mergers have been implemented by one firm folding into another. Simplistically, this involves two steps: the transfer by the LLP or the partners of one firm of assets and undertaking to the other by means of a merger or business transfer agreement, and the partners of that transferring firm becoming partners of the other. The merger agreement may plan for the convergence of the two firms over time, but this is comparatively unusual.

And although there are many ways in which these two steps can be taken, they are often in fact relatively informally done; many smaller mergers will not comprise much more than an exchange of letters, although of course the mergers between larger firms require fuller documentation and external advice.

The merger agreement, apart from the transfer of assets and undertaking, will deal with particular liabilities which are identified in due diligence, such as:

- the treatment of retired or about to retire partners who have a right to an annuity – there are still some – or a consultancy;
- the treatment of pension schemes in the merging firm. This is a particular issue if that firm has, or has had, a final salary scheme, whether or not it has a pension fund deficit;
- how the liability for particular leasehold interests might be dealt with;
- any particular employee claims which, by virtue of TUPE, will pass to the merged firm – the merger agreement will seek by means of an indemnity to leave the liability where it arose, at least if it exceeds an identified level.

The merger agreement will deal with other more routine matters, such as the effective date of the merger and arrangements for run-off professional indemnity insurance for the merging firm. It would also be expected to have a few, basic warranties which are mutual, ie each firm gives certain warranties to the other. These will generally be concerned with liabilities and would cover:

- each firm's accounts and management accounts;
- its claims and complaints record;
- the extent and cost of its professional indemnity over.

The merger agreement should also make clear how the merger is to be communicated to both firms' key constituencies of staff and clients – although planning for this will have started a great deal earlier in the process and the communications strategy will be well under way before the agreement is signed.

The second leg of the merger arrangements deals with the position of each partner of the merging firm in the larger firm he is joining. At the simplest level, this will be a deed of adherence to the other firm's partnership or membership deed. This will set out where the partner is to slot in – whether he will remain an equity or fixed-share partner and, assuming there is some form of lockstep, at what level the partner is to join. This sensitive area is the one which is perhaps most likely to derail merger negotiations, particularly in smaller firm mergers.

One striking feature is that it has been comparatively rare for any payment to be made to the joining partners for what they bring with them – their reward for doing so is deemed to be satisfied by fulfilling the strategic logic of the merger. We consider below whether this may change.

The joining partners may also wish to vary the partnership agreement in relation to restrictive covenants by, for example, seeking a carve-out for clients of their existing firm for when they have worked up to the time of the merger. Giving such a carve-out, even if for a relatively limited time to allow the merger to bed down, is a useful and easy gesture for the other firm to make.

Almost as important is what role the merging partners will have in the management of the merged firm. One would expect those who had such a role in the merging firm and have led it into the merger to be given a role in management going forward, but this will depend on the relative sizes and strengths of the two firms to the merger. There are arguments both ways; keeping the merging firm's partners involved in the management of the merged firm ought to give comfort to their other partners and professionals that their voice will be heard and that the merger is not in fact – as many of them fear – a takeover. Equally, if the larger firm's management has a successful track record, particularly in making mergers work, finding a management slot for some of the incoming partners may disrupt a successful team and actually hold back the integration of the merging firm by encouraging its partners to hold on to their old ways. Certainly it is not hard to think of examples of where partners from the merging firm have joined the other firm's management but have not survived, even though the merger as a whole has been considered a success. This is a difficult area where the solution in a particular case will be a pragmatic one.

Salaried partners, and salaried members of an LLP, will be TUPEed across to the other firm[1]. But although as a matter of law they are easily dealt with, they are often key to the success of the merger; they and the senior associates are the 'marzipan layer' from which the future success of the practice is often derived and they have to be kept happy. There is a tension in merger negotiations between the need for confidentiality and the need to keep key players, who may well be salaried partners, happy about their prospects. This pushes towards keeping them in the loop, but the risks of premature disclosure of a merger are so great that generally the negotiations are kept on a strictly need-to-know basis, and salaried partners and other professionals are kept in the dark.

Most of the salaried partners would recognise the need for this; what they need to feel is that the merger makes strategic sense to them when it is eventually revealed to them, and they have a worthwhile role to play in the merged firm.

1 Although LLPA 2000, s 4 provides that members of an LLP are not to be regarded as employees, there is a carve out in s 4(4) which in effect preserves the employment status of salaried members if they are members on terms that are consistent with an employment contract.

MERGERS – THE FUTURE

9.6 How will the implementation of the Act change any of this?

Of course, many mergers will continue to happen – indeed many commentators see this as an inevitable consequence of the Act. Professor Stephen Mayson, in his slightly chilling article published in March 2007, 'Legal Services Reforms; Catalyst, Cataclysm or Catastrophe?'[1], which favours cataclysm but warns of catastrophe, anticipates 3,000 of the 8,500 firms with fewer than ten partners disappearing in the five to ten years from 2007, with most lawyers in these firms having a place in a smaller number of larger firms[2].

We discuss in Chapter 11 the increasing pressures being brought to bear on smaller high street firms by the Act, which could well push them towards merger. This assumes that the options of outside investment in the firm, in the form of a listing or private equity investment discussed in Chapter 9, are not readily available to them. A merger may seem the best way forward.

There is likely to be increased merger activity amongst larger firms too, for the mixture of reasons discussed above, with perhaps a desire for 'critical mass' fuelled by the changes in the market place encouraged by the Act.

Will the way in which mergers happen change? Certainly, it could. The introduction of outside capital into law firms could well allow firms to merge with others by acquisition. Up until now, it has been difficult and expensive for firms to build a reserve to fund acquisitions; this would have to be funded out of after-tax earnings. So without a war chest it has been difficult for a firm to acquire a successful firm or part of a firm, but the position could well change, with the acquiring firm able to tempt with substantial cash sums being offered to the partners in the target firm.

Once cash is on the table the mechanics of the merger will change – it will move towards a straight acquisition of one firm by the other. And the injection of hard cash into the deal (particularly as it is likely to be someone else's, such as a private equity investor's) will move the transaction closer to a private company or business acquisition. The present often rather informal arrangements may well move to the model typically used for a business or share acquisition and, for example, involve the merging or selling partners to give a raft of warranties and indemnities. This model is of course well understood by lawyers in advising their own clients, but they are not be used to applying it to their own affairs.

The change in the nature of the transaction could have an effect on two other key constituencies who are vital to the success of the merger – the 'marzipan layer' of salaried parties and senior associates, and clients. The former can of course be offered incentives by the acquiring firm, which will be anxious to ensure that they retain the 'good guys'; clients may be a bit more difficult to please if they thought their lawyers were in any sense cashing in on them. This may lead to a more structured deal, with the cash consideration being paid out against delivery and performance criteria to be met over time. But, of course, the more conditional the deal becomes, the less interesting it will be for partners to sell in the first place.

So, cash payments as an inducement to merge could well be a consequence of the Act.

Another force blowing through the legal world is the credit crunch which, in a very short space of time, has changed dramatically the outlook for law firms. We have daily examples of law firms downsizing, with the legal press keeping track of each newly announced 'restructuring' or 'scaling back'. Clearly firms are not cutting back with a view to a return in the short term to the boom times many corporate and commercial lawyers have enjoyed almost without a break since the mid-1990s. Cutbacks are being made because the firms cannot see that significant areas of practice are likely to return to previous levels of activity within the foreseeable future.

Against this background mergers will be for more defensive reasons. The legal world is not immune from the rest of business life; as its clients suffer so will the pressure on costs increase, giving us all the dismal prospect of chasing harder for less work at a worse rate. It is this pressure which will lead to more defensive mergers.

Some firms will merge in the perhaps mistaken belief that bigger is better and safer: that will not be enough. Such mergers may save some overhead costs, but mergers can produce higher costs, at least in the short term – the costs of the merger, or redundancies of duplicated staff, or integrating IT systems and the like. But the biggest costs are to be found in professional staff, partners and assistants, and a merger triggered by the credit crunch will doubtless focus on these as a means of driving down costs.

Mergers done against this background are also likely to be more bloody; although a merger is an opportunity to sort out issues within a partnership, in good times there has been some tolerance in dealing with these. In tougher times mergers will be harsher with the weaker, smaller partnership being offered a worse deal all round. The larger firm driving the merger may expect to take on fewer of the partners and professional and support staff of the other, and be more concerned to leave behind problems, for example, relating to properties, pensions, employees, etc.

This is not much of a prospect, but the credit crunch could well have a more severe impact on mergers in the short and medium term than the more positive opportunities promised by the Act.

1 Given as his inaugural address as Director of the College of Law's Legal Services Policy Institute.

2 This is perhaps a brighter outlook than then portrayed in Chapter 7, which foresees many practitioners facing insolvency at the end of their careers – see para 7.6 above.

Chapter 10

OUTSIDE INVESTMENT – LISTINGS AND PRIVATE EQUITY

James Thorne

INTRODUCTION

10.1 This chapter considers the two principal means by which law firms will be able to raise external capital after the LSA 2007 is fully implemented. There are of course means by which firms can be supported by external finance at present – in particular bank debt and convertible debt[1], which itself anticipates the implementation of the Act – but here we focus on what new channels of finance will be available to law firms.

To raise external finance will require the firm to become an alternative business structure (ABS)[2]. The formalities of this will not be considered further here, but any investor who acquires 10% or more of the firm's capital will need to be approved as a fit and proper person to do so by the appropriate regulatory authority.

1 See Chapter 8.
2 See Chapter 4.

When?

10.2 As to when listings of law firms and outside investment will be permitted, the timetable is, as always, uncertain. The Government originally indicated 2010, then moved this back to 2011. The head of the Legal Services Board on appointment expressed the hope that the process could be accelerated, but the prospects of this are not good. The comparatively straightforward step of allowing non-solicitors to become partners in legal disciplinary practices (LDPs) was planned for 1 March 2009, but by that date the regulations to allow this to happen had not been approved in accordance with statutory procedures nor had a commencement date been set by the Lord Chancellor. This is a small issue. The larger picture of the Act's implementation could well be held up by the Law Society sponsored reviews of the regulatory process by the Hunt[1] and Rodgers[2] Committees and, whatever their outcome, the oddly timed enthusiasm of the Law Society for these reviews, particularly of Lord Hunt, has not smoothed the way forward.

And all this before we know whether the credit crunch is likely to increase pressure from law firms and others for a speedy implementation of the Act, or the reverse[3].

For present purposes we assume that ABSs will be allowed in 2011.

1 The Independent Review of Legal Regulation of Law Firms led by Lord Hunt.
2 Regulation of Corporate Legal Work Review, lead by Nick Smedley, a 'sub-strand' of the Hunt Review.
3 As at 12 February 2009, according to the Law Society *Gazette*, only four firms had applied to LDP status, suggesting floodgates were not then about to be opened. Equally, law firms were slow in adopting LLP status although most larger firms, eight years on, now have.

Stick to your knitting?

10.3 There are compelling reasons for law firms to look for outside capital in the form of a private equity investment or listing. But it is not the only option. One of the fallacies of the White Paper on which the LSA 2007 is based is that firms are uncompetitive because of a lack of access to capital; this is undoubtedly true of a number of firms but, with respect to them, they may not be the prime targets for outside investment. Certainly up to the credit crunch many firms had ready access to sufficient capital for their needs in the form of bank debt, often supplied in the simplest form of an overdraft or term loan and often without security, either from a limited liability partnership (if the firm was incorporated) or the partners themselves. Even with the credit crunch, law firms remain attractive borrowers to banks, for the same reasons they are attractive to private equity investors and, potentially, a listing. We return to why this is below.

Bank debt is relatively cheap and leaves the structure, ownership and management of law firms undisturbed. If available, many firms will continue to rely on this.

Firms may also look at other internal sources of finance; perhaps the disposal of a non-core business[1] or property.

Private equity investment in and listing of law firms is likely to remain the exception, either because it is not needed or firms will not meet the demanding requirements of either.

1 Such as the disposals by Addleshaw Goddard and Hammonds of their conveyancing businesses; that of Hammonds failed in early 2009.

Outside investment – reasons for

10.4 There will be a good deal of overlap between the reasons for seeking either a private equity investment or listing, and we consider these here.

(a) Access to money seems the most obvious reason for taking an outside investment or listing, and clearly it is the prime mover. There does, though, need to be a good reason for this and one which could be transformational for the firm. Examples are:

(i) to fund significant investment in IT. Not only are commoditised services such as residential conveyancing and personal injury claims susceptible to legal services becoming very largely IT-driven, but so are parts of larger, more complex transactions such as mergers and acquisitions where electronic data rooms and document management systems require significant IT systems;

(ii) to fund acquisitions of legal firms and teams. It is anticipated that outside investors will fund firms to go on the acquisition trail, based on the belief that the legal market is ready and suitable for consolidation. US law firms have in the last decade shown how relatively easily partners can be persuaded to move by guaranteed profit shares and the like; might the same be applied on a broader canvas? Yes, probably, though the case for this is not as persuasive as it would have been a year or so before the credit crunch – which has stymied much acquisition activity.

(iii) to take advantage of the new ABSs by recruiting non-lawyers to the firm, so that it can offer a full range of professional services;

(iv) to fund a firm's expansion in other ways, for example, into other parts of the country or to set up abroad;

(v) to replace funding from other sources. For example, in November 2007 *The Lawyer* reported that Irwin Mitchell had very successfully built up its personal injury practice, based partly on the payment of referral fees. It was thought then that the SRA might prohibit the contentious practice of paying referral fees and, although in the event it did not, the miners' compensation scheme saga has called the practice of paying referral fees into question. To fuel the Irwin Mitchel engine, *The Lawyer* speculated that outside capital would be welcomed by the firm;

(vi) to fund the retirement of senior partners. In the minds of some younger partners and senior assistants this has become a bogeyman, but it is not going to happen. It is quite clear that no outside investor would invest in a firm if it saw a substantial part of its investment walking out the door; nor would the funding of retiring partners be a sufficient reason to justify a listing.

But funding is not the only reason to look outside.

(b) Private equity investors believe they can be the catalyst for change within a firm. They invest with a view to their eventual exit, and during the period of involvement wish to make things happen. They will often have skills – perhaps not otherwise available within law firms – of driving revenue and profits and improving cash flow, of managing change within the practice and helping in the completion and integration of acquisitions. They also often will have contacts in different areas not available to the firm itself, which can be used for the firm's benefit.

(c) The experience of listing or a private equity investment can clearly be liberating for those within the traditional, professional partnership structure. For younger partners in particular, the consensual approach to decision-taking within partnerships can be irksome; with outside investment, particularly a listing, this is necessarily removed. The company becomes more focussed on profit generation; glass ceilings to ownership are removed (making it easier to recruit those subject to such restrictions in other firms); the company is seen to become more meritocratic and attracts good people from outside the firm to manage it. It even has a client benefit in that clients believe that, as a listed company, their advisers have more empathy with the client's own position.

Many of us perhaps romanticise the partnership ideal (even in LLP form), savouring its consensual approach, collegiality and culture. Of course, the size of a firm militates against these values, but it is worth remembering that they can be seen as shackles to the development of a firm, and outside investment is an opportunity to shake them off.

We have considered why a firm might choose a private equity investment or listing. We now look at these in turn.

PRIVATE EQUITY INVESTMENT

10.5 What is attractive to a private equity investor in the legal market?

As we have seen from Michael McLaren QC and Marianne Butler[1] and Tony Williams[2] the legal profession has grown strongly in the last 20 years, producing excellent income and profit growth for those working within it. (It is too early to judge, but it may become even more attractive in comparison to other areas during the credit crunch era, assuming of course that this does not kill off all forms of outside investment whilst it lasts.) The profession has had strong and generally growing earnings, but at the same time there is huge potential for change by reason of the fragmentation of the legal services market, much of which is perceived to be poorly managed. The threats and opportunities created by technology, the continued commoditisation of many legal services, the financial backing available to firms even before the full implementation of the LSA 2007, and increasing cost pressures from clients all make the market an attractive one to private equity investors who believe they can make a difference[3].

The private equity investor will look for a firm with a clear and plausible strategy of where it wants to get to and a management committed to that. The business will be expected to be well established with strong client relationships and, preferably, a strong brand. Above all, it must have potential for development.

Does it need to be broken in some way so that the private equity investor, using his alchemy, can fix it? Certainly this view has been expressed[4], but is not a necessary element. In short, the private equity investor will not have a template as to which firms it will invest in, or the terms on which he will do so. His investment will be earmarked for specific projects, mentioned above.

There may also be the possibility of paying out some senior partners in full. In this the investor may help not only the leaving partner of achieving the holy grail of converting income into capital for tax purposes, but also help those who remain within the firm in this respect.

As to the deal itself, the value put on the investor's stake is obviously important, if not key. This will be based on the firm's profits, adjusted for the equity partners' profit shares and substituting an appropriate salary for them. A multiple will be applied based on comparable transactions and the price–earnings ratios of listed professional firms, discounted to reflect the lack of market for the investment. To produce the enterprise value of the firm, surplus cash and assets in the business will be added to this with all non-trading debt deducted, as will be incentives thought necessary for the marzipan layer below equity partners. That's the process; it clearly is a flexible one and will have to satisfy the firm, which will not wish to sell a stake in the firm too cheaply, and the investor, who will not want to pay too much.

The structure of the deal will be along the lines of any private equity investment. The investment will require regulatory clearance, with the firm being approved as an ABS and the investor being an approved person to hold a stake within it. Subject to this, the formalities will probably be along conventional lines for a private equity investment and involve[5]:

- the establishment of Newco, which will acquire the business of the firm. This will be along the lines of a conventional acquisition with a sale and purchase agreement and a set of warranties given by at least the existing LLP and probably its members, or by the partners of an unlimited partnership. This would follow conventional due diligence;
- the partners will receive their stakes in Newco along with service agreements;
- the investor will invest in Newco by subscribing shares and loan notes.

The shares will probably be a form of cumulative participating redeemable preference shares with conventional loan stock. A subscription and shareholders agreement, with matching new articles of association for Newco, will be put in place. The rights attaching to the investors' shares will give it a preferential share of profits and certain negative controls – its consent will be required to key decision – as well as a place on Newco's board.

The articles will also cater for good and bad leaver provisions for departing partners.

The investor's exit provisions will also be covered; these are of key significance to the investor. The idea of the investor's exit will be of concern to the professional firm, but the investor has to make a capital return so it can reward its own investors. The exit will usually be planned for three to five years after the investment is made, and is more likely to take the form of a sale to another private equity investor rather than a sale to another firm or a listing, but all of this is some time off.

10.5 *Outside Investment – Listings and Private Equity*

Will private equity investment in law firms happen and be a success? There seems to be an appetite for it; Lyceum Capital has been reported to have a £50 million fund ready for investment in law firms. Also, other professional practices have gone down this route successfully – see the GVA Grimley case study below.

The challenges for private equity may be in finding suitable firms in which to invest, with many firms being adequately capitalised and unwilling to divest any part of its ownership to a third party.

1 See Chapter 1.
2 See Chapter 7.
3 I am grateful to Jeremy Hand and Humphrey Baker of Lyceum Capital for sharing the views of a private equity investor in this field.
4 Not by Lyceum Capital but others, generally before the credit crunch. Now the prospect of investing in a basket case may be less attractive.
5 See Chapter 17 for more sophisticated structures. The nature of the rights given to the investor will be much the same.

LISTING

10.6 We have not had listed law firms in this country previously, but other professional firms have listed here in the past, and law firms have done so in Australia. Here we look briefly at the experience of four of them:

- Savills, the surveyors firm, which listed on the full market in the UK on 21 July 1988;
- Murgitroyd Group plc, a Scottish patent agency, which listed on AIM in November 2001;
- Slater & Gordon Limited, a Australian law firm which listed on the Australian Stock Exchange in May 2007; and
- Tenon, 'advisers to entrepreneurs' providing financial, taxation and business advice, which was admitted to AIM in March 2000.

They have been selected fairly randomly and of course their past performance is no guide to what might happen to others in the future. But here are some hard facts.

Savills plc (property)	
Date when first listed:	21 July 1988
Proportion of company listed:	27.1%
Market capitalisation on listing:	£44,000,000
Market capitalisation on 14 April 2009:	£380,030,000
Listing price:	£1.25 per share
Earnings per share at 31 December 2007:	£44.30
Number of offices at listing:	22
Number of offices at 31 December 2007:	195
Number of employees on listing:	507
Number of employees 31 December 2007:	18,000
Turnover for year end pre-listing 31 December 1996:	£9,644,000
Turnover for year to 31 December 2007:	£650,000,000
Profits for year end pre-listing 31 December 2006:	£2,516,000
Profits for year to 31 December 2007*:	£57,900,000
* Date of most up-to-date audited accounts	

Murgitroyd Group plc (patent agents)	
Date when first listed:	30 November 2001
Proportion of company listed:	29.95%
Market capitalisation on listing:	£10,000,000
Market capitalisation on 14 April 2009:	£21,000,000
Listing price:	£1.21 per share
Earnings per share at 31 May 2008:	29.6p
Number of offices at listing:	7
Number of offices at January 2009:	14
Number of employees on listing:	110
Number of employees latest:	226
Turnover for year end pre-listing 31 May 2001:	£7,750,000
Turnover for latest year end 31 May 2008:	£25,700,000
Profits for year end pre-listing 31 May 2001:	£391,000
Profits for 31 May 2008*:	£2,000,000
* *Date of most up-to-date audited accounts*	

Slater & Gordon Limited (**Australian law firm**)	
Date when first listed:	21 May 2007
Proportion of company listed:	32.5%
Market capitalisation on listing:	Aus $107,800,000
Market capitalisation on 14 April 2009	Aus $184,900,000
Listing price:	Aus $1
Earnings per share at 30 June 2008:	15.3 cents
Number of offices at listing:	15
Number of offices at January 2009:	27
Number of employees on listing:	400
Number of employees at January 2009:	500+
Turnover for year end pre-listing 31 December 2006:	Aus $43,149,000
Turnover for latest year end 30 June 2008:	Aus $79,715,000
Profits for year end pre-listing 31 December 2006:	Aus $5,113
Profits for year to 30 June 2008:	Aus $15,104,000

Tenon (**business services**)	
Date when first listed:	20 March 2000
Proportion of company listed:	99%
Market capitalisation on listing:	£10,000,000
Market capitalisation on 14 April 2009:	£74,820,000
Listing price:	10p per share
Earnings per share at 30 June 2008:	6.11p
Turnover for latest year end 30 June 2008:	£160,300,000
Profits for year to 30 June 2008:	£17,636,000

What is striking is that up to the onset of the credit crunch, growth in turnover and profits, and number of offices and employees was impressive, and the listing had achieved a fundamental, seismic shift in those firms from successful professional partnership (other than Tenon, which was a start-up), to fully fledged listed companies[1].

Of course, transformational shifts can happen in other ways – Clifford Chance and Eversheds, for example, achieved it by merger[2], and they and others have shown an equally impressive growth in turnover and profits. But Murgitroyd and Slater & Gordon Limited since listing have acquired a number of other firms, and opened a number of other offices, and Tenon has sustained an acquisition spree, none of which is likely to have happened without those firms listing, bearing in mind that these three businesses had not been sector leaders in their fields before listing.

But listing is not a panacea; it did not work for Numerica, an accountancy practice which was subsumed into Tenon, and other listed professional firms are clearly struggling.

Around the time that the LSA 2007 was passed, there was a fair amount of enthusiasm amongst law firms to be the first to list, or at least to be in the first wave. This enthusiasm has clearly diminished in light of the impact of the credit crunch on stock markets generally; valuations are poor, investor enthusiasm for listing uncertain and partners in unlisted firms have not surprisingly taken a more cautious approach to plunging into a listing of their firms, with turnover and profits both in decline and the prospects of a return to the long-running bull market (which law firms have enjoyed almost unbroken for nearly 20 years) uncertain. At the time of writing, no firms are trumpeting their desire to list as soon as it is permitted. A comparison of the share prices of the four example companies on 1 August 2007 and 19 March 2009 helps explain this lack of enthusiasm:

	1 August 2007	19 March 2009
Savills	516p	227.25p
Murgitroyd	450p	260p
Slater & Gordon Limited	Aus $1.68	Aus $1.54
Tenon	60.25p	46p

The desire to list, which was in some firms so strong, will return when the markets eventually find their confidence.

1 My thanks to my colleague Patrick Tolhurst for his research into these companies.
2 See Chapter 9 on mergers.

Reasons for listing

10.7 It is interesting to see what reasons these examples of listed professional practices put forward for listing, and to what extent their intentions have been fulfilled.

Back in 1988, Savills set out[1] its reasons for placing as follows:

- To enhance the status and corporate profile of Savills amongst its existing and potential clients – the listing of shares of itself would not have achieved this, but clearly Savills now has an international standing which the listing almost certainly helped to establish.
- To have greater access to capital – this undoubtedly has been realised; in straightforward terms, on completion of the listing its issued share capital was £1.77 million with a market capitalisation of £44.2 million and by March 2009 its issued share capital had grown to £3.3 million with a market capitalisation of £305.8 million.
- This increased access to capital was to 'finance future growth' by 'internal development' and 'acquisition of related businesses'. We have noted above the number of employees and offices Savills now has.
- To develop the 'principle of employee share ownership'. The company ceased to be owned by the former equity partners.

Over a long period of 21 years Savills has adhered to and fulfilled these criteria. What is equally striking is that it has, over that time, maintained its independence, unlike a number of lending commercial property practices from 20 years ago, or opticians' practices, where almost all of the top 20 firms have given up their independence.

The reasons set out by Savills for listing will be reflected by most professional practices going for a listing. Looking at more recent examples, what other, more specific goals have the listed practices had in view?

- Murgitroyd had in 2001 a growth plan centring on the 'development of a pan-European expansion strategy'[2], specifically by obtaining representation rights in Germany, Italy and Sweden within four years, the recruitment of local patent agents and establishing a desk in each country. By May 2008 it had offices in Germany and Italy but not Sweden, but new offices elsewhere in France and the USA.
- Slater & Gordon Limited wanted in April 2007[3] to take advantage of a 'tougher personal injuries legislative environment' and of consolidation opportunities in its sector; it also wanted to grow outside the personal injury sector. In the year to 30 June 2008, it acquired four personal injury specialist practices and three practices focused on other areas – seven acquisitions in one year – and established three family law offices.
- Tenon was formed specifically to acquire 'high quality accountancy practices'[4] outside the five firms with the highest turnover, but not their audit practices, focusing instead on business services. It had no pre-existing business. Since then it has acquired at least 20 practices, five in 2007/08.

Broadly then, at least in relation to these companies, the aims of the listing have been fulfilled. And although they may have made progress towards achieving their goals of acquisitions without listing – both Murgitroyd and Slater & Gordon had already grown substantially before listing, albeit from a relatively small base – it seems clear that listing sped them along their chosen paths. Further, the goal of spreading ownership beyond the confines of the equity partnership is much more easily achieved with a listing.

1 In its Placing document of 21 July 1988.
2 Murgitroyd Group plc Placing document dated 24 November 2001.
3 Slater & Gordon Prospectus dated 2 April 2007.
4 Tenon Group plc Placing document dated March 2000.

Risks relating to listing

10.8 A bombed-out share price with little immediate prospect of growth will not have the same allure for would-be recruits to the ranks of listed firms, although it may well be that shares are in any event regarded as bunce by many employees, and the prospect of longer term capital growth, and a more favourable tax treatment, will even now hold some attraction.

The various placing documents highlight some particular issues for both the listed entity and investors in it. These include:

- The market in which the company operates. Will the market appreciate the opportunity to invest in law practices? Certainly in the depths of the credit crunch it is difficult to see any share in any company operating in any market being in demand, but we assume this is a timing issue only. There is evidence of successful IPOs of a variety of professional practices over the years. The listing of Slater & Gordon and Integrated Legal Holdings Limited, another Australian law practice but one which, like Tenon, was starting from scratch, suggests there is a demand at the commoditised end of the market and it would be surprising if bigger, better established and more profitable City practices were not at least equally attractive.

- The lack of barriers to entry to the intellectual property were cited by Murgitroyd as a risk. The same will be true of most legal practices, at least for those practices offering commoditised services such as personal injury and residential conveyancing services. At the top end of the City the opposite is true; the Magic Circle has retained its pre-eminence for a long time, despite being assailed first by regional (later national) firms and then by US ones. That said, there could well be an early mover advantage in getting to the market first.
- Tenon identified the risk inherent in coming to the market with an untested strategy of buying up medium-sized accountancy practices. The accountancy profession has over a generation seen a great deal of consolidation, producing the Big Four accountancy practices, which in terms of turnover dominate the accountancy market both in this country and globally to an extent a beyond the reach of Magic Circle firms in the legal market. There had not, however, been the model of a successful new entrant to the market previously. Slater & Gordon identified the same risk of target practices being unwilling to sell; in practice this risk was avoided before the present recession started.
- Tenon's cherry-picking approach of leaving behind the audit practice of acquired firms was identified as putting at risk the integration of the acquired practices.
- The risk factors identified by Slater & Gordon are most pertinent to a law firm. These rightly stressed that a lawyer's duty is to the court rather than their clients. This conflict could affect the interests of clients, the company's business and indirectly its shareholders.
- The regulatory environment in which Slater & Gordon operates could change adversely, particularly as the firm was looking to extend the jurisdictions in which it operates. The same risk would apply to international firms based here looking to list indeed, local jurisdictions may well prohibit the local practice from having any outside ownership. Germany and Belgium, for example, are reluctant to allow this.
- Equally, losing high-profile cases could damage the company's reputation.
- The risk of losing key lawyers in what was a very competitive market was highlighted. The loss of 'star' lawyers is clearly an issue – and has been in relation to fund management, where a star manager leaving can adversely affect fund withdrawals. Some protection can be had by imposing enforceable restrictive covenants and lock-ins, and more so by management managing the stars or the fall-out from their departure.

- Changes in the law in the areas in which the firm specialises are, slightly oddly, also identified as a risk. This is as likely to be as much an opportunity for a market leader as not.

Of course other risks will arise from the particular nature of the applicant for listing. In addition there are generic risks applying to all listed companies:

- the discipline of a listing and the seemingly insatiable appetite of the market for information. Close public security of a business is a demanding taskmaster, particularly if the market is disappointed in a company's performance;
- likewise, having multiple shareholders involves a good deal of administrative effort, and expense;
- listings/admissions to the London Stock Exchange and AIM are expensive;
- the shares, particularly in the early days and in relation to AIM companies, may well be very illiquid, with the bulk of shares held by directors and employees of the firm;
- shareholders in public companies obviously expect an income stream in the form of dividends. The need to provide this may constrain what management of the listed company can do;
- shareholders often, of course, invest in the hope or expectation of realising a capital gain on a takeover. Regulation of ABS's may limit the opportunities by limiting who can own the company and the size of their shareholding.

All of that said, there was a good deal of initial enthusiasm amongst law firms to list, and also enthusiasm from private equity investors to take a stake in such firms. This enthusiasm is undoubtedly dimmer at present; will it have returned by the time the LSA 2007 is fully implemented in 2011?

Chapter 11

CONSOLIDATORS AND TESCO LAW

James Thorne

INTRODUCTION

11.1 Consolidators and Tesco Law are the big beasts stalking the high street lawyers, the decimators of legal practice as it has been since time immemorial, about to leave the centres of towns bare of solicitors, a veritable wasteland of the unlawyered, or so many practitioners and commentators would have us believe. We explore here what lies behind these concepts, the market opportunities allowed by the LSA 2007 in this area and what threat they pose to traditional legal practice, as well as unresolved issues.

THE CONCEPTS

11.2 Consolidators are those firms who set out to increase their share of a particular sector of the market by acquiring other practices operating in that area. In the Chapter 10 we have seen an example of consolidators in the field of business services to entrepreneurs in the form of Tenon. In Australia, Slater & Gordon Limited sought to build its position after listing in the legal practice area of personal injury, and Integrated Legal Holdings Limited, which was set up there to 'establish a model by which the ownership of existing independent law firms and related business can be consolidated under one listed legal services entity'.

In Tesco Law[1] (the increasingly hackneyed expression applied to the 'one-stop shop') the idea is that the consumer can have all his legal needs met – conveyancing, wills and probate, personal injury, divorce, simple business issues – as well as his other needs as a consumer.

A flavour of this is given by Tesco's website (www.tesco.com) which has a link to its Legal Store amongst a number of other links to Flowers, Gas & Electricity, Travel, Clearance and Nurture (its fruit and vegetable suppliers policy), as well as the mainstream links to groceries, wine, entertainment, finance and insurance and phones and broadband[2]. This is not an advertisement for Tesco, but an indication of how legal services might be packaged up with other consumer services going forward, being just one of a number of services which the one-stop shop seeks to provide.

The White Paper which was a precursor of the LSA 2007 was an enthusiast for the one-stop shop, believing these commoditised services could be provided more cheaply and efficiently by new and non-traditional entrants into the field of supplying legal services.

It is striking that the move towards Tesco Law has already started, even before the full implementation of the Act; indeed Tesco's Legal Store website was set up in 2004. Tesco and other brands offering legal services do it perfectly legitimately by contracting with a law firm for the supply of legal services in a specific area – for example, the AA offers personal injury, conveyancing, wills and trust and inheritance tax services to users of its website (www.theaa.com/legal-services) and makes clear there that these services are provided by third-party suppliers – Irwin Mitchell for wills and family; a panel of law firms for personal injury work.

However, the Act is expected to accelerate this process by removing the need for these third-party arrangements to be in place and allowing the retailer, insurance company,etc to own in whole or part the provider of the legal services.

Another striking feature of the Tesco offering is that it is an online one without a physical manifestation on the high street or the out-of-town superstore. Although Professor Richard Susskind[3] foresees the move towards much greater use of IT by lawyers and consumers, it may well be that many, indeed most, one-stop shops do not have a physical presence.

1 'Tesco Law' here is applied as if it were the proper name of a one-stop shop legal services provider and is taken as the exemplar of all such would-be providers.
2 The subjects covered by its Legal Store including starting a company, making a will, making a tenancy agreement, divorce, family trees, unmarried persons' rights, making complaints and dealing with noisy neighbours, as well as do-it-yourself guidance on school appeals, selling a house and appealing against motoring tickets.
3 In 'The End of Lawyers?' and his earlier works.

ADVANTAGES

11.3 Underpinning both these concepts is that the legal services provided are 'commoditised', i e relatively simple legal processes which need not involve the expertise of a highly trained and expensively educated qualified lawyer. We have already identified what these services are – conveyancing, personal injury claims, will preparation etc. The attraction of this area to would-be providers is that the services are delivered with relatively light involvement of any solicitor. The contact with clients may be with junior clerks, with or without formal legal training, who report to team leaders who themselves may not be solicitors, who in turn are supervised by a solicitor whose involvement in certain of these areas is required as a matter of law. This model provides a high degree of leverage with much fewer qualified lawyers involved in the process than under the model traditionally used in high street firms, even after taking into account that such firms have often made good use of unqualified staff in certain processes, such as competent secretaries dealing with the mechanics of residential conveyancing. In turn, this leverage allows costs to be much reduced, particularly if a great deal of the process can be one subject of sophisticated software packages.

It is worth considering what the advantages the consolidators and Tesco Law might have to the consumer. First and foremost is the belief that these commoditised legal services can be delivered just as effectively but much more cheaply[1] by the consolidators and the one-stop shop, not as a result of predatory pricing but because of economies of scale. These would be derived from the provider's commitment to and heavy investment in sophisticated IT systems and software covering not only the process involved in the service being provided but also know-how and knowledge management. This would be combined with a heavily leveraged staffing model of the type described in para 11.2 above, with the minimum number of legally qualified professionals involved to supervise the provision of advice in relation to reserved legal matters. With the focus on commoditised services these providers may also become more specialised and focused than a high street practitioner can be and, it is argued, provide a better service as a result.

The scale at which these providers can operate may itself help reduce costs by economies of scale in management and administration. In addition, it is conceivable that in using these commoditised services the consumer might consider transacting via a screen to be rather more convenient than a visit to a solicitor's office or even a telephone conversation with his lawyer. Other consumer services – motor insurance, for example – has moved substantially away from any form of personal service, where the consumer in the past used his insurance broker to advise on the best policy to one which is web-based or arranged through a call to a centre in this country or abroad. Not many consumers think this is a turn for the worse.

The ready availability of other services provided by Tesco Law beyond the purely legal may well also be attractive to consumers; when buying a house, will they not also be happy to buy insurance for that house from the same shop? Issues about conflicts of interest will trouble them less than getting a decent, comprehensive service at a competitive cost.

1 Too cheaply on occasion. A letter from an anonymous practitioner appeared in the Law Society *Gazette* of 5 February 2009 after a residential conveyancing practice failed:

> 'I cannot recall an occasion when I have gleaned any pleasure from someone else's misery, but I confess to feeling a certain amount of schadenfreude at the news last week of the demise of another "conveyancing farm". These "businesses" have devalued conveyancing to the lowest possible level, operating tick-box systems, and have denigrated the role of property lawyer to such an extent that I have almost become embarrassed to tell people what I do for a living ... Do we have so little regard for the value of our own skills that we are prepared to give them away? Is our job so easy that it can be done by anyone with minimal training but state-of-the-art software?'

This schadenfreude will doubtless have been shared by others, although it was probably a collapse in the property market rather than a fundamentally flawed business model which led to the collapse of the property practices.

THE MARKET OPPORTUNITIES

11.4 We identified in para 11.2 above a number of consolidators, here or abroad, operating in their chosen fields: Tenon, Slater & Gordon and Integrated Legal Holdings. The LSA 2007, by allowing alternative business structures (ABSs), whereby non-lawyers can own legal practices[1], will undoubtedly see consolidators and Tesco Law moving into the area of providing commoditised legal services.

The example of Vantis plc is an instructive one, operating as it does in the UK rather than Australia. Its experience in its field shows how consolidators might operate in the legal market when the Act is fully implemented.

Vantis plc is a company listed on AIM, being within the top 15 accounting, tax and business advisory practices measured by the income. It was admitted to AIM in 2002.

Four firms came together at the time of the listing to form Vantis. In its first year to April 2003, its turnover was £18.6 million, increasing to £94.3 million to April 2008, and £48.3 million in the six months to 31 October 2008. Although its profitability has not grown so fast, from £3.9 million profit before tax in the year to April 2003, £7.1 million to 30 April 2008 and £7.2 million in the six months to 31 October 2009, the growth is still respectable. Its business model has been to be acquire other practices quite aggressively, looking at literally hundreds of targets since its listing, and buying a significant number in that time, averaging two or three a year, targeting those which service the small to medium-sized enterprise sector of the market.

Like other professional practices that chose the listing route, part of the attraction of doing so was to leave behind the consensual decision-making of a partnership. Its business model was, first, to integrate the four founding firms and others subsequently acquired; secondly, to acquire and consolidate other small and medium-sized accountancy practices; and thirdly, to provide value-added services to clients of the company.

Its consolidation and integration strategy is dependent on the stringent application of an acquisition plan. It has a strategy and modus operandi that it sticks to remorselessly, and focuses as much on integration of the target as on the acquisition itself. It would be surprising if consolidators in the legal market did not look to go down a similar route.

This model may be what solicitors' firms are facing; a well funded conquistador that has a clear strategy of consolidating its position in the marketplace by adopting a hard-nosed, take-it-or-leave-it approach to targets. If it happens it will be very different experience to the gentler, consensual mergers described in Chapter 9. And it's not to say that a more robust approach is not appropriate or effective; it certainly would be different, however.

Will law firms be ready, willing and able to accept the consolidator's embrace?

An acquisition is of course a two-way process; the acquired has the option of whether or not to sell. There are and will continue to be good reasons for doing so:

- to hide from the icy blasts of competition in the safe harbour of the larger firm;
- to give senior partners a chance to exit with something paid for the goodwill they have helped develop;
- to help the business forward by taking advantage of the support and systems the larger firm can offer, and creating new cross-selling opportunities for the firm; and
- to create new and better career opportunities for those in the firm.

The LSA 2007 cannot be looked at merely in terms of what the Act itself allows; it does not compel or require any legal firm to adopt any different structure to the one it has now. Legal disciplinary practices (LDPs) and ABSs are options. But the Act's impact will be affected by the economic circumstances in which it operates, and a long and deep recession, which at the time of writing is possible, will make a difference to all practitioners, but perhaps particularly those on the high street.

In this chastened world perhaps a worse prospect for high street practitioners is that both these forces in the marketplace will pass them by. The consolidator may not wish to acquire their practice. And Tesco Law, the one-stop shop, may equally not want to take them on board.

This is because of the business model of the one-stop-shop. It seeks to provide the commoditised services at a relatively low cost; these expectations cannot readily by met if they take over a number of high street solicitors, many of whom are still relatively well paid. The prospect, then, is bleak: Tesco Law, perhaps exclusively web-based, setting up a legal practice which will be promoted heavily on cost grounds. If this happens then the prospects of high street solicitors are gloomier even than that foreseen by Professor Stephen Mayson[2], who predicted a substantial reduction in the number of independent law firms but with many of those engaged in those firms finding a position elsewhere.

1 See Chapter 4; the extent of ownership is to be established by regulations in due course.
2 Referred to in para 9.6 above.

UNRESOLVED ISSUES

11.5 The impact of the Act is most difficult to predict in relation to consolidators – at least, those who are not themselves lawyers – and Tesco Law. This is because both will be subject to the ABS regime[1], the start date for which is not yet known (we assume here it will be in 2011); nor have the regulations under which they will be established and operate yet been issued. The Clementi Review anticipated that there would be a proper bedding-down process, a trial run with LDPs, before ABSs would be established. The Act itself does not contemplate the introduction of ABSs being in any way conditional on the performance of LDPs, although the LDP experience will no doubt inform the regulation of ABSs. So, there is necessarily more speculation in this area as to what the impact of the Act will be.

That said, issues[2] have been raised in relation to ABSs which will affect the willingness and ability of consolidators and Tesco Law to adopt and use the ABS model:

(i) There is the question of whether the one-stop shop really will improve the choice and quality of service available to consumers. The Forum of Private Businesses said in relation to the prospect of the Legal Services Bill in 2005, 'We feel deeply uneasy about the monstrous supermarkets like Tesco and we are very concerned about the dominance it has over independent businesses.' Even allowing for the self-interest of the Forum's members here, it is not difficult to share some concern that commoditised legal services will become a more homogenised and inflexible product than is available to consumers at present. This may well not be in the interests of consumers as a whole.

(ii) Equally, there is a concern that the consolidator will be profit-driven to the extent of compromising professional standards. Provisions in the Act are designed to prevent this. For example a non-lawyer is prohibited from interfering with a lawyer's observance of his professional duties[3], and an obligation is placed on the lawyer to comply with these professional rules[4]. Similarly, the individual appointed to the new role of Head of Legal Practice has the duty placed on him to ensure the ABS acts and behaves within the terms of its licence[5]. How all of this will work in practice remains to be seen.

(iii) Professor Mayson[6] has highlighted the potential conflict between certain of the regulatory objectives of the Act, in particular, that those of promoting competition and the interests of consumers (embodied in LSA 2007, s 1(1)(d), (e)) could conflict with the promotion of the public interest and access to justice (s 1(1)(a), (c)). He cites in support the danger of ABSs leading to the reduction in the number of rural law firms, and an increased difficulty for the elderly in particular in getting access to legal advice. The aptitude of 'silver surfers' in using the internet may mean his latter concern is exaggerated but fewer, larger providers of a more uniform type of legal service could well create real difficulties here.

(iv) Professor Mayson also raises the question of whether certain combinations of services create particular concerns. For example, would it be right for a consolidator in the audit sphere to provide legal services as well? Enron ended the Arthur Andersen experiment of combining the two, but the Act might allow them to be combined in the future. Would it be right for an insurance company to own a personal injury practice, or a bank a residential conveyancing and mortgage practice? Careful regulation will be needed to strike the right balance of interests.

(v) What is permitted in this jurisdiction may well not be permitted abroad. The Sarbannes-Oxley Act 2002 in the USA would certainly prevent any compromise of auditor independence, and a number of European jurisdictions would not allow non-lawyers to own any part of a legal practice.

(vi) There are also concerns about inherent conflicts of interest within an ABS between the owners, clients and lawyers engaged by the ABS. This could give rise to 'ethical strain', in the words of Timothy Dutton QC, former head of the Bar Council (and contributor of Chapter 12). Slater & Gordon Limited recognised this conflict in its prospectus and expressly placed the duties owed to the company's shareholders behind those owed to the court and clients of the company. This formulation had the support of the local law regulator, the Legal Services Commissioner of New South Wales. This precedent could well be followed by the licensing authority for ABSs here. The formulation is relatively easy; again, the practice may be more difficult.

(vii) There are concerns too about the standard of service provided by the consolidators and Tesco Law. Some protection against unacceptable standards are catered for in the Act, by providing that reserved legal matters must in effect be at least supervised by a suitably qualified person, and having a Head of Legal Practice in place with a responsibility in this area. As important will be the brand of the legal services provider. Tesco, AA, the RAC, the Co-op or any other business that goes down this route will be very conscious of the value of their brands and will not want to risk damage to them by persistent complaints about poor legal service.

(viii) Will the ABS be guilty of abusing its dominant market position by, for example, predatory pricing and the cross-subsidising of the provision of legal services from its other resources? Of course the danger is there, but this should be a particular concern of the regulator and the Office of Fair Trading. Merely by virtue of being licensed as an ABS will not take the provider outside the realm of competition law.

The regulatory framework itself will help on a number of these issues – the owner of Tesco Law must be approved as a fit and proper person by the appropriate licensing authority, although what standards it will impose are not yet known. As mentioned above, the LDP experience could well inform the debate about this framework. In short, much is still in play before those big beasts of consolidators and Tesco Law are let loose on their high street prey.

1 See Chapter 4.
2 See, for example, the thoughtful analysis of the issues by Stephen Mayson in the discussion paper produced for the College of Law: Legal Services Policy Institute, 'External Ownership and Investment: Issues and Challenges', published in December 2008.
3 LSA 1007, s 90.
4 Section 176.
5 Section 91(1).
6 See note 1 above.

Chapter 12

THE FUTURE OF THE BAR AFTER THE LSA 2007

Timothy Dutton QC

INTRODUCTION

12.1 Barristers have been permitted to provide legal services under the Bar Code of Conduct in three ways: as self-employed sole traders via referrals from solicitors with practising certificates; as employees on behalf of their employers; or under limited direct access arrangements. Of the 15,000 practising barristers in England and Wales, about 12,000[1] provide their services as self-employed barristers, and the balance is employed. Barristers are restricted in the functions they can perform to pleading, advisory and advocacy services.

The justification, in the public interest, for these restrictions lies in the belief that advocacy is a specialist skill which requires concentration by those who undertake it on its core elements of written and oral submissions, examination in chief, cross-examination and legal/forensic analysis, in the same way that brain surgery requires specialist skills which are obtained through a referral mechanism.

The separation of the advocate's functions from the solicitor's or litigator's functions has traditionally been considered also to be in the public interest because it fosters independence: the barrister is not close to the litigant, cannot gather evidence, and (in criminal cases) appears for the Crown one week and the defence the next. The sole trader status of barristers is considered to be in the interests of those seeking specialist advocates in particular fields (eg defamation, Chancery, commercial, crime, family), as they are not conflicted from acting if members of the same specialist set of chambers are on the other side – precisely because they are self-employed and not working for the same employer or business.

Before turning to predictions as to how the market may develop it is necessary to set the regulatory framework into context. Both the Solicitors Regulation Authority (SRA) and the Bar Standards Board (BSB) conducted consultations in 2007–08 as to whether their respective Codes should be changed so as to permit them to become entity regulators, and if so what type of entity. The SRA has an agenda to turn itself into the entity regulator for legal disciplinary partnerships (LDPs) in 2009 and for ABSs in 2011–12. The BSB is attempting to maintain the same pace and embarked on a consultation in February 2008 as to whether the Bar Code of Conduct should be changed and, if so, how. The Bar Council set up a working group which produced a detailed response to the BSB's paper in May 2008. Broadly speaking, that working group recommended that:

- Rule 205 of the Code of Conduct which prohibits barristers from practising save as self-employed barristers or as employees should not be fundamentally altered except to the extent necessary to permit barristers to take part in bids for work jointly with solicitors if block procurement comes into the system.
- There should be modest changes to other parts of the Code so as to permit barristers to expand their functions slightly, for example those operating with a Direct Access Licence should now be permitted to conduct correspondence in respect only of direct access work and barristers should now be able to take witness statements should they be asked to do so.

The BSB in its consultation paper started from the proposition that the LSA 2007 promotes LDPs and alternative business structures (ABSs). This starting proposition may be wrong. What the Act does is to create a legislative environment in which it will be possible for LDPs and ABSs to be created and regulated: nowhere does the Act suggest that LDPs or ABSs are the appropriate model by which advocacy services should be delivered in the public interest. The BSB's paper appeared to presuppose that barristers should be permitted to practise in partnership and that the market, not the regulator, should decide whether or not such partnerships are better models for the delivery of advocacy services than the current structure of self-employment or employment for barristers. In a second consultation paper issued in November 2008, the BSB stated that it was contemplating permitting barristers to form partnerships both of barristers/barristers and barristers/solicitors and that it, the BSB, would be the entity regulator for barrister-only partnerships whilst the SRA should be the entity regulator for structures which included non-barristers. The BSB would retain jurisdiction for the individual members of the barrister profession.

Solicitors' practices have developed through a partnership (or LLP) model for the delivery of their services because of the security which such a model provides to solicitors, partly in their own self-interest. The partnership or LLP model provides to solicitors the opportunity to maximise profits by the work of others, a larger, more corporate structure, and a larger method of capitalisation so that services can be provided on a grander scale than is provided by the profession of advocates.

The Bar, by contrast, has a number of interrelated features which have hitherto ensured that it provides its services to the public at large irrespective of the means of those who need such services. There are key features within the Bar Code of Conduct which ensure that there is this provision. Those features are the cab rank 'rule' contained in paragraphs 601–602, which contains three interlocking parts, namely:

- a barrister in independent practice must accept instructions if available, provided the instructions are offered at a 'proper' fee;
- a barrister is not permitted to decline instructions simply because he or his chambers would normally be acting for the opposing side in a particular type of case; and
- a barrister is not entitled to withhold advocacy services on the grounds that the nature of the case or the conduct or the opinion of the client are objectionable.

Under paragraph 205 of the Code barristers can only provide their services through self-employment or as employees on behalf of their employer.

The result of the observation by the profession of these provisions and other parts of the Code, coupled with strength of recruitment and a reputation for rigour, is that the Bar enjoys a high reputation nationally and internationally for the quality of its services and the independence of barristers in their work. In a commercial context by far the best defence of the cab rank rule is that attempts to conflict barristers out of cases on purely commercial grounds – i e the 'commercial conflict' point so frequently raised by clients with solicitors – not only fails but it is recognised to be an inappropriate basis on which to attempt to prevent a barrister from providing his services. Increasingly, solicitors recognise that their own acceptance that they should not act for clients where a larger client creates a 'commercial' as opposed to 'legal' conflict has led them into difficulties and may restrict access to high quality services in the market place.

The advantages of self-employed specialist practice at the referral Bar are therefore strong both from the public's and the practitioner's perspective. The common belief that 'surely costs rise because you employ two people rather than one' ignores the fact that in any case which requires advocacy an advocate will have to be instructed to prepare the advocacy work – whether the advocate be in-house or external. The Bar has, through keeping a reasonably high volume of work, and through low overheads, managed to be less expensive than its solicitor-advocate competitors. Typically, the Bar's overheads will be in the 20–30% bracket of turnover whereas a solicitor's practice will be in the region of 70%.

In its paper to the BSB the Bar Council Working Group devoted a chapter (Chapter 5) to the legal and practical consequences of using alternative structures through which legal services could be delivered by barristers. In short, the group argued that if barristers formed partnerships, or LDPs, through which they provided their services they would be conflicted out from acting on both sides of the case from within the same set of chambers or partnership. Institutional barriers to protect confidential information would have to be established within partnerships or sets of chambers. There would be an increasing demand from large clients not to accept other clients on the 'commercial conflict' basis. If barristers were structured around LDPs, partnerships, LLPs, or ABSs, choice would be massively restricted to clients, as whole sets of chambers would be conflicted from acting against other members of the partnership, LDP, etc.

The working group concluded that the Bar, and particularly the commercial and Chancery Bars, would be disinclined, even if permitted, to enter into structures which restricted the sources of supply of work. Partnerships, LDPs or ABSs will all have this restricting effect. It follows that the inclination of the Bar will be towards not forming such structures as they will damage both the Bar's self-interest and the public's choice of advocate. Such structures would be damaging to the public interest because the specialist Bar's services would be restricted to those who got through the door first, and conflicted all others out. All of the indications are therefore that the civil, commercial and Chancery Bars will wish to continue to operate through sets of chambers which provide self-employed practitioners as specialists for the work.

It does not follow that the Bar's working models will not change or improve. Indeed they will need to improve in certain areas; for example, special arrangements need to be put in place for institutional barriers to protect confidential information. The Bar has some way to go before these barriers are sufficiently robust. Also, the costs of qualification as a barrister is becoming prohibitive and there is an urgent need for the profession to manage the costs and process of entry better if it is to remain ahead of any competition whilst also fulfilling the oft-stated desire to be an open, diverse and inclusive profession of specialist advocates.

There will be an increase in supply of work coming through 'direct access'. In an age of increasingly sophisticated commercial clients the need for clients always to come to the Bar via solicitors is likely to reduce and it is expected that the BSB will relax some of the rules which restrict direct access.

The Bar's work will increase internationally as the common law becomes attractive in new and developing commercial centres. The Gulf States, for example, are turning to English law as the choice of law, and are using common law forms of dispute resolution. This means that the Bar's antennae should lift beyond the immediate domestic horizon to a more international one. Geographical boundaries are increasingly diminishing in a hyper-electronic age, which should mean that the Bar's services in its traditional functions should remain in demand.

It follows from this that the self-employed civil, commercial and Chancery Bars should be confident of their futures because of a natural desire to maintain access for all, not to be conflicted out of cases, and to be able to respond to market pressures so that they invest in recruitment exercises which ensure that the Bar attracts the best future advocates with high academic standards.

The next question is whether or not commercial pressures would be imposed upon the commercial Bar through solicitors or other forms of structure which could have some kind of domino effect on the self-employed practitioner. An answer to this question may be found in the Bar's post-1990 history. The Courts and Legal Services Act 1990 created an environment in which solicitors could acquire Higher Rights, and solicitors have been able to appear as advocates in the higher courts. A number of have done so, and there are approximately 4,700 such practitioners. But the Bar's pre-eminence in the field of advisory and advocacy work remains relatively undiminished. The few firms practising civil law who have set up in-house advocacy departments still refer their difficult work to the Bar and many firms have simply refused to go down the route of in-house advocacy. There has been some removal of preparatory work for the junior Bar, which is a cause for concern. If too much pleading and advisory work is done in-house the specialist skills which need to be developed at a referral Bar could be put at risk. Some solicitors are recognising the need to involve their litigator and advocacy teams from the very beginning of a case, and the reduction of pleading work or keeping too much pleading work in-house do not seem, in and of themselves, to be likely to prevent the referral Bar from being able to survive. It follows that it is unlikely that the commercial pressures which have been around now for more than 18 years will somehow, as a result of the LSA 2007, be brought to bear again and cause a domino effect whereby barristers are either taken over or succumb to the temptation to join LDPs or ABSs. Neither seems likely in the privately funded civil/commercial end of the Bar. The converse is just as, if not more, likely: that as new structures develop the need for specialist outside advice and representation may increase certainly in the regulatory field, if not in all areas of civil work. However, all of the foregoing assumes that there will remain a ready source of supply of work for the referral Bar in a changing market for legal services. *If* the supply of work remains strong then there is little reason to suppose that the referral Bar would want to operate through structures such as LDPs and ABSs. This, however, begs the question as to whether or not the traditional sources of supply of work will remain strong. That requires consideration of the wider context in which legal services will be supplied in a changing marketplace.

1 Source: Bar Council, Chambers annual returns.

WIDER CONTEXT

12.2 The ratio of lawyers per head of population in the UK has increased in the last 20 years from approximately 1:1,000 to about 1:400 today. There has been a significant increase in the number of solicitors and barristers. Twenty years ago there were less than 60,000 solicitors with practising certificates and less than 7,000 barristers. There are now approximately 120,000 solicitors (of whom 108,000 have practising certificates at any one time) and 15,000 barristers.

Professor Stephen Mayson, Professor of Strategy and Director of the Legal Services Policy Institute, has examined the market in which legal services are provided in this country. He concludes that there has been a massive increase in the knowledge base through which clients are serviced, where at the same time there is a growing perception that not all legal services require an expert knowledge base in order to be delivered to a high standard. For example, in 1985 the Council for Licensed Conveyancers was established so that licensed conveyancers as well as solicitors could undertake conveyancing work. Banks have started to undertake routine will-writing work. Banks and insurance companies have begun to outsource at low cost blocks of legal work to firms of solicitors expecting that work in effect to appear to be undertaken by the bank or insurance company.

Mayson argues that there has been an over-expansion in the knowledge base of legal services, whereas what clients may well require, certainly in the more commoditised area of work (such as will-writing, routine conveyancing, etc) is a decent customer service for a reasonable price; good technical knowledge is not what the customer is actually interested in purchasing provided, of course, that the client has no cause to question the outcome.

A large firm of solicitors turning over £110 million per annum may receive two thirds or three quarters of its income generating work by means of block referrals. Such a firm may receive through claims, intermediaries or insurance companies whole tranches comprising thousands of cases of accident work, will-writing work and so on. What is the likely effect of this 'commoditisation' on the Bar?

It does not seem likely that the commoditisation of some forms of legal work will have a dramatic impact on the specialist, privately funded, civil Bar. The likelihood is that those firms or organisations embarking on block forms of work, which do after all carry risks, will require outside advice and will need to obtain advocacy services for some of these blocks of work. The choice for such firms or organisations will be whether to develop a specialist advisory and advocacy service for such commoditised work in-house for the comparatively rare occasions when it is required. The greater likelihood is that sets of chambers will tailor the way they work, and will be required to indulge more in block bidding for such work – such as is already occurring in some employment and public law chambers who work for public authorities. Such work requires chambers to operate to high standards with proper diversity practices in place as part of their own procurement exercises. This does not require a radical or fundamental change to the methodology of working by the Bar, and if it is introduced in some areas of commercial practice it is doubtful that it will alter the basic model of working, although it may require chambers as a whole to be more corporate in the way they approach their larger institutional clients.

THE DEMISE OF THE 'HIGH STREET SOLICITOR' AND THEREFORE THE BAR?

12.3 Small firms of solicitors have traditionally managed to provide their clients with specialist advisory and advocacy services by purchasing them from the referral Bar as and when required. It seems unlikely that such firms will survive the changes which are taking place in the market. First, pressure on public funding will make the undertaking of legal aid work less and less viable for such small firms. Other traditional forms of work will not be undertaken by small high street firms as the source of supply for them will not be the individual private client but a referrer – bank, insurer or claims management company. The signs are therefore that the traditional high street firm will become part of a chain or may in some areas disappear as, say, a local supermarket, the AA or the RAC, offers a conveyancing, will-writing, or accident claim service. It is of course possible that the owners of such volume businesses will want to offer all services, including advocacy, as part of their 'in-house' package and will therefore want to employ their advocates in-house. However, it is more likely that a referral Bar will, with adaptation, emerge stronger from these changes for two reasons. First, specialist advocacy and advisory work is comparatively rare, so gearing up to provide them in-house may not make economic sense. Second, this new marketplace will be highly competitive. A selling point for an insurance or will-writing product is likely to be that the provider of the service will use specialist advocates and advisers if the case requires it. Using only an in-house team may prevent such a claim being made. Provided therefore that the Bar remains competitively priced and keeps the quality of its services high the risk of a massive in-house recruitment exercise in newly formed legal 'businesses' which have taken over the work of the traditional high street solicitor, seems, to this writer at least, unlikely.

PUBLIC PROCUREMENT AS THE DRIVER OF CHANGE?

12.4 There has in recent years been a significant shift in attitude by the Government towards procurement of legal services. Until about 2004 the legal aid budget was largely demand-driven. Since then it has been effectively capped and is now being reduced, with the Government increasingly looking towards procurement through means of price-competitive tendering or, as they would now prefer to call it, 'best value tendering'.

At the same time, the Crown Prosecution Service has been undertaking a well publicised programme which involves shifting work from the self-employed Bar to employed Crown advocates. It has also been attempting to obtain through legislative change greater powers for designated caseworkers with no legal qualifications to prosecute cases in the magistrates courts. In order to achieve this, the Crown Prosecution Service has entered into an agreement with the Institute of Legal Executives for it to act as regulator of the advocacy of designated caseworkers. The overall indications are that government, which is a major procurer of litigation services, wishes to move towards forms of block procurement, block contracting, and a level of deskilling.

These developments are of real concern not just for the profession but for the public at large. The more publicly funded cases are 'commoditised', the less skill will be applied to them. This gives rise to greater risk of injustice or miscarriage of justice in individual cases.

If the publicly funded Bar were to be driven into price-competitive tendering on terms which require the publicly funded Bar to conduct cases from beginning to end, pressure would be imposed on the publicly funded Bar to form LDPs or other such structures so as to be able to undertake cases from beginning to end. That in turn would dilute the quality of the advocacy service since that service would be pooled under one roof with a variety of other tasks being undertaken, all under enormous financial pressures. In turn, in this scenario the publicly funded Bar may have to look to an entity regulator which is not the BSB in order for the LDP or the ABS under which it was operating to be regulated under the LSA 2007. Were this to happen one can envisage that those advocates who are undertaking publicly funded work – predominantly legal aid work in crime and family law – would need to move to another regulator. In turn, this would reduce the income and resources for the BSB, which could, on this hypothetical scenario, become the regulator for a much smaller specialist profession.

HOW LIKELY IS THIS SCENARIO?

12.5 The publicly funded area is undoubtedly the area most at risk so far as the referral Bar is concerned. Whilst the Bar does not want 'fusion', it is ultimately government which will decide. The combination of a desire to drive down legal aid costs and a severe economic recession may cause government to create a scenario which leads to a significant number of specialist advocates being forced into models for delivery of service that restrict the choice of advocate, and the numbers available, ie into a one-stop shop for publicly funded work.

At present the Government is proposing to block contract police and magistrates court work in June 2009 with two pilot Crown Court projects in 2010–11. There will be a general election before the Crown Court project can get under way. Both the Law Society and the Bar Council have strenuously objected to best value tendering as it is so called – all experiences of it in North America, for example, where it was tried for defence services showed it to be an abject failure. Thus far it has only ever worked for things like refuse collection – not a complex personal service such as legal advice and advocacy!

So far as family law is concerned the Legal Services Commission is involved in a step-by-step approach towards best value tendering. Step 1 is to attempt to cut the fees of the family Bar followed by a one case, one fee scheme (OCOF) whereby a single pot of money would be handed over to solicitors or the entity which supplies the service. If the Legal Services Commission can make OCOF work it will proceed to best value tendering in 2013. This approach to procurement in family work is riddled with dangers. A swings-and-roundabouts principle will not ensure that, for example, vulnerable children will obtain representation of the quality required in the now many thousands of cases involving child abuse that take place up and down the country. Judges are likely to speak out strongly against such crude mechanisms of procurement. Whilst the Legal Services Commission may therefore have plans to proceed down this route, neither the profession, the judiciary nor wiser counsel in political services ought to support these ideas. But the tough economic conditions post the financial collapse in the latter part of 2008 may mean that government will face down its critics. If not defeated, the Bar, the judiciary and those involved in wider aspects of social welfare may hope that the more extreme of the Government's proposals could be moderated significantly.

RECRUITMENT TO THE BAR

12.6 A profession that trades on excellence, as the Bar does, will only ever thrive if the best advocates of the future are recruited into its ranks. Indeed it will only thrive if the best are recruited no matter what their social background, or ethnic origin. The Bar has for over a decade been addressing the need for inclusiveness – the most recent manifestation of this being the report by Lord Neuberger of Abbotsbury published in November 2007 which made 57 recommendations for furthering the Bar's work in this area. The Bar Council is committed to implementing the Neuberger recommendations and in November 2008 he reported to the Bar Conference that he was pleased with progress. But the backdrop is one of ever increasing financial burdens on those who wish to come to the Bar, and these burdens will most severely affect the less well off. It is now quite common to hear of a person leaving university with debts of approx £25,000, and for those debts to rise to over £40,000 by the time Bar finals have been undertaken, rising still further even after a funded pupillage. Thus, the Bar is pursuing a diversity agenda whilst the costs of qualification are having the opposite effect. The question is whether the Bar can adapt so as to be able to continue to attract the best despite these pressures?

Again, the divide is likely to occur between the privately funded and the publicly funded sectors. Successful commercial sets of chambers are recruiting their future pupils from the top universities and are able to offer funding through Bar School and through pupillage which matches or betters what is on offer in solicitor firms or other walks of life. But the publicly funded sector is not so well placed. A pupillage in a publicly funded set of chambers is funded only up to £10,000. Practice in the first few years is tough and it is becoming ever more difficult for a barrister to pay off student debt.

CONCLUSION

12.7 Whilst the Bar remains strong, and unified in its desire to provide advocacy services on a largely referral basis, the real question is whether or not government will through a new procurement methodology and cost-cutting achieve a restructuring of the models through which advocacy services are provided. The strength of purpose across the Bar as a whole ensured that this did not happen in 1990. In the early 1990s the combination of a squeeze on public funding and high student debts had not occurred. It is still too early to say what the future shape of the Bar is to be. However, the greatest danger of change driven by government procurement and cost-cutting measures is that two forms of service will emerge: a high quality referral Bar for those who pay privately, and a one-stop shop or LDP model for those who cannot afford to do so. This two tier system becomes increasingly likely as the depression of late 2008 causes the Government to cut budgets yet further. We face one form of legal service for the rich and another for the poor, something which in the post-war, post-Beveridge-era successive governments have claimed firmly to resist but which looks, in a post-LSA 2007 landscape, to be what we will have.

Chapter 13

IMPACT OF LSA 2007 ON PROVISION OF LEGAL SERVICES IN PUBLIC SECTOR

Bethan Evans

THE CURRENT LANDSCAPE OF PUBLIC SECTOR LEGAL PROVISION

13.1 Organisations in the public sector currently source and commission legal services in a number of ways. Many organisations such as central government departments, non-departmental public bodies and local authorities directly employ teams of in-house lawyers who provide legal support direct to their employer client, in the same way as in-house counsel in the private commercial sector.

Given the scope and range of legal services required by complex public sector organisations, it is unusual for such a body to be completely self-sufficient in their legal supply and many therefore commission external legal support from the private sector. This can be done simply by commissioning legal support on a project-by-project basis, often through the competitive tendering of the work in accordance with the organisation's Financial Regulations and Standing Orders. Some public sector bodies enter long-term arrangements which enable them to call off work on individual projects and appoint those lawyers best suited to that particular commission.

Many public sector organisations have no in-house legal resource at all. For example, most NHS Trusts, whilst significant employers, land owners and providers of complex services, will contract with private sector lawyers for the provision of all their legal services. These range from routine property or debt transactions, through to major commercial private finance initiative projects or High Court litigation.

Where public sector bodies have an in-house legal team, the most common organisational approach is for these lawyers to be directly employed by the organisation which they are advising. In the case, for example, of local authorities, every authority has at least one employed qualified solicitor. Smaller district councils may have a team of one or two lawyers; large metropolitan and city authorities would have legal departments the size of major private practice law firms with up to 100 employed legal staff.

STATUTORY REQUIREMENTS OF PUBLIC SECTOR LEGAL SERVICES

13.2 Certain public sector bodies have specific statutory requirements which they need to take into account in the provision of their legal services. Local authorities are each required to appoint one of their staff as the authority's Monitoring Officer[1].

The Monitoring Officer has personal statutory responsibilities to report to the local authority any contravention of any enactment or rule of law or any maladministration or injustice, and must investigate and deal with allegations of misconduct by local councillors.

At present it is not a requirement that the Monitoring Officer of an authority must be legally qualified although, in practice, the vast majority of them are solicitors.

The Law Society issued a consultation paper in January 2009 to seek views on whether a change to the legislation should be sought which would require each authority to appoint a Chief Legal Officer (CLO), rather then an Monitoring Officer. The proposal envisages that the CLO would need to be a person regulated by the SRA, the Bar Council or the Institute of Legal Executives. The new role would absorb the current responsibilities of the Monitoring Officer.

1 Local Government and Housing Act 1989, s 5.

APPLICATION OF THE CODE OF CONDUCT TO SOLICITORS IN THE PUBLIC SECTOR

13.3 The provisions of the new Code of Conduct introduced in 2007 made certain changes to the provisions relating to employed solicitors. The new conduct rule relating to in-house solicitors is Conduct Rule 13, which replaced the former Practice Rule 4 and the separate Employed Solicitors Code. The conduct requirements imposed on in-house solicitors (including those employed in the public sector) can be divided into two categories:

- those relating to in-house solicitors who provide legal services to their employer only; and
- those relating to in-house solicitors providing legal advice to persons other than their employer, including members of the public.

In-house solicitors in this latter category (ie providing legal services to other bodies and entities) are subject to greater obligations under Conduct Rule 13. For example, any solicitor wishing to take advantage of the wider opportunities is required under r 13.01 not to do so if it would compromise professional independence and integrity, the duty to act in the best interest of clients, the duty not to act in a conflict of interest situation, the duty to keep information about clients' affairs confidential from the employer and the solicitor's ability to discharge any other duty owed to clients under the Code of Conduct. It may well also be necessary to have professional indemnity cover in such situations.

PROVISION OF LEGAL SERVICES TO PERSONS OTHER THAN THE EMPLOYER

13.4 A number of in-house legal teams are increasingly seeking to use the wider opportunities to provide legal services under r 13 to broaden their client base beyond that of their direct employer.

This is facilitated by the provisions of the new Code. For example, in relation to local government solicitors, r 13.08 states that:

> 'If you are employed in local government, you may act ...for another organisation or person to which or to whom your employer is statutorily empowered to provide legal services.'

Because of the wider statutory powers which were introduced for local authorities in 2000[1], it is arguable that this provides a very wide gateway for local government solicitors to act for a whole range of clients, well beyond the previously accepted broader client group of other public bodies.

With the introduction of the new Code and the increasing interest of a number of public sector legal teams in providing legal services beyond their own employer, the issue of alternative business models for these services has come onto the agenda as the same time as the LSA 2007 introduces the prospect of alternative business structures potentially helping this agenda.

1 Local Government Act 2000, s 2 (the promotion of well-being).

SHARED LEGAL SERVICES

13.5 One very current issue is the ability of public sector legal teams to collaborate with each other in order to assist in the cost-effective provision of legal services. There has, traditionally, been much informal co-operation between legal departments in the same sector. For example, local authority legal departments will often make staff available to neighbouring authorities who may have a workload peak or a staff shortage which can be covered on a temporary basis. Other local authorities have moved to making joint appointments to cover certain posts. This might enable them each to have the services of a specialist lawyer in circumstances where the authority's individual workload would not sustain this. Greater scale in a larger legal team can also offer greater career opportunity and assist with retention and recruitment.

These measures have worked to a limited extent, but the current rules relating to the running of legal practices have constrained more innovative sharing of legal resource.

The pressures on budgets in the public sector has led to many organisations exploring different models of providing support services (including legal). Some of these options involve collaboration with the private sector. Other models have explored the establishment of a public sector-owned vehicle from which the constituent authorities then purchase back according to their needs. This has enabled authorities to collaborate and make economies of scale, whilst still retaining control over the arrangements for the services, ie not contracting them out to the private sector.

Some local authorities have wished to explore this concept not just for, for example, HR, IT and finance services, but also for their legal services.

Under the current professional regulatory regime, it would not be possible for a number of local authorities, or other public bodies, to set up a wholly owned entity, transfer a number of legal teams into that body and then buy services back. This is because of the current limitations of the ownership and control of legal services providers. The rules relating to employed solicitors do not assist as once the lawyers are transferred to the wholly owned entity, it is that entity which is their employer. However, the whole purpose of the exercise is to enable the lawyers to continue to provide legal advice direct to local authorities, which is not currently feasible.

As an alternative, a number of authorities have therefore set up a model of shared services which essentially involve lawyers in a number of bodies transferring to a lead authority or being seconded to that authority and setting up the necessary government law and governance arrangements to enable this arrangement to work. This can operate satisfactorily on a practical level, but does have certain limitations. In particular, it requires one of the authorities to take the lead as the lead employer and contractor with other bodies and this can create the perception that all of the clients receiving the benefit of legal services are not being treated the same and raise concerns about preferential treatment.

If it was possible to establish an arm's-length publicly owned body which could then provide legal services to its founding local authorities (and other defined public sector clients) this could be a very effective way of providing high quality, cost-effective legal services to a range of public sector bodies.

IMPACT OF THE LSA 2007

13.6 Set against the above background, the introduction of ABSs may provide a way of achieving the existing underlying commercial needs within the public sector. The ABS model would enable public sector organisations to share legal services within an ABS jointly owned by various public bodies. The prospect may also be raised of new ABSs being structured as joint venture enterprises with public sector bodies coming together with other authorised persons in a public/private enterprise.

However, one should not underestimate the practical difficulties that may be faced. The current experience of public bodies collaborating on shared service enterprises has shown that these involve considerable political and organisational complexities and can therefore take significant time to establish. Even though ABSs will not be allowed until at least 2011, and public organisation wishing to take early advantage of the new structure would need to start planning now.

In relation to ABSs there is the additional complexity involved in complying with the regulatory framework set out in the LSA 2007 and in the licensing rules which are yet to be developed by the LSB and licensing authorities. However, LSA 2007, ss 106–108 do provide for 'low risk' ABSs that will be subject to a more light-touch regulatory framework. These include a 'not-for-profit body' and a 'community interest company'. It may well be that these provisions will reduce the regulatory burdens for establishing a public sector ABS. It may also be that certain licensing authorities will have arrangements that specifically address the nature of ABSs controlled by public bodies.

Chapter 14

THE LSA 2007 AND THE IN-HOUSE LAWYER

Ian Jones

INTRODUCTION

14.1

> 'I'm an in-house lawyer – will anything change for me?
>
> 'The Legal Services Act amends the statutory powers of existing regulators so that they can develop firm-based regulation. Firm-based regulation is unlikely to affect in-house lawyers who provide legal services mainly to their employer. It may affect in-house lawyers who currently provide services to the public under rule 13 of the Solicitors' Code of Conduct 2007, but not until the advent of the licensing regime for ABSs, when they may need to seek a licence and be regulated as an ABS.'[1]

And with that brief, technically accurate, workmanlike response, this chapter could end. In the context of the website on which the answer is published, the logic is unimpeachable and its simplicity reassuring. In-house lawyers need not worry about the LSA 2007 until the introduction of alternative business structures (ABSs) in 2011. It is suggested, though, that the reader reflects on the broader context in which the question is being asked. That context is the world inhabited by the most sophisticated consumer of legal services: the in-house lawyer. It is a world seldom considered when assessing the legal consumer market, yet one which many law firms approach relentlessly as a source of work and thus income. Can the answer really be so simple?

As Oscar Wilde once said: 'Life is rarely pure and never simple'. So, following Wilde's logic, the answer is not simple. The advent of legal disciplinary partnerships (LDPs) and then ABSs will be recognisable milestones in the development of the legal services market, but all law firms, at different levels in that market, will have to adjust their trading models to meet the demands of their clients in a cost-effective and flexible way. It will not be argued here that the LSA 2007 is the sole catalyst for change. The way in which firms will have to adjust is driven by three factors: the current economic situation, the increasing use of technology and finally (but by no means least) the LSA 2007. The Act builds on developments in the marketplace during the last 20 years. It will be an accelerant and further catalyst to those developments. In-house lawyers will play a part in that rapidly increasing transformation and that role could be substantial. To understand why that is the case, it is necessary to take a further step back and look at the issues faced by in-house lawyers.

The LSA 2007 is designed to give the consumer greater access to cheaper legal services. The 'consumer' in the mind of the Department of Constitutional Affairs was the individual, but in-house legal functions are consumers as well. Nearly a quarter of solicitors in England and Wales work outside private practice[2]. That number has dramatically increased in the last ten years[3]. In addition, there are barristers, trade mark and patent attorneys, contract managers, regulatory experts, legal executives and licensed conveyancers who make up the in-house legal community. In-house lawyers want to able to obtain legal services on a cost-efficient basis, and for them to be delivered in a way that is compatible with their business requirements. They have substantial buying power. Recent figures suggest that a FTSE 100 company will spend an average of £14.9 million a year, with the variety of legal work being purchased being greater than five years ago[4]. There has been a recent trend to bring more work back in-house, but the need for external suppliers will continue to exist. Even if there is less transactional work, the increasing freeze on legal recruitment will be in place for some time as companies pull in their horns, and therefore external resource will be required.

1 Solicitors Regulatory Authority, Legal Services Act FAQ (13 February 2009): http://www.sra.org.uk/sra/legal-services-act/lsa-questions-faqs.page.
2 Law Society of England and Wales Annual Statistical Survey 2007.
3 For example, the number of solicitors in England and Wales outside private practice has risen from 18.5% to 23.8% in the period 1997–2007 (Law Society of England and Wales Annual Statistical Survey 2007). Similar figures apply in Scotland.
4 FTSE/Client Satisfaction Report, *Legal Week Intelligence* (November 2008).

RESPONSIBILITIES OF IN-HOUSE LAWYERS

14.2 In-house lawyers have four key responsibilities. They provide legal advice to their employer based on a sophisticated understanding of their business; they are business managers who use their legal skills to help shape the right commercial outcome. Secondly, they have a governance responsibility which, regardless of the nature of their sector or jurisdiction, is to act in the best interests of their shareholders. A major part of that responsibility is risk management. Thirdly, they are responsible for managing the corporate knowledge of legal matters, whether that be feeding in developments in legal and regulatory policy to their company's business strategy, training the employees in legal matters or managing the wealth of legal documents created by their organisation[1]. Finally, they are responsible for procuring legal services for their company.

To fulfil their first three key responsibilities, in-house counsel have two choices when buying legal services. Either they will be 'bought' by recruiting lawyers into the in-house team to 'self provide' or they will buy services from an external law firm. In reality, services are purchased on a hybrid basis; part self-provided, part externally sourced. In-house legal teams face a myriad of complex legal problems. The decision to purchase externally will be driven by the shape, size and expertise of the in-house team. An in-house counsel may need niche advice or alternatively armies of lawyers (particularly when executing major corporate transactions) or access to up-to-date legal advice on everyday, mainstream legal topics or any combination of the above. Sometimes the decision will be purely a cost-based one.

1 Companies retain huge amounts of legal materials: board papers and minutes, title documents for property ownership, commercial contracts and business agreements, to give just a few examples.

EXTERNAL LAW FIRMS

14.3 During the past 20 years or so, the trend of companies has been to create panel arrangements with external law firms and call on legal services as and when they are needed. The theory is that by providing volumes of work to firms, discounted rates can be achieved and a deeper relationship established with the suppliers, resulting in value-added services being supplied either at low cost or free of charge. However, such arrangements can be unsophisticated. The distribution of work is not always directed to the best provider because personal relationships still hold sway, genuine service level agreements are not industry practice and the tyranny of the 'billable' hour still prevails[1]. The types of cost-efficiencies that General Counsel are required to achieve in external legal budgets are often only partially achieved and then, only after considerable wrangling to the detriment of relationship building.

Even if all of those things could be got right, there is still a fundamental mismatch between the demands of in-house counsel and what is provided by the external law firm. This is a major obstacle in reaching the goal of the deeper relationship. In-house lawyers look to external law firms to be part of their armoury of getting the job done for the business. In addition to the fees, they do not want to have to pay either in terms of excessive time taken to execute a task or risk the opportunity of mistakes being made because of a lengthy internal supply chain as work is delegated downwards in the firm. The holy grail is the ability of the client to decide how legal service is provided rather than the law firm.

Mark Chandler, the General Counsel of Cisco, spelled out a vision of legal services that is compelling[2]. He said, 'From the law firm think perspective, "sales" too often means a one-to-one relationship with a lawyer who bills by the hour. As a client, I can tell you what I want to buy is access to information, strategy, and negotiation, and, in the case of litigation, to courtroom skill as well.' He continued by saying, 'the very source of success for firms today – the ability to manage client access to information and require clients to use bespoke 1–1 systems – will be the source of the issue of failure in future.[3]'

1 For evidence that the tyranny of hourly billing remains at the top of in-house legal teams thinking, see http://www.lawgazette.co.uk/news/in-house-lawyers-call-billing-revolution – although it would appear that there are some law firms that see it as a tyranny too: http://www.forbes.com/forbes/2009/0112/026.html.

2 http://blogs.cisco.com/news/comments/cisco_general_counsel_on_state_of_technology_in_the_law/ Whilst the speech may have even greater resonance with those of us in the ICT sector, its message is impossible to ignore for anyone in modern legal business.

[3] For further and deeper understanding of this school of thought see Richard Susskind: 'The Future of Law' (1996) and more recently 'The End of Lawyers'.

INFORMATION TECHNOLOGY

14.4 This desire to put the client rather than the lawyer first is reflected in the approach of the LSA 2007. 'Consumers have the right to expect services to be delivered in a way that suits them, not the provider'[1]. In tune with Mark Chandler's theme, the Government concluded that it is information technology that will drive the ability of the consumer – including the in-house lawyer – to have greater and faster access to legal services.

The pages of evidence put in front of Sir David Clementi, the Department of Constitutional Affairs (and its predecessor, the Lord Chancellor's Department) and finally Parliament in the evolution of the LSA 2007 are peppered with references to the importance of information technology in the future provision of legal services[2]. Investment in information technology by organisations providing access to legal services is an essential factor in opening up the market. The creation of ABSs under the Act is an enabler for technology investment. I will return to this below when looking at the possible impact of the ABS.

But information technology is not the only factor in deciding on the services an in -house team requires. It can help in providing flexible access for the in-house lawyer to the right source of legal advice and information, but the culture of law firms and the way in which they structures their businesses will have to change in advance of 2011. In my view, this is why the change will occur before the advent of the ABS.

[1] Ministry of Justice 'Legal Services Reform Update' (February 2009).
[2] For example, Chapter 5, Paragraphs 311 and 312 of the Joint Committee on the Draft Legal Services Bill, Session 2005 – 2006 http://www.publications.parliament.uk/pa/jt200506/jtselect/jtlegal/232/232i.pdf.

THE ADVENT OF THE ABS

14.5 In July 1999, KPMG established the law firm of KLegal. KLegal wanted to create a business that was 'not merely ... the provision of legal advice, but as part of a range of integrated business services which have been developed with one clear vision – to deliver clear, commercial advantage to our clients.' By providing a multi-disciplinary partnership, the KPMG organisation was hoping to provide a 'corporate one-stop shop' for its clients providing accounting, legal and consultancy services. In 2002, it merged with McGrigor Donald and things appeared to be set fair for the enhanced law firm. However the model was never to mature. Enron highlighted the problems of audit firms providing consultancy services to corporate organisations and the introduction in the US of the Sarbanes-Oxley Act 2002 spelled the end for the KLegal experiment[1].

However the experiment provides an interesting template for law firms and the use of legal disciplinary partnerships (LDPs), which are permitted from March 2009. In the case of KLegal, it was an accountancy firm that established a law firm. However there is no reason, subject to compliance with the appropriate regulations and professional rules, why a law firm cannot bring in other professionals from other professional disciplines that can own a stake in the business and develop consultancy services in ancillary legal services that the law firm could offer. In fact the LDP is a precursor to the ABS and firms that may want to develop into an ABS could use this as a route to preparing to do so[2].

It is not just the 'one-stop' shop for corporate clients that the LSA 2007 fosters. Although not immediately obvious to the outside observer, the ability to bring non-lawyers into the legal firm's structure and give them a share in the business will be of great interest to in-house counsel. To more closely align to the needs of the in-house lawyer, law firms need people who can look at their internal firm supply chains and 'unbundle' the traditional offering made by external lawyers. Furthermore, those who come into legal firms from outside businesses will have had exposure to commercial drivers outside of the profession, but will increasingly be part of it. In-house lawyers spend a considerable part of their lives dealing with contracts sourcing services from many sectors and suppliers. They work with businesses for which performance metrics, service levels and key performance indicators are a way of life. Service credits and guarantees, financial incentives and sanctions are also part of that world. Indeed many in-house lawyers will themselves have to act in accordance with performance scorecards at unit and personal level. In the main, these things are alien to the engagement terms of private practice lawyers. There is no reason why they should be. Law firms who bring in non-lawyer managers and experts used to operating in such environments will be equipped to meet the demands of their corporate clients; it would be a substantial business development opportunity. Furthermore, the ability to introduce outside capital through ABSs will provide a further catalyst.

Larger law firms

14.6 There is a certain degree of complacency amongst law firms who deal with corporate clients, particularly amongst the larger law firms, as to the applicability of the LSA 2007 to them[3]. Much has been made of the 'Tesco Law' aspect of the ABS structure. However 'Tesco Law' does not depend on the development of ABSs. Will-writing, employment law and personal injury claims have all been accessible through the less traditional routes for some time and, in particular, personal injury claims organisations' adverts are established staple fare of daytime television. More recently, virtual law firms and law firm networks have begun to spring up on the internet[4]. ABSs will increase the proliferation of these types of companies by allowing investment by third parties to provide capital for their development. The economics of the ABS approach were considered in some detail by experts reporting to the Department of Constitutional Affairs. They tend to point to the ABS offering more in the area of commoditised legal services rather than the more complex corporate transactions[5].

However, this again is overly simplistic for two reasons. First, to achieve the appropriate levels of investment the law firms will need capital and the ABS provides a mechanism for obtaining that capital in a sustainable economic model. In good times, law firms have been able to rely on revenue assurance to fund investment. In lean times, even those businesses who have hedged against downturn in specific sectors may find themselves eventually turning to outside capital for investment. The idea that this model applies only to 'Tesco Law' is misleading. A well placed General Counsel will see that in respect of their suppliers and this presents further opportunities to encourage law firms to 'productise', namely specialise in certain areas of work. A good comparison has been the complete change in the nature of financial services since reform of the markets in the mid 1980s.

Secondly, creating products in the law firm will promote 'unbundling' of services. In-house lawyers want to be able to ensure that they are getting cost-efficient service. That does not mean the cheapest service, but the service that provides the most for each pound spent with the law firm. Legal 'products' are not the sole preserve of the individual consumer. It is perfectly possible to break down complex transactions into a combination of 'products' and bespoke parts. For example, in a mergers and acquisitions transaction, due diligence could be carried out by specialist teams. In new businesses developed under the Act, due diligence carried out by a law firm could extend to other specialists and thus go wider than traditional legal due diligence. At the same time, an in-house counsel may look to source that through other routes, including a law firm that specialises in carrying out due diligence or post-completion implementation.

Traditional 'bundling' pushes up fee rates and militates against cost-efficiency. In 'unbundling' services and providing a menu of services that the in-house lawyer can choose from, a law firm can achieve a significant advantage. A good analogy of unbundling of services is that of a hotel[6]. In-house lawyers do not always want to stay in a five star hotel; sometimes they are quite happy to stay in an economy hotel and bring their own consumables. Traditional bundling does not provide choice. The in-house lawyer may not want all the services in the bundle. Indeed their company may already have volume-based discounts for these activities for other parts of its business (for example; searches, company incorporation, tax advice, photocopying and document production) and therefore be able to 'self-provide' more cheaply.

LDPs and ABSs will create business models that reward non-lawyers who have the skills to unbundle ancillary services and offer them on a menu basis by giving them an interest in the business. Consequently an LDP could have a department that manages company incorporations and filings and other registrar type activities. Tax and insolvency advice is another discreet area which is an opportunity. Furthermore with the ability to reward through equity stakes key operating personnel such as financial directors and chief operating officers, law firms can compete to recruit the best business people from other areas of commerce who are experienced in client relations management, supply chain management, change management etc[7].

1 http://www.tax-news.com/archive/story/KPMG_Ditches_KLegal_xxxx13977.html

[2] Professor Stephen Mayson's address at the launch of MyLawyer.co.uk http://www.lawgazette.co.uk/news/firms-will-need-more-non-lawyers-post-legal-services-act-world

[3] 'Firms Lukewarm as LDPs loom' Law Society Gazette February 2009 – only 4 firms have registered to become LDPs.

[4] A good example is https://mylawyer.secureclient.co.uk/ml, which Professor Stephen Mayson was speaking at the launch of when he made his remarks about more non-lawyers being needed (see para 14.4, note 2). See also http://business.timesonline.co.uk/tol/business/law/article1699474.ece.

[5] See 'The Benefits Of Multiple Ownership Models In Law Services' (July 2005) by James Dow and Carlos Lapuerta (http://www.dca.gov.uk/legalsys/dow-lapuerta.pdf) and 'The Organisational Structure of Legal Firms; a Discussion of the Recommendations of the 2004 Review of the Regulatory Framework for Legal Services in England and Wales' by Richard A Brealey and Julian R Franks (http://www.dca.gov.uk/legalsys/brealey-franks.pdf).

[6] And not just hotels, airlines too: http://www.thelawyer.com/cgi-bin/item.cgi?id=135700&d=415&h=417&f=416.

[7] Tasks traditionally carried out by partners in addition to their 'day job' earning fees thereby relegating vital business tasks to the status of ancillary tasks. Only in partnerships can vital business tasks be assigned to people with little relevant experience, deflecting them from the role for which they were first engaged.

OTHER ISSUES

14.7 There are several other issues that arise from the Act concerning ABSs which will be important for in-house lawyers. The formal legal requirements of ABSs are dealt with elsewhere in this book and therefore there is no need to repeat them in this chapter. If an in-house Counsel is involved with an ABS, either by engaging them or working for them, three areas stand out: conflict of interest, legal privilege and 'fitness to own'.

Conflict of interest

14.8 In-house lawyers have considerable experience of dealing with conflicts of interest in corporate life. Rule 13 of the Code of Conduct, which principally governs the conduct of in-house solicitors, requires them to comply with Rule 3 on Conflict of Interest. They also have to ensure that they act in the best interest of their client. In-house solicitors have to navigate each day the complex series of relationships and interests that enliven corporate life. Anyone who has had to deal with cut and thrust of the sales end of the business will be very aware of the issue of conflicts, particularly if they are standing between a manager and the manager's large bonus.

Generally speaking, conflicts of interests can be theoretically hard to define, but actually, like elephants and obscenity, easy to spot when you see them. Furthermore, within an ABS the requirement for there to be a Head of Legal Practice will be of considerable assistance when dealing with conflicts of interest. There will be many General Counsel in-house who will be able to identify and resolve conflict experience on past experience of corporate life.

Nevertheless, in-house counsel will need to ensure that employees understand fully the nature of conflicts of interest. The KLegal example at para 14.5

above also highlights the issues around Sarbanes-Oxley. However, since 2002 and the introduction of Sarbanes-Oxley, accountancy firms have successfully navigated the conflicts between compliance and business development.

Legal privilege

14.9 A major issue for in-house lawyers at present is the issue of legal professional privilege. First, the *Three Rivers* case[1] has gone some way to clarifying the extent of legal privilege in protecting the right to receive legal advice in confidence. However, a major question mark still hangs over the distinction between advice of a legal nature and commercial advice. As Lord Scott observed:

> 'If a solicitor becomes the client's "man of business", and some solicitors do, responsible for advising the client on all matters of business, including investment policy, finance policy and other business matters, the advice may lack a relevant legal context. There is, in my opinion, no way of avoiding difficulty in deciding in marginal cases whether the seeking of advice from or the giving of advice by lawyers does or does not take place in a relevant legal context so as to attract legal advice privilege.[2]'

Indeed, an in-house lawyer advising its ABS employee on the application of regulations under the LSA 2007 in respect of a new legal product could find themselves involved in some knotty problems. Furthermore, the question, even after consideration by the House of Lords, as to the true identity of the 'client' remains. Potentially within an ABS this situation could prove even more problematic for an in-house lawyer.

The other case is the *Akzo Nobel Chemicals Ltd* case[3] decided last year by the European Court of First Instance, which has further restricted the ability of in-house lawyers involved in competition cases and investigations involving the European Commission from claiming legal privilege.

Although these are not issues generated by the LSA 2007, they are nevertheless areas which could be further complicated when applied in respect of an ABS.

1 *Three Rivers District Council and others (Respondents) v Governor and Company of the Bank of England (Appellants)* [2004] UKHL 48.
2 [2004] UKHL 48, para 38.
3 *Akzo Nobel Chemicals Ltd v European Commission: T-125/03 and T-253/03* [2008] All ER (EC) 1, [2008] 4 CMLR 97, [2007] All ER (D) 97 (Sep).

'Fitness to own'

14.10 Quite rightly, the issue is one of concern[1]. However, in debates and evidence given to the Joint Committee on the Draft Bill, there seemed to be some confusion between the fitness of an owner because they were able to provide services in a competitive way and somebody who is unfit by virtue of criminal activity or similar lack of integrity. In fact, many organisations mentioned as being potential investors in ABSs (the RAC, the Co-operative

Society and the AA, to take three examples) are organisations with instantly recognisable brands that are synonymous with good service and integrity. Major corporate organisations are consistently working to ensure that their brands are not only protected, but are readily identifiable with ethical stances and integrity. In-house counsels have considerable experience of working to ensure that their businesses fully comply with regulation and governance far more reaching on occasion than their own professional rules. A Head of Legal Practice in an ABS should be experienced in ensuring that this fundamental regulatory requirement is complied with.

1 *Three Rivers District Council and others (Respondents) v Governor and Company of the Bank of England (Appellants)* [2004] UKHL 48, paras 282–284.

CONCLUSION

14.11 Writing this chapter has not been easy as there is little by way of regulatory guidance in the form of draft regulations available for looking at the LSA 2007 and specifically ABSs, let alone how in-house counsel may be involved with them. However, if nothing else, it has hopefully left the reader with the view that although correct, the answer of the SRA is limited in its scope. I would argue that, unlike the implications of the SRA's answer, in-house lawyers should be thinking about the LSA 2007 and its implications for the procurement of legal services *now*. We do not have to wait for the arrival of ABSs. A combination of IT, current economic circumstances and the advent of LDPs will cause the market to begin to change. Already those firms with mixed client bases (ie private and corporate clients) have to compete against organisations carrying out non-reserved activities[2]. As they are adopting new systems to compete, they will be able to adapt their systems to provide better working methods and efficiencies for their corporate clients and, most importantly, potential corporate clients. In fact, this may be a situation that change is driven from the bottom of the market rather than the top. Also it is not beyond the realms of possibility that in-house lawyers from different companies may join together either to buy services from new organisations or even self-provide themselves. The 'big bang' in the corporate legal services market is unlikely. Rather, there is an earthquake coming, the first tremors of which are now being felt. In-house lawyers should be in the vanguard of driving these changes. For the in-house lawyer these are exciting times.

1 *Three Rivers District Council and others (Respondents) v Governor and Company of the Bank of England (Appellants)* [2004] UKHL 48, para 290.

Chapter 15

COMPLAINTS HANDLING

Iain Miller

INTRODUCTION

15.1

> 'I hope that those of you who have ever been asked for an explanation by The Law Society on any matter at all, however insignificant, will be encouraged by the knowledge that there are roughly 200 complaints a week, year in and year out. It may also cheer you up to know that the vast majority of these complaints are either from people who are mentally unbalanced or from clients who do not really, I think, intend to complain but from ignorance of legal procedure and practice write and ask whether something is right or wrong.'

These words were written by Sir Thomas Lund in the first Guide to the Professional Conduct of Solicitors in 1960. Between 1 April 2007 and 31 March 2008 the Legal Complaints Service received 14,514 complaints and these are no longer considered to be the preserve of the mentally unbalanced and the ignorant. Chapter 5 sets out in careful detail the unequal struggle between the Law Society and the rising tide of complaints that led to the establishment under the LSA 2007 of the Office for Legal Complaints (OLC), which is modelled on the Financial Services Ombudsman. In contrast to the discipline and regulation of the legal profession, complaints have been taken away and given to this independent statutory body. Whilst the difficulties with complaints in relation to the solicitors' profession led to the establishment of the OLC, it will cover complaints for the legal profession as a whole.

At the time of writing the OLC has yet to be fully established and it is far from clear has to how it will interpret its own statutory powers. It will need, of course, to consult on and then implement more detailed rules. However, the existence of an independent statutory body that deals with all the complaints in relation to the legal profession will have a significant impact on the legal market and the regulation of the legal market.

THE ROOTS OF THE PROBLEM

15.2 The idea is, of course, that by being independent the OLC will command the respect of consumers dealing with complaints in relation to the legal professions and be a power for good. The availability of fair redress in the eyes of consumers will serve the public interest and improve the standing of the profession as a whole. The hope must be in time that the rate of complaints will reduce as firms, encouraged by the OLC, become more effective at dealing with complaints. However, substantial efforts have been made by the Law Society to try and manage complaints and, more importantly, to force the profession to manage its own complaints more effectively. As we have seen from Chapter 5, the Law Society has had a statutory power to compensate since 1985. Is the Law Society's inability to stem the tide of complaints entirely down to a lack of adequate funding and a lack of independence? It may well be that the biggest cause of the problem is the structure of the solicitors' profession, and in this respect the OLC may be assisted by the changes to the legal profession by the LSA 2007 more generally. In 2007, 87% of law firms had four partners or fewer, and 44% were sole practitioners. This group also accounted for 31% of all solicitors. It is this group which is the main source of complaints. This for two reasons: first, some of these firms are not effective at dealing with complaints; second, the client base of some of these firms is more likely to complain than, say, larger corporate clients. In either case, a smaller business unit has fewer resources to deal with complaints.

One of the reasons for such a large number of smaller firms is the current ownership restrictions whereby only solicitors can own law firms. By the introduction of outside investment in law firms through alternative business structures (ABSs), this is likely in time to reduce the number of smaller firms as they may find it more difficult to compete with larger brands providing legal services to individual clients. At the same time the increase in the complexity of regulation will place an additional cost burden on small firms which will impact on their viability. As described below, part of this regulatory burden will be the OLC itself.

If in ten years' time the number of complaints about legal professionals has significantly reduced it may be that this is because there are fewer small firms, not because of the OLC. It is always better to be lucky than good. However, there are other issues that arise from the new complaints regime.

PROBLEMS WITH THE NEW REGIME

15.3 In a self-regulated profession the professional body deals with all issues arising from that profession. This has historically been the case with the legal professions. For example, until very recently, the Law Society dealt with both service complaints and conduct complaints. Over the years this has been through bodies called the Law Society, The Office for the Supervision of Solicitors and the Solicitors' Complaints Bureau. There are advantages in this approach. It is not always easy to distinguish between conduct and service. Often the same facts give rise to both. For example, if a solicitor fails to register a charge (in breach of an undertaking) he or she is prima facie guilty of misconduct, but the client who cannot then sell the property may also suffer a loss as a result of the inadequacy of the service provided by the solicitor and for which an order for compensation is available. When these two matters are separated out into different organisations there are a number of consequences. First, two separate investigations of the facts takes place. This is likely to cost more. It may be that the complainant will be asked to produce the same information twice. There could be an inconsistency of outcome if different views are taken of the same facts.

The separation of roles also diffuses the information available to one regulator about a firm. A poor complaints record is an indicator that there may be other regulatory failings within an organisation. In future, the flow of this intelligence will be inhibited as it is no longer contained within one organisation. Clearly, and for understandable reasons, the decision has been taken that there has to be separation of roles, but this is not without these disadvantages.

As suggested in para 15.2, the OLC will add to the regulatory burden of legal professionals. This is because it will be a source of greater costs and risk. Prior to the Administration of Justice Act 1985, the only 'liability' of legal professionals was through established causes of action enforceable through a court of law. In relation to solicitors' practices these have normally been claims for breach of contract or negligence brought by clients of solicitors. The principles for such claims are well established. The claimant must, amongst other things, show that they suffered a loss and that the loss was caused by the solicitor. Clients who bring such claims are at risk on costs if they fail in their claim. Solicitors are required to have in place professional indemnity insurance. Whilst premiums and claims fluctuate with market conditions, the management of the professional negligence claims risk is well developed.

The powers of the OLC are contained in LSA 2007, s 137. Broadly, these include a direction that the legal practitioner apologises, pays compensation, reduces a bill or works to 'secure the rectification' of some act or omission. These directions are similar to those previously vested in the Law Society in respect of Inadequate Professional Service under the Solicitors Act 1974, Sch 1A (as amended). However, for the Law Society to make such directions it needed to establish that there had been a service which was not of a 'quality' expected by a solicitor[1]. There are no such limitations to the OLC's powers to make a direction. These arise when the ombudsman determines that it is 'fair and reasonable in all of the circumstances of the case'. This is a much softer concept than the hard legal liability or the current Inadequate Professional Service regime. There is ostensibly no need to show causation or, indeed, loss, or an inadequate (let alone negligent) level of service.

The limit under the LSA 2007 for a determination is a total value of £30,000[2]. In contrast to legal proceedings a complainant will not be exposed to adverse costs consequences. Indeed, the legal practitioner may well be ordered to pay costs unless it can be demonstrated that all reasonable steps were taken to resolve the complaint. Having the complaint dismissed may not be enough.

In practice, the effect of these provisions is that if a complainant considers that they have suffered loss as a result of the acts of a legal practitioner and that loss is not significantly more than £30,000 then they will pursue the claim through to the OLC. Professional negligence claims will be limited to claims over £30,000 or claims brought by organisations that fall outside the scheme. The costs regime for complaints to the OLC is less of an impediment than legal proceedings.

1 Solicitors Act 1974, Sch 1A, para 1(1).
2 Section 138.

IMPLICATIONS OF THE NEW REGIME

15.4 It is likely that the above changes with have the following effect. First, professional indemnity premiums will rise to cover the greater risk being taken on by insurers for OLC determinations. This is because such determinations are almost certain to fall within the minimum terms of insurance imposed by approved regulators as it is in the public interest that it is so. Second, legal practitioners will need to allocate even greater resources in managing complaints. This is not only because it makes business sense to do so, but insurers will also require it. However, the risk is not likely to fall evenly across the profession. Complaints to the OLC can only be made by an individual or an organisation prescribed by order made by the Lord Chancellor[1]. If this provision accords with the approach taken by the Financial Ombudsman Service then complaints are likely to be restricted to individuals, small companies and the like. Bigger firms who have a client base of large corporate entities may have very limited risk as only a small proportion of their client base will fall within the jurisdiction of the OLC. All of this will place greater pressure on small firms.

Finally, it is not clear from the LSA 2007 as to how proactive the OLC will be in ensuring that firms manage their own complaints. It is clearly right that the public interest is best served if firms deal with their own complaints effectively. The statutory scheme encourages firms to do so not least because this is the only way to avoid an adverse costs order. However, there is nothing in the LSA 2007 that obliges the OLC to provide guidance as to best practice. Previously, the Law Society has taken a proactive role in trying to assist with such matters. However, it is not only a regulatory but also a representative professional body. The OLC may consider that such matter remain the concern of the Law Society as a representative body rather than the OLC itself.

1 Section 128(3).

Chapter 16

TRAINING

Melissa Hardee

INTRODUCTION

16.1 The impact on training of the Clementi Review and the LSA 2007, which put the Review into effect, is likely to be as great as it was unexpected.

The LSA 2007 does not address training or specify any requirements for training, other than to say in s 4 that the Legal Services Board:

> 'must assist in the maintenance and development of standards in relation to–
> (a) the regulation by approved regulators of persons authorised by them to carry on activities which are reserved legal activities, and
> (b) the education and training of persons so authorised.'

However, changes being made by the Solicitors Regulation Authority (SRA) and Bar Standards Board (BSB) to the training of solicitors and barristers, coupled with the new market created by the LSA 2007 and its new business structures, have a potential impact for both the solicitors' and barristers' professions which may not have been anticipated or possibly even intended. What this chapter attempts to do is to describe the possible manifestations of that impact.

THE LEGAL TRAINING FRAMEWORK

16.2 In the post-Clementi era, the SRA is the independent body to which the Law Society of England and Wales has delegated regulatory responsibility for the pre- and post-qualification training of solicitors. The BSB has had similar responsibility delegated to it by the Bar Council for the training of barristers.

Training for barristers and solicitors consists of a framework of formal academic education in law, compulsory vocational training, a period of work-based learning and, then, ongoing continuing professional development. The term 'training' is used in this chapter as an umbrella term to cover all of these stages of legal education, training and development at both pre- and post-qualification stages.

16.2 *Training*

The various stages of the legal training framework are more commonly referred to as the 'academic', 'vocational' and 'work-based learning' stages of training.

The academic stage is common to both solicitors and barristers, and consists of either the Qualifying Law Degree (QLD), or the Graduate Diploma in Law (GDL) which is a year-long postgraduate course for non-law graduates who wish to 'convert' to law. The vocational and work-based learning stages which follow the academic stage are different according to whether one wishes to qualify as a solicitor or a barrister.

The vocational stage for both professions acts a bridge between the academic stage and the work-based learning stage by introducing would-be solicitors and barristers to the practical knowledge and skills they will require for practice. For solicitors, the vocational stage comprises the year-long Legal Practice Course (LPC), and for barristers, the year-long Bar Vocational Course (BVC).

Barristers, unlike solicitors, qualify at the end of the vocational stage by being called to the Bar by one of the Inns of Court after successfully completing the BVC[1]. The work-based learning stage for barristers, which consists of two six-month pupillages, is therefore post-qualification but needs to be completed in order to practise in one's own right, that is to say, without supervision and with full rights of audience.

Solicitors, on the other hand, need to complete the work-based learning stage in order to qualify, which means a two-year training contract and successful completion of the Professional Skills Course (PSC).

1 And also having joined one of the Inns and attended the educational sessions which the Inn requires.

SOLICITORS

16.3 The domestic[1] paths to qualification as a solicitor in England and Wales are:

- a QLD, followed by the LPC, a two-year training contract (subject to any 'time to count' allowance[2]) and the PSC;
- a non-law honours degree, followed by the GDL, the LPC, a two-year training contract (subject to 'time to count' allowances) and the PSC; or
- as a fellow of the Institute of Legal Executives (the FILEX route), Institute of Legal Executives (ILEX) exams while in qualifying legal employment followed by the LPC.

1 There are also routes for EU nationals and other lawyers to qualify as solicitors in England and Wales under the Establishment Directive and Qualified Lawyers Transfer Test, which is not discussed here.

2 At present, the two-year period for the training contract may be reduced if the trainee has had relevant experience in legal practice in a non-qualified position. A maximum of six months may be deducted on the basis of at least 12 months' experience.

SRA changes to training

16.4 These domestic paths to qualification will be subject to change in the near future through reform by the SRA of the LPC and the training contract.

The LPC will change from September 2010 (although some courses will change from September 2009[1]) to a more flexible course based on achievement of 'outcomes'[2] rather than prescription of process[3]. The aim of the SRA in introducing these changes is to provide greater flexibility for students, providers and firms. This new flexibility will be important for firms in the post-LSA 2007 world, for reasons which are explained below.

Changes to the training contract are not as advanced as reform of the LPC, although the same driver of achieving more flexibility for those who want to qualify has influenced proposed reform in this area. A further driver for the training contract reforms, however, has been the desire to overcome the existing bottleneck at entry to the training contract. According to the Law Society's 2007 annual statistical report[4], there were 12,858 law graduates in 2006, with possibly a further 4,000 from joint honours or modular degrees. The number of LPC enrolments in 2006/07 was 11,351 with a pass rate of 75.6% – in other words, around 8,500 LPC graduates, and 6,012 traineeships registered in the same period. The LPC graduates from previous years still looking for training contracts also need to be factored in, and one estimate is that this means there are some 16,000 LPC graduates in the market for some 6,000 training contracts. Whichever way one looks at it, there is a substantial oversupply of potential trainee solicitors compared with the number of training contracts available. Consequently, the SRA is piloting a new 'work-based learning' stage over two years which would enable LPC graduates not in a training contract but doing equivalent work to qualify.

1 LPC providers were given the option by the SRA to offer the 'new' LPC from September 2009.
2 Essentially descriptions of competence.
3 Such as prescription of the particular course which must be studied (eg the LPC) or prescription of duration (eg two years for the training contract).
4 'Trends in the solicitors' profession – Annual statistical report 2007'.

The LSA 2007's implications

16.5 Chapter 4 explained the new structures of legal disciplinary practices (LDPs) and alternative business structures (ABSs), which have been introduced by the LSA 2007. The features of these new business structures relevant for training are to do with allowing non-solicitors to become partners – 'owners' or 'managers' in the LSA 2007's terminology – of an LDP or an ABS and the fact that an ABS may offer services other than legal services, and may have non-lawyer owners and managers. This potentially means that the skills and knowledge required for the business of an ABS may be more than is currently provided in traditional solicitor training.

Possible consequences

16.6 There are a number of possible consequences arising from the confluence of the SRA's reforms and the implications of the LSA 2007, particularly in relation to:

- career paths (see para 16.7 below);
- recruitment (see para 16.8 below);
- required skills and expertise (see para 16.9 below);
- investment by firms in training (see para 16.10 below); and
- perception of the law degree (see para 16.11 below).

Career paths

16.7 By following either of the QLD/GDL routes to qualification, someone who wants to become a solicitor is looking at three years of the QLD (four years for the non-law degree plus GDL route) and tuition fees, followed by a further year on the LPC with course fees of around £10,000 on top – and no guarantee of a training contract at the end. Not surprisingly, perhaps, a trend which has been increasing is for LPC graduates to take paralegal positions in firms with the promise or hope, depending on the firm, of the paralegal position leading to a training contract[1]. If the training contract is reformed along the lines of the SRA's work-based learning proposals described at para 16.4 above, then the way will be opened up to qualify without a training contract (although a similar period of practice experience is still likely to be required, and probably at lower salary levels.) With the possibility of new business models under the LSA 2007, coupled with the impact of the current economic downturn on career prospects, the likelihood is that more paralegal positions than training contracts will be available, and qualification may be able to be obtained without a training contract by using external supervision and assessment.

However, that assumes that qualification will remain the be-all and end-all, when the real question is: why should it? Even now, qualification is only needed to practise in reserved areas – that is all. So, the question for students who wish to enter the legal services market is whether in fact they need to qualify, particularly if opportunity is opened up to them by the dynamic firms and new entrants described in Chapter 6.

This is not a prediction that anyone who has done a law degree and the LPC and who is otherwise thinking of becoming a solicitor will suddenly decide to junk that and become a paralegal, just because they can become a manager in an ABS without being a solicitor. Would a non-law graduate, for example, who might be considering whether to become a solicitor, find a paralegal position that could lead to partnership in an ABS more attractive than qualifying on the basis that it saved further time studying and further debt? Possibly, if the main driver for moving into the area of legal services was the attraction of becoming a partner. But is it? Chapter 6 has discussed the change in approach of the next generation of solicitors to their careers who: do not expect to stay with one firm for the whole of their career; see their career as consisting of different stages; may or may not have partnership as a goal, and will have a more short-term view, influenced by specific (financial or other) objectives. This change in approach had started even before the LSA 2007. For many, the attraction in becoming qualified as a solicitor is a matter of status – having the title of lawyer – rather than the attraction of becoming a partner, which would tie them to a firm as well as opening up the prospect of potential personal liability[2], which the new generation of lawyers may regard as something to avoid. In the end, whether a career as a paralegal or a non-solicitor manager in a firm will be attractive will be down to individual motivation.

1 Whether working as a paralegal does in fact enhance an LPC graduate's CV is moot. What it does do, however, is allow the trainee to get a foot in the door for a potential training contract.

2 Subject to the vehicle used for the business.

Recruitment

16.8 If a non-qualified career path were to become an attractive option for those who might otherwise choose to qualify as a solicitor, then there could be a potential impact for firms which chose to retain the traditional model of the single disciplinary business, namely that their potential pool for recruitment might be more limited in future. Not all firms are moving towards commoditisation or 'process re-engineering'[1], nor will wish to do so. Many firms will choose to remain at the high-value end of the market – high profit but high overheads, for which sort of practice the demand is likely to continue to be for qualified solicitors whose expertise will justify the higher costs to the client (assuming, of course, that clients are prepared to bear those higher costs). The problem firms may have in recruiting solicitors is if potential solicitors are discouraged from entering the profession, as opposed to the legal services market. For instance, they could be discouraged by the bottleneck at entry to the training contract, and attracted by the prospect of a non-qualified career path within new business structures. The result of this could be that, without appropriate inducements, the profession could miss out on the bright, motivated lawyers it needs.

The flipside of the question of why someone needs to qualify is: to what extent does a firm need to recruit qualified staff? Again, qualification as a solicitor is only needed to practise the reserved areas. However, even these reserved areas are being eroded by paralegal advisory service firms and the commoditisation of areas of practice. Consequently, the extent to which a firm needs to recruit qualified solicitors is going to depend on its business needs and client expectation. If the client is happy to rely on the firm holding out its employee as competent, then the employee's qualification status may be irrelevant – particularly if there is a knock-on benefit to the client in terms of charge-out rates, for example. If qualification is not relevant for the client, then a firm may decide to concentrate on attracting the best quality recruits, irrespective of solicitor, or even legal, qualification.

It may also reconsider recruiting trainees at all if it finds the SRA's proposals for work-based learning increase the supervisory burden to a point that makes the balance between training, supervision and fee earning unrealistic.

1 See Chapter 6.

Investment in training

16.9 Many, particularly larger, firms invest a lot of money in recruiting their future trainee solicitors, and recruitment of the best quality students is highly competitive. Many firms will look to recruit law students in the penultimate year of their degree, and will then sponsor them on the LPC, some firms paying living expenses as well.

However, it is not just law graduates who are attractive to firms; the advantages of languages or other specialist ability, or just a wider perspective, lead firms to recruit capable non-law graduates, some firms even having a preference for sponsoring non-law students through the GDL as well as the LPC. Given that trainees are rarely profitable for firms (firms will normally only start to recoup on their investment in their trainees some two years after qualification – which is why they tend to be used as cannon fodder), the earlier a trainee is able to start being productive is of great commercial interest to firms. The problem comes, though if, having paid for the LPC (and possibly GDL), the firm finds when trainees start the training contract that they are still not up to speed for practice and need more training, which the firm, again, will have to pay for. This can rankle, particularly where the further training required is in core skills such as writing, drafting and research skills – commonly cited culprits. Where this happens, it is not difficult to imagine a firm reconsidering its financial investment.

One thing the new LPC will do is provide firms with far greater opportunity than they have at present to be involved in the design of the course they are paying to put their future trainees through. Some firms started along this track some time back when the City LPC emerged, followed by themed LPCs, compulsory electives, and, most recently, exclusive tie-ups by firms with an LPC provider. However, with the new LPC and the 'headroom' in the curriculum for tailoring[1], described in para 16.4 above, this means that the range of involvement a firm may have with the LPC can vary considerably. At one end of the spectrum is the firm which has little or no involvement (the situation for most firms at present), particularly where the firm recruits the finished product off the LPC rather than recruiting a couple of years in advance. In this scenario, the firm is happy for the trainee to choose the particular LPC he wishes to attend, and the elective subjects. Further along the spectrum, a firm may direct its future trainees to a particular LPC, either because of the specific focus of the course, or because of the elective subjects on offer. Then, towards the other end of the spectrum, is the firm which is actively involved in designing the course. At the extreme end, a firm could deliver the electives in-house – or even the whole course itself. Consequently, the firm that has been spending substantially to subsidise its future trainees through the LPC and possibly the GDL, and then has to invest in top-up

students attending the GDL and BVC, and a small number of individual sets of chambers also make awards to enable students to study for the GDL and BVC.

In terms of pupillage, there is a difference in the level of prescription for training between pupillage and the training contract, with the BSB's regulatory regime not specifying the training a pupil is required to undergo during pupillage. Pupil supervisors are, however, required to be approved by the Inns of Court and each pupil is required to complete a checklist of designated subjects before they complete pupillage. Further changes to the manner in which pupillage is delivered are likely to take place following the completion of the review of pupillage being carried out by Derek Wood on behalf of the BSB.

1 See para 16.2 above.

BSB changes to training

16.13 The issue for many students aspiring to join the Bar is the bottleneck at the point of entry to pupillage. Although this does not lead directly to qualification, it does lead to employment and the ability to practise as a barrister in one's own right. This was a central issue in the BSB's recent review of the BVC, and a reason why the BSB has retained the practice of allowing a student barrister to be called at the end of the BVC without requiring completion of pupillage.

To give some idea of the size of the problem, there were 1,953 students enrolled on the BVC in 2007/08 and 561 pupillages registered for the same period. This picture is not completely accurate, since approximately 23% of BVC students are from overseas and intend to return to their home jurisdiction to practise. However, as the Wood Report states, 'even if one discounts the number of overseas students ... it is plain that in any given year the number of people in search of pupillage greatly exceeds the number of pupillages available,'[1] and the gap between supply and demand is, 'a cause for considerable concern.'

A related concern identified by the Wood Report is in relation to the quality of some BVC students, the Report's view being that some would be unlikely to acquire a pupillage even if it were the case that a pupillage was available, simply because they do not have the necessary level of ability required for the profession.

In response to these dual problems of number and quality of students, the Wood Report made proposals that have been approved in principle by the BSB and are being taken forward by the BSB's education and training committee. In particular, the Report proposed the introduction of an aptitude test at the point of entry to the BVC in order to manage student expectation and the standards of entry to the barrister profession.

1 Para 27, p18.

LSA implications

16.14 Chapter 12 describes the implications for the Bar arising from the LSA 2007. An implication for the training of barristers particularly arises from the possibility of barristers being able to become managers of ABSs, should this be allowed by the BSB. The issues relating to alternative career paths for paralegals, although relevant for solicitors, is not as relevant for barristers, who do not tend to use paralegals in the same way as solicitors do as a way of offering more competitive costs and reducing overheads.

Possible consequences

16.15 Although much of the legal education and training framework for both barristers and solicitors is common or equivalent, the differences between the two, some of which are outlined above, mean that not all of the issues described in para 16.3 ff above for solicitors are relevant for the barristers' profession, and others, such as career paths and additional training needs, may have different consequences.

Career paths

16.16 One particular consequence of the LSA 2007 is the impact ABSs could have on both potential future entrants to the Bar in deciding which career path to pursue and, in the case of those already called to the Bar, in deciding on a change of career.

Given the shortage in the number of pupillages available, and the likely ongoing decrease in that number due to pressures on publicly funded work, some students who would otherwise choose to qualify as barristers may reconsider. One possibility is that they may instead decide to qualify as solicitors, particularly with the increasing advent of the solicitor advocate qualification. In principle, if this reduced the mismatch between the number of potential pupils and actual pupillages, it would be difficult to see the problem (putting aside for a moment the potential impact on the solicitors' profession of an increase in the number of potential entrants). However, it could have access-to-justice issues which are central to the Bar and its identity.

The considerations that tend to influence someone in deciding to become a solicitor rather than a barrister generally relate to availability of sponsorship, salary and retention. For instance, training contracts, generally speaking, although for two years (compared to one year of pupillage), are usually considered to be better paid.

Even without the LSA 2007, these considerations are not always clear-cut. Taking the issue of retention by way of example, until the recent downturn in the economic climate it has been the exception rather than the rule not to be kept on after qualification as a solicitor. This is because law firms often sponsor their trainees through the LPC and even GDL. However, even without that investment, the firm which spends two years training its trainees, who are rarely profitable at that stage (see para 16.9 above), will wish to get a return on the two years at least, on the basis that law firms are businesses, not nurseries. Until the BSB required all pupillages to be funded, tenancy after pupillage was very difficult to obtain because fewer tenancies were offered by chambers compared to pupillages. A result of the requirement for funded pupillages has been a decrease in the number of pupillages offered by chambers but a rise, comparatively speaking, in the number of tenancies available in order to match the requirements of chambers for tenants. Over recent years the number of tenancies available in any given year is broadly equivalent to the number of pupillages and reflects the pattern that most pupils are taken on in the set of chambers in which pupillage has been undertaken, and if not, find a tenancy in another set of chambers. The reason for this is that the Bar, increasingly, is taking a relatively similar approach to that of solicitors' firms, recognising that a pupil in a set of chambers represents a significant investment for chambers both in terms of time, particularly on the part of the pupil supervisor, and also money[1].

There may now be new considerations for someone deciding whether to qualify as a solicitor or a barrister, which arise out of the BSB's and SRA's respective reforms, as well as the LSA 2007.

Following the Wood Report, a consideration which may weigh is that there is no aptitude test to enter onto the LPC. For some students, 'aptitude' as a professional increases with maturity and exposure: closer knowledge and understanding of what practice and being a practitioner entails. Consequently, some may be concerned that they would not pass an aptitude test at this early point, and may therefore deselect themselves from pursuing the barrister route out of lack of confidence rather than any question of ability.

In terms of pure numbers, there are more training contracts available than pupillages. However, as has been discussed in para 16.4 above, this perceived advantage may be illusory given the number of LPC graduates compared to the number of training contracts available. If the SRA's proposed reforms to work-based learning make completion of a formal training contract unnecessary to qualify as a solicitor – provided the individual can find employment doing equivalent work[2] – then the bottleneck becomes less important.

Then there is the opportunity opened up by the LSA 2007, subject to the BSB's own regulations, for barristers both to be employed in and managers of LDPs and ABSs[3]. If the BSB's current proposals to allow barristers to be managers in ABSs do not proceed, then those who wish to take advantage of the opportunities offered by the LSA 2007with ABSs may see this as a reason to qualify as a solicitor.

This may also be a consideration for a barrister who is already qualified but who wishes to do advocacy within an ABS and who may decide to requalify as a solicitor (something the OFT has identified as undesirable)[4]. To date, barristers have been able to requalify as a solicitor with relative ease by way of the Qualified Lawyers' Transfer Test (QLTT) – a test administered by the SRA for non-domestically qualified or non-solicitor qualified lawyers who wish to qualify as solicitors in England and Wales. However, the QLTT has itself been the subject of recent review by the SRA and proposed changes could have the effect of making requalification by a barrister more difficult, particularly if there is a requirement as has been proposed[5] that eligibility to sit the transfer test depends on having the entitlement to practise. For barristers, this would mean completion of pupillage. This may weigh with BVC students, who, up until now, have been able to do the BVC, knowing that if they were still unable to obtain pupillage at the end of the course, they could use the QLTT route to requalify as a solicitor. This would no longer be possible under the proposed reforms without completion of pupillage. Even if the entitlement-to-practise requirement could be met, the barrister may then be faced with having to do the full set of exams without exemption under the proposals that have been put out to consultation.

Irrespective of the introduction of an aptitude test for entry onto the BVC, the proposed changes to the QLTT, if adopted, could have a deterrent effect on students considering enrolling on the BVC who may no longer have an easy way of requalifying as a solicitor via the QLTT if they are not able to obtain pupillage.

The BSB has observed in its two consultation documents to date that there does not appear to be much appetite from the profession to join ABSs. However, this may change if pressures on the Bar make traditional work more difficult and less attractive. With the other pressures which exist, being able to form partnerships or enter into LDPs and ultimately ABSs could be the lifeline many in this part of the legal profession feel is needed.

If there was a trend away from the Bar, irrespective of ability, and towards qualification as a solicitor advocate or of barristers moving to work in ABSs, which reduced the size of the self-employed Bar, this could be a matter of concern if the effect was to reduce access to, and choice of, a barrister[6]. As discussed above, solicitors working in firms are bound by rules as to conflicts of interest; barristers, although subject to the same ethical considerations, being self-employed, are not affected as a member of a set of chambers. By logical extension, a barrister who is an employee or a manager in an ABS would be similarly constrained by the rule to avoid a conflict of interest. This means that the firm or ABS could not act for someone where it would mean a conflict of interest within the firm or ABS. Consequently, the client's choice of representation could be considerably reduced, which would have implications for access to justice.

The other possible issue which may arise from a reduction in the number of entrants to the Bar could be a reduction in the pool from which future barristers were 'recruited' by chambers. An overall reduction in the number of entrants to the Bar may not be of concern, given the mismatch between the number of BVC graduates and the number of pupillages as has been discussed above – provided those who decide not to go to the Bar are the ones the Bar would not wish to have enter because of their level of ability. The objective underpinning the aptitude test is to remove from entry to the BVC those students who do not have the qualities for successful practice at the Bar so as to leave a large pool of able students from which pupils are selected. In order to meet concerns that 'less well-off students of high ability will be deterred from choosing a career at the Bar'[7], implementation of the proposals contained in the Neuberger Report through initiatives and schemes by the Bar Council and Inns of Court with schools will be very important. The Bar does not see any indication of a reduction in absolute numbers, or indeed, able students wanting to come to the Bar. In fact, the current economic downturn and its effect on firms of solicitors both in and outside London leading to programmes of redundancies, could make a tenancy in a set of chambers a safer and securer place, subject of course to the ability of the barrister to build a practice, and putting aside the publicly funded bar which may see a reduction in its numbers in the future because of current pressures on publicly funded work.

The risk the Bar runs in having a reduced pool for suitable entrants is that the considerations outlined above may weigh equally with those whom the Bar would otherwise wish to attract, and not just those who would be unlikely to succeed.

1 During pupillage the pupil makes no contribution to the operating costs of chambers and this usually remains the position during the first year of tenancy.
2 If the predicted increase in paralegal positions is correct, gaining employment as a paralegal may be less difficult than either obtaining a training contract or finding pupillage.
3 See Chapter 4.
4 'The Legal Services Act 2007 Implications for the regulation of the Bar of England and Wales – Second consultation paper – Legal Disciplinary Practices and Partnerships of Barristers' (December 2008) p6.
5 SRA consultation paper 'Arrangements for qualified lawyers transferring to become solicitors in England and Wales' (November 2008).
6 'The Legal Services Act 2007 Implications for the regulation of the Bar of England and Wales – Second consultation paper – Legal Disciplinary Practices and Partnerships of Barristers' (December 2008).
7 Paragraph 30, p19.

Chapter 17

STRUCTURES AND TAXATION

Colin Ives

GENERAL

17.1 The concept of alternative business structures (ABSs) already exists and is in common use outside the legal sphere; other professions already use a wide variety of business structures, including traditional partnerships, limited liability partnerships (LLPs), unlisted private companies, listed entities and foreign-owned entities. From a taxation and accounting perspective this variety has at its core two particular structures: that of a partnership/LLP and a limited liability company.

These structures are taxed very differently and this often influences the commercial decision as to which type of structure is used; tax, however, is not seen as the only influencing factor here.

Before considering the impact of the LSA 2007, it is worth setting out the tax regime that applies to each structure.

Partnership/LLP

17.2 The partnership/LLP is referred to as being 'transparent' for tax purposes with the partners themselves being individually responsible for paying all taxation on the profits arising. The partners are required to report their share of the profits of the business on their personal tax return and paying the tax thereon through the self-assessment system. There is also a reporting requirement for the partnership/LLP to submit a return to HM Revenue and Customs (HMRC) annually and this reflects the tax adjusted result of the firm and allocates the taxable profits and proceeds of any capital disposals amongst the partners.

In general, the tax liability of partners in a partnership is paid much later than that of equivalent employees in a limited company structure. The tax liability is, in general, paid in three instalments: on 31 January during the tax year, 31 July following the end of the tax year and the following 31 January. The first two instalments are normally based on 50% of the individual partner's previous year tax liability with the balance of the liability being paid as the final instalment. The first two instalments may be reduced where profits have decreased and the individual partner's expected tax liability reduces from that of the previous year. There are complex rules affecting the commencement and retirement of a partner and how this impacts their tax payment profile.

An equity partner is liable to two types of National Insurance (NI): Class II and Class IV. The Class II liability is a fixed weekly amount not dependant upon profitability and is normally paid by the partner via direct debit on a monthly or quarterly basis. The Class IV liability is calculated based on the partner's profit share and paid via the self-assessment system at the same time as the personal income tax liabilities.

Limited company

17.3 For a limited company, it is the company itself that is liable to tax in the first instance. A company has a responsibility to submit an annual tax return to HMRC, reporting its taxable profits and chargeable gains, and is required to settle any corporation tax due on those profits. Any remuneration paid out to employees, which would normally include the equivalent of equity partners in a partnership/LLP, will be liable to payroll taxes through the firm's PAYE scheme, and this tax and NI liability is paid each month on the amounts paid to the individuals concerned. The salaries are a tax deductible expense for the company so that these payments do not suffer corporation tax.

Employees are also liable to NI contributions and these are based entirely upon the level of remuneration paid to the employee. In general, employee NI contributions are marginally more than those of the self-employed although this difference is being eroded with the intention that the employee and self-employed NI contributions will equalise in future years. At the time of writing, the NI contributions of a typical equity partner are £920 less than that of a salaried individual on the same salary.

Payments by way of salary are also liable to pay employer's NI contributions and the current rates of employer's NI is 12.8%. This is set to rise to 13.3% in April 2011 as announced in the Pre-Budget Report in November 2008. No equivalent to employer's NIC exists for profits paid to equity partners.

As an alternative to paying salary, a company may pay profits as a dividend to shareholders. The dividend is payable to the shareholders pro rata to their shareholding. Any amounts paid as dividend are not deducted from taxable profits of the company and is therefore subject to corporation tax. The dividend is taxed on the recipient as dividend income and for individual higher rate shareholders a further amount of tax arises at the rate of 32.5%, which after credit for a notional tax credit of 10%, equates to a further 25% of the net dividend received by the shareholder.

Taxation comparison between partnership/LLPs and limited companies

17.4 The tables below demonstrate the effective tax rates, inclusive of NI contributions, that is suffered on profits that are paid out to directors/ partners. The tables show the position for individuals whose top tax rate is either 40% or 50% and, as can be seen, it is only the smallest of companies where the extraction of profits is more tax efficient in a limited company in comparison with that of a partnership or LLP. In the context of a professional practice, it is normal to expect a high level of profit distribution such that the partnership or LLP structure provides the most favourable tax position. It is for this reason that a number of limited company businesses have, in recent years, sought to convert their structure so that it includes a LLP. It can be said that under the recent UK tax regime there has been a general move away from limited companies for 'people businesses' when there is a high level of profit distribution. Following the 2009 Budget, this may alter as the tax and NI differential will reduce. However, the flexibility of a partnership or LLP structure is likely to remain a considerable attraction.

Individual taxpayer top tax rate 50%	**Effective rate 2008/09 and 2009/10**	**Effective rate 2010/11**	**Effective rate 2011/12**
Dividend			
Small company	40.75%	49.53%	49.53%
Marginal rate company	47.31%	55.12%	55.12%
Large company	46.00%	54.00%	54.00%
Remuneration	47.70%	56.57%	57.19%
LLP or partnership (ignoring tax on disallowables)	41.00%	51.00%	51.50%

Individual taxpayer top tax rate 40%	**Effective rate 2008/09 and 2009/10**	**Effective rate 2010/11**	**Effective rate 2011/12**
Dividend			
Small company	40.75%	49.53%	49.53%
Marginal rate company	47.31%	55.12%	55.12%
Large company	46.00%	54.00%	54.00%
Remuneration	47.70%	56.57%	57.19%
LLP or partnership (ignoring tax on disallowables)	41.00%	51.00%	51.50%

Notes

1. The tax rates for limited companies are 21% on the first £300,000; 29.75% on profits between £300,000 and £1,500,000; and 28% on profits in excess of £1,500,000.
2. The rates reflected for the years 2010/11 and 2011/12 are those announced in the Pre-Budget Report in November 2008 as amended by the Budget in April 2009.

Where the business does not intend to distribute the majority of its profits then a limited company structure may be preferable as this allows funds to be accumulated at the lower corporation tax rates and therefore enhance the capital value of the business. For example, if a large company were to retain profits these would be retained after corporation tax at 28%. However, if these were merely to be distributed by way of dividends then the combined effective tax rate as shown in the table above would apply.

Where profits are to be retained it would be essential for the company to have some form of mechanism whereby the increased value of the company would result in a capital gain for shareholders rather than either remuneration or dividend. This may be achieved by creating either an internal market for company shares or an external market such as a flotation. The problem here is that any growth on value will be attributable to the shareholders in shareholding ratios and not necessarily reflective of those whose performance has earned or created the increase in value.

Where employees are rewarded by way of share options or share allocations then consideration needs to be given to the taxation position and in particular the employment-related securities legislation. This legislation seeks to tax any award of shares or share options as though it were remuneration resulting from the individuals' employment and in such cases employment taxes including employer's NI may apply. There are a number of favoured share schemes for employees approved by the tax legislation, but this topic is beyond the scope of this chapter.

LEGAL DISCIPLINARY PRACTICES

17.5 The LSA 2007 envisages a two-stage process resulting in external or non-lawyer ownership of law firms. The first step is the introduction of legal disciplinary practices (LDPs), which it was planned would be available from March 2009. These LDPs are law firms where the substantial ownership remains vested with qualified solicitors. However, a LDP will be able to admit appropriate persons to the business ownership despite them not being qualified solicitors. Typically, this may involve the admission of barristers, patent attorneys, a chief executive, finance director or marketing director as a partner in the business. Where the business is an existing partnership or LLP, this will be treated just the same as an admission of a new partner to the partnership[1].

In this context, for a partnership/LLP the only person affected by the admission for income tax and NI purposes is the individual himself, who will be subject to the opening year rules that apply to new partners. For a limited company, assuming the individual works in the business, the new shareholder will either be a continuing employee or a new employee such that they will be taxed via the firm's PAYE scheme.

LDPs – capital interests

17.6 The position for capital gains tax purposes depends on how the firm has been dealing with capital interests. It is common for legal partnerships/LLPs to ignore the value of goodwill on their balance sheet and transactions between partners. In this case, HMRC Statement of Practice D12 can apply such that the admission or retirement of a partner from a partnership/LLP will be treated as a no gain/no loss transaction for all partners. Alternatively, where a firm does recognise the value of goodwill at other than cost or has other chargeable assets not held at cost, there will be multiple transactions for capital gains tax purposes reflecting the changing participation interests in each asset. For example, if a four-partner firm admits a new partner, with all partners having equal interests, the existing partners will each be disposing of ⅕th of their interest in each partnership/LLP asset and the new partner will be treated as acquiring a 20% interest in each asset.

The position is generally more complex if the legal practice is being conducted via a limited company. In this case, the admission of the non-solicitor member into the ownership of the business may be reflected by the issue of shares to a new participant or alternatively the sale by some stakeholders of an interest in their shares to the new stakeholder. As mentioned above, if this allocation of shares is to an existing employee, then the employment-related security legislation may apply such that the individual concerned is likely to be deemed to receive additional employment income, equivalent to the market value of the shares being acquired, resulting in payroll taxes and NI contributions becoming due for payment. This may also be the case for a new employee particularly where it can be shown that the acquisition of shares is by reason of the new employee's employment.

Any stakeholder selling shares to the individual concerned will be deemed to be making a capital gains tax disposal such that they may have a capital gains tax liability.

A partner who disposes of an interest in a legal practice operating through a LLP or partnership may be able to obtain Entrepreneurs Relief (Taxation of Chargeable Gains Act 1992, ss 169H–P) such that up to £1 million of the chargeable gain may be taxed at the reduced rate of 10%. This contrasts with shareholders of a company, where only those individual shareholders holding an interest of at least 5% may qualify for Entrepreneurs Relief.

International aspects of LDPs

17.7 The admission of non-qualified solicitors into legal practices may cause some difficulties for UK law firms who operate in overseas jurisdictions through branch offices of the main partnership/LLP or limited company. It is likely that a number of local legal authorities will not allow law firms with non-solicitor partners to practice law in their jurisdiction. Where this is the case, to enable such firms to become LDPs, alternative structures will be required such that the overseas branch office remains part of a partnership/ LLP or company, with only qualified solicitors as partners. It is therefore likely that such arrangements will be achieved for partnerships/LLPs by way of a dual partnership/LLP structures such that the branch activities are carried out by a partnership where all partners are qualified solicitors whilst only the UK activities for the law firm are carried out by the LDP, which includes the non-solicitor partners. The solution for a limited company legal practice would probably be more dependent upon the ability of legal practices to operate in those jurisdictions via a limited company and is beyond the scope of this chapter.

The creation of a dual partnership arrangement could be viewed in a number of ways by HMRC in the UK. Firstly, the restructuring could be viewed as a cessation of the old business and the commencement of two new separate businesses. This would mean that each individual partner would be treated as though his self-employment with the old firm had come to an end and that they had commenced two new businesses, such that the self-assessment opening and closing year rules applied. This could have significant cash flow consequences for such firms.

Alternatively, firms may be able to organise the restructuring in such a way that the UK activities were, in effect, treated as a continuation with the only change applying to the new non-solicitor partners and for the overseas activities. HMRC Statement of Practice 9/86 may apply in such circumstances and where it can be substantiated the 'the business' from a UK tax position continues into one of the successor LLPs, then a continuation for the UK business may be achieved. The overseas operations would be treated as coming to an end and recommencing. It is probable that the impact of this latter version would be less significant due to the way tax is administered in foreign jurisdictions and how the offset of foreign taxes against the UK tax liability can apply. However, great care should be exercised in such circumstances as the overseas rules may result in additional taxes becoming due for payment.

As an alternative, it may be possible to have a clause inserted into the partnership/LLP agreement to preclude non-solicitor partners participating in the profits of any overseas branch. Whilst this may seem a simple solution to this issue, it remains to be seen whether this would be acceptable to a foreign jurisdiction legal authority and it would be wise to seek the agreement of the overseas legal regulatory body before relying on such an alternative. Whilst this may be a solution in respect of individuals taking a stakeholder interest in a UK law firm, it is unlikely to be a solution in respect of a corporate investor.

Separating the business of the overseas branches into a separate partnership may also give rise to capital gains tax issues. Care needs to be taken that by transferring the trade of the overseas branch to a new partnership a gain is not triggered either in the UK or overseas. It should be possible to structure this without triggering a chargeable capital gain in the UK providing that the business is transferred prior to the admission into the UK partnership/LLP of any new partners and that the partners hold identical interests in the new overseas partnership. If structured in this way each partner will continue to hold the same interest before and after the restructuring.

ABSS – 2011/12

17.8 The LSA 2007 envisages the formation of ABSs. These are, in effect, organisations where both qualified solicitors and others provide legal services in a regulated manner in the UK. The LSA 2007 does not require that an ABS is either a partnership, LLP or limited company as it focuses more on the regulatory issues rather than the structural. Therefore, an ABS can be a partnership, LLP or limited company or even a combination of these, or a multiple of such structures. Ultimately, the structure from a tax and accounting perspective of an ABS will be determined by financial and commercial considerations both as to the international implications (see above), distribution of current year profit, the accumulation and investment of funds, the objectives of the shareholders and their existing structures and the potential increase in value of the business as a whole.

Many businesses, particularly partnerships and LLPs, converting to an ABS will need to deal with the challenges that such businesses will encounter when they move from the distribution of the whole of their profits year on year to the position where the partners' reward package does not include full participation in the profits of the business going forward. This is likely to result in partners of ABS vehicles exchanging annual income for potential capital growth. This may well provide many challenges to such firms as they will be competing in the open market with firms that remain as partnerships or LLPs and continue to have a full distribution policy, which may appear more attractive to existing talent.

As a result, even where firms do not intend to distribute the whole of its profits after becoming an ABS, it is likely that they will still distribute a large proportion of the profits of the firm to the partners. In these cases, it is likely to still be beneficial to have an LLP as a party of the ABS structure so that the profit share being distributed to partners can be distributed in the most tax-efficient manner.

Diagrams A and B provide two alternative structures where a LLP can be used in conjunction with a limited company.

In diagram A the existing legal practice has merely introduced the third party investor as a new partner in the legal practice. For this purpose it is assumed that the investor is investing via a limited company. Whilst the admission of a limited company as a partner in the partnership has some taxation consequences (see below), these should be relatively minor to the existing partners and in the context of the potential new funding being available to the practice.

Diagram A

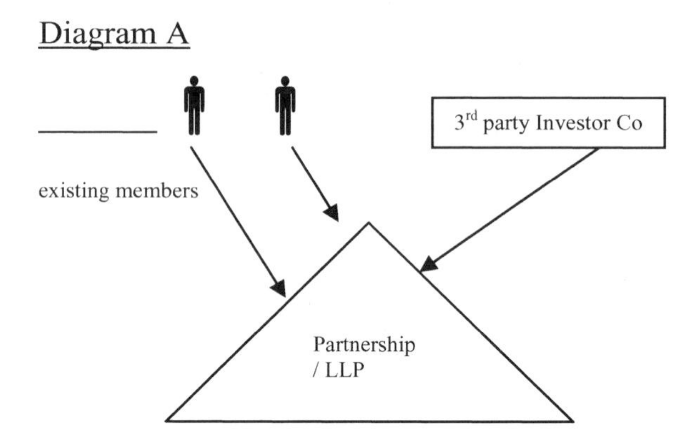

Diagram B

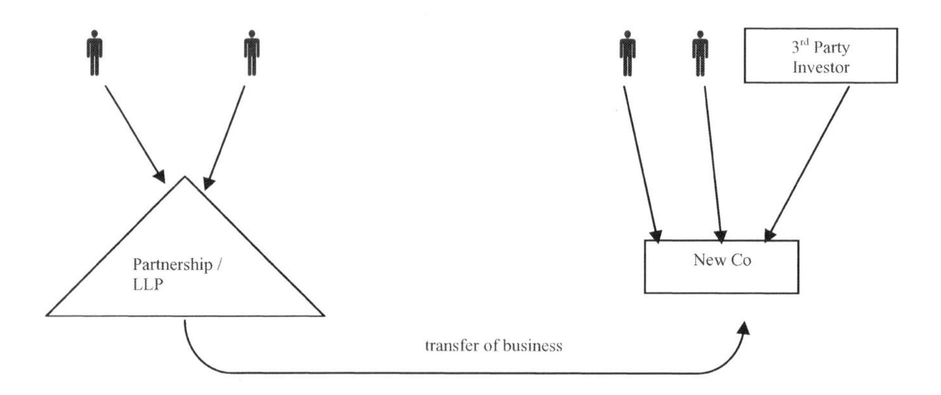

Diagram A also envisages that the limited company will be entitled to a certain percentage of the profits of the business, which it may or may not draw out of the firm. As long as the individual partners are not connected for tax purposes with the limited company partner then it is possible for such funds to be retained within the LLP for future investment in the business. The company will still be taxed on its share of the profits, even if they are retained within the LLP; however, this will be at the lower rates of corporation tax. In this scenario there would be some arrangement between the individual partners and the limited company partner concerning future ownership and how any increase in value of the business is reflected between all parties.

In diagram B it is envisaged that the legal practice itself has been incorporated into a limited company. In this scenario a separate LLP can either be established or the old LLP used to provide the services of the partners to the limited company. The company will enter into an agreement with the LLP for the services of the LLP partners and other services as appropriate. It would then be the profitability of the LLP which would be used to reward the partners and thus take advantage of the lower tax rates for profits distributed to stakeholders that applies to LLP structures.

INCORPORATION AS A LIMITED COMPANY

17.9 Where the business of a partnership/LLP is transferred to a limited company this will cause the business to have a cessation for income tax purposes with each individual partner being treated as having a cessation for income tax purposes.

Where the partners become employees of the new company, their self-employment will come to an end and they will be paid via the firm's PAYE scheme net of taxes deducted at source.

In the scenario outlined in diagram B at para 17.8 above, it may be difficult to argue that the existing partnership/LLP activities had not ceased for income tax purposes, although self-employment may be preserved.

For capital gains tax purposes, specific tax reliefs apply to enable partners of a partnership/LLP to incorporate the practice without triggering an immediate capital gains tax liability. The Taxation of Chargeable Gains Act 1992, s 162 provides automatic relief where the whole of the business of the partnership/LLP is transferred as a going concern (although cash may be excluded) to the company in exchange for shares. In this case the gains arising on the disposal are automatically rolled over into the base cost of the shares. Where appropriate, it is possible for individual partners to elect for s 162 relief to be disclaimed, resulting in the gain being chargeable. In effect the gain is calculated at the date of the transfer but does not crystallise until the shares in the company are eventually sold (or a chargeable event triggered).

As an alternative to relief under s 162, s 165 may be claimed on the gift of business assets to a company. Under this section, if the partner and the company jointly elect, the gain is held over against the individual base cost of each asset in the company's hands, therefore delaying the gain until the individual assets are disposed of. When the gain is triggered it is payable by the company rather than the individual. Under this route the shares issued by the company to the former partners/members are likely to have little or no base cost for capital gains tax purposes. This relief is generally used where it is not intended to transfer the whole of the assets and activities of the partnership/LLP as, for example, in the structure outlined in diagram B above.

Each partner may individually decide whether an election under s 162 or s 165 is beneficial in relation to his share in the business.

As mentioned at para 17.6 above, the incorporation may result in the individual shareholders no longer being able to obtain Entrepreneurs Relief.

Consideration should also be given regarding the availability of Business Property Relief (BPR) for inheritance tax (IHT) purposes if a business were to float at some later stage. 100% relief from IHT is available on an interest in a professional partnership or LLP, and equally for unquoted shares of a professional business providing that the interest or the shares have been held for a period of two years or more and the legislative criteria is met. However, quoted shares only qualify for 50% BPR if the transfer is out of a controlling holding. For a minority quoted holding no BPR at all is available. Quoted shares excludes shares listed on AIM and it is perhaps likely that most law firms seeking a listing will, at least initially, go for an AIM listing.

Admission of a limited company partner

17.10 As mentioned above, many partnerships/LLPs currently choose to ignore the value of goodwill on the balance sheet and retain this and other assets in their books at original cost value. However, if a limited company is admitted as a partner into the business it may be preferable for the partners to recognise the value of goodwill for future transactions between partners. If this position is adopted, Statement of Practice D12 will no longer apply such that any changes in the partners and the partnership capital sharing ratios will trigger capital gains tax disposals and acquisitions between partners.

In a simple limited company scenario it is only possible to vary a stakeholder's interest by transferring shareholdings in the company. This will trigger capital gains tax disposals and acquisitions based on the shares being sold or transferred between owners.

By retaining the partnership/LLP and using this as a vehicle to remunerate partners it may be possible to retain some of the goodwill within the partnership/LLP. Much will depend upon how much of the goodwill attaches to the business or the individual partners.

Limited company partner

17.11 The corporate member must declare its share of partnership income on its corporation tax return CT600.

The presence of a corporate member may also affect the deadline for filing the partnership/LLP tax return. For periods ending between 6 April and 31 January the filing deadline remains the same as for a normal partnership (ie 31 October for non-electronic filing and 31 January for electronic filing); however, if the period end is between 1 February and 5 April the filing deadline for a LLP with a corporate member will be nine months after the end of the relevant period for non-electronic returns and 12 months after the end of the relevant period for returns submitted electronically.

Where a limited company partner is admitted into a partnership/LLP there are detailed rules relating to the taxation of the limited company's share of profits from the partnership/LLP. The partnership/LLP will prepare tax computations based upon income tax principles for the individual members. However, the limited company member must calculate its share of the profits by reference to corporation tax principles. It is therefore necessary to prepare two separate tax computations.

Whilst the majority of rules for calculating the profits under either income or corporation tax rules will be the same, there are some differences, notably the treatment of interest paid and received, capital allowances, charges and distributions. It is therefore possible that the taxable profits shared between the individual partners and the corporate member will not add up to the total taxable income shown in the income or corporation tax computation.

There are two particular areas affecting the position of a limited company partner relating to the availability of loss relief and how the corporation is taxed.

The Income and Corporation Taxes Act 1988, s 118 restricts the quantum of loss relief available to a corporation to the company's contribution to the partnership at the appropriate time of the claim. This will invariably be the capital contributed by the company to the partnership. This may therefore restrict the availability of loss relief for a limited company partner and it is important to ensure that any funding contributed by the limited company partner is recognised as contributed capital such that increased loss relief can be achieved if needed.

If the legal practice has been incorporated as shown in diagram B at para 17.8 above there is a possibility that losses may be ring-fenced within the corporate vehicle and cannot be accessed by the individual partners. It is unlikely in this scenario for losses to be capable of being passed to the LLP and therefore the individual partners. If this is the case, losses may only be relieved at corporation tax rates; this could be a significant disadvantage as profits passed up to the members would be taxed at up to 41%, or 51% in 2010/11, but losses would only obtain tax relief at a maximum rate of 28%.

It is not unusual in the scenario in diagram A at para 17.8 above for services to be provided between the LLP and the corporate member. Transfer pricing rules apply not only to overseas companies, but also in respect of UK-to-UK services. It is therefore necessary to have a robust transfer pricing policy in place and ensure that all services are carried out at an appropriate arm's-length price. This may in fact be advantageous as the tax deduction in the partnership/LLP would be relieved at up to 41%, or 51% in 2010/11, whereas the corresponding adjustment in the limited company would only be taxed at up to 28%.

APPENDIX

LEGAL SERVICES ACT 2007

LEGAL SERVICES ACT 2007

2007 CHAPTER 29

An Act to make provision for the establishment of the Legal Services Board and in respect of its functions; to make provision for, and in connection with, the regulation of persons who carry on certain legal activities; to make provision for the establishment of the Office for Legal Complaints and for a scheme to consider and determine legal complaints; to make provision about claims management services and about immigration advice and immigration services; to make provision in respect of legal representation provided free of charge; to make provision about the application of the Legal Profession and Legal Aid (Scotland) Act 2007; to make provision about the Scottish legal services ombudsman; and for connected purposes.

[30th October 2007]

Be it enacted by the Queen's most Excellent Majesty, by and with the advice and consent of the Lords Spiritual and Temporal, and Commons, in this present Parliament assembled, and by the authority of the same, as follows:—

PART 1
THE REGULATORY OBJECTIVES

1 The regulatory objectives

(1) In this Act a reference to "the regulatory objectives" is a reference to the objectives of—

(a) protecting and promoting the public interest;
(b) supporting the constitutional principle of the rule of law;
(c) improving access to justice;
(d) protecting and promoting the interests of consumers;
(e) promoting competition in the provision of services within subsection (2);
(f) encouraging an independent, strong, diverse and effective legal profession;
(g) increasing public understanding of the citizen's legal rights and duties;
(h) promoting and maintaining adherence to the professional principles.

(2) The services within this subsection are services such as are provided by authorised persons (including services which do not involve the carrying on of activities which are reserved legal activities).

(3) The "professional principles" are—

(a) that authorised persons should act with independence and integrity,
(b) that authorised persons should maintain proper standards of work,
(c) that authorised persons should act in the best interests of their clients,

(d) that persons who exercise before any court a right of audience, or conduct litigation in relation to proceedings in any court, by virtue of being authorised persons should comply with their duty to the court to act with independence in the interests of justice, and
(e) that the affairs of clients should be kept confidential.

(4) In this section "authorised persons" means authorised persons in relation to activities which are reserved legal activities.

Initial Commencement
To be appointed: see s 211(2).
Appointment
Appointment: 7 March 2008: see SI 2008/222, art 2(a); for transitional provisions see art 7(1) thereof.
Extent
This section does not extend to Scotland: see s 212(1).

PART 2
THE LEGAL SERVICES BOARD

Constitution

2 The Legal Services Board

(1) There is to be a body corporate called the Legal Services Board ("the Board").

(2) Schedule 1 is about the Board.

Initial Commencement
To be appointed: see s 211(2).
Appointment
Appointment: 7 March 2008: see SI 2008/222, art 2(b).
Extent
This section does not extend to Scotland: see s 212(1).

General functions

3 The Board's duty to promote the regulatory objectives etc

(1) In discharging its functions the Board must comply with the requirements of this section.

(2) The Board must, so far as is reasonably practicable, act in a way—

(a) which is compatible with the regulatory objectives, and
(b) which the Board considers most appropriate for the purpose of meeting those objectives.

(3) The Board must have regard to—

(a) the principles under which regulatory activities should be transparent, accountable, proportionate, consistent and targeted only at cases in which action is needed, and
(b) any other principle appearing to it to represent the best regulatory practice.

Initial Commencement
To be appointed: see s 211(2).
Appointment
Appointment: 7 March 2008: see SI 2008/222, art 2(b).
Extent
This section does not extend to Scotland: see s 212(1).

---

4 Standards of regulation, education and training

The Board must assist in the maintenance and development of standards in relation to—

(a) the regulation by approved regulators of persons authorised by them to carry on activities which are reserved legal activities, and
(b) the education and training of persons so authorised.

Initial Commencement
To be appointed: see s 211(2).
Extent
This section does not extend to Scotland: see s 212(1).

---

5 Corporate governance

In managing its affairs, the Board must have regard to such generally accepted principles of good corporate governance as it is reasonable to regard as applicable to it.

Initial Commencement
To be appointed: see s 211(2).
Appointment
Appointment: 7 March 2008: see SI 2008/222, art 2(b).
Extent
This section does not extend to Scotland: see s 212(1).

---

6 Annual report

(1) The Board must prepare a report ("the annual report") for each financial year.

(2) The annual report must deal with—

(a) the discharge of the Board's functions,
(b) the extent to which, in the Board's opinion, the Board has met the regulatory objectives, and
(c) such other matters as the Lord Chancellor may from time to time direct.

(3) As soon as reasonably practicable after the end of each financial year, the Board must give the Lord Chancellor a copy of the annual report prepared for that year.

(4) The Lord Chancellor must lay a copy of the annual report before Parliament.

(5) In this section "financial year" means—

(a) the period beginning with the day on which the Board is established and ending with the next following 31 March, and
(b) each successive period of 12 months.

Initial Commencement
To be appointed: see s 211(2).
Appointment
Appointment: 7 March 2008: see SI 2008/222, art 2(b).
Extent
This section does not extend to Scotland: see s 212(1).

---

7 Supplementary powers

The Board may do anything calculated to facilitate, or incidental or conducive to, the carrying out of any of its functions.

Initial Commencement
To be appointed: see s 211(2).

Appointment
Appointment: 7 March 2008: see SI 2008/222, art 2(b).
Extent
This section does not extend to Scotland: see s 212(1).

Consumer Panel

8 The Consumer Panel

(1) The Board must establish and maintain a panel of persons (to be known as "the Consumer Panel") to represent the interests of consumers.

(2) The Consumer Panel is to consist of such consumers, or persons representing the interests of consumers, as the Board may appoint with the approval of the Lord Chancellor.

(3) The Board must appoint one of the members of the Consumer Panel to be the chairman of the Panel.

(4) The Board must secure that the membership of the Consumer Panel is such as to give a fair degree of representation to both—

(a) those who are using (or are or may be contemplating using), in connection with businesses carried on by them, services provided by persons who are authorised persons in relation to activities which are reserved legal activities, and
(b) those who are using (or are or may be contemplating using) such services otherwise than in connection with businesses carried on by them.

(5) The Consumer Panel must not include any person who is—

(a) a member of the Board or of its staff;
(b) a member of the Office for Legal Complaints (see Part 6), an ombudsman appointed by it or a member of its staff appointed under paragraph 13 of Schedule 15;
(c) a member of the governing body, or of the staff, of an approved regulator;
(d) an authorised person in relation to an activity which is a reserved legal activity;
(e) a person authorised, by a person designated under section 5(1) of the Compensation Act 2006 (c 29), to provide services which are regulated claims management services (within the meaning of that Act);
(f) an advocate in Scotland;
(g) a solicitor in Scotland;
(h) a member of the Bar of Northern Ireland; or
(i) a solicitor of the Court of Judicature of Northern Ireland.

(6) The chairman and other members of the Consumer Panel are to be—

(a) appointed for a fixed period, and on other terms and conditions, determined by the Board, and
(b) paid by the Board in accordance with provision made by or under the terms of appointment.

(7) But a person may be removed from office in accordance with those terms and conditions only with the approval of the Lord Chancellor.

(8) A person who ceases to be chairman or another member of the Consumer Panel may be re-appointed.

Initial Commencement
To be appointed: see s 211(2).
Appointment
Appointment: 1 January 2009: see SI 2008/3149, art 2(a); for transitional provisions see art 3(1) thereof.
Extent
This section does not extend to Scotland: see s 212(1).

---

9 Committees and the procedure of the Consumer Panel

(1) The Consumer Panel may make such arrangements as it thinks fit for committees established by the Panel to give advice to the Panel about matters relating to the carrying out of the Panel's functions.

(2) The Consumer Panel may make such other arrangements for regulating its own procedure, and for regulating the procedure of the committees established by it, as it thinks fit.

(3) Those arrangements may include arrangements as to quorums and as to the making of decisions by a majority.

(4) The committees established by the Consumer Panel may include committees the membership of which includes persons who are not members of the Panel.

(5) The membership of every committee established by the Consumer Panel must contain at least one person who is a member of the Panel.

(6) Where a person who is not a member of the Consumer Panel is a member of a committee established by it, the Board may pay to that person such remuneration and expenses as the Board may determine.

Initial Commencement
To be appointed: see s 211(2).
Appointment
Appointment: 1 January 2009: see SI 2008/3149, art 2(a).
Extent
This section does not extend to Scotland: see s 212(1).

---

10 Representations by the Consumer Panel

(1) The Board must consider any representations made to it by the Consumer Panel.

(2) If the Board disagrees with a view expressed, or proposal made, in the representations, it must give the Consumer Panel a notice to that effect stating its reasons for disagreeing.

(3) The Consumer Panel may publish such information as it thinks fit about any representations made by it to the Board.

(4) Where the Consumer Panel publishes information about any representations made by it, the Board must publish any notice it gives under subsection (2) in respect of those representations.

Initial Commencement
To be appointed: see s 211(2).
Appointment
Appointment: 1 January 2009: see SI 2008/3149, art 2(a).
Extent
This section does not extend to Scotland: see s 212(1).

---

11 Advice and research functions of the Consumer Panel

(1) The Consumer Panel may, at the request of the Board—

(a) carry out research for the Board;
(b) give advice to the Board.

(2) The Board must consider any advice given and the results of any research carried out under this section.

(3) The Consumer Panel may publish such information as it thinks fit about advice it gives, and about the results of research carried out by it, under this section.

Initial Commencement
To be appointed: see s 211(2).

Appointment
Appointment: 1 January 2009: see SI 2008/3149, art 2(a).
Extent
This section does not extend to Scotland: see s 212(1).

PART 3
RESERVED LEGAL ACTIVITIES

Reserved legal activities

12 Meaning of "reserved legal activity" and "legal activity"

(1) In this Act "reserved legal activity" means—

(a) the exercise of a right of audience;
(b) the conduct of litigation;
(c) reserved instrument activities;
(d) probate activities;
(e) notarial activities;
(f) the administration of oaths.

(2) Schedule 2 makes provision about what constitutes each of those activities.

(3) In this Act "legal activity" means—

(a) an activity which is a reserved legal activity within the meaning of this Act as originally enacted, and
(b) any other activity which consists of one or both of the following—
 (i) the provision of legal advice or assistance in connection with the application of the law or with any form of resolution of legal disputes;
 (ii) the provision of representation in connection with any matter concerning the application of the law or any form of resolution of legal disputes.

(4) But "legal activity" does not include any activity of a judicial or quasi-judicial nature (including acting as a mediator).

(5) For the purposes of subsection (3) "legal dispute" includes a dispute as to any matter of fact the resolution of which is relevant to determining the nature of any person's legal rights or liabilities.

(6) Section 24 makes provision for adding legal activities to the reserved legal activities.

Initial Commencement
To be appointed: see s 211(2).
Appointment
Appointment (for certain purposes): 7 March 2008: see SI 2008/222, art 3.
Extent
This section does not extend to Scotland: see s 212(1).

Carrying on the activities

13 Entitlement to carry on a reserved legal activity

(1) The question whether a person is entitled to carry on an activity which is a reserved legal activity is to be determined solely in accordance with the provisions of this Act.

(2) A person is entitled to carry on an activity ("the relevant activity") which is a reserved legal activity where—

(a) the person is an authorised person in relation to the relevant activity, or
(b) the person is an exempt person in relation to that activity.

(3) Subsection (2) is subject to section 23 (transitional protection for non-commercial bodies).

(4) Nothing in this section or section 23 affects section 84 of the Immigration and Asylum Act 1999 (c 33) (which prohibits the provision of immigration advice and immigration services except by certain persons).

Initial Commencement
To be appointed: see s 211(2).
Extent
This section does not extend to Scotland: see s 212(1).

Offences

14 Offence to carry on a reserved legal activity if not entitled

(1) It is an offence for a person to carry on an activity ("the relevant activity") which is a reserved legal activity unless that person is entitled to carry on the relevant activity.

(2) In proceedings for an offence under subsection (1), it is a defence for the accused to show that the accused did not know, and could not reasonably have been expected to know, that the offence was being committed.

(3) A person who is guilty of an offence under subsection (1) is liable—

- (a) on summary conviction, to imprisonment for a term not exceeding 12 months or a fine not exceeding the statutory maximum (or both), and
- (b) on conviction on indictment, to imprisonment for a term not exceeding 2 years or a fine (or both).

(4) A person who is guilty of an offence under subsection (1) by reason of an act done in the purported exercise of a right of audience, or a right to conduct litigation, in relation to any proceedings or contemplated proceedings is also guilty of contempt of the court concerned and may be punished accordingly.

(5) In relation to an offence under subsection (1) committed before the commencement of section 154(1) of the Criminal Justice Act 2003 (c 44), the reference in subsection (3)(a) to 12 months is to be read as a reference to 6 months.

Initial Commencement
To be appointed: see s 211(2).
Extent
This section does not extend to Scotland: see s 212(1).

---

15 Carrying on of a reserved legal activity: employers and employees etc

(1) This section applies for the interpretation of references in this Act to a person carrying on an activity which is a reserved legal activity.

(2) References to a person carrying on an activity which is a reserved legal activity include a person ("E") who—

- (a) is an employee of a person ("P"), and
- (b) carries on the activity in E's capacity as such an employee.

(3) For the purposes of subsection (2), it is irrelevant whether P is entitled to carry on the activity.

(4) P does not carry on an activity ("the relevant activity") which is a reserved legal activity by virtue of E carrying it on in E's capacity as an employee of P, unless the provision of relevant services to the public or a section of the public (with or without a view to profit) is part of P's business.

(5) Relevant services are services which consist of or include the carrying on of the relevant activity by employees of P in their capacity as employees of P.

(6) Where P is an independent trade union, persons provided with relevant services do not constitute the public or a section of the public where—

- (a) the persons are provided with the relevant services by virtue of their membership or former membership of P or of another person's membership or former membership of P, and
- (b) the services are excepted membership services.

(7) Subject to subsection (8), "excepted membership services" means relevant services which relate to or have a connection with—

- (a) relevant activities of a member, or former member, of the independent trade union;
- (b) any other activities carried on for the purposes of or in connection with, or arising from, such relevant activities;
- (c) any event which has occurred (or is alleged to have occurred) in the course of or in connection with such relevant activities or activities within paragraph (b);
- (d) activities carried on by a person for the purposes of or in connection with, or arising from, the person's membership of the independent trade union;

and such other relevant services as the Lord Chancellor may by order specify.

(8) The Lord Chancellor may by order make provision about the circumstances in which relevant services do or do not relate to, or have a connection with, the matters mentioned in paragraphs (a) to (d) of subsection (7).

(9) Subject to that, the Lord Chancellor may by order make provision about—

- (a) what does or does not constitute a section of the public;
- (b) the circumstances in which the provision of relevant services to the public or a section of the public does or does not form part of P's business.

(10) The Lord Chancellor may make an order under subsection (7), (8) or (9) only on the recommendation of the Board.

(11) If P is a body, references to an employee of P include references to a manager of P.

(12) In subsection (7), "relevant activities", in relation to a person who is or was a member of an independent trade union, means any employment (including self-employment), trade, occupation or other activity to which the person's membership of the trade union relates or related.

Initial Commencement

To be appointed: see s 211(2).

Extent

This section does not extend to Scotland: see s 212(1).

---

16 Offence to carry on reserved legal activity through person not entitled

(1) Where subsection (2) applies it is an offence for a person ("P") to carry on an activity ("the relevant activity") which is a reserved legal activity, despite P being entitled to carry on the relevant activity.

(2) This subsection applies if—

- (a) P carries on the relevant activity by virtue of an employee of P ("E") carrying it on in E's capacity as such an employee, and
- (b) in carrying on the relevant activity, E commits an offence under section 14.

(3) If P is a body, references in subsection (2) to an employee of P include references to a manager of P.

(4) In proceedings for an offence under subsection (1), it is a defence for the accused to show that the accused took all reasonable precautions and exercised all due diligence to avoid committing the offence.

(5) A person who is guilty of an offence under subsection (1) is liable—

- (a) on summary conviction, to imprisonment for a term not exceeding 12 months or a fine not exceeding the statutory maximum (or both), and

(b) on conviction on indictment, to imprisonment for a term not exceeding 2 years or a fine (or both).

(6) A person who is guilty of an offence under subsection (1) by reason of an act done in the purported exercise of a right of audience, or a right to conduct litigation, in relation to any proceedings or contemplated proceedings is also guilty of contempt of the court concerned and may be punished accordingly.

(7) In relation to an offence under subsection (1) committed before the commencement of section 154(1) of the Criminal Justice Act 2003 (c 44), the reference in subsection (5)(a) to 12 months is to be read as a reference to 6 months.

Initial Commencement
To be appointed: see s 211(2).
Extent
This section does not extend to Scotland: see s 212(1).

---

17 Offence to pretend to be entitled

(1) It is an offence for a person—

(a) wilfully to pretend to be entitled to carry on any activity which is a reserved legal activity when that person is not so entitled, or
(b) with the intention of implying falsely that that person is so entitled, to take or use any name, title or description.

(2) A person who is guilty of an offence under subsection (1) is liable—

(a) on summary conviction, to imprisonment for a term not exceeding 12 months or a fine not exceeding the statutory maximum (or both), and
(b) on conviction on indictment, to imprisonment for a term not exceeding 2 years or a fine (or both).

(3) In relation to an offence under subsection (1) committed before the commencement of section 154(1) of the Criminal Justice Act 2003 (c 44), the reference in subsection (2)(a) to 12 months is to be read as a reference to 6 months.

Initial Commencement
To be appointed: see s 211(2).
Extent
This section does not extend to Scotland: see s 212(1).

Interpretation

18 Authorised persons

(1) For the purposes of this Act "authorised person", in relation to an activity ("the relevant activity") which is a reserved legal activity, means—

(a) a person who is authorised to carry on the relevant activity by a relevant approved regulator in relation to the relevant activity (other than by virtue of a licence under Part 5), or
(b) a licensable body which, by virtue of such a licence, is authorised to carry on the relevant activity by a licensing authority in relation to the reserved legal activity.

(2) A licensable body may not be authorised to carry on the relevant activity as mentioned in subsection (1)(a).

(3) But where a body ("A") which is authorised as mentioned in subsection (1)(a) becomes a licensable body, the body is deemed by virtue of this subsection to continue to be so authorised from that time until the earliest of the following events—

(a) the end of the period of 90 days beginning with the day on which that time falls;

(b) the time from which the relevant approved regulator determines this subsection is to cease to apply to A;
(c) the time when A ceases to be a licensable body.

(4) Subsection (2) is subject to Part 2 of Schedule 5 (by virtue of which licensable bodies may be deemed to be authorised as mentioned in subsection (1)(a) in relation to certain activities during a transitional period).

(5) A person other than a licensable body may not be authorised to carry on the relevant activity as mentioned in subsection (1)(b).

(6) But where a body ("L") which is authorised as mentioned in subsection (1)(b) ceases to be a licensable body, the body is deemed by virtue of this subsection to continue to be so authorised from that time until the earliest of the following events—

(a) the end of the period of 90 days beginning with the day on which that time falls;
(b) the time from which the relevant licensing authority determines this subsection is to cease to apply to L;
(c) the time when L becomes a licensable body.

Initial Commencement
To be appointed: see s 211(2).
Extent
This section does not extend to Scotland: see s 212(1).

---

19 Exempt persons

In this Act, "exempt person", in relation to an activity ("the relevant activity") which is a reserved legal activity, means a person who, for the purposes of carrying on the relevant activity, is an exempt person by virtue of—

(a) Schedule 3 (exempt persons), or
(b) paragraph 13 or 18 of Schedule 5 (additional categories of exempt persons during transitional period).

Initial Commencement
To be appointed: see s 211(2).
Extent
This section does not extend to Scotland: see s 212(1).

---

20 Approved regulators and relevant approved regulators

(1) In this Act, the following expressions have the meaning given by this section—

"approved regulator";
"relevant approved regulator".

(2) "Approved regulator" means—

(a) a body which is designated as an approved regulator by Part 1 of Schedule 4 or under Part 2 of that Schedule (or both) and whose regulatory arrangements are approved for the purposes of this Act, and
(b) if an order under section 62(1)(a) has effect, the Board.

(3) An approved regulator is a "relevant approved regulator" in relation to an activity which is a reserved legal activity if—

(a) the approved regulator is designated by Part 1, or under Part 2, of Schedule 4 in relation to that reserved legal activity, or
(b) where the approved regulator is the Board, it is designated in relation to that reserved legal activity by an order under section 62(1)(a).

(4) An approved regulator is a "relevant approved regulator" in relation to a person if the person is authorised by the approved regulator to carry on an activity which is a reserved legal activity.

(5) Schedule 4 makes provision with respect to approved regulators other than the Board.

In that Schedule—

- (a) Part 1 designates certain bodies as approved regulators in relation to certain reserved legal activities,
- (b) Part 2 makes provision for bodies to be designated by order as approved regulators in relation to one or more reserved legal activities, and
- (c) Part 3 makes provision relating to the approval of changes to an approved regulator's regulatory arrangements.

(6) An approved regulator may authorise persons to carry on any activity which is a reserved legal activity in respect of which it is a relevant approved regulator.

Initial Commencement

To be appointed: see s 211(2).

Appointment

Sub-s (2): Appointment (for certain purposes): 7 March 2008: see SI 2008/222, art 3.

Sub-s (5): Appointment: 1 January 2009: see SI 2008/3149, art 2(b)(i).

Extent

This section does not extend to Scotland: see s 212(1).

---

21 Regulatory arrangements

(1) In this Act references to the "regulatory arrangements" of a body are to—

- (a) its arrangements for authorising persons to carry on reserved legal activities,
- (b) its arrangements (if any) for authorising persons to provide immigration advice or immigration services,
- (c) its practice rules,
- (d) its conduct rules,
- (e) its disciplinary arrangements in relation to regulated persons (including its discipline rules),
- (f) its qualification regulations,
- (g) its indemnification arrangements,
- (h) its compensation arrangements,
- (i) any of its other rules or regulations (however they may be described), and any other arrangements, which apply to or in relation to regulated persons, other than those made for the purposes of any function the body has to represent or promote the interests of persons regulated by it, and
- (j) its licensing rules (if any), so far as not within paragraphs (a) to (i),

(whether or not those arrangements, rules or regulations are contained in, or made under, an enactment).

(2) In this Act—

"compensation arrangements", in relation to a body, means arrangements to provide for grants or other payments for the purposes of relieving or mitigating losses or hardship suffered by persons in consequence of—

- (a) negligence or fraud or other dishonesty on the part of any persons whom the body has authorised to carry on activities which constitute a reserved legal activity, or of employees of theirs, in connection with their activities as such authorised persons, and
- (b) failure, on the part of regulated persons, to account for money received by them in connection with their activities as such regulated persons;

"conduct rules", in relation to a body, means any rules or regulations (however they may be described) as to the conduct required of regulated persons;

"discipline rules", in relation to a body, means any rules or regulations (however they may be described) as to the disciplining of regulated persons;

"indemnification arrangements", in relation to a body, means arrangements for the purpose of ensuring the indemnification of those who are or were regulated persons against losses arising from claims in relation to any description of civil liability incurred by them, or by employees or former employees of theirs, in connection with their activities as such regulated persons;

"practice rules", in relation to a body, means any rules or regulations (however they may be described) which govern the practice of regulated persons;

"qualification regulations", in relation to a body, means—

(a) any rules or regulations relating to—
  (i) the education and training which persons must receive, or
  (ii) any other requirements which must be met by or in respect of them,

  in order for them to be authorised by the body to carry on an activity which is a reserved legal activity,

(b) any rules or regulations relating to—
  (i) the education and training which persons must receive, or
  (ii) any other requirements which must be met by or in respect of them,

  in order for them to be authorised by the body to provide immigration advice or immigration services, and

(c) any other rules or regulations relating to the education and training which regulated persons must receive or any other requirements which must be met by or in respect of them,

(however they may be described).

(3) In this section "regulated persons", in relation to a body, means any class of persons which consists of or includes—

(a) persons who are authorised by the body to carry on an activity which is a reserved legal activity;
(b) persons who are not so authorised, but are employees of a person who is so authorised.

(4) In relation to an authorised person other than an individual, references in subsection (2) and (3) to employees of the person include managers of the person.

Initial Commencement
To be appointed: see s 211(2).
Extent
This section does not extend to Scotland: see s 212(1).

Continuity of existing rights and transitional protection

22 Continuity of existing rights to carry on reserved legal activities

Schedule 5 makes provision for the continuity of existing rights and for certain persons to be deemed, during a transitional period, to be authorised by approved regulators to carry on certain activities.

Initial Commencement
To be appointed: see s 211(2).
Extent
This section does not extend to Scotland: see s 212(1).

---

23 Transitional protection for non-commercial bodies

(1) During the transitional period, a body within subsection (2) is entitled to carry on any activity which is a reserved legal activity.

(2) The bodies are—

(a) a not for profit body,
(b) a community interest company, or
(c) an independent trade union.

(3) The transitional period is the period which—

(a) begins with the day appointed for the coming into force of section 13, and
(b) ends with the day appointed by the Lord Chancellor by order for the purposes of this paragraph.

(4) Different days may be appointed under subsection (3)(b) for different purposes.

(5) An order may be made under subsection (3)(b) only on the recommendation of the Board.

Initial Commencement
To be appointed: see s 211(2).
Extent
This section does not extend to Scotland: see s 212(1).

Alteration of reserved legal activities

24 Extension of the reserved legal activities

(1) The Lord Chancellor may, by order, amend section 12 or Schedule 2 (reserved legal activities) so as to add any legal activity to the activities which are reserved legal activities for the purposes of this Act.

(2) An order under subsection (1) may be made only on the recommendation of the Board.

(3) Schedule 6 makes provision about the making of recommendations for the purposes of this section.

(4) Where a recommendation is made in relation to an activity, the Lord Chancellor must—

(a) consider the report containing the recommendation given to the Lord Chancellor under paragraph 16(3)(a) of that Schedule,
(b) decide whether or not to make an order under this section in respect of the activity, and
(c) publish a notice of that decision,

within the period of 90 days beginning with the day on which the report was given to the Lord Chancellor.

(5) Where the Lord Chancellor decides not to make an order under this section in respect of an activity, the notice under subsection (4)(c) must state the reasons for that decision.

Initial Commencement
To be appointed: see s 211(2).
Appointment
Sub-s (3): Appointment: 1 January 2009: see SI 2008/3149, art 2(b)(i).
Extent
This section does not extend to Scotland: see s 212(1).

---

25 Provisional designation as approved regulators and licensing authorities

(1) The Lord Chancellor may, by order, make provision—

(a) enabling applications to be made, considered and determined under Part 2 of Schedule 4 or Part 1 of Schedule 10 in relation to a provisional reserved activity, as if the activity were a reserved legal activity;
(b) enabling provisional designation orders to be made by the Lord Chancellor in respect of a provisional reserved activity, as if the activity were a reserved legal activity.

(2) An order under subsection (1) may, in particular, provide that Part 2 of Schedule 4 or Part 1 of Schedule 10 is to apply, in relation to such cases as may be specified by the order, with such modifications as may be so specified.

(3) The Lord Chancellor may also, by order, make provision—

(a) for the purpose of enabling applications for authorisation to carry on an activity which is a provisional reserved activity to be made to and considered and determined by—
 (i) a body in respect of which a provisional designation order is made, or
 (ii) the Board in its capacity as a licensing authority;

(b) for the purpose of enabling persons to be deemed to be authorised to carry on an activity which is a new reserved legal activity by a relevant approved regulator in relation to the activity, or by the Board in its capacity as a licensing authority, for a period specified in the order.

(4) For this purpose—

"provisional reserved activity" means an activity in respect of which a provisional report under paragraph 10 of Schedule 6 states that the Board is minded to make a recommendation for the purposes of section 24;

"provisional designation order" means an order made by the Lord Chancellor under Part 2 of Schedule 4 or Part 1 of Schedule 10 which is conditional upon the Lord Chancellor making an order under section 24 in respect of the provisional reserved activity, pursuant to a recommendation made by the Board following the provisional report;

"new reserved legal activity" means a legal activity which has become a reserved legal activity by virtue of an order under section 24.

Initial Commencement
To be appointed: see s 211(2).
Extent
This section does not extend to Scotland: see s 212(1).

---

26 Recommendations that activities should cease to be reserved legal activities

(1) The Board may recommend that an activity should cease to be a reserved legal activity.

(2) Schedule 6 makes provision about the making of recommendations for the purposes of this section.

(3) The Lord Chancellor must consider any recommendation made by the Board for the purposes of this section (but nothing in section 208 (minor and consequential provision etc) authorises the Lord Chancellor to give effect to such a recommendation).

(4) Where the Lord Chancellor disagrees with a recommendation (or any part of it), the Lord Chancellor must publish a notice to that effect which must include the Lord Chancellor's reasons for disagreeing.

Initial Commencement
To be appointed: see s 211(2).
Appointment
Sub-s (2): Appointment: 1 January 2009: see SI 2008/3149, art 2(b)(i).
Extent
This section does not extend to Scotland: see s 212(1).

PART 4
REGULATION OF APPROVED REGULATORS

Introductory

27 Regulatory and representative functions of approved regulators

(1) In this Act references to the "regulatory functions" of an approved regulator are to any functions the approved regulator has—

(a) under or in relation to its regulatory arrangements, or
(b) in connection with the making or alteration of those arrangements.

(2) In this Act references to the "representative functions" of an approved regulator are to any functions the approved regulator has in connection with the representation, or promotion, of the interests of persons regulated by it.

Initial Commencement
To be appointed: see s 211(2).
Appointment
Appointment: 1 January 2009: see SI 2008/3149, art 2(c).
Extent
This section does not extend to Scotland: see s 212(1).

General duties of approved regulators

28 Approved regulator's duty to promote the regulatory objectives etc

(1) In discharging its regulatory functions (whether in connection with a reserved legal activity or otherwise) an approved regulator must comply with the requirements of this section.

(2) The approved regulator must, so far as is reasonably practicable, act in a way—

- (a) which is compatible with the regulatory objectives, and
- (b) which the approved regulator considers most appropriate for the purpose of meeting those objectives.

(3) The approved regulator must have regard to—

- (a) the principles under which regulatory activities should be transparent, accountable, proportionate, consistent and targeted only at cases in which action is needed, and
- (b) any other principle appearing to it to represent the best regulatory practice.

Initial Commencement
To be appointed: see s 211(2).
Extent
This section does not extend to Scotland: see s 212(1).

Separation of regulatory and representative functions

29 Prohibition on the Board interfering with representative functions

(1) Nothing in this Act authorises the Board to exercise its functions in relation to any representative function of an approved regulator.

(2) But subsection (1) does not prevent the Board exercising its functions for the purpose of ensuring—

- (a) that the exercise of an approved regulator's regulatory functions is not prejudiced by its representative functions, or
- (b) that decisions relating to the exercise of an approved regulator's regulatory functions are, so far as reasonably practicable, taken independently from decisions relating to the exercise of its representative functions.

Initial Commencement
To be appointed: see s 211(2).
Appointment
Appointment: 1 January 2009: see SI 2008/3149, art 2(c)(i).
Extent
This section does not extend to Scotland: see s 212(1).

---

30 Rules relating to the exercise of regulatory functions

(1) The Board must make rules ("internal governance rules") setting out requirements to be met by approved regulators for the purpose of ensuring—

(a) that the exercise of an approved regulator's regulatory functions is not prejudiced by its representative functions, and
(b) that decisions relating to the exercise of an approved regulator's regulatory functions are so far as reasonably practicable taken independently from decisions relating to the exercise of its representative functions.

(2) The internal governance rules must require each approved regulator to have in place arrangements which ensure—

(a) that the persons involved in the exercise of its regulatory functions are, in that capacity, able to make representations to, be consulted by and enter into communications with the Board, the Consumer Panel, the OLC and other approved regulators, and
(b) that the exercise by those persons of those powers is not prejudiced by the approved regulator's representative functions and is, so far as reasonably practicable, independent from the exercise of those functions.

(3) The internal governance rules must also require each approved regulator—

(a) to take such steps as are reasonably practicable to ensure that it provides such resources as are reasonably required for or in connection with the exercise of its regulatory functions;
(b) to make such provision as is necessary to enable persons involved in the exercise of its regulatory functions to be able to notify the Board where they consider that their independence or effectiveness is being prejudiced.

(4) The first set of rules under this section must be made before the day appointed by the Lord Chancellor by order for the purposes of this section.

Initial Commencement
To be appointed: see s 211(2).
Appointment
Appointment: 1 January 2009: see SI 2008/3149, art 2(c)(i).
Extent
This section does not extend to Scotland: see s 212(1).

Performance targets

31 Performance targets and monitoring

(1) The Board may—

(a) set one or more performance targets relating to the performance by an approved regulator of any of its regulatory functions, or
(b) direct an approved regulator to set one or more performance targets relating to the performance by the approved regulator of any of its regulatory functions,

if the Board is satisfied that the conditions in subsection (2) are satisfied.

(2) Those conditions are—

(a) that an act or omission of the approved regulator (or a series of such acts or omissions) has had, or is likely to have, an adverse impact on one or more of the regulatory objectives, and
(b) that it is appropriate to take the action proposed under subsection (1) in all the circumstances of the case (including in particular the impact of taking the action on the other regulatory objectives).

(3) A direction under subsection (1)(b) may impose conditions with which the performance targets must conform.

(4) If the Board proposes to take action under this section in respect of an approved regulator it must give notice to the approved regulator—

(a) describing the action it proposes to take,
(b) specifying the acts or omissions to which the proposed action relates and any other facts which, in the opinion of the Board, justify the taking of that action, and
(c) specifying the time (not being earlier than the end of the period of 28 days beginning with the day on which the notice is given) before which representations with respect to that action may be made.

(5) Before taking action under this section, the Board must consider any representations which are duly made.

(6) In exercising its regulatory functions, an approved regulator must seek to meet any performance target set for or by it under this section.

(7) The Board must publish any target set or direction given by it under this section.

(8) An approved regulator must publish any target set by it pursuant to a direction under subsection (1)(b).

(9) The Board may take such steps as it regards as appropriate to monitor the extent to which any performance target set under this section is being, or has been, met.

Initial Commencement
To be appointed: see s 211(2).
Extent
This section does not extend to Scotland: see s 212(1).

Directions

32 Directions

(1) This section applies if the Board is satisfied—

(a) that an act or omission of an approved regulator (or a series of such acts or omissions) has had, or is likely to have, an adverse impact on one or more of the regulatory objectives,
(b) that an approved regulator has failed to comply with any requirement imposed on it by or under this Act (including this section) or any other enactment, or
(c) that an approved regulator—
  (i) has failed to ensure that the exercise of its regulatory functions is not prejudiced by any of its representative functions, or
  (ii) has failed to ensure that decisions relating to the exercise of its regulatory functions are, so far as reasonably practicable, taken independently from decisions relating to the exercise of its representative functions.

(2) If, in all the circumstances of the case, the Board is satisfied that it is appropriate to do so, it may direct the approved regulator to take—

(a) in a case within subsection (1)(a), such steps as the Board considers will counter the adverse impact, mitigate its effect or prevent its occurrence or recurrence;
(b) in a case within subsection (1)(b) or (c), such steps as the Board considers will remedy the failure, mitigate its effect or prevent its recurrence.

(3) In a case within subsection (1)(a), before giving a direction under subsection (2) the Board must in particular consider the impact of giving the direction on the other regulatory objectives.

(4) A direction under subsection (2)—

(a) may only require an approved regulator to take steps which it has power to take;
(b) may require an approved regulator to take steps with a view to the modification of any part of its regulatory arrangements.

(5) The Board may not exercise its powers under this section so as to give a direction requiring an approved regulator to take steps in respect of a specific disciplinary case or other specific regulatory proceedings (as opposed to all, or a specified class of, such cases or proceedings).

(6) For the purposes of this section a direction to take steps includes a direction which requires an approved regulator to refrain from taking a particular course of action.

(7) The power to give a direction under this section is subject to any provision made by or under any other enactment.

(8) The Board may take such steps as it regards as appropriate to monitor the extent to which a direction under this section is being, or has been, complied with.

(9) Where the Board revokes a direction under this section, it must—

(a) give the approved regulator to whom the direction was given notice of the revocation, and

(b) publish that notice.

Initial Commencement

To be appointed: see s 211(2).

Extent

This section does not extend to Scotland: see s 212(1).

---

33 Directions: procedure

Schedule 7 makes provision about the procedure which must be complied with before a direction is given under section 32.

Initial Commencement

To be appointed: see s 211(2).

Appointment

Appointment: 1 January 2009: see SI 2008/3149, art 2(c)(i).

Extent

This section does not extend to Scotland: see s 212(1).

---

34 Enforcement of directions

(1) If at any time it appears to the Board that an approved regulator has failed to comply with a direction given under section 32, the Board may make an application to the High Court under this section.

(2) If, on an application under this section, the High Court decides that the approved regulator has failed to comply with the direction in question, it may order the approved regulator to take such steps as the High Court directs for securing that the direction is complied with.

(3) This section is without prejudice to any other powers conferred on the Board by this Part.

Initial Commencement

To be appointed: see s 211(2).

Extent

This section does not extend to Scotland: see s 212(1).

Censure

35 Public censure

(1) This section applies if the Board is satisfied—

(a) that an act or omission of an approved regulator (or a series of such acts or omissions) has had, or is likely to have, an adverse impact on one or more of the regulatory objectives, and

(b) that it is appropriate to act under this section in all the circumstances of the case (including in particular the impact of so acting on the other regulatory objectives).

(2) The Board may publish a statement censuring the approved regulator for the act or omission (or series of acts or omissions).

Initial Commencement
To be appointed: see s 211(2).
Extent
This section does not extend to Scotland: see s 212(1).

---

36 Public censure: procedure

(1) If the Board proposes to publish a statement under section 35 in respect of an approved regulator, it must give notice to the approved regulator—

- (a) stating that the Board proposes to publish such a statement and setting out the terms of the proposed statement,
- (b) specifying the acts or omissions to which the proposed statement relates, and
- (c) specifying the time (not being earlier than the end of the period of 28 days beginning with the day on which the notice is given to the approved regulator) before which representations with respect to the proposed statement may be made.

(2) Before publishing the statement, the Board must consider any representations which are duly made.

(3) Before varying any proposed statement set out in a notice under subsection (1)(a), the Board must give notice to the approved regulator—

- (a) setting out the proposed variation and the reasons for it, and
- (b) specifying the time (not being earlier than the end of the period of 28 days beginning with the day on which the notice is given to the approved regulator) before which representations with respect to the proposed variation may be made.

(4) Before varying the proposal, the Board must consider any representations which are duly made.

Initial Commencement
To be appointed: see s 211(2).
Extent
This section does not extend to Scotland: see s 212(1).

Financial penalties

37 Financial penalties

(1) This section applies if the Board is satisfied—

- (a) that an approved regulator has failed to comply with a requirement to which this section applies, and
- (b) that, in all the circumstances of the case, it is appropriate to impose a financial penalty on the approved regulator.

(2) This section applies to any requirement imposed on the approved regulator—

- (a) by rules under section 30 (internal governance rules),
- (b) by a direction given under section 32 (Board directions), or
- (c) by section 51 (control of practising fees charged by approved regulators) or by rules under that section.

(3) The Board may impose a penalty, in respect of the failure, of such an amount as it considers appropriate, but not exceeding the maximum amount prescribed under subsection (4).

(4) The Board must make rules prescribing the maximum amount of a penalty which may be imposed under this section.

(5) Rules may be made only under subsection (4) with the consent of the Lord Chancellor.

(6) A penalty under this section is payable to the Board.

(7) In sections 38 to 40 references to a "penalty" are to a penalty under this section.

Initial Commencement
To be appointed: see s 211(2).
Appointment
Sub-ss (4), (5): Appointment: 1 January 2009: see SI 2008/3149, art 2(c)(i).
Extent
This section does not extend to Scotland: see s 212(1).

38 Financial penalties: procedure

(1) If the Board proposes to impose a penalty on an approved regulator, it must give notice to the approved regulator—

- (a) stating that the Board proposes to impose a penalty and the amount of the penalty proposed to be imposed,
- (b) specifying the failure to which the proposed penalty relates,
- (c) specifying the other facts which, in the Board's opinion, justify the imposition of a penalty and the amount of the penalty, and
- (d) specifying the time (not being earlier than the end of the period of 21 days beginning with the day on which the notice is published under subsection (8)) before which representations with respect to the proposed penalty may be made.

(2) Before imposing a penalty on an approved regulator, the Board must consider any representations which are duly made.

(3) Where the Board proposes to vary the amount of a proposed penalty stated in a notice under subsection (1)(a), the Board must give notice to the approved regulator—

- (a) setting out the proposed variation and the reasons for it, and
- (b) specifying the time (not being earlier than the end of the period of 21 days beginning with the day on which the notice is published under subsection (8)) before which representations with respect to the proposed variation may be made.

(4) Before varying the proposal, the Board must consider any representations which are duly made.

(5) As soon as practicable after imposing a penalty, the Board must give notice to the approved regulator—

- (a) stating that it has imposed a penalty on the approved regulator and its amount,
- (b) specifying the failure to which the penalty relates,
- (c) specifying the other facts which, in the Board's opinion, justify the imposition of the penalty and its amount, and
- (d) specifying a time (not being earlier than the end of the period of 3 months beginning with the day on which the notice is given to the approved regulator), before which the penalty is required to be paid.

(6) The approved regulator may, within the period of 21 days beginning with the day on which it is given the notice under subsection (5), make an application to the Board for it to specify different times by which different portions of the penalty are to be paid.

(7) If an application is made under subsection (6) in relation to a penalty, the penalty is not required to be paid until the application has been determined.

(8) The Board must publish any notice given under this section.

Initial Commencement
To be appointed: see s 211(2).
Extent
This section does not extend to Scotland: see s 212(1).

39 Appeals against financial penalties

(1) An approved regulator on whom a penalty is imposed may appeal to the court on one or more of the appeal grounds.

(2) The appeal grounds are—

- (a) that the imposition of the penalty was not within the power of the Board under section 37;
- (b) that any of the requirements of section 38 have not been complied with in relation to the imposition of the penalty and the interests of the approved regulator have been substantially prejudiced by the non-compliance;
- (c) that the amount of the penalty is unreasonable;
- (d) that it was unreasonable of the Board to require the penalty imposed or any portion of it to be paid by the time or times by which it was required to be paid.

(3) An appeal under subsection (1) must be made—

- (a) within the period of 3 months beginning with the day on which the notice under section 38(5) is given to the approved regulator in respect of the penalty, or
- (b) where the appeal relates to a decision of the Board on an application by the approved regulator under section 38(6), within the period of 3 months beginning with the day on which the approved regulator is notified of the decision.

(4) On any such appeal, where the court considers it appropriate to do so in all the circumstances of the case and is satisfied of one or more of the appeal grounds, the court may—

- (a) quash the penalty,
- (b) substitute a penalty of such lesser amount as the court considers appropriate, or
- (c) in the case of the appeal ground in subsection (2)(d), substitute for any time imposed by the Board a different time or times.

(5) Where the court substitutes a penalty of a lesser amount it may require the payment of interest on the substituted penalty at such rate, and from such time, as it considers just and equitable.

(6) Where the court specifies as a time by which the penalty, or a portion of the penalty, is to be paid a time before the determination of the appeal under this section, it may require the payment of interest on the penalty, or portion, from that time at such rate as it considers just and equitable.

(7) Except as provided by this section, the validity of a penalty is not to be questioned by any legal proceedings whatever.

(8) In this section "the court" means the High Court.

Initial Commencement

To be appointed: see s 211(2).

Extent

This section does not extend to Scotland: see s 212(1).

---

40 Recovery of financial penalties

(1) If the whole or any part of a penalty is not paid by the time by which it is required to be paid, the unpaid balance from time to time carries interest at the rate for the time being specified in section 17 of the Judgments Act 1838 (c 110).

(2) If an appeal is made under section 39 in relation to a penalty, the penalty is not required to be paid until the appeal has been determined or withdrawn.

(3) If the Board grants an application under subsection (6) of section 38 in relation to a penalty but any portion of the penalty is not paid by the time specified in relation to it by the Board under that subsection, the Board may where it considers it appropriate require so much of the penalty as has not already been paid to be paid immediately.

(4) Where a penalty, or any portion of it, has not been paid by the time when it is required to be paid and—

(a) no appeal relating to the penalty has been made under section 39 during the period within which such an appeal can be made, or
(b) an appeal has been made under that section and determined or withdrawn,

the Board may recover from the approved regulator, as a debt due to the Board, any of the penalty and any interest which has not been paid.

Initial Commencement
To be appointed: see s 211(2).
Extent
This section does not extend to Scotland: see s 212(1).

Intervention

41 Intervention directions

(1) The Board may give an approved regulator an intervention direction in relation to any of the approved regulator's regulatory functions if the Board is satisfied—

(a) that an act or omission of an approved regulator (or a series of such acts or omissions) has had, or is likely to have, an adverse impact on one or more of the regulatory objectives, and
(b) that it is appropriate to give the intervention direction in all the circumstances of the case (including in particular the impact of giving the direction on the other regulatory objectives).

(2) An intervention direction, in relation to a regulatory function of an approved regulator, is a direction—

(a) that the regulatory function is to be exercised by the Board or a person nominated by it, and
(b) that the approved regulator must comply with any instructions of the Board or its nominee in relation to the exercise of the function.

(3) The Board may not determine that it is appropriate to give an intervention direction unless it is satisfied that the matter cannot be adequately addressed by the Board exercising the powers available to it under sections 31 to 40.

(4) Part 1 of Schedule 8 makes provision about the procedure which must be complied with before an intervention direction is given and the manner in which such a direction is to be given.

(5) The Board must make rules as to the persons it may nominate for the purposes of subsection (2)(a).

Initial Commencement
To be appointed: see s 211(2).
Appointment
Sub-ss (4), (5): Appointment: 1 January 2009: see SI 2008/3149, art 2(c)(i).
Extent
This section does not extend to Scotland: see s 212(1).

---

42 Intervention directions: further provision

(1) This section applies where an intervention direction has effect in respect of a function of an approved regulator ("the relevant function").

(2) The approved regulator must give the specified person all such assistance, in connection with the proposed exercise of the relevant function by the specified person in pursuance of the direction, as the approved regulator is reasonably able to give.

(3) On an application by the specified person (or a person appointed by the specified person to act on its behalf) a judge of the High Court, Circuit judge or justice of the peace may issue a warrant authorising that person to—

(a) enter and search the premises of the approved regulator, and
(b) take possession of any written or electronic records found on the premises.

(4) The person so authorised may, for the purpose of the exercise by the specified person of the relevant function, take copies of written or electronic records found on a search carried out by virtue of the warrant.

(5) The judge or justice of the peace may not issue the warrant unless satisfied that its issue is necessary or desirable for the exercise by the specified person of the relevant function.

(6) The Lord Chancellor must make regulations—

(a) specifying further matters which a judge or justice of the peace must be satisfied of, or matters which a judge or justice of the peace must have regard to, before issuing a warrant, and
(b) regulating the exercise of a power conferred by a warrant issued under subsection (3) or by subsection (4) (whether by restricting the circumstances in which a power may be exercised, by specifying conditions to be complied with in the exercise of a power, or otherwise).

(7) Regulations under subsection (6)(b) must in particular make provision as to the circumstances in which written or electronic records of which a person has taken possession by virtue of a warrant issued under subsection (3) may be copied or must be returned.

(8) But the Lord Chancellor may not make regulations under subsection (6) unless—

(a) they are made in accordance with a recommendation made by the Board, or
(b) the Lord Chancellor has consulted the Board about the making of the regulations.

(9) In this section "the specified person" means the Board or, where a person is nominated by it as mentioned in section 41(2), that person.

(10) The Board must make rules as to the persons a specified person may appoint for the purposes of subsection (3).

Initial Commencement
To be appointed: see s 211(2).
Appointment
Sub-ss (6)–(10): Appointment: 1 January 2009: see SI 2008/3149, art 2(c)(i).
Extent
This section does not extend to Scotland: see s 212(1).

---

43 Intervention directions: enforcement

(1) If at any time it appears to the Board that an approved regulator has failed to comply with an obligation imposed on it by, or by virtue of, an intervention direction or section 42(2), the Board may make an application to the High Court under this section.

(2) If, on an application under subsection (1), the High Court decides that the approved regulator has failed to comply with the obligation in question, it may order the approved regulator to take such steps as the High Court directs for securing that the obligation is complied with.

(3) This section is without prejudice to any other powers conferred on the Board by this Part.

Initial Commencement
To be appointed: see s 211(2).
Extent
This section does not extend to Scotland: see s 212(1).

---

44 Revocation of intervention directions

(1) An intervention direction has effect until such time as it is revoked by the Board (whether on the application of the approved regulator or otherwise).

(2) Part 2 of Schedule 8 makes provision about the procedure which must be complied with before an intervention direction is revoked and the manner in which notice of the revocation is to be given.

Initial Commencement
To be appointed: see s 211(2).
Appointment
Sub-s (2): Appointment: 1 January 2009: see SI 2008/3149, art 2(c)(i).
Extent
This section does not extend to Scotland: see s 212(1).

Cancellation of approval

45 Cancellation of designation as approved regulator

(1) The Lord Chancellor may by order cancel a body's designation as an approved regulator—

(a) in relation to all the reserved legal activities in relation to which it is an approved regulator, or
(b) in relation to one or more, but not all, of those reserved legal activities,

with effect from a date specified in the order.

(2) But the Lord Chancellor may only make an order under subsection (1) in accordance with a recommendation made by the Board under subsection (3) or (5).

(3) The Board must recommend that an order is made cancelling a body's designation as an approved regulator in relation to one or more reserved legal activities, if—

(a) the body applies to the Board for such a recommendation to be made,
(b) the application is made in such form and manner as may be prescribed by rules made by the Board, and is accompanied by the prescribed fee, and
(c) the body publishes a notice giving details of the application in accordance with such requirements as may be specified in rules made by the Board.

(4) In this section "the prescribed fee", in relation to an application, means the fee specified in, or determined in accordance with, rules made by the Board, with the consent of the Lord Chancellor.

(5) The Board may recommend that an order is made cancelling a body's designation as an approved regulator in relation to one or more reserved legal activities if it is satisfied—

(a) that an act or omission of an approved regulator (or a series of such acts or omissions) has had, or is likely to have, an adverse impact on one or more of the regulatory objectives, and
(b) that it is appropriate to cancel the body's designation in relation to the activity or activities in question in all the circumstances of the case (including in particular the impact of cancelling the designation on the other regulatory objectives).

(6) The Board may not determine that it is appropriate to cancel a body's designation in relation to an activity or activities unless it is satisfied that the matter cannot be adequately addressed by the Board exercising the powers available to it under sections 31 to 43.

(7) Schedule 9 makes further provision about the making of recommendations under subsection (5).

(8) If the Lord Chancellor decides not to make an order in response to a recommendation made under subsection (3) or (5), the Lord Chancellor must give the Board notice of the decision and the reasons for it.

(9) The Lord Chancellor must publish a notice given under subsection (8).

(10) The Board may not make a recommendation under subsection (5) in respect of a body's designation as an approved regulator in relation to a reserved legal activity at any time when, by virtue of Part 2 of Schedule 5 (protection of rights during a transitional period), any person is being treated as authorised by the body to carry on that activity.

Initial Commencement
To be appointed: see s 211(2).
Appointment
Sub-ss (3)(b), (c), (4), (7): Appointment: 1 January 2009: see SI 2008/3149, art 2(c)(i).
Extent
This section does not extend to Scotland: see s 212(1).

---

46 Cancellation of designation: further provision

(1) This section applies where a body ("the former regulator") has its designation in relation to one or more reserved legal activities cancelled by an order under section 45.

(2) The Lord Chancellor may by order make—

(a) such modifications of provisions made by or under any enactment (including this Act or any enactment passed after this Act), prerogative instrument or other instrument or document, and
(b) such transitional or consequential provision,

as the Lord Chancellor considers necessary or expedient in consequence of the cancellation.

(3) The Lord Chancellor may, by order, make transfer arrangements.

(4) "Transfer arrangements" are arrangements in accordance with which each person authorised by the former regulator who consents to the arrangements is, from the time the cancellation takes effect, treated as being authorised to carry on each protected activity by either—

(a) a relevant approved regulator, in relation to the protected activity, who consents to the transfer arrangements, or
(b) the Board acting in its capacity as a relevant approved regulator in relation to the protected activity by virtue of an order made under section 62.

(5) The transfer arrangements—

(a) must make such provision as is necessary to ensure that, where a person is treated under those arrangements as being authorised to carry on a protected activity by the new regulator, that person is subject to the regulatory arrangements of the new regulator;
(b) may make provision requiring amounts held by the former regulator which represent amounts paid to it by way of practising fees by the persons to whom the transfer arrangements apply (or a part of the amounts so held) to be paid to the new regulator and treated as if they were amounts paid by those persons by way of practising fees to the new regulator.

(6) Subsection (5)(a) is subject to any transitional provision which may be made by the transfer arrangements, including provision modifying the regulatory arrangements of the new regulator as they apply to persons to whom the transfer arrangements apply.

(7) The Lord Chancellor may make an order under this section only if—

(a) the Board has made a recommendation in accordance with section 47, and
(b) the order is in the same form as, or in a form which is not materially different from, the draft order annexed to that recommendation.

(8) For the purposes of this section—

(a) a person is "authorised by the former regulator" if immediately before the time the cancellation takes effect the person is authorised by the former regulator (other than by virtue of a licence under Part 5) to carry on an activity which is a reserved legal activity to which the cancellation relates, and
(b) in relation to that person—
   (i) the activity which that person is authorised to carry on as mentioned in paragraph (a) is a "protected activity", and
   (ii) "the new regulator" means the approved regulator within paragraph (a) or (b) of subsection (4).

(9) In this section "practising fee", in relation to an approved regulator, means a fee payable by a person under the approved regulator's regulatory arrangements in circumstances where the payment of the fee is a condition which must be satisfied for that person to be authorised by the approved regulator to carry on one or more activities which are reserved legal activities.

(10) But for the purposes of this section "practising fee" does not include a fee payable by a licensed body to its licensing authority under licensing rules.

Initial Commencement
To be appointed: see s 211(2).
Extent
This section does not extend to Scotland: see s 212(1).

---

47 The Board's power to recommend orders made under section 46

(1) The Board may recommend to the Lord Chancellor that the Lord Chancellor make an order under section 46 in the form of a draft order prepared by the Board and annexed to the recommendation.

(2) Before making a recommendation under this section, the Board must publish a draft of—

- (a) the proposed recommendation, and
- (b) the proposed draft order.

(3) The draft must be accompanied by a notice which states that representations about the proposals may be made to the Board within a specified period.

(4) Before making the recommendation, the Board must have regard to any representations duly made.

(5) If the draft order to be annexed to the recommendation differs from the draft published under subsection (2)(b) in a way which in the opinion of the Board is material, the Board must, before making the recommendation, publish the draft order along with a statement detailing the changes made and the reasons for those changes.

Initial Commencement
To be appointed: see s 211(2).
Extent
This section does not extend to Scotland: see s 212(1).

---

48 Cancellation of designation: powers of entry etc

(1) This section applies where a body ("the former regulator") has its designation in relation to one or more reserved legal activities cancelled by an order under section 45.

(2) The Board may request the former regulator to provide assistance to the new regulator and the Board, for the purpose of continuing regulation.

(3) On an application by a person appointed by the Board to act on its behalf, a judge of the High Court, Circuit judge or justice of the peace may issue a warrant authorising that person to—

- (a) enter and search the premises of the former regulator, and
- (b) take possession of any written or electronic records found on the premises.

(4) A person so authorised may, for the purpose of continuing regulation, take copies of written or electronic records found on a search carried out by virtue of the warrant.

(5) The judge or justice of the peace may not issue the warrant unless satisfied that its issue is necessary or desirable for the purpose of continuing regulation.

(6) The Lord Chancellor must make regulations—

- (a) specifying further matters which a judge or justice of the peace must be satisfied of, or matters which a judge or justice of the peace must have regard to, before issuing a warrant, and

(b) regulating the exercise of a power conferred by a warrant issued under subsection (3) or by subsection (4) (whether by restricting the circumstances in which a power may be exercised, by specifying conditions to be complied with in the exercise of a power, or otherwise).

(7) Regulations under subsection (6)(b) must in particular make provision as to circumstances in which written or electronic records of which a person has taken possession by virtue of a warrant issued under subsection (3) may be copied or must be returned.

(8) But the Lord Chancellor may not make regulations under subsection (6) unless—

(a) they are made in accordance with a recommendation made by the Board, or
(b) the Lord Chancellor has consulted the Board about the making of the regulations.

(9) The Board must make rules as to the persons it may appoint for the purposes of subsection (3).

(10) For the purposes of this section—

"authorised by the former regulator", "protected activity" and "new regulator" have the same meaning as for the purposes of section 46;
"the purpose of continuing regulation" means the purpose of enabling persons authorised by the former regulator to continue to be authorised and regulated in relation to the protected activity.

Initial Commencement
To be appointed: see s 211(2).
Appointment
Sub-ss (6)–(9): Appointment: 1 January 2009: see SI 2008/3149, art 2(c)(i).
Extent
This section does not extend to Scotland: see s 212(1).

Policy statements

49 The Board's policy statements

(1) The Board must prepare and issue a statement of policy with respect to the exercise of its functions under—

(a) section 31 (performance targets and monitoring);
(b) section 32 (directions);
(c) section 35 (public censure);
(d) section 37 (financial penalties);
(e) section 41 (intervention directions);
(f) section 45 (cancellation of designation as approved regulator);
(g) section 76 (cancellation of designation as licensing authority by order).

(2) The Board may prepare and issue a statement of policy with respect to any other matter.

(3) In preparing a statement of policy, the Board must have regard to the principle that its principal role is the oversight of approved regulators.

(4) The statement of policy prepared under subsection (1) must—

(a) take account of the desirability of resolving informally matters which arise between the Board and an approved regulator, and
(b) specify how, in exercising the functions mentioned in that subsection, the Board will comply with the requirements of section 3(3) (regulatory activities to be proportionate, consistent and targeted only at cases in which action is needed, etc),

and, in preparing that statement, the Board must have regard to the principle that the Board should not exercise any of those functions by reason of an act or omission of an approved regulator unless the act or omission was unreasonable.

(5) The Board's policy in determining what the amount of a penalty under section 37 should be must include having regard to—

(a) the seriousness of the failure in question, and
(b) the extent to which it was deliberate or reckless.

(6) The Board may at any time alter or replace any statement issued under this section.

(7) If a statement is altered or replaced, the Board must issue the altered or replacement statement.

(8) In exercising or deciding whether to exercise any of its functions, the Board must have regard to any relevant policy statement published under this section.

(9) The Board must publish a statement issued under this section.

(10) The Board may make a reasonable charge for providing a person with a copy of a statement.

Initial Commencement
To be appointed: see s 211(2).
Appointment
Appointment: 1 January 2009: see SI 2008/3149, art 2(c)(i).
Extent
This section does not extend to Scotland: see s 212(1).

---

50 Policy statements: procedure

(1) Before issuing a statement under section 49, the Board must publish a draft of the proposed statement.

(2) The draft must be accompanied by a notice which states that representations about the proposals may be made to the Board within a specified period.

(3) Before issuing the statement, the Board must have regard to any representations duly made.

(4) If the statement differs from the draft published under subsection (1) in a way which is, in the opinion of the Board, material, the Board must publish details of the differences.

(5) The Board may make a reasonable charge for providing a person with a copy of a draft published under subsection (1).

Initial Commencement
To be appointed: see s 211(2).
Appointment
Appointment: 1 January 2009: see SI 2008/3149, art 2(c)(i).
Extent
This section does not extend to Scotland: see s 212(1).

Practising fees

51 Control of practising fees charged by approved regulators

(1) In this section "practising fee", in relation to an approved regulator, means a fee payable by a person under the approved regulator's regulatory arrangements in circumstances where the payment of the fee is a condition which must be satisfied for that person to be authorised by the approved regulator to carry on one or more activities which are reserved legal activities.

(2) An approved regulator may only apply amounts raised by practising fees for one or more of the permitted purposes.

(3) The Board must make rules specifying the permitted purposes.

(4) Those rules must, in particular, provide that the following are permitted purposes—

(a) the regulation, accreditation, education and training of relevant authorised persons and those wishing to become such persons, including—
(i) the maintaining and raising of their professional standards, and

(ii) the giving of practical support, and advice about practice management, in relation to practices carried on by such persons;

(b) the payment of a levy imposed on the approved regulator under section 173;

(c) the participation by the approved regulator in law reform and the legislative process;

(d) the provision by relevant authorised persons, and those wishing to become relevant authorised persons, of reserved legal services, immigration advice or immigration services to the public free of charge;

(e) the promotion of the protection by law of human rights and fundamental freedoms;

(f) the promotion of relations between the approved regulator and relevant national or international bodies, governments or the legal professions of other jurisdictions.

(5) A practising fee is payable under the regulatory arrangements of an approved regulator only if the Board has approved the level of the fee.

(6) The Board must make rules containing provision—

(a) about the form and manner in which applications for approval for the purposes of subsection (5) must be made and the material which must accompany such applications;

(b) requiring applicants to have consulted such persons as may be prescribed by the rules in such manner as may be so prescribed before such an application is made;

(c) about the procedures and criteria that will be applied by the Board when determining whether to approve the level of a fee for the purposes of subsection (5).

(7) Rules under subsection (6)(c) must, in particular, contain—

(a) provision requiring the Board, before it determines an application for approval of the level of a fee, to consult such persons as it considers appropriate about the impact of the proposed fee on persons providing non-commercial legal services;

(b) provision about the time limit for the determining of an application.

(8) In this section "relevant authorised persons", in relation to an approved regulator, means persons who are authorised by the approved regulator to carry on activities which are reserved legal activities.

Initial Commencement

To be appointed: see s 211(2).

Appointment

Sub-ss (1), (3), (4), (6)–(8): Appointment: 1 January 2009: see SI 2008/3149, art 2(c)(i).

Extent

This section does not extend to Scotland: see s 212(1).

Regulatory conflict

52 Regulatory conflict with approved regulators

(1) The regulatory arrangements of an approved regulator must make such provision as is reasonably practicable to prevent regulatory conflicts.

(2) For the purposes of this section and section 53, a regulatory conflict is a conflict between—

(a) a requirement of the approved regulator's regulatory arrangements, and

(b) a requirement of the regulatory arrangements of another approved regulator.

(3) Subsection (4) applies where a body is authorised by an approved regulator ("the entity regulator") to carry on an activity which is a reserved legal activity.

(4) If a conflict arises between—

(a) a requirement of the regulatory arrangements of the entity regulator, in relation to the body authorised by the entity regulator or an employee or manager of the body ("an entity requirement"), and

(b) a requirement of the regulatory arrangements of another approved regulator in relation to an employee or manager of the body who is authorised by it to carry on a reserved legal activity ("an individual requirement"),

the entity requirement prevails over the individual requirement.

Initial Commencement
To be appointed: see s 211(2).
Extent
This section does not extend to Scotland: see s 212(1).

53 Modification of provision made about regulatory conflict

(1) An approved regulator ("the applicant regulator") may make an application under this section if it considers that the regulatory arrangements of another approved regulator ("the conflicting regulator") do not make appropriate provision to prevent a regulatory conflict with the applicant regulator.

(2) An application under this section is an application made to the Board for the Board to exercise its powers under section 32 to direct the conflicting regulator—

- (a) to take steps to modify, in such manner as may be specified in the direction, the provision made by its regulatory arrangements to prevent a regulatory conflict with the applicant regulator, or
- (b) if its regulatory arrangements do not make any such provision, to make such provision as may be specified in the direction to prevent such a conflict.

(3) An approved regulator must consider any request made by an affected person—

- (a) for the approved regulator to reconsider the provision made by its regulatory arrangements to prevent a regulatory conflict with another approved regulator, or
- (b) for the approved regulator to make an application under this section.

(4) An "affected person", in relation to an approved regulator, means—

- (a) a person authorised by the approved regulator to carry on a reserved legal activity;
- (b) an employee or manager of such a person.

(5) Where an application is made under this section, the Board—

- (a) must give the applicant regulator and the conflicting regulator an opportunity to make representations, and
- (b) may consult any persons it considers appropriate.

(6) The Board must decide whether or not to give a warning notice in response to the application.

(7) The Board must make that decision before the end of the period of 6 months beginning with the day on which the application is received by it.

(8) The Board must give notice of its decision, and the reasons for it, to the applicant regulator and the conflicting regulator.

(9) For the purposes of this section "warning notice" means a notice given under paragraph 2(1) of Schedule 7 (warning of proposed direction under section 32).

Initial Commencement
To be appointed: see s 211(2).
Extent
This section does not extend to Scotland: see s 212(1).

54 Regulatory conflict with other regulatory regimes

(1) The regulatory arrangements of an approved regulator must make such provision as is reasonably practicable and, in all the circumstances, appropriate—

- (a) to prevent external regulatory conflicts,
- (b) to provide for the resolution of any external regulatory conflicts which arise, and
- (c) to prevent unnecessary duplication of regulatory provisions made by an external regulatory body.

(2) For the purposes of this section, an external regulatory conflict is a conflict between—

(a) a requirement of the regulatory arrangements of the approved regulator, and
(b) a requirement of any regulatory provision made by an external regulatory body.

(3) For this purpose "external regulatory body" means a person (other than an approved regulator) who exercises regulatory functions in relation to a particular description of persons with a view to ensuring compliance with rules (whether statutory or non-statutory) by those persons.

(4) Regulatory arrangements made for the purposes of subsection (1)(b) may, with the consent of the Board, provide for the Board to exercise functions in connection with the resolution of conflicts.

Initial Commencement
To be appointed: see s 211(2).
Extent
This section does not extend to Scotland: see s 212(1).

Information

55 Provision of information to the Board

(1) The Board may, by notice, require an approved regulator—

(a) to provide any information, or information of a description, specified in the notice, or
(b) to produce documents, or documents of a description, specified in the notice.

(2) A notice under subsection (1)—

(a) may specify the manner and form in which any information is to be provided;
(b) must specify the period within which any information is to be provided or document is to be produced;
(c) may require any information to be provided, or document to be produced, to the Board or to a person specified in the notice.

(3) The Board may, by notice, require a person representing the approved regulator to attend at a time and place specified in the notice to provide an explanation of any information provided or document produced under this section.

(4) The Board may pay to any person such reasonable costs as may be incurred by that person in connection with—

(a) the provision of any information, or the production of any document, by that person pursuant to a notice under subsection (1), or
(b) that person's compliance with a requirement imposed under subsection (3).

(5) The Board, or a person specified under subsection (2)(c), may take copies of or extracts from a document produced pursuant to a notice under subsection (1).

(6) For the purposes of this section and section 56, references to an approved regulator include a body which was, but is no longer, an approved regulator.

Initial Commencement
To be appointed: see s 211(2).
Extent
This section does not extend to Scotland: see s 212(1).

---

56 Enforcement of notices under section 55

(1) Where an approved regulator is unable to comply with a notice given to it under section 55(1), it must give the Board a notice to that effect stating the reasons why it cannot comply.

(2) If an approved regulator refuses, or otherwise fails, to comply with a notice under section 55(1), the Board may apply to the High Court for an order requiring the approved regulator to comply with the notice or with such directions for the like purpose as may be contained in the order.

(3) This section applies in relation to a person to whom a notice is given under section 55(3) as it applies in relation to an approved regulator to whom a notice is given under section 55(1).

Initial Commencement
To be appointed: see s 211(2).
Extent
This section does not extend to Scotland: see s 212(1).

Competition

57 Reports by the OFT

(1) If the OFT is of the opinion that the regulatory arrangements of an approved regulator (or any part of them) prevent, restrict or distort competition within the market for reserved legal services to any significant extent, or are likely to do so, the OFT may prepare a report to that effect.

(2) A report under subsection (1)—

- (a) must state what, in the OFT's opinion, is the effect, or likely effect, on competition of the regulatory arrangements or part of them to which the report relates, and
- (b) may contain recommendations as to the action which the Board should take for the purpose of ensuring that the regulatory arrangements of the approved regulator do not prevent, restrict or distort competition.

(3) Where the OFT makes a report under subsection (1), it must—

- (a) give a copy of the report to the Board, the Consumer Panel and the approved regulator, and
- (b) publish the report.

(4) Before publishing a report under subsection (3)(b), the OFT must, so far as practicable, exclude any matter which relates to the private affairs of a particular individual the publication of which, in the opinion of the OFT, would or might seriously and prejudicially affect the interests of that individual.

(5) The OFT may exercise any of the powers conferred on it by section 174(3) to (5) of the Enterprise Act 2002 (c 40) (investigation powers) for the purpose of assisting it in exercising its functions under this section.

(6) For the purposes of the law of defamation, absolute privilege attaches to any report of the OFT under this section.

Initial Commencement
To be appointed: see s 211(2).
Extent
This section does not extend to Scotland: see s 212(1).

---

58 The Board's response to OFT report

(1) This section applies where a report is made by the OFT under section 57 in respect of an approved regulator.

(2) The Board must allow the approved regulator a period of 28 days beginning with the day on which the copy of the report is given to the approved regulator under section 57, or such longer period as the Board may specify in a particular case, to make representations to the Board about the OFT's report.

(3) The Consumer Panel may give the Board such advice as the Consumer Panel thinks fit regarding the OFT's report.

(4) Having considered any representations made under subsection (2) and any advice given under subsection (3), the Board must notify the OFT of the action (if any) it proposes to take in response to the report.

Initial Commencement
To be appointed: see s 211(2).
Extent
This section does not extend to Scotland: see s 212(1).

---

59 Referral of report by the Lord Chancellor to the Competition Commission

(1) This section applies where the OFT is satisfied that the Board has failed to give full and proper consideration to a report made by the OFT, in respect of an approved regulator, under section 57.

(2) The OFT may give a copy of its report to the Lord Chancellor.

(3) The OFT must notify the Board and the approved regulator if it gives a copy of its report to the Lord Chancellor.

(4) On receiving a report under subsection (2), the Lord Chancellor must—

- (a) give the Competition Commission a copy of the report, and
- (b) seek its advice on what action (if any) should be taken by the Lord Chancellor under section 61.

Initial Commencement
To be appointed: see s 211(2).
Extent
This section does not extend to Scotland: see s 212(1).

---

60 Duties of the Competition Commission

(1) Where the Lord Chancellor seeks the advice of the Competition Commission under section 59, the Commission must investigate the matter.

(2) The Commission must then make its own report on the matter unless it considers that, as a result of any change of circumstances, no useful purpose would be served by a report.

(3) If the Commission decides in accordance with subsection (2) not to make a report, it must make a statement setting out the change of circumstances which resulted in that decision.

(4) The Commission must comply with subsection (2) or (3) within the period of 3 months beginning with the day on which it receives a copy of the OFT's report under section 59(4)(a).

(5) A report made under this section must state the Commission's conclusion as to whether any of the matters which is the subject of the report has or is likely to have the effect of preventing, restricting or distorting competition within the market for reserved legal services to a significant extent.

(6) A report under this section stating the Commission's conclusion that there is, or is likely to be, such an effect must also—

- (a) state whether or not the Commission considers that that effect is justified, and
- (b) if it states that the Commission considers that it is not justified, state its conclusion as to what action, if any, ought to be taken by the Board.

(7) When determining under subsection (6)(b) any action to be taken by the Board, the Commission must ensure—

- (a) that the action stated is action which the Board has power to take, and
- (b) so far as reasonably possible, that the action stated is compatible with the functions conferred, and obligations imposed, on the Board by or under this Act.

(8) A report under this section must contain such an account of the Commission's reasons for its conclusions as is expedient, in the opinion of the Commission, for facilitating proper understanding of them.

(9) Sections 109 to 115 of the Enterprise Act 2002 (c 40) (investigation powers) apply in relation to an investigation under this section as they apply in relation to an investigation made on a reference made to the Commission under Part 3 of that Act (mergers), but as if—

(a) in section 110(4) of that Act, the reference to the publication of the report of the Commission on the reference concerned were a reference to the Commission making a report under subsection (2) or a statement under subsection (3), and
(b) in section 111(5)(b)(ii) of that Act the day referred to were the day on which the Commission makes that report or statement.

(10) If the Commission makes a report or a statement under this section it must—

(a) give a copy to the Lord Chancellor, the Board, the Consumer Panel and the approved regulator to which the OFT's report relates, and
(b) publish the report or statement.

Initial Commencement
To be appointed: see s 211(2).
Extent
This section does not extend to Scotland: see s 212(1).

---

61 Lord Chancellor's power to give directions

(1) The Lord Chancellor may direct the Board to take such action as the Lord Chancellor considers appropriate in connection with any matter raised in a report made by the OFT under section 57.

(2) Before giving a direction under subsection (1), the Lord Chancellor must consider any report from the Competition Commission under section 60 on that matter.

(3) When exercising the power to give a direction under subsection (1), the Lord Chancellor must ensure—

(a) that the action stated is action which the Board has power to take, and
(b) so far as reasonably possible, that the action stated in any direction is compatible with the functions conferred, and obligations imposed, on the Board by or under this Act.

(4) The Lord Chancellor must publish a direction given under this section.

Initial Commencement
To be appointed: see s 211(2).
Extent
This section does not extend to Scotland: see s 212(1).

The Board as approved regulator

62 The Board as an approved regulator

(1) The Lord Chancellor may by order—

(a) designate the Board as an approved regulator in relation to one or more reserved legal activities;
(b) modify the functions of the Board, and make such other provision relating to those functions as the Lord Chancellor considers necessary or expedient, with a view to enabling the Board to discharge its functions as an approved regulator effectively and efficiently;
(c) cancel the Board's designation as an approved regulator in relation to one or more reserved legal activities.

(2) But the Lord Chancellor may make an order under subsection (1) only if—

(a) the Board has made a recommendation in accordance with section 66, and
(b) the order is in the same form as, or in a form which is not materially different from, the draft order annexed to that recommendation.

(3) If the Lord Chancellor decides not to make an order pursuant to a recommendation made under section 66, the Lord Chancellor must—

(a) give the Board a notice stating the reasons for that decision, and
(b) publish the notice.

(4) In discharging its functions as an approved regulator the Board must take such steps as are necessary to ensure an appropriate financial and organisational separation between the activities of the Board that relate to the carrying out of those functions and the other activities of the Board.

(5) An order under this section may make such modifications of provision made by or under any enactment (including this Act or any Act passed after this Act) as the Lord Chancellor considers necessary or expedient.

Initial Commencement
To be appointed: see s 211(2).
Extent
This section does not extend to Scotland: see s 212(1).

---

63 The Board's designation under section 62(1)(a)

(1) This section applies in relation to an order under section 62(1)(a) (an order designating the Board as an approved regulator).

(2) Subject to subsection (3), the order may designate the Board as an approved regulator in relation to a reserved legal activity only where—

(a) a body's designation as an approved regulator in relation to the activity is cancelled under section 45, or
(b) the activity becomes a reserved legal activity by virtue of an order under section 24.

(3) Subsection (2) does not prevent the order having effect in advance of an event within paragraph (a) or (b) of that subsection for the purpose of enabling the Board to authorise persons to carry on activities which constitute the reserved legal activity in question with effect from the occurrence of the event.

(4) The order must ensure that the Board, acting as an approved regulator, may make regulatory arrangements or modify its regulatory arrangements only with the approval of the Board (acting otherwise than in its capacity as an approved regulator or as a licensing authority under Part 5).

Initial Commencement
To be appointed: see s 211(2).
Extent
This section does not extend to Scotland: see s 212(1).

---

64 Modification of the Board's functions under section 62(1)(b)

(1) This section applies in relation to an order under section 62(1)(b) (an order modifying the functions of the Board).

(2) The order may include (among other things) provision conferring on the Board powers to do any of the following—

(a) to authorise (otherwise than by the grant of a licence under Part 5) persons or any category of persons (whether corporate or unincorporate) to carry on one or more activities which are reserved legal activities in relation to which the Board is designated as an approved regulator;
(b) to make qualification regulations;
(c) to make provision as to the educational, training and other requirements to be met by regulated persons who are not relevant authorised persons;

(d) to make practice rules and conduct rules;
(e) to make disciplinary arrangements in relation to regulated persons (including discipline rules);
(f) to make rules requiring the payment of fees specified in or determined in accordance with the rules;
(g) to make indemnification arrangements;
(h) to make compensation arrangements;
(i) to make rules as to the treatment of money (including money held in trust) which is received, held or dealt with for clients, or other persons, by regulated persons, and as to the keeping by such persons of accounts in respect of such money;
(j) to take steps for the purpose of ascertaining whether or not the provisions of rules or regulations made, or any code or guidance issued, by the Board in its capacity as an approved regulator are being complied with, and to make rules requiring relevant authorised persons to produce documents and provide information for that purpose;
(k) to delegate any of the functions exercisable by the Board in its capacity as an approved regulator to such persons as it considers appropriate;
(l) to make regulations or rules providing for appeals to the High Court or another body against decisions made by the Board in its capacity as an approved regulator (including regulations or rules providing for a decision on such an appeal to be final and for orders as to payment of costs).

(3) The order may—

(a) provide for any provision of Schedule 14 (licensing authority's powers of intervention)—
  (i) to apply in relation to the Board (in its capacity as an approved regulator) and regulated persons as it applies in relation to a licensing authority and licensed bodies (or managers or employees of such bodies), or
  (ii) to so apply with such modifications as are prescribed by the order, or
(b) make provision, in relation to the Board (in that capacity) and regulated persons, corresponding to any of the provisions made, in relation to licensing authorities and licensed bodies (or managers or employees of such bodies), by that Schedule.

(4) For the purposes of giving effect to indemnification arrangements and compensation arrangements, the order may authorise the Board to make rules—

(a) authorising or requiring the Board to establish and maintain a fund or funds;
(b) authorising or requiring the Board to take out and maintain insurance with authorised insurers;
(c) requiring relevant authorised persons or relevant authorised persons of any specific description to take out and maintain insurance with authorised insurers.

(5) In this section—

"authorised insurer" means a person within any of the following paragraphs—
  (a) a person who has permission under Part 4 of the Financial Services and Markets Act 2000 (c 8) to effect or carry out contracts of insurance of a relevant class;
  (b) an EEA firm (within the meaning of that Act) of the kind mentioned in paragraph 5(d) of Schedule 3 to that Act, which has permission under paragraph 15 of that Schedule (as a result of qualifying for authorisation under paragraph 12 of that Schedule) to effect or carry out contracts of a relevant class;
  (c) a person who does not fall within paragraph (a) or (b) and who may lawfully effect or carry out contracts of insurance of a relevant class in a member State other than the United Kingdom;

"regulated person" has the meaning given by section 21;

"relevant authorised person" means a person authorised by the Board (other than by the grant of a licence under Part 5) to carry on one or more activities which are reserved legal activities.

(6) For the purposes of this section—

(a) a contract of insurance is of a relevant class if it insures against a risk arising from accident, credit, legal expenses, general liability to third parties, sickness, suretyship or miscellaneous financial loss, and

(b) the definition of "authorised insurer" in subsection (5) must be read with section 22 of the Financial Services and Markets Act 2000, and any relevant order under that section, and with Schedule 2 to that Act.

Initial Commencement
To be appointed: see s 211(2).
Extent
This section does not extend to Scotland: see s 212(1).

---

65 Cancellation of the Board's designation under section 62(1)(c)

(1) This section applies in relation to an order under section 62(1)(c) (cancellation of Board's designation as an approved regulator).

(2) Where such an order is made, section 46 (other than subsection (4)(b)) and section 47 (transfer arrangements etc on cancellation of approved regulator's designation) apply in relation to the Board and relevant authorised persons as they apply to an approved regulator whose designation is cancelled under section 45 and persons authorised by that approved regulator to carry on activities which are reserved legal activities.

(3) In this section "relevant authorised persons" has the same meaning as in section 64.

Initial Commencement
To be appointed: see s 211(2).
Extent
This section does not extend to Scotland: see s 212(1).

---

66 The Board's power to recommend orders made under section 62

(1) The Board may recommend to the Lord Chancellor that the Lord Chancellor make an order under section 62 in the form of a draft order prepared by the Board and annexed to the recommendation.

(2) Before making a recommendation under this section, the Board must give each of the persons listed in subsection (3) a notice containing—

(a) a copy of the proposed recommendation,
(b) a copy of the proposed draft order, and
(c) a statement specifying a period within which representations may be made about the proposals.

(3) Those persons are—

(a) the Lord Chancellor,
(b) the OFT,
(c) the Consumer Panel,
(d) the Lord Chief Justice, and
(e) such other persons as the Board considers it reasonable to consult regarding the proposals.

(4) The Board must publish a notice given under subsection (2).

(5) Before making the recommendation, the Board must have regard to any representations duly made (whether by persons within subsection (3) or otherwise).

(6) If the draft order to be annexed to the recommendation differs from the draft contained in the notice under subsection (2) in a way which is, in the opinion of the Board, material, the Board must, before making the recommendation, publish the draft order along with a statement detailing the changes made and the reasons for those changes.

Initial Commencement
To be appointed: see s 211(2).
Extent

This section does not extend to Scotland: see s 212(1).

---

67 Effect of the Board's designation as an approved regulator

(1) The powers of the Board under sections 31 to 51 and 55 (regulatory powers in respect of approved regulators) are not exercisable by it in relation to the Board in its capacity as an approved regulator.

(2) In section 53 references to an approved regulator do not include the Board in its capacity as an approved regulator.

(3) Sections 57 to 61 (reports by OFT etc) do not apply in relation to the Board in its capacity as an approved regulator.

Initial Commencement
To be appointed: see s 211(2).
Extent
This section does not extend to Scotland: see s 212(1).

---

68 Regulatory conflict and the Board as approved regulator

(1) An approved regulator may make a request under subsection (4) if it considers that the regulatory arrangements of the Board (in its capacity as an approved regulator) do not make appropriate provision to prevent a conflict between—

(a) a requirement of those regulatory arrangements, and
(b) a requirement of the regulatory arrangements of the approved regulator.

(2) An affected person in relation to an approved regulator may request the approved regulator to exercise its powers under subsection (1).

(3) An affected person in relation to the Board may make a request under subsection (4) if the person considers that the regulatory arrangements of the Board (in its capacity as an approved regulator) do not make appropriate provision to prevent a conflict between—

(a) a requirement of those regulatory arrangements, and
(b) a requirement of the regulatory arrangements of an approved regulator.

(4) The request is a request made to the Board (in its capacity as an approved regulator) that it reconsider the provision made by its regulatory arrangements to prevent a regulatory conflict with the conflicting regulator.

(5) An affected person in relation to the Board may make an application under subsection (6) if the person considers that the regulatory arrangements of an approved regulator do not make appropriate provision to prevent a conflict between—

(a) a requirement of those regulatory arrangements, and
(b) a requirement of the regulatory arrangements of the Board (in its capacity as an approved regulator).

(6) The application is an application to the Board for it to exercise its powers under section 32 to direct the approved regulator—

(a) to take steps to modify, in such manner as may be specified in the direction, the provision made by its regulatory arrangements to prevent a regulatory conflict with the Board (in its capacity as an approved regulator), or
(b) if its regulatory arrangements do not make any such provision, to make such provision as may be specified in the direction to prevent such a conflict.

(7) An affected person in relation to an approved regulator (other than the Board) may make a request under subsection (8) if the person considers that the regulatory arrangements of the approved regulator do not make appropriate provision to prevent a conflict between—

(a) a requirement of those regulatory arrangements, and
(b) a requirement of the regulatory arrangements of the Board (in its capacity as an approved regulator).

(8) The request is a request to the approved regulator that it reconsider the provision made by its regulatory arrangements to prevent a regulatory conflict with the Board.

(9) The Board (in its capacity as an approved regulator) and any other approved regulator must consider any request made to it under this section.

(10) Subsections (5) to (8) of section 53 apply in relation to an application under subsection (6) as they apply in relation to an application under that section, except that—

- (a) references to the applicant regulator are to be read as references to the person who made the application, and
- (b) references to the conflicting regulator are to be construed in accordance with this section.

(11) In this section—

"affected person" in relation to the Board or any other approved regulator, means—
- (a) any person authorised by the body to carry on a reserved legal activity, or
- (b) an employee or manager of such a person;

"conflicting regulator" means—
- (a) in a case within subsection (1), the approved regulator making the request, and
- (b) in a case within subsection (3) or (5), the approved regulator whose regulatory arrangements are considered to conflict with those of the Board.

Initial Commencement
To be appointed: see s 211(2).
Extent
This section does not extend to Scotland: see s 212(1).

Functions of approved regulators etc

69 Modification of the functions of approved regulators etc

(1) The Lord Chancellor may by order modify, or make other provision relating to, the functions of an approved regulator or any other body (other than the Board).

(2) The Lord Chancellor may make an order under subsection (1) only if—

- (a) the Board has made a recommendation under this section,
- (b) a draft order was annexed to the recommendation, and
- (c) the order is in the same form as, or a form not materially different from, that draft order.

(3) The Board may make a recommendation under this section only with a view to an order being made which enables the body to which it relates to do one or more of the following—

- (a) to become designated by an order under Part 2 of Schedule 4 as an approved regulator, or designated by an order under Part 1 of Schedule 10 as a licensing authority, in relation to one or more reserved legal activities;
- (b) to authorise persons or any category of persons (whether corporate or unincorporate) to carry on one or more activities which are reserved legal activities in relation to which the body is (at the time the authorisation has effect) designated as an approved regulator, or to make regulatory arrangements;
- (c) to carry out its role as an approved regulator (including its role, if any, as a licensing authority) more effectively or efficiently;
- (d) to become a qualifying regulator under Part 1 of Schedule 18;
- (e) if it is a designated qualifying regulator under section 86A of the Immigration and Asylum Act 1999 (c 33), to authorise persons to provide any additional advice or services the provision of which amounts to the provision of immigration advice or immigration services.

(4) Subsections (2) (other than paragraph (a)), (3) and (4) of section 64 apply in relation to an order under this section as they apply in relation to an order under section 62(1)(b) in relation to the Board.

(5) An order under this section also may make provision in relation to—

(a) the provision of immigration advice or immigration services, and
(b) persons authorised to provide such advice and services by the body to which the order relates,

corresponding to the provision which may be made by virtue of section 64(2) to (4) in relation to reserved legal activities and persons authorised to carry on those activities.

(6) An order under this section may modify provisions made by or under any enactment (including this Act or any Act passed after this Act), prerogative instrument or other instrument or document.

(7) Any provision made by an order under this section may be expressed to be conditional upon—

(a) the body to which the order relates being designated by an order under Part 2 of Schedule 4 as an approved regulator, or by an order under Part 1 of Schedule 10 as a licensing authority, in relation to one or more reserved legal activities specified in the proposed draft order, or
(b) the body to which the order relates becoming a designated qualifying regulator under section 86A of the Immigration and Asylum Act 1999 (c 33).

(8) The powers to make an order conferred by this section are without prejudice to any powers (statutory or non-statutory) which an approved regulator or other body may have apart from this section.

Initial Commencement
To be appointed: see s 211(2).
Appointment
Appointment: 7 March 2008: see SI 2008/222, art 2(c); for transitional modifications see art 4 thereof.
Extent
This section does not extend to Scotland: see s 212(1).

---

70 Procedural requirements relating to recommendations under section 69

(1) A recommendation may be made under section 69 only with the consent of the approved regulator or other body to which the recommendation relates.

(2) Before making a recommendation under that section, the Board must publish a draft of—

(a) the proposed recommendation, and
(b) the proposed draft order.

(3) The draft must be accompanied by a notice which states that representations about the proposals may be made to the Board within a specified period.

(4) Before making the recommendation, the Board must have regard to any representations duly made.

(5) If the draft order to be annexed to the recommendation differs from the draft published under subsection (2)(b) in a way which is, in the opinion of the Board, material, the Board must, before making the recommendation, publish the draft order along with a statement detailing the changes made and the reasons for those changes.

Initial Commencement
To be appointed: see s 211(2).
Appointment
Appointment: 7 March 2008: see SI 2008/222, art 2(c); for transitional modifications see art 5 thereof.
Extent
This section does not extend to Scotland: see s 212(1).

PART 5
ALTERNATIVE BUSINESS STRUCTURES

Introductory

71 Carrying on of activities by licensed bodies

(1) The provisions of this Part have effect for the purpose of regulating the carrying on of reserved legal activities and other activities by licensed bodies.

(2) In this Act "licensed body" means a body which holds a licence in force under this Part.

Initial Commencement
To be appointed: see s 211(2).
Extent
This section does not extend to Scotland: see s 212(1).

---

72 "Licensable body"

(1) A body ("B") is a licensable body if a non-authorised person—

(a) is a manager of B, or
(b) has an interest in B.

(2) A body ("B") is also a licensable body if—

(a) another body ("A") is a manager of B, or has an interest in B, and
(b) non-authorised persons are entitled to exercise, or control the exercise of, at least 10% of the voting rights in A.

(3) For the purposes of this Act, a person has an interest in a body if—

(a) the person holds shares in the body, or
(b) the person is entitled to exercise, or control the exercise of, voting rights in the body.

(4) A body may be licensable by virtue of both subsection (1) and subsection (2).

(5) For the purposes of this Act, a non-authorised person has an indirect interest in a licensable body if the body is licensable by virtue of subsection (2) and the non-authorised person is entitled to exercise, or control the exercise of, voting rights in A.

(6) In this Act "shares" means—

(a) in relation to a body with a share capital, allotted shares (within the meaning of the Companies Acts);
(b) in relation to a body with capital but no share capital, rights to share in the capital of the body;
(c) in relation to a body without capital, interests—
 (i) conferring any right to share in the profits, or liability to contribute to the losses, of the body, or
 (ii) giving rise to an obligation to contribute to the debts or expenses of the body in the event of a winding up;

and references to the holding of shares, or to a shareholding, are to be construed accordingly.

Initial Commencement
To be appointed: see s 211(2).
Extent
This section does not extend to Scotland: see s 212(1).

Licensing authorities

73 Licensing authorities and relevant licensing authorities

(1) In this Act "licensing authority" means—

(a) the Board, or
(b) an approved regulator which is designated as a licensing authority under Part 1 of Schedule 10 and whose licensing rules are approved for the purposes of this Act.

(2) For the purposes of this Act—

(a) the Board is a licensing authority in relation to all reserved legal activities, and
(b) an approved regulator within subsection (1)(b) is a licensing authority in relation to any reserved legal activity in relation to which the designation is made.

(3) The Board—

(a) may delegate any of its functions as a licensing authority to such persons as it considers appropriate;
(b) must take such steps as are necessary to ensure an appropriate financial and organisational separation between the activities of the Board that relate to the carrying out of its functions as a licensing authority and the other activities of the Board.

(4) In this Part "relevant licensing authority"—

(a) in relation to a licensed body, means the licensing authority by which the licensed body is authorised to carry on an activity which is a reserved legal activity;
(b) in relation to an applicant for a licence, means the licensing authority to which the application is made.

Initial Commencement
To be appointed: see s 211(2).
Appointment
Sub-s (1): Appointment (for certain purposes): 7 March 2008: see SI 2008/222, art 3.
Extent
This section does not extend to Scotland: see s 212(1).

---

74 Designation of approved regulator as licensing authority

Part 1 of Schedule 10 makes provision for approved regulators to be designated, by order, as licensing authorities in relation to one or more reserved legal activities.

Initial Commencement
To be appointed: see s 211(2).
Appointment
Appointment: 1 January 2009: see SI 2008/3149, art 2(d)(i).
Extent
This section does not extend to Scotland: see s 212(1).

---

75 Automatic cancellation of designation as licensing authority

(1) This section applies where a body is designated—

(a) as an approved regulator in relation to a reserved legal activity ("the activity"), and
(b) as a licensing authority in relation to the activity.

(2) If the Lord Chancellor makes an order under section 45 cancelling the body's designation as an approved regulator in relation to the activity, the body's designation as a licensing authority in relation to the activity is also cancelled.

(3) The cancellation takes effect at the same time as cancellation of the body's designation as an approved regulator.

Initial Commencement
To be appointed: see s 211(2).
Extent
This section does not extend to Scotland: see s 212(1).

---

76 Cancellation of designation as licensing authority by order

(1) The Lord Chancellor may by order cancel an approved regulator's designation as a licensing authority—

(a) in relation to all the reserved legal activities in relation to which it is designated, or
(b) in relation to one or more, but not all, of those reserved legal activities,

with effect from a date specified in the order.

(2) But the Lord Chancellor may only make an order under subsection (1) in accordance with a recommendation made by the Board under subsection (3) or (5).

(3) The Board must recommend that an order is made cancelling an approved regulator's designation as a licensing authority in relation to one or more reserved legal activities, if—

(a) the approved regulator applies to the Board for such a recommendation to be made,
(b) the application is made in such form and manner as may be prescribed by rules made by the Board, and is accompanied by the prescribed fee, and
(c) the approved regulator publishes a notice giving details of the application in accordance with such requirements as may be specified in rules made by the Board.

(4) In this section "the prescribed fee", in relation to an application, means the fee specified in or determined in accordance with rules made by the Board, with the consent of the Lord Chancellor.

(5) The Board may recommend that an order is made cancelling an approved regulator's designation as a licensing authority in relation to one or more reserved legal activities if it is satisfied—

(a) that an act or omission of the licensing authority (or a series of such acts or omissions) has had, or is likely to have, an adverse impact on one or more of the regulatory objectives, and
(b) that it is appropriate to cancel the approved regulator's designation in relation to the activity or activities in question in all the circumstances of the case (including in particular the impact of cancelling the designation on the other regulatory objectives).

(6) The Board may not determine that it is appropriate to cancel an approved regulator's designation as a licensing authority in relation to an activity or activities unless it is satisfied that the matter cannot be adequately addressed by the Board exercising the powers available to it under sections 31 to 43.

(7) Part 2 of Schedule 10 makes further provision about the making of recommendations under subsection (5).

(8) If the Lord Chancellor decides not to make an order in response to a recommendation made under subsection (3) or (5), the Lord Chancellor must give the Board notice of the decision and the reasons for it.

(9) The Lord Chancellor must publish a notice given under subsection (8).

Initial Commencement
To be appointed: see s 211(2).
Appointment
Sub-ss (3)(b), (c), (4), (7): Appointment: 1 January 2009: see SI 2008/3149, art 2(d)(i).
Extent
This section does not extend to Scotland: see s 212(1).

---

77 Cancellation of designation: further provision

(1) This section applies where an approved regulator ("the former authority") has its designation as a licensing authority in relation to one or more reserved legal activities cancelled—

(a) by virtue of section 75, or
(b) by an order under section 76.

(2) The Lord Chancellor may by order make—

(a) such modifications of provisions made by or under any enactment (including this Act or any enactment passed after this Act), prerogative instrument or other instrument or document, and
(b) such transitional or consequential provision,

as the Lord Chancellor considers necessary or expedient in consequence of the cancellation.

(3) The Lord Chancellor may, by order, make transfer arrangements.

(4) "Transfer arrangements" are arrangements in accordance with which each consenting licensed body is, from the time the cancellation takes effect, treated as being authorised to carry on each protected activity by virtue of a licence issued under this Part by a licensing authority, in relation to the protected activity, which consents to the transfer arrangements.

(5) "Consenting licensed body" means a licensed body authorised by the former authority which consents to the transfer arrangements.

(6) The transfer arrangements—

(a) must make such provision as is necessary to ensure that, where a licensed body is treated under those arrangements as being authorised to carry on a protected activity by the new authority, that licensed body is subject to the licensing rules of the new authority;
(b) may make provision requiring amounts held by the former authority which represent amounts paid to it by way of licensing fees by the consenting licensed bodies (or a part of the amounts so held) to be paid to the new authority and treated as if they were amounts paid by those licensed bodies by way of licensing fees to the new authority.

(7) Subsection (6)(a) is subject to any transitional provision which may be made by the transfer arrangements, including provision modifying the licensing rules of the new authority as they apply to the bodies to whom the transfer arrangements apply.

(8) The Lord Chancellor may make an order under this section only if—

(a) the Board has made a recommendation in accordance with section 78, and
(b) the order is in the same form as, or in a form which is not materially different from, the draft order annexed to that recommendation.

(9) For the purposes of this section—

(a) a licensed body is "authorised by the former authority" if immediately before the time the cancellation takes effect the body is, by virtue of a licence under this Part, authorised by the former authority to carry on an activity which is a reserved legal activity to which the cancellation relates, and
(b) in relation to that body—
    (i) the activity which the body is authorised to carry on as mentioned in paragraph (a) is a "protected activity", and
    (ii) "the new authority" means the licensing authority by which (in accordance with transfer arrangements under subsection (4)) the body is treated as authorised to carry on a protected activity.

(10) In this section "licensing fee", in relation to a licensing authority, means a fee payable by a licensed body under the authority's licensing rules made in accordance with paragraph 21 of Schedule 11.

Initial Commencement
To be appointed: see s 211(2).
Extent
This section does not extend to Scotland: see s 212(1).

---

78 The Board's power to recommend orders made under section 77

(1) The Board may recommend to the Lord Chancellor that the Lord Chancellor make an order under section 77 in the form of a draft order prepared by the Board and annexed to the recommendation.

(2) Before making a recommendation under this section, the Board must publish a draft of—

(a) the proposed recommendation, and
(b) the proposed draft order.

(3) The draft must be accompanied by a notice which states that representations about the proposals may be made to the Board within a specified period.

(4) Before making the recommendation, the Board must have regard to any representations duly made.

(5) If the draft order to be annexed to the recommendation differs from the draft published under subsection (2)(b) in a way which is, in the opinion of the Board, material, the Board must, before making the recommendation, publish the draft order along with a statement detailing the changes made and the reasons for those changes.

Initial Commencement
To be appointed: see s 211(2).
Extent
This section does not extend to Scotland: see s 212(1).

---

79 Cancellation of designation: powers of entry etc

(1) This section applies where an approved regulator ("the former authority") has its designation in relation to one or more reserved legal activities cancelled by by virtue of section 75 or an order under section 76.

(2) The Board may request the former authority to provide assistance to the new authority and the Board, for the purpose of continuing regulation.

(3) On an application by a person appointed by the Board to act on its behalf, a judge of the High Court, Circuit judge or justice of the peace may issue a warrant authorising that person to—

(a) enter and search the premises of the former authority, and
(b) take possession of any written or electronic records found on the premises.

(4) A person so authorised may, for the purpose of continuing regulation, take copies of written or electronic records found on a search carried out by virtue of the warrant.

(5) The judge or justice of the peace may not issue the warrant unless satisfied that its issue is necessary or desirable for the purpose of continuing regulation.

(6) The Lord Chancellor must make regulations—

(a) specifying further matters which a judge or justice of the peace must be satisfied of, or matters which a judge or justice of the peace must have regard to, before issuing a warrant, and
(b) regulating the exercise of a power conferred by a warrant issued under subsection (3) or by subsection (4) (whether by restricting the circumstances in which a power may be exercised, by specifying conditions to be complied with in the exercise of a power, or otherwise).

(7) Regulations under subsection (6)(b) must in particular make provision as to circumstances in which written or electronic records of which a person has taken possession by virtue of a warrant issued under subsection (3) may be copied or must be returned.

(8) But the Lord Chancellor may not make regulations under subsection (6) unless—

(a) they are made in accordance with a recommendation made by the Board, or
(b) the Lord Chancellor has consulted the Board about the making of the regulations.

(9) The Board must make rules as to the persons it may appoint for the purposes of subsection (3).

(10) For the purposes of this section—

"authorised by the former authority", "protected activity" and "new authority" have the same meaning as for the purposes of section 77;

"the purpose of continuing regulation" means the purpose of enabling bodies authorised by the former authority to continue to be authorised and regulated in relation to the protected activity.

Initial Commencement
To be appointed: see s 211(2).
Appointment
Sub-ss (6)–(10): Appointment: 1 January 2009: see SI 2008/3149, art 2(d)(i).
Extent
This section does not extend to Scotland: see s 212(1).

Appeals

80 Functions of appellate bodies

(1) The Lord Chancellor may by order—

(a) establish a body to hear and determine appeals from decisions, made by a person specified in the order in the person's capacity as a licensing authority, which are appealable under this Part or licensing rules made by the person;
(b) modify, or make any other provision relating to, the functions of a body within subsection (2) or any other body, for the purpose of enabling the body to hear and determine appeals from such decisions.

(2) The bodies mentioned in subsection (1)(b) are—

(a) the Solicitors Disciplinary Tribunal;
(b) the Discipline and Appeals Committee established by the Council of Licensed Conveyancers under section 25 of the Administration of Justice Act 1985 (c 61).

(3) The Lord Chancellor may make an order under subsection (1) only if—

(a) the Board has made a recommendation in accordance with section 81,
(b) a draft order was annexed to the recommendation, and
(c) the order is in the same form as, or not materially different from, that draft order.

(4) An order under this section may—

(a) make provision as to the payment of fees, and award of costs, in relation to such appeals;
(b) modify provisions made by or under any enactment (including this Act or any Act passed after this Act), prerogative instrument or other instrument or document.

(5) Any provision made by an order under this section may be expressed to be conditional upon the person specified in the order being designated by an order under Part 1 of Schedule 10 as a licensing authority in relation to one or more reserved legal activities.

(6) The powers to make an order conferred by this section are without prejudice to any powers (statutory or non-statutory) which a body may have apart from this section.

Initial Commencement
To be appointed: see s 211(2).
Extent
This section does not extend to Scotland: see s 212(1).

---

81 Procedural requirements relating to recommendations under section 80

(1) A recommendation may be made under section 80 only with the consent of—

(a) the person from whose decisions the appeals are to be made, and
(b) where the recommendation is for an order under section 80(1)(b), the body to which appeals are to be made.

(2) Before making a recommendation under that section, the Board must publish a draft of—

(a) the proposed recommendation, and
(b) the proposed draft order.

(3) The draft must be accompanied by a notice which states that representations about the proposals may be made to the Board within a specified period.

(4) Before making any recommendation, the Board must have regard to any representations duly made.

(5) If the draft order to be annexed to the recommendation differs from the draft published under subsection (2)(b) in a way which is, in the opinion of the Board, material, the Board must, before making the recommendation, publish the draft order along with a statement detailing the changes made and the reasons for those changes.

Initial Commencement
To be appointed: see s 211(2).
Extent
This section does not extend to Scotland: see s 212(1).

Policy statement

82 Licensing authority policy statement

(1) Each licensing authority must prepare and issue a statement of policy as to how, in exercising its functions under this Part, it will comply with the requirements of section 28 (or, in the case of the Board, section 3) (duties to promote regulatory objectives etc).

(2) A licensing authority may issue a statement under subsection (1) only with the approval of the Board (acting otherwise than in its capacity as a licensing authority or as an approved regulator).

(3) A licensing authority may, with the approval of the Board (acting otherwise than in its capacity as a licensing authority or as an approved regulator), alter or replace a statement issued under this section.

(4) If it does so, it must issue the altered or replacement statement.

(5) In exercising its functions under this Part, a licensing authority must have regard to the statement issued by it under this section.

(6) A licensing authority must publish a statement issued by it under this section.

Initial Commencement
To be appointed: see s 211(2).
Extent
This section does not extend to Scotland: see s 212(1).

Licensing rules

83 Licensing rules

(1) The Board (acting in its capacity as a licensing authority)—

(a) must make suitable licensing rules before the end of the period of 12 months beginning with the day on which a licensable body first becomes entitled to make an application to it for a licence by virtue of a decision of the Board (acting otherwise than in its capacity as a licensing authority or as an approved regulator) under Schedule 12;
(b) may make or modify its licensing rules only with the approval of the Board (acting otherwise than in its capacity as a licensing authority or as an approved regulator).

(2) In subsection (1)(a), "suitable licensing rules" means licensing rules which constitute suitable regulatory arrangements (within the meaning of Schedule 12) in respect of licensable bodies entitled by virtue of a decision under that Schedule to make an application to the Board for a licence.

(3) Licensing rules made by an approved regulator have effect only at a time when the approved regulator is a licensing authority (subject to any provision made by an order under section 25).

(4) Licensing rules of a licensing authority are rules as to—

- (a) the licensing by the authority of licensable bodies, and
- (b) the regulation by the licensing authority of licensable bodies licensed by it, and their managers and employees.

(5) Licensing rules of a licensing authority must contain—

- (a) appropriate qualification regulations in respect of licensable bodies to which the licensing authority proposes to issue licences under this Part,
- (b) provision as to how the licensing authority, when considering the regulatory objectives (in compliance with its duties under section 3(2) or 28(2)) in connection with an application for a licence, should take account of the objective of improving access to justice,
- (c) appropriate arrangements (including conduct rules, discipline rules and practice rules) under which the licensing authority will be able to regulate the conduct of bodies licensed by it, and their managers and employees,
- (d) appropriate indemnification arrangements,
- (e) appropriate compensation arrangements,
- (f) the provision required by sections 52 and 54 (resolution of regulatory conflict) (including those provisions as applied by section 103),
- (g) the provision required by sections 112 and 145 (requirements imposed in relation to the handling of complaints), and
- (h) any other provision required to be contained in licensing rules by this Act.

(6) Without prejudice to the generality of subsection (4), licensing rules of a licensing authority may contain any provision authorised by this Act.

(7) Schedule 11 makes further provision as to the contents of licensing rules.

(8) Subsections (5) to (7) are subject to—

- (a) section 105 (which exempts trade unions from certain provisions), and
- (b) section 106 (which provides for the modification of licensing rules in their application to bodies to which that section applies).

(9) Licensing rules may not apply to bodies to which section 106 applies in a way which is different from the way they apply to other bodies, except by virtue of an order under that section.

Initial Commencement
To be appointed: see s 211(2).
Extent
This section does not extend to Scotland: see s 212(1).

Licensing

84 Application for licence

(1) A licensing authority other than the Board must determine any application for a licence which is made to it.

(2) The Board (acting in its capacity as a licensing authority) may determine an application for a licence which is made to it only if the applicant is entitled to make the application by virtue of a decision of the Board (acting otherwise than in its capacity as a licensing authority) under Schedule 12.

(3) A licensing authority may not grant an application for a licence unless it is satisfied that if the licence is granted the applicant will comply with its licensing rules.

(4) If the licensing authority grants an application for a licence, it must issue the licence as soon as reasonably practicable.

(5) The licence has effect from the date on which it is issued.

(6) References in this section to an application for a licence are to an application for a licence which is—

(a) made to a licensing authority by a licensable body, in accordance with the authority's licensing rules, and
(b) accompanied by the required application fee (if any).

Initial Commencement
To be appointed: see s 211(2).
Appointment
Sub-s (2): Appointment (for certain purposes): 1 January 2009: see SI 2008/3149, art 2(d)(i).
Extent
This section does not extend to Scotland: see s 212(1).

85 Terms of licence

(1) A licence issued under section 84 must specify—

(a) the activities which are reserved legal activities and which the licensed body is authorised to carry on by virtue of the licence, and
(b) any conditions subject to which the licence is granted.

(2) If an order under section 106 has been made in relation to the licensed body, the licence must also specify the terms of the order.

(3) In the case of a licensing authority other than the Board, the licence may authorise the licensed body to carry on activities which are reserved legal activities only if the licensing authority is designated in relation to the reserved legal activities in question.

(4) A licence must be granted subject to the condition that—

(a) any obligation which may from time to time be imposed on the licensed body or a person within subsection (5) by or under the licensing authority's licensing rules is complied with, and
(b) any other obligations imposed on the licensed body or a person within that subsection by or under this or any other enactment (whether passed before or after this Act) are complied with.

(5) The persons mentioned in subsection (4) are the managers and employees of a licensed body, and non-authorised persons having an interest or an indirect interest, or holding a material interest, in the licensed body (in their capacity as such).

(6) A licence may be granted subject to such other conditions as the licensing authority considers appropriate.

(7) Those conditions may include conditions as to the non-reserved activities which the licensed body may or may not carry on.

(8) In this Part references to the terms of the licence are to the matters listed in subsections (1) and (2).

Initial Commencement
To be appointed: see s 211(2).
Extent
This section does not extend to Scotland: see s 212(1).

86 Modification of licence

(1) A licensing authority may modify the terms of a licence granted by it—

(a) if the licensed body applies to the licensing authority, in accordance with its licensing rules, for it to do so;
(b) in such other circumstances as may be specified in its licensing rules.

(2) If a licensed body is a body to which section 106 applies, the licensing authority may modify the terms of its licence in accordance with sections 106 and 107.

(3) A licensing authority modifies the terms of a licensed body's licence by giving the licensed body notice in writing of the modifications; and the modifications have effect from the time the licensing authority gives the licensed body the notice or such later time as may be specified in the notice.

(4) The licensing authority's power under this section is subject to—

(a) section 85(3) and (4), and
(b) licensing rules made under paragraph 6 of Schedule 11.

Initial Commencement
To be appointed: see s 211(2).
Extent
This section does not extend to Scotland: see s 212(1).

---

87 Registers of licensed bodies

(1) Each licensing authority must keep a register containing the names and places of business of all bodies which hold or have held licences granted by the licensing authority.

(2) Where any licence held by a body is for the time being suspended, the licensing authority shall cause that fact to be noted in the register in the entry for that body.

(3) A licensing authority must provide facilities for making the information contained in the entries in its register available for inspection by any person during office hours and without payment.

(4) The Board may make rules about—

(a) the register to be kept by the Board under this section, and
(b) the register to be kept under this section by each licensing authority designated under Part 1 of Schedule 10.

(5) Rules under subsection (4) may in particular prescribe any further information which must be contained in an entry in the register in relation to a licensed body or former licensed body.

Initial Commencement
To be appointed: see s 211(2).
Appointment
Sub-ss (4), (5): Appointment: 1 January 2009: see SI 2008/3149, art 2(d)(i).
Extent
This section does not extend to Scotland: see s 212(1).

---

88 Evidence of status

(1) A certificate signed by an officer of a licensing authority appointed for the purpose and stating one of the matters within subsection (2) is, unless the contrary is proved, evidence of the facts stated in the certificate.

(2) The matters are that any person does or does not, or did or did not at any time, hold a licence granted by the licensing authority under this Part.

(3) A certificate purporting to be so signed is to be taken to have been so signed unless the contrary is proved.

Initial Commencement
To be appointed: see s 211(2).
Extent
This section does not extend to Scotland: see s 212(1).

Ownership of licensed bodies

89 Ownership of licensed bodies

Schedule 13 makes provision about the holding of certain interests in licensed bodies by non-authorised persons.

Initial Commencement
To be appointed: see s 211(2).
Appointment
Appointment: 1 January 2009: see SI 2008/3149, art 2(d)(i).
Extent
This section does not extend to Scotland: see s 212(1).

Regulation of licensed bodies

90 Duties of non-authorised persons

A non-authorised person who is an employee or manager of a licensed body, or has an interest or an indirect interest, or holds a material interest, in a licensed body, must not do anything which causes or substantially contributes to a breach by—

(a) the licensed body, or
(b) an employee or manager of the licensed body who is an authorised person in relation to an activity which is a reserved legal activity,

of the duties imposed on them by section 176.

Initial Commencement
To be appointed: see s 211(2).
Extent
This section does not extend to Scotland: see s 212(1).

---

91 Duties of Head of Legal Practice

(1) The Head of Legal Practice of a licensed body must—

(a) take all reasonable steps to ensure compliance with the terms of the licensed body's licence, and
(b) as soon as reasonably practicable, report to the licensing authority any failure to comply with the terms of the licence.

(2) Subsection (1) does not apply to the terms of the licence so far as they require compliance with licensing rules made under paragraph 20 of Schedule 11 (accounts) (as to which see section 92).

(3) The Head of Legal Practice of a licensed body must—

(a) take all reasonable steps to ensure that the licensed body, and any of its employees or managers who are authorised persons in relation to an activity which is a reserved legal activity, comply with the duties imposed by section 176, and
(b) as soon as reasonably practicable, report to the licensing authority such failures by those persons to comply with those duties as may be specified in licensing rules.

(4) The Head of Legal Practice of a licensed body must—

(a) take all reasonable steps to ensure that non-authorised persons subject to the duty imposed by section 90 in relation to the licensed body comply with that duty, and
(b) as soon as reasonably practicable, report to the licensing authority any failure by a non-authorised person to comply with that duty.

Initial Commencement
To be appointed: see s 211(2).

Extent
This section does not extend to Scotland: see s 212(1).

---

92 Duties of Head of Finance and Administration

(1) The Head of Finance and Administration of a licensed body must take all reasonable steps to ensure compliance with licensing rules made under paragraph 20 of Schedule 11 (accounts).

(2) The Head of Finance and Administration must report any breach of those rules to the licensing authority as soon as reasonably practicable.

Initial Commencement
To be appointed: see s 211(2).
Extent
This section does not extend to Scotland: see s 212(1).

---

93 Information

(1) The relevant licensing authority in relation to a licensed body may by notice require a person within subsection (2)—

- (a) to provide information, or information of a description, specified in the notice, or
- (b) produce documents, or documents of a description, specified in the notice,

for the purpose of enabling the licensing authority to ascertain whether the terms of the licensed body's licence are being, or have been, complied with.

(2) The persons are—

- (a) the licensed body;
- (b) any manager or employee (or former manager or employee) of the licensed body;
- (c) any non-authorised person who has an interest or an indirect interest, or holds a material interest, in the licensed body.

(3) A notice under subsection (1)—

- (a) may specify the manner and form in which any information is to be provided;
- (b) must specify the period within which the information is to be provided or the document produced;
- (c) may require the information to be provided, or the document to be produced, to the licensing authority or to a person specified in the notice.

(4) The licensing authority may, by notice, require a person within subsection (2) (or a representative of such a person) to attend at a time and place specified in the notice to provide an explanation of any information provided or document produced under this section.

(5) The licensing authority may pay to any person such reasonable costs as may be incurred by that person in connection with—

- (a) the provision of any information, or production of any document, by that person pursuant to a notice under subsection (1), or
- (b) that person's compliance with a requirement imposed under subsection (4).

(6) The licensing authority, or a person specified under subsection (3)(c) in a notice, may take copies of or extracts from a document produced pursuant to a notice under subsection (1).

(7) For the purposes of this section and section 94, references to a licensed body include a body which was, but is no longer, a licensed body.

Initial Commencement
To be appointed: see s 211(2).
Extent
This section does not extend to Scotland: see s 212(1).

---

94 Enforcement of notices under section 93

(1) Where a person is unable to comply with a notice given to the person under section 93, the person must give the licensing authority a notice to that effect stating the reasons why the person cannot comply.

(2) If a person refuses or otherwise fails to comply with a notice under section 93, the licensing authority may apply to the High Court for an order requiring the person to comply with the notice or with such directions for the like purpose as may be contained in the order.

Initial Commencement
To be appointed: see s 211(2).
Extent
This section does not extend to Scotland: see s 212(1).

---

95 Financial penalties

(1) A licensing authority may, in accordance with its licensing rules, impose on a licensed body, or a manager or employee of a licensed body, a penalty of such amount as it considers appropriate.

(2) The amount must not exceed the maximum amount prescribed under subsection (3).

(3) The Board must make rules prescribing the maximum amount of a penalty which may be imposed under this section.

(4) Rules may be made under subsection (3) only with the consent of the Lord Chancellor.

(5) A penalty under this section is payable to the licensing authority.

(6) For the purposes of this section—

(a) references to a licensed body are to a body which was a licensed body at the time the act or omission in respect of which the penalty is imposed occurred, and
(b) references to a manager or employee of a licensed body are to a person who was a manager or employee of a licensed body at that time,

(whether or not the body subsequently ceased to be a licensed body or the person subsequently ceased to be a manager or employee).

(7) In sections 96 and 97 references to a "penalty" are to a penalty under this section.

Initial Commencement
To be appointed: see s 211(2).
Appointment
Sub-ss (3), (4): Appointment: 1 January 2009: see SI 2008/3149, art 2(d)(i).
Extent
This section does not extend to Scotland: see s 212(1).

---

96 Appeals against financial penalties

(1) A person on whom a penalty is imposed under section 95 may, before the end of such period as may be prescribed by rules made by the Board, appeal to the relevant appellate body on one or more of the appeal grounds.

(2) The appeal grounds are—

(a) that the imposition of the penalty is unreasonable in all the circumstances of the case;
(b) that the amount of the penalty is unreasonable;
(c) that it is unreasonable of the licensing authority to require the penalty imposed or any portion of it to be paid by the time or times by which it was required to be paid.

(3) On any such appeal, where the relevant appellate body considers it appropriate to do so in all the circumstances of the case and is satisfied of one or more of the appeal grounds, that body may—

(a) quash the penalty,
(b) substitute a penalty of such lesser amount as it considers appropriate, or
(c) in the case of the appeal ground in subsection (2)(c), substitute for any time imposed by the licensing authority a different time or times.

(4) Where the relevant appellate body substitutes a penalty of a lesser amount it may require the payment of interest on the substituted penalty at such rate, and from such time, as it considers just and equitable.

(5) Where the relevant appellate body specifies as a time by which the penalty, or a portion of the penalty, is to be paid a time before the determination of the appeal under this section it may require the payment of interest on the penalty, or portion, from that time at such rate as it considers just and equitable.

(6) A party to the appeal may appeal to the High Court on a point of law arising from the decision of the relevant appellate body, but only with the permission of the High Court.

(7) The High Court may make such order as it thinks fit.

(8) Except as provided by this section, the validity of a penalty is not to be questioned by any legal proceedings whatever.

Initial Commencement
To be appointed: see s 211(2).
Appointment
Sub-s (1): Appointment: 1 January 2009: see SI 2008/3149, art 2(d)(i).
Extent
This section does not extend to Scotland: see s 212(1).

---

97 Recovery of financial penalties

(1) If the whole or any part of a penalty is not paid by the time by which, in accordance with licensing rules, it is required to be paid, the unpaid balance from time to time carries interest at the rate for the time being specified in section 17 of the Judgments Act 1838 (c 110).

(2) Where a penalty, or any portion of it, has not been paid by the time by which, in accordance with licensing rules, it is required to be paid and—

(a) no appeal relating to the penalty has been made under section 96 during the period within which such an appeal can be made, or
(b) an appeal has been made under that section and determined or withdrawn,

the licensing authority may recover from the person on whom the penalty was imposed, as a debt due to the licensing authority, any of the penalty and any interest which has not been paid.

(3) A licensing authority must pay into the Consolidated Fund any sum received by it as a penalty (or as interest on a penalty).

Initial Commencement
To be appointed: see s 211(2).
Extent
This section does not extend to Scotland: see s 212(1).

---

98 Referral of employees etc to appropriate regulator

(1) The relevant licensing authority may refer to an appropriate regulator any matter relating to the conduct of—

(a) an employee or manager of a licensed body;
(b) a person designated as a licensed body's Head of Legal Practice or Head of Finance and Administration.

(2) The licensing authority may also refer any matter relating to the conduct of such a person to the Board.

(3) Appropriate regulators are—

(a) if the person is an authorised person in relation to a reserved legal activity, any relevant approved regulator in relation to that person, and
(b) if the person carries on non-reserved activities, any person who exercises regulatory functions in relation to the carrying on of such activities by the person.

Initial Commencement
To be appointed: see s 211(2).
Extent
This section does not extend to Scotland: see s 212(1).

---

99 Disqualification

(1) A licensing authority may in accordance with its licensing rules disqualify a person from one or more of the activities mentioned in subsection (2) if—

(a) the disqualification condition is satisfied in relation to the person, and
(b) the licensing authority is satisfied that it is undesirable for the person to engage in that activity or those activities.

(2) The activities are—

(a) acting as Head of Legal Practice of any licensed body,
(b) acting as Head of Finance and Administration of any licensed body,
(c) being a manager of any licensed body, or
(d) being employed by any licensed body.

(3) The disqualification condition is satisfied in relation to a person if, in relation to a licensed body licensed by the licensing authority, the person (intentionally or through neglect)—

(a) breaches a relevant duty to which the person is subject, or
(b) causes, or substantially contributes to, a significant breach of the terms of the licensed body's licence.

(4) The relevant duties are—

(a) the duties imposed on a Head of Legal Practice by section 91,
(b) the duties imposed on a Head of Finance and Administration by section 92,
(c) the duties imposed by section 176 on regulated persons (within the meaning of that section), and
(d) the duty imposed on non-authorised persons by section 90.

Initial Commencement
To be appointed: see s 211(2).
Extent
This section does not extend to Scotland: see s 212(1).

---

100 Lists of disqualified persons

(1) The Board must keep lists of persons who are disqualified from—

(a) acting as Head of Legal Practice of any licensed body,
(b) acting as Head of Finance and Administration of any licensed body,
(c) being a manager of any licensed body, or
(d) being employed by any licensed body.

(2) A person is disqualified from acting in a way mentioned in subsection (1) if—

(a) the person has been disqualified from so acting by a licensing authority under section 99, and
(b) the disqualification continues in force.

(3) The disqualification ceases to be in force if the appropriate licensing authority so determines, on a review or otherwise, in accordance with licensing rules made under paragraph 23 of Schedule 11.

(4) The appropriate licensing authority is—

(a) the licensing authority which disqualified the person, or
(b) if the person was disqualified by an approved regulator which is no longer designated as a licensing authority, the successor licensing authority.

(5) The successor licensing authority is—

(a) the licensing authority which licenses the body in relation to which the disqualification condition (within the meaning of section 99) was satisfied in respect of the person, or
(b) if there is no such licensing authority, the licensing authority designated by the Board on an application by the disqualified person.

(6) The Board must publish the lists kept by it under subsection (1).

Initial Commencement
To be appointed: see s 211(2).
Extent
This section does not extend to Scotland: see s 212(1).

---

101 Suspension and revocation of licence

(1) A licensing authority may, in accordance with its licensing rules, suspend or revoke any licence granted by it under this Part.

(2) A licence is to be treated as not being in force at any time while it is suspended under this section.

Initial Commencement
To be appointed: see s 211(2).
Extent
This section does not extend to Scotland: see s 212(1).

---

102 Intervention

Schedule 14 confers powers of intervention on licensing authorities.

Initial Commencement
To be appointed: see s 211(2).
Extent
This section does not extend to Scotland: see s 212(1).

---

103 Regulatory conflict and the Board as licensing authority

(1) Sections 52 and 54 (regulatory conflict between approved regulators and between approved regulators and other regulators) apply in relation to the Board in its capacity as a licensing authority and its licensing rules as they apply in relation to an approved regulator (including the Board in its capacity as approved regulator) and its regulatory arrangements.

(2) Section 68 (regulatory conflict and the Board as approved regulator) applies in relation to the Board in its capacity as a licensing authority and its licensing rules as it applies in relation to the Board in its capacity as an approved regulator and its regulatory arrangements.

Initial Commencement
To be appointed: see s 211(2).
Extent
This section does not extend to Scotland: see s 212(1).

104 Prevention of regulatory conflict: accounts rules

(1) Where a licensed body carries on an activity through a solicitor, the rules made under paragraph 20 of Schedule 11 apply instead of those made under sections 32 to 34 of the Solicitors Act 1974 (c 47).

(2) Where a licensed body carries on an activity through a licensed conveyancer, the rules made under paragraph 20 of Schedule 11 apply instead of those made under sections 22 and 23 of the Administration of Justice Act 1985 (c 61).

Initial Commencement
To be appointed: see s 211(2).
Extent
This section does not extend to Scotland: see s 212(1).

Special kinds of body

105 Trade union exemptions

(1) Paragraphs 11 to 14 of Schedule 11 (Head of Legal Practice and Head of Finance and Administration) do not apply in relation to a licensed body which is an independent trade union.

(2) Schedule 13 (ownership) does not apply in relation to an applicant for a licence, or a licensed body, which is an independent trade union.

Initial Commencement
To be appointed: see s 211(2).
Extent
This section does not extend to Scotland: see s 212(1).

106 Power to modify application of licensing rules etc to special bodies

(1) This section applies to a licensed body (or an applicant for a licence) which is—

- (a) an independent trade union,
- (b) a not for profit body,
- (c) a community interest company,
- (d) a low-risk body (see section 108), or
- (e) a body of such other description as may be prescribed by order made by the Lord Chancellor on the recommendation of the Board.

(2) A body to which this section applies may apply to the relevant licensing authority, in accordance with its licensing rules, for the authority to make an order under this section.

(3) The licensing authority may make one or both of the following orders—

- (a) that the authority's licensing rules apply in relation to the body with such modifications as may be specified in the order;
- (b) that Schedule 13 does not apply in relation to the body, or applies in relation to the body with such modifications as may be specified in the order.

(4) On an application under subsection (2), the licensing authority may make any order which the authority—

- (a) has power to make under subsection (3), and
- (b) considers appropriate in all the circumstances of the case,

whether or not it is the order for which the applicant applied.

(5) In deciding what order (if any) is appropriate in all the circumstances of the case, the licensing authority must in particular have regard to—

(a) the reserved legal activities and non-reserved activities which the body carries on (or proposes to carry on),
(b) the nature of the persons to whom the body provides (or proposes to provide) services,
(c) any non-authorised persons who have an interest or an indirect interest in the licensed body or hold a material interest in the licensed body, or are managers of the body, and
(d) any other matter specified in the authority's licensing rules.

(6) If the licensing authority makes an order under subsection (3), the authority's licensing rules or Schedule 13 or both (as the case may be) have effect in relation to that body in accordance with that order.

(7) The licensing authority may not make an order under subsection (3)(a) in relation to provisions of its licensing rules made in accordance with the following paragraphs of Schedule 11—

(a) paragraphs 2 and 3 (determination and review of applications for a licence);
(b) paragraphs 7 and 8 (applications under this section);
(c) paragraphs 9(3), 18 and 23 (disqualifications);
(d) paragraph 10(2) (management);
(e) paragraph 16 (carrying on of licensed activities);
(f) paragraph 24(1), (2), (3) and (8) (grounds for suspending and revoking licences);
(g) paragraph 24(10) and (11) (procedure for suspending or revoking licence);
(h) paragraph 26(2) (review of decision to suspend or revoke licence).

(8) The licensing authority may not make an order under subsection (3)(a) which results in its licensing rules, as they apply in relation to the body to which the order relates, not making the provision required by—

(a) section 83(5)(a) to (g);
(b) paragraph 1 of Schedule 11 (applications for licences);
(c) paragraph 4(3) of that Schedule (renewal of licences);
(d) paragraph 6 of that Schedule (modification of licence);
(e) paragraph 20 of that Schedule (accounts).

(9) If the licensing authority's licensing rules, as they apply in relation to a body to which an order under subsection (3)(a) relates, make provision requiring the body to have—

(a) a Head of Legal Practice approved by the licensing authority, or
(b) a Head of Finance and Administration approved by the licensing authority,

they must also provide for a review by the licensing authority of any decision by it to refuse or withdraw that approval.

Initial Commencement
To be appointed: see s 211(2).
Extent
This section does not extend to Scotland: see s 212(1).

---

107 Modifications under section 106: supplementary

(1) This section applies where a licensing authority has made an order under section 106 in relation to a body to which that section applies.

(2) The licensing authority must revoke the order under section 106 if it becomes aware that the body in respect of which the order was made is no longer a body to which that section applies.

(3) The licensing authority may revoke or otherwise modify an order under section 106—

(a) on the application of the body in relation to which the order was made, or
(b) of its own motion.

(4) It may do so only if it considers it appropriate to do so in all the circumstances of the case, having regard to the matters mentioned in section 106(5).

Initial Commencement
To be appointed: see s 211(2).

Extent
This section does not extend to Scotland: see s 212(1).

108 "Low risk body"

(1) A body ("B") is a low risk body if the management condition and the ownership condition are satisfied in relation to it.

(2) The management condition is that the number of managers of the body who are within subsection (4) is less than 10% of the total number of managers.

(3) The ownership condition is that—

- (a) the proportion of shares in B held by persons within subsection (4) is less than 10%, and
- (b) the proportion of the voting rights in B which such persons are entitled to exercise, or control the exercise of, is less than 10%, and
- (c) if B has a parent undertaking ("P")—
  - (i) the proportion of shares in P held by such persons is less than 10%, and
  - (ii) the proportion of the voting rights in P which such persons are entitled to exercise, or control the exercise of, is less than 10%.

(4) The persons within this subsection are—

- (a) non-authorised persons;
- (b) licensed bodies.

(5) For the purposes of this section "parent undertaking" has the same meaning as in the Financial Services and Markets Act 2000 (c 8) (see section 420 of that Act).

Initial Commencement
To be appointed: see s 211(2).
Extent
This section does not extend to Scotland: see s 212(1).

109 Foreign bodies

The Lord Chancellor may by order make provision for the modification of any provision of this Part in its application to a body of persons formed under, or in so far as the body is recognised by, law having effect outside England and Wales.

Initial Commencement
To be appointed: see s 211(2).
Extent
This section does not extend to Scotland: see s 212(1).

Supplementary provision

110 Reporting requirements relating to Part 5

(1) The Board's annual report must deal with how, in the Board's opinion, the activities of licensing authorities and licensed bodies have affected the regulatory objectives.

(2) This section does not apply to an annual report for a financial year before the first financial year in which a licence is issued under this Part.

(3) In this section "annual report" and "financial year" have the same meaning as in section 6.

Initial Commencement
To be appointed: see s 211(2).
Extent
This section does not extend to Scotland: see s 212(1).

111 Interpretation of Part 5

(1) In this Part—

"licensed activity", in relation to a licensed body, means an activity—
(a) which is a reserved legal activity, and
(b) which the licensed body is authorised to carry on by virtue of its licence;
"non-authorised person" means a person who is not within subsection (2);
"non-reserved activity" means an activity which is not a reserved legal activity;
"relevant appellate body", in relation to decisions made by a licensing authority under this Part, means the body having power to hear appeals from those decisions (whether by virtue of an order under section 80 or otherwise).

(2) The following persons are within this subsection—

(a) an authorised person in relation to an activity which constitutes a reserved legal activity,
(b) a registered foreign lawyer (within the meaning of section 89 of the Courts and Legal Services Act 1990 (c 41)),
(c) a person entitled to pursue professional activities under a professional title to which the Directive applies in a state to which the Directive applies (other than the title of barrister or solicitor in England and Wales),
(d) a body which provides professional services such as are provided by persons within paragraph (a) or lawyers of other jurisdictions, and all the managers of which and all the persons with an interest in which—
(i) are within paragraphs (a) to (c), or
(ii) are bodies in which persons within paragraphs (a) to (c) are entitled to exercise, or control the exercise of, more than 90% of the voting rights.

(3) In subsection (2)(c) "the Directive" means Directive 98/5/EC of the European Parliament and the Council, to facilitate practice of the profession of lawyer on a permanent basis in a Member State other than that in which the qualification was obtained.

Initial Commencement
To be appointed: see s 211(2).
Extent
This section does not extend to Scotland: see s 212(1).

PART 6
LEGAL COMPLAINTS

Complaints procedures of authorised persons

112 Complaints procedures of authorised persons

(1) The regulatory arrangements of an approved regulator must make provision requiring each relevant authorised person—

(a) to establish and maintain procedures for the resolution of relevant complaints, or
(b) to participate in, or make arrangements to be subject to, such procedures established and maintained by another person,

and provision for the enforcement of that requirement.

(2) The provision made for the purposes of subsection (1) must satisfy such requirements as the Board may, from time to time, specify for the purposes of that subsection.

(3) In this section—

"relevant authorised person", in relation to an approved regulator, means a person in relation to whom the approved regulator is a relevant approved regulator;
"relevant complaint", in relation to a relevant authorised person, means a complaint which—
(a) relates to an act or omission of that person, and
(b) may be made under the scheme provided for by this Part.

(4) The Board must publish any requirements specified by it for the purposes of subsection (2).

(5) This section applies in relation to the licensing rules of the Board as it applies in relation to the regulatory arrangements of an approved regulator except that subsection (3) has effect as if for the definition of "relevant authorised person" there were substituted—

"”relevant authorised person", in relation to the Board, means a person licensed by the Board under Part 5;".

Initial Commencement
To be appointed: see s 211(2).
Appointment
Sub-ss (2), (4): Appointment: 1 January 2009: see SI 2008/3149, art 2(e)(i).
Extent
This section does not extend to Scotland: see s 212(1).

Overview of the scheme

113 Overview of the scheme

(1) This Part provides for a scheme under which complaints which—

- (a) relate to an act or omission of a person ("the respondent") in carrying on an activity, and
- (b) are within the jurisdiction of the scheme (see section 125),

may be resolved quickly and with minimum formality by an independent person.

(2) Under the scheme—

- (a) redress may be provided to the complainant, but
- (b) no disciplinary action may be taken against the respondent.

(3) Section 157 prevents provision relating to redress being included in the regulatory arrangements of an approved regulator, or licensing rules made by the Board in its capacity as a licensing authority.

(4) But neither the scheme nor any provision made by this Part affects any power of an approved regulator, or the Board in its capacity as a licensing authority, to take disciplinary action.

(5) "Disciplinary action" means the imposition of sanctions, in respect of a breach of conduct rules or discipline rules, on a person who is an authorised person in relation to an activity which is a reserved legal activity.

Initial Commencement
To be appointed: see s 211(2).
Extent
This section does not extend to Scotland: see s 212(1).

The Office for Legal Complaints

114 The Office for Legal Complaints

(1) There is to be a body corporate called the Office for Legal Complaints (in this Act referred to as "the OLC").

(2) Schedule 15 is about the OLC

Initial Commencement
To be appointed: see s 211(2).
Appointment
Appointment: 7 March 2008: see SI 2008/222, art 2(d).

Extent
This section does not extend to Scotland: see s 212(1).

---

115 The ombudsman scheme

(1) The scheme provided for by this Part is to be administered by the OLC in accordance with this Part and with scheme rules made under this Part.

(2) In this Part "scheme rules" means rules made by the OLC

(3) The scheme is to be operated under a name (which must include the word "ombudsman") chosen by the OLC, and is referred to in this Act as "the ombudsman scheme".

Initial Commencement
To be appointed: see s 211(2).
Appointment
Appointment: 1 January 2009: see SI 2008/3149, art 2(e)(i).
Extent
This section does not extend to Scotland: see s 212(1).

---

116 General obligations

(1) In discharging its functions the OLC must comply with the requirements of this section.

(2) The OLC must, so far as is reasonably practicable, act in a way—

(a) which is compatible with the regulatory objectives, and
(b) which it considers most appropriate for the purpose of meeting those objectives.

(3) The OLC must have regard to any principles appearing to it to represent the best practice of those who administer ombudsman schemes.

Initial Commencement
To be appointed: see s 211(2).
Appointment
Appointment: 1 January 2009: see SI 2008/3149, art 2(e)(i).
Extent
This section does not extend to Scotland: see s 212(1).

---

117 Corporate governance

In managing its affairs, the OLC must have regard to such generally accepted principles of good corporate governance as it is reasonable to regard as applicable to it.

Initial Commencement
To be appointed: see s 211(2).
Appointment
Appointment: 1 January 2009: see SI 2008/3149, art 2(e)(i).
Extent
This section does not extend to Scotland: see s 212(1).

---

118 Annual report

(1) The OLC must prepare a report ("the annual report") for each financial year.

(2) The annual report must deal with—

(a) the discharge of the functions of the OLC,
(b) the extent to which, in the OLC's opinion, the OLC has met the regulatory objectives, and
(c) such other matters as the Board may from time to time direct.

(3) The OLC must include in the annual report a copy of the report prepared by the Chief Ombudsman under section 123 for the financial year in question.

(4) As soon as reasonably practicable after the end of each financial year, the OLC must give the Board a copy of the annual report prepared for that year.

(5) The Board must give a copy of the annual report to the Lord Chancellor.

(6) The Lord Chancellor must lay a copy of the annual report before Parliament.

(7) In this section "financial year" means—

- (a) the period beginning with the day on which the OLC is established and ending with the next following 31 March, and
- (b) each successive period of 12 months.

Initial Commencement
To be appointed: see s 211(2).
Appointment
Appointment: 1 January 2009: see SI 2008/3149, art 2(e)(i).

Extent

This section does not extend to Scotland: see s 212(1).

119 Supplementary powers

The OLC may do anything calculated to facilitate, or incidental or conducive to, the carrying out of any of its functions.

Initial Commencement
To be appointed: see s 211(2).
Appointment
Appointment: 1 January 2009: see SI 2008/3149, art 2(e)(i).
Extent
This section does not extend to Scotland: see s 212(1).

---

120 Reporting to the Board

(1) The Board may require the OLC to prepare and give the Board, within a specified period, a report in respect of any specified matter relating to the functions of the OLC

(2) In subsection (1) "specified" means specified in the requirement.

(3) The Board must publish any report given to it under this section.

Initial Commencement
To be appointed: see s 211(2).
Appointment
Appointment: 1 January 2009: see SI 2008/3149, art 2(e)(i).
Extent
This section does not extend to Scotland: see s 212(1).

---

121 Performance targets and monitoring

(1) The Board may—

- (a) set one or more performance targets relating to the performance by the OLC of any of its functions, or
- (b) direct the OLC to set one or more performance targets relating to the performance by the OLC of any of its functions.

(2) A direction under subsection (1)(b) may impose conditions with which the performance targets must conform.

(3) The Board must publish any target set or direction given by it under this section.

(4) The OLC must publish any target set by it pursuant to a direction under subsection (1)(b).

(5) The Board may take such steps as it regards as appropriate to monitor the extent to which any performance target set under this section is being, or has been, met.

Initial Commencement
To be appointed: see s 211(2).
Appointment
Appointment: 1 January 2009: see SI 2008/3149, art 2(e)(i).
Extent
This section does not extend to Scotland: see s 212(1).

The ombudsmen

122 Appointment of the Chief Ombudsman and assistant ombudsmen

(1) The OLC—

(a) must appoint a person to act as Chief Ombudsman for the purposes of the ombudsman scheme, and
(b) may, with the consent of the Chief Ombudsman, appoint one or more other persons to act as assistant ombudsmen for those purposes.

(2) The person appointed under subsection (1)(a) must be a lay person.

(3) It is a condition of an appointment under subsection (1)(b) that the person appointed must not during the appointment carry on any activity which is a reserved legal activity for or in expectation of any fee, gain or reward.

(4) Each person appointed under subsection (1)(a) or (b) must be a person appearing to the OLC to have appropriate qualifications and experience to act as an ombudsman for the purposes of the ombudsman scheme.

(5) In this Act a reference to an "ombudsman" (except in the expressions "ombudsman scheme", "Chief Ombudsman" and "assistant ombudsman") is a reference to the Chief Ombudsman or an assistant ombudsman.

(6) A person's appointment as Chief Ombudsman ceases if that person ceases to be a lay person.

(7) The terms and conditions on which a person is appointed as an assistant ombudsman must specify the consequences of a breach of the condition imposed by subsection (3).

(8) Subject to that, a person's appointment as an ombudsman is to be on such terms and conditions (including terms as to the duration and termination of a person's appointment and as to remuneration) as the OLC considers—

(a) consistent with ensuring the independence of the person appointed, and
(b) otherwise appropriate.

(9) Appointment as an ombudsman does not confer the status of Crown servant.

(10) In this section "lay person" has the same meaning as in Schedule 15.

Initial Commencement
To be appointed: see s 211(2).
Appointment
Appointment: 1 January 2009: see SI 2008/3149, art 2(e)(i).
Extent
This section does not extend to Scotland: see s 212(1).

---

123 Annual report of Chief Ombudsman

(1) The Chief Ombudsman must prepare a report for each financial year on the discharge of the functions of the ombudsmen.

(2) A report under this section must comply with any requirements specified by the OLC

(3) The OLC must publish any requirements specified for the purposes of subsection (2).

(4) As soon as reasonably practicable after the end of each financial year, the Chief Ombudsman must give the OLC a copy of the report prepared under this section for the year.

(5) In this section "financial year" has the meaning given by section 118(7).

Initial Commencement
To be appointed: see s 211(2).
Appointment
Appointment: 1 January 2009: see SI 2008/3149, art 2(e)(i).
Extent
This section does not extend to Scotland: see s 212(1).

---

124 Additional reports of Chief Ombudsman

(1) The OLC may require the Chief Ombudsman to prepare and give the OLC, within a specified period, a report in respect of any specified matter relating to the functions of the ombudsmen.

(2) In subsection (1) "specified" means specified in the requirement.

Initial Commencement
To be appointed: see s 211(2).
Appointment
Appointment: 1 January 2009: see SI 2008/3149, art 2(e)(i).
Extent
This section does not extend to Scotland: see s 212(1).

Jurisdiction and operation of the ombudsman scheme

125 Jurisdiction of the ombudsman scheme

(1) A complaint which relates to an act or omission of a person ("the respondent") in carrying on an activity is within the jurisdiction of the ombudsman scheme if—

- (a) the complaint is not excluded from the jurisdiction of the scheme by section 126, or by scheme rules made under section 127,
- (b) the respondent is within section 128, and
- (c) the complainant is within section 128 and wishes to have the complaint dealt with under the scheme.

(2) In subsection (1) references to an act or omission include an act or omission which occurs before the coming into force of this section.

(3) The right of a person to make a complaint under the ombudsman scheme, and the jurisdiction of an ombudsman to investigate, consider and determine a complaint, may not be limited or excluded by any contract term or by notice.

Initial Commencement
To be appointed: see s 211(2).
Extent
This section does not extend to Scotland: see s 212(1).

---

126 Complaints excluded because respondent's complaints procedures not used

(1) A complaint is excluded from the jurisdiction of the ombudsman scheme if the complainant has not first used the respondent's complaints procedures in relation to the complaint.

(2) The respondent's complaints procedures are the procedures established by the respondent, or which the respondent participates in or is subject to, in accordance with regulatory arrangements (or licensing rules of the Board) made in accordance with section 112.

(3) Scheme rules may provide that subsection (1) does not apply in specified circumstances.

Initial Commencement
To be appointed: see s 211(2).
Appointment
Sub-s (3): Appointment: 1 January 2009: see SI 2008/3149, art 2(e)(i).
Extent
This section does not extend to Scotland: see s 212(1).

---

127 Complaints excluded by scheme rules

(1) Scheme rules may make provision excluding complaints of a description specified in the rules from the jurisdiction of the ombudsman scheme.

(2) But they may not make provision excluding a complaint from the jurisdiction of the ombudsman scheme on the ground that it relates to a matter which has been or could be dealt with under the disciplinary arrangements of the respondent's relevant authorising body.

Initial Commencement
To be appointed: see s 211(2).
Appointment
Appointment: 1 January 2009: see SI 2008/3149, art 2(e)(i).
Extent
This section does not extend to Scotland: see s 212(1).

---

128 Parties

(1) The respondent is within this section if, at the relevant time, the respondent was an authorised person in relation to an activity which was a reserved legal activity (whether or not the act or omission relates to a reserved legal activity).

(2) The complainant ("C") is within this section if C—

(a) meets the first and second conditions, and
(b) is not excluded by subsection (5).

(3) The first condition is that C is—

(a) an individual, or
(b) a person (other than an individual) of a description prescribed by order made by the Lord Chancellor in accordance with a recommendation made under section 130.

(4) The second condition is that—

(a) the services to which the complaint relates were provided by the respondent to C;
(b) the services to which the complaint relates were provided by the respondent to an authorised person who procured them on C's behalf;
(c) the services to which the complaint relates were provided by the respondent—
(i) in the respondent's capacity as a personal representative or trustee, or
(ii) to a person acting as a personal representative or trustee,
and C is a beneficiary of the estate or trust in question; or
(d) C satisfies such other conditions, in relation to the services to which the complaint relates, as may be prescribed by order made by the Lord Chancellor in accordance with a recommendation made under section 130.

(5) C is excluded if, at the relevant time—

(a) C was an authorised person in relation to an activity which was a reserved legal activity and the services to which the complaint relates were procured by C on behalf of another person,
(b) C was a public body or was acting on behalf of such a body in relation to the services to which the complaint relates, or
(c) C was a person prescribed, or of a description prescribed, as excluded by order made by the Lord Chancellor in accordance with a recommendation made under section 130.

(6) In subsection (4)(b) "authorised person" means an authorised person in relation to any activity which is a reserved legal activity.

(7) In this section—

"public body" means any government department, local authority or other body constituted for purposes of the public services, local government or the administration of justice;
"relevant time", in relation to a complaint, means the time when the act or omission to which the complaint relates took place.

Initial Commencement
To be appointed: see s 211(2).
Appointment
Sub-ss (3)(b), (4)(d), (5)(c): Appointment: 1 January 2009: see SI 2008/3149, art 2(e)(i).
Extent
This section does not extend to Scotland: see s 212(1).

---

129 Pre-commencement acts and omissions

(1) For the purposes of section 128 a person is to be regarded as an authorised person in relation to an activity which is a reserved legal activity, at a time before section 125 comes into force, if the person was at that time—

(a) a person of the kind mentioned in paragraph 2(4) of Schedule 15,
(b) a body recognised under section 9 or 32 of the Administration of Justice Act 1985 (c 61) (recognised bodies), or
(c) a legal partnership, a conveyancing partnership, a patent attorney body or a trade mark attorney body.

(2) In this section—

"conveyancing partnership" has the meaning given by paragraph 11(5) of Schedule 5;
"legal partnership" has the meaning given by paragraph 7(4) of that Schedule;
"patent attorney body" has the meaning given by paragraph 14(7) of that Schedule;
"trade mark attorney body" has the meaning given by paragraph 16(7) of that Schedule.

Initial Commencement
To be appointed: see s 211(2).
Extent
This section does not extend to Scotland: see s 212(1).

---

130 Orders under section 128

(1) An interested body may, at any time, recommend to the Lord Chancellor that the Lord Chancellor make an order under section 128(3)(b), (4)(d) or (5)(c).

(2) An interested body must, if requested to do so by the Lord Chancellor, consider whether or not it is appropriate to make a recommendation under subsection (1).

(3) An interested body must, before making a recommendation under subsection (1)—

(a) publish a draft of the proposed recommendation,
(b) invite representations regarding the proposed recommendation, and
(c) consider any such representations which are made.

(4) Where the Lord Chancellor receives a recommendation under subsection (1), the Lord Chancellor must consider whether to follow the recommendation.

(5) If the Lord Chancellor decides not to follow the recommendation, the Lord Chancellor must publish a notice to that effect which includes the Lord Chancellor's reasons for the decision.

(6) In this section "interested body" means—

(a) the OLC,
(b) the Board, or
(c) the Consumer Panel.

Initial Commencement
To be appointed: see s 211(2).
Appointment
Appointment: 1 January 2009: see SI 2008/3149, art 2(e)(i).
Extent
This section does not extend to Scotland: see s 212(1).

---

131 Acts and omissions by employees etc

(1) For the purposes of this Part and the ombudsman scheme, any act or omission by a person in the course of the person's employment is to be treated as also an act or omission by the person's employer, whether or not it was done with the employer's knowledge or approval.

(2) For the purposes of this Part and the ombudsman scheme, any act or omission by a partner in a partnership in the course of carrying on, in the usual way, business of the kind carried on by the partnership is to be treated as also an act or omission by the partnership.

(3) But subsection (2) does not apply if the partner had no authority to act for the partnership and the person purporting to rely on that subsection knew, at the time of the act or omission, that the partner had no such authority.

Initial Commencement
To be appointed: see s 211(2).
Extent
This section does not extend to Scotland: see s 212(1).

---

132 Continuity of complaints

(1) The ability of a person to make a complaint about an act or omission of a partnership or other unincorporated body is not affected by any change in the membership of the partnership or body.

(2) Scheme rules must make provision determining the circumstances in which, for the purposes of the ombudsman scheme, an act or omission of a person ("A") is, where A ceases to exist and another person ("B") succeeds to the whole or substantially the whole of the business of A, to be treated as an act or omission of B.

(3) Rules under subsection (2) must, in relation to cases where an act or omission of A is treated as an act or omission of B, make provision about the treatment of complaints under the ombudsman scheme which are outstanding against A at the time A ceases to exist.

(4) Scheme rules must make provision permitting such persons as may be specified in the rules to continue a complaint made by a person who has died or is otherwise unable to act; and for that purpose may modify references to the complainant in this Part and in scheme rules.

Initial Commencement
To be appointed: see s 211(2).
Appointment
Appointment: 1 January 2009: see SI 2008/3149, art 2(e)(i).
Extent

This section does not extend to Scotland: see s 212(1).

133 Operation of the ombudsman scheme

(1) Scheme rules must set out the procedure for—

(a) the making of complaints under the ombudsman scheme, and
(b) the investigation, consideration and determination of complaints by an ombudsman.

(2) Scheme rules—

(a) must provide that a complaint is to be entertained under the ombudsman scheme only if the complainant has made the complaint under that scheme before the applicable time limit (determined in accordance with the scheme rules) has expired, and
(b) may provide that an ombudsman may extend that time limit in specified circumstances.

(3) Scheme rules made under subsection (1) may (among other things) make provision—

(a) for the whole or part of a complaint to be dismissed, in specified circumstances, without consideration of its merits;
(b) for the reference of a complaint, in specified circumstances and with the consent of the complainant, to another body with a view to it being determined by that body instead of by an ombudsman;
(c) for a person who, at the relevant time (within the meaning of section 128(7)) was an authorised person in relation to an activity to be treated in specified circumstances, for the purposes of the scheme and this Part, as if that person were a co-respondent in relation to a complaint;
(d) about the evidence which may be required or admitted and the extent to which it should be oral or written;
(e) for requiring parties to the complaint to attend to give evidence and produce documents, and for authorising the administration of oaths by ombudsmen;
(f) about the matters which are to be taken into account in determining whether an act or omission was fair and reasonable;
(g) for an ombudsman, in such circumstances as may be specified, to award expenses to persons in connection with attendance at a hearing before an ombudsman;
(h) for an ombudsman to award costs against the respondent in favour of the complainant;
(i) for an ombudsman to award costs against the complainant or the respondent in favour of the OLC for the purpose of providing a contribution to resources deployed in dealing with the complaint, if in the ombudsman's opinion that person acted so unreasonably in relation to the complaint that it is appropriate in all the circumstances of the case to make such an award;
(j) for the purpose of facilitating the settlement of a complaint with the agreement of the parties to it;
(k) for specified persons to be notified of complaints, determinations and directions under the ombudsman scheme.

(4) The circumstances specified under subsection (3)(a) may include the following—

(a) the ombudsman considers the complaint or part to be frivolous or vexatious or totally without merit;
(b) the ombudsman considers that the complaint or part would be better dealt with under another ombudsman scheme, by arbitration or by other legal proceedings;
(c) the ombudsman considers that there has been undue delay in the making of the complaint or part, or the provision of evidence to support it;
(d) the ombudsman is satisfied that the matter which is the subject of the complaint or part has previously been dealt with under another ombudsman scheme, by arbitration or by other legal proceedings;
(e) the ombudsman considers that there are other compelling reasons why it is inappropriate for the complaint or part to be dealt with under the ombudsman scheme.

(5) No person may be required by scheme rules—

(a) to provide any information or give any evidence which that person could not be compelled to provide or give in evidence in civil proceedings before the High Court, or
(b) to produce any document which that person could not be compelled to produce in such proceedings.

(6) Scheme rules may authorise an ombudsman making an award of costs in accordance with rules within subsection (3)(h) or (i) to order that the amount payable under the award bears interest, from a time specified in or determined in accordance with the order, at a rate specified in or determined in accordance with the rules.

(7) An amount due under an award made in favour of a person by virtue of provision made under subsection (3)(g), (h) or (i) is recoverable as a debt due to that person.

(8) In this section—

"party", in relation to a complaint, means—

(a) the complainant,

(b) the respondent, and

(c) any other person who in accordance with scheme rules is to be regarded as a party to the complaint;

"specified" means specified in scheme rules.

Initial Commencement

To be appointed: see s 211(2).

Appointment

Appointment: 1 January 2009: see SI 2008/3149, art 2(e)(i).

Extent

This section does not extend to Scotland: see s 212(1).

---

134 Delegation of an ombudsman's functions

(1) An ombudsman may delegate to a member of the OLC's staff appointed under paragraph 13 of Schedule 15—

(a) any function of the ombudsman in relation to the making, investigation or consideration of a complaint;

(b) any other function conferred on the ombudsman by or by virtue of this Part.

(2) Nothing in subsection (1) applies to the following functions—

(a) the function of determining a complaint;

(b) the function of deciding that a complaint should be dismissed by virtue of rules under section 133(3)(a);

(c) the Chief Ombudsman's power to consent to the appointment of an assistant ombudsman under section 122;

(d) the duties imposed on the Chief Ombudsman by section 123 (Chief Ombudsman's report).

Initial Commencement

To be appointed: see s 211(2).

Extent

This section does not extend to Scotland: see s 212(1).

---

135 Notification requirements

(1) This section applies where a complaint—

(a) is excluded from the jurisdiction of the ombudsman scheme under section 126, or by virtue of scheme rules made under section 127;

(b) is dismissed, or referred to another body, by virtue of scheme rules;

(c) is settled, withdrawn or abandoned (or treated as withdrawn or abandoned by virtue of scheme rules).

(2) The ombudsman must notify—

(a) the complainant;

(b) the respondent;

(c) any relevant authorising body, in relation to the respondent, notified of the complaint in accordance with rules within section 133(3)(k), and, in a case within subsection (1)(a) or (b), must give reasons for the exclusion, dismissal or referral.

Initial Commencement
To be appointed: see s 211(2).
Extent
This section does not extend to Scotland: see s 212(1).

---

136 Charges payable by respondents

(1) Scheme rules must require respondents, in relation to complaints under the ombudsman scheme, to pay to the OLC such charges as may be specified in the rules.

(2) The rules must provide for charges payable in relation to a complaint to be waived (or wholly refunded) where—

- (a) the complaint is determined or otherwise resolved in favour of the respondent, and
- (b) the ombudsman is satisfied that the respondent took all reasonable steps to try to resolve the complaint under the respondent's complaints procedures.

(3) The rules may make provision as to—

- (a) the circumstances in which a complaint is to be treated as determined or otherwise resolved in favour of the respondent (which may include circumstances where a complaint is settled, withdrawn or abandoned (or treated as withdrawn or abandoned by virtue of scheme rules));
- (b) matters to be taken into account by the ombudsman for the purposes of subsection (2)(b).

(4) The respondent's complaints procedures are the procedures established by the respondent, or which the respondent participates in or is subject to, in accordance with regulatory arrangements (or licensing rules of the Board) made in accordance with section 112.

(5) The rules may, among other things—

- (a) provide for the OLC to reduce or waive a charge in such other circumstances as may be specified;
- (b) set different charges for different stages of the proceedings on a complaint;
- (c) provide for charges to be wholly or partly refunded in such other circumstances as may be specified;
- (d) provide that if the whole or any part of a charge is not paid by the time by which it is required to be paid under the rules, the unpaid balance from time to time carries interest at the rate specified in, or determined in accordance with, the rules.

(6) Any charge which is owed to the OLC by virtue of rules made under this section may be recovered as a debt due to the OLC

Initial Commencement
To be appointed: see s 211(2).
Appointment
Appointment: 1 January 2009: see SI 2008/3149, art 2(e)(i).
Extent
This section does not extend to Scotland: see s 212(1).

Determinations under the scheme

137 Determination of complaints

(1) A complaint is to be determined under the ombudsman scheme by reference to what is, in the opinion of the ombudsman making the determination, fair and reasonable in all the circumstances of the case.

(2) The determination may contain one or more of the following—

(a) a direction that the respondent make an apology to the complainant;
(b) a direction that—
  (i) the fees to which the respondent is entitled in respect of the services to which the complaint relates ("the fees") are limited to such amount as may be specified in the direction, and
  (ii) the respondent comply, or secure compliance, with such one or more of the permitted requirements as appear to the ombudsman to be necessary in order for effect to be given to the direction under sub-paragraph (i);
(c) a direction that the respondent pay compensation to the complainant of such an amount as is specified in the direction in respect of any loss which has been suffered by, or any inconvenience or distress which has been caused to, the complainant as a result of any matter connected with the complaint;
(d) a direction that the respondent secure the rectification, at the expense of the respondent, of any such error, omission or other deficiency arising in connection with the matter in question as the direction may specify;
(e) a direction that the respondent take, at the expense of the respondent, such other action in the interests of the complainant as the direction may specify.

(3) For the purposes of subsection (2)(b) "the permitted requirements" are—

(a) that the whole or part of any amount already paid by or on behalf of the complainant in respect of the fees be refunded;
(b) that the whole or part of the fees be remitted;
(c) that the right to recover the fees be waived, whether wholly or to any specified extent.

(4) Where—

(a) a direction is made under subsection (2)(b) which requires that the whole or part of any amount already paid by or on behalf of the complainant in respect of the fees be refunded, or
(b) a direction is made under subsection (2)(c),

the direction may also provide for the amount payable under the direction to carry interest from a time specified in or determined in accordance with the direction, at the rate specified in or determined in accordance with scheme rules.

(5) The power of the ombudsman to make a direction under subsection (2) is not confined to cases where the complainant may have a cause of action against the respondent for negligence.

Initial Commencement
To be appointed: see s 211(2).
Appointment
Sub-s (4): Appointment: 1 January 2009: see SI 2008/3149, art 2(e)(i).
Extent
This section does not extend to Scotland: see s 212(1).

---

138 Limitation on value of directions under the ombudsman scheme

(1) Where a determination is made under the ombudsman scheme in respect of a complaint, the total value of directions under section 137(2)(c) to (e) contained in the determination must not exceed £30,000.

(2) For this purpose the total value of such directions is the aggregate of—

(a) the amount of any compensation specified in a direction under subsection (2)(c) of section 137, and
(b) the amount of any expenses reasonably incurred by the respondent when complying with a direction under subsection (2)(d) or (e) of that section.

(3) For the purposes of determining that total value, any interest payable on an amount within subsection (2)(a) of this section, by virtue of section 137(4), is to be ignored.

Initial Commencement
To be appointed: see s 211(2).

Extent
This section does not extend to Scotland: see s 212(1).

139 Alteration of limit

(1) The Lord Chancellor may by order amend section 138(1) in accordance with a recommendation made by an interested body under subsection (2).

(2) An interested body may, at any time, recommend to the Lord Chancellor that section 138(1) should be amended so as to substitute the amount specified in the recommendation for the amount for the time being specified in that provision.

(3) An interested body must, if requested to do so by the Lord Chancellor, consider whether or not it is appropriate to make a recommendation under subsection (2).

(4) An interested body must, before making a recommendation under subsection (2)—

(a) publish a draft of the proposed recommendation,
(b) invite representations regarding the proposed recommendation, and
(c) consider any such representations which are made.

(5) Where the Lord Chancellor receives a recommendation under subsection (2), the Lord Chancellor must consider whether to follow the recommendation.

(6) If the Lord Chancellor decides not to follow the recommendation, the Lord Chancellor must publish a notice to that effect which includes the Lord Chancellor's reasons for the decision.

(7) In this section "interested body" means—

(a) the OLC,
(b) the Board, or
(c) the Consumer Panel.

Initial Commencement
To be appointed: see s 211(2).
Extent
This section does not extend to Scotland: see s 212(1).

140 Acceptance or rejection of determination

(1) When an ombudsman has determined a complaint the ombudsman must prepare a written statement of the determination.

(2) The statement must—

(a) give the ombudsman's reasons for the determination,
(b) be signed by the ombudsman, and
(c) require the complainant to notify the ombudsman, before a time specified in the statement ("the specified time"), whether the complainant accepts or rejects the determination.

(3) The ombudsman must give a copy of the statement to—

(a) the complainant,
(b) the respondent, and
(c) any relevant authorising body in relation to the respondent.

(4) If the complainant notifies the ombudsman that the determination is accepted by the complainant, it is binding on the respondent and the complainant and is final.

(5) If, by the specified time, the complainant has not notified the ombudsman of the complainant's acceptance or rejection of the determination, the complainant is to be treated as having rejected it.

(6) But if—

(a) the complainant notifies the ombudsman after the specified time that the determination is accepted by the complainant,

(b) the complainant has not previously notified the ombudsman of the complainant's rejection of the determination, and
(c) the ombudsman is satisfied that such conditions as may be prescribed by the scheme rules for the purposes of this subsection are satisfied,

the determination is treated as if it had never been rejected by virtue of subsection (5).

(7) The ombudsman must give notice of the outcome to—

(a) the complainant,
(b) the respondent, and
(c) any relevant authorising body in relation to the respondent.

(8) Where a determination is rejected by virtue of subsection (5), that notice must contain a general description of the effect of subsection (6).

(9) A copy of the determination on which appears a certificate signed by an ombudsman is evidence that the determination was made under the scheme.

(10) Such a certificate purporting to be signed by an ombudsman is to be taken to have been duly signed unless the contrary is shown.

(11) Neither the complainant nor the respondent, in relation to a complaint, may institute or continue legal proceedings in respect of a matter which was the subject of a complaint, after the time when a determination by an ombudsman of the complaint becomes binding and final in accordance with this section.

Initial Commencement
To be appointed: see s 211(2).
Appointment
Sub-s (6)(c): Appointment: 1 January 2009: see SI 2008/3149, art 2(e)(i).
Extent
This section does not extend to Scotland: see s 212(1).

---

141 Enforcement by complainant of directions under section 137

(1) This section applies where—

(a) a determination is made in respect of a complaint under the ombudsman scheme,
(b) one or more directions are made under section 137(2), and
(c) the determination is final by virtue of section 140(4).

(2) An amount payable in accordance with—

(a) a direction under subsection (2)(b) of section 137 which requires that the whole or part of any amount already paid by or on behalf of the complainant in respect of the fees be refunded, or
(b) a direction under subsection (2)(c) of that section,

including any interest payable by virtue of subsection (4) of that section, is recoverable, if a court so orders on the application of the complainant or an ombudsman, as if it were payable under an order of that court.

(3) If the respondent fails to comply with any other direction under section 137(2), the complainant or an ombudsman may make an application to the court under this subsection.

(4) If, on an application under subsection (3), the court decides that the respondent has failed to comply with the direction in question, it may order the respondent to take such steps as the court directs for securing that the direction is complied with.

(5) An ombudsman may make an application under subsection (2) or (3) only in such circumstances as may be specified in scheme rules, and with the complainant's consent.

(6) If the court makes an order under subsection (2) on the application of an ombudsman, the ombudsman may in such circumstances as may be specified in scheme rules and with the complainant's consent recover the amount mentioned in that subsection on behalf of the complainant.

(7) In this section "court" means the High Court or a county court.

Initial Commencement
To be appointed: see s 211(2).
Appointment
Sub-ss (5)–(7): Appointment: 1 January 2009: see SI 2008/3149, art 2(e)(i).
Extent
This section does not extend to Scotland: see s 212(1).

---

142 Reporting court orders made against authorised persons

(1) Where a court makes an order under section 141, it must give the OLC notice to that effect.

(2) Where the order is made against a person who is an authorised person in relation to any activity which is a reserved legal activity, the OLC must make arrangements to ensure that an ombudsman gives to each relevant authorising body, in relation to that person, a report which states that the order has been made.

(3) A report under subsection (2) may require the relevant authorising body to report to the ombudsman the action which has been or is to be taken by it in response to the report under subsection (2) and the reasons for that action being taken.

(4) If an ombudsman, having regard to any report produced by the relevant authorising body in compliance with a requirement imposed under subsection (3), or any failure to comply with such a requirement, considers—

- (a) that there has been a serious failure by the relevant authorising body to discharge its regulatory functions, or
- (b) if such a requirement has been imposed on the body on more than one occasion, that the relevant authorising body has persistently failed adequately to discharge its regulatory functions,

the ombudsman may make a report to that effect to the Board.

Initial Commencement
To be appointed: see s 211(2).
Extent
This section does not extend to Scotland: see s 212(1).

Reporting misconduct

143 Reporting possible misconduct to approved regulators

(1) This section applies where—

- (a) an ombudsman is dealing, or has dealt, with a complaint under the ombudsman scheme, and
- (b) the ombudsman is of the opinion that the conduct of the respondent or any other person in relation to any matter connected with the complaint is such that a relevant authorising body in relation to that person should consider whether to take action against that person.

(2) The ombudsman must give the relevant authorising body a report which—

- (a) states that the ombudsman is of that opinion, and
- (b) gives details of that conduct.

(3) The ombudsman must give the complainant a notice stating that a report under subsection (2) has been given to the relevant authorising body.

(4) A report under subsection (2) may require the relevant authorising body to report to the ombudsman the action which has been or is to be taken by it in response to the report and the reasons for that action being taken.

(5) The duty imposed by subsection (2) is not affected by the withdrawal or abandonment of the complaint.

(6) If an ombudsman, having regard to any report produced by the relevant authorising body in compliance with a requirement imposed under subsection (4), or any failure to comply with such a requirement, considers—

(a) that there has been a serious failure by the relevant authorising body to discharge its regulatory functions, or
(b) if such a requirement has been imposed on the body on more than one occasion, that the relevant authorising body has persistently failed adequately to discharge its regulatory functions,

the ombudsman may make a report to that effect to the Board.

Initial Commencement
To be appointed: see s 211(2).
Extent
This section does not extend to Scotland: see s 212(1).

Co-operation with investigations

144 Duties to share information

(1) Scheme rules must make provision requiring persons within subsection (3) to disclose to an approved regulator information of such description as may be specified in the rules, in such circumstances as may be so specified.

(2) The regulatory arrangements of an approved regulator must make provision requiring the approved regulator to disclose to persons within subsection (3) information of such description as may be specified in the arrangements, in such circumstances as may be so specified.

(3) The persons are—

(a) the OLC;
(b) an ombudsman;
(c) a member of the OLC's staff appointed under paragraph 13 of Schedule 15.

(4) Provision made under subsection (1) or (2) must satisfy such requirements as the Board may, from time to time, specify.

(5) In specifying requirements under subsection (4) the Board must have regard to the need to ensure that, so far as reasonably practicable—

(a) duplication of investigations is avoided;
(b) the OLC assists approved regulators to carry out their regulatory functions, and approved regulators assist with the investigation, consideration and determination of complaints under the ombudsman scheme.

(6) The Board must publish any requirements specified by it under subsection (4).

(7) The OLC must—

(a) before publishing under section 205(2) a draft of rules it proposes to make under subsection (1), consult each approved regulator to which the proposed rules apply, and
(b) when seeking the Board's consent to such rules under section 155, identify any objections made by an approved regulator to the rules and not withdrawn.

(8) An approved regulator must—

(a) consult the OLC before making provisions in its regulatory arrangements of the kind mentioned in subsection (2), and
(b) where an application is made for the Board's approval of such provisions, identify any objections made by the OLC to the provisions and not withdrawn.

(9) This section applies to the Board in its capacity as a licensing authority and licensing rules made by the Board as it applies to an approved regulator and its regulatory arrangements; and for

this purpose the reference in subsection (5)(b) to "regulatory functions" is to be read as a reference to the Board's functions under its licensing rules.

Initial Commencement
To be appointed: see s 211(2).
Appointment
Sub-ss (1), (3)–(7): Appointment: 1 January 2009: see SI 2008/3149, art 2(e)(i); for transitional provisions see art 3(2) thereof.
Extent
This section does not extend to Scotland: see s 212(1).

---

145 Duties of authorised persons to co-operate with investigations

(1) The regulatory arrangements of an approved regulator, and licensing rules made by the Board in its capacity as a licensing authority, must make—

- (a) provision requiring each relevant authorised person to give ombudsmen all such assistance requested by them, in connection with the investigation, consideration or determination of complaints under the ombudsman scheme, as that person is reasonably able to give, and
- (b) provision for the enforcement of that requirement.

(2) The provision made for the purposes of subsection (1) must satisfy such requirements as the Board may, from time to time, specify for the purposes of that subsection.

(3) The Board must publish any requirements specified by it under subsection (2).

(4) In this section "relevant authorised person"—

- (a) in relation to an approved regulator, has the same meaning as in section 112, and
- (b) in relation to the Board in its capacity as a licensing authority, means a person licensed by the Board under Part 5.

Initial Commencement
To be appointed: see s 211(2).
Appointment
Sub-ss (2), (3): Appointment: 1 January 2009: see SI 2008/3149, art 2(e)(i).
Extent
This section does not extend to Scotland: see s 212(1).

---

146 Reporting failures to co-operate with an investigation to approved regulators

(1) This section applies where an ombudsman is of the opinion that an authorised person has failed to give an ombudsman all such assistance requested by the ombudsman, in connection with the investigation, consideration or determination of a complaint under the ombudsman scheme, as that person is reasonably able to give.

(2) The ombudsman must give each relevant authorising body, in relation to that person, a report which—

- (a) states that the ombudsman is of that opinion, and
- (b) gives details of the failure.

(3) A report under subsection (2) may require the relevant authorising body to report to the ombudsman the action which has been or is to be taken by it in response to the report under that subsection and the reasons for that action being taken.

(4) The duty imposed by subsection (2) is not affected by the withdrawal or abandonment of the complaint.

(5) If an ombudsman, having regard to any report produced by the relevant authorising body in compliance with a requirement imposed under subsection (3), or any failure to comply with such a requirement, considers—

(a) that there has been a serious failure by the relevant authorising body to discharge its regulatory functions, or
(b) if such a requirement has been imposed on the body on more than one occasion, that the relevant authorising body has persistently failed adequately to discharge its regulatory functions,

the ombudsman may make a report to that effect to the Board.

(6) In this section "authorised person" means an authorised person in relation to any activity which is a reserved legal activity.

Initial Commencement
To be appointed: see s 211(2).
Extent
This section does not extend to Scotland: see s 212(1).

Information

147 Information and documents

(1) An ombudsman may, by notice, require a party to a complaint under the ombudsman scheme—

(a) to produce documents, or documents of a description, specified in the notice, or
(b) to provide information, or information of a description, specified in the notice.

(2) A notice under subsection (1) may require the information or documents to be provided or produced—

(a) before the end of such reasonable period as may be specified in the notice, and
(b) in the case of information, in such manner or form as may be so specified.

(3) This section applies only to information and documents the provision or production of which the ombudsman considers necessary for the determination of the complaint.

(4) An ombudsman may—

(a) take copies of or extracts from a document produced under this section, and
(b) require the person producing the document to provide an explanation of it.

(5) If a person who is required under this section to produce a document fails to do so, an ombudsman may require that person to state, to the best of that person's knowledge and belief, where the document is.

(6) No person may be required under this section—

(a) to provide any information which that person could not be compelled to provide or give in evidence in civil proceedings before the High Court, or
(b) to produce any document which that person could not be compelled to produce in such proceedings.

(7) In this section "party", in relation to a complaint, means—

(a) the complainant;
(b) the respondent;
(c) any other person who in accordance with the scheme rules is to be regarded as a party to the complaint.

Initial Commencement
To be appointed: see s 211(2).
Extent
This section does not extend to Scotland: see s 212(1).

---

148 Reporting failures to provide information or produce documents

(1) This section applies where an ombudsman is of the opinion that an authorised person has failed to comply with a requirement imposed under section 147(1).

(2) The ombudsman must give each relevant authorising body, in relation to that person, a report which—

(a) states that the ombudsman is of that opinion, and
(b) gives details of the failure.

(3) A report under subsection (2) may require the relevant authorising body to report to the ombudsman the action which has been or is to be taken by it in response to the report under that subsection and the reasons for that action being taken.

(4) The duty imposed by subsection (2) is not affected by the withdrawal or abandonment of the complaint in relation to which the requirement was imposed under section 147(1).

(5) If an ombudsman, having regard to any report produced by the relevant authorising body in compliance with a requirement imposed under subsection (3), or any failure to comply with such a requirement, considers—

(a) that there has been a serious failure by the relevant authorising body to discharge its regulatory functions, or
(b) if such a requirement has been imposed on the body on more than one occasion, that the relevant authorising body has persistently failed adequately to discharge its regulatory functions,

the ombudsman may make a report to that effect to the Board.

(6) In this section "authorised person" means an authorised person in relation to any activity which is a reserved legal activity.

Initial Commencement
To be appointed: see s 211(2).
Extent
This section does not extend to Scotland: see s 212(1).

---

149 Enforcement of requirements to provide information or produce documents

(1) This section applies where an ombudsman is of the opinion that a person ("the defaulter") has failed to comply with a requirement imposed under section 147(1).

(2) The ombudsman may certify the defaulter's failure to comply with the requirement to the court.

(3) Where an ombudsman certifies a failure to the court under subsection (2), the court may enquire into the case.

(4) If the court is satisfied that the defaulter has failed without reasonable excuse to comply with the requirement, it may deal with—

(a) the defaulter, and
(b) in the case of a body, any manager of the body,

as if that person were in contempt.

(5) Subsection (6) applies in a case where the defaulter is an authorised person in relation to any activity which is a reserved legal activity.

(6) The ombudsman ("the enforcing ombudsman") may not certify the defaulter's failure to the court until a report by that or another ombudsman has been made as required by section 148(2) and the enforcing ombudsman is satisfied—

(a) that each relevant authorising body to whom such a report was made has been given a reasonable opportunity to take action in respect of the defaulter's failure, and
(b) that the defaulter has continued to fail to provide the information or produce the documents to which the requirement under section 147 related.

(7) In this section "court" means the High Court.

Initial Commencement
To be appointed: see s 211(2).
Extent
This section does not extend to Scotland: see s 212(1).

---

150 Reports of investigations

(1) The OLC may, if it considers it appropriate to do so in any particular case, publish a report of the investigation, consideration and determination of a complaint made under the ombudsman scheme.

(2) A report under subsection (1) must not (unless the complainant consents)—

(a) mention the name of the complainant, or
(b) include any particulars which, in the opinion of the OLC, are likely to identify the complainant.

Initial Commencement
To be appointed: see s 211(2).
Extent
This section does not extend to Scotland: see s 212(1).

---

151 Restricted information

(1) Except as provided by section 152, restricted information must not be disclosed—

(a) by a restricted person, or
(b) by any person who receives the information directly or indirectly from a restricted person.

(2) In this section and section 152—

"restricted information" means information (other than excluded information) which is obtained by a restricted person in the course of, or for the purposes of, an investigation into a complaint made under the ombudsman scheme (including information obtained for the purposes of deciding whether to begin such an investigation or in connection with the settlement of a complaint);
"restricted person" means—
(a) the OLC,
(b) an ombudsman, or
(c) a person who exercises functions delegated under paragraph 22 of Schedule 15.

(3) For the purposes of subsection (2) "excluded information" means—

(a) information which is in the form of a summary or collection of information so framed as not to enable information relating to any particular person to be ascertained from it;
(b) information which at the time of the disclosure is or has already been made available to the public from other sources;
(c) information which was obtained more than 70 years before the date of the disclosure.

Initial Commencement
To be appointed: see s 211(2).
Extent
This section does not extend to Scotland: see s 212(1).

---

152 Disclosure of restricted information

(1) A restricted person may disclose restricted information to another restricted person.

(2) Restricted information may be disclosed for the purposes of the investigation in the course of which, or for the purposes of which, it was obtained.

(3) Section 151 also does not preclude the disclosure of restricted information—

- (a) in a report made under—
  - (i) section 143(2) (report of possible misconduct to approved regulators),
  - (ii) section 146(2) (report of failure to co-operate with investigation),
  - (iii) section 148 (reporting failures to provide information or produce documents), or
  - (iv) section 150 (reports of investigations),
- (b) for the purposes of enabling or assisting the Board to exercise any of its functions,
- (c) to an approved regulator for the purposes of enabling or assisting the approved regulator to exercise any of its regulatory functions,
- (d) with the consent of the person to whom it relates and (if different) the person from whom the restricted person obtained it,
- (e) for the purposes of an inquiry with a view to the taking of any criminal proceedings or for the purposes of any such proceedings,
- (f) where the disclosure is required by or by virtue of any provision made by or under this Act or any other enactment or other rule of law,
- (g) to such persons (other than approved regulators) who exercise regulatory functions as may be prescribed by order made by the Lord Chancellor, for such purposes as may be so prescribed.

(4) Subsections (2) and (3) are subject to subsection (5).

(5) The Lord Chancellor may by order prevent the disclosure of restricted information by virtue of subsection (2) or (3) in such circumstances, or for such purposes, as may be prescribed in the order.

Initial Commencement
To be appointed: see s 211(2).
Extent
This section does not extend to Scotland: see s 212(1).

---

153 Data protection

In section 31 of the Data Protection Act 1998 (c 29) (regulatory activity), after subsection (4B) (inserted by section 170) insert—

"(4C) Personal data processed for the purposes of the function of considering a complaint under the scheme established under Part 6 of the Legal Services Act 2007 (legal complaints) are exempt from the subject information provisions in any case to the extent to which the application of those provisions to the data would be likely to prejudice the proper discharge of the function."

Initial Commencement
To be appointed: see s 211(2).

Defamation

154 Protection from defamation claims

For the purposes of the law of defamation—

- (a) proceedings in relation to a complaint under the ombudsman scheme are to be treated as if they were proceedings before a court, and
- (b) the publication of any matter by the OLC under this Part is absolutely privileged.

Initial Commencement
To be appointed: see s 211(2).
Extent
This section does not extend to Scotland: see s 212(1).

Scheme rules

155 Consent requirements for rules

(1) Before making scheme rules under any provision of this Part, the OLC must obtain—

- (a) the consent of the Board, and
- (b) in the case of rules under section 136 (charges payable by respondents), the consent of the Lord Chancellor.

(2) In subsection (1) the reference to making rules includes a reference to modifying rules.

Initial Commencement
To be appointed: see s 211(2).
Appointment
Appointment: 1 January 2009: see SI 2008/3149, art 2(e)(i).
Extent
This section does not extend to Scotland: see s 212(1).

---

156 The Board's powers in respect of rules

(1) The Board may direct the OLC to take such steps as are necessary—

- (a) to modify its scheme rules in accordance with such general requirements as are specified in the direction, or
- (b) to make a specified modification to its scheme rules.

(2) Before giving a direction under subsection (1)(b), the Board must—

- (a) give the OLC a notice giving details of the proposed modification and containing a statement that representations about the proposal may be made to the Board within a period specified in the notice,
- (b) publish a copy of that notice, and
- (c) have regard to any representations duly made.

(3) The following provisions do not apply in relation to any modification made by the OLC to its rules in compliance with a direction under subsection (1)(b)—

- (a) section 155(1)(a) (requirement to obtain the Board's consent to rules);
- (b) section 205 (requirement to consult before making rules).

(4) Where the Board revokes a direction, it must—

- (a) give the OLC notice of the revocation, and
- (b) publish that notice.

Initial Commencement
To be appointed: see s 211(2).
Appointment
Appointment: 1 January 2009: see SI 2008/3149, art 2(e)(i).
Extent
This section does not extend to Scotland: see s 212(1).

Effect on existing arrangements for redress etc

157 Approved regulators not to make provision for redress

(1) The regulatory arrangements of an approved regulator must not include any provision relating to redress.

(2) If at the time this subsection comes into force the regulatory arrangements of an approved regulator contravene subsection (1), any provision relating to redress included in those regulatory arrangements ceases to have effect at that time, subject to subsection (3).

(3) An order under section 211 which appoints a day for the coming into force of subsection (2) may include transitional provision in respect of any proceedings which, immediately before that day are awaiting determination under any provision relating to redress made by an approved regulator.

This subsection is without prejudice to any other transitional provision which may be made by or under this Act.

(4) For the purposes of this section "provision relating to redress" means any provision made in regulatory arrangements (whether it is statutory or non-statutory) for redress in respect of acts or omissions of authorised persons and any provision connected with such provision.

(5) Nothing in this section prevents an approved regulator making—

- (a) provision in its regulatory arrangements of the kind required by section 112 (requirement for authorised persons to have complaints procedures etc),
- (b) indemnification arrangements or compensation arrangements, or
- (c) provision which by virtue of section 158 is not prohibited by this section.

(6) In subsection (4) "authorised person" means an authorised person in relation to any activity which is a reserved legal activity.

(7) This section applies to licensing rules made by the Board in its capacity as a licensing authority as it applies in relation to the regulatory arrangements of an approved regulator.

Initial Commencement
To be appointed: see s 211(2).
Extent
This section does not extend to Scotland: see s 212(1).

---

158 Regulatory arrangements not prohibited by section 157

(1) Section 157 does not prohibit the regulatory arrangements of an approved regulator from making provision requiring, or authorising the approved regulator to require, a relevant authorised person—

- (a) to investigate whether there are any persons who may have a claim against the relevant authorised person in relation to a matter specified by the approved regulator;
- (b) to provide the approved regulator with a report on the outcome of the investigation;
- (c) to identify persons ("affected persons") who may have such a claim;
- (d) to notify affected persons that they may have such a claim;
- (e) to provide affected persons with information about the relevant authorised person's complaints procedures and the ombudsman scheme;
- (f) to ensure that the relevant authorised person's complaints procedures operate as if an affected person had made a complaint against the relevant authorised person in respect of the act or omission to which the claim relates.

(2) For the purposes of subsection (1) "claim", in relation to a relevant authorised person, means a claim for redress resulting from an act or omission of that person.

(3) For the purposes of this section—

- (a) "relevant authorised person", in relation to an approved regulator, means a person authorised by that approved regulator to carry on an activity which is a reserved legal activity, and
- (b) a relevant authorised person's complaints procedures are the procedures established by that person, or which that person participates in or is subject to, in accordance with regulatory arrangements made in accordance with section 112.

(4) This section applies in relation to the Board in its capacity as a licensing authority as it applies in relation to an approved regulator, and in relation to the Board references to regulatory arrangements are to be read as references to the Board's licensing rules.

Initial Commencement
To be appointed: see s 211(2).
Extent
This section does not extend to Scotland: see s 212(1).

---

159 Legal Services Complaints Commissioner and Legal Services Ombudsman

(1) The offices of Legal Services Complaints Commissioner and Legal Services Ombudsman are abolished.

(2) Accordingly—

- (a) sections 51 and 52 of, and Schedule 8 to, the Access to Justice Act 1999 (c 22), and
- (b) sections 21 to 26 of, and Schedule 3 to, the Courts and Legal Services Act 1990 (c 41),

are repealed.

Initial Commencement
To be appointed: see s 211(2).
Extent
This section does not extend to Scotland: see s 212(1).

Interpretation

160 Interpretation of Part 6

In this Part—

"complainant", in relation to a complaint, means the person who makes the complaint;
"relevant authorising body", in relation to a person, means—

- (a) an approved regulator by which the person is authorised to carry on an activity which is a reserved legal activity, or
- (b) where the person is authorised to carry on such an activity by the Board in its capacity as a licensing authority, the Board;

"respondent", in relation to a complaint, is to be construed in accordance with section 125 (except that, where scheme rules of the kind mentioned in section 133(3)(c) have effect, references to the "respondent" include a person treated as a co-respondent under those rules).

Initial Commencement
To be appointed: see s 211(2).
Appointment
Appointment: 1 January 2009: see SI 2008/3149, art 2(e)(i).
Extent
This section does not extend to Scotland: see s 212(1).

Claims management services

161 Extension of Part 6 to claims management services

(1) For the purposes of this Part (and sections 1, 21 and 27 as they apply in relation to this Part)—

- (a) the Claims Management Services Regulator is to be treated as an approved regulator;
- (b) regulated claims management services are to be treated as a reserved legal activity;
- (c) a person authorised by the Claims Management Services Regulator, under Part 2 of the Compensation Act 2006 (c 29), to provide regulated claims management services is to be treated as an authorised person in relation to that activity;

(d) the Claims Management Services Regulator is to be treated as a relevant authorising body in relation to such a person; and
(e) regulations under section 9 of, and the Schedule to, the Compensation Act 2006 (regulations about the functions of the Claims Management Services Regulator etc) are to be treated as regulatory arrangements of the Claims Management Services Regulator.

(2) For the purposes of sections 112 and 145 (as extended by this section) a person authorised by the Claims Management Services Regulator under Part 2 of the Compensation Act 2006 to provide regulated claims management services is to be treated as a "relevant authorised person" in relation to the Regulator.

(3) Section 9 of, and the Schedule to, the Compensation Act 2006 (regulations about the functions of the Claims Management Regulator etc) are subject to any requirements imposed by this Part in relation to the regulatory arrangements of the Claims Management Regulator.

(4) In this section—

"Claims Management Services Regulator" means—
(a) the person designated under section 5(1) of the Compensation Act 2006, or
(b) at a time when no person is so designated, the Board;

"regulated claims management services" has the same meaning as in Part 2 of the Compensation Act 2006.

Initial Commencement
To be appointed: see s 211(2).
Extent
This section does not extend to Scotland: see s 212(1).

PART 7
FURTHER PROVISIONS RELATING TO THE BOARD AND THE OLC

Guidance

162 Guidance

(1) The Board may give guidance—

(a) about the operation of this Act and of any order made under it;
(b) about the operation of any rules made by the Board under this Act;
(c) about any matter relating to the Board's functions;
(d) for the purpose of meeting the regulatory objectives;
(e) about the content of licensing rules;
(f) about any other matters about which it appears to the Board to be desirable to give guidance.

(2) Guidance under this section may consist of such information and advice as the Board considers appropriate.

(3) The Board may give financial or other assistance to persons giving information or advice of a kind which the Board could give under this section.

(4) The Board may—

(a) publish its guidance,
(b) offer copies of its published guidance for sale at a reasonable price, and
(c) if it gives guidance in response to a request made by any person, make a reasonable charge for that guidance.

(5) When exercising its functions, the Board may have regard to the extent to which an approved regulator has complied with any guidance issued under this section which is applicable to the approved regulator.

(6) When exercising its functions—

(a) in its capacity as an approved regulator by virtue of an order under section 62(1)(a), or
(b) in its capacity as a licensing authority under Part 5,

the Board must have regard to any guidance it has issued under this section.

Initial Commencement
To be appointed: see s 211(2).
Appointment
Appointment: 1 January 2009: see SI 2008/3149, art 2(f).
Extent
This section does not extend to Scotland: see s 212(1).

Voluntary arrangements

163 Voluntary arrangements

(1) The Board may enter into arrangements with any person under which the Board is to provide assistance for the purpose of improving standards of service and promoting best practice in connection with the carrying on of any legal activity.

(2) These arrangements may (among other things) provide for the Board to give advice on—

(a) the best regulatory practice, or
(b) the contents of codes of practice or other voluntary arrangements.

(3) Arrangements under this section may include provision as to the terms on which assistance is to be provided by the Board (including provision as to payment).

(4) Where the Board enters into arrangements under this section, it must publish a statement giving details of the arrangements and explaining what they are intended to achieve.

Initial Commencement
To be appointed: see s 211(2).
Extent
This section does not extend to Scotland: see s 212(1).

---

164 Power to establish voluntary scheme for resolving complaints

(1) This section and section 166 provide for a scheme under which legal services complaints may be resolved quickly and with minimum formality by an independent person.

(2) The OLC may make rules ("voluntary scheme rules") establishing such a scheme ("the voluntary scheme"), but only in relation to such kinds of legal services complaints as may be specified by order made by the Lord Chancellor for the purposes of this section.

(3) An order under subsection (2) may in particular specify a kind of legal services complaint by reference to the description of the complainant, of the respondent, or of the legal services to which the complaint relates.

(4) "Legal services complaint" means a complaint which relates to an act or omission of an eligible person ("the respondent") in the course of that person providing legal services.

(5) For that purpose a person is eligible if at the time the act or omission took place there was no activity in relation to which the person—

(a) was an authorised person, or
(b) is to be regarded as having been such a person by virtue of section 129.

(6) Under the voluntary scheme—

(a) redress may be provided to the complainant, but
(b) no disciplinary action may be taken against the respondent.

(7) Voluntary scheme rules may confer functions on ombudsmen for the purposes of the voluntary scheme.

(8) Section 131 applies for the purposes of the voluntary scheme as it applies for the purposes of the ombudsman scheme.

(9) Sections 155 and 156 apply in relation to voluntary scheme rules as they apply in relation to scheme rules.

(10) In this section—

"legal services" means services provided by a person which consist of or include legal activities carried on by, or on behalf of, that person;

"the voluntary scheme" and "voluntary scheme rules" have the meaning given by subsection (2).

Initial Commencement
To be appointed: see s 211(2).
Extent
This section does not extend to Scotland: see s 212(1).

---

165 Procedure for making orders under section 164

(1) The Lord Chancellor may make an order under section 164(2) only on the recommendation of an interested body.

(2) An interested body must, if requested to do so by the Lord Chancellor, consider whether or not it is appropriate to make a recommendation for such an order.

(3) An interested body must, before making a recommendation for such an order—

(a) publish a draft of the proposed recommendation,
(b) invite representations regarding the proposed recommendation, and
(c) consider any such representations which are made.

(4) Where the Lord Chancellor receives a recommendation from an interested body for an order under section 164(2), the Lord Chancellor must consider whether to follow the recommendation.

(5) If the Lord Chancellor decides not to follow the recommendation, the Lord Chancellor must publish a notice to that effect which includes the Lord Chancellor's reasons for the decision.

(6) In this section "interested body" means—

(a) the OLC,
(b) the Board, or
(c) the Consumer Panel.

Initial Commencement
To be appointed: see s 211(2).
Extent
This section does not extend to Scotland: see s 212(1).

---

166 Operation of voluntary scheme

(1) A complaint may be determined under the voluntary scheme only if—

(a) the complainant falls within a class of persons specified in voluntary scheme rules as qualified to make a complaint,
(b) the complainant wishes to have the complaint dealt with under the scheme,
(c) at the time of the act or omission to which the complaint relates, the respondent was participating in the scheme and voluntary scheme rules were in force in relation to the legal services in question, and
(d) at the time the complaint is made under the scheme the respondent has not withdrawn from the scheme in accordance with its provisions.

(2) A person qualifies for participation in the voluntary scheme if the person falls within a class of persons specified as qualified in voluntary scheme rules.

(3) In such circumstances as may be specified in voluntary scheme rules, a complaint may be dealt with under the voluntary scheme even though subsection (1)(c) would otherwise prevent that.

(4) Subsection (3) applies only if the respondent participates in the voluntary scheme on the basis that complaints of that kind are to be dealt with under the scheme.

(5) Complaints are to be dealt with and determined under the voluntary scheme on standard terms fixed by the OLC with the consent of the Board.

(6) The OLC may modify standard terms only with the consent of the Board.

(7) Section 204(3) applies to standard terms as it applies to rules made by the OLC

(8) The standard terms may in particular make provision—

(a) requiring the making of payments to the OLC by persons participating in the scheme of such amounts, at such times and in such circumstances, as may be determined by the OLC;
(b) as to the award of costs on the determination of a complaint (including provision for an award of costs in favour of the OLC for the purpose of providing a contribution to resources deployed in dealing with the complaint).

(9) In this section "legal services", "the voluntary scheme" and "voluntary scheme rules" have the same meaning as in section 164.

Initial Commencement
To be appointed: see s 211(2).
Extent
This section does not extend to Scotland: see s 212(1).

Disclosure and use of information

167 Restricted information

(1) Except as provided by section 168, restricted information must not be disclosed—

(a) by a restricted person, or
(b) by any person who receives the information directly or indirectly from a restricted person.

(2) In this section and section 168—

"restricted information" means information (other than excluded information) which is obtained by the Board in the exercise of its functions;
"restricted person" means—
(a) the Board (including the Board in its capacity as an approved regulator or a licensing authority),
(b) a person who exercises functions delegated under paragraph 23 of Schedule 1 or section 73 or by virtue of section 64(2)(k).

(3) For the purposes of subsection (2) "excluded information" means—

(a) information which is in the form of a summary or collection of information so framed as not to enable information relating to any particular person to be ascertained from it;
(b) information which at the time of the disclosure is or has already been made available to the public from other sources;
(c) information which was obtained more than 70 years before the date of the disclosure.

Initial Commencement
To be appointed: see s 211(2).
Extent
This section does not extend to Scotland: see s 212(1).

---

168 Disclosure of restricted information

(1) A restricted person may disclose restricted information to another restricted person.

(2) Restricted information may be disclosed for the purposes of enabling or assisting the Board to exercise its functions (whether as an approved regulator, a licensing authority or otherwise).

(3) Section 167 also does not preclude the disclosure of restricted information—

- (a) where the disclosure is a result of the Board exercising any power to publish information under this Act;
- (b) for the purposes of enabling or assisting the OLC, ombudsmen or persons who exercise functions delegated under paragraph 22 of Schedule 15, to exercise any of its or their functions,
- (c) to an approved regulator for the purposes of enabling or assisting the approved regulator to exercise any of its functions,
- (d) with the consent of the person to whom it relates and (if different) the person from whom the restricted person obtained it,
- (e) for the purposes of an inquiry with a view to the taking of any criminal proceedings or for the purposes of any such proceedings,
- (f) where the disclosure is required by or by virtue of any provision made by or under this Act or any other enactment or other rule of law, or
- (g) to such persons (other than approved regulators) who exercise regulatory functions as may be prescribed by order made by the Lord Chancellor, for such purposes as may be so prescribed.

(4) Subsections (2) and (3) are subject to subsection (5).

(5) The Lord Chancellor may by order prevent the disclosure of restricted information by virtue of subsection (2) or (3) in such circumstances, or for such purposes, as may be prescribed in the order.

Initial Commencement
To be appointed: see s 211(2).
Extent
This section does not extend to Scotland: see s 212(1).

---

169 Disclosure of information to the Board

(1) Information which is held by or on behalf of a permitted person (whether obtained before or after this section comes into force) may be disclosed to the Board for the purposes of enabling or assisting the Board to exercise its functions (whether as an approved regulator, a licensing authority or otherwise).

(2) A disclosure under this section is not to be taken to breach any restriction on the disclosure of information (however imposed).

(3) But nothing in this section authorises the making of a disclosure—

- (a) which contravenes the Data Protection Act 1998 (c 29), or
- (b) which is prohibited by Part 1 of the Regulation of Investigatory Powers Act 2000 (c 23).

(4) This section does not affect a power to disclose which exists apart from this section.

(5) The following are permitted persons—

- (a) a chief officer of police of a police force in England and Wales;
- (b) a chief constable of a police force in Scotland;
- (c) the Chief Constable of the Police Service of Northern Ireland;
- (d) the Director General of the Serious Organised Crime Agency;
- (e) the Commissioners for Her Majesty's Revenue and Customs;
- (f) the Financial Services Authority.

(6) The Lord Chancellor may by order designate as permitted persons other persons who exercise functions which the Lord Chancellor considers are of a public nature (including a person discharging regulatory functions in relation to any description of activities).

(7) Information must not be disclosed under this section on behalf of the Commissioners for Her Majesty's Revenue and Customs unless the Commissioners authorise the disclosure.

(8) The power to authorise a disclosure under subsection (7) may be delegated (either generally or for a specific purpose) to an officer of Revenue and Customs.

Initial Commencement
To be appointed: see s 211(2).
Extent
This section does not extend to Scotland: see s 212(1).

---

170 Data protection

In section 31 of the Data Protection Act 1998 (c 29) (regulatory activity), after subsection (4A) insert—

"(4B) Personal data processed for the purposes of discharging any function of the Legal Services Board are exempt from the subject information provisions in any case to the extent to which the application of those provisions to the data would be likely to prejudice the proper discharge of the function."

Initial Commencement
To be appointed: see s 211(2).

---

171 Use of information

Information obtained by the Board (whether in its capacity as an approved regulator or licensing authority or otherwise) may be used by the Board for the purposes of, or for any purpose connected with or incidental to, the exercise of its functions.

Initial Commencement
To be appointed: see s 211(2).
Extent
This section does not extend to Scotland: see s 212(1).

Payments by Lord Chancellor

172 Funding

(1) The Lord Chancellor may—

(a) pay to the Board such sums as the Lord Chancellor may determine as appropriate for the purpose of meeting the expenditure of the Board incurred under or for the purposes of this Act or any other enactment (including any expenditure incurred by it in its capacity as an approved regulator or its capacity as a licensing authority), and

(b) pay to the OLC such sums as the Lord Chancellor may determine as appropriate for the purposes of meeting the expenditure of the OLC incurred under or for the purposes of this Act.

(2) The Lord Chancellor may—

(a) determine the manner in which and times at which the sums mentioned in subsection (1) are to be paid, and

(b) impose conditions on the payment of those sums.

Initial Commencement
To be appointed: see s 211(2).
Appointment
Appointment: 7 March 2008: see SI 2008/222, art 2(e).
Extent
This section does not extend to Scotland: see s 212(1).

The levy

173 The levy

(1) The Board must make rules providing for the imposition of a levy on leviable bodies for the purpose of raising an amount corresponding to the aggregate of—

(a) the leviable Board expenditure,
(b) the leviable OLC expenditure, and
(c) the leviable Lord Chancellor expenditure.

(2) A levy imposed under this section is payable to the Board.

(3) Before making rules under this section, the Board must satisfy itself that the apportionment of the levy as between different leviable bodies will be in accordance with fair principles.

(4) The Board may not make rules under this section except with the consent of the Lord Chancellor.

(5) "Leviable body" means—

(a) an approved regulator,
(b) the person designated under section 5(1) of the Compensation Act 2006 (c 29) (the Regulator in relation to claims management services), or
(c) any other person prescribed by the Lord Chancellor by order.

(6) The "leviable Board expenditure" means the difference between—

(a) the expenditure of the Board incurred under or for the purposes of this Act or any other enactment (including any expenditure incurred in connection with its establishment and any expenditure incurred by it in its capacity as an approved regulator or its capacity as a licensing authority), and
(b) the aggregate of the amounts which the Board pays into the Consolidated Fund under section 175(1)(a), (c) to (e) and (k) to (m) or by virtue of regulations under paragraph 7(g) of the Schedule to the Compensation Act 2006.

(7) The "leviable OLC expenditure" means the difference between—

(a) the expenditure of the OLC incurred under or for the purposes of this Act (including any expenditure incurred in connection with its establishment), and
(b) the aggregate of the amounts which the OLC pays into the Consolidated Fund under section 175(1)(g), (h) or (n).

(8) But subsection (7)(a) does not include such proportion of the expenditure of the OLC incurred under or for the purposes of this Act as may reasonably be attributed to the exercise of its functions under sections 164 to 166.

(9) The "leviable Lord Chancellor expenditure" means any expenditure incurred by the Lord Chancellor in connection with the establishment of the Board or the OLC (including expenditure incurred under or for the purposes of paragraph 10 of Schedule 22 (Interim Chief Executive of the OLC)).

(10) But the leviable Lord Chancellor expenditure does not include any expenditure under section 172 (funding of Board and OLC).

(11) In subsection (5) the reference to "an approved regulator" does not include the Board where it is designated as an approved regulator under section 62.

Initial Commencement
To be appointed: see s 211(2).
Appointment
Sub-ss (1), (3)–(11): Appointment: 1 January 2009: see SI 2008/3149, art 2(f); for transitional provisions see art 3(3) thereof.
Extent
This section does not extend to Scotland: see s 212(1).

---

174 The levy: supplementary provisions

(1) In this section—

"leviable body" has the meaning given by section 173;
"the levy" means the levy payable by virtue of that section;
"the levy rules" means the rules made in accordance with that section.

(2) The levy is to be payable at such rate and at such times as may be specified in the levy rules.

(3) The provision made in the levy rules for determining the amount of the levy payable in respect of a particular period—

(a) may require account to be taken of estimated as well as actual expenditure and receipts, and
(b) must require the Board to obtain the Lord Chancellor's agreement to the amount payable in respect of a particular period.

(4) The levy rules may provide for different parts of the levy to be payable at different rates.

(5) Any amount which is owed to the Board in accordance with the levy rules may be recovered as a debt due to the Board.

(6) The levy rules must require the Board—

(a) to calculate the amount of the levy payable by each leviable body,
(b) to notify each leviable body of its liability to pay an amount of levy and the time or times at which it becomes payable.

(7) Without prejudice to subsections (2) to (6), the levy rules may—

(a) make provision about the collection and recovery of the levy;
(b) make provision about the circumstances in which any amount of the levy payable may be waived;
(c) provide that if the whole or any part of an amount of the levy payable under the levy rules is not paid by the time when it is required to be paid under the rules, the unpaid balance from time to time carries interest at the rate determined by or in accordance with the levy rules.

Initial Commencement
To be appointed: see s 211(2).
Appointment
Sub-ss (1), (3), (4), (6), (7): Appointment: 1 January 2009: see SI 2008/3149, art 2(f); for transitional provisions see art 3(3) thereof.
Extent
This section does not extend to Scotland: see s 212(1).

Payments into the Consolidated Fund

175 Amounts payable into the Consolidated Fund

(1) The following must be paid into the Consolidated Fund—

(a) any application fee received by the Board;
(b) any sum received by the Board under sections 37 to 40 (financial penalties and interest);
(c) amounts paid to the Board under section 49(10) or 50(5) (charges for providing draft and final policy statements);
(d) any sums received by the Board in its capacity as an approved regulator by virtue of rules within section 64(2)(f) (practising fees etc);
(e) any sums received by the Board in its capacity as a licensing authority by virtue of its licensing rules within paragraph 1, 4, 6, 7 or 21 of Schedule 11 or by virtue of paragraph 17 or 18 of Schedule 14;
(f) any sums received by the Board in its capacity as a licensing authority under sections 95 to 97 (financial penalties and interest);
(g) any charges received by the OLC by virtue of rules under section 136 (charges payable by respondents), together with any interest payable in accordance with those rules;

(h) any amount payable to the OLC in accordance with scheme rules within subsection (3)(i) of section 133 (costs of OLC payable by the complainant or the respondent in relation to a complaint), together with any interest payable on such an amount under subsection (6) of that section;
(i) any amount payable to the OLC by virtue of standard terms within section 166(8);
(j) any sum received by the Board in accordance with rules under section 173 (the levy);
(k) amounts paid to the Board under section 162(4)(c) (charges for providing copies of guidance);
(l) any amount payable to the Board under arrangements entered into under section 163 (voluntary arrangements);
(m) amounts paid to the Board under subsection (8) of section 205 (charges for providing copies of rules and draft rules);
(n) amounts paid to the OLC under that subsection.

(2) In this section "application fee" means a fee within—

(a) paragraph 3(3)(d) of Schedule 4 (application fees in respect of designation as approved regulator);
(b) section 45(3)(b) (application fees in respect of cancellation of designation as approved regulator);
(c) paragraph 1(4)(d) of Schedule 10 (application fees in respect of designation as licensing authority);
(d) section 76(3)(b) (application fees in respect of cancellation of designation as licensing authority);
(e) paragraph 3(4)(c) of Schedule 18 (application fees in respect of designation as qualifying regulator for the purposes of Part 5 of the Immigration and Asylum Act 1999 (c 33)).

Initial Commencement
To be appointed: see s 211(2).
Appointment
Sub-ss (1)(c), (k), (m), (n): Appointment: 1 January 2009: see SI 2008/3149, art 2(f).
Extent
This section does not extend to Scotland: see s 212(1).

PART 8
MISCELLANEOUS PROVISIONS ABOUT LAWYERS ETC

Duties of regulated persons

176 Duties of regulated persons

(1) A person who is a regulated person in relation to an approved regulator has a duty to comply with the regulatory arrangements of the approved regulator as they apply to that person.

(2) A person is a regulated person in relation to an approved regulator if the person—

(a) is authorised by the approved regulator to carry on an activity which is a reserved legal activity, or
(b) is not so authorised, but is a manager or employee of a person who is so authorised.

(3) This section applies in relation to the Board in its capacity as a licensing authority and its licensing rules, as it applies in relation to an approved regulator and its regulatory arrangements.

Initial Commencement
To be appointed: see s 211(2).
Extent
This section does not extend to Scotland: see s 212(1).

Solicitors, the Law Society and the Disciplinary Tribunal

177 The Law Society, solicitors, recognised bodies and foreign lawyers

Schedule 16 contains amendments of—

(a) the Solicitors Act 1974 (c 47),
(b) Part 1 of the Administration of Justice Act 1985 (c 61) (recognised bodies), and
(c) section 89 of, and Schedule 14 to, the Courts and Legal Services Act 1990 (c 41) (foreign lawyers: partnerships and recognised bodies).

Initial Commencement
To be appointed: see s 211(2).
Appointment
Appointment: 7 March 2008: see SI 2008/222, art 2(f).
Extent
This section does not extend to Scotland: see s 212(1).

---

178 The Solicitors Disciplinary Tribunal: approval of rules

(1) If the Solicitors Disciplinary Tribunal ("the Tribunal") makes an alteration of its rules under section 46(9)(b) of the Solicitors Act 1974 ("the tribunal rules"), the alteration does not have effect unless it is approved for the purposes of this Act.

(2) An alteration is approved for the purposes of this Act if—

(a) it is approved by the Board under Part 3 of Schedule 4 (alteration of approved regulator's regulatory arrangements),
(b) it is an exempt alteration, or
(c) it is an alteration made in compliance with a direction under section 32 (given by virtue of section 179).

(3) For the purposes of subsection (2)(a), paragraphs 20 to 27 of Schedule 4 (procedure for approval of alterations of regulatory arrangements) apply in relation to an application by the Tribunal for approval of an alteration or alterations of the tribunal rules as they apply in relation to an application by an approved regulator for approval of an alteration or alterations of its regulatory arrangements, but as if—

(a) paragraph 23 of that Schedule applied in relation to the Law Society as well as the Tribunal,
(b) in paragraph 25(3) (grounds for refusal of application), paragraphs (d) and (e) were omitted, and
(c) in paragraph 27(3) the reference to section 32 were a reference to that section as applied (with modifications) by section 179.

(4) For the purposes of subsection (2)(b), an exempt alteration is an alteration which the Board has directed is to be treated as exempt for the purposes of this section.

(5) A direction under subsection (4) may be specific or general, and must be published by the Board.

(6) In this section references to an "alteration" of the tribunal rules include the making of such rules and the modification of such rules.

Initial Commencement
To be appointed: see s 211(2).
Extent
This section does not extend to Scotland: see s 212(1).

---

179 Board's power to give directions to the Tribunal

Sections 32 to 34 and Schedule 7 (Board's powers to give directions) apply in relation to the Tribunal as they apply in relation to an approved regulator, but as if—

(a) in section 32(1)—
  (i) paragraphs (a) and (c) were omitted, and
  (ii) in paragraph (b) after "failed" there were inserted "to perform any of its functions to an adequate standard (or at all) or",
(b) in subsection (4)(b) of that section for "regulatory arrangements" there were substituted "rules under section 46(9)(b) of the Solicitors Act 1974",
(c) section 34(3) were omitted, and
(d) paragraphs 2 and 10 of Schedule 7 applied in relation to the Law Society, as well as the Tribunal, where it is proposed to give the Tribunal a direction under section 32.

Initial Commencement
To be appointed: see s 211(2).
Extent
This section does not extend to Scotland: see s 212(1).

---

180 Functions of the Tribunal

Sections 69 and 70 (modification of functions of approved regulators) apply in relation to the Tribunal as they apply in relation to an approved regulator, but as if—

(a) for section 69(3) (purpose for which modifying order may be made) there were substituted—

"(3) The Board may make a recommendation under this section only with a view to an order being made which enables the Tribunal to carry out its role more effectively or efficiently.", and

(b) subsections (4), (5) and (7) of that section were omitted

---

Initial Commencement
To be appointed: see s 211(2).
Appointment
Appointment: 7 March 2008: see SI 2008/222, art 2(f); for transitional modifications see art 6 thereof.
Extent
This section does not extend to Scotland: see s 212(1).

Other lawyers

181 Unqualified person not to pretend to be a barrister

(1) It is an offence for a person who is not a barrister—

(a) wilfully to pretend to be a barrister, or
(b) with the intention of implying falsely that that person is a barrister to take or use any name, title or description.

(2) A person who is guilty of an offence under subsection (1) is liable—

(a) on summary conviction, to imprisonment for a term not exceeding 12 months or a fine not exceeding the statutory maximum (or both), and
(b) on conviction on indictment, to imprisonment for a term not exceeding 2 years or a fine (or both).

(3) In relation to an offence under subsection (1) committed before the commencement of section 154(1) of the Criminal Justice Act 2003 (c 44), the reference in subsection (2)(a) to 12 months is to be read as a reference to 6 months.

Initial Commencement
To be appointed: see s 211(2).
Extent
This section does not extend to Scotland: see s 212(1).

---

182 Licensed conveyancers

Schedule 17 contains amendments relating to the Council for Licensed Conveyancers, licensed conveyancers and bodies recognised under section 32 of the Administration of Justice Act 1985 (c 61).

Initial Commencement
To be appointed: see s 211(2).
Appointment
Appointment: 7 March 2008: see SI 2008/222, art 2(f).
Extent
This section does not extend to Scotland: see s 212(1).

---

183 Commissioners for oaths

(1) For the purposes of any enactment or instrument (including an enactment passed or instrument made after the passing of this Act) "commissioner for oaths" includes an authorised person in relation to the administration of oaths ("a relevant authorised person").

(2) A relevant authorised person has the right to use the title "Commissioner for Oaths".

(3) A relevant authorised person may not carry on the administration of oaths in any proceedings in which that person represents any of the parties or is interested.

(4) A relevant authorised person before whom an oath or affidavit is taken or made must state in the jurat or attestation at which place and on what date the oath or affidavit is taken or made.

(5) A document containing such a statement and purporting to be sealed or signed by a relevant authorised person must be admitted in evidence without proof of the seal or signature, and without proof that that person is a relevant authorised person.

(6) The Lord Chancellor may by order prescribe the fees to be charged by relevant authorised persons in respect of the administration of an oath or the taking of an affidavit.

(7) The Lord Chancellor may make an order under subsection (6) only—

(a) after consultation with the Board, and
(b) with the consent of the Lord Chief Justice and the Master of the Rolls.

(8) In this section "affidavit" has the same meaning as in the Commissioners for Oaths Act 1889 (c 10).

Initial Commencement
To be appointed: see s 211(2).
Extent
This section does not extend to Scotland: see s 212(1).

---

184 Trade mark attorneys

(1) The Trade Marks Act 1994 (c 26) is amended as follows.

(2) In section 82 (recognition of agents) after "rules" insert "and subject to the Legal Services Act 2007".

(3) For section 83 (the register of trade mark agents) substitute—

"83 The register of trade mark attorneys

(1) There is to continue to be a register of persons who act as agent for others for the purpose of applying for or obtaining the registration of trade marks.

(2) In this Act a registered trade mark attorney means an individual whose name is entered on the register kept under this section.

(3) The register is to be kept by the Institute of Trade Mark Attorneys.

(4) The Secretary of State may, by order, amend subsection (3) so as to require the register to be kept by the person specified in the order.

(5) Before making an order under subsection (4), the Secretary of State must consult the Legal Services Board.

(6) An order under this section must be made by statutory instrument.

(7) An order under this section may not be made unless a draft of it has been laid before, and approved by a resolution of, each House of Parliament.

83A Regulation of trade mark attorneys

(1) The person who keeps the register under section 83 may make regulations which regulate—

(a) the keeping of the register and the registration of persons;
(b) the carrying on of trade mark agency work by registered persons.

(2) Those regulations may, amongst other things, make—

(a) provision as to the educational and training qualifications, and other requirements, which must be satisfied before an individual may be registered or for an individual to remain registered;
(b) provision as to the requirements which must be met by a body (corporate or unincorporate) before it may be registered or for it to remain registered, including provision as to the management and control of the body;
(c) provision as to the educational, training or other requirements to be met by regulated persons;
(d) provision regulating the practice, conduct and discipline of registered persons or regulated persons;
(e) provision authorising in such cases as may be specified in the regulations the erasure from the register of the name of any person registered in it, or the suspension of a person's registration;
(f) provision requiring the payment of such fees as may be specified in or determined in accordance with the regulations;
(g) provision about the provision to be made by registered persons in respect of complaints made against them;
(h) provision about the keeping of records and accounts by registered persons or regulated persons;
(i) provision for reviews of or appeals against decisions made under the regulations;
(j) provision as to the indemnification of registered persons or regulated persons against losses arising from claims in respect of civil liability incurred by them.

(3) Regulations under this section may make different provision for different purposes.

(4) Regulations under this section which are not regulatory arrangements within the meaning of the Legal Services Act 2007 are to be treated as such arrangements for the purposes of that Act.

(5) Before the appointed day, regulations under this section may be made only with the approval of the Secretary of State.

(6) The powers conferred to make regulations under this section are not to be taken to prejudice—

(a) any other power which the person who keeps the register may have to make rules or regulations (however they may be described and whether they are made under an enactment or otherwise);
(b) any rules or regulations made by that person under any such power.

(7) In this section—

"appointed day" means the day appointed for the coming into force of paragraph 1 of Schedule 4 to the Legal Services Act 2007;
"manager", in relation to a body, has the same meaning as in the Legal Services Act 2007 (see section 207);
"registered person" means—
(a) a registered trade mark attorney, or
(b) a body (corporate or unincorporate) registered in the register kept under section 83;

(6) In section 280 (privilege for communications with patent agents), in subsection (3), at the end of paragraph (b) insert—

"(ba) an unincorporated body (other than a partnership) entitled to describe itself as a patent attorney, or".

Initial Commencement
To be appointed: see s 211(2).

---

186 Immigration advisers and immigration service providers

(1) Schedule 18 makes provision relating to Part 5 of the Immigration and Asylum Act 1999 (c 33) (immigration advisers and immigration service providers).

(2) In that Schedule—

(a) Part 1 makes provision for approved regulators to become qualifying regulators for the purposes of Part 5 of the Immigration and Asylum Act 1999,
(b) Part 2 contains amendments of that Act (which amongst other things enable persons authorised by qualifying regulators to provide immigration advice and immigration services in England and Wales), and
(c) Part 3 makes provision for certain persons to be treated, during a transitional period, as authorised by qualifying regulators to provide such advice and services.

Initial Commencement
To be appointed: see s 211(2).
Extent
This section does not extend to Scotland: see s 212(1).

---

187 Claims management services

Schedule 19 contains amendments of Part 2 of the Compensation Act 2006 (c 29) (claims management services).

Initial Commencement
To be appointed: see s 211(2).
Appointment
Appointment: 7 March 2008: see SI 2008/222, art 2(f).
Extent
This section does not extend to Scotland: see s 212(1).

Advocates and litigators

188 Duties of advocates and litigators

(1) This section applies to a person who—

(a) exercises before any court a right of audience, or
(b) conducts litigation in relation to proceedings in any court,

by virtue of being an authorised person in relation to the activity in question.

(2) A person to whom this section applies has a duty to the court in question to act with independence in the interests of justice.

(3) That duty, and the duty to comply with relevant conduct rules imposed on the person by section 176(1), override any obligations which the person may have (otherwise than under the criminal law) if they are inconsistent with them.

(4) "Relevant conduct rules" are the conduct rules of the relevant authorising body which relate to the exercise of a right of audience or the conduct of litigation.

(5) The relevant authorising body is—

(a) the approved regulator by which the person is authorised to exercise the right of audience or conduct the litigation, or
(b) where the person is authorised to exercise the right of audience or conduct the litigation by the Board in its capacity as a licensing authority, the Board.

Initial Commencement
To be appointed: see s 211(2).
Extent
This section does not extend to Scotland: see s 212(1).

---

189 Employed advocates

(1) This section applies where an authorised person in relation to the exercise of a right of audience is employed as a Crown Prosecutor or in any other description of employment.

(2) Qualification regulations or conduct rules of the approved regulator by whom the person is authorised to carry on that activity which relate to the right of audience do not have effect in relation to the person if—

(a) they—
  (i) limit the courts before which, or proceedings in which, that activity may be carried on by persons who are employed, or
  (ii) limit the circumstances in which that activity may be carried on by persons who are employed by requiring such persons to be accompanied by some other person when carrying on that activity, and
(b) they do not impose the same limitation on persons who are authorised persons in relation to the activity in question but are not employed.

Initial Commencement
To be appointed: see s 211(2).
Extent
This section does not extend to Scotland: see s 212(1).

Legal professional privilege

190 Legal professional privilege

(1) Subsection (2) applies where an individual ("P") who is not a barrister or solicitor—

(a) provides advocacy services as an authorised person in relation to the exercise of rights of audience,
(b) provides litigation services as an authorised person in relation to the conduct of litigation,
(c) provides conveyancing services as an authorised person in relation to reserved instrument activities, or
(d) provides probate services as an authorised person in relation to probate activities.

(2) Any communication, document, material or information relating to the provision of the services in question is privileged from disclosure in like manner as if P had at all material times been acting as P's client's solicitor.

(3) Subsection (4) applies where—

(a) a licensed body provides services to a client, and
(b) the individual ("E") through whom the body provides those services—
  (i) is a relevant lawyer, or
  (ii) acts at the direction and under the supervision of a relevant lawyer ("the supervisor").

(4) Any communication, document, material or information relating to the provision of the services in question is privileged from disclosure only if, and to the extent that, it would have been privileged from disclosure if—

- (a) the services had been provided by E or, if E is not a relevant lawyer, by the supervisor, and
- (b) at all material times the client had been the client of E or, if E is not a relevant lawyer, of the supervisor.

(5) "Relevant lawyer" means an individual who is—

- (a) a solicitor;
- (b) a barrister;
- (c) a solicitor in Scotland;
- (d) an advocate in Scotland;
- (e) a solicitor of the Court of Judicature of Northern Ireland;
- (f) a member of the Bar of Northern Ireland;
- (g) a registered foreign lawyer (within the meaning of section 89 of the Courts and Legal Services Act 1990 (c 41));
- (h) an individual not within paragraphs (a) to (g) who is an authorised person in relation to an activity which is a reserved legal activity; or
- (i) a European lawyer (within the meaning of the European Communities (Services of Lawyers) Order 1978 (SI 1978/1910)).

(6) In this section—

"advocacy services" means any services which it would be reasonable to expect a person who is exercising, or contemplating exercising, a right of audience in relation to any proceedings, or contemplated proceedings, to provide;

"litigation services" means any services which it would be reasonable to expect a person who is exercising, or contemplating exercising, a right to conduct litigation in relation to any proceedings, or contemplated proceedings, to provide;

"conveyancing services" means the preparation of transfers, conveyances, contracts and other documents in connection with, and other services ancillary to, the disposition or acquisition of estates or interests in land;

"probate services" means the preparation of any papers on which to found or oppose a grant of probate or a grant of letters of administration and the administration of the estate of a deceased person.

(7) This section is without prejudice to any other enactment or rule of law by virtue of which a communication, a document, material or information is privileged from disclosure.

Initial Commencement

To be appointed: see s 211(2).

Extent

This section does not extend to Scotland: see s 212(1).

Employees of housing management bodies

191 Rights of audience etc of employees of housing management bodies

After section 60 of the County Courts Act 1984 (c 28) insert—

"60A Rights of audience etc of employees of housing management bodies

(1) An employee of a housing management body who is authorised by that body for the purposes of this section has—

- (a) a right of audience in relation to any proceedings to which this section applies, and
- (b) a right to conduct litigation in relation to any such proceedings.

(2) This section applies to relevant housing proceedings in a county court before a district judge which are brought—

- (a) in the name of a local housing authority, and

(b) by the housing management body in the exercise of functions of that local housing authority delegated to that body under a housing management agreement.

(3) "Relevant housing proceedings" are—

(a) proceedings under section 82A of the Housing Act 1985 (demotion because of anti-social behaviour);
(b) proceedings for possession of a dwelling-house subject to a secure tenancy, where possession is sought on ground 2 in Part 1 of Schedule 2 to that Act (anti-social behaviour);
(c) proceedings for possession of a dwelling-house subject to a demoted tenancy;
(d) proceedings for a suspension order under section 121A of the Housing Act 1985 (suspension of right to buy);
(e) proceedings under section 153A, 153B or 153D of the Housing Act 1996 (injunctions against anti-social behaviour);
(f) proceedings for the attachment of a power of arrest to an injunction by virtue of section 91(2) of the Anti-social Behaviour Act 2003 or section 27(2) of the Police and Justice Act 2006 (proceedings under section 222 of the Local Government Act 1972: power of arrest attached to injunction);
(g) at a hearing at which a decision is made in relation to proceedings within paragraphs (a) to (f), proceedings for permission to appeal against that decision;
(h) such other proceedings as the Lord Chancellor may prescribe by order.

(4) An authorisation for the purposes of this section must be in writing.

(5) The power to make an order under subsection (3)(h) is exercisable by statutory instrument subject to annulment by resolution of either House of Parliament.

(6) In subsection (3)(e) the reference to section 153A of the Housing Act 1996 is a reference to that section—

(a) as inserted by section 13 of the Anti-social Behaviour Act 2003, or
(b) as substituted by section 26 of the Police and Justice Act 2006.

(7) In this section—

"dwelling-house" has the same meaning as in Part 4 of the Housing Act 1985;
"housing management agreement" means an agreement under section 27 of the Housing Act 1985 (including an agreement to which section 27B(2) or (3) of that Act applies);
"housing management body" means a person who exercises management functions of a local housing authority by virtue of a housing management agreement;
"local housing authority" has the same meaning as in section 27 of the Housing Act 1985;
"right of audience" means the right to appear before and address a court, including the right to call and examine witnesses;
"right to conduct litigation" means the right—
(a) to issue proceedings before any court in England and Wales,
(b) to commence, prosecute and defend such proceedings, and
(c) to perform any ancillary functions in relation to such proceedings (such as entering appearances to actions);
"secure tenancy" has the same meaning as in Part 4 of the Housing Act 1985."

Initial Commencement
To be appointed: see s 211(2).

Savings

192 Powers of court in respect of rights of audience and conduct of litigation

(1) Nothing in this Act affects the power of any court in any proceedings to refuse to hear a person (for reasons which apply to that person as an individual) who would otherwise have a right of audience before the court in relation to those proceedings.

(2) Where a court refuses to hear a person as mentioned in subsection (1), it must give its reasons for refusing.

(3) Where—

- (a) immediately before the commencement of section 13 (entitlement to carry on reserved legal activities), or
- (b) by virtue of any provision made by or under an enactment passed subsequently,

a court does not permit the appearance of advocates, or permits the appearance of advocates only with leave, no person may exercise a right of audience before the court, in relation to any proceedings, solely by virtue of being entitled to do so under this Act.

(4) But a court may not limit the right to appear before the court in any proceedings to only some of those who are entitled to exercise that right by virtue of this Act.

(5) A court may not limit the right to conduct litigation in relation to proceedings before the court to only some of those who are entitled to exercise that right by virtue of this Act.

(6) In this section "advocate", in relation to any proceedings, means a person exercising a right of audience as a representative of, or on behalf of, any party to the proceedings.

Initial Commencement
To be appointed: see s 211(2).
Extent
This section does not extend to Scotland: see s 212(1).

---

193 Solicitors to public departments and the City of London

(1) Nothing in this Act is to prejudice or affect any rights or privileges of—

- (a) the Treasury Solicitor,
- (b) the solicitor to any other public department,
- (c) the solicitor to the Church Commissioners, or
- (d) the solicitor to the Duchy of Cornwall.

(2) Nothing in this Act requires a person to whom subsection (1) applies, or any clerk or officer appointed to act for such a person, to be entitled to carry on an activity which is a reserved legal activity in any case where, by virtue of section 88(1) of the Solicitors Act 1974 (c 47), it would not have been necessary for that person to be admitted and enrolled and to hold a practising certificate under that Act if this Act had not been passed.

(3) Nothing in this Act is to prejudice or affect any rights or privileges which immediately before the commencement of this Act attached to the office of Solicitor of the City of London.

(4) Nothing in section 17 (offence to pretend to be entitled) applies to a person to whom subsection (1) applies, or any clerk or officer appointed to act for such a person, or to the Solicitor of the City of London.

(5) A person who—

- (a) exercises before any court a right of audience, or
- (b) conducts litigation in relation to proceedings in any court,

by virtue of this section has a duty to the court in question to act with independence in the interests of justice.

(6) That duty overrides any obligations which the person may have (otherwise than under the criminal law) if it is inconsistent with them.

Initial Commencement
To be appointed: see s 211(2).
Extent
This section does not extend to Scotland: see s 212(1).

Pro bono representation

194 Payments in respect of pro bono representation

(1) This section applies to proceedings in a civil court in which—

(a) a party to the proceedings ("P") is or was represented by a legal representative ("R"), and
(b) R's representation of P is or was provided free of charge, in whole or in part.

(2) This section applies to such proceedings even if P is or was also represented by a legal representative not acting free of charge.

(3) The court may order any person to make a payment to the prescribed charity in respect of R's representation of P (or, if only part of R's representation of P was provided free of charge, in respect of that part).

(4) In considering whether to make such an order and the terms of such an order, the court must have regard to—

(a) whether, had R's representation of P not been provided free of charge, it would have ordered the person to make a payment to P in respect of the costs payable to R by P in respect of that representation, and
(b) if it would, what the terms of the order would have been.

(5) The court may not make an order under subsection (3) against a person represented in the proceedings if the person's representation was at all times within subsection (6).

(6) Representation is within this subsection if it is—

(a) provided by a legal representative acting free of charge, or
(b) funded by the Legal Services Commission as part of the Community Legal Service.

(7) Rules of court may make further provision as to the making of orders under subsection (3), and may in particular—

(a) provide that such orders may not be made in civil proceedings of a description specified in the rules;
(b) make provision about the procedure to be followed in relation to such orders;
(c) specify matters (in addition to those mentioned in subsection (4)) to which the court must have regard in deciding whether to make such an order, and the terms of any order.

(8) "The prescribed charity" means the charity prescribed by order made by the Lord Chancellor.

(9) An order under subsection (8) may only prescribe a charity which—

(a) is registered in accordance with section 3A of the Charities Act 1993 (c 10), and
(b) provides financial support to persons who provide, or organise or facilitate the provision of, legal advice or assistance (by way of representation or otherwise) which is free of charge.

(10) In this section—

"legal representative", in relation to a party to proceedings, means a person exercising a right of audience or conducting litigation on the party's behalf;
"civil court" means the civil division of the Court of Appeal, the High Court, or any county court;
"free of charge" means otherwise than for or in expectation of fee, gain or reward.

(11) The court may not make an order under subsection (3) in respect of representation if (or to the extent that) it is provided before this section comes into force.

Initial Commencement

To be appointed: see s 211(2).

Appointment

Sub-ss (1)–(7), (11): Appointment: 1 October 2008: see SI 2008/1436, art 3(a).

Sub-ss (8), (9): Appointment: 30 June 2008: see SI 2008/1436, art 2(a).

Sub-s (10): Appointment (for certain purposes): 30 June 2008: see SI 2008/1436, art 2(a).
Sub-s (10): Appointment (for remaining purposes): 1 October 2008: see SI 2008/1436, art 3(a).

Extent

This section does not extend to Scotland: see s 212(1).

See Further

See further, in relation to the application of sub-s (9)(a) above, with modifications until such time as the Charities Act 1993, 3A comes into force: the Legal Services Act 2007 (Transitory Provision) Order 2008, SI 2008/1779, art 2.

Subordinate Legislation

Legal Services Act 2007 (Prescribed Charity) Order 2008, SI 2008/2680 (made under sub-s (8)).

Scotland

195 Application of the Legal Profession and Legal Aid (Scotland) Act 2007

(1) The Legal Profession and Legal Aid (Scotland) Act 2007 (asp 5) ("the 2007 Act") applies to—

(a) any element of a complaint relating to,
(b) the provision by a practitioner of,

the advice, services and activities mentioned in subsection (2) as it applies to any other advice, services and activities provided by a practitioner.

(2) The advice, services and activities are—

(a) activities carried out by virtue of a group licence issued under section 22(1)(b) of the Consumer Credit Act 1974 (c 39);
(b) activities of an insolvency practitioner within the meaning of Part 13 of the Insolvency Act 1986 (c 45);
(c) activities mentioned in paragraph (a) of paragraph 5(1) of Schedule 3 to the Financial Services Act 1986 (c 60);
(d) immigration advice or immigration services;
(e) regulated activity within the meaning of section 22 of the Financial Services and Markets Act 2000 (c 8), other than activity falling within paragraph (f) below, in respect of which the Financial Services Authority has by virtue of Part 20 of that Act arranged for its regulatory role to be carried out by the Law Society of Scotland;
(f) exempt regulated activities within the meaning of section 325(2) of the Financial Services and Markets Act 2000.

(3) In subsection (1), "complaint" and "practitioner" have the same meaning as in Part 1 of the 2007 Act.

(4) Omit section 77 of the 2007 Act (advice services and activities to which Act does not apply).

(5) Schedule 20 contains minor and consequential amendments in connection with the application of the 2007 Act by virtue of this section.

Initial Commencement

To be appointed: see s 211(2).

Appointment

Appointment: 1 October 2008: see SI 2008/1436, art 3(a).

---

196 Scottish legal services ombudsman: functions

(1) The functions of the Scottish legal services ombudsman cease to be exercisable in relation to the advice, services and activities mentioned in section 195(2).

(2) In the Immigration and Asylum Act 1999 (c 33)—

(a) in section 86(4)(c) (designated professional bodies), for "Scottish Legal Services Ombudsman" substitute "Scottish Legal Complaints Commission", and

(b) in paragraph 4(2)(c) of Schedule 5 (the Immigration Services Commissioner), for "Scottish Legal Services Ombudsman" substitute "Scottish Legal Complaints Commission".

Initial Commencement
To be appointed: see s 211(2).
Appointment
Appointment: 1 October 2008: see SI 2008/1436, art 3(a).

PART 9
GENERAL

Offences

197 Offences committed by bodies corporate and unincorporated bodies

(1) Where an offence committed by a body corporate is proved to have been committed with the consent or connivance of or to be attributable to any neglect on the part of an officer of the body corporate, that officer (as well as the body corporate) is guilty of the offence and is liable to be proceeded against and punished accordingly.

(2) Where the affairs of a body corporate are managed by its members, subsection (1) applies in relation to the acts and defaults of a member in connection with the member's functions of management as it applies to an officer of the body corporate.

(3) Proceedings for an offence alleged to have been committed by an unincorporated body are to be brought in the name of that body (and not in that of any of its members) and, for the purposes of any such proceedings, any rules of court relating to the service of documents have effect as if that body were a corporation.

(4) A fine imposed on an unincorporated body on its conviction of an offence is to be paid out of the funds of that body.

(5) If an unincorporated body is charged with an offence, section 33 of the Criminal Justice Act 1925 (c 86) and Schedule 3 to the Magistrates' Courts Act 1980 (c 43) (procedure on charge of an offence against a corporation) have effect in like manner as in the case of a corporation so charged.

(6) Where an offence committed by an unincorporated body (other than a partnership) is proved to have been committed with the consent or connivance of, or to be attributable to any neglect on the part of, any officer of the body or any member of its governing body, that officer or member as well as the unincorporated body is guilty of the offence and liable to be proceeded against and punished accordingly.

(7) Where an offence committed by a partnership is proved to have been committed with the consent or connivance of, or to be attributable to any neglect on the part of, a partner, that partner as well as the partnership is guilty of the offence and liable to be proceeded against and punished accordingly.

(8) In this section—

"offence" means an offence under this Act;
"officer", in relation to a body corporate, means—
(a) any director, secretary or other similar officer of the body corporate, or
(b) any person who was purporting to act in any such capacity.

Initial Commencement
To be appointed: see s 211(2).

---

198 Local weights and measures authorities

(1) A local weights and measures authority may institute proceedings for an offence under section 14 if the activity which it is alleged that the accused was not entitled to carry on constitutes reserved instrument activities.

(2) A local weights and measures authority may institute proceedings for an offence under section 16 if the activity which it is alleged that E was not entitled to carry on constitutes reserved instrument activities.

"E" has the same meaning as in that section.

(3) In this section—

"relevant offence" means an offence in relation to which proceedings may be instituted by virtue of subsection (1) or (2);
"weights and measures officer" means an officer of a local weights and measures authority who is authorised by the authority to exercise the powers conferred by subsection (4).

(4) A weights and measures officer who has reasonable cause to suspect that a relevant offence may have been committed may, at any reasonable time—

(a) enter any premises which are not used solely as a dwelling;
(b) require any officer, agent or other competent person on the premises who is, or may be, in possession of information relevant to an investigation of the suspected offence to provide such information;
(c) require the production of any document which may be relevant to such an investigation;
(d) take copies, or extracts, of any such documents;
(e) seize and retain any document which the weights and measures officer has reason to believe may be required as evidence in proceedings for a relevant offence.

(5) Any person exercising a power given by subsection (4) must, if asked to do so, produce evidence that that person is a weights and measures officer.

(6) A justice of the peace may issue a warrant under this section if satisfied, on information on oath given by a weights and measures officer, that there is reasonable cause to believe that a relevant offence may have been committed and that—

(a) entry to the premises concerned, or production of any documents which may be relevant to an investigation of the relevant offence, has been or is likely to be refused to a weights and measures officer, or
(b) there is reasonable cause to believe that, if production of any such document were to be required by the weights and measures officer without a warrant having been issued under this section, the document would not be produced but would be removed from the premises or hidden, tampered with or destroyed.

(7) A warrant issued under this section must authorise the weights and measures officer accompanied, where that officer considers it appropriate, by a constable or other person—

(a) to enter the premises specified in the information, using such force as is reasonably necessary, and
(b) to exercise any of the powers given to the weights and measures officer by subsection (4).

(8) It is an offence for a person ("P")—

(a) intentionally to obstruct a weights and measures officer in the exercise of any power under this section;
(b) intentionally to fail to comply with any requirement properly imposed on P by a weights and measures officer in the exercise of any such power;
(c) to fail, without reasonable excuse, to give a weights and measures officer any assistance or information which the weights and measures officer may reasonably require of P for the purpose of exercising any such power; or
(d) in giving to a weights and measures officer any information which P has been required to give a weights and measures officer exercising any such power, to make any statement which P knows to be false or misleading in a material particular.

(9) A person who is guilty of an offence under subsection (8) is liable on summary conviction to a fine not exceeding level 3 on the standard scale.

(10) Nothing in this section is to be taken to require any person to answer any question put to that person by a weights and measures officer, or to give any information to such an officer, if to do so might incriminate that person.

Initial Commencement
To be appointed: see s 211(2).

Protected functions of the Lord Chancellor

199 Protected functions of the Lord Chancellor

(1) Schedule 7 to the Constitutional Reform Act 2005 (c 4) (protected functions of the Lord Chancellor) is amended as follows.

(2) After paragraph 3 insert—

"**3A** Any function of the Lord Chancellor under the Legal Services Act 2007."

(3) Part A of paragraph 4 is amended in accordance with subsections (4) to (7).

(4) After the entry for the Juries Act 1974 (c 23), insert—

"*Solicitors Act 1974 (c 47)*

Section 56".

(5) After the entry for the Reserve Forces (Safeguard of Employment) Act 1985 (c 17), insert—

"*Administration of Justice Act 1985 (c 61)*

Section 9(7)

Section 69(2)

Schedule 3".

(6) In the entry for the Courts and Legal Services Act 1990 (c 41)—

(a) after "Section 1" insert—

"Section 53

Section 60", and

(b) after "Section 72" insert—

"Section 89

Section 125(4)

Schedule 19, paragraph 17".

(7) After the entry for the Finance Act 1999 (c 16), insert—

"*Access to Justice Act 1999 (c 22)*

Section 45".

Initial Commencement
To be appointed: see s 211(2).
Appointment
Sub-ss (1), (2): Appointment: 7 March 2008: see SI 2008/222, art 2(g).
Sub-s (4): Appointment: 30 June 2008: see SI 2008/1436, art 2(b).
Sub-ss (5), (6)(b): Appointment (for certain purposes): 30 June 2008: see SI 2008/1436, art 2(b).

Notices etc

200 Notices and directions

(1) A requirement or power under this Act to give a notice (or to notify) is a requirement or power to give notice in writing.

(2) A requirement or power under this Act to give a direction (or to direct) is a requirement or power to give a direction in writing.

(3) Any power conferred by this Act to give a direction includes power to revoke the direction.

(4) Subsection (3) does not apply to the power conferred on an ombudsman to give a direction under section 137 (directions on a determination of a complaint).

Initial Commencement
To be appointed: see s 211(2).
Appointment
Sub-s (1): Appointment: 7 March 2008: see SI 2008/222, art 2(g).
Sub-ss (2)–(4): Appointment: 1 January 2009: see SI 2008/3149, art 2(g).

---

201 Documents

(1) In this Act "document" includes anything in which information is recorded in any form.

(2) In relation to a document in which information is recorded otherwise than in a legible form, any reference to the production of the document is a reference to the production of the information in a legible form or in a form from which it can readily be produced in a legible form.

Initial Commencement
To be appointed: see s 211(2).
Appointment
Appointment: 1 January 2009: see SI 2008/3149, art 2(g).

---

202 The giving of notices, directions and other documents

(1) This section applies where provision made (in whatever terms) by or under this Act authorises or requires a notice, direction or any other document (including a copy of a document) to be given to a person.

(2) The notice, direction or document may be given to the person—

(a) by delivering it to the person,
(b) by leaving it at the person's proper address, or
(c) by sending it by post to the person at that address.

(3) The notice, direction or document may be given to a body corporate by being given to the secretary or clerk of that body.

(4) The notice, direction or document may be given to a partnership by being given to—

(a) a partner in the partnership, or
(b) a person having the control or management of the partnership business.

(5) The notice, direction or document may be given to any other unincorporated body by being given to a member of the governing body of the unincorporated body.

(6) For the purposes of this section, and section 7 of the Interpretation Act 1978 (c 30) (service of documents by post) in its application to this section, the proper address of a person is—

(a) in the case of a body corporate, the address of the registered or principal office of the body;
(b) in the case of a partnership, or any other unincorporated body, the address of the principal office of the partnership or body;

(c) in the case of a person to whom the notice or other document is given in reliance on any of subsections (3) to (5), the proper address of the body corporate, partnership or other unincorporated body in question;
(d) in any other case, the last known address of the person in question.

(7) In the case of—

(a) a company registered outside the United Kingdom,
(b) a partnership carrying on business outside the United Kingdom, or
(c) any other unincorporated body with offices outside the United Kingdom,

the references in subsection (6) to its principal office include references to its principal office within the United Kingdom (if any).

(8) This section has effect subject to section 203 (notices, directions and documents in electronic form).

Initial Commencement
To be appointed: see s 211(2).
Appointment
Appointment: 1 January 2009: see SI 2008/3149, art 2(g).

---

203 The giving of notices, directions and other documents in electronic form

(1) This section applies where—

(a) section 202 authorises the giving of a notice, direction or other document by its delivery to a particular person ("the recipient"), and
(b) the notice, direction or other document is transmitted to the recipient—
  (i) by means of an electronic communications network, or
  (ii) by other means but in a form that nevertheless requires the use of apparatus by the recipient to render it intelligible.

(2) The transmission has effect for the purposes of this Act as a delivery of the notice, direction or other document to the recipient, but only if the requirements imposed by or under this section are complied with.

(3) Where the recipient is the Board, the OLC or an ombudsman—

(a) the recipient must have indicated its willingness to receive the notice, direction or other document in a manner mentioned in subsection (1)(b),
(b) the transmission must be made in such manner, and satisfy such other conditions as the recipient may require, and
(c) the notice, direction or other document must take such form as the recipient may require.

(4) Where the person making the transmission is the Board, the OLC or an ombudsman, that person may (subject to subsection (5)) determine—

(a) the manner in which the transmission is made, and
(b) the form in which the notice, direction or other document is transmitted.

(5) Where the recipient is a person other than the Board, the OLC or an ombudsman—

(a) the recipient, or
(b) the person on whose behalf the recipient receives the notice, direction or other document,

must have indicated to the person making the transmission the recipient's willingness to receive notices, directions or other documents transmitted in the form and manner used.

(6) An indication to any person for the purposes of subsection (5)—

(a) must be given to that person in such manner as that person may require;
(b) may be a general indication or one that is limited to notices or documents of particular descriptions;
(c) must state the address to be used and must be accompanied by such other information as that person requires for the making of the transmission;

(d) may be modified or withdrawn at any time by a notice given to that person in such manner as that person may require.

(7) An indication, requirement or determination given, imposed or made by the Board, the OLC or an ombudsman for the purposes of this section is to be given, imposed or made by being published by that person.

(8) In this section "electronic communications network" has the same meaning as in the Communications Act 2003 (c 21).

Initial Commencement
To be appointed: see s 211(2).
Appointment
Appointment: 1 January 2009: see SI 2008/3149, art 2(g).

Orders, rules etc

204 Orders, regulations and rules

(1) Any order or regulations made by the Lord Chancellor under this Act must be made by statutory instrument.

(2) Any rules made by the Board under section 37(4), 95(3) or 173 must be made by statutory instrument, and the Statutory Instruments Act 1946 (c 36) applies to the Board's powers to make rules under those sections as if the Board were a Minister of the Crown.

(3) An instrument to which this subsection applies may—

(a) provide for a person to exercise a discretion in dealing with any matter;
(b) include incidental, supplementary and consequential provision;
(c) make transitory or transitional provision and savings;
(d) make provision generally or subject to exceptions or only in relation to specified cases;
(e) make different provision for different cases or circumstances or for different purposes.

(4) Subsection (3) applies to—

(a) any order or regulations made by the Lord Chancellor,
(b) any rules or regulations made by the Board, and
(c) any rules made by the OLC,

under or by virtue of this Act.

Initial Commencement
To be appointed: see s 211(2).
Appointment
Sub-ss (1), (3), (4)(a): Appointment: 7 March 2008: see SI 2008/222, art 2(g).
Sub-ss (2), (4)(b), (c): Appointment: 1 January 2009: see SI 2008/3149, art 2(g).

---

205 Consultation requirements for rules

(1) This section applies in relation to—

(a) rules made by the Board under this Act, and
(b) rules made by the OLC under Part 6,

other than excluded rules.

(2) If the Board or the OLC ("the rule-making body") proposes to make any rules, it must publish a draft of the proposed rules.

(3) The draft must be accompanied by a notice which states that representations about the proposals may be made to the rule-making body within the period specified in the notice.

(4) Before making the rules, the rule-making body must have regard to any representations duly made.

(5) If the rules differ from the draft published under subsection (2) in a way which is, in the opinion of the rule-making body, material, it must publish details of the differences.

(6) The rule-making body must publish any rules it makes, and rules may not take effect before the time they are published.

(7) Subsection (6) does not apply to rules made by the Board under section 37(4), 95(3) or 173.

(8) The rule-making body may make a reasonable charge for providing a person with a copy of—

(a) a draft published under subsection (2), or
(b) rules published under subsection (6).

(9) In this section "excluded rules" means—

(a) rules of procedure made by the Board for the purposes of paragraph 21 of Schedule 1,
(b) rules made by the Board in its capacity as an approved regulator or a licensing authority, and
(c) rules of procedure made by the OLC for the purposes of paragraph 20 of Schedule 15;

and references to making rules include references to modifying the rules and, in relation to any modifications of rules, references to the proposed rules are to be read as references to the proposed modifications.

(10) This section is subject to section 156(3) (which disapplies this section to OLC rules made in response to a Board direction under section 156(1)(b)).

Initial Commencement
To be appointed: see s 211(2).
Appointment
Appointment: 1 January 2009: see SI 2008/3149, art 2(g).

---

206 Parliamentary control of orders and regulations

(1) A statutory instrument containing an order or regulations made by the Lord Chancellor under this Act is subject to annulment in pursuance of a resolution of either House of Parliament.

(2) Subsection (1) is subject to subsections (3) and (4).

(3) Subsection (1) does not apply to an order if it contains only provision made under one or more of the following—

(a) section 23(3)(b) (day appointed as end of transitional period relating to non-commercial bodies);
(b) section 30(4) (appointed day before which first set of rules must be made under section 30);
(c) section 211 (commencement);
(d) paragraph 3(1)(b) of Schedule 5 (day appointed as end of transitional period during which rights conferred by virtue of Part 2 of that Schedule);
(e) paragraph 18(1)(b) of Schedule 18 (day appointed as end of transitional period during which rights conferred by virtue of Part 3 of that Schedule).

(4) Subsection (1) does not apply to an order or regulations which contains (whether alone or together with other provision) provision made under any of the following—

(a) section 24(1) (orders adding to reserved legal activities);
(b) section 25(1) or (3) (provisional designation of approved regulators);
(c) section 42(6) (regulations relating to warrants under section 42);
(d) section 45(1) (cancellation of designation as approved regulator);
(e) section 46 (transitional arrangements following cancellation under section 45);
(f) section 48(6) (regulations relating to warrants under section 48);
(g) section 62(1) (power to designate Board as an approved regulator, modify its functions or cancel its designation);
(h) section 69(1) (modification of functions of approved regulators etc);
(i) section 76(1) (cancellation of designation as licensing authority);
(j) section 77 (transitional arrangements following cancellation under section 76);

(k) section 79(6) (regulations relating to warrants under section 79);
(l) section 80(1) (order establishing appellate body etc);
(m) section 106(1)(e) (power to prescribe bodies as bodies to which section 106 applies);
(n) section 109 (power to modify application of Part 5 to foreign bodies);
(o) section 173(5)(c) (power to prescribe persons as leviable bodies);
(p) section 207(5) (power to modify definition of "manager" in its application to foreign bodies);
(q) section 208(3) (power to make consequential provision etc by amending enactments);
(r) paragraph 9(1) of Schedule 3 (modification of exempt persons);
(s) paragraph 17 of Schedule 4 (designation of approved regulators);
(t) paragraph 9 of Schedule 13 (power to modify definitions of "material interest" and "associates");
(u) paragraph 2 of Schedule 22 (transitory power to modify functions of designated regulators etc).

(5) An order or regulations within subsection (4) may not be made unless a draft of the order or regulations has been laid before, and approved by a resolution of, each House of Parliament.

(6) A statutory instrument containing rules made by the Board under section 37(4), 95(3) or 173 is subject to annulment in pursuance of a resolution of either House of Parliament.

Initial Commencement
To be appointed: see s 211(2).
Appointment
Appointment: 7 March 2008: see SI 2008/222, art 2(g).

Interpretation

207 Interpretation

(1) In this Act, except where the context otherwise requires—

"barrister" means an individual who—
(a) has been called to the Bar by an Inn of Court, and
(b) is not disbarred by order of an Inn of Court;

"consumers" means (subject to subsection (3)) persons—
(a) who use, have used or are or may be contemplating using, services within subsection (2),
(b) who have rights or interests which are derived from, or are otherwise attributable to, the use of such services by other persons, or
(c) who have rights or interests which may be adversely affected by the use of such services by persons acting on their behalf or in a fiduciary capacity in relation to them;

"conveyancing services" has the same meaning as in Part 2 of the Administration of Justice Act 1985 (c 61) (licensed conveyancing) (see section 11(3) of that Act);

"court" includes—
(a) a tribunal that is (to any extent) a listed tribunal for, or for any of, the purposes of Schedule 7 to the Tribunals, Courts and Enforcement Act 2007 (functions etc of Administrative Justice and Tribunals Council);
(b) a court-martial;
(c) a statutory inquiry within the meaning of section 16(1) of the Tribunals and Inquiries Act 1992 (c 53);
(d) an ecclesiastical court (including the Court of Faculties);

"functions" includes powers and duties;

"immigration advice" and "immigration services" have the meaning given by section 82 of the Immigration and Asylum Act 1999 (c 33) (interpretation of Part 5) (see also subsection (4) below);

"independent trade union" has the same meaning as in the Trade Union and Labour Relations (Consolidation) Act 1992 (c 52) (see section 5 of that Act);

"manager", in relation to a body, means (subject to subsection (5)) a person who—
(a) if the body is a body corporate whose affairs are managed by its members, is a member of the body,

(b) if the body is a body corporate and paragraph (a) does not apply, is a director of the body,
(c) if the body is a partnership, is a partner, and
(d) if the body is an unincorporated body (other than a partnership), is a member of its governing body;

"modify" includes amend, add to or revoke, and references to "modifications" are to be construed accordingly;

"non-commercial legal services" means—

(a) legal services carried on otherwise than with a view to profit;
(b) legal services carried on by a not for profit body, a community interest company or an independent trade union;

"not for profit body" means a body which, by or by virtue of its constitution or any enactment—

(a) is required (after payment of outgoings) to apply the whole of its income, and any capital which it expends, for charitable or public purposes, and
(b) is prohibited from directly or indirectly distributing amongst its members any part of its assets (otherwise than for charitable or public purposes);

"the OFT" means the Office of Fair Trading;

"person" includes a body of persons (corporate or unincorporate);

"reserved legal services" means services provided by a person which consist of or include reserved legal activities carried on by, or on behalf of, that person;

"solicitor" means solicitor of the Senior Courts.

(2) The services within this subsection are—

(a) any services provided by a person who is an authorised person in relation to an activity which is a reserved legal activity, and
(b) any other services provided by a person which consist of or include a legal activity carried on by, or on behalf of, that person.

(3) For the purposes of the definition of "consumers" in subsection (1)—

(a) if a person ("A") is carrying on an activity in A's capacity as a trustee, the persons who are, have been or may be beneficiaries of the trust are to be treated as persons who use, have used or are or may be contemplating using services provided by A in A's carrying on of that activity, and
(b) a person who deals with another person ("B") in the course of B's carrying on of an activity is to be treated as using services provided by B in carrying on that activity.

(4) The references in this Act (other than section 195) to the provision of immigration advice or immigration services are to the provision of such advice or services by a person—

(a) in England and Wales (regardless of whether the persons to whom they are provided are in England and Wales or elsewhere), and
(b) in the course of a business carried on (whether or not for profit) by the person or another person.

(5) The Lord Chancellor may by order make provision modifying the definition of "manager" in its application to a body of persons formed under, or in so far as the body is recognised by, law having effect outside England and Wales.

(6) In this section "enactment" means a provision of—

(a) an Act of Parliament;
(b) an Act of the Scottish Parliament;
(c) a Measure or Act of the National Assembly for Wales;
(d) Northern Ireland legislation.

Initial Commencement

To be appointed: see s 211(2).

Appointment

Appointment (in relation to definitions "barrister", "consumers", "court", "functions", "immigration advice", "immigration services", "modify" and "solicitor"): 7 March 2008: see SI 2008/222, art 2(g); for transitional provisions see art 7(1) thereof.

Appointment (for certain purposes): 7 March 2008: see SI 2008/222, art 3.

Sub-s (1): Appointment (in relation to definition "manager"): 30 June 2008: see SI 2008/1436, art 2(c).
Sub-s (5): Appointment: 30 June 2008: see SI 2008/1436, art 2(c).

Miscellaneous and supplementary

208 Minor and consequential provision etc

(1) Schedule 21 contains minor and consequential amendments.

(2) The Lord Chancellor may by order make any supplementary, incidental or consequential provision and any transitory, transitional or saving provision which the Lord Chancellor considers necessary or expedient—

- (a) for the general purposes, or any particular purpose, of this Act, or
- (b) in consequence of any provision made by or under it or for giving full effect to it.

(3) An order under this section may make provision amending, repealing or revoking (with or without savings) any provision of—

- (a) an Act passed before or in the same session as this Act, or
- (b) an instrument made under an Act before the passing of this Act.

(4) An order under this section may make such adaptations of provisions of this Act brought into force as appear to be necessary or expedient in consequence of other provisions of this Act not yet having come into force.

(5) Provision made under this section is additional, and without prejudice, to that made by or under any other provision of this Act.

Initial Commencement
Sub-ss (2)–(5): Specified date: 30 October 2007: see s 211(1).
To be appointed: Sub-s (1): To be appointed: see s 211(2).
Subordinate Legislation
Legal Services Act 2007 (Commencement No 1 and Transitory Provisions) Order 2008, SI 2008/222 (made under sub-ss (2), (4)).
Legal Services Act 2007 (Commencement No 2 and Transitory Provisions) Order 2008, SI 2008/1436 (made under sub-ss (2), (4)).
Legal Services Act 2007 (Transitory Provision) Order 2008, SI 2008/1799 (made under sub-s (2)).
Legal Services Act 2007 (Transitional, Savings and Consequential Provisions) (Scotland) Order 2008, SI 2008/2341 (made under sub-s (2)).
Legal Services Act 2007 (Commencement No 3 and Transitory Provisions) Order 2008, SI 2008/3149 (made under sub-ss (2), (4)).

---

209 Transitional and transitory provision

Schedule 22 contains transitional and transitory provision.

Initial Commencement
To be appointed: see s 211(2).
Appointment
Appointment: 7 March 2008: see SI 2008/222, art 2(g).

---

210 Repeals

Schedule 23 contains repeals (including repeals of spent provisions).

Initial Commencement
To be appointed: see s 211(2).
Appointment
Appointment: 7 March 2008: see SI 2008/222, art 2(g).

---

211 Commencement

(1) This section and sections 208(2) to (5), 212 and 214 come into force on the day this Act is passed.

(2) Subject to that, the provisions of this Act come into force on such day as may be appointed by order of the Lord Chancellor.

Initial Commencement
Specified date: 30 October 2007: see para (1) above.
Subordinate Legislation
Legal Services Act 2007 (Commencement No 1 and Transitory Provisions) Order 2008, SI 2008/222.
Legal Services Act 2007 (Commencement No 2 and Transitory Provisions) Order 2008, SI 2008/1436 (made under sub-s (2)).
Legal Services Act 2007 (Commencement No 2 and Transitory Provisions) (Amendment) Order 2008, SI 2008/1591 (made by sub-s (2)).
Legal Services Act 2007 (Commencement No 3 and Transitory Provisions) Order 2008, SI 2008/3149 (made under sub-s (2)).

---

212 Extent

(1) Subject to subsections (2) and (3), this Act extends to England and Wales only.

(2) Sections 195 and 196(1) and Schedule 20 extend to Scotland only (and, for the purposes of those provisions, this Part also extends there).

(3) An amendment or repeal contained in this Act (and, for the purposes of such an amendment or repeal, this Part) has the same extent as the enactment or relevant part of the enactment to which the amendment or repeal relates.

Initial Commencement
Specified date: 30 October 2007: see s 211(1).

---

213 Index of defined expressions

Schedule 24 lists the places where expressions used in this Act are defined or otherwise explained.

Initial Commencement
To be appointed: see s 211(2).

---

214 Short title

This Act may be cited as the Legal Services Act 2007.

Initial Commencement
Specified date: 30 October 2007: see s 211(1).

SCHEDULE 1
THE LEGAL SERVICES BOARD

Section 2

Membership

1 (1) The Board is to consist of the following members—

(a) a chairman appointed by the Lord Chancellor,
(b) the Chief Executive of the Board (see paragraph 13), and
(c) at least 7, but not more than 10, other persons appointed by the Lord Chancellor.

(2) In this Schedule a reference to an "ordinary member" is a reference to a member of the Board other than the Chief Executive.

(3) Before appointing an ordinary member, the Lord Chancellor must consult the Lord Chief Justice about the process for appointment of the member and about the person selected for appointment.

(4) The Lord Chancellor may by order amend sub-paragraph (1) by substituting for the limit on the maximum number of persons for the time being specified in paragraph (c) of that sub-paragraph a different limit.

2 (1) In appointing persons as ordinary members the Lord Chancellor must ensure that a majority of the members of the Board are lay persons.

(2) The chairman must be a lay person.

(3) It is a condition of the appointment of the chairman that the person appointed must not during the appointment—

- (a) carry on any activity which is a reserved legal activity,
- (b) provide regulated claims management services (within the meaning of Part 2 of the Compensation Act 2006 (c 29)), or
- (c) provide immigration advice or immigration services,

for or in expectation of any fee, gain or reward.

(4) In this Schedule a reference to a "lay person" is a reference to a person who has never been—

- (a) an authorised person in relation to an activity which is a reserved legal activity;
- (b) a person authorised, by a person designated under section 5(1) of the Compensation Act 2006, to provide services which are regulated claims management services (within the meaning of that Act);
- (c) an advocate in Scotland;
- (d) a solicitor in Scotland;
- (e) a member of the Bar of Northern Ireland;
- (f) a solicitor of the Court of Judicature of Northern Ireland.

(5) For the purposes of sub-paragraph (4), a person is deemed to have been an authorised person in relation to an activity which is a reserved legal activity if that person has before the appointed day been—

- (a) a barrister;
- (b) a solicitor;
- (c) a public notary;
- (d) a licensed conveyancer;
- (e) granted a certificate issued by the Institute of Legal Executives authorising the person to practise as a legal executive;
- (f) a registered patent attorney, within the meaning given by section 275(1) of the Copyright, Designs and Patents Act 1988 (c 48);
- (g) a registered trade mark attorney, within the meaning of the Trade Marks Act 1994 (c 26); or
- (h) granted a right of audience or a right to conduct litigation in relation to any proceedings by virtue of section 27(2)(a) or section 28(2)(a) of the Courts and Legal Services Act 1990 (c 41) (rights of audience and rights to conduct litigation).

(6) For the purpose of sub-paragraph (5)—

"appointed day" means the day appointed for the coming into force of section 13;
"licensed conveyancer" has the meaning given by section 11(2) of the Administration of Justice Act 1985 (c 61).

3 In appointing persons to be ordinary members, the Lord Chancellor must have regard to the desirability of securing that the Board includes members who (between them) have experience in or knowledge of—

- (a) the provision of legal services;
- (b) legal education and legal training;
- (c) consumer affairs;
- (d) civil or criminal proceedings and the working of the courts;

(e) competition matters;
(f) the maintenance of the professional standards of persons who provide legal services;
(g) the maintenance of standards in professions other than the legal profession;
(h) the handling of complaints;
(i) commercial affairs;
(j) non-commercial legal services;
(k) the differing needs of consumers;
(l) the provision of claims management services (within the meaning of Part 2 of the Compensation Act 2006 (c 29)).

Terms of appointment and tenure of members

4 An ordinary member is to hold and vacate office in accordance with the terms and conditions of that member's appointment (subject to this Schedule).

5 (1) An ordinary member must be appointed for a fixed period.

(2) The period for which an ordinary member is appointed must not exceed 5 years.

(3) A person who has held office as an ordinary member may be re-appointed, once only, for a further period (whether consecutive or not) not exceeding 5 years.

6 If an ordinary member who is a lay person becomes a person within paragraphs (a) to (f) of paragraph 2(4) that person ceases to be a member of the Board.

7 (1) An ordinary member may at any time—

(a) resign from office by giving notice to the Lord Chancellor;
(b) be removed from office by the Lord Chancellor.

(2) The Lord Chancellor may not under sub-paragraph (1)(b) remove an ordinary member from office unless sub-paragraph (3) or (4) applies.

(3) This sub-paragraph applies if the Lord Chancellor is satisfied that the member—

(a) has failed without reasonable excuse to discharge the functions of the office for a continuous period of at least 6 months,
(b) has been convicted of an offence,
(c) is an undischarged bankrupt, or
(d) is otherwise unfit to hold the office or unable to discharge its functions.

(4) This sub-paragraph applies if the member is the chairman and has breached the condition imposed on his appointment by paragraph 2(3).

(5) Before removing any ordinary member under sub-paragraph (1)(b), the Lord Chancellor must consult—

(a) the Lord Chief Justice, and
(b) if the ordinary member is not the chairman, the chairman.

(6) The Lord Chancellor may not remove an ordinary member on the ground mentioned in paragraph (a) of sub-paragraph (3) more than 3 months after the end of the period mentioned in that paragraph.

8 The chairman ceases to be chairman upon ceasing to be a member of the Board.

9 Where a person ceases to be employed as Chief Executive, that person ceases to be a member of the Board.

Remuneration etc of members

10 The chairman and other ordinary members are to be paid by the Board in accordance with provision made by or under their terms of appointment.

11 The terms of appointment of the chairman or any other ordinary member may provide for the Board to pay, or make payments towards the provision of, a pension, allowance or gratuity to or in respect of that person.

12 If the Lord Chancellor thinks there are circumstances that make it right for a person ceasing to hold office as chairman or another ordinary member to receive compensation, the Board may pay that person such compensation as the Lord Chancellor may determine.

Staff

13 The Board must appoint a person as its Chief Executive.

14 The Board may appoint such other staff as it considers appropriate to assist in the performance of its functions.

15 The Chief Executive and other staff are to be—

(a) appointed on terms and conditions determined by the Board, and
(b) paid by the Board in accordance with provision made by or under the terms of appointment.

16 The terms and conditions on which the Chief Executive or any other member of staff is appointed may provide for the Board to pay, or make payments towards the provision of, a pension, allowance or gratuity to or in respect of that person.

17 The Board may pay compensation for loss of employment to or in respect of a member (or former member) of staff.

18 A member of staff appointed under paragraph 14 may be a member (but not chairman) of the Board.

Arrangements for assistance

19 (1) The Board may make arrangements with such persons as it considers appropriate for assistance to be provided to it.

(2) Arrangements may include the paying of fees to such persons.

Committees

20 (1) The Board may establish committees.

(2) Any committee so established may establish sub-committees.

(3) Only members of the Board may be members of a committee or sub-committee.

(4) A majority of the members of a committee or sub-committee must be lay persons.

Proceedings

21 (1) The Board may regulate its own procedure, and the procedure of its committees and sub-committees, including quorum.

(2) But the quorum of a committee or sub-committee must not be less than 3.

(3) The Board must publish any rules of procedure made under this paragraph.

(4) This paragraph is without prejudice to any other power the Board has under this Act to make rules.

22 The validity of any act of the Board is not affected—

(a) by a vacancy in the office of chairman or amongst the other members, or
(b) by a defect in the appointment or any disqualification of a person as chairman or another member of the Board.

Delegation of functions

23 (1) The Board may authorise—

(a) the chairman, the Chief Executive or any other member of the Board,
(b) a committee or sub-committee of the Board, or
(c) a member of staff appointed under paragraph 14,

to exercise, on behalf of the Board, such of its functions, in such circumstances, as it may determine.

(2) A committee may delegate functions (including functions delegated to the committee) to—

(a) a sub-committee,
(b) the chairman, the Chief Executive or any other member of the Board, or

(c) a member of staff appointed under paragraph 14.

(3) Sub-paragraphs (1) and (2) are subject to—

(a) any provision made by an order under section 62 by virtue of section 64(2)(k) (powers to authorise the Board to delegate to any person functions conferred on it in its capacity as an approved regulator), and
(b) section 73(3)(a) (power to delegate to any person functions conferred on the Board in its capacity as a licensing authority).

(4) Sub-paragraph (1) does not apply to any power or duty the Board has to make rules (other than excluded rules) under this Act.

(5) In sub-paragraph (4) "excluded rules" means—

(a) rules of procedure made under paragraph 21 in relation to any committee or sub-committee of the Board, and
(b) rules made by the Board in its capacity as an approved regulator or a licensing authority.

Borrowing

24 The Board is not to borrow money, except—

(a) with the consent of the Lord Chancellor, or
(b) in accordance with a general authorisation given by the Lord Chancellor.

Accounts

25 (1) The Board must—

(a) keep proper accounts and proper records in relation to the accounts, and
(b) prepare in respect of each financial year a statement of accounts.

(2) Each statement of accounts must comply with any directions given by the Lord Chancellor, with the approval of the Treasury, as to—

(a) the information to be contained in it and the manner in which it is to be presented;
(b) the methods and principles according to which the statement is to be prepared;
(c) the additional information (if any) which is to be provided for the information of Parliament.

(3) The Board must give a copy of each statement of accounts—

(a) to the Lord Chancellor, and
(b) to the Comptroller and Auditor General,

before the end of the month of August next following the financial year to which the statement relates.

(4) The Comptroller and Auditor General must—

(a) examine, certify and report on each statement of accounts which is received under sub-paragraph (3), and
(b) give a copy of the Comptroller and Auditor General's report to the Lord Chancellor.

(5) In respect of each financial year, the Lord Chancellor must lay before Parliament a document consisting of—

(a) a copy of the statement of accounts for that year, and
(b) a copy of the Comptroller and Auditor General's report on that statement.

(6) "Financial year" means—

(a) the period beginning with the day on which the Board is established and ending with the next following 31 March, and
(b) each successive period of 12 months.

Status

26 (1) The Board is not to be regarded—

(a) as the servant or agent of the Crown, or
(b) as enjoying any status, immunity or privilege of the Crown.

(2) Accordingly—

(a) the Board's property is not to be regarded as property of or held on behalf of the Crown, and
(b) the Board's staff are not to be regarded as servants or agents of the Crown or as enjoying any status, immunity or privilege of the Crown.

Application of seal and proof of instruments

27 The application of the seal of the Board is to be authenticated by the signature of any member of the Board, or of its staff, who has been authorised (whether generally or specifically) by the Board for the purpose.

28 Any contract or instrument which, if entered into or executed by an individual, would not need to be under seal may be entered into or executed on behalf of the Board by any person who has been authorised (whether generally or specifically) by the Board for the purpose.

29 A document purporting to be duly executed under the seal of the Board or signed on its behalf—

(a) is to be received in evidence, and
(b) is to be taken to be executed or signed in that way, unless the contrary is proved.

Disqualification

30 (1) In Part 2 of Schedule 1 to the House of Commons Disqualification Act 1975 (c 24) (bodies of which all members are disqualified) at the appropriate place insert—

"The Legal Services Board."

(2) In Part 2 of Schedule 1 to the Northern Ireland Assembly Disqualification Act 1975 (c 25) (bodies of which all members are disqualified) at the appropriate place insert—

"The Legal Services Board."

Freedom of information

31 In Part 6 of Schedule 1 to the Freedom of Information Act 2000 (c 36) (other public bodies and offices which are public authorities) at the appropriate place insert—

"The Legal Services Board."

Public records

32 In Schedule 1 to the Public Records Act 1958 (c 51) (definition of public records) at the appropriate place in Part 2 of the Table at the end of paragraph 3 insert—

"The Legal Services Board."

Exemption from liability in damages

33 (1) This paragraph applies to—

(a) the Board,
(b) a member of the Board,
(c) a member of the Board's staff appointed under paragraph 14,
(d) a person to whom the Board (in its capacity as an approved regulator) delegates any of its functions by virtue of provision made under section 64(2)(k), and
(e) a person to whom the Board (in its capacity as a licensing authority) delegates any of its functions by virtue of section 73(3)(a).

(2) A person to whom this paragraph applies is not liable in damages for anything done or omitted in the exercise or purported exercise of the functions of the Board conferred by or by virtue of this or any other enactment.

(3) But sub-paragraph (1) does not apply—

(a) if it is shown that the act or omission was in bad faith, or
(b) so as to prevent an award of damages made in respect of an act or omission on the ground that the act or omission was unlawful as a result of section 6(1) of the Human Rights Act 1998 (c 42).

Initial Commencement
To be appointed: see s 211(2).
Appointment
Appointment: 7 March 2008: see SI 2008/222, art 2(h); for transitional provisions see art 8 thereof.
Extent
This Schedule does not extend to Scotland: see s 212(1).

SCHEDULE 2
THE RESERVED LEGAL ACTIVITIES

Section 12

Introduction

1 This Schedule makes provision about the reserved legal activities.

2 In this Schedule "the appointed day" means the day appointed for the coming into force of section 13 (entitlement to carry on reserved legal activities).

Rights of audience

3 (1) A "right of audience" means the right to appear before and address a court, including the right to call and examine witnesses.

(2) But a "right of audience" does not include a right to appear before or address a court, or to call or examine witnesses, in relation to any particular court or in relation to particular proceedings, if immediately before the appointed day no restriction was placed on the persons entitled to exercise that right.

Conduct of litigation

4 (1) The "conduct of litigation" means—

(a) the issuing of proceedings before any court in England and Wales,
(b) the commencement, prosecution and defence of such proceedings, and
(c) the performance of any ancillary functions in relation to such proceedings (such as entering appearances to actions).

(2) But the "conduct of litigation" does not include any activity within paragraphs (a) to (c) of sub-paragraph (1), in relation to any particular court or in relation to any particular proceedings, if immediately before the appointed day no restriction was placed on the persons entitled to carry on that activity.

Reserved instrument activities

5 (1) "Reserved instrument activities" means—

(a) preparing any instrument of transfer or charge for the purposes of the Land Registration Act 2002 (c 9);
(b) making an application or lodging a document for registration under that Act;
(c) preparing any other instrument relating to real or personal estate for the purposes of the law of England and Wales or instrument relating to court proceedings in England and Wales.

(2) But "reserved instrument activities" does not include the preparation of an instrument relating to any particular court proceedings if, immediately before the appointed day, no restriction was placed on the persons entitled to carry on that activity.

(3) In this paragraph "instrument" includes a contract for the sale or other disposition of land (except a contract to grant a short lease), but does not include—

(a) a will or other testamentary instrument,
(b) an agreement not intended to be executed as a deed, other than a contract that is included by virtue of the preceding provisions of this sub-paragraph,
(c) a letter or power of attorney, or
(d) a transfer of stock containing no trust or limitation of the transfer.

(4) In this paragraph a "short lease" means a lease such as is referred to in section 54(2) of the Law of Property Act 1925 (c 20) (short leases).

Probate activities

6 (1) "Probate activities" means preparing any probate papers for the purposes of the law of England and Wales or in relation to any proceedings in England and Wales.

(2) In this paragraph "probate papers" means papers on which to found or oppose—

(a) a grant of probate, or
(b) a grant of letters of administration.

Notarial activities

7 (1) "Notarial activities" means activities which, immediately before the appointed day, were customarily carried on by virtue of enrolment as a notary in accordance with section 1 of the Public Notaries Act 1801 (c 79).

(2) Sub-paragraph (1) does not include activities carried on—

(a) by virtue of section 22 or 23 of the Solicitors Act 1974 (c 47) (reserved instrument activities and probate activities), or
(b) by virtue of section 113 of the Courts and Legal Services Act 1990 (c 41) (administration of oaths).

Administration of oaths

8 The "administration of oaths" means the exercise of the powers conferred on a commissioner for oaths by—

(a) the Commissioners for Oaths Act 1889 (c 10);
(b) the Commissioners for Oaths Act 1891 (c 50);
(c) section 24 of the Stamp Duties Management Act 1891 (c 38).

Initial Commencement
To be appointed: see s 211(2).
Appointment
Appointment (for certain purposes): 7 March 2008: see SI 2008/222, art 3.
Extent
This Schedule does not extend to Scotland: see s 212(1).

SCHEDULE 3
EXEMPT PERSONS

Section 19

Rights of audience

1 (1) This paragraph applies to determine whether a person is an exempt person for the purpose of exercising a right of audience before a court in relation to any proceedings (subject to paragraph 7).

(2) The person is exempt if the person—

(a) is not an authorised person in relation to that activity, but
(b) has a right of audience granted by that court in relation to those proceedings.

(3) The person is exempt if the person—

(a) is not an authorised person in relation to that activity, but
(b) has a right of audience before that court in relation to those proceedings granted by or under any enactment.

(4) The person is exempt if the person is the Attorney General or the Solicitor General and—

(a) the name of the person is on the roll kept by the Law Society under section 6 of the Solicitors Act 1974 (c 47), or
(b) the person has been called to the Bar by an Inn of Court.

(5) The person is exempt if the person is the Advocate General for Scotland and is admitted—

(a) as a solicitor in Scotland under section 6 of the Solicitors (Scotland) Act 1980 (c 46), or
(b) to practise as an advocate before the courts of Scotland.

(6) The person is exempt if the person—

(a) is a party to those proceedings, and
(b) would have a right of audience, in the person's capacity as such a party, if this Act had not been passed.

(7) The person is exempt if—

(a) the person is an individual whose work includes assisting in the conduct of litigation,
(b) the person is assisting in the conduct of litigation—
 (i) under instructions given (either generally or in relation to the proceedings) by an individual to whom sub-paragraph (8) applies, and
 (ii) under the supervision of that individual, and
(c) the proceedings are being heard in chambers in the High Court or a county court and are not reserved family proceedings.

(8) This sub-paragraph applies to—

(a) any authorised person in relation to an activity which constitutes the conduct of litigation;
(b) any person who by virtue of section 193 is not required to be entitled to carry on such an activity.

(9) The person is an exempt person in relation to the exercise of a right of audience in proceedings on an appeal from the Comptroller-General of Patents, Designs and Trade Marks to the Patents Court under the Patents Act 1977 (c 37), if the person is a solicitor of the Court of Judicature of Northern Ireland.

(10) For the purposes of this paragraph—

"family proceedings" has the same meaning as in the Matrimonial and Family Proceedings Act 1984 (c 42) and also includes any other proceedings which are family proceedings for the purposes of the Children Act 1989 (c 41);
"reserved family proceedings" means such category of family proceedings as the Lord Chancellor may, after consulting the President of the Law Society and with the concurrence of the President of the Family Division, by order prescribe;

and any order made under section 27(9) of the Courts and Legal Services Act 1990 (c 41) before the day appointed for the coming into force of this paragraph is to have effect on and after that day as if it were an order made under this sub-paragraph.

Conduct of litigation

2 (1) This paragraph applies to determine whether a person is an exempt person for the purpose of carrying on any activity which constitutes the conduct of litigation in relation to any proceedings (subject to paragraph 7).

(2) The person is exempt if the person—

(a) is not an authorised person in relation to that activity, but
(b) has a right to conduct litigation granted by a court in relation to those proceedings.

(3) The person is exempt if the person—

(a) is not an authorised person in relation to that activity, but

(b) has a right to conduct litigation in relation to those proceedings granted by or under any enactment.

(4) The person is exempt if the person—

(a) is a party to those proceedings, and
(b) would have a right to conduct the litigation, in the person's capacity as such a party, if this Act had not been passed.

(5) The person is an exempt person in relation to any activity which is carried on in or in connection with proceedings on an appeal from the Comptroller-General of Patents, Designs and Trade Marks to the Patents Court under the Patents Act 1977 (c 37), if the person is a solicitor of the Court of Judicature of Northern Ireland.

Reserved instrument activities

3 (1) This paragraph applies to determine whether a person is an exempt person for the purpose of carrying on any activity which constitutes reserved instrument activities (subject to paragraph 7).

(2) The person is exempt if the person prepares the instruments or applications in the course of the person's duty as a public officer.

(3) The person ("E") is exempt if—

(a) E is an individual,
(b) E carries on the activity at the direction and under the supervision of another individual ("P"),
(c) when E does so, P and E are connected, and
(d) P is entitled to carry on the activity, otherwise than by virtue of sub-paragraph (10).

(4) For the purposes of sub-paragraph (3), P and E are connected if—

(a) P is E's employer,
(b) P is a fellow employee of E,
(c) P is a manager or employee of a body which is an authorised person in relation to the activity, and E is also a manager or employee of that body.

(5) If the person is an accredited person, the person is exempt to the extent that the activity consists of the preparation of any instrument—

(a) which creates, or which the person believes on reasonable grounds will create, a farm business tenancy (within the meaning of the Agricultural Tenancies Act 1995 (c 8)), or
(b) which relates to an existing tenancy which is, or which the person believes on reasonable grounds to be, such a tenancy.

(6) In sub-paragraph (5) "accredited person" means a person who is—

(a) a Fellow of the Central Association of Agricultural Valuers, or
(b) a Member or Fellow of the Royal Institution of Chartered Surveyors.

(7) The person is exempt to the extent that the activity carried on by the person is also a reserved legal activity within sub-paragraph (8) and the person is—

(a) authorised to carry on that activity (other than under Part 5) by a relevant approved regulator in relation to the activity,
(b) authorised to carry on that activity by a licence under Part 5, or
(c) an exempt person in relation to that activity by virtue of paragraph 1 or 2 of this Schedule.

(8) The activities are—

(a) the exercise of a right of audience;
(b) the conduct of litigation.

(9) The person is exempt if the person is employed merely to engross the instrument or application.

(10) The person is exempt if the person is an individual who carries on the activity otherwise than for, or in expectation of, any fee, gain or reward.

(11) The person is exempt if—

(a) the person is a person qualified to practise as a solicitor in Scotland in accordance with section 4 of the Solicitors (Scotland) Act 1980 (c 46), and

(b) the reserved instrument activities fall within paragraph 5(1)(c) of Schedule 2 (preparation of certain instruments relating to real or personal property or legal proceedings).

Probate activities

4 (1) This paragraph applies to determine whether a person is an exempt person for the purpose of carrying on any activity which constitutes probate activities (subject to paragraph 7).

(2) The person ("E") is an exempt person if—

(a) E is an individual,

(b) E provides the probate activities at the direction and under the supervision of another individual ("P"),

(c) when E does so, P and E are connected, and

(d) P is entitled to carry on the activity, otherwise than by virtue of sub-paragraph (4).

(3) For the purposes of sub-paragraph (2), P and E are connected if—

(a) P is E's employer,

(b) P is a fellow employee of E,

(c) P is a manager or employee of a body which is an authorised person in relation to the activity, and E is also a manager or employee of that body.

(4) The person is exempt if the person is an individual who carries on the activity otherwise than for, or in expectation of, any fee, gain or reward.

Notarial activities

5 (1) This paragraph applies to determine whether a person is an exempt person for the purpose of carrying on any activity which constitutes notarial activities (subject to paragraph 7).

(2) The person is exempt if the person is not an authorised person in relation to that activity under this Act, but is authorised to carry on that activity by or by virtue of any other enactment.

(3) The person is exempt if section 14 of the Public Notaries Act 1801 (c 79) applies to the person, and—

(a) where that section applies by virtue of the person holding or exercising an office or appointment, the person carries on the activity for ecclesiastical purposes;

(b) where that section applies by virtue of the person performing a public duty or service under government, the person carries on the activity in the course of performing that duty or service.

(4) The person is exempt if the person is an individual who carries on the notarial activities otherwise than for or in expectation of a fee, gain or reward.

Administration of oaths

6 (1) This paragraph applies to determine whether a person is an exempt person for the purpose of carrying on any activity which constitutes the administration of oaths (subject to paragraph 7).

(2) The person is exempt if the person is not an authorised person in relation to that activity under this Act, but is authorised to carry on that activity by or by virtue of any other enactment.

(3) The person is exempt if the person has a commission under section 1(1) of the Commissioners for Oaths Act 1889 (c 10).

European lawyers

7 A European lawyer (within the meaning of the European Communities (Services of Lawyers) Order 1978 (SI 1978/1910)) is an exempt person for the purposes of carrying on an activity which is a reserved legal activity and which the European lawyer is entitled to carry on by virtue of that order.

Employers etc acting through exempt person

8 (1) This paragraph applies where—

(a) a person ("P") carries on an activity ("the relevant activity") which is a reserved legal activity,
(b) P carries on the relevant activity by virtue of an employee of P ("E") carrying it on in E's capacity as such an employee, and
(c) E is an exempt person in relation to the relevant activity.

(2) P is an exempt person in relation to the relevant activity to the extent that P carries on that activity by virtue of E so carrying it on.

(3) This paragraph does not apply where E—

(a) carries on the relevant activity at the direction and under the supervision of an authorised person in relation to that activity, and
(b) is exempt in relation to that activity by virtue of paragraph 1(7), 3(3) or 4(2).

(4) If P is a body, in this paragraph references to an employee of P include references to a manager of P.

Further exempt persons

9 (1) The Lord Chancellor may, by order, amend this Schedule so as to provide—

(a) for persons to be exempt persons in relation to any activity which is a reserved legal activity (including any activity which is a reserved legal activity by virtue of an order under section 24 (extension of reserved legal activities)),
(b) for persons to cease to be such persons, or
(c) for the amendment of any provision made in respect of an exempt person.

(2) The Lord Chancellor may make an order under sub-paragraph (1) only on the recommendation of the Board.

Initial Commencement
To be appointed: see s 211(2).
Extent
This Schedule does not extend to Scotland: see s 212(1).

SCHEDULE 4
APPROVED REGULATORS

Section 20

PART 1
EXISTING REGULATORS

1 (1) Each body listed in the first column of the Table in this paragraph is an approved regulator.

(2) Each body so listed is an approved regulator in relation to the reserved legal activities listed in relation to it in the second column of the Table.

Approved regulator	*Reserved legal activities*
The Law Society	The exercise of a right of audience. The conduct of litigation. Reserved instrument activities. Probate activities. The administration of oaths.

Approved regulator	*Reserved legal activities*
The General Council of the Bar	The exercise of a right of audience. The conduct of litigation. Reserved instrument activities. Probate activities. The administration of oaths.
The Master of the Faculties	Reserved instrument activities. Probate activities. Notarial activities. The administration of oaths.
The Institute of Legal Executives	The exercise of a right of audience. The administration of oaths.
The Council for Licensed Conveyancers	Reserved instrument activities. The administration of oaths.
The Chartered Institute of Patent Attorneys	The exercise of a right of audience. The conduct of litigation. Reserved instrument activities. The administration of oaths.
The Institute of Trade Mark Attorneys	The exercise of a right of audience. The conduct of litigation. Reserved instrument activities. The administration of oaths.
The Association of Law Costs Draftsmen	The exercise of a right of audience. The conduct of litigation. The administration of oaths.

2 (1) The regulatory arrangements of a listed body, as they have effect immediately before paragraph 1 comes into force, are to be treated as having been approved by the Board for the purposes of this Act at the time that paragraph comes into force.

(2) "Listed body" means a body listed in the first column of the Table in paragraph 1 as that Table has effect at the time that paragraph comes into force.

(3) Sub-paragraph (1) is without prejudice to the Board's power to give directions under section 32 (powers to direct an approved regulator to take steps in certain circumstances, including steps to amend its regulatory arrangements).

Initial Commencement
To be appointed: see s 211(2).
Extent
This part of this Schedule does not extend to Scotland: see s 212(1).

PART 2
DESIGNATION OF BODIES BY ORDER

Application to the Board

3 (1) This paragraph applies where a body wishes to authorise persons to carry on one or more activities which constitute one or more reserved legal activities.

(2) The body may apply to the Board for the Board—

(a) to recommend that an order be made by the Lord Chancellor designating the body as an approved regulator in relation to the reserved legal activity or activities in question, and

(b) to approve what the body proposes as its regulatory arrangements if such an order is made ("the proposed regulatory arrangements").

(3) An application under this paragraph must be made in such form and manner as the Board may specify in rules and must be accompanied by—

(a) a statement of the reserved legal activity or activities to which it relates,
(b) details of the applicant's proposed regulatory arrangements,
(c) such explanatory material (including material about the applicant's constitution and activities) as the applicant considers is likely to be needed for the purposes of this Part of this Schedule, and
(d) the prescribed fee.

(4) The prescribed fee is the fee specified in, or determined in accordance with, rules made by the Board with the consent of the Lord Chancellor.

(5) The proposed regulatory arrangements must, in particular, include—

(a) details of the authority which the applicant proposes to give persons to carry on activities which are reserved legal activities and of the nature of the persons to whom the authority is to be given,
(b) regulations (however they may be described) as to the education and training which persons must receive, and any other requirements which must be met by or in respect of them, in order for them to be authorised, and
(c) rules (however they may be described) as to the conduct required of persons in carrying on any activity by virtue of the authority.

(6) An applicant may, at any time, withdraw the application by giving notice to that effect to the Board.

Dismissal of application

4 (1) The Board may refuse to consider, or to continue its consideration of, an application.

(2) The Board must make rules about the procedures and criteria that it will apply when determining whether to refuse to consider, or to continue its consideration of, an application under sub-paragraph (1).

(3) Where the Board decides to refuse to consider, or to continue its consideration of, an application it must give the applicant notice of that decision and of its reasons for it.

(4) The Board must publish a notice given under sub-paragraph (3).

Board's duty to seek advice

5 (1) The Board must give each of the persons listed in sub-paragraph (2)—

(a) a copy of the application and accompanying material, and
(b) a notice specifying a period within which any advice given under paragraphs 6 to 8 must be given.

(2) Those persons are—

(a) the OFT,
(b) the Consumer Panel,
(c) the Lord Chief Justice, and
(d) such other persons as the Board considers it reasonable to consult regarding the application.

(3) In this Part of this Schedule, in relation to an application, "selected consultee" means a person within sub-paragraph (2)(d).

Advice of Office of Fair Trading

6 (1) The OFT must give the Board such advice as the OFT thinks fit regarding whether the application should be granted.

(2) In deciding what advice to give, the OFT must, in particular, have regard to whether making an order under paragraph 17 in accordance with the recommendation applied for would (or would be likely to) prevent, restrict or distort competition within the market for reserved legal services to any significant extent.

Advice of the Consumer Panel

7 (1) The Consumer Panel must give the Board such advice as the Consumer Panel thinks fit regarding whether the application should be granted.

(2) In deciding what advice to give, the Consumer Panel must, in particular, have regard to the likely impact on consumers of the making of an order under paragraph 17 in accordance with the recommendation applied for.

Advice of selected consultees

8 A selected consultee may give the Board such advice as the selected consultee thinks fit in respect of the application.

Advice of the Lord Chief Justice

9 (1) The Board must give the Lord Chief Justice—

(a) a copy of any advice duly given under paragraphs 6 to 8, and
(b) a notice specifying a period within which any advice under this paragraph must be given.

(2) The Lord Chief Justice must then give such advice to the Board as the Lord Chief Justice thinks fit regarding whether the application should be granted.

(3) In deciding what advice to give, the Lord Chief Justice must, in particular, have regard to the likely impact on the courts in England and Wales of the making of an order under paragraph 17 in accordance with the recommendation applied for.

Information obtained by consultees

10 A person ("the consultee") to whom a copy of the application is given under paragraph 5(1) may, for the purposes of giving advice under paragraphs 6 to 9, request the applicant or any other person to provide the consultee with such additional information as may be specified by the consultee.

Representations by applicant

11 (1) The Board must give the applicant a copy of any advice duly given under paragraphs 6 to 9.

(2) The applicant may make to the Board—

(a) written representations, and
(b) if the Board authorises it to do so, oral representations,

about the advice.

(3) The Board must make rules governing the making of oral and written representations.

(4) Representations under this paragraph must be made within—

(a) the period of 28 days beginning with the day on which the copy of the advice is given to the applicant, or
(b) such longer period as the Board may specify in a particular case.

(5) Where oral representations are made, the Board must prepare a report of those representations.

(6) Before preparing that report, the Board must—

(a) give the applicant a reasonable opportunity to comment on a draft of the report, and
(b) have regard to any comments duly made.

Publication of advice and representations etc

12 (1) The Board must, as soon as practicable after the end of the period within which representations under paragraph 11 may be made, publish—

(a) any advice duly given under paragraphs 6 to 9, and
(b) any written representations duly made under paragraph 11 and the report (if any) prepared under that paragraph.

(2) Nothing in sub-paragraph (1) operates—

(a) to prevent a person who gives advice under paragraphs 6 to 9 from publishing that advice, or
(b) to prevent a person who makes representations under paragraph 11 from publishing those representations.

(3) A person ("the publisher") publishing any such material (whether under sub-paragraph (1) or otherwise) must, so far as practicable, exclude any matter which relates to the private affairs of a particular individual the publication of which, in the opinion of the publisher, would or might seriously and prejudicially affect the interests of that individual.

Rules governing decisions by the Board

13 (1) The Board must make rules specifying how it will determine applications.

(2) Rules under sub-paragraph (1) must, in particular, provide that the Board may grant an application in relation to a particular reserved legal activity only if it is satisfied—

(a) that, if an order were to be made under paragraph 17 designating the body in relation to that activity, the applicant would have appropriate internal governance arrangements in place at the time the order takes effect,
(b) that, if such an order were to be made, the applicant would be competent, and have sufficient resources, to perform the role of approved regulator in relation to the reserved legal activity at that time,
(c) that the applicant's proposed regulatory arrangements make appropriate provision,
(d) that the applicant's proposed regulatory arrangements comply with the requirement imposed by sections 52 and 54 (resolution of regulatory conflict), and
(e) that those arrangements comply with the requirements imposed by sections 112 and 145 (requirements imposed in relation to the handling of complaints).

(3) The rules made for the purposes of sub-paragraph (2)(a) must in particular require the Board to be satisfied—

(a) that the exercise of the applicant's regulatory functions would not be prejudiced by any of its representative functions, and
(b) that decisions relating to the exercise of its regulatory functions would so far as reasonably practicable be taken independently from decisions relating to the exercise of its representative functions.

Determination of applications

14 (1) After considering—

(a) the application and accompanying material,
(b) any other information provided by the applicant,
(c) any advice duly given under paragraphs 6 to 9,
(d) any representations duly made under paragraph 11, and
(e) any other information which the Board considers relevant to the application,

the Board must decide whether to grant the application.

(2) Where the application relates to more than one reserved legal activity, the Board may grant the application in relation to all or any of them.

(3) The Board must give notice of its decision to the applicant ("the decision notice").

(4) Where the Board decides to refuse the application (in whole or in part), the decision notice must specify the reasons for that decision.

(5) The Board must publish the decision notice.

15 (1) Where an application is made under this Part, the Board must give the decision notice under paragraph 14 within the decision period.

(2) The "decision period" is the period of 12 months beginning with the day on which the application is made to the Board.

(3) The Board may, before the end of the decision period, issue a notice extending that period by a period specified in the notice.

(4) More than one notice may be issued under sub-paragraph (3), but the decision period must not exceed 16 months.

(5) The Board may issue a notice under sub-paragraph (3) only after it has consulted—

(a) the OFT,
(b) the Consumer Panel, and
(c) the Lord Chief Justice.

(6) A notice under sub-paragraph (3) must state the Board's reasons for extending the decision period.

(7) The Board must publish any notice issued under sub-paragraph (3).

Effect of grant of application

16 (1) This paragraph applies where an application is granted in relation to a reserved legal activity or activities.

(2) The Board must recommend to the Lord Chancellor that an order be made designating the applicant as an approved regulator in relation to the reserved legal activity or activities in question.

(3) The Board must publish any recommendation made under sub-paragraph (2).

(4) The Board must make available to the Lord Chancellor—

(a) any advice duly given under paragraphs 6 to 9,
(b) any written representations duly made under paragraph 11 and the report (if any) prepared under that paragraph, and
(c) any other material considered by the Board for the purpose of determining the application.

Lord Chancellor's decision to make an order

17 (1) Where a recommendation is made to the Lord Chancellor under paragraph 16, the Lord Chancellor may—

(a) make an order in accordance with the recommendation, or
(b) refuse to make such an order.

(2) Where the recommendation relates to more than one reserved legal activity, the Lord Chancellor may make an order under sub-paragraph (1)(a) in relation to all or any of them.

(3) The Lord Chancellor must—

(a) decide whether to make an order under this paragraph, and
(b) give notice of that decision ("the decision notice") to the applicant,

within the period of 90 days beginning with the day on which the recommendation was made.

(4) If the Lord Chancellor decides not to make an order in accordance with the whole or part of the recommendation, the decision notice must state the reasons for the decision.

(5) The Lord Chancellor must publish the decision notice.

Approval of regulatory arrangements

18 (1) Where an order is made by the Lord Chancellor under paragraph 17, the applicant's proposed regulatory arrangements are at the same time treated as having been approved by the Board.

(2) But where the order relates to one or more (but not all) of the reserved legal activities to which the application related, sub-paragraph (1) has effect as if the reference to the applicant's proposed regulatory arrangements were a reference to those arrangements excluding any provision made in respect of any activities excluded from the order.

(3) Sub-paragraph (1) is without prejudice to the Board's power to give directions under section 32 (powers to direct an approved regulator to take steps in certain circumstances, including steps to amend its regulatory arrangements).

Initial Commencement
To be appointed: see s 211(2).
Appointment
Paras 3(1), (3), (4), 4(2), 11(3), 13: Appointment: 1 January 2009: see SI 2008/3149, art 2(b)(ii).
Extent
This part of this Schedule does not extend to Scotland: see s 212(1).

PART 3
ALTERATION OF APPROVED REGULATOR'S REGULATORY ARRANGEMENTS

Requirement for approval

19 (1) If an alteration is made of the regulatory arrangements of an approved regulator, the alteration does not have effect unless it is approved for the purposes of this Act.

(2) An alteration is approved for the purposes of this Act if—

- (a) it is approved by virtue of paragraph 18 (approval of proposed regulatory arrangements on designation by order as approved regulator),
- (b) it is approved by the Board under this Part of this Schedule,
- (c) it is an exempt alteration,
- (d) it is an alteration made in compliance with a direction under section 32,
- (e) it is approved by virtue of paragraph 16 of Schedule 10 (approval of licensing rules on designation by order as licensing authority), or
- (f) it is approved by virtue of paragraph 7 of Schedule 18 (approval of proposed regulatory arrangements when granting "qualifying regulator" status for the purposes of Part 5 of the Immigration and Asylum Act 1999 (c 33)).

(3) An exempt alteration is an alteration which the Board has directed is to be treated as exempt for the purposes of this paragraph.

(4) A direction under sub-paragraph (3) may be specific or general and must be published by the Board.

(5) In this Part of this Schedule, references to an "alteration" of regulatory arrangements include an addition to, or the revocation of any part of, the arrangements.

(6) If a question arises whether approval is required by virtue of this Part of this Schedule, it is for the Board to decide.

(7) Nothing in this Part of this Schedule applies in relation to any alteration of the regulatory arrangements of the Board in its capacity as an approved regulator (or of its licensing rules).

Application to Board

20 (1) An application by an approved regulator for the Board to approve an alteration or alterations of its regulatory arrangements must be made in such form and manner as the Board may specify in rules.

(2) The application must be accompanied by—

- (a) details of such of the approved regulator's regulatory arrangements as are relevant to the application,
- (b) details of the alteration or alterations, and
- (c) such explanatory material as the approved regulator considers is likely to be needed for the purposes of this Part of this Schedule.

Initial determination

21 (1) Where the Board has received an application under paragraph 20 it may—

(a) grant the application and give the approved regulator a notice to that effect, or
(b) give the approved regulator a notice stating that the Board is considering whether to refuse the application (a "warning notice").

(2) The Board must publish any notice given by it under sub-paragraph (1)(a) or (b).

(3) If the Board does not give the approved regulator a notice under sub-paragraph (1)(a) or (b) within the initial decision period, the application is deemed to have been granted by the Board.

(4) The "initial decision period" means the period of 28 days beginning with the day on which the application was received by the Board.

(5) The Board may extend the initial decision period—

(a) with the consent of the approved regulator, or
(b) by giving an extension notice to the approved regulator,

before the end of that period (or if it has previously been extended under this sub-paragraph, that period as so extended).

(6) An extension notice—

(a) must specify the period of the extension, and
(b) must state the Board's reasons for extending the initial decision period.

(7) The period specified in the notice under sub-paragraph (6)(a) must end no later than the end of the period of 90 days beginning with the date on which the application was made under paragraph 20.

Advice

22 (1) Where the Board has given the approved regulator a warning notice, the Board may invite such persons as it considers appropriate to give the Board advice regarding whether the application should be granted.

(2) A person ("the consultee") to whom an invitation is given under sub-paragraph (1) may, for the purposes of giving advice to the Board under this paragraph, request the approved regulator or any other person to provide the consultee with such additional information as may be specified by the consultee.

Representations by applicant

23 (1) The Board must give the approved regulator a copy of any advice obtained under paragraph 22.

(2) The approved regulator may make to the Board—

(a) written representations, and
(b) if the Board authorises it to do so, oral representations,

about the advice.

(3) The Board must make rules governing the making of oral and written representations.

(4) Representations under this paragraph must be made within—

(a) the period of 28 days beginning with the day on which the copy of the advice is given to the approved regulator, or
(b) such longer period as the Board may specify in a particular case.

(5) Where oral representations are made, the Board must prepare a report of those representations.

(6) Before preparing that report, the Board must—

(a) give the approved regulator a reasonable opportunity to comment on a draft of the report, and
(b) have regard to any comments duly made.

Publication of advice and representations etc

24 (1) The Board must, as soon as practicable after the end of the period within which representations under paragraph 23 may be made, publish—

- (a) any advice given under paragraph 22, and
- (b) any written representations duly made under paragraph 23 and the report (if any) prepared under that paragraph.

(2) Nothing in sub-paragraph (1) operates—

- (a) to prevent a person who gives advice under paragraph 22 from publishing that advice, or
- (b) to prevent a person who makes representations under paragraph 23 from publishing those representations.

(3) A person ("the publisher") publishing any such material (whether under sub-paragraph (1) or otherwise) must, so far as practicable, exclude any matter which relates to the private affairs of a particular individual the publication of which, in the opinion of the publisher, would or might seriously and prejudicially affect the interests of that individual.

Decision by the Board

25 (1) After considering—

- (a) the application and any accompanying material,
- (b) any other information provided by the approved regulator,
- (c) any advice obtained under paragraph 22,
- (d) any representations duly made under paragraph 23, and
- (e) any other information which the Board considers relevant to the application,

the Board must decide whether to grant the application.

(2) The Board may grant the application in whole or in part.

(3) The Board may refuse the application only if it is satisfied that—

- (a) granting the application would be prejudicial to the regulatory objectives,
- (b) granting the application would be contrary to any provision made by or by virtue of this Act or any other enactment or would result in any of the designation requirements ceasing to be satisfied in relation to the approved regulator,
- (c) granting the application would be contrary to the public interest,
- (d) the alteration would enable the approved regulator to authorise persons to carry on activities which are reserved legal activities in relation to which it is not a relevant approved regulator,
- (e) the alteration would enable the approved regulator to license persons under Part 5 to carry on activities which are reserved legal activities in relation to which it is not a licensing authority, or
- (f) the alteration has been or is likely to be made otherwise than in accordance with the procedures (whether statutory or otherwise) which apply in relation to the making of the alteration.

(4) For the purposes of sub-paragraph (3)(b) the designation requirements are—

- (a) a requirement that the approved regulator has appropriate internal governance arrangements in place,
- (b) a requirement that the applicant is competent, and has sufficient resources to perform the role of approved regulator in relation to the reserved legal activities in respect of which it is designated, and
- (c) the requirements of paragraph 13(2)(c) to (e).

(5) Sub-paragraph (3) applies in relation to any part of an application as if references to the application were to the part.

(6) The Board must give notice of its decision ("the decision notice") to the approved regulator.

(7) Where the Board decides to refuse the application (in whole or in part), the decision notice must specify the reasons for that decision.

(8) The Board must publish the decision notice.

Failure to decide application during decision period

26 (1) This paragraph applies where the Board gives an approved regulator a warning notice under paragraph 21 in respect of the approved regulator's application.

(2) If the Board does not give the approved regulator notice of its decision under paragraph 25 within the decision period, the application is deemed to have been granted by the Board at the end of that period.

(3) Subject to sub-paragraphs (4) and (5), "the decision period" means the period of 12 months beginning with the day on which the approved regulator received the warning notice.

(4) The Board may, on one or more occasions, give the approved regulator a notice (an "extension notice") extending the decision period.

(5) But—

(a) an extension notice may only be given before the time when the decision period would end, but for the extension notice, and
(b) the total decision period must not exceed 18 months.

(6) The Board must publish any extension notice given by it.

Effect of grant of application

27 (1) Where an application is granted under paragraph 21(1)(a) or (3), 25(1) or 26(2), the alteration or alterations of the regulatory arrangements to which the application relates are approved.

(2) Where a part of an application is granted under paragraph 25(1), the alteration or alterations of the regulatory arrangements to which the part relates are approved.

(3) Sub-paragraphs (1) and (2) are without prejudice to the Board's power to give directions under section 32 (power to direct an approved regulator to take steps in certain circumstances, including steps to amend its regulatory arrangements).

Initial Commencement
To be appointed: see s 211(2).
Appointment
Paras 20, 23(3): Appointment: 1 January 2009: see SI 2008/3149, art 2(b)(ii).
Extent
This part of this Schedule does not extend to Scotland: see s 212(1).

SCHEDULE 5
AUTHORISED PERSONS

Section 22

PART 1
CONTINUITY OF RIGHTS

Rights of audience and conduct of litigation

1 (1) For the purposes of section 18 (authorised persons), in the case of a person who is authorised by a listed body—

(a) to exercise a right of audience before a court in relation to any proceedings, or
(b) to conduct litigation in relation to any proceedings,

it is irrelevant whether the person's authorisation was granted before or on or after the appointed day.

(2) The "listed bodies" are—

(a) The Law Society,
(b) The General Council of the Bar,
(c) The Chartered Institute of Patent Attorneys,

(d) The Institute of Trade Mark Attorneys,
(e) The Association of Law Costs Draftsmen, and
(f) for the purposes of sub-paragraph (1)(a) only, The Institute of Legal Executives.

(3) For the purposes of sub-paragraph (1), any authority conferred by section 31 of the Courts and Legal Services Act 1990 (c 41) (barristers and solicitors deemed to have rights of audience and rights to conduct litigation) is to be disregarded (see paragraphs 4 and 7 below).

Conveyancing services

2 (1) For the purposes of section 18, in the case of a licensed conveyancer who is authorised to carry on an activity which is a reserved instrument activity by a conveyancing licence, it is irrelevant whether the licence was granted before or on or after the appointed day.

(2) For the purposes of this paragraph "conveyancing licence" means a licence to practise as a licensed conveyancer granted under Part 2 of the Administration of Justice Act 1985 (c 61).

Initial Commencement
To be appointed: see s 211(2).
Extent
This part of this Schedule does not extend to Scotland: see s 212(1).

PART 2
RIGHTS DURING TRANSITIONAL PERIOD

The transitional period

3 (1) In this Part of this Schedule references to "the transitional period" are to the period which—

(a) begins with the appointed day (within the meaning given by paragraph 19), and
(b) ends with the day appointed by the Lord Chancellor by order for the purposes of this paragraph.

(2) Different days may be appointed under sub-paragraph (1)(b) for different purposes.

(3) An order may be made under sub-paragraph (1)(b) only on the recommendation of the Board.

Barristers etc

4 (1) During the transitional period, every barrister is deemed to be authorised by the General Council of the Bar to carry on the activities in sub-paragraph (2).

(2) Those activities are—

(a) the exercise of a right of audience before every court in relation to all proceedings;
(b) reserved instrument activities;
(c) probate activities;
(d) the administration of oaths.

(3) The authority conferred on a barrister by this paragraph is exercisable in accordance with, and subject to, the regulatory arrangements of the General Council of the Bar.

(4) A person is not authorised under sub-paragraph (1) unless the person has in force a certificate issued by the General Council of the Bar authorising the person to practise as a barrister.

5 (1) During the transitional period, every registered European lawyer registered with the Inns of Court and the General Council of the Bar is deemed to be authorised by the General Council of the Bar to carry on activities which—

(a) are within paragraph 4(2), and
(b) the registered European lawyer is entitled to carry on under his home professional title by virtue of the European regulations.

(2) The authority conferred on a registered European lawyer by virtue of this paragraph is exercisable in accordance with, and subject to, the regulatory arrangements of the General Council of the Bar (as they apply to the registered European lawyer by virtue of the European regulations).

(3) In this paragraph—

"European regulations" means the European Communities (Lawyer's Practice) Regulations 2000 (SI 2000/1119);

"home professional title" and "registered European lawyer" have the same meaning as in the European regulations.

6 During the transitional period members of the Bar not in actual practice are to continue to have the rights conferred by section 102A(2) of the Patents Act 1977 (c 37) (right of audience, etc in proceedings on appeal from the comptroller).

Solicitors etc

7 (1) During the transitional period—

(a) every qualified solicitor,
(b) every legal partnership, and
(c) every body recognised under section 9 of the Administration of Justice Act 1985 (c 61) (incorporated practices) ("a recognised body"),

is deemed to be authorised by the Law Society to carry on the activities in sub-paragraph (2).

(2) Those activities are—

(a) the exercise of a right of audience before every court in relation to all proceedings;
(b) the conduct of litigation in relation to every court and all proceedings;
(c) reserved instrument activities;
(d) probate activities;
(e) the administration of oaths.

(3) The authority conferred on a qualified solicitor, legal partnership or recognised body by this paragraph is exercisable in accordance with, and subject to, the regulatory arrangements of the Law Society.

(4) In this paragraph—

"legal partnership" means a partnership in which a qualified solicitor, a registered European Lawyer or a body recognised under section 9 of the Administration of Justice Act 1985 (c 61) is permitted to practise by virtue of rules made under that section or section 31 of the Solicitors Act 1974 (c 47);

"qualified solicitor" means a person who is qualified under section 1 of the Solicitors Act 1974 to act as a solicitor;

"registered European lawyer" means a registered European lawyer within the meaning of the European Communities (Lawyer's Practice) Regulations 2000 (SI 2000/1119) who is registered with the Law Society.

8 (1) During the transitional period, every registered European lawyer registered with the Law Society is deemed to be authorised by the Law Society to carry on activities which—

(a) are within paragraph 7(2), and
(b) the registered European lawyer is entitled to carry on under his home professional title by virtue of the European regulations.

(2) The authority conferred on a registered European lawyer by virtue of this paragraph is exercisable in accordance with, and subject to, the regulatory arrangements of the Law Society (as they apply to the registered European lawyer by virtue of the European regulations).

(3) In this paragraph—

"European regulations" means the European Communities (Lawyer's Practice) Regulations 2000 (SI 2000/1119);

"home professional title" and "registered European lawyer" have the same meaning as in the European regulations.

9 (1) During the transitional period, solicitors are to continue to have the rights conferred on them by subsection (1) of section 102A of the Patents Act 1977 (c 37) (rights of audience, etc in proceedings on appeal from the comptroller).

(2) During that period, registered European lawyers are to continue to have the rights conferred on them by that subsection by virtue of the European regulations.

(3) In this paragraph "European regulations" and "registered European lawyer" have the same meaning as in paragraph 8.

Legal Executives

10 (1) During the transitional period, a person authorised by the Institute of Legal Executives to practise as a member of the profession of legal executives is deemed to be authorised by that Institute to administer oaths.

(2) The authority conferred by sub-paragraph (1) is exercisable in accordance with and subject to the regulatory arrangements of the Institute of Legal Executives.

(3) A person is not authorised under sub-paragraph (1) unless the person has in force a certificate issued by the Institute of Legal Executives authorising the person to practise as a legal executive.

Licensed conveyancers

11 (1) During the transitional period every individual who holds a conveyancing licence is deemed to be authorised by the Council for Licensed Conveyancers to administer oaths.

(2) The authority conferred by sub-paragraph (1) is exercisable in accordance with and subject to the regulatory arrangements of the Council.

(3) During that period, every conveyancing partnership and every body recognised under section 32 of the Administration of Justice Act 1985 (c 61) (bodies corporate entitled to provide conveyancing services) is deemed to be authorised by the Council—

(a) to carry on conveyancing services, and
(b) to administer oaths.

(4) The authority conferred by sub-paragraph (3) is exercisable in accordance with and subject to—

(a) in the case of a body recognised under section 32 of the Administration of Justice Act 1985, any condition subject to which its recognition has effect, and
(b) the regulatory arrangements of the Council.

(5) In this section "conveyancing partnership" means a partnership at least some of the members of which are licensed conveyancers.

(6) For the purposes of this paragraph a conveyancing licence is to be treated as not in force during any period when it is suspended.

Notaries public

12 (1) During the transitional period, every duly certificated notary is deemed to be authorised by the Master of the Faculties to carry on the activities in sub-paragraph (2).

(2) Those activities are—

(a) reserved instrument activities;
(b) probate activities;
(c) notarial activities;
(d) the administration of oaths.

(3) The authority conferred by sub-paragraph (1) is exercisable in accordance with and subject to the regulatory arrangements of the Master of the Faculties.

(4) In this paragraph "duly certificated notary" means a notary who either—

(a) has in force a practising certificate as a solicitor issued under the Solicitors Act 1974 (c 47), and is duly entered in the Court of Faculties of the Archbishop of Canterbury in accordance with rules made by the Master of the Faculties, or
(b) has in force a practising certificate as a public notary issued by the said Court of Faculties in accordance with rules so made.

13 (1) During the transitional period, a person ("P") is an exempt person in relation to the carrying on of an activity ("the relevant activity") which is a notarial activity if—

(a) P carries on the relevant activity by virtue of an employee of P ("E") carrying it on in E's capacity as such an employee, and
(b) E is an authorised person in relation to the relevant activity.

(2) If P is a body, in this paragraph references to an employee of P include references to a manager of P.

Patent attorneys

14 (1) During the transitional period, every registered patent attorney is deemed to be authorised by the Chartered Institute of Patent Attorneys to carry on reserved instrument activities.

(2) During that period, every authorised patent attorney is deemed to be authorised by the Chartered Institute of Patent Attorneys to administer oaths.

(3) During that period, every patent attorney body is deemed to be authorised by the Chartered Institute of Patent Attorneys to carry on the activities in sub-paragraph (4).

(4) Those activities are any activities which are reserved legal activities within sub-paragraph (5) and which—

(a) if the body is a partnership, any partner who is a registered patent attorney is authorised to carry on;
(b) if the body is a body corporate, any director who is a registered patent attorney is authorised to carry on.

(5) Those activities are—

(a) the exercise of a right of audience;
(b) the conduct of litigation;
(c) reserved instrument activities;
(d) the administration of oaths.

(6) The authority conferred by any of sub-paragraphs (1) to (3) is exercisable in accordance with and subject to the regulatory arrangements of the Chartered Institute of Patent Attorneys.

(7) In this paragraph—

"authorised patent attorney" means a registered patent attorney who is authorised by the Chartered Institute of Patent Attorneys to carry on one or both of the following activities—
(a) the exercise of a right of audience;
(b) the conduct of litigation;

"patent attorney body" means—
(a) a partnership all the partners of which are registered patent attorneys,
(b) a body corporate all the directors of which are registered patent attorneys,
(c) a partnership or body corporate which satisfies the conditions prescribed under section 279 of the Copyright, Designs and Patents Act 1988 (c 48), or
(d) a body corporate to which section 276(4) of that Act applies;

"registered patent attorney" has the meaning given by section 275(2) of that Act;

and, in the case of a patent attorney body to which section 276(4) of that Act applies, the reference in sub-paragraph (4)(b) to a director includes a reference to the manager (within the meaning of section 276(4) of that Act) of the company.

15 (1) During the transitional period registered patent attorneys are to continue to have the rights conferred by section 102A(2) of the Patents Act 1977 (c 37) and section 292 of the Copyright, Designs and Patents Act 1988 (c 48).

(2) In this paragraph "registered patent attorney" has the same meaning as in paragraph 14.

Trade mark attorneys

16 (1) During the transitional period, every registered trade mark attorney is deemed to be authorised by the Institute of Trade Mark Attorneys to carry on reserved instrument activities.

(2) During that period, every authorised trade mark attorney is deemed to be authorised by the Institute of Trade Mark Attorneys to administer oaths.

(3) During that period, every trade mark attorney body is deemed to be authorised by the Institute of Trade Mark Attorneys to carry on the activities in sub-paragraph (4).

(4) Those activities are any activities which are reserved legal activities within sub-paragraph (5) and which—

- (a) if the body is a partnership, any partner who is a registered trade mark attorney is authorised to carry on, or
- (b) if the body is a body corporate, any director who is a registered trade mark attorney is authorised to carry on.

(5) Those activities are—

- (a) the exercise of a right of audience;
- (b) the conduct of litigation;
- (c) reserved instrument activities;
- (d) the administration of oaths.

(6) The authority conferred by any of sub-paragraphs (1) to (3) is exercisable in accordance with and subject to the regulatory arrangements of the Institute of Trade Mark Attorneys.

(7) In this paragraph—

"authorised trade mark attorney" means a registered trade mark attorney who is authorised by the Institute of Trade Mark Attorneys to carry on one or both of the following activities—
- (a) the exercise of a right of audience;
- (b) the conduct of litigation;

"trade mark attorney body" means—
- (a) a partnership all the partners of which are registered trade mark attorneys,
- (b) a body corporate all the directors of which are registered trade mark attorneys, or
- (c) a partnership or body corporate which satisfies the conditions prescribed under section 85 of the Trade Marks Act 1994 (c 26);

"registered trade mark attorney" has the same meaning as in the Trade Marks Act 1994.

Law costs draftsmen

17 (1) During the transitional period, every authorised member of the Association of Law Costs Draftsmen is deemed to be authorised by that Association to administer oaths.

(2) In this paragraph, "authorised member of the Association of Law Costs Draftsmen" means a member of that Association who has been authorised by that Association to carry on one or both of the following activities—

- (a) the exercise of a right of audience;
- (b) the conduct of litigation.

(3) The authority conferred by sub-paragraph (1) is exercisable in accordance with and subject to the regulatory arrangements of the Association of Law Costs Draftsmen.

18 (1) During the transitional period, a person ("P") is an exempt person in relation to the carrying on of an activity ("the relevant activity") which is a reserved legal activity within sub-paragraph (2), if—

- (a) P carries on the relevant activity by virtue of an employee of P ("E") carrying it on in E's capacity as such an employee, and
- (b) E is an authorised member of the Association of Law Costs Draftsmen (within the meaning of paragraph 17(2) of this Schedule).

(2) The reserved legal activities mentioned in sub-paragraph (1) are—

(a) the exercise of a right of audience;
(b) the conduct of litigation;
(c) the administration of oaths.

(3) If P is a body, in this paragraph references to an employee of P include references to a manager of P.

Initial Commencement
To be appointed: see s 211(2).
Extent
This part of this Schedule does not extend to Scotland: see s 212(1).

PART 3
INTERPRETATION

19 In this Schedule—

"the appointed day" means the day appointed for the coming into force of section 13 (entitlement to carry on a reserved legal activity);
"conveyancing licence" has the meaning given by paragraph 2.

Initial Commencement
To be appointed: see s 211(2).
Extent
This part of this Schedule does not extend to Scotland: see s 212(1).

SCHEDULE 6
ALTERATION OF RESERVED LEGAL ACTIVITIES

Sections 24 and 26

Introductory

1 In this Schedule, in relation to an activity—

"section 24 investigation" means an investigation held with a view to determining whether or not the Board should make a recommendation in respect of the activity for the purposes of section 24 (recommendations and orders to extend the reserved legal activities);
"section 26 investigation" means an investigation held with a view to determining whether or not the Board should make a recommendation in respect of the activity for the purposes of section 26 (recommendations that an activity should cease to be a reserved legal activity).

Requests for Board to hold a full investigation

2 (1) A person may—

(a) request the Board to hold a section 24 investigation in respect of an activity, or
(b) request the Board to hold a section 26 investigation in respect of an activity.

(2) A request under sub-paragraph (1) must be in writing and specify the activity to which it relates.

(3) In the case of a request for a section 24 investigation, the activity in respect of which the request is made must be a legal activity.

Board's duty to hold preliminary inquiries in certain cases

3 (1) This paragraph applies where the Board receives a request under paragraph 2, in respect of an activity, from—

(a) the Lord Chancellor,
(b) the OFT,
(c) the Consumer Panel, or

(d) the Lord Chief Justice.

(2) The Board must—

(a) carry out such inquiries as it considers appropriate to enable it to determine whether it is appropriate to hold a section 24 investigation or, as the case may be, a section 26 investigation in respect of the activity, and
(b) make that determination within the preliminary inquiry period.

(3) "The preliminary inquiry period" means the period of 3 months beginning with the day on which the request under paragraph 2 was received by the Board.

(4) The Board may, before the end of the preliminary inquiry period in relation to a request, issue a notice extending that period by a period specified in the notice.

(5) More than one notice may be issued under sub-paragraph (4), but the total preliminary inquiry period must not exceed 4 months.

(6) A notice under sub-paragraph (4) must state the Board's reasons for extending the preliminary inquiry period.

(7) The Board must publish a notice issued under sub-paragraph (4).

Board's power to hold preliminary inquiries in other cases

4 (1) The Board may—

(a) where it receives a request under paragraph 2 to which paragraph 3 does not apply, or
(b) in any other case where it considers it appropriate to do so,

carry out such inquiries as it considers appropriate to enable it to determine whether it is appropriate to hold a section 24 investigation or a section 26 investigation in respect of an activity.

(2) In the case of a section 24 investigation, that activity must be a legal activity.

Advice

5 (1) Before determining whether it is appropriate to hold a section 24 investigation or a section 26 investigation in respect of an activity, the Board may seek the advice of one or both of the following bodies—

(a) the OFT;
(b) the Consumer Panel.

(2) The OFT or the Consumer Panel must, if its advice is sought, give the Board such advice as it thinks fit, within such reasonable period as the Board may specify.

(3) In deciding what advice to give—

(a) the OFT must, in particular, consider whether making an order under section 24 or (as the case may be) provision in accordance with a recommendation under section 26, in respect of the activity would (or would be likely to) prevent, restrict or distort competition within the market for reserved legal services to any significant extent, and
(b) the Consumer Panel must have regard to the likely impact which making that order or (as the case may be) provision would have on consumers.

(4) The OFT or the Consumer Panel may, for the purposes of giving advice under this paragraph, request any person to provide it with such information as may be specified by it.

6 (1) Before determining whether it is appropriate to hold a section 24 investigation or a section 26 investigation in respect of an activity the Board may also seek the advice of the Lord Chief Justice.

(2) If the Board has sought advice under paragraph 5, the Board may not seek advice from the Lord Chief Justice until—

(a) the period for giving advice under paragraph 5 has ended, and
(b) it has given the Lord Chief Justice a copy of any advice duly given under that paragraph.

(3) If advice is sought under sub-paragraph (1), the Lord Chief Justice—

(a) must give the Board such advice as the Lord Chief Justice thinks fit, within such reasonable period as may be specified by the Board, and
(b) may, for the purposes of giving that advice, request any person to provide the Lord Chief Justice with such information as may be specified by the Lord Chief Justice.

(4) In deciding what advice to give, the Lord Chief Justice must, in particular, have regard to the likely impact on the courts in England and Wales of the making of an order under section 24 or (as the case may be) provision in accordance with a recommendation under section 26, in respect of the activity in question.

7 (1) The Board must consider, and publish, any advice given under paragraph 5 or 6.

(2) Nothing in this paragraph operates to prevent a person who gives such advice from publishing it.

Restrictions on refusing a paragraph 2 request

8 (1) This paragraph applies where—

(a) a request has been made under paragraph 2, and
(b) paragraph 3 applies to that request.

(2) The Board may refuse the request only if—

(a) the consultation requirements are satisfied, and
(b) either the consent requirement is satisfied or the request was made by the Lord Chancellor.

(3) The consultation requirements are—

(a) that the Board has consulted the OFT, the Consumer Panel and the Lord Chief Justice under paragraphs 5 and 6, and
(b) that—
(i) the Board has obtained advice from the OFT and the Consumer Panel or the period within which that advice is required to be given has expired, and
(ii) the Board has obtained advice from the Lord Chief Justice or the period within which that advice is required to be given has expired.

(4) The consent requirement is that—

(a) the Board has given the Lord Chancellor a copy of any advice given under paragraph 5 or 6, and
(b) the Lord Chancellor has consented to the Board's refusal of the request.

Decision to hold investigation

9 (1) This paragraph applies where the Board has decided, following inquiries under paragraph 3 or 4, to hold a section 24 investigation or a section 26 investigation in respect of an activity.

(2) The Board must, as soon as reasonably practicable, give notice of its decision to—

(a) the Lord Chancellor,
(b) the OFT,
(c) the Consumer Panel, and
(d) the Lord Chief Justice,

and publish the notice.

(3) The notice must—

(a) state the Board's reasons for its decision to hold the investigation, and
(b) contain a description (in general terms) of the procedure set out in paragraphs 10 to 17 and in rules under this Schedule, including any relevant time limits.

Duty to investigate and produce a provisional report within the investigation period

10 (1) This paragraph applies where the Board has given notice under paragraph 9(2) of—

(a) a decision to hold a section 24 investigation, or

(b) a decision to hold a section 26 investigation,

in respect of an activity.

(2) The Board must within the investigation period—

(a) carry out such investigations as it considers appropriate for the purposes of enabling it to produce a provisional report in respect of the activity, and
(b) produce and publish such a report.

(3) A provisional report is a report stating—

(a) in a case within sub-paragraph (1)(a), whether or not the Board is minded to make a recommendation for the purposes of section 24 (recommendation that activity should become a reserved legal activity);
(b) in a case within sub-paragraph (1)(b), whether or not the Board is minded to make a recommendation for the purposes of section 26 (recommendation that activity should cease to be a reserved legal activity).

(4) A provisional report must also state the Board's reasons for it being, or not being, minded to make the recommendation in question.

"The investigation period"

11 (1) "The investigation period" means the period of 12 months beginning with the day on which the notice was given under paragraph 9(2).

(2) The Board may, before the end of the investigation period, issue a notice extending that period by a period specified in the notice.

(3) More than one notice may be issued under sub-paragraph (2) but the total investigation period must not exceed 16 months.

(4) The Board may issue a notice under sub-paragraph (2) only after it has consulted—

(a) the OFT,
(b) the Consumer Panel, and
(c) the Lord Chief Justice.

(5) A notice under sub-paragraph (2) must state the Board's reasons for extending the investigation period.

(6) The Board must publish any notice issued under sub-paragraph (2).

Supplementary provisions about the investigation

12 (1) This paragraph applies for the purposes of investigations under paragraph 10(2)(a).

(2) The Board may make rules governing the making of oral and written representations, and the giving of oral and written evidence, to the Board.

(3) Rules under sub-paragraph (2) may (among other things) include—

(a) provision about the time and place at which any oral evidence is to be given or oral representations are to be heard;
(b) provision about the period within which any written evidence is to be given or written representations are to be made.

(4) In relation to each investigation, the Board must determine if, and to what extent—

(a) oral evidence or representations should be heard, and
(b) written evidence or representations should be received.

(5) The Board must, so far as is reasonably practicable, consider any written or oral representations duly made under this paragraph.

Consideration of the provisional report

13 (1) The Board may make rules governing the making to the Board of oral and written representations in respect of provisional reports.

(2) Rules under sub-paragraph (1) may (among other things) include—

(a) provision about the time and place at which any oral representations are to be heard;
(b) provision about the period within which any written representations are to be made.

(3) The Board must exercise the power conferred by sub-paragraph (1) to make provision—

(a) enabling written representations and, so far as is reasonably practicable, oral representations to be made by affected practitioners, and
(b) enabling written or oral representations to be made by bodies which represent affected practitioners.

(4) An "affected practitioner" is a person carrying on the activity in respect of which the investigation is being held.

14 (1) For the purpose of making a decision under paragraph 16(1)(a) or (b), the Board must, after publication of a provisional report, determine if and to what extent further evidence should be heard or received.

(2) The Board may make rules governing the giving of such evidence.

(3) Rules under sub-paragraph (2) may (among other things) include—

(a) provision about the time and place at which any oral evidence is to be given;
(b) provision about the period within which any written evidence is to be given.

15 The Board must, so far as is reasonably practicable, consider—

(a) any written or oral representations made in accordance with rules to which paragraph 13(3) applies, and
(b) any other representations made in accordance with rules under paragraph 13(1), and any written or oral evidence given in accordance with rules under paragraph 14(2), which the Board considers relevant.

Duty to prepare final report within the final reporting period

16 (1) After complying with paragraph 15, the Board must decide—

(a) in the case of a section 24 investigation, whether or not to make a recommendation for the purposes of that section, and
(b) in the case of a section 26 investigation, whether or not to make a recommendation for the purposes of that section.

(2) The Board must prepare a report ("the final report") which sets out—

(a) its decision and the reasons for it,
(b) where it decides to make a recommendation for the purposes of section 24 or 26, that recommendation, and
(c) where it decides to make a recommendation for the purposes of section 24, a statement of the provision which, in the Board's opinion, will need to be made by virtue of section 204(3) or in an order under section 208 (power to make consequential provision, transitional provision etc) if an order is made under section 24 in accordance with that recommendation.

(3) The Board must—

(a) give a copy of the final report to the Lord Chancellor, and
(b) publish that report.

(4) The Board must comply with the obligations imposed by this paragraph within the final reporting period.

"The final reporting period"

17 (1) "The final reporting period" means the period of 3 months beginning with the date on which the provisional report was published under paragraph 10(2).

(2) The Board may, before the end of the final reporting period, issue a notice extending that period by a period specified in the notice.

(3) More than one notice may be issued under sub-paragraph (2), but the total final reporting period must not exceed 5 months.

(4) The Board may issue a notice under sub-paragraph (2) only after it has consulted—

(a) the OFT,
(b) the Consumer Panel, and
(c) the Lord Chief Justice.

(5) A notice under sub-paragraph (2) must state the Board's reasons for extending the final reporting period.

(6) The Board must publish a notice issued under sub-paragraph (2).

Costs

18 The Board may pay such costs of a person as the Board considers reasonable for the purpose of facilitating the giving of oral evidence or the making of oral representations, by or on behalf of that person, in accordance with rules made under this Schedule.

Initial Commencement
To be appointed: see s 211(2).
Appointment
Paras 12(1)–(3), 13, 14: Appointment: 1 January 2009: see SI 2008/3149, art 2(b)(iii).
Extent
This Schedule does not extend to Scotland: see s 212(1).

SCHEDULE 7
DIRECTIONS: PROCEDURE

Section 33

Introductory

1 This Schedule applies where the Board proposes giving a direction to an approved regulator under section 32.

Notification of the approved regulator

2 (1) The Board must give the approved regulator a notice ("a warning notice") accompanied by a copy of the proposed direction.

(2) The warning notice must—

(a) state that the Board proposes to give the approved regulator a direction in the form of the accompanying draft,
(b) specify why the Board is satisfied as mentioned in section 32(1) and (2), and
(c) specify a period within which the approved regulator may make representations with respect to the proposal.

(3) The period specified under sub-paragraph (2)(c)—

(a) must begin with the date on which the warning notice is given to the approved regulator, and
(b) must not be less than 14 days.

(4) The approved regulator may make to the Board—

(a) written representations, and
(b) if the Board authorises it to do so, oral representations,

about the proposed direction.

(5) The Board must make rules governing the making of oral and written representations.

(6) The Board must consider any representations duly made by the approved regulator.

(7) Where oral representations are duly made, the Board must prepare a report of those representations.

(8) Before preparing that report, the Board must—

(a) give the approved regulator a reasonable opportunity to comment on a draft of the report, and
(b) have regard to any comments duly made.

Board's duty to seek advice

3 (1) After complying with paragraph 2, the Board must give each of the persons listed in sub-paragraph (2)—

(a) a copy of the warning notice and the accompanying draft direction,
(b) a copy of any written representations duly made under paragraph 2 and a copy of the report (if any) prepared under that paragraph, and
(c) a notice specifying a period within which any advice under paragraphs 4 to 7 must be given.

(2) Those persons are—

(a) the Lord Chancellor,
(b) the OFT,
(c) the Consumer Panel,
(d) the Lord Chief Justice, and
(e) such other persons as the Board considers it reasonable to consult in respect of the proposed direction.

(3) In this Schedule, in relation to a proposed direction, "selected consultee" means a person within sub-paragraph (2)(e).

Advice of the Lord Chancellor

4 The Lord Chancellor must give the Board such advice as the Lord Chancellor thinks fit in respect of the proposed direction.

Advice of Office of Fair Trading

5 (1) The OFT must give the Board such advice as it thinks fit regarding whether the proposed direction should be given.

(2) In deciding what advice to give, the OFT must, in particular, have regard to whether giving the proposed direction would (or would be likely to) prevent, restrict or distort competition within the market for reserved legal services to any significant extent.

Advice of the Consumer Panel

6 (1) The Consumer Panel must give the Board such advice as it thinks fit regarding whether the proposed direction should be given.

(2) In deciding what advice to give, the Consumer Panel must, in particular, have regard to the likely impact of the proposed direction on consumers.

Advice of selected consultees

7 A selected consultee may give the Board such advice as the selected consultee thinks fit in respect of the proposed direction.

Advice of the Lord Chief Justice

8 (1) The Board must give the Lord Chief Justice—

(a) a copy of any advice duly given under paragraphs 4 to 7, and
(b) a notice specifying a period within which any advice under this paragraph must be given.

(2) The Lord Chief Justice must then give such advice as the Lord Chief Justice thinks fit regarding whether the proposed direction should be given.

(3) In deciding what advice to give, the Lord Chief Justice must, in particular, have regard to the likely impact of the proposed direction on the courts in England and Wales.

Consultees' powers to request information

9 A person ("the consultee") to whom a copy of the warning notice is given under paragraph 3(1) may, for the purposes of giving advice under paragraphs 4 to 8, request the approved regulator or any other person to provide the consultee with such additional information as may be specified by the consultee.

Representations by approved regulator

10 (1) The Board must give the approved regulator a copy of any advice duly given under paragraphs 4 to 8.

(2) The approved regulator may make to the Board—

(a) written representations, and
(b) if the Board authorises it to do so, oral representations,

about the advice.

(3) The Board must make rules governing the making of oral and written representations.

(4) Representations under this paragraph must be made within—

(a) the period of 28 days beginning with the day on which the copy of the advice is given to the approved regulator, or
(b) such longer period as the Board may specify in a particular case.

(5) Where oral representations are made, the Board must prepare a report of those representations.

(6) Before preparing that report, the Board must—

(a) give the approved regulator a reasonable opportunity to comment on a draft of the report, and
(b) have regard to any comments duly made.

Publication of advice etc

11 (1) The Board must, as soon as practicable after the end of the period within which representations under paragraph 10 may be made, publish—

(a) any advice duly given under paragraphs 4 to 8, and
(b) any written representations duly made under paragraph 10 and the report (if any) prepared under that paragraph.

(2) Nothing in sub-paragraph (1) operates—

(a) to prevent a person who gives advice under paragraphs 4 to 8 from publishing that advice, or
(b) to prevent a person who makes representations under paragraph 10 from publishing those representations.

(3) A person ("the publisher") publishing any such material (whether under sub-paragraph (1) or otherwise) must, so far as practicable, exclude any matter which relates to the private affairs of a particular individual the publication of which, in the opinion of the publisher, would or might seriously and prejudicially affect the interests of that individual.

Decision by the Board

12 (1) After considering—

(a) any advice duly given under paragraphs 4 to 8,
(b) any representations duly made under paragraph 10, and
(c) any other information which the Board considers relevant,

the Board must decide whether to give the approved regulator the proposed direction.

(2) The Board must give notice of its decision ("the decision notice") to the approved regulator.

(3) Where the Board decides to give the proposed direction, the decision notice must—

(a) contain the direction,

(b) state the time at which the direction is to take effect, and
(c) specify the Board's reasons for the decision to give the direction.

(4) The Board must publish the decision notice.

Initial Commencement
To be appointed: see s 211(2).
Appointment
Paras 1, 2(5), 10(3): Appointment: 1 January 2009: see SI 2008/3149, art 2(c)(ii).
Extent
This Schedule does not extend to Scotland: see s 212(1).

SCHEDULE 8
INTERVENTION DIRECTIONS: PROCEDURE

Sections 41 and 44

PART 1
GIVING INTERVENTION DIRECTIONS

Introductory

1 (1) This Part of this Schedule applies where the Board proposes giving an intervention direction to an approved regulator in respect of a regulatory function.

(2) In this Schedule "intervention direction" has the same meaning as in section 41.

Notification of the approved regulator

2 (1) The Board must give the approved regulator a notice ("a warning notice") accompanied by a draft of the proposed intervention direction.

(2) The warning notice must—

(a) state that the Board proposes to give the approved regulator an intervention direction in the form of the accompanying draft and the time when it is proposed that direction should take effect, and
(b) state the reasons why the Board is satisfied of the matters mentioned in section 41(1)(a) and (b).

(3) The Board must publish a copy of the warning notice.

(4) The approved regulator may make to the Board—

(a) written representations, and
(b) if the Board authorises it to do so, oral representations,

about the proposed intervention direction.

(5) The Board must make rules governing the making of written and oral representations.

(6) Any representations under sub-paragraph (4) must be made before the end of—

(a) the period of 28 days beginning with the day on which the warning notice is given to the approved regulator, or
(b) such longer period as the Board may specify in a particular case.

(7) Where oral representations are duly made under this paragraph, the Board must prepare a report of those representations.

(8) Before preparing that report, the Board must—

(a) give the approved regulator a reasonable opportunity to comment on a draft of the report, and
(b) have regard to any comments duly made.

Board's duty to seek advice

3 (1) After complying with paragraph 2, the Board must give each of the persons listed in sub-paragraph (2)—

(a) a copy of the warning notice and the accompanying draft,
(b) a copy of any written representations duly made under paragraph 2 and a copy of the report (if any) prepared under that paragraph, and
(c) a notice specifying a period within which any advice under paragraphs 4 to 7 must be given.

(2) Those persons are—

(a) the Lord Chancellor,
(b) the OFT,
(c) the Consumer Panel,
(d) the Lord Chief Justice, and
(e) such other persons as the Board considers it reasonable to consult in respect of the proposed intervention direction.

(3) In this Part of this Schedule, in relation to a proposed intervention direction, "selected consultee" means a person within sub-paragraph (2)(e).

Advice of the Lord Chancellor

4 The Lord Chancellor must give the Board such advice as the Lord Chancellor thinks fit in respect of the proposed intervention direction.

Advice of Office of Fair Trading

5 (1) The OFT must give the Board such advice as it thinks fit regarding whether the proposed intervention direction should be given.

(2) In deciding what advice to give, the OFT must, in particular, have regard to whether giving the proposed intervention direction would (or would be likely to) prevent, restrict or distort competition within the market for reserved legal services to any significant extent.

Advice of the Consumer Panel

6 (1) The Consumer Panel must give the Board such advice as it thinks fit regarding whether the proposed intervention direction should be given.

(2) In deciding what advice to give, the Consumer Panel must, in particular, have regard to the likely impact of the proposed direction on consumers.

Advice of selected consultees

7 A selected consultee may give the Board such advice as the selected consultee thinks fit in respect of the proposed intervention direction.

Advice of the Lord Chief Justice

8 (1) The Board must give the Lord Chief Justice—

(a) a copy of any advice duly given under paragraphs 4 to 7, and
(b) a notice specifying a period within which any advice under this paragraph must be given.

(2) The Lord Chief Justice must then give such advice as the Lord Chief Justice thinks fit regarding whether the proposed intervention direction should be given.

(3) In deciding what advice to give, the Lord Chief Justice must, in particular, have regard to the likely impact of the proposed intervention direction on the courts in England and Wales.

Consultees' powers to request information

9 A person ("the consultee") to whom a copy of the warning notice is given under paragraph 3(1) may, for the purposes of giving advice under paragraphs 4 to 8, request the approved regulator or any other person to provide the consultee with such additional information as may be specified by the consultee.

Representations by the approved regulator etc

10 (1) The Board must—

(a) give the approved regulator a copy of any advice duly given under paragraphs 4 to 8, and
(b) publish that advice together with any written representations duly made by the approved regulator under paragraph 2 and the report (if any) prepared under that paragraph.

(2) The approved regulator and any body within sub-paragraph (3) may make to the Board—

(a) written representations, and
(b) if the Board authorises it to do so, oral representations,

about the advice.

(3) A body is within this sub-paragraph if it represents persons authorised by the approved regulator to carry on activities which are reserved legal activities.

(4) The Board may allow any other person to make written or oral representations about the advice.

(5) The Board must make rules governing the making of oral and written representations.

(6) Representations under this paragraph must be made within—

(a) the period of 28 days beginning with the day on which the representations and advice are published under sub-paragraph (1)(b), or
(b) such longer period as the Board may specify in a particular case.

(7) Where oral representations are made, the Board must prepare a report of those representations.

(8) Before preparing that report, the Board must—

(a) give each person who made oral representations a reasonable opportunity to comment on a draft of the report of those representations, and
(b) have regard to any comments duly made.

(9) The Board must, as soon as reasonably practicable after the end of the period within which representations may be made under this paragraph, publish any written representations duly made and the report (if any) prepared under sub-paragraph (7).

Further provision about publishing of advice and representations

11 (1) Nothing in paragraph 10 operates—

(a) to prevent a person who gives advice under paragraphs 4 to 8 from publishing that advice, or
(b) to prevent a person who makes representations under paragraph 2 or 10 from publishing those representations.

(2) A person ("the publisher") publishing any such material (whether under paragraph 10 or otherwise) must, so far as practicable, exclude any matter which relates to the private affairs of a particular individual the publication of which, in the opinion of the publisher, would or might seriously and prejudicially affect the interests of that individual.

Decision by the Board

12 (1) After considering—

(a) any advice duly given under paragraphs 4 to 8,
(b) any representations duly made under paragraph 2 or 10, and

(c) any other information which the Board considers relevant,

the Board must decide whether to give an intervention direction.

(2) Where it decides to give an intervention direction, it may decide—

(a) to give an intervention direction in the form of the proposed intervention direction, or
(b) to amend the form of the proposed intervention direction and give an intervention direction in that amended form.

(3) The Board must give notice of its decision ("the decision notice") to the approved regulator.

(4) Where the Board decides to give an intervention direction, the decision notice must—

(a) contain the intervention direction,
(b) state the time at which the intervention direction is to take effect,
(c) specify the reasons why the Board is satisfied of the matters mentioned in section 41(1)(a) and (b), and
(d) if the decision is under sub-paragraph (2)(b), set out the nature of any amendments made and the reasons for them.

(5) The time specified under sub-paragraph (4)(b) must not be before—

(a) the time specified in the warning notice in accordance with paragraph 2(2)(a), or
(b) the time the decision notice is given to the approved regulator.

(6) The Board must publish the decision notice.

Initial Commencement
To be appointed: see s 211(2).
Appointment
Paras 1, 2(5), 10(5): Appointment: 1 January 2009: see SI 2008/3149, art 2(c)(iii).
Extent
This part of this Schedule does not extend to Scotland: see s 212(1).

PART 2
REVOKING INTERVENTION DIRECTIONS

Introductory

13 (1) Where an intervention direction has effect in respect of a regulatory function of an approved regulator—

(a) the approved regulator may apply to the Board for the Board to revoke the direction, or
(b) the Board may give the approved regulator a notice stating the Board's intention to revoke the direction.

(2) An application under sub-paragraph (1)(a) must—

(a) be made in the form and manner specified by the Board, and
(b) be accompanied by such material as the applicant considers is likely to be needed for the purposes of this Part of this Schedule.

Board's duty to seek advice

14 (1) Where the Board has received an application under paragraph 13(1)(a), it must give each of the persons listed in sub-paragraph (3)—

(a) a copy of the application,
(b) a copy of any material which accompanied it, and
(c) a notice specifying a period within which any advice under paragraphs 15 to 18 must be given.

(2) Where the Board has given a notice under paragraph 13(1)(b), it must give each of the persons listed in sub-paragraph (3)—

(a) a copy of the notice, and

(b) a notice specifying a period within which any advice under paragraphs 15 to 18 must be given.

(3) The persons are—

(a) the Lord Chancellor,
(b) the OFT,
(c) the Consumer Panel,
(d) the Lord Chief Justice, and
(e) such other persons as the Board considers it reasonable to consult in respect of the proposed revocation.

(4) In this Part of this Schedule, in relation to an application or notice, "selected consultee" means a person within sub-paragraph (3)(e).

Advice of the Lord Chancellor

15 The Lord Chancellor must give the Board such advice as the Lord Chancellor thinks fit in respect of the proposed revocation.

Advice of Office of Fair Trading

16 (1) The OFT must give the Board such advice as it thinks fit regarding the proposed revocation.

(2) In deciding what advice to give, the OFT must, in particular, have regard to whether revoking the intervention direction would (or would be likely to) prevent, restrict or distort competition within the market for reserved legal services to any significant extent.

Advice of the Consumer Panel

17 (1) The Consumer Panel must give the Board such advice as it thinks fit regarding the proposed revocation.

(2) In deciding what advice to give, the Consumer Panel must, in particular, have regard to the likely impact which revoking the intervention direction would have on consumers.

Advice of the selected consultees

18 A selected consultee may give the Board such advice as the selected consultee thinks fit in respect of the proposed revocation.

Advice of the Lord Chief Justice

19 (1) The Board must give the Lord Chief Justice—

(a) a copy of any advice duly given under paragraphs 15 to 18, and
(b) a notice specifying a period within which any advice under this paragraph must be given.

(2) The Lord Chief Justice must then give the Board such advice as the Lord Chief Justice thinks fit in respect of the proposed revocation.

(3) In deciding what advice to give, the Lord Chief Justice must, in particular, have regard to the likely impact which revoking the intervention direction would have on the courts in England and Wales.

Information obtained by consultees

20 A person to whom a copy of the application or notice is given under paragraph 14(1) or (2) may, for the purposes of giving advice under paragraphs 15 to 19, request the approved regulator or any other person to provide that person with such additional information as may be specified by that person.

Representations by approved regulator etc

21 (1) The Board must—

(a) give the approved regulator a copy of any advice duly given under paragraphs 15 to 19, and
(b) publish that advice.

(2) The approved regulator and any body within sub-paragraph (3) may make to the Board—

(a) written representations, and
(b) if the Board authorises it to do so, oral representations,

about the advice.

(3) A body is within this sub-paragraph if it represents persons authorised by the approved regulator to carry on activities which are reserved legal activities.

(4) The Board may allow any other person to make written or oral representations about the advice.

(5) The Board must make rules governing the making of oral and written representations.

(6) Representations under this paragraph must be made within—

(a) the period of 28 days beginning with the day on which the advice is published under sub-paragraph (1), or
(b) such longer period as the Board may specify in a particular case.

(7) Where oral representations are made, the Board must prepare a report of those representations.

(8) Before preparing that report, the Board must—

(a) give each person who made oral representations a reasonable opportunity to comment on a draft of the report of those representations, and
(b) have regard to any comments duly made.

(9) The Board must, as soon as practicable after the end of the period within which representations may be made under this paragraph, publish any written representations duly made and the report (if any) prepared under sub-paragraph (7).

Further provision about publishing advice and representations

22 (1) Nothing in paragraph 21 operates—

(a) to prevent a person who gives advice under paragraphs 15 to 19 from publishing that advice, or
(b) to prevent a person who makes representations under paragraph 21 from publishing those representations.

(2) A person ("the publisher") publishing any such material (whether under paragraph 21 or otherwise) must, so far as practicable, exclude any matter which relates to the private affairs of a particular individual the publication of which, in the opinion of the publisher, would or might seriously and prejudicially affect the interests of that individual.

Decision by the Board

23 (1) After considering—

(a) in a case within paragraph 13(1)(a), the application and any accompanying material,
(b) any advice duly given under paragraphs 15 to 19,
(c) any representations duly made under paragraph 21, and
(d) any other information which the Board considers relevant to the application or notice,

the Board must decide whether to revoke the intervention direction in accordance with the application or notice.

(2) The Board must give notice of its decision ("the decision notice") to the approved regulator.

(3) Where the Board decides to revoke the intervention direction, the decision notice must state the time the revocation is to take effect.

(4) Where the Board decides not to revoke the intervention direction, the decision notice must specify the reasons for that decision.

(5) The Board must publish the decision notice.

Initial Commencement
To be appointed: see s 211(2).
Appointment
Paras 13(2)(a), 21(5): Appointment: 1 January 2009: see SI 2008/3149, art 2(c)(iii).
Extent
This part of this Schedule does not extend to Scotland: see s 212(1).

SCHEDULE 9
CANCELLATION OF DESIGNATION AS APPROVED REGULATOR

Section 45

Introductory

1 This Schedule applies where the Board considers that it may be appropriate for it to make a recommendation under section 45(5).

Notification of the approved regulator

2 (1) The Board must give the approved regulator a notice ("a warning notice") accompanied by a draft of the proposed recommendation.

(2) The warning notice must—

(a) state that the Board proposes to make a recommendation under subsection (5) of section 45 in the form of the accompanying draft, and
(b) state the reasons why the Board is satisfied of the matters mentioned in paragraphs (a) and (b) of that subsection.

(3) The Board must publish a copy of the warning notice.

(4) The approved regulator may make to the Board—

(a) written representations, and
(b) if the Board authorises it to do so, oral representations,

about the proposed recommendation.

(5) The Board must make rules governing the making of oral and written representations.

(6) Representations under this paragraph must be made within—

(a) the period of 28 days beginning with the day on which the warning notice is given to the approved regulator, or
(b) such longer period as the Board may specify in a particular case.

(7) The Board must consider any representations duly made by the approved regulator.

(8) Where oral representations are duly made, the Board must prepare a report of those representations.

(9) Before preparing that report, the Board must—

(a) give the approved regulator a reasonable opportunity to comment on a draft of the report, and
(b) have regard to any comments duly made.

Board's duty to seek advice

3 (1) After complying with paragraph 2, the Board must give each of the persons listed in sub-paragraph (2)—

(a) a copy of the warning notice and the accompanying draft,
(b) a copy of any written representations duly made by the approved regulator under paragraph 2 and a copy of the report (if any) prepared under that paragraph, and

(c) a notice specifying a period within which any advice under paragraphs 4 to 6 must be given.

(2) Those persons are—

(a) the OFT,
(b) the Consumer Panel,
(c) the Lord Chief Justice, and
(d) such other persons as the Board considers it reasonable to consult in respect of the proposed recommendation.

(3) In this Schedule, in relation to a proposed recommendation, "selected consultee" means a person within sub-paragraph (2)(d).

Advice of Office of Fair Trading

4 (1) The OFT must give the Board such advice as it thinks fit regarding whether the proposed recommendation should be made.

(2) In deciding what advice to give, the OFT must, in particular, have regard to whether making an order under section 45 in accordance with the proposed recommendation would (or would be likely to) prevent, restrict or distort competition within the market for reserved legal services to any significant extent.

Advice of the Consumer Panel

5 (1) The Consumer Panel must give the Board such advice as it thinks fit regarding whether the proposed recommendation should be made.

(2) In deciding what advice to give, the Consumer Panel must, in particular, have regard to the likely impact on consumers of making an order under section 45 in accordance with the proposed recommendation.

Advice of selected consultees

6 A selected consultee may give the Board such advice as the selected consultee thinks fit in respect of the proposed recommendation.

Advice of the Lord Chief Justice

7 (1) The Board must give the Lord Chief Justice—

(a) a copy of any advice duly given under paragraphs 4 to 6, and
(b) a notice specifying a period within which advice under this paragraph must be given.

(2) The Lord Chief Justice must then give such advice as the Lord Chief Justice thinks fit in respect of the proposed recommendation.

(3) In deciding what advice to give, the Lord Chief Justice must, in particular, have regard to the likely impact on the courts in England and Wales of making an order under section 45 in accordance with the proposed recommendation.

Information obtained by consultees

8 A person ("the consultee") to whom a copy of the warning notice is given under paragraph 3(1) may, for the purposes of giving advice under paragraphs 4 to 7, request the approved regulator or any other person to provide the consultee with such additional information as may be specified by the consultee.

Representations by the approved regulator etc

9 (1) The Board must—

(a) give the approved regulator a copy of any advice duly given under paragraphs 4 to 7, and
(b) publish that advice together with any written representations duly made by the approved regulator under paragraph 2 and the report (if any) prepared under that paragraph.

(2) The approved regulator and any body within sub-paragraph (3) may make to the Board—

(a) written representations, and
(b) if authorised to do so by the Board, oral representations,

about the advice.

(3) A body is within this sub-paragraph if it represents persons authorised by the approved regulator to carry on activities which are reserved legal activities.

(4) The Board may allow any other person to make written or oral representations about the advice.

(5) The Board may make rules governing the making to the Board of written or oral representations.

(6) Representations under this paragraph must be made within—

(a) the period of 28 days beginning with the day on which the representations and advice are published under sub-paragraph (1)(b), or
(b) such longer period as the Board may specify in a particular case.

(7) Where oral representations are made, the Board must prepare a report of those representations.

(8) Before preparing that report, the Board must—

(a) give each person who made oral representations a reasonable opportunity to comment on a draft of the report of those representations, and
(b) have regard to any comments duly made.

(9) The Board must, as soon as reasonably practicable after the end of the period within which representations under this paragraph may be made, publish any written representations duly made and the report (if any) prepared under sub-paragraph (7).

Publication of advice etc

10 (1) Nothing in paragraph 9 operates—

(a) to prevent a person who gives advice under paragraphs 4 to 7 from publishing that advice, or
(b) to prevent a person who makes representations under paragraph 2 or 9 from publishing those representations.

(2) A person ("the publisher") publishing any such material (whether under paragraph 9 or otherwise) must, so far as practicable, exclude any matter which relates to the private affairs of a particular individual the publication of which, in the opinion of the publisher, would or might seriously and prejudicially affect the interests of that individual.

Decision by the Board

11 (1) After considering—

(a) any advice duly given under paragraphs 4 to 7,
(b) any representations duly made under paragraph 2 or 9, and
(c) any other information which the Board considers relevant,

the Board must decide whether to make the proposed recommendation.

(2) The Board must give notice of its decision ("the decision notice") to the approved regulator and to the Lord Chancellor.

(3) If the Board decides to make the proposed recommendation, the decision notice must—

(a) contain the recommendation, and
(b) state why the Board is satisfied of the matters mentioned in section 45(5)(a) and (b).

(4) The Board must publish the decision notice.

Initial Commencement
To be appointed: see s 211(2).

Appointment
Paras 1, 2(5), 9(5): Appointment: 1 January 2009: see SI 2008/3149, art 2(c)(iv).
Extent
This Schedule does not extend to Scotland: see s 212(1).

SCHEDULE 10
DESIGNATION OF APPROVED REGULATORS AS LICENSING AUTHORITIES

Sections 74 and 76

PART 1
DESIGNATION OF APPROVED REGULATORS BY ORDER

Application to the Board

1 (1) This paragraph applies where a body wishes to become a licensing authority in relation to one or more activities which constitute one or more reserved legal activities.

(2) The body may apply to the Board for the Board—

(a) to recommend that an order be made by the Lord Chancellor designating the applicant as a licensing authority in relation to the reserved legal activity or activities in question, and
(b) to approve what the applicant proposes as its licensing rules if such an order is made ("the proposed licensing rules").

(3) But the body may make an application under this paragraph in relation to a reserved legal activity only if—

(a) it is a relevant approved regulator in relation to the activity, or
(b) it has made an application under Part 2 of Schedule 4 (designation of approved regulators) for the Board to recommend that an order be made by the Lord Chancellor designating the body as an approved regulator in relation to the activity.

(4) An application under this paragraph must be made in such form and manner as the Board may specify in rules and must be accompanied by—

(a) a statement of the reserved legal activity or activities to which it relates,
(b) details of the applicant's proposed licensing rules,
(c) such explanatory material as the applicant considers is likely to be needed for the purposes of this Part of this Schedule, and
(d) the prescribed fee.

(5) The prescribed fee is the fee specified in, or determined in accordance with, rules made by the Board with the consent of the Lord Chancellor.

(6) An applicant may, at any time, withdraw the application by giving notice to that effect to the Board.

Dismissal of application

2 (1) The Board may refuse to consider, or to continue its consideration of, an application.

(2) The Board must make rules about the procedures and criteria that it will apply when determining whether to refuse to consider, or to continue its consideration of, an application under sub-paragraph (1).

(3) Where the Board decides to refuse to consider, or to continue its consideration of, an application it must give the applicant notice of that decision and of its reasons for it.

(4) The Board must publish a notice given under sub-paragraph (3).

Board's duty to seek advice

3 (1) The Board must give each of the persons listed in sub-paragraph (2)—

(a) a copy of the application and accompanying material, and

(b) a notice specifying a period within which any advice given under paragraphs 4 to 6 must be given.

(2) Those persons are—

(a) the OFT,
(b) the Consumer Panel,
(c) the Lord Chief Justice, and
(d) such other persons as the Board considers it reasonable to consult regarding the application.

(3) In this Part of this Schedule, in relation to an application, "selected consultee" means a person within sub-paragraph (2)(d).

Advice of Office of Fair Trading

4 (1) The OFT must give the Board such advice as the OFT thinks fit regarding whether the application should be granted.

(2) In deciding what advice to give, the OFT must, in particular, have regard to whether making an order under paragraph 15 in accordance with the recommendation applied for would (or would be likely to) prevent, restrict or distort competition within the market for reserved legal services to any significant extent.

Advice of the Consumer Panel

5 (1) The Consumer Panel must give the Board such advice as the Consumer Panel thinks fit regarding whether the application should be granted.

(2) In deciding what advice to give, the Consumer Panel must, in particular, have regard to the likely impact on consumers of the making of an order under paragraph 15 in accordance with the recommendation applied for.

Advice of selected consultees

6

A selected consultee may give the Board such advice as the selected consultee thinks fit in respect of the application.

Advice of the Lord Chief Justice

7 (1) The Board must give the Lord Chief Justice—

(a) a copy of any advice duly given under paragraphs 4 to 6, and
(b) a notice specifying a period within which any advice under this paragraph must be given.

(2) The Lord Chief Justice must then give such advice to the Board as the Lord Chief Justice thinks fit regarding whether the application should be granted.

(3) In deciding what advice to give, the Lord Chief Justice must, in particular, have regard to the likely impact on the courts in England and Wales of the making of an order under paragraph 15 in accordance with the recommendation applied for.

Information obtained by consultees

8 A person ("the consultee") to whom a copy of the application is given under paragraph 3(1) may, for the purposes of giving advice under paragraphs 4 to 7, request the applicant or any other person to provide the consultee with such additional information as may be specified by the consultee.

Representations by applicant

9 (1) The Board must give the applicant a copy of any advice duly given under paragraphs 4 to 7.

(2) The applicant may make to the Board—

(a) written representations, and
(b) if the Board authorises it to do so, oral representations,

about the advice.

(3) The Board must make rules governing the making of oral and written representations.

(4) Representations under this paragraph must be made within—

(a) the period of 28 days beginning with the day on which the copy of the advice is given to the applicant, or
(b) such longer period as the Board may specify in a particular case.

(5) Where oral representations are made, the Board must prepare a report of those representations.

(6) Before preparing that report, the Board must—

(a) give the applicant a reasonable opportunity to comment on a draft of the report, and
(b) have regard to any comments duly made.

Publication of advice and representations etc

10 (1) The Board must, as soon as practicable after the end of the period within which representations under paragraph 9 may be made, publish—

(a) any advice duly given under paragraphs 4 to 7,
(b) any written representations duly made under paragraph 9 and the report (if any) prepared under that paragraph.

(2) Nothing in sub-paragraph (1) operates—

(a) to prevent a person who gives advice under paragraphs 4 to 7 from publishing that advice, or
(b) to prevent a person who makes representations under paragraph 9 from publishing those representations.

(3) A person ("the publisher") publishing any such material (whether under sub-paragraph (1) or otherwise) must, so far as practicable, exclude any matter which relates to the private affairs of a particular individual the publication of which, in the opinion of the publisher, would or might seriously and prejudicially affect the interests of that individual.

Rules governing decisions by the Board

11 (1) The Board must make rules specifying how it will determine applications.

(2) Rules under sub-paragraph (1) must, in particular, provide that the Board may grant an application in relation to a particular reserved legal activity only if it is satisfied—

(a) that the applicant's proposed licensing rules in relation to the activity comply with the requirements of section 83;
(b) that, if an order were to be made under paragraph 15 designating the body in relation to the activity, there would be a body with power to hear and determine appeals which, under this Part or the applicant's proposed licensing rules, may be made against decisions of the applicant;
(c) that, if an order were to be made under paragraph 15 designating the body in relation to the activity, the applicant would have appropriate internal governance arrangements in place at the time the order takes effect;
(d) that, if an order were made under paragraph 15 designating the body in relation to the activity, the applicant would be competent, and have sufficient resources, to perform the role of licensing authority in relation to the activity at the time the order takes effect.

(3) The rules made for the purposes of sub-paragraph (2)(c) must in particular require the Board to be satisfied—

(a) that the exercise of the applicant's regulatory functions would not be prejudiced by any of its representative functions, and
(b) that decisions relating to the exercise of its regulatory functions would so far as reasonably practicable be taken independently from decisions relating to the exercise of its representative functions.

Determination of applications

12 (1) After considering—

(a) the application and accompanying material,
(b) any other information provided by the applicant,
(c) any advice duly given under paragraphs 4 to 7,
(d) any representations duly made under paragraph 9, and
(e) any other information which the Board considers relevant to the application,

the Board must decide whether to grant the application.

(2) Where the application relates to more than one reserved legal activity, the Board may grant the application in relation to all or any of them.

(3) The Board must give notice of its decision to the applicant ("the decision notice").

(4) Where the Board decides to refuse the application (in whole or in part), the decision notice must specify the reasons for that decision.

(5) The Board must publish the decision notice.

13 (1) Where an application is made under this Part, the Board must give the decision notice under paragraph 12 within the decision period.

(2) The "decision period" is the period of 12 months beginning with the day on which the application is made to the Board.

(3) The Board may, before the end of the decision period, issue a notice extending that period by a period specified in the notice.

(4) More than one notice may be issued under sub-paragraph (3), but the decision period must not exceed 16 months.

(5) The Board may issue a notice under sub-paragraph (3) only after it has—

(a) consulted the OFT, the Consumer Panel and the Lord Chief Justice, and
(b) obtained the Lord Chancellor's consent to the extension.

(6) A notice under sub-paragraph (3) must state the Board's reasons for extending the decision period.

(7) The Board must publish any notice issued under sub-paragraph (3).

Effect of grant of application

14 (1) This paragraph applies where an application is granted in relation to a reserved legal activity or activities.

(2) The Board must recommend to the Lord Chancellor that an order be made designating the applicant as a licensing authority in relation to the reserved legal activity or activities in question.

(3) The Board must publish any recommendation made under sub-paragraph (2).

(4) The Board must make available to the Lord Chancellor—

(a) any advice duly given under paragraphs 4 to 7,
(b) any written representations duly made under paragraph 9 and the report (if any) prepared under that paragraph, and
(c) any other material considered by the Board for the purpose of determining the application.

Lord Chancellor's decision to make an order

15 (1) Where a recommendation is made to the Lord Chancellor under paragraph 14, the Lord Chancellor may—

(a) make an order in accordance with the recommendation, or
(b) refuse to make such an order.

(2) Where the recommendation relates to more than one reserved legal activity, the Lord Chancellor may make an order under sub-paragraph (1)(a) in relation to all or any of them.

(3) But if the application, in relation to a particular reserved legal activity, was made in reliance on paragraph 1(3)(b), the Lord Chancellor must not make an order in relation to that activity unless the Lord Chancellor has made an order under Part 2 of Schedule 4 designating the body as an approved regulator in relation to that activity.

(4) The Lord Chancellor must—

- (a) decide whether to make an order under this paragraph, and
- (b) give notice of that decision ("the decision notice") to the applicant,

within the period of 90 days beginning with the day on which the recommendation was made.

(5) If the Lord Chancellor decides not to make an order in accordance with the whole or part of the recommendation, the decision notice must state the reasons for the decision.

(6) The Lord Chancellor must publish the decision notice.

Approval of licensing rules

16 (1) Where an order is made by the Lord Chancellor under paragraph 15, the applicant's proposed licensing rules are at the same time treated as having been approved by the Board.

(2) But where the order relates to one or more (but not all) of the reserved legal activities to which the application related, sub-paragraph (1) has effect as if the reference to the applicant's proposed licensing rules were a reference to those rules excluding any provision made in respect of any activities excluded from the order.

(3) Sub-paragraph (1) is without prejudice to the Board's power to give directions under section 32 (powers to direct an approved regulator to take steps in certain circumstances, including steps to amend its regulatory arrangements).

Initial Commencement
To be appointed: see s 211(2).
Appointment
Paras 1(1), (4), (5), 2(2), 9(3), 11: Appointment: 1 January 2009: see SI 2008/3149, art 2(d)(ii).
Extent
This part of this Schedule does not extend to Scotland: see s 212(1).

PART 2
CANCELLATION OF DESIGNATION BY ORDER

Introductory

17 This Part of this Schedule applies where the Board considers that it may be appropriate for it to make a recommendation under section 76(5).

Notification of the licensing authority

18 (1) The Board must give the licensing authority a notice ("a warning notice") accompanied by a draft of the proposed recommendation.

(2) The warning notice must—

- (a) state that the Board proposes to make a recommendation under subsection (5) of section 76 in the form of the accompanying draft, and
- (b) state the reasons why the Board is satisfied of the matters mentioned in paragraphs (a) and (b) of that subsection.

(3) The Board must publish a copy of the warning notice.

(4) The licensing authority may make to the Board—

- (a) written representations, and
- (b) if the Board authorises it to do so, oral representations,

about the proposed recommendation.

(5) The Board must make rules governing the making of oral and written representations.

(6) Representations under this paragraph must be made within—

(a) the period of 28 days beginning with the day on which the warning notice is given to the licensing authority, or
(b) such longer period as the Board may specify in a particular case.

(7) The Board must consider any representations duly made by the licensing authority.

(8) Where oral representations are duly made, the Board must prepare a report of those representations.

(9) Before preparing that report, the Board must—

(a) give the licensing authority a reasonable opportunity to comment on a draft of the report, and
(b) have regard to any comments duly made.

Board's duty to seek advice

19 (1) After complying with paragraph 18, the Board must give each of the persons listed in sub-paragraph (2)—

(a) a copy of the warning notice and the accompanying draft,
(b) a copy of any written representations duly made by the licensing authority under paragraph 18 and a copy of the report (if any) prepared under that paragraph, and
(c) a notice specifying a period within which any advice under paragraphs 20 to 22 must be given.

(2) Those persons are—

(a) the OFT,
(b) the Consumer Panel,
(c) the Lord Chief Justice, and
(d) such other persons as the Board considers it reasonable to consult in respect of the proposed recommendation.

(3) In this Part of this Schedule, in relation to a proposed recommendation, "selected consultee" means a person within sub-paragraph (2)(d).

Advice of Office of Fair Trading

20 (1) The OFT must give the Board such advice as it thinks fit regarding whether the proposed recommendation should be made.

(2) In deciding what advice to give, the OFT must, in particular, have regard to whether making an order under section 76 in accordance with the proposed recommendation would (or would be likely to) prevent, restrict or distort competition within the market for reserved legal services to any significant extent.

Advice of the Consumer Panel

21 (1) The Consumer Panel must give the Board such advice as it thinks fit regarding whether the proposed recommendation should be made.

(2) In deciding what advice to give, the Consumer Panel must, in particular, have regard to the likely impact on consumers of making an order under section 76 in accordance with the proposed recommendation.

Advice of selected consultees

22 A selected consultee may give the Board such advice as the selected consultee thinks fit in respect of the proposed recommendation.

Advice of the Lord Chief Justice

23 (1) The Board must give the Lord Chief Justice—

(a) a copy of any advice duly given under paragraphs 20 to 22, and

(b) a notice specifying a period within which advice under this paragraph must be given.

(2) The Lord Chief Justice must then give such advice as the Lord Chief Justice thinks fit in respect of the proposed recommendation.

(3) In deciding what advice to give, the Lord Chief Justice must, in particular, have regard to the likely impact on the courts in England and Wales of making an order under section 76 in accordance with the proposed recommendation.

Information obtained by consultees

24 A person ("the consultee") to whom a copy of the warning notice is given under paragraph 19(1) may, for the purposes of giving advice under paragraphs 20 to 23, request the licensing authority or any other person to provide the consultee with such additional information as may be specified by the consultee.

Representations by the approved regulator etc

25 (1) The Board must—

(a) give the licensing authority a copy of any advice duly given under paragraphs 20 to 23, and
(b) publish that advice together with any written representations duly made by the licensing authority under paragraph 18 and the report (if any) prepared under that paragraph.

(2) The licensing authority and any body within sub-paragraph (3) may make to the Board—

(a) written representations, and
(b) if authorised to do so by the Board, oral representations,

about the advice.

(3) A body is within this sub-paragraph if it represents licensed bodies authorised by the licensing authority to carry on activities which are reserved legal activities.

(4) The Board may allow any other person to make written or oral representations about the advice.

(5) The Board may make rules governing the making to the Board of written or oral representations.

(6) Representations under this paragraph must be made within—

(a) the period of 28 days beginning with the day on which the representations and advice are published under sub-paragraph (1)(b), or
(b) such longer period as the Board may specify in a particular case.

(7) Where oral representations are made, the Board must prepare a report of those representations.

(8) Before preparing that report, the Board must—

(a) give each person who made oral representations a reasonable opportunity to comment on a draft of the report of those representations, and
(b) have regard to any comments duly made.

(9) The Board must, as soon as reasonably practicable after the end of the period within which representations under this paragraph may be made, publish any written representations duly made and the report (if any) prepared under sub-paragraph (7).

Publication of advice etc

26 (1) Nothing in paragraph 25 operates—

(a) to prevent a person who gives advice under paragraphs 20 to 23 from publishing that advice, or
(b) to prevent a person who makes representations under paragraph 18 or 25 from publishing those representations.

(2) A person ("the publisher") publishing any such material (whether under paragraph 25 or otherwise) must, so far as practicable, exclude any matter which relates to the private affairs of a

particular individual the publication of which, in the opinion of the publisher, would or might seriously and prejudicially affect the interests of that individual.

Decision by the Board

27 (1) After considering—

(a) any advice duly given under paragraphs 20 to 23,
(b) any representations duly made under paragraph 18 or 25, and
(c) any other information which the Board considers relevant,

the Board must decide whether to make the proposed recommendation.

(2) The Board must give notice of its decision ("the decision notice") to the licensing authority and to the Lord Chancellor.

(3) If the Board decides to make the proposed recommendation, the decision notice must—

(a) contain the recommendation, and
(b) state why the Board is satisfied of the matters mentioned in section 76(5)(a) and (b).

(4) The Board must publish the decision notice.

Initial Commencement
To be appointed: see s 211(2).
Appointment
Paras 17, 18(5), 25: Appointment: 1 January 2009: see SI 2008/3149, art 2(d)(ii).
Extent
This part of this Schedule does not extend to Scotland: see s 212(1).

SCHEDULE 11
LICENSING RULES

Section 83

PART 1
LICENSING PROCEDURE

Applications for licences

1 (1) Licensing rules must make provision about the form and manner in which applications for licences are to be made, and the fee (if any) which is to accompany an application.

(2) They may make provision about—

(a) the information which applications must contain, and
(b) the documents which must accompany applications.

Determination of applications

2 (1) Licensing rules must make the following provision about the determination of applications for licences.

(2) Before the end of the decision period the licensing authority must—

(a) decide the application,
(b) notify the applicant of its decision, and
(c) if it decides to refuse the application, set out in the notice the reasons for the refusal.

(3) The decision period is the period of 6 months beginning with the day on which the application is made to the licensing authority in accordance with its licensing rules.

(4) The licensing authority may, on one or more occasions, give the applicant a notice (an "extension notice") extending the decision period by a period specified in the notice.

(5) But—

(a) an extension notice may only be given before the time when the decision period would end, but for the extension notice, and
(b) the total decision period must not exceed 9 months.

(6) An extension notice must set out the reasons for the extension.

Review of determination

3 Licensing rules must make provision for review by the licensing authority of—

(a) a decision to refuse an application for a licence;
(b) if a licence is granted, the terms of the licence.

Period of licence and renewal

4 (1) The licensing rules may make provision—

(a) limiting the period for which any licence is (subject to the provision of this Part of this Schedule and of the licensing rules) to remain in force;
(b) about the renewal of licences, including provision about the form and manner in which an application for the renewal is to be made, and the fee (if any) which is to accompany an application.

(2) The licensing rules may make provision about—

(a) the information which applications for renewal must contain, and
(b) the documents which must accompany applications.

(3) Licensing rules must provide that a licence issued to a licensed body by the licensing authority ceases to have effect if the licensed body is issued with a licence by another licensing authority.

Continuity of licences

5 (1) Licensing rules may make provision about the effect, on a licence issued to a partnership or other unincorporated body ("the existing body"), of any change in the membership of the existing body.

(2) The provision which may be made includes provision for the existing body's licence to be transferred where the existing body ceases to exist and another body succeeds to the whole or substantially the whole of its business.

Modification of licences

6 (1) Licensing rules must make provision about the form and manner in which applications are to be made for modification of the terms of a licence under section 86, and the fee (if any) which is to accompany the application.

(2) They may make provision as to the circumstances in which the licensing authority may modify the terms of a licence under section 86 without an application being made.

(3) They must make provision for review by the licensing authority of—

(a) a decision to refuse an application for modification of the terms of a licence;
(b) if the licensing authority makes licensing rules under sub-paragraph (2), a decision under those rules to modify the terms of a licence.

Modifications under section 106 or 107

7 (1) Licensing rules must make provision about the form and manner in which applications are to be made under section 106 or 107, and the fee (if any) which is to accompany the application.

(2) They may make provision as to the matters to which the licensing authority must have regard in determining whether to make an order under section 106, or to revoke or modify such an order.

(3) They must make provision for review by the licensing authority of—

(a) a decision to refuse an application under those sections;

(b) the terms of any order made under section 106 or any decision under section 107.

8 (1) Licensing rules must make the following provision in relation to licensed bodies to which section 106 applies ("special bodies"), and in relation to which an order under section 106 has been made.

(2) If a special body becomes a special body of a different kind, it must notify the licensing authority of that fact before the end of the relevant period.

(3) If a special body ceases to be a special body, it must notify the licensing authority of that fact before the end of the relevant period.

(4) The relevant period is the period of 30 days (or such longer period as may be specified in licensing rules) beginning with the day on which the body first became a special body of a different kind, or ceased to be a special body.

(5) Licensing rules may make provision requiring a special body to provide the licensing authority with such information relevant to the matters mentioned in section 106(5) as may be specified in the licensing rules.

Initial Commencement
To be appointed: see s 211(2).
Extent
This part of this Schedule does not extend to Scotland: see s 212(1).

PART 2
STRUCTURAL REQUIREMENTS

Management

9 (1) Licensing rules must require a licensed body to comply with the following requirement at all times.

(2) At least one of the licensed body's managers must be a person (other than a licensed body) who is an authorised person in relation to a licensed activity.

(3) No manager of the licensed body may be a person who under this Part of this Act is disqualified from acting as a manager of a licensed body.

10 (1) Licensing rules may make further provision as to—

(a) the managers of licensed bodies, and
(b) the arrangements for the management by them of the licensed body and its activities.

(2) They must not require all the managers of a licensed body to be authorised persons in relation to a reserved legal activity.

Head of Legal Practice

11 (1) Licensing rules must include the following requirements.

(2) A licensed body must at all times have an individual—

(a) who is designated as Head of Legal Practice, and
(b) whose designation is approved by the licensing authority.

(3) A designation of an individual as Head of Legal Practice has effect only while the individual—

(a) consents to the designation,
(b) is an authorised person in relation to one or more of the licensed activities, and
(c) is not under this Part of this Act disqualified from acting as Head of Legal Practice of a licensed body.

(4) The licensing authority may approve a person's designation only if it is satisfied that the person is a fit and proper person to carry out the duties imposed by section 91 in relation to that body.

(5) The licensing authority may approve a person's designation in the course of determining an application for a licence under section 84.

(6) If the licensing authority is satisfied that the person designated as a licensed body's Head of Legal Practice has breached a duty imposed by section 91, it may withdraw its approval of that person's designation.

12 (1) Licensing rules must make provision—

(a) about the procedures and criteria that will be applied by the licensing authority when determining under paragraph 11(4) whether an individual is a fit and proper person;
(b) for a review by the licensing authority of a determination under that paragraph that an individual is not a fit and proper person;
(c) about the procedures and criteria that will be applied by the licensing authority in determining under paragraph 11(6) whether to withdraw its approval;
(d) for a review by the licensing authority of a determination under that paragraph to withdraw its approval;
(e) about the procedure which is to apply where a licensed body ceases to comply with the requirement imposed by virtue of paragraph 11(2).

(2) Rules made in accordance with sub-paragraph (1)(e) may in particular provide that the requirement imposed by virtue of paragraph 11(2) is suspended until such time as may be specified by the licensing authority if the licensed body complies with such other requirements as may be specified in the rules.

Head of Finance and Administration

13 (1) Licensing rules must include the following requirements.

(2) A licensed body must at all times have an individual—

(a) who is designated as Head of Finance and Administration, and
(b) whose designation is approved by the licensing authority.

(3) A designation of an individual as Head of Finance and Administration has effect only while the individual—

(a) consents to the designation, and
(b) is not under this Part of this Act disqualified from acting as Head of Finance and Administration of a licensed body.

(4) The licensing authority may approve a person's designation only if it is satisfied that the person is a fit and proper person to carry out the duties imposed by section 92 in relation to that body.

(5) The licensing authority may approve a person's designation in the course of determining an application for a licence under section 84.

(6) If the licensing authority is satisfied that the person designated as a licensed body's Head of Finance and Administration has breached a duty imposed by section 92, it may withdraw its approval of that person's designation.

14 (1) Licensing rules must make provision—

(a) about the procedures and criteria that will be applied by the licensing authority when determining under paragraph 13(4) whether an individual is a fit and proper person;
(b) for a review by the licensing authority of a determination under that paragraph that an individual is not a fit and proper person;
(c) about the procedures and criteria that will be applied by the licensing authority in determining under paragraph 13(6) whether to withdraw its approval;
(d) for a review by the licensing authority of a determination under that paragraph to withdraw its approval;
(e) about the procedure which is to apply where a licensed body ceases to comply with the requirement imposed by virtue of paragraph 13(2).

(2) The rules made in accordance with sub-paragraph (1)(e) may in particular provide that the requirement imposed by virtue of sub-paragraph 13(2) is suspended until such time as may be specified by the licensing authority if the licensed body complies with such other requirements as may be specified in the rules.

Initial Commencement
To be appointed: see s 211(2).
Extent
This part of this Schedule does not extend to Scotland: see s 212(1).

PART 3
PRACTICE REQUIREMENTS

Practising address

15 (1) Licensing rules must require a licensed body, other than one to which sub-paragraph (3) applies, at all times to have a practising address in England and Wales.

(2) For this purpose "practising address", in relation to a licensed body, means an address from which the body provides services which consist of or include the carrying on of reserved legal activities.

(3) This sub-paragraph applies to a licensed body—

(a) which is a company or limited liability partnership, and
(b) the registered office of which is situated in England and Wales (or in Wales).

Licensed activities

16 Licensing rules must provide that a licensed body may carry on a licensed activity only through a person who is entitled to carry on the activity.

Compliance with regulatory arrangements etc

17 (1) Licensing rules must include the following provision.

(2) A licensed body must at all times have suitable arrangements in place to ensure that—

(a) it, and its managers and employees, comply with the duties imposed by section 176, and
(b) it, and any person to whom sub-paragraph (3) applies, maintain the professional principles set out in section 1(3).

(3) This sub-paragraph applies to any manager or employee of the licensed body who is an authorised person in relation to an activity which is a reserved legal activity.

(4) A licensed body must at all times have suitable arrangements in place to ensure that non-authorised persons subject to the duty imposed by section 90 in relation to the licensed body comply with that duty.

(5) Licensing rules may make provision as to the arrangements which are suitable for the purposes of rules made under sub-paragraphs (2) and (4).

Disqualified employees

18 (1) Licensing rules must include the following requirement.

(2) A licensed body may not employ a person who under this Part of this Act is disqualified from being an employee of a licensed body.

Indemnification arrangements and compensation arrangements

19 (1) For the purpose of giving effect to indemnification arrangements and compensation arrangements, licensing rules may—

(a) authorise or require the licensing authority to establish and maintain a fund or funds;
(b) authorise or require the licensing authority to take out and maintain insurance with authorised insurers;
(c) require licensed bodies or licensed bodies of any specific description to take out and maintain insurance with authorised insurers.

(2) In this paragraph "authorised insurer" has the same meaning as in section 64.

Accounts

20 (1) The licensing rules must make provision as to the treatment of money within sub-paragraph (2), and the keeping of accounts in respect of such money.

(2) The money referred to in sub-paragraph (1) is money (including money held on trust) which is received, held or dealt with by the licensed body, its managers and employees for clients or other persons.

Initial Commencement
To be appointed: see s 211(2).
Extent
This part of this Schedule does not extend to Scotland: see s 212(1).

PART 4
REGULATION

Fees

21 (1) The licensing rules must require licensed bodies to pay periodical fees to the licensing authority.

(2) The rules may provide for the payment of different fees by different descriptions of licensed body.

Financial penalties

22 The licensing rules must make provision as to—

(a) the acts and omissions in respect of which the licensing authority may impose a penalty under section 95, and
(b) the criteria and procedure to be applied by the licensing authority in determining whether to impose a penalty under that section, and the amount of any penalty.

Disqualifications

23 (1) Licensing rules must make provision as to the criteria and procedure to be applied by the licensing authority in determining whether a person should be disqualified under section 99.

(2) Licensing rules must make provision—

(a) for a review by the licensing authority of a determination by the licensing authority that a person should be disqualified;
(b) as to the criteria and procedure to be applied by the licensing authority in determining whether a person's disqualification should cease to be in force;
(c) requiring the licensing authority to notify the Board of any determination by the licensing authority that a person should be disqualified, of the results of any review of that determination, and of any decision by the licensing authority that a person's disqualification should cease to be in force.

Suspension or revocation of licence under section 101

24 (1) Licensing rules must make the following provision.

(2) The licensing authority may suspend or revoke a licensed body's licence under section 101 in the following cases.

(3) The first case is that the licensed body becomes a body which is not a licensable body.

(4) The second case is that the licensed body fails to comply with licensing rules made under paragraph 16 (carrying on of licensed activities).

(5) The third case is that—

(a) a non-authorised person holds a restricted interest in the licensed body—

(i) as a result of the person taking a step in circumstances where that constitutes an offence under paragraph 24(1) of Schedule 13 (whether or not the person is charged with or convicted of an offence under that paragraph),
(ii) in breach of conditions imposed under paragraph 17, 28, or 33 of that Schedule, or
(iii) the person's holding of which is subject to an objection by the licensing authority under paragraph 31 or 36 of that Schedule,

(b) if the relevant licensing rules make the provision mentioned in paragraph 38(1)(a) of that Schedule, a non-authorised person has under those rules a shareholding in the licensed body, or a parent undertaking of the licensed body, which exceeds the share limit,
(c) if the relevant licensing rules make the provision mentioned in paragraph 38(1)(b) of that Schedule, a non-authorised person has under those rules an entitlement to exercise, or control the exercise of, voting rights in the licensed body or a parent undertaking of the licensed body which exceeds the voting limit,
(d) if the relevant licensing rules make the provision mentioned in paragraph 38(1)(c) of that Schedule, the total proportion of shares in the licensed body or a parent undertaking of the licensed body held by non-authorised persons exceeds the limit specified in the rules, or
(e) if the relevant licensing rules make the provision mentioned in paragraph 38(1)(d) of that Schedule, the total proportion of voting rights in the licensed body or a parent undertaking of the licensed body which non-authorised persons are entitled to exercise, or control the exercise of, exceeds the limit specified in the rules.

(6) The fourth case is that a non-authorised person subject to the duty in section 90 in relation to the licensed body fails to comply with that duty.

(7) The fifth case is that the licensed body, or a manager or employee of the licensed body, fails to comply with the duties imposed by section 176.

(8) The sixth case is that—

(a) the licensed body fails to comply with licensing rules made under paragraph 9(3) or 18 (prohibition on disqualified managers and employees), and
(b) the manager or employee concerned was disqualified as a result of breach of a duty within section 99(4)(c) or (d).

(9) The seventh case is that the licensed body is unable to comply with licensing rules made under—

(a) paragraph 11 (requirement for Head of Legal Practice), or
(b) paragraph 13 (requirement for Head of Finance and Administration).

(10) Before suspending or revoking a licence in accordance with sub-paragraph (2), the licensing authority must give the licensed body notice of its intention.

(11) The licensing authority may not suspend or revoke the licence before the end of the period of 28 days beginning with the day on which the notice is given to the licensed body (or any longer period specified in the notice).

25 Licensing rules may make provision about other circumstances in which the licensing authority may exercise its power under section 101 to suspend or revoke a licence.

26 (1) Licensing rules must make provision about the criteria and procedure the licensing authority will apply in deciding whether to suspend or revoke a licence, or to end the suspension of a licence, under section 101.

(2) They must make provision for a review by the licensing authority of a decision by the licensing authority to suspend or revoke a licence.

Initial Commencement
To be appointed: see s 211(2).
Extent
This part of this Schedule does not extend to Scotland: see s 212(1).

SCHEDULE 12
ENTITLEMENT TO MAKE AN APPLICATION FOR A LICENCE TO THE BOARD

Section 84

Application to Board

1 (1) A licensable body may apply to the Board for a decision that the body is entitled to make an application for a licence to the Board acting in its capacity as a licensing authority.

(2) An application under sub-paragraph (1) may be made only on one of the grounds specified in this paragraph.

(3) The first ground is that—

(a) there is no competent licensing authority, and
(b) there is no potentially competent licensing authority.

(4) The second ground is that—

(a) each competent licensing authority has determined that it does not have suitable regulatory arrangements,
(b) if one or more competent licensing authorities have made an application to the Board under Part 3 of Schedule 4 for the approval of alterations of their regulatory arrangements, each of those authorities has determined that it will not have suitable regulatory arrangements if the application is granted, and
(c) each potentially competent licensing authority has determined that it will not have suitable regulatory arrangements if it becomes a competent licensing authority.

(5) The third ground applies only in relation to a licensable body within sub-paragraph (6), and is that—

(a) the body has made an application for a licence to each competent licensing authority which has suitable regulatory arrangements, and
(b) no such licensing authority is prepared to grant the body a licence on terms which are appropriate to that body, having regard to the matters in section 106(5)(a) to (c) and any other matter specified in rules made by the Board for the purposes of this sub-paragraph.

(6) The licensable bodies within this sub-paragraph are—

(a) a not for profit body;
(b) a community interest company;
(c) an independent trade union;
(d) if an order under section 106(1)(e) so provides in relation to a description of body prescribed under that section, a body of that description.

Board's decision on an application under paragraph 1

2 (1) On an application under paragraph 1 the Board must, before the end of the decision period, decide whether the licensable body is entitled to make an application for a licence to the Board acting in its capacity as a licensing authority.

(2) The decision period is—

(a) in relation to an application on the first ground, the period of 14 days beginning with the day on which the application is made,
(b) in relation to an application on the second ground, the period of 28 days beginning with the day on which the application is made, and
(c) in relation to an application on the third ground, the period of 60 days beginning with the day on which the application is made.

(3) The Board must give a notice to the licensable body—

(a) stating its decision, and
(b) giving reasons for its decision.

(4) The Board must make rules providing for a review of any decision made by it under this paragraph.

(5) The rules may in particular provide that if the Board decides to grant the application, the Board may review that decision if the ground on which the application was granted ceases to be made out before the Board (in its capacity as a licensing authority) determines any application for a licence made by the licensable body.

Licensing authority's duty to make relevant determinations

3 (1) A licensable body may apply to each competent licensing authority for—

(a) a determination as to whether the authority has suitable regulatory arrangements;
(b) a statement as to whether the authority has made an application as mentioned in paragraph 1(4)(b) and if it has, a determination as to whether, if the application is granted, the authority will have suitable regulatory arrangements.

(2) A licensable body may apply to each potentially competent licensing authority for a determination as to whether it will have suitable regulatory arrangements in place if it becomes a competent licensing authority.

(3) A competent (or potentially competent) licensing authority to which a licensable body makes an application under sub-paragraph (1) or (2) may require the licensable body to provide it with such information in relation to the licensable body as it may specify.

(4) The authority may specify only information which it reasonably requires for the purpose of making the determination applied for.

(5) A competent (or potentially competent) licensing authority to which an application is made under sub-paragraph (1) or (2) must make the determination before the end of—

(a) the decision period, or
(b) if it requires the licensable body to provide it with information under sub-paragraph (3), the period of 28 days beginning with the day on which the information is provided.

(6) The decision period, in relation to an application under sub-paragraph (1) or (2), is the period of 28 days beginning with the day on which the application is made.

"The Board"

4 In this Schedule references to the Board, unless otherwise stated, are to the Board acting otherwise than in its capacity as a licensing authority or an approved regulator.

"Competent licensing authority"

5 "Competent licensing authority", in relation to a licensable body, means an approved regulator designated as a licensing authority in relation to each reserved legal activity which the licensable body proposes to carry on.

"Potentially competent licensing authority"

6 (1) "Potentially competent licensing authority", in relation to a licensable body, means an approved regulator—

(a) which has made an application to the Board under Part 1 of Schedule 10 for a recommendation that the Lord Chancellor make a relevant designation order, and whose application has not been determined, or
(b) in respect of which the Board has made such a recommendation, but in respect of which no relevant designation order (or decision not to make such an order) has been made by the Lord Chancellor.

(2) A relevant designation order is an order—

(a) designating the approved regulator as a licensing authority in respect of one or more reserved legal activities, and
(b) the effect of which will be that the approved regulator becomes a competent licensing authority in relation to the licensable body.

"Suitable regulatory arrangements"

7 (1) "Suitable regulatory arrangements", in relation to a licensable body and a competent licensing authority, means regulatory arrangements which are suitable in relation to the licensable body, having regard to—

- (a) the composition of the licensable body, including in particular the matters in sub-paragraph (2);
- (b) the services the licensable body proposes to provide;
- (c) if the licensable body proposes to carry on non-reserved activities, any regulation to which the carrying on of such activities is subject;
- (d) the persons to whom the licensable body proposes to provide services.

(2) The matters are—

- (a) the kinds of authorised persons who are managers of, or have an interest in, the licensable body,
- (b) the proportion of persons who are managers of, or have an interest in, the licensable body who are authorised persons or authorised persons of a particular kind,
- (c) the kinds of non-authorised persons who are managers of, or have an interest in, the licensable body,
- (d) the proportion of persons who are managers of, or have an interest in, the licensable body who are non-authorised persons or non-authorised persons of a particular kind, and
- (e) the kinds of non-authorised persons who have an indirect interest in the licensable body.

(3) In sub-paragraph (2)—

- (a) "authorised person" means a person who is an authorised person in relation to any activity which is a reserved legal activity, and
- (b) authorised persons are of different kinds if they are authorised to carry on such activities by different approved regulators.

Initial Commencement
To be appointed: see s 211(2).
Appointment
Paras 2(4), (5), 4: Appointment: 1 January 2009: see SI 2008/3149, art 2(d)(iii).
Extent
This Schedule does not extend to Scotland: see s 212(1).

SCHEDULE 13
OWNERSHIP OF LICENSED BODIES

Section 89

PART 1
INTRODUCTORY

Restricted interests subject to approval

1 (1) The holding by a non-authorised person of a restricted interest in a licensed body is subject to the approval of the relevant licensing authority in accordance with the provisions of this Schedule.

(2) In relation to a licensed body which is a partnership, for the purposes of section 34 of the Partnership Act 1890 (c 39) (dissolution by illegality) the holding by a non-authorised person of a restricted interest in the body without the approval of the relevant licensing authority does not make it unlawful for the business of the partnership to be carried on, or for the partners to carry it on in partnership.

Restricted interest

2 (1) "Restricted interest" means each of the following—

(a) a material interest;
(b) if licensing rules are made by the relevant licensing authority under sub-paragraph (2), a controlled interest.

(2) Licensing rules may specify that a controlled interest is a restricted interest for the purposes of this Schedule.

Material interest

3 (1) For the purposes of this Part of this Act, a person holds a material interest in a body ("B") if the person—

(a) holds at least 10% of the shares in B,
(b) is able to exercise significant influence over the management of B by virtue of the person's shareholding in B,
(c) holds at least 10% of the shares in a parent undertaking ("P") of B,
(d) is able to exercise significant influence over the management of P by virtue of the person's shareholding in P,
(e) is entitled to exercise, or control the exercise of, voting power in B which, if it consists of voting rights, constitutes at least 10% of the voting rights in B,
(f) is able to exercise significant influence over the management of B by virtue of the person's entitlement to exercise, or control the exercise of, voting rights in B,
(g) is entitled to exercise, or control the exercise of, voting power in P which, if it consists of voting rights, constitutes at least 10% of the voting rights in P,
(h) is able to exercise significant influence over the management of P by virtue of the person's entitlement to exercise, or control the exercise of, voting rights in P.

(2) Licensing rules made by the relevant licensing authority may provide—

(a) that the references in sub-paragraph (1) to 10% are to have effect as references to such lesser percentage as may be specified in the rules;
(b) that in relation to a partnership, for the purposes of this Part a person has a material interest in the partnership if he is a partner (whether or not the person has a material interest by virtue of sub-paragraph (1)).

(3) For the purposes of sub-paragraph (1) "the person" means—

(a) the person,
(b) any of the person's associates, or
(c) the person and any of the person's associates taken together.

(4) For the purposes of this Schedule, material interests held by virtue of different paragraphs of sub-paragraph (1) are restricted interests of different kinds.

Controlled interest

4 (1) For the purposes of this Schedule, a person holds a controlled interest in a body ("B") if the person—

(a) holds at least x% of the shares in B,
(b) holds at least x% of the shares in a parent undertaking ("P") of B,
(c) is entitled to exercise, or control the exercise of, at least x% of the voting rights in B, or
(d) is entitled to exercise, or control the exercise of, at least x% of the voting rights in P.

(2) For the purposes of sub-paragraph (1) "the person" means—

(a) the person,
(b) any of the person's associates, or
(c) the person and any of the person's associates taken together.

(3) In sub-paragraph (1), "x" means such percentage as may be specified in licensing rules made by the relevant licensing authority under paragraph 2(2).

(4) Licensing rules made under paragraph 2(2) may specify more than one percentage.

(5) Any percentage specified by licensing rules made under paragraph 2(2) must be greater than—

(a) 10%, or

(b) if the relevant licensing authority makes licensing rules under paragraph 3(2)(a), the percentage specified in those rules.

(6) For the purposes of this Schedule—

(a) controlled interests held by virtue of different paragraphs of sub-paragraph (1) are restricted interests of different kinds;
(b) if licensing rules made under paragraph 2(2) specify more than one percentage, controlled interests held by virtue of each of those percentages are restricted interests of different kinds.

Associates, parent undertakings and voting power

5 (1) For the purposes of this Schedule "associate", in relation to a person ("A") and—

(a) a shareholding in a body ("S"), or
(b) an entitlement to exercise or control the exercise of voting power in a body ("V"),

means a person listed in sub-paragraph (2).

(2) The persons are—

(a) the spouse or civil partner of A,
(b) a child or stepchild of A (if under 18),
(c) the trustee of any settlement under which A has a life interest in possession (in Scotland a life interest),
(d) an undertaking of which A is a director,
(e) an employee of A,
(f) a partner of A (except, where S or V is a partnership in which A is a partner, another partner in S or V),
(g) if A is an undertaking—
 (i) a director of A,
 (ii) a subsidiary undertaking of A, or
 (iii) a director or employee of such a subsidiary undertaking,
(h) if A has with any other person an agreement or arrangement with respect to the acquisition, holding or disposal of shares or other interests in S or V (whether or not they are interests within the meaning of section 72(3)), that other person, or
(i) if A has with any other person an agreement or arrangement under which they undertake to act together in exercising their voting power in relation to S or V, that person.

(3) In sub-paragraph (2)(c), "settlement" means any disposition or arrangement under which property is held on trust (or subject to a comparable obligation).

(4) For the purposes of this Schedule—

"parent undertaking" and "subsidiary undertaking" have the same meaning as in the Financial Services and Markets Act 2000 (c 8) (see section 420 of that Act);
"voting power", in relation to a body which does not have general meetings at which matters are decided by the exercise of voting rights, means the right under the constitution of the body to direct the overall policy of the body or alter the terms of its constitution.

The approval requirements

6 (1) For the purposes of this Schedule, the approval requirements are met in relation to a person's holding of a restricted interest if—

(a) the person's holding of that interest does not compromise the regulatory objectives,
(b) the person's holding of that interest does not compromise compliance with the duties imposed by section 176 by the licensed body or persons to whom sub-paragraph (2) applies, and
(c) the person is otherwise a fit and proper person to hold that interest.

(2) This sub-paragraph applies to any employee or manager of the licensed body who is an authorised person in relation to an activity which is a reserved legal activity.

(3) In determining whether it is satisfied of the matters mentioned in sub-paragraph (1)(a) to (c), the licensing authority must in particular have regard to—

(a) the person's probity and financial position,
(b) whether the person is disqualified as mentioned in section 100(1), or included in the list kept by the Board under paragraph 51,
(c) the person's associates, and
(d) any other matter which may be specified in licensing rules.

(4) Licensing rules must make provision about the procedures that will be applied by the licensing authority when determining whether it is satisfied of the matters mentioned in sub-paragraph (1)(a) to (c).

Approval of multiple restricted interests

7 (1) This paragraph applies if a person ("P") holds a kind of restricted interest in a body ("B") by virtue of—

(a) holding a particular percentage of the shares in B or a parent undertaking of B, or
(b) an entitlement to exercise, or control the exercise of, a particular percentage of the voting rights in B or a parent undertaking of B.

(2) If the relevant licensing authority approves P's holding of that interest, it is to be treated as also approving P's holding of any lesser restricted interest in B held by P.

(3) A lesser restricted interest is a kind of restricted interest held by P by virtue of—

(a) holding a smaller percentage of the shares mentioned in sub-paragraph (1)(a), or
(b) an entitlement to exercise, or control the exercise of, a smaller percentage of the voting rights mentioned in sub-paragraph (1)(b).

Board's power to prescribe rules

8 In this Schedule "prescribed" means prescribed by rules made by the Board for the purposes of this Schedule.

Lord Chancellor's power to modify

9 The Lord Chancellor may, on the recommendation of the Board, by order modify—

(a) paragraph 3 (material interest);
(b) paragraphs 4(2), 5, 6(3)(c), 38(3), 41(3) and 42(3) (associates).

Initial Commencement
To be appointed: see s 211(2).
Appointment
Para 8: Appointment: 1 January 2009: see SI 2008/3149, art 2(d)(iv).
Extent
This part of this Schedule does not extend to Scotland: see s 212(1).

PART 2
APPROVAL OF RESTRICTED INTERESTS ON APPLICATION FOR LICENCE

Requirement to identify non-authorised persons

10 (1) Where a body applies to a licensing authority for a licence, it must identify in its application—

(a) any non-authorised person who holds a restricted interest in the body, or whom the body expects to hold such an interest when the licence is issued, and
(b) the kind of restricted interest held, or expected to be held, by that person.

(2) If, before the licence is issued, there is any change in—

(a) the identity of the non-authorised persons within sub-paragraph (1)(a), or
(b) the kind of restricted interest held, or expected to be held, by a person identified to the licensing authority under that sub-paragraph,

the applicant must inform the relevant licensing authority within such period as may be specified by order made by the Lord Chancellor on the recommendation of the Board.

11 (1) It is an offence for a person to fail to comply with a requirement imposed on the person by paragraph 10.

(2) A person who is guilty of an offence under sub-paragraph (1) is liable on summary conviction to a fine not exceeding level 5 on the standard scale.

(3) It is a defence for a person charged with an offence under sub-paragraph (1) to show that at the time of the alleged offence the person had no knowledge of the facts by virtue of which the duty to notify arose.

12 (1) This paragraph applies if a person under a duty to notify imposed by paragraph 10—

(a) had no knowledge of the facts by virtue of which that duty arose, but
(b) subsequently becomes aware of those facts.

(2) The person must give the licensing authority the required notification within such period, after the person becomes so aware, as may be specified by order made by the Lord Chancellor on the recommendation of the Board.

(3) A person who fails to comply with the duty to notify imposed by sub-paragraph (2) is guilty of an offence.

(4) A person who is guilty of an offence under sub-paragraph (3) is liable on summary conviction to a fine not exceeding level 5 on the standard scale.

Requirement to notify non-authorised persons

13 (1) Where an applicant for a licence identifies a non-authorised person to a licensing authority in accordance with paragraph 10 or 12, it must give that person a notice—

(a) stating that it has applied for a licence and identified the person to the licensing authority in accordance with paragraph 10 or 12, and
(b) explaining the effect of paragraph 14.

(2) It is an offence for a person to fail to comply with a requirement imposed on it by sub-paragraph (1).

(3) A person who is guilty of an offence under sub-paragraph (2) is liable on summary conviction to a fine not exceeding level 5 on the standard scale.

Licensing authority's power to require information

14 (1) A licensing authority may require a non-authorised person identified to it in accordance with paragraph 10 or 12 to provide it with such documents and information as it may require.

(2) It is an offence for a person who is required to provide information or documents under sub-paragraph (1) knowingly to provide false or misleading information or documents.

(3) A person who is guilty of an offence under sub-paragraph (2) is liable—

(a) on summary conviction, to a fine not exceeding the statutory maximum, and
(b) on conviction on indictment, to a term of imprisonment not exceeding 2 years or a fine (or both).

Licence may not be granted unless non-authorised persons approved

15 (1) This paragraph applies where an applicant for a licence ("the applicant") gives the licensing authority notification under paragraph 10 or 12 in relation to one or more non-authorised persons.

(2) The licensing authority may not grant the application for a licence unless, in relation to each non-authorised person in respect of which notification is given ("the investor"), it approves the investor's holding of the restricted interest to which the notification relates ("the notified interest").

(3) Sub-paragraph (2) does not apply in relation to a non-authorised person who does not hold the notified interest when the licence is issued.

(4) In this Part of this Schedule, "the applicant", "the investor" and "the notified interest" are to be construed in accordance with this paragraph.

Unconditional approval of notified interest

16 (1) If the licensing authority is satisfied that the approval requirements are met in relation to the investor's holding of the notified interest, it must approve the investor's holding of that interest without conditions.

(2) If the licensing authority approves the investor's holding of the notified interest without conditions, it must notify the investor and the applicant of its approval as soon as reasonably practicable.

Conditional approval of notified interest

17 (1) If the licensing authority is not satisfied that the approval requirements are met in relation to the investor's holding of the notified interest, it may approve the investor's holding of the notified interest subject to conditions.

(2) It may do so only if it considers that, if the conditions are complied with, it will be appropriate for the investor to hold the notified interest without the approval requirements being met.

(3) If the licensing authority proposes to approve the investor's holding of the notified interest subject to conditions it must give the investor and the applicant a warning notice.

(4) The warning notice must—

(a) specify the nature of the conditions proposed and the reasons for their imposition, and
(b) state that representations may be made to the licensing authority within the prescribed period.

(5) The licensing authority must consider any representations made within the prescribed period.

(6) If the licensing authority approves the investor's holding of the notified interest subject to conditions, it must notify the investor and the applicant of its approval as soon as reasonably practicable.

(7) The notice must—

(a) specify the reasons for the imposition of the conditions, and
(b) explain the effect of Part 5 of this Schedule.

18 (1) The investor and the applicant may before the end of the prescribed period appeal to the relevant appellate body against the imposition of any or all of the conditions.

(2) The relevant appellate body may dismiss the appeal, or allow the appeal and—

(a) order the licensing authority to approve the investor's holding of the notified interest without conditions, or subject to such conditions as may be specified in the order, or
(b) remit the matter to the licensing authority.

(3) A party to the appeal may before the end of the prescribed period appeal to the High Court on a point of law arising from the decision of the relevant appellant body, but only with the permission of the High Court.

(4) The High Court may make such order as it thinks fit.

(5) If the investor's holding of the notified interest is subject to conditions as a result of an order made on an appeal under this paragraph, for the purposes of this Schedule the conditions are to be treated as having been imposed under paragraph 17.

Objection to notified interest

19 (1) If the licensing authority is not satisfied that the approval requirements are met in relation to the investor's holding of the notified interest, it may object to the investor's holding of that interest.

(2) If the licensing authority proposes to object to the investor's holding of the notified interest, it must give the investor and the applicant a warning notice.

(3) The warning notice must—

- (a) specify the reasons for the proposed objection, and
- (b) state that representations may be made to the licensing authority within the prescribed period.

(4) The licensing authority must consider any representations made within the prescribed period.

(5) If the licensing authority objects to the investor's holding of the notified interest, it must notify the investor and the applicant of its objection as soon as reasonably practicable.

(6) The notice must—

- (a) specify the reasons for the objection, and
- (b) explain the effect of Part 5 of this Schedule.

20 (1) The investor and the applicant may before the end of the prescribed period appeal to the relevant appellate body against the objection.

(2) The relevant appellate body may dismiss the appeal, or allow the appeal and—

- (a) order the licensing authority to approve the investor's holding of the notified interest without conditions, or subject to such conditions as may be specified in the order, or
- (b) remit the matter to the licensing authority.

(3) A party to the appeal may before the end of the prescribed period appeal to the High Court on a point of law arising from the decision of the relevant appellate body, but only with the permission of the High Court.

(4) The High Court may make such order as it thinks fit.

(5) If the investor's holding of the notified interest is subject to conditions as a result of an order made on an appeal under this paragraph, for the purposes of this Schedule the conditions are to be treated as having been imposed under paragraph 17.

Initial Commencement

To be appointed: see s 211(2).

Appointment

Paras 17(4)(b), (5), 18(1), (3), 19(3)(b), (4), 20(1), (3): Appointment (in so far as relating to the exercise of powers by virtue of Pt 1, para 8 hereto): 1 January 2009: see SI 2008/3149, art 2(d)(iv).

Extent

This part of this Schedule does not extend to Scotland: see s 212(1).

PART 3
APPROVAL OF RESTRICTED INTERESTS AFTER LICENCE IS ISSUED

Powers of licensing authority in relation to change of interests

Continuing notification requirements

21 (1) This paragraph applies where a non-authorised person ("the investor")—

- (a) proposes to take a step which would result in the investor acquiring a restricted interest in a licensed body (or, if the investor already has one or more kinds of restricted interest, acquiring an additional kind of restricted interest), or
- (b) acquires such an interest in a licensed body without taking such a step.

(2) In a case within sub-paragraph (1)(a) the investor must notify the licensed body and the relevant licensing authority of the proposal.

(3) In a case within sub-paragraph (1)(b) the investor must notify the licensed body and the relevant licensing authority of the acquisition within such period, after the investor becomes aware of it, as may be specified by order made by the Lord Chancellor on the recommendation of the Board.

(4) In this Part of this Schedule—

(a) references to "the investor" are to be construed in accordance with this paragraph, and
(b) references to a notifiable interest are to the restricted interest which the investor will have as a result of the step the investor proposes to take (or has as a result of the acquisition which has taken place).

Offences in connection with paragraph 21

22 (1) It is an offence for a person to fail to comply with a requirement imposed by—

(a) paragraph 21(2), or
(b) paragraph 21(3).

(2) A person who is guilty of an offence under sub-paragraph (1) is liable on summary conviction to a fine not exceeding level 5 on the standard scale.

(3) It is a defence for a person charged with an offence under sub-paragraph (1)(a) to show that at the time of the alleged offence the person had no knowledge of the facts by virtue of which the duty to notify arose.

23 (1) This paragraph applies if a person under the duty to notify imposed by paragraph 21(2)—

(a) had no knowledge of the facts by virtue of which that duty arose, but
(b) subsequently becomes aware of those facts.

(2) The person must give the licensed body and the licensing authority the required notification within such period, after the person becomes so aware, as may be specified by order made by the Lord Chancellor on the recommendation of the Board.

(3) A person who fails to comply with the duty to notify imposed by sub-paragraph (2) is guilty of an offence.

(4) A person who is guilty of an offence under sub-paragraph (3) is liable on summary conviction to a fine not exceeding level 5 on the standard scale.

24 (1) It is an offence for a non-authorised person, who under paragraph 21(2) is required to notify the licensed body and the relevant licensing authority of a proposal to take a step, to take the step, unless the relevant licensing authority has approved the investor's holding of the notifiable interest under paragraph 27 or 28.

(2) If paragraph 22(3) applies, the reference in sub-paragraph (1) to paragraph 21(2) is to be read as a reference to paragraph 23(2).

(3) A person who is guilty of an offence under sub-paragraph (1) is liable—

(a) on summary conviction, to a fine not exceeding the statutory maximum, and
(b) on conviction on indictment, to a term of imprisonment not exceeding 2 years or a fine (or both).

Duty of licensing authority following notification etc

25 (1) The relevant licensing authority must—

(a) following receipt of a notification under paragraph 21(2) or (3) or 23(2), or
(b) if the licensing authority becomes aware that an investor has failed to comply with a notification requirement imposed by paragraph 21(2) or (3) or 23(2),

determine which of the steps in sub-paragraph (3) to take.

(2) The licensing authority must make the determination within such period as may be prescribed.

(3) The steps are—

(a) to approve the investor's holding of the notifiable interest unconditionally under paragraph 27,
(b) to warn the investor under paragraph 28(3) that it proposes to approve the investor's holding of the notifiable interest subject to conditions,
(c) to approve under paragraph 28(4) the investor's holding of the notifiable interest subject to conditions,
(d) to warn the investor under paragraph 31(2) that it proposes to object to the investor's holding of the notifiable interest, or
(e) to object under paragraph 31(3) to the investor's holding of the notifiable interest.

Licensing authority's power to require information

26 (1) A licensing authority may require the investor to provide it with such documents and information as it may require.

(2) It is an offence for a person who is required to provide information or documents under sub-paragraph (1) knowingly to provide false or misleading information or documents.

(3) A person who is guilty of an offence under sub-paragraph (2) is liable—

(a) on summary conviction, to a fine not exceeding the statutory maximum, and
(b) on conviction on indictment, to a term of imprisonment not exceeding 2 years or a fine (or both).

Unconditional approval of notifiable interest

27 (1) If the licensing authority is satisfied that the approval requirements are met in relation to the investor's holding of the notifiable interest, it must approve the investor's holding of that interest without conditions.

(2) If the licensing authority approves the investor's holding of the notifiable interest without conditions, it must notify the investor and the licensed body of its approval as soon as reasonably practicable.

Conditional approval of notifiable interest

28 (1) If the licensing authority is not satisfied that the approval requirements are met in relation to the investor's holding of the notifiable interest, it may approve the investor's holding of that interest subject to conditions.

(2) It may do so only if it considers that, if the conditions are complied with, it will be appropriate for the investor to hold the notifiable interest without the approval requirements being met.

(3) If the licensing authority proposes to approve the investor's holding of the notifiable interest subject to conditions it must give the investor and the licensed body a warning notice.

(4) But the licensing authority may approve the investor's holding of the notifiable interest subject to conditions without giving a warning notice if it considers it necessary or desirable to do so for the purpose of protecting any of the regulatory objectives.

(5) The warning notice must—

(a) specify the nature of the conditions proposed and the reasons for their imposition, and
(b) state that representations may be made to the licensing authority within the prescribed period.

(6) The licensing authority must consider any representations made within the prescribed period.

(7) If the licensing authority approves the investor's holding of the notifiable interest subject to conditions, it must notify the investor and the licensed body of its approval as soon as reasonably practicable.

(8) The notice must—

(a) specify the reasons for the imposition of the conditions and (if the investor already holds the notifiable interest) the time from which they have effect, and
(b) explain the effect of Part 5 of this Schedule.

29 (1) The investor and the licensed body may before the end of the prescribed period appeal to the relevant appellate body against the imposition of any or all the conditions.

(2) The relevant appellate body may dismiss the appeal, or allow the appeal and—

(a) order the licensing authority to approve the investor's holding of the notifiable interest without conditions, or subject to such conditions as may be specified in the order, or
(b) remit the matter to the licensing authority.

(3) A party to the appeal may before the end of the prescribed period appeal to the High Court on a point of law arising from the decision of the relevant appellate body, but only with the permission of the High Court.

(4) The High Court may make such order as it thinks fit.

(5) If the investor's holding of the notifiable interest is subject to conditions as a result of an order made on an appeal under this paragraph, for the purposes of this Schedule the conditions are to be treated as having been imposed under paragraph 28.

Duration of unconditional or conditional approval

30 In a case within paragraph 21(1)(a), the licensing authority's approval under paragraph 27 or 28 remains effective only if the investor acquires the notifiable interest—

(a) before the end of such period as may be specified in the notice under paragraph 27(2) or 28(7), or
(b) if no such period is specified, before the end of the period of one year beginning with the date of that notice.

Objection to acquisition of notifiable interest

31 (1) If the licensing authority is not satisfied that the approval requirements are met in relation to the investor's holding of the notifiable interest, it may object to the investor's holding of that interest.

(2) If the licensing authority proposes to object to the investor's holding of the notifiable interest, it must give the investor and the licensed body a warning notice.

(3) But the licensing authority may object to the investor's holding of the notifiable interest without giving a warning notice if it considers it necessary or desirable to do so for the purpose of protecting any of the regulatory objectives.

(4) The warning notice must—

(a) specify the reasons for the proposed objection, and
(b) state that representations may be made to the licensing authority within the prescribed period.

(5) The licensing authority must consider any representations made within the prescribed period.

(6) If the licensing authority objects to the investor's holding of the notifiable interest, it must notify the investor and the licensed body of its objection as soon as reasonably practicable.

(7) The notice must—

(a) specify the reasons for the objection, and
(b) explain the effect of Part 5 of this Schedule.

32 (1) The investor and the licensed body may before the end of the prescribed period appeal to the relevant appellate body against the objection.

(2) The relevant appellate body may dismiss the appeal, or allow the appeal and—

(a) order the licensing authority to approve the investor's holding of the notifiable interest without conditions, or subject to such conditions as may be specified in the order, or
(b) remit the matter to the licensing authority.

(3) A party to the appeal may before the end of the prescribed period appeal to the High Court on a point of law arising from the decision of the relevant appellant body, but only with the permission of the High Court.

(4) The High Court may make such order as it thinks fit.

(5) If the investor's holding of the notifiable interest is subject to conditions as a result of an order made on an appeal under this paragraph, for the purposes of this Schedule the conditions are to be treated as having been imposed under paragraph 28.

Powers of licensing authority where no change of interests

Imposition of conditions (or further conditions) on existing restricted interest

33 (1) The relevant licensing authority may impose conditions (or further conditions) on a person's holding of a restricted interest in a licensed body (or a restricted interest of a particular kind) if—

(a) it is not satisfied that the approval requirements are met in relation to the person's holding of that interest, or
(b) it is satisfied that a condition imposed under paragraph 17 or 28 or this paragraph on the person's holding of that interest has not been, or is not being, complied with.

(2) The licensing authority may act under sub-paragraph (1) only—

(a) if it considers that, if the conditions are complied with, it will be appropriate for the investor to hold the restricted interest without the approval requirements being met, and
(b) before the end of such period (beginning with the time when the licensing authority becomes aware of the matters in question) as may be prescribed.

(3) If the licensing authority proposes to impose conditions (or further conditions) on the person's holding of the restricted interest, it must give the person and the licensed body a warning notice.

(4) But the licensing authority may impose conditions (or further conditions) on the person's holding of the restricted interest without giving a warning notice if it considers it necessary or desirable to do so for the purpose of protecting any of the regulatory objectives.

(5) The warning notice must—

(a) specify the nature of the conditions proposed and the reasons for their imposition, and
(b) state that representations may be made to the licensing authority within the prescribed period.

(6) The licensing authority must consider any representations made within the prescribed period.

(7) If the licensing authority imposes conditions (or further conditions) on the person's holding of the restricted interest, it must notify the person and the licensed body as soon as reasonably practicable.

(8) The notice must—

(a) specify the reasons for the imposition of the conditions, and the time from which they are to take effect, and
(b) explain the effect of Part 5 of this Schedule.

34 (1) The person and the licensed body may before the end of the prescribed period appeal to the relevant appellate body against any or all of the conditions (or further conditions).

(2) The relevant appellate body may dismiss the appeal, or allow the appeal and—

(a) modify or quash the conditions imposed by the licensing authority under paragraph 33, or
(b) remit the matter to the licensing authority.

(3) A party to the appeal may before the end of the prescribed period appeal to the High Court on a point of law arising from the decision of the relevant appellate body, but only with the permission of the High Court.

(4) The High Court may make such order as it thinks fit.

(5) If the person's holding of the restricted interest is subject to any conditions as a result of an order made on an appeal under this paragraph, for the purposes of this Schedule those conditions are to be treated as having been imposed under paragraph 33.

Variation and cancellation of conditions

35 (1) A person whose holding of a restricted interest in a licensed body is subject to a condition imposed under paragraph 17, 28 or 33 may apply to the relevant licensing authority—

- (a) for the condition to be varied, or
- (b) for the condition to be cancelled.

(2) The licensing authority may, on its own initiative, cancel a condition imposed under one of those paragraphs.

(3) If the licensing authority varies or cancels a condition under this paragraph, it must notify the person and the licensed body as soon as reasonably practicable.

Objection to existing restricted interest

36 (1) The relevant licensing authority may object to a person's holding of a restricted interest in a licensed body (or a restricted interest of a particular kind) if—

- (a) it is not satisfied that the approval requirements are met in relation to the person's holding of that interest, or
- (b) it is satisfied that a condition imposed under paragraph 17, 28 or 33 on the person's holding of the interest has not been, or is not being, complied with.

(2) The licensing authority may act under sub-paragraph (1) only before the end of such period (beginning with the time when the licensing authority becomes aware of the matters in question) as may be prescribed.

(3) If the licensing authority proposes to object to a person's holding of the restricted interest, it must give the person and the licensed body a warning notice.

(4) But the licensing authority may object to the person's holding of the restricted interest without giving a warning notice if it considers it necessary or desirable to do so for the purpose of protecting any of the regulatory objectives.

(5) The warning notice must—

- (a) specify the reasons for the proposed objection, and
- (b) state that representations may be made to the licensing authority within the prescribed period.

(6) The licensing authority must consider any representations made within the prescribed period.

(7) If the licensing authority objects to the person's holding of the restricted interest, it must notify the person and the licensed body of its objection as soon as reasonably practicable.

(8) The notice must—

- (a) specify the reasons for the objection, and
- (b) explain the effect of Part 5 of this Schedule.

37 (1) The person and the licensed body may before the end of the prescribed period appeal to the relevant appellate body against the objection.

(2) The relevant appellate body may dismiss or allow the appeal.

(3) If the relevant appellate body allows the appeal it may also—

- (a) order the licensing authority to impose under paragraph 33 such conditions on the person's holding of the restricted interest as may be specified in the order, or
- (b) remit the matter to the licensing authority.

(4) A party to the appeal may before the end of the prescribed period appeal to the High Court on a point of law arising from the decision of the relevant appellant body, but only with the permission of the High Court.

(5) The High Court may make such order as it thinks fit.

(6) If the person's holding of the restricted interest is subject to conditions as a result of an order made on an appeal under this paragraph, for the purposes of this Schedule the conditions are to be treated as having been imposed under paragraph 33.

Initial Commencement
To be appointed: see s 211(2).
Appointment
Paras 25(2), 28(5)(b), (6), 29(1), (3), 31(4)(b), (5), 32(1), (3), 33(2)(b), (5)(b), (6), 34(1), (3), 36(2), (5)(b), (6), 37(1), (4): Appointment (in so far as relating to the exercise of powers by virtue of Pt 1, para 8 hereto): 1 January 2009: see SI 2008/3149, art 2(d)(iv).
Extent
This part of this Schedule does not extend to Scotland: see s 212(1).

PART 4
ADDITIONAL RESTRICTIONS

Power to impose share limit, voting limit etc

38 (1) Licensing rules may provide that—

(a) a non-authorised person may not have a shareholding in a licensed body, or in a parent undertaking of a licensed body, which exceeds a limit specified in the rules ("the share limit");
(b) a non-authorised person may not have an entitlement to exercise, or control the exercise of, voting rights in a licensable body, or a parent undertaking of a licensable body, which exceeds a limit specified in the rules ("the voting limit");
(c) the total proportion of shares in a licensed body, or a parent undertaking of a licensed body, held by non-authorised persons may not exceed a limit specified in the rules;
(d) the total proportion of voting rights in a licensed body, or a parent undertaking of a licensed body, which non-authorised persons are entitled to exercise or control the exercise of, may not exceed a limit specified in the rules.

(2) Rules made under any paragraph of sub-paragraph (1) in relation to a licensed body and a parent undertaking may specify different limits in relation to the licensed body and the parent undertaking.

(3) Licensing rules made under sub-paragraph (1)(a) or (b) may provide that references in those rules to a person, in relation to a person's shareholding or entitlement to exercise or control the exercise of voting rights, are to—

(a) the person,
(b) any of the person's associates, or
(c) the person and any of the person's associates taken together.

(4) In relation to a licensed body which is a partnership, for the purposes of section 34 of the Partnership Act 1890 (c 39) (dissolution by illegality) a breach of licensing rules made under sub-paragraph (1) does not make it unlawful for the business of the partnership to be carried on, or for the partners to carry it on in partnership.

Obligation to notify where share limit or voting limit exceeded

39 (1) This paragraph applies in relation to a licensed body, or a parent undertaking of a licensed body, if licensing rules made by the relevant licensing authority make the provision mentioned in paragraph 38(1)(a) or (b) in relation to the body.

(2) Any non-authorised person who acquires—

(a) a shareholding in the body which exceeds the share limit, or
(b) an entitlement to exercise, or control the exercise of, voting rights in the body which exceeds the voting limit,

must notify the body (and, if the body is a parent undertaking of a licensed body, the licensed body) and the licensing authority of the acquisition within such period, after the person becomes aware of it, as may be specified by order made by the Lord Chancellor on the recommendation of the Board.

(3) It is an offence for a person to fail to comply with a requirement imposed by sub-paragraph (2).

(4) A person who is guilty of an offence under sub-paragraph (3) is liable on summary conviction to a fine not exceeding level 5 on the standard scale.

(5) It is a defence for a person charged with an offence under sub-paragraph (3) to show that at the time of the alleged offence the person had no knowledge of the facts by virtue of which the duty to notify arose.

40 (1) This paragraph applies if a person under the duty to notify imposed by paragraph 39(2)—

(a) had no knowledge of the facts by virtue of which that duty arose, but
(b) subsequently becomes aware of those facts.

(2) The person must give the body (and, if the body is a parent undertaking of a licensed body, the licensed body) and the licensing authority the required notification within such period, after the person becomes so aware, as may be specified by order made by the Lord Chancellor on the recommendation of the Board.

(3) A person who fails to comply with the duty to notify imposed by sub-paragraph (2) is guilty of an offence.

(4) A person who is guilty of an offence under sub-paragraph (3) is liable on summary conviction to a fine not exceeding level 5 on the standard scale.

Initial Commencement
To be appointed: see s 211(2).
Extent
This part of this Schedule does not extend to Scotland: see s 212(1).

PART 5
ENFORCEMENT

Divestiture

The divestiture condition

41 (1) The divestiture condition is satisfied in relation to a non-authorised person and a licensed body if—

(a) the person holds a restricted interest in the licensed body in the circumstances mentioned in sub-paragraph (2), and
(b) the person holds that interest, in whole or in part, by virtue of the person's shareholding in a body corporate with a share capital (in this Part of this Schedule referred to as "the relevant shares").

(2) The circumstances are that the person holds the restricted interest—

(a) as a result of the person taking a step in circumstances in which that constitutes an offence under paragraph 24(1) (whether or not the person is charged with or convicted of an offence under that paragraph),
(b) in breach of conditions imposed under paragraph 17, 28, or 33, or
(c) in contravention of an objection by the licensing authority under paragraph 31 or 36.

(3) In sub-paragraph (1)(b), references to a person's shareholding are to be read in accordance with paragraph 3(3) or 4(2) (as the case may be).

42 (1) If the relevant licensing rules make the provision mentioned in paragraph 38(1)(a) or (b), the divestiture condition is also satisfied in relation to a non-authorised person and a licensed body if—

(a) the person's shareholding in the body, or a parent undertaking of the body, exceeds the share limit, and the body or parent undertaking (as the case may be) is a body corporate with a share capital, or
(b) the person's entitlement to exercise or control the exercise of voting rights in the body, or a parent undertaking of the body, exceeds the voting limit by virtue of the person holding shares in a body corporate with a share capital.

(2) In this Part of this Schedule, "excess shares" means

(a) in a case within sub-paragraph (1)(a), the number of shares by which the person's shareholding exceeds the share limit, and
(b) in a case within sub-paragraph (1)(b), the number of shares held by the person in excess of the number of shares the person could hold without the person's entitlement to exercise, or control the exercise of, voting rights exceeding the voting limit.

(3) References in this paragraph to a person's shareholding (or holding of shares) or entitlement are to be read in accordance with any applicable licensing rules made under paragraph 38(3).

Application for divestiture

43 (1) If the divestiture condition is satisfied in relation to a non-authorised person and a licensed body, the licensing authority may give the person a restriction notice under paragraph 44 and apply to the High Court for an order under paragraph 45.

(2) The licensing authority may not make an application to the High Court for an order under paragraph 45 unless—

(a) it has notified the person that it intends to do so if the divestiture condition is satisfied in relation to the person and the body at the end of the relevant period, and
(b) the relevant period has expired.

(3) The relevant period is such period (not less than the prescribed period) as may be specified in the notice.

Restriction notice

44 (1) A restriction notice is a notice directing that such of the relevant shares or excess shares (as the case may be) as are specified in the notice are, until further notice, subject to one or more of the following restrictions.

(2) The restrictions are—

(a) a transfer of (or agreement to transfer) those shares, or in the case of unissued shares a transfer of (or agreement to transfer) the right to be issued with them, is void;
(b) no voting rights are to be exercisable in respect of the shares;
(c) no further shares are to be issued in right of them or in pursuance of any offer made to their holder;
(d) except in a liquidation, no payment is to be made of any sums due from the company on the shares, whether in respect of capital or otherwise.

(3) A copy of the restriction notice must be given to the body to whose shares it relates.

(4) A restriction notice ceases to have effect—

(a) in accordance with an order of the High Court under paragraph 45(4);
(b) if no application has been made to the High Court for an order under paragraph 45 before the end of such period as may be prescribed, at the end of that period;
(c) if the licensed body ceases to be licensed by the licensing authority.

Divestiture by High Court

45 (1) If the divestiture condition is satisfied by virtue of paragraph 41 the High Court may, on the application of the licensing authority, order the sale of the appropriate number of the relevant shares.

(2) The appropriate number of the relevant shares is the number of those shares, the sale of which will result in the non-authorised person no longer holding—

(a) a restricted interest in the licensed body, or

(b) if the non-authorised person holds more than one kind of restricted interest, a restricted interest the person's holding of which is within paragraph 41(2).

(3) If the divestiture condition is satisfied by virtue of paragraph 42 the High Court may, on the application of the licensing authority, order the sale of the excess shares.

(4) If shares are for the time being subject to any restriction under paragraph 44, the court may order that they are to cease to be subject to that restriction.

(5) If the divestiture condition is satisfied by virtue of paragraph 41(2)(b) or (c), no order may be made under sub-paragraph (1) or (4)—

(a) until the end of the period within which an appeal may be made against the imposition of the conditions or the objection, or
(b) if an appeal is made, until the appeal has been determined or withdrawn.

(6) If an order has been made under sub-paragraph (1) or (3) the court may, on the application of the licensing authority, make such further order relating to the sale or transfer of the shares as it thinks fit.

(7) If shares are sold in pursuance of an order under this paragraph, the proceeds of sale, less the costs of sale, must be paid into court for the benefit of the persons beneficially interested in them.

(8) Any such person may apply to the court for the whole or part of the proceeds to be paid to the person.

Conditions

Enforcement of conditions

46 (1) If a person holds a restricted interest in a licensed body in breach of conditions imposed under paragraph 17, 28 or 33, the licensing authority may make an application to the High Court for an order under this paragraph.

(2) The licensing authority may not make such an application unless—

(a) it has notified the person that it intends to do so if the conditions are not complied with before the end of the relevant period, and
(b) the relevant period has expired.

(3) The relevant period is such period (not less than the prescribed period) as may be specified in the notice.

(4) The High Court may, on the application of the licensing authority, make such order as the court thinks fit to secure compliance with the conditions to which the person's holding of the restricted interest is subject.

(5) No order may be made under this paragraph—

(a) until the end of the period within which an appeal may be made against the imposition of the conditions, or
(b) if an appeal is made, until the appeal has been determined or withdrawn.

Records of decisions

Duty to notify Board of decisions under this Schedule

47 (1) The relevant licensing authority must notify the Board where—

(a) it has objected under paragraph 19, 31, or 36 to a person's holding of a restricted interest, or
(b) it has imposed conditions under paragraph 17, 28, or 33 on a person's holding of a restricted interest.

(2) The notification must state—

(a) the reasons for the objection or imposition of conditions, and
(b) the kind of restricted interest to which the objection or conditions related.

(3) If the licensing authority takes any action under paragraph 43 in relation to a person notified to the Board under sub-paragraph (1), it must notify the Board of that fact.

(4) If there is an appeal to the relevant appellate body against the objection or imposition of conditions, the licensing authority must notify the Board of the outcome of that appeal (and any subsequent appeal to the High Court).

(5) If the licensing authority has imposed conditions on a person's holding of a restricted interest, it must notify the Board of any decision taken by it under paragraph 35 (variation and cancellation of conditions).

(6) The licensing authority must give the person and the licensed body concerned a copy of any notification it gives the Board under this paragraph.

48 (1) A licensing authority must notify the Board where under paragraph 16, 17, 27 or 28 it approves the holding of a restricted interest in a licensed body by a person included in the list kept by the Board under paragraph 51.

(2) The notification must state—

- (a) if the approval was under paragraph 17 or 28, the conditions to which the approval was subject, and
- (b) the reasons for the licensing authority's decision to approve the person's holding of the interest.

(3) If the approval was under paragraph 17 or 28 and there is an appeal to the relevant appellate body against the imposition of conditions, the licensing authority must notify the Board of the outcome of that appeal (and any subsequent appeal to the High Court).

(4) If the approval was under paragraph 17 or 28, the licensing authority must notify the Board of any decision taken by it under paragraph 35 (variation and cancellation of conditions).

(5) The licensing authority must give the person and the licensed body concerned a copy of any notification it gives the Board under this paragraph.

Power to notify Board where share limit or voting limit breached

49 (1) This paragraph applies if the relevant licensing rules make the provision mentioned in paragraph 38(1)(a) or (b).

(2) The licensing authority may, if it considers it appropriate to do so in all the circumstances of the case, notify the Board where a non-authorised person acquires—

- (a) a shareholding in a licensed body or parent undertaking of a licensed body which exceeds the share limit, or
- (b) an entitlement to exercise, or control the exercise of, voting rights in a licensed body or parent undertaking of a licensed body which exceeds the voting limit.

(3) If the licensing authority proposes to make a notification under sub-paragraph (2), it must give the person and the licensed body a warning notice.

(4) The warning notice must—

- (a) specify the reasons for the proposed notification, and
- (b) state that representations may be made to the licensing authority within the prescribed period.

(5) The licensing authority must consider any representations made within the prescribed period.

(6) If the licensing authority notifies the Board under sub-paragraph (2), it must give the person concerned and the licensed body a copy of the notification and a notice stating the reasons for the notification.

(7) If the share limit or voting limit is breached in relation to a parent undertaking of a licensed body, references in sub-paragraphs (3) and (6) to the licensed body include the parent undertaking.

50 (1) The person concerned and the licensed body may before the end of the prescribed period appeal to the relevant appellate body against the notification.

(2) The relevant appellate body may—

- (a) dismiss the appeal, or

(b) allow the appeal and order the person's name to be removed from the list kept by the Board under paragraph 51.

(3) A party to the appeal may before the end of the prescribed period appeal to the High Court on a point of law arising from the decision of the relevant appellant body, but only with the permission of the High Court.

(4) The High Court may make such order as it thinks fit.

(5) The licensing authority must notify the Board of the outcome of any appeal under this paragraph, and give the person concerned and the licensed body a copy of the notification.

(6) If the share limit or voting limit is breached in relation to a parent undertaking of a licensed body, references in sub-paragraphs (1) and (5) to the licensed body include the parent undertaking.

Board's list of persons subject to objections and conditions

51 (1) The Board must keep a list of the persons in respect of which it receives a notification under paragraph 47(1) or 49(2).

(2) The list must record—

(a) in relation to a person notified to the Board under paragraph 47(1), the information included in the notification by virtue of paragraph 47(2) and any notification under paragraph 47(3), and
(b) in relation to any person included in the list, the information included in any notification relating to that person under paragraph 48.

(3) If the Board receives a notification under paragraph 47(4) or (5), 48(3) or (4) or 50(5) it must make such alterations to the list as it considers appropriate having regard to the decision of the licensing authority or the outcome of the appeal (which may include removing a person from the list).

(4) The Board must make the list kept by it under this paragraph available to every licensing authority.

Initial Commencement
To be appointed: see s 211(2).
Appointment
Paras 43(3), 44(4)(b), 46(3), 49(4)(b), (5), 50(1), (3): Appointment (in so far as relating to the exercise of powers by virtue of Pt 1, para 8 hereto): 1 January 2009: see SI 2008/3149, art 2(d)(iv).
Extent
This part of this Schedule does not extend to Scotland: see s 212(1).

SCHEDULE 14
LICENSING AUTHORITY'S POWERS OF INTERVENTION

Section 102

Introductory

1 (1) This Schedule applies—

(a) where, in relation to a licensed body and the relevant licensing authority, one or more of the intervention conditions is satisfied;
(b) where a licence granted to a body has expired (and has not been renewed or replaced by the relevant licensing authority).

(2) The intervention conditions are—

(a) that the licensing authority is satisfied that one or more of the terms of the licensed body's licence have not been complied with;
(b) that a person has been appointed receiver or manager of property of the licensed body;
(c) that a relevant insolvency event has occurred in relation to the licensed body;

(d) that the licensing authority has reason to suspect dishonesty on the part of any manager or employee of the licensed body in connection with—
  (i) that body's business,
  (ii) any trust of which that body is or was a trustee,
  (iii) any trust of which the manager or employee of the body is or was a trustee in that person's capacity as such a manager or employee, or
  (iv) the business of another body in which the manager or employee is or was a manager or employee, or the practice (or former practice) of the manager or employee;

(e) that the licensing authority is satisfied that there has been undue delay—
  (i) on the part of the licensed body in connection with any matter in which it is or was acting for a client or with any trust of which it is or was a trustee, or
  (ii) on the part of a person who is or was a manager or employee of the licensed body in connection with any trust of which that person is or was a trustee in that person's capacity as such a manager or employee,

and the notice conditions are satisfied;

(f) that the licensing authority is satisfied that it is necessary to exercise the powers conferred by this Schedule (or any of them) in relation to a licensed body to protect—
  (i) the interests of clients (or former or potential clients) of the licensed body,
  (ii) the interests of the beneficiaries of any trust of which the licensed body is or was a trustee, or
  (iii) the interests of the beneficiaries of any trust of which a person who is or was a manager or employee of the licensed body is or was a trustee in that person's capacity as such a manager or employee.

(3) For the purposes of sub-paragraph (2) a relevant insolvency event occurs in relation to a licensed body if—

(a) a resolution for a voluntary winding-up of the body is passed without a declaration of solvency under section 89 of the Insolvency Act 1986 (c 45);
(b) the body enters administration within the meaning of paragraph 1(2)(b) of Schedule B1 to that Act;
(c) an administrative receiver within the meaning of section 251 of that Act is appointed;
(d) a meeting of creditors is held in relation to the body under section 95 of that Act (creditors' meeting which has the effect of converting a members' voluntary winding up into a creditors' voluntary winding up);
(e) an order for the winding up of the body is made.

(4) The notice conditions referred to in sub-paragraph (2)(e) are—

(a) that the licensing authority has given the licensed body a notice inviting it to give an explanation within such period (of not less than 8 days) following the giving of the notice as may be specified in it;
(b) that the licensed body has failed within that period to give an explanation which the licensing authority regards as satisfactory; and
(c) that the licensing authority gives notice of the failure to the licensed body and (at the same time or later) notice that this Schedule applies in its case by virtue of sub-paragraph (2)(e).

(5) Where this Schedule applies in relation to a licensed body by virtue of sub-paragraph (1)(a) it continues to apply after the body's licence has been revoked or has otherwise ceased to have effect.

(6) For the purposes of this Schedule "licensed body" includes—

(a) a body whose licence is suspended;
(b) a body to whom this Schedule continues to apply by virtue of sub-paragraph (5);
(c) except in this paragraph, a body whose licence has ceased to have effect as mentioned in sub-paragraph (1)(b).

Money: prohibition on payment

2 (1) The licensing authority may apply to the High Court for an order under sub-paragraph (2), and the High Court may make the order if it thinks fit.

(2) The order is that a person holding money on behalf of the licensed body may not make any payment of the money, except with the leave of the court.

(3) An order under sub-paragraph (2) may take effect in relation to a person—

(a) whether or not the person is named in the order;
(b) however the money is held;
(c) whether the money was received before or after the order was made.

(4) But an order under sub-paragraph (2) does not take effect in relation to a person until the licensing authority—

(a) has given the person a copy of the order, and
(b) (in the case of a bank or other financial institution) has indicated the branches at which it believes money to which the order relates is held.

(5) A person is not to be treated as having disobeyed an order under sub-paragraph (2) by making a payment of money if the court is satisfied that the person—

(a) exercised due diligence to ascertain whether it was money to which the order related, and
(b) failed to ascertain that the order related to it.

Money etc: vesting in licensing authority

3 (1) The sums of money to which this paragraph applies, and the right to recover or receive them, vest in the licensing authority if the licensing authority decides that they should do so.

(2) This paragraph applies to all sums of money held by or on behalf of the licensed body in connection with—

(a) its activities as a licensed body,
(b) any trust of which it is or was a trustee, or
(c) any trust of which a person who is or was a manager or employee of the licensed body is or was a trustee in that person's capacity as such a manager or employee.

(3) Sub-paragraph (1) applies whether the sums were received by the person holding them before or after the licensing authority's decision.

(4) Those sums and that right are held by the licensing authority—

(a) on trust to exercise the powers conferred by this Schedule in relation to them, and
(b) subject to that and to rules under paragraph 6, on trust for the persons beneficially entitled.

(5) The licensing authority must give the licensed body, and any other person in possession of sums of money to which this paragraph applies—

(a) a copy of the licensing authority's decision, and
(b) a notice prohibiting the payment out of those sums.

(6) A person to whom a notice under sub-paragraph (5) is given may apply to the High Court for an order directing the licensing authority to withdraw the notice.

(7) An application under sub-paragraph (6) must be made within 8 days of the licensing authority giving the person notice under sub-paragraph (5).

(8) The person must give not less than 48 hours notice of any application under sub-paragraph (6)—

(a) to the licensing authority, and
(b) if the notice under sub-paragraph (5) gives the name of a solicitor instructed by the licensing authority, to that solicitor.

(9) If the court makes the order, it may make any other order it thinks fit with respect to the matter.

(10) It is an offence for a person to whom a notice has been given under sub-paragraph (5) to pay out sums of money at a time when such payment is prohibited by the notice.

(11) A person who is guilty of an offence under sub-paragraph (10) is liable on summary conviction to a fine not exceeding level 3 on the standard scale.

4 (1) Any rights to which this paragraph applies shall vest in the licensing authority if the licensing authority decides that they should do so.

(2) This paragraph applies to any right to recover or receive debts due to the licensed body in connection with its business.

(3) Any sums recovered by the licensing authority by virtue of the exercise of rights vested under sub-paragraph (1) vest in the licensing authority and are held by it—

- (a) on trust to exercise the powers conferred by this Schedule in relation to them, and
- (b) subject to that and to rules under paragraph 6, on trust for the persons beneficially entitled.

(4) The licensing authority must give the licensed body, and any other person who owes a debt to which the order applies a copy of the licensing authority's decision.

5 (1) If the licensing authority takes possession of any sum of money to which paragraph 3 applies or by virtue of paragraph 4, it must pay it into a special account in the name of the licensing authority or a person nominated on its behalf.

(2) A person nominated under sub-paragraph (1) holds that sum—

- (a) on trust to permit the licensing authority to exercise the powers conferred by this Schedule in relation to it, and
- (b) subject to that and rules under paragraph 6, on trust for the persons beneficially entitled.

(3) A bank or other financial institution at which a special account is kept is under no obligation to ascertain whether it is being dealt with properly.

6 (1) The licensing authority may make rules governing its treatment of sums vested in it under paragraph 3 or 4(3).

(2) The rules may, in particular, make provision in respect of cases where the licensing authority, having taken such steps to do so as are reasonable in all the circumstances of the case, is unable to trace the person or persons beneficially entitled to any sum vested in the licensing authority under paragraph 3 or 4(3) (including provision which requires amounts to be paid into or out of any fund maintained by the licensing authority in connection with its compensation arrangements).

Money: information

7 (1) The licensing authority may apply to the High Court for an order requiring a person to give the licensing authority—

- (a) information about any money held by the person on behalf of the licensed body, and the accounts in which it is held, or
- (b) information relevant to identifying any money held by the licensed body or by another person on its behalf.

(2) The High Court may make the order if it is satisfied that there is reason to suspect—

- (a) in a case within sub-paragraph (1)(a), that the person holds money on behalf of the licensed body, and
- (b) in a case within sub-paragraph (1)(b), that the person has the information in question.

(3) This paragraph is without prejudice to paragraphs 2 to 6.

Notice to produce or deliver documents

8 (1) The licensing authority may give notice to the licensed body requiring it to produce or deliver all documents in its possession or under its control in connection with—

- (a) its activities as a licensed body,
- (b) any trust of which it is or was a trustee, or
- (c) any trust of which a person who is or was a manager or employee of the licensed body is or was a trustee in that person's capacity as such a manager or employee.

(2) The notice may require the documents to be produced—

- (a) to any person appointed by the licensing authority;
- (b) at a time and place to be fixed by the licensing authority.

(3) The person appointed by the licensing authority may take possession of any such documents on behalf of the licensing authority.

(4) It is an offence for a person having possession of such documents to refuse, neglect or otherwise fail to comply with a notice under sub-paragraph (1).

(5) Sub-paragraph (4) does not apply where an application has been made to the High Court under paragraph 9(1)(a).

(6) A person who is guilty of an offence under sub-paragraph (4) is liable on summary conviction to a fine not exceeding level 3 on the standard scale.

Order to produce or deliver documents

9 (1) The High Court may, on the application of the licensing authority, make an order for production or delivery—

- (a) in relation to a person required to produce documents under paragraph 8 and the documents the person was required to produce;
- (b) if it is satisfied that there is reason to suspect that documents in relation to which the powers in paragraph 8 are exercisable have come into the possession or under the control of some person other than the licensed body, in relation to that person and those documents.

(2) An order for production or delivery is an order—

- (a) requiring a person to produce or deliver documents to any person appointed by the licensing authority, at a time and place specified in the order, and
- (b) authorising the appointed person to take possession of the documents on behalf of the licensing authority.

(3) The court may, on the application of the licensing authority, authorise a person appointed by the licensing authority to enter any premises (using such force as is reasonably necessary) to search for and take possession of—

- (a) any documents to which an order for production or delivery relates;
- (b) any property—
  - (i) in the possession of or under the control of the licensed body, or
  - (ii) in the case of an order under sub-paragraph (1)(b), which was in the possession or under the control of that body and has come into the possession or under the control of the person in respect of whom the order is made,

  which the licensing authority reasonably requires for the purpose of accessing information contained in any such documents,

and to use property obtained under paragraph (b) for that purpose.

(4) It may do so on making the order for production or delivery, or at any later time.

Taking possession of documents etc under notice or order

10 (1) This paragraph applies where the licensing authority takes possession of documents or any other property under paragraph 8 or 9.

(2) On taking possession, it must give a notice to—

- (a) the licensed body, and
- (b) any other person from whom the documents or property were received or from whose possession they were taken.

(3) The notice must state that possession has been taken and specify the date on which possession was taken.

(4) A person to whom a notice under sub-paragraph (2) is given may apply to the High Court for an order directing the licensing authority to deliver the documents or other property to such person as the applicant requires.

(5) An application under sub-paragraph (4) must be made within 8 days of the licensing authority giving the person notice under sub-paragraph (2).

(6) The person must give not less than 48 hours notice of the application—

(a) to the licensing authority, and
(b) if the notice under sub-paragraph (2) gives the name of a solicitor instructed by the licensing authority, to that solicitor.

(7) The court may make any order it thinks fit.

Mail and other forms of communication

11 (1) The High Court, on the application of the licensing authority, may from time to time make a communications redirection order.

(2) A communications redirection order is an order that specified communications to the licensed body are to be directed, in accordance with the order, to the licensing authority or any person appointed by the licensing authority.

(3) For the purposes of this paragraph—

(a) "specified communications" means communications of such description as are specified in the order;
(b) the descriptions of communications which may be so specified include—
  (i) communications in the form of a postal packet;
  (ii) electronic communications;
  (iii) communications by telephone.

(4) A communications redirection order has effect for such time not exceeding 18 months as is specified in the order.

(5) Where a communications redirection order has effect, the licensing authority or the person appointed by the licensing authority may take possession or receipt of the communications redirected in accordance with the order.

(6) Where a communications redirection order is made the licensing authority must pay to the designated payee the like charges (if any) as would have been payable for the redirection of the communications to which the order relates if the addressee—

(a) had permanently ceased to occupy or use the premises or other destination of the communications, and
(b) had applied to the designated payee to redirect the communications as mentioned in the order.

(7) For this purpose "the designated payee" means—

(a) in the case of an order relating to postal packets, the postal operator concerned, and
(b) in any other case, the person specified in the order as the designated payee.

(8) The High Court may, on the application of the licensing authority, authorise the licensing authority, or a person appointed by it, to take such steps as may be specified in the order in relation to any website purporting to be or have been maintained by or on behalf of the licensed body, if the High Court is satisfied that the taking of those steps is necessary to protect the public interest or the interests of clients (or potential or former clients) of the licensed body.

(9) In this paragraph "postal operator" and "postal packet" have the meaning given by section 125(1) of the Postal Services Act 2000 (c 26).

(10) This paragraph does not apply where the powers conferred by this Part of this Schedule are exercisable by virtue of paragraph 1(2)(e).

Use of documents in licensing authority's possession

12 (1) The licensing authority may apply to the High Court for an order as to the disposal or destruction of any document or other property in its possession by virtue of paragraph 8, 9 or 11.

(2) The court may make any order it thinks fit.

13 (1) The licensing authority may take copies of or extracts from any documents in its possession by virtue of paragraph 8, 9 or 11.

(2) If the licensing authority proposes to deliver such documents to any person, it may make the delivery conditional on the person giving a reasonable undertaking to supply copies or extracts to the licensing authority.

(3) Sub-paragraphs (1) and (2) are subject to any order made by the court under paragraph 10 or 12.

Trusts

14 (1) If the licensed body is a trustee of any trust, the licensing authority may apply to the High Court for an order for the appointment of a new trustee in substitution for it.

(2) If a person who is a manager or employee of the licensed body is a trustee of any trust in that person's capacity as such a manager or employee, the licensing authority may apply to the High Court for an order for the appointment of a new trustee in substitution for that person.

(3) The Trustee Act 1925 (c 19) has effect in relation to an appointment of a new trustee under this paragraph as it has effect in relation to an appointment under section 41 of that Act.

General powers of licensing authority

15 The powers conferred by this Schedule in relation to sums of money, documents or other property may be exercised despite any lien on them or right to their possession.

16 The licensing authority may do all things which are reasonably necessary to facilitate the exercise of its powers under this Schedule.

Licensing authority's costs

17 (1) Any costs incurred by the licensing authority for the purposes of this Schedule (including the costs of any person exercising powers under this Schedule on behalf of the licensing authority)—

- (a) are to be paid by the licensed body, and
- (b) may be recovered from the licensed body as a debt owing to the licensing authority.

(2) Sub-paragraph (1) is subject to any order for payment of costs that may be made on an application to the court under this Schedule.

18 (1) The High Court, on the application of the licensing authority, may order a liable party to pay a specified proportion of the costs mentioned in paragraph 17.

(2) For this purpose a "liable party" means—

- (a) if the licensed body is a partnership, any former partner in the licensed body,
- (b) in any other case, any manager or former manager of the licensed body.

(3) The High Court may make an order under this paragraph in respect of a liable party only if it is satisfied that the conduct (or any part of the conduct) by reason of which this Schedule applies was conduct carried on with the consent or connivance of, or was attributable to any neglect on the part of, the liable party.

(4) In this paragraph "specified" means specified in the order made by the High Court.

Initial Commencement
To be appointed: see s 211(2).
Extent
This Schedule does not extend to Scotland: see s 212(1).

SCHEDULE 15
THE OFFICE FOR LEGAL COMPLAINTS

Section 114

Membership

1 (1) The OLC is to consist of the following members—

- (a) a chairman appointed by the Board with the approval of the Lord Chancellor, and
- (b) at least 6, but not more than 8, other persons appointed by the Board after consultation with the chairman.

(2) The Lord Chancellor may by order amend sub-paragraph (1) by substituting, for the limit on the maximum number of persons for the time being specified in paragraph (b) of that sub-paragraph, a different limit.

2 (1) In appointing members of the OLC, the Board must ensure that a majority of the members of the OLC are lay persons.

(2) The chairman must be a lay person.

(3) In this Schedule a reference to a "lay person" is a reference to a person who has never been—

(a) an authorised person in relation to an activity which is a reserved legal activity,
(b) an advocate in Scotland,
(c) a solicitor in Scotland,
(d) a member of the Bar of Northern Ireland, or
(e) a solicitor of the Court of Judicature of Northern Ireland.

(4) For the purposes of sub-paragraph (3), a person is deemed to have been an authorised person in relation to an activity which is a reserved legal activity if that person has before the appointed day been—

(a) a barrister,
(b) a solicitor,
(c) a public notary,
(d) a licensed conveyancer,
(e) granted a certificate issued by the Institute of Legal Executives authorising the person to practise as a legal executive,
(f) a registered patent attorney, within the meaning given by section 275(1) of the Copyright, Designs and Patents Act 1988 (c 48),
(g) a registered trade mark attorney, within the meaning of the Trade Marks Act 1994 (c 26), or
(h) granted a right of audience or right to conduct litigation in relation to any proceedings by virtue of section 27(2)(a) or section 28(2)(a) of the Courts and Legal Services Act 1990 (c 41) (rights of audience and rights to conduct litigation).

(5) For the purpose of sub-paragraph (4)—

"appointed day" means the day appointed for the coming into force of section 13;
"licensed conveyancer" has the meaning given by section 11(2) of the Administration of Justice Act 1985 (c 61).

3 (1) An ombudsman may be a member (but not chairman) of the OLC

(2) In appointing members of the OLC, the Board must ensure that a majority of the members of the OLC are not ombudsmen.

4 In appointing members of the OLC, the Board must have regard to the desirability of securing that the OLC includes members who (between them) have experience in or knowledge of—

(a) the handling of complaints,
(b) the provision of legal services,
(c) legal education and legal training,
(d) consumer affairs,
(e) civil or criminal proceedings and the working of the courts,
(f) the maintenance of the professional standards of persons who provide legal services,
(g) non-commercial legal services,
(h) the differing needs of consumers, and
(i) the provision of claims management services (within the meaning of Part 2 of the Compensation Act 2006 (c 29)).

Terms of appointment and tenure of members

5 A member of the OLC is to hold and vacate office in accordance with the terms and conditions of the member's appointment (subject to this Schedule).

6 (1) A member of the OLC must be appointed for a fixed period.

(2) The period for which a member is appointed must not exceed 5 years.

(3) A person who has held office as a member may be re-appointed once only, for a further period (whether consecutive or not) not exceeding 5 years.

7 If a member of the OLC who is a lay person becomes a person within paragraph (a) to (e) of paragraph 2(3), that person ceases to be a member of the OLC

8 (1) A member may at any time—

(a) resign from office by giving notice to the Board;
(b) be removed from office by the Board.

(2) The Board may not under sub-paragraph (1)(b) remove a member (including the chairman) from office unless the Board is satisfied that the member—

(a) has failed without reasonable excuse to discharge the functions of the office for a continuous period of at least 6 months,
(b) has been convicted of an offence,
(c) is an undischarged bankrupt, or
(d) is otherwise unfit to hold the office or unable to discharge its functions.

(3) The chairman may be removed from office under sub-paragraph (1)(b) only with the consent of the Lord Chancellor.

(4) The Board must consult the chairman before removing a member (other than the chairman) under sub-paragraph (1)(b).

(5) The Board may not remove an ordinary member on the ground mentioned in paragraph (a) of sub-paragraph (2) more than 3 months after the end of the period mentioned in that paragraph.

9 The chairman ceases to be chairman upon ceasing to be a member of the OLC

Remuneration etc of members

10 The chairman and other members of the OLC are to be paid by the Board in accordance with provision made by or under their terms of appointment.

11 The terms of appointment of the chairman or any other member may provide for the Board to pay, or make payments towards the provision of, a pension, allowance or gratuity to or in respect of that person.

12 If the Board thinks there are circumstances that make it right for a person ceasing to hold office as chairman or another member to receive compensation, the OLC may pay that person such compensation as the Board may determine.

Staff

13 The OLC may appoint such staff as it considers appropriate to assist in the performance of its functions.

14 Staff appointed under paragraph 13 are to be—

(a) appointed on terms and conditions determined by the OLC, and
(b) paid by the OLC in accordance with provision made by or under the terms of appointment.

15 A member of staff appointed under paragraph 13 may be a member (but not chairman) of the OLC

16 The terms and conditions on which an ombudsman, or any member of staff appointed under paragraph 13, is appointed may provide for the OLC to pay, or make payments towards the provision of, a pension, allowance or gratuity to or in respect of that person.

17 The OLC may pay compensation for loss of employment to or in respect of an ombudsman (or former ombudsman), or a member (or former member) of staff appointed under paragraph 13.

Arrangements for assistance

18 (1) The OLC may make arrangements with such persons as it considers appropriate for assistance to be provided to it or to an ombudsman.

(2) Arrangements may include the paying of fees to such persons.

(3) The persons with whom the OLC may make arrangements include approved regulators; and the arrangements it may make include arrangements for assistance to be provided to an ombudsman in relation to the investigation and consideration of a complaint.

Committees

19 (1) The OLC may establish committees.

(2) Any committee so established may establish sub-committees.

(3) Only members of the OLC may be members of a committee or sub-committee.

(4) A majority of the members of a committee or sub-committee must be lay persons.

Proceedings

20 (1) The OLC may regulate its own procedure, and the procedure of its committees and sub-committees, including quorum.

(2) But the quorum of a committee or sub-committee must not be less than 3.

(3) The OLC must publish any rules of procedure made under this paragraph.

(4) This paragraph is without prejudice to any other power the OLC has under this Act to make rules.

21 The validity of any act of the OLC is not affected—

(a) by a vacancy in the office of chairman or amongst the other members, or
(b) by a defect in the appointment or any disqualification of a person as chairman or another member of the OLC

Delegation of functions

22 (1) The OLC may authorise—

(a) the chairman or any other member of the OLC,
(b) a committee or sub-committee of the OLC,
(c) an ombudsman, or
(d) a member of the OLC's staff appointed under paragraph 13,

to exercise, on behalf of the OLC, such of its functions, in such circumstances, as it may determine.

(2) Sub-paragraph (1) does not apply to—

(a) the OLC's functions under section 118(1) (annual report),
(b) the OLC's functions under section 122 (appointment of Chief Ombudsman and assistant ombudsmen),
(c) the OLC's functions under paragraph 20 or 23 of this Schedule, or
(d) any power or duty the OLC has to make rules under this Part of this Act.

(3) A committee may delegate functions (including functions delegated to the committee) to—

(a) a sub-committee,
(b) the chairman or any other member of the OLC,
(c) an ombudsman, or
(d) a member of the OLC's staff appointed under paragraph 13.

Budget

23 (1) The OLC must, before the start of each financial year, adopt an annual budget which has been approved by the Board.

(2) The OLC may, with the approval of the Board, vary the budget for a financial year at any time after its adoption.

(3) The annual budget must include an indication of—

(a) the distribution of resources deployed in the operation of the ombudsman scheme, and
(b) the amounts of income of the OLC arising or expected to arise from the operation of the scheme.

Land

24 (1) During the initial 5 year period, the OLC must not acquire or dispose of an interest in land, except with the approval of the Lord Chancellor.

(2) The initial 5 year period is the period of 5 years beginning with the day on which the appointment of the first Interim Chief Executive under paragraph 10 of Schedule 22 takes effect or the day on which the first appointment of a member of the OLC takes effect, whichever first occurs.

Borrowing

25 (1) The OLC must not borrow money, except—

(a) with the consent of the Board, or
(b) in accordance with a general authorisation given by the Board.

(2) The Board may not consent or give a general authorisation for the purposes of sub-paragraph (1), except with the consent of the Lord Chancellor.

Accounts

26 (1) The OLC must—

(a) keep proper accounts and proper records in relation to the accounts, and
(b) prepare in respect of each financial year a statement of accounts.

(2) Each statement of accounts must comply with any directions given by the Lord Chancellor, with the approval of the Treasury, as to—

(a) the information to be contained in it and the manner in which it is to be presented;
(b) the methods and principles according to which the statement is to be prepared;
(c) the additional information (if any) which is to be provided for the information of Parliament.

(3) The OLC must give a copy of each statement of accounts to the Board before the end of the month of August next following the financial year to which the statement relates.

(4) The Board must give a copy of each statement received under sub-paragraph (3)—

(a) to the Lord Chancellor, and
(b) to the Comptroller and Auditor General.

(5) The Comptroller and Auditor General must—

(a) examine, certify and report on each statement of accounts which is received under sub-paragraph (4), and
(b) give a copy of the Comptroller and Auditor General's report to the Lord Chancellor.

(6) In respect of each financial year, the Lord Chancellor must lay before Parliament a document consisting of—

(a) a copy of the statement of accounts for that year, and
(b) a copy of the Comptroller and Auditor General's report on that statement.

(7) "Financial year" means—

(a) the period beginning with the day on which the OLC is established and ending with the next following 31 March, and
(b) each successive period of 12 months.

Status

27 (1) The OLC is not to be regarded—

(a) as the servant or agent of the Crown, or
(b) as enjoying any status, immunity or privilege of the Crown.

(2) Accordingly—

(a) the OLC's property is not to be regarded as property of or held on behalf of the Crown, and
(b) the staff appointed under paragraph 13 are not to be regarded as servants or agents of the Crown or as enjoying any status, immunity or privilege of the Crown.

Application of seal and proof of instruments

28 The application of the seal of the OLC is to be authenticated by the signature of any member of the OLC, or of its staff, who has been authorised (whether generally or specifically) by the OLC for the purpose.

29 Any contract or instrument which, if entered into or executed by an individual, would not need to be under seal, may be entered into or executed on behalf of the OLC by any person who has been authorised (whether generally or specifically) by the OLC for the purpose.

30 A document purporting to be duly executed under the seal of the OLC, or signed on its behalf—

(a) is to be received in evidence, and
(b) is to be taken to be executed or signed in that way, unless the contrary is proved.

Disqualification

31 (1) In Part 2 of Schedule 1 to the House of Commons Disqualification Act 1975 (c 24) (bodies of which all members are disqualified) at the appropriate place insert—

"The Office for Legal Complaints."

(2) In Part 3 of that Schedule (other disqualifying offices) at the appropriate place insert—

"The Chief Ombudsman or an assistant ombudsman appointed under section 122 of the Legal Services Act 2007 (Chief Ombudsman and assistant ombudsmen appointed for the purposes of the ombudsman scheme)."

(3) In Part 2 of Schedule 1 to the Northern Ireland Assembly Disqualification Act 1975 (c 25) (bodies of which all members are disqualified) at the appropriate place insert—

"The Office for Legal Complaints."

(4) In Part 3 of that Schedule (other disqualifying offices) at the appropriate place insert—

"The Chief Ombudsman or an assistant ombudsman appointed under section 122 of the Legal Services Act 2007 (Chief Ombudsman and assistant ombudsmen appointed for the purposes of the ombudsman scheme)."

Freedom of information

32 In Part 6 of Schedule 1 to the Freedom of Information Act 2000 (c 36) (other public bodies and offices which are public authorities) at the appropriate place insert—

"The Office for Legal Complaints."

Public records

33 In Schedule 1 to the Public Records Act 1958 (c 51) (definition of public records) at the appropriate place in Part 2 of the Table at the end of paragraph 3 insert—

"The Office for Legal Complaints."

Exemption from liability in damages

34 (1) This paragraph applies to—

(a) the OLC,
(b) a member of the OLC,
(c) an ombudsman, and
(d) a member of the OLC's staff appointed under paragraph 13.

(2) A person to whom this paragraph applies is not liable in damages for anything done or omitted in the exercise or purported exercise of the functions conferred on the person concerned by or by virtue of this or any other enactment.

(3) But sub-paragraph (2) does not apply—

(a) if it is shown that the act or omission was in bad faith, or
(b) so as to prevent an award of damages made in respect of an act or omission on the ground that the act or omission was unlawful as a result of section 6(1) of the Human Rights Act 1998 (c 42).

Initial Commencement
To be appointed: see s 211(2).
Appointment
Paras 1–12: Appointment: 7 March 2008: see SI 2008/222, art 2(i); for transitional provisions see art 8 thereof.
Paras 13–34: Appointment: 1 January 2009: see SI 2008/3149, art 2(e)(ii).
Extent
This Schedule does not extend to Scotland: see s 212(1).

SCHEDULE 16
THE LAW SOCIETY, SOLICITORS, RECOGNISED BODIES AND FOREIGN LAWYERS

Section 177

PART 1
THE SOLICITORS ACT 1974 (C 47)

1 The Solicitors Act 1974 is amended in accordance with this Part of this Schedule.

2 In section 1A (practising certificates: employed solicitors)—

(a) omit "or" at the end of paragraph (b),
(b) in paragraph (c) omit "by the Council of the Law Society", and
(c) at the end of that paragraph insert
"or
(d) by any other person who, for the purposes of the Legal Services Act 2007, is an authorised person in relation to an activity which is a reserved legal activity (within the meaning of that Act)."

3 After section 1A insert—

"1B Restriction on practice as sole solicitor

(1) Rules under section 31 (rules as to professional practice etc) must provide that a solicitor may not practise as a sole solicitor unless he has in force—

(a) a practising certificate, and
(b) an endorsement of that certificate by the Society authorising him to practise as a sole solicitor (a "sole solicitor endorsement").

(2) The rules may provide that, for the purposes of the rules and this Act, a solicitor is not to be regarded as practising as a sole solicitor in such circumstances as may be prescribed by the rules.

(3) The rules must prescribe the circumstances in which a solicitor may be regarded by the Society as suitable to be authorised to practise as a sole solicitor."

4 In section 2 (training regulations)—

(a) in subsection (1) omit ", with the concurrence of the Secretary of State, the Lord Chief Justice and the Master of the Rolls,",
(b) in subsection (3)(a)—

(i) in sub-paragraph (i) omit ", whether by service under articles or otherwise,",
(ii) in sub-paragraph (v) omit "articles may be discharged or", and
(iii) in that sub-paragraph after "be" (in the second place) insert "started or", and
(c) omit subsections (4) and (5).

5 In section 3 (admission as solicitor), in subsection (2)—

(a) for "Master of the Rolls" (in each place) substitute "Society", and
(b) for "his" substitute "its".

6 In section 6 (keeping of the roll) omit subsections (2) to (4).

7 In section 7 (entry of name and restoration of name struck off)—

(a) for paragraph (a) substitute—
"(a) of written evidence of admission of any person as a solicitor by the Society,", and
(b) for "Council" substitute "Society".

8 (1) Section 8 (removal or restoration of name at solicitor's request) is amended as follows.

(2) In subsection (2) for "Council" substitute "Society".

(3) In subsection (4) for "Master of the Rolls" substitute "High Court".

(4) After that subsection insert—

"(4A) In relation to an appeal under subsection (4) the High Court may make such order as it thinks fit as to payment of costs.

(4B) The decision of the High Court on an appeal under subsection (4) shall be final."

(5) Omit subsection (5).

9 For sections 9 and 10 (applications for and issue of practising certificates) substitute—

"9 Applications for practising certificates

(1) A person whose name is on the roll may apply to the Society to be issued with a practising certificate.

(2) An application under this section may include an application for a sole solicitor endorsement.

(3) An application under this section must be—

(a) made in accordance with regulations under section 28, and
(b) accompanied by the appropriate fee.

(4) "The appropriate fee", in relation to an application, means—

(a) any fee payable under subsection (1) of section 11 in respect of the practising certificate applied for, and
(b) any additional fee payable under subsection (4) of that section in respect of the application.

10 The issue of practising certificates

(1) Subject to the following provisions of this section, where an application is made in accordance with section 9, the Society must issue a practising certificate to the applicant if it is satisfied that the applicant—

(a) is not suspended from practice, and
(b) is complying with any prescribed requirements imposed on the applicant.

(2) A practising certificate issued to an applicant of a prescribed description must be issued subject to any conditions prescribed in relation to applicants of that description.

(3) In such circumstances as may be prescribed, the Society must, if it considers it is in the public interest to do so—

(a) refuse to issue a practising certificate under this section, or
(b) where it decides to issue a practising certificate, issue it subject to one or more conditions.

(4) The conditions which may be imposed include—

(a) conditions requiring the person to whom the certificate is issued to take specified steps that will, in the opinion of the Society, be conducive to the carrying on by that person of an efficient practice as a solicitor (including, if the certificate has a sole solicitor endorsement, an efficient practice as a sole solicitor);

(b) conditions which prohibit that person from taking any specified steps, except with the approval of the Society.

(5) In this section—

"prescribed" means prescribed by regulations under section 28;

"specified", in relation to a condition imposed on a practising certificate, means specified in the condition."

10 After section 10 (as inserted by paragraph 9) insert—

"10A Register of holders of practising certificates

(1) The Society must keep a register of all solicitors who hold practising certificates.

(2) The register must contain—

(a) the full name of each solicitor who holds a practising certificate,

(b) in relation to each solicitor who holds a practising certificate, a statement as to whether there is in force a sole solicitor endorsement, and

(c) such other information as may be specified in regulations under section 28(1)(d)."

11 For section 11 (fee payable on issue of practising certificate) substitute—

"11 Fee payable on issue of practising certificates

(1) Before a practising certificate is issued, there must be paid to the Society in respect of the certificate a fee of such amount as the Society may from time to time determine.

(2) Different fees may be specified for different categories of applicant and in respect of different circumstances.

(3) Subsection (4) applies where a solicitor makes an application for a practising certificate if—

(a) the solicitor has failed to deliver an accountant's report required by rules under section 34(1) by such time or in such circumstances as may be prescribed by those rules, and

(b) a practising certificate has not been issued by the Society to the solicitor since the Society became aware of the failure.

(4) Where this subsection applies, the solicitor's application must be accompanied by an additional fee of such amount as the Society from time to time determines."

12 Omit section 12 (discretion of Society with respect to issue of practising certificates in special cases).

13 Omit section 12A (additional fee payable by certain solicitors on applying for practising certificates).

14 For section 13 (appeals in connection with issue of practising certificates) substitute—

"13 Appeals etc in connection with the issue of practising certificates

(1) A person who makes an application under section 9 may appeal to the High Court against—

(a) a decision to refuse the application for a practising certificate,

(b) if the application included an application for a sole solicitor endorsement, a decision to refuse the application for the endorsement, or

(c) a decision to impose a condition on a practising certificate issued in consequence of the application.

(2) A person who holds a practising certificate subject to a condition within section 10(4)(b) may appeal to the High Court against any decision by the Society to refuse to approve the taking of any step for the purposes of that condition.

(3) The Society may make rules which provide, as respects any application under section 9 that is neither granted nor refused by the Society within such period as may be specified in the rules, for enabling an appeal to be brought under this section in relation to the application as if it had been refused by the Society.

(4) On an appeal under subsection (1), the High Court may—

(a) affirm the decision of the Society,
(b) direct the Society to make a sole solicitor endorsement on the applicant's practising certificate and to issue that certificate subject to such conditions (if any) as the High Court may think fit,
(c) direct the Society to issue a certificate to the applicant free from conditions or subject to such conditions as the High Court may think fit,
(d) direct the Society not to issue a certificate,
(e) if a certificate has been issued, by order suspend it,
(f) if the certificate has been endorsed with a sole solicitor endorsement, by order suspend the endorsement, or
(g) make such other order as the High Court thinks fit.

(5) On an appeal under subsection (2), the High Court may—

(a) affirm the decision of the Society,
(b) direct the Society to approve the taking of one or more steps for the purposes of a condition within section 10(4)(b), or
(c) make such other order as the High Court thinks fit.

(6) In relation to an appeal under this section the High Court may make such order as it thinks fit as to payment of costs.

(7) The decision of the High Court on an appeal under subsection (1) or (2) shall be final."

15 After section 13 insert—

"13ZA Application to practise as sole practitioner while practising certificate in force

(1) A solicitor whose practising certificate for the time being in force (his "current certificate") does not have a sole solicitor endorsement, may apply to the Society for such an endorsement.

(2) For the purposes of subsection (1) a practising certificate with a sole solicitor endorsement which is suspended is to be treated as having such an endorsement.

(3) A solicitor may not apply under subsection (1) if he is suspended from practice as a sole solicitor.

(4) An application must be—

(a) made in accordance with regulations under section 28, and
(b) accompanied by any fee payable under section 13ZB in respect of the endorsement applied for.

(5) Where a sole solicitor endorsement is granted to an applicant of a prescribed description, the applicant's practising certificate shall have effect subject to any conditions prescribed in relation to applicants of that description.

"Prescribed" means prescribed by regulations under section 28(3B)(f).

(6) A person who makes an application under this section may appeal to the High Court against—

(a) a decision to refuse the application, or
(b) a decision to impose a condition on a practising certificate in accordance with subsection (5).

(7) The Society may by rules make provision, as respects any application under this section that is neither granted nor refused by the Society within such period as may be specified in the rules, for enabling an appeal to be brought under this section in relation to the application as if it had been refused by the Society.

(8) On an appeal under this section the High Court may—

(a) affirm the decision of the Society,

(b) direct the Society to grant a sole solicitor endorsement,
(c) direct that the applicant's practising certificate is to have effect subject to such conditions (if any) as the High Court thinks fit, or
(d) make such other order as the High Court thinks fit.

(9) In relation to an appeal under this section the High Court may make such order as it thinks fit as to payment of costs.

(10) The decision of the High Court on an appeal under this section shall be final.

13ZB Fee payable on making of sole solicitor endorsement

(1) Before a sole solicitor endorsement is granted under section 13ZA, there must be paid to the Society in respect of the endorsement a fee of such amount as the Society may from time to time determine.

(2) Different fees may be specified for different categories of applicant and in different circumstances.

(3) If a fee payable under this section would not otherwise be a practising fee for the purposes of section 51 of the Legal Services Act 2007, it is to be treated for the purposes of that section as such a fee.

(4) In subsection (3) "practising fee" has the meaning given by that section."

16 (1) Section 13A (imposition of conditions while practising certificates are in force) is amended as follows.

(2) For subsections (2) to (5) substitute—

"(2) The power conferred by subsection (1) is exercisable in relation to a solicitor at any time during the period for which the solicitor's current certificate is in force if—

(a) under section 13ZA the Society grants a sole solicitor endorsement, or
(b) it appears to the Society that the case is of a prescribed description.

(3) "Prescribed" means prescribed by regulations under section 28."

(3) In subsection (6) for "Master" to the end substitute "High Court against the decision of the Society."

(4) In subsection (7)—

(a) for "Master of the Rolls" (in both places) substitute "High Court", and
(b) for "he" substitute "it".

(5) After that subsection insert—

"(7A) The decision of the High Court on an appeal under subsection (6) shall be final."

(6) For subsection (8) substitute—

"(8) Subsections (4) and (5) of section 10 apply for the purposes of subsection (1) of this section as they apply for the purposes of that section."

(7) After that subsection insert—

"(9) A solicitor who holds a practising certificate subject to a condition imposed under subsection (1) which prohibits that solicitor from taking any steps specified in the condition, except with the approval of the Society, may appeal to the High Court against any decision by the Society to refuse to approve the taking of any step for the purposes of that condition.

(10) On an appeal under subsection (9), the High Court may—

(a) affirm the decision of the Society,
(b) direct the Society to approve the taking of one or more steps for the purposes of the condition, or
(c) make such other order as the High Court thinks fit.

(11) The decision of the High Court on an appeal under subsection (9) shall be final.

(12) In relation to an appeal under this section the High Court may make such order as it thinks fit as to payment of costs."

17 In section 13B (suspension of practising certificates where solicitors convicted of fraud or serious crime)—

(a) in subsection (1), after "practising certificate" insert "or sole solicitor endorsement",
(b) in subsection (6), after "practice" insert "or from practice as a sole solicitor",
(c) in subsection (7) for "Master of the Rolls" substitute "High Court",
(d) in subsection (8)—
  (i) for "Master of the Rolls" (in both places) substitute "High Court",
  (ii) in paragraph (b), for "shall not be suspended but" substitute "or sole solicitor endorsement shall not be suspended, but that the appellant's certificate", and
  (iii) in paragraph (d) for "he" substitute "it", and
(e) after that subsection insert—

"(9) In relation to an appeal under subsection (7) the High Court may make such order as it thinks fit as to payment of costs.

(10) The decision of the High Court on an appeal under subsection (7) shall be final."

18 Omit section 14 (commencement, expiry and replacement of practising certificates).

19 In section 15 (suspension of practising certificates), in subsection (1A)—

(a) after "6(1)" insert ", 6A(1)",
(b) after "1(1)(a)(i)," insert "(aa),", and
(c) after "section" insert "31 or".

20 (1) Section 16 (duration of suspension of practising certificates) is amended as follows.

(2) For subsection (1) substitute—

"(1) Where a practising certificate is suspended, it expires on such date as may be prescribed by regulations under section 28."

(3) In subsection (3)(c) for "the replacement date of the certificate" substitute "the date on which his certificate will expire".

(4) In subsection (5)—

(a) for "Master of the Rolls, who" substitute "High Court, which", and
(b) in paragraph (b) for "he" substitute "it".

(5) After that subsection insert—

"(6) In relation to an appeal under subsection (5) the High Court may make such order as it thinks fit as to payment of costs.

(7) The decision of the High Court on an appeal under subsection (5) shall be final."

21 In section 17 (publicity in relation to suspension of practising certificates), in subsections (1) and (2) omit "in the London Gazette".

22 After section 17 insert—

"17A Suspension of sole solicitor endorsement

(1) The making by the Tribunal or by the court of an order suspending a solicitor from practice as a sole solicitor shall operate to suspend any sole solicitor endorsement of that solicitor for the time being in force.

(2) For the purposes of this Act, a sole solicitor endorsement shall be deemed not to be in force at any time while it is suspended.

(3) Subsection (2) is subject to section 13ZA(2).

17B Duration and publicity of suspension of sole solicitor endorsement

(1) Where a sole solicitor endorsement is suspended, it expires on such date as may be prescribed by regulations under section 28.

(2) Where a solicitor's sole solicitor endorsement is suspended—

(a) by an order under section 13(4), or

(b) by virtue of section 17A(1) in circumstances where the period of that suspension expires before the date on which his endorsement will expire,

the solicitor may at any time before the endorsement expires apply to the Society to terminate the suspension.

(3) Section 16(4) to (7) apply in relation to an application under subsection (2) as they apply in relation to an application under section 16(3).

(4) Where a solicitor's sole solicitor endorsement is suspended by an order under section 13(4) or by virtue of section 17A(1), the Society shall forthwith cause notice of that suspension to be published and a note of it to be entered against the name of the solicitor on the roll.

(5) Where any suspension is terminated by virtue of section 16(4) or (5), as applied by subsection (3) of this section, the Society shall forthwith cause a note of that termination to be entered against the name of the solicitor on the roll and, if so requested in writing by the solicitor, a notice of it to be published."

23 For section 18 (evidence as to holding of practising certificates) substitute—

"18 Extracts from the roll or register etc as evidence

(1) An extract from the roll, or an extract from the register kept under section 10A, which is certified as correct by the Society is evidence of the matters mentioned in it.

(2) A certificate from the Society stating that—

(a) a person's name is or was on the roll, or
(b) a person is or was registered in the register kept under section 10A,

is evidence of the matters stated."

24 Omit section 19 (rights of practising and rights of audience).

25 For section 20 (unqualified person not to act as solicitor) substitute—

"20 Unqualified person not to act as solicitor

(1) No unqualified person is to act as a solicitor.

(2) Any person who contravenes subsection (1) is guilty of an offence and liable on conviction on indictment to imprisonment for not more than 2 years or to a fine, or to both."

26 Omit—

(a) sections 22 and 22A (unqualified person not to prepare certain instruments etc), and
(b) section 23 (unqualified person not to prepare papers for probate etc).

27 In section 24 (application of penal provisions to body corporate), in subsection (2) from "sections" to the end substitute "section 20 the reference to an unqualified person and the reference to a person both include a reference to a body corporate."

28 In section 26 (time limit for commencement of certain proceedings) omit ", 22 or 23".

29 Omit section 27 (saving for persons authorised to conduct legal proceedings).

30 (1) Section 28 (regulations) is amended as follows.

(2) In subsection (1)—

(a) for "Master of the Rolls" substitute "Society",
(b) omit ", with the concurrence of the Secretary of State and the Lord Chief Justice,",
(c) in paragraph (c) omit "and applications for them",
(d) after that paragraph insert—
"(ca) sole solicitor endorsements and applications for them,", and
(e) in paragraph (d) for "section 9" substitute "section 10A".

(3) Omit subsections (2) and (3).

(4) In subsection (3A)—

(a) for "may—" insert

"may (among other things)—

(za) make provision about the form in which the roll is to be kept and the manner in which entries are to be made, altered and removed;",
(b) omit "and" at the end of paragraph (b), and
(c) after paragraph (d) insert—
"(e) require the information on the roll to be made available to the public;
(f) specify the manner in which information is to be made so available and require it to be made so available during office hours and without charge."

(5) After that subsection insert—

"(3B) Regulations about practising certificates or sole solicitor endorsements may (among other things)—

(a) prescribe the form and manner in which applications for, or relating to, practising certificates or sole solicitor endorsements are to be made;
(b) prescribe information which must be included in or accompany such applications;
(c) make provision about time limits for dealing with such applications, and confer on a person power to extend or bring forward such a time limit in prescribed circumstances;
(d) prescribe the requirements which applicants for practising certificates must satisfy before they may be issued with a practising certificate;
(e) prescribe descriptions of applicants, and conditions in relation to them, for the purposes of section 10(2) (circumstances in which practising certificates must be issued subject to prescribed conditions);
(f) prescribe descriptions of applicants, and conditions in relation to them, for the purposes of section 13ZA(5) (circumstances in which a practising certificate endorsed with a sole solicitor endorsement after it was issued must be made subject to prescribed conditions);
(g) prescribe circumstances for the purposes of section 10(3) (circumstances in which application may be refused etc in the public interest);
(h) make provision about when conditions imposed on practising certificates take effect (including provision conferring power on the Society to direct that a condition is not to have effect until the conclusion of any appeal in relation to it);
(i) make provision for the commencement, duration, replacement, withdrawal and expiry of practising certificates or sole solicitor endorsements;
(j) prescribe circumstances for the purposes of section 13A(2) (circumstances in which conditions can be imposed during period of practising certificate);
(k) require solicitors who hold practising certificates to notify the Society of such matters as may be prescribed, at such times, or in such circumstances as may be prescribed.

(3C) Regulations about the keeping of the register under section 10A may (among other things)—

(a) make provision about the form in which the register is to be kept and the manner in which entries are to be made, altered and removed;
(b) require information of a specified kind to be included in entries in the register;
(c) require information (or information of a specified description) on the register to be made available to the public;
(d) specify the manner in which it is to be made so available and require it to be made so available during office hours and without charge.

(3D) Regulations under this section may make provision for appeals to the High Court against decisions made by the Society under the regulations.

(3E) In relation to an appeal under regulations made by virtue of subsection (3D), the High Court may make such order as it thinks fit as to payment of costs.

(3F) The decision of the High Court on such an appeal shall be final.

(3G) Regulations under this section may—

(a) provide for a person to exercise a discretion in dealing with any matter;
(b) include incidental, supplementary and consequential provision;
(c) make transitory or transitional provision and savings;
(d) make provision generally or only in relation to specified cases or subject to specified exceptions;
(e) make different provision for different cases."

(6) Omit subsections (4) and (5).

31 (1) Section 31 (rules as to professional practice, conduct and discipline) is amended as follows.

(2) In subsection (1)—

(a) for "Council may, if they think fit," substitute "Society may",
(b) omit ", with the concurrence of the Master of the Rolls,",
(c) after "conduct" insert ", fitness to practise",
(d) for "Council" (in the second place) substitute "Society", and
(e) after "being" insert ", or have been,".

(3) After that subsection insert—

"(1A) The powers conferred on the Society by subsection (1) include power to make, in relation to solicitors, provision of a kind which the Society would be prohibited from making but for section 157(5)(c) of the Legal Services Act 2007 (exception from prohibition on approved regulators making provision for redress)."

(4) Omit subsections (3) and (4).

32 (1) Section 32 (accounts rules and trust accounts rules) is amended as follows.

(2) In subsection (1)—

(a) for "Council" (in the first place) substitute "Society",
(b) omit ", with the concurrence of the Master of the Rolls",
(c) for paragraphs (a) and (b) substitute—
"(a) as to the opening and keeping by solicitors of accounts at banks or with building societies for money within subsection (1A);
(aa) as to the operation by solicitors of accounts kept by their clients or other persons at banks or with building societies or other financial institutions;
(b) as to the keeping by solicitors of accounts containing information as to money received, held or paid by them for or on account of their clients or other persons (including money received, held or paid under a trust); and",
(d) in paragraph (c) of that subsection—
(i) for "Council" substitute "Society",
(ii) for "them" substitute "it", and
(iii) after "being" insert ", or have been,", and
(e) omit from "and the rules" to the end.

(3) After that subsection insert—

"(1A) The money referred to in subsection (1) is money (including money held on trust) which is received, held or dealt with for clients or other persons."

(4) Omit subsection (2).

(5) In subsection (4)—

(a) for "Council" substitute "Society",
(b) omit "or (2)", and
(c) after "solicitor" (in both places) insert "or any of his employees".

(6) In subsection (5) for "by virtue" to the end substitute "or a part of the rules."

(7) Omit subsection (6).

33 (1) Section 33 (interest on clients' money) is amended as follows.

(2) For subsection (1) substitute—

"(1) Rules under section 32 may require a solicitor to pay interest, or sums in lieu of and equivalent to interest, to a client, any other person or any trust, for whom the solicitor holds money."

(3) In subsection (2), omit from "and the rules" to the end.

(4) For subsection (3) substitute—

"(3) Except as provided by the rules, a solicitor is not liable to account to any client, other person or trust for interest received by the solicitor on money held at a bank or building society in an account which is for money received or held for, or on account of—

(a) the solicitor's clients, other persons or trusts, generally, or
(b) that client, person or trust, separately."

(5) For subsection (4) substitute—

"(4) Rules under section 32 may—

(a) prescribe the circumstances in which a solicitor may make arrangements to limit or exclude an obligation imposed on the solicitor by rules made by virtue of this section, and
(b) prescribe the requirements to be met by and in relation to those arrangements."

34 (1) Section 33A (inspection of practice bank accounts etc) is amended as follows.

(2) In subsection (1)—

(a) for "Council" (in each place) substitute "Society", and
(b) omit ", with the concurrence of the Master of the Rolls,".

(3) In subsection (2) for "Council" substitute "Society".

35 (1) Section 34 (accountants' reports) is amended as follows.

(2) For subsections (1) to (5A) substitute—

"(1) The Society may make rules requiring solicitors to provide the Society with reports signed by an accountant (in this section referred to as an "accountant's report") at such times or in such circumstances as may be prescribed by the rules.

(2) The rules may specify requirements to be met by, or in relation to, an accountant's report (including requirements relating to the accountant who signs the report)."

(3) In subsection (6) for "this section or of any rules made under it" substitute "any rules made under this section".

(4) Omit subsections (7) and (8).

(5) At the end insert—

"(9) Where an accountant, during the course of preparing an accountant's report—

(a) discovers evidence of fraud or theft in relation to money held by a solicitor for a client or any other person (including money held on trust) or money held in an account of a client of a solicitor, or an account of another person, which is operated by the solicitor, or
(b) obtains information which the accountant has reasonable cause to believe is likely to be of material significance in determining whether a solicitor is a fit and proper person to hold money for clients or other persons (including money held on trust) or to operate an account of a client of the solicitor or an account of another person,

the accountant must immediately give a report of the matter to the Society.

(10) No duty to which an accountant is subject is to be regarded as contravened merely because of any information or opinion contained in a report under subsection (9)."

36 After section 34 insert—

"Sole solicitors

34A Employees of solicitors

(1) Rules made by the Society may provide for any rules made under section 31, 32, 33A or 34 to have effect in relation to employees of solicitors with such additions, omissions or other modifications as appear to the Society to be necessary or expedient.

(2) If any employee of a solicitor fails to comply with rules made under section 31 or 32, as they have effect in relation to the employee by virtue of subsection (1), any person may make a complaint in respect of that failure to the Tribunal.

(3) If any employee of a solicitor fails to comply with rules made under section 34, as they have effect in relation to the employee by virtue of subsection (1), a complaint in respect of that failure may be made to the Tribunal by or on behalf of the Society.

34B Employees of solicitors: accounts rules etc

(1) Where rules made under section 32(1) have effect in relation to employees of solicitors by virtue of section 34A(1), section 85 applies in relation to an employee to whom the rules have effect who keeps an account with a bank or building society in pursuance of such rules as it applies in relation to a solicitor who keeps such an account in pursuance of rules under section 32.

(2) Subsection (3) applies where rules made under section 32—

(a) contain any such provision as is referred to in section 33(1), and
(b) have effect in relation to employees of solicitors by virtue of section 34A(1).

(3) Except as provided by the rules, an employee to whom the rules are applied is not liable to account to any client, other person or trust for interest received by the employee on money held at a bank or building society in an account which is for money received or held for, or on account of—

(a) clients of the solicitor, other persons or trusts, generally, or
(b) that client, person or trust, separately.

(4) Subsection (5) applies where rules made under section 33A(1) have effect in relation to employees of solicitors by virtue of section 34A(1).

(5) The Society may disclose a report on or information about the accounts of any employee of a solicitor obtained in pursuance of such rules for use—

(a) in investigating the possible commission of an offence by the solicitor or any employees of the solicitor, and
(b) in connection with any prosecution of the solicitor or any employees of the solicitor consequent on the investigation.

(6) Where rules made under section 34 have effect in relation to employees of solicitors by virtue of section 34A(1), section 34(9) and (10) apply in relation to such an employee as they apply in relation to a solicitor."

37 For section 36 (compensation fund) substitute—

"36 Compensation grants

(1) The Society may make rules concerning the grant of compensation by the Society in respect of loss that a person has suffered, or is likely to suffer, as a result of—

(a) an act or omission of a solicitor or former solicitor;
(b) an act or omission of an employee or former employee of a solicitor or former solicitor;
(c) the exercise by the Society of any of its powers under Part 2 of Schedule 1.

(2) The rules may (among other things) make provision—

(a) as to the circumstances in which such grants may and may not be made;
(b) as to the form and manner in which a compensation claim is to be made;
(c) as to the procedure for determining compensation claims;
(d) for the making of grants in respect of a compensation claim before it is finally determined;
(e) for a grant to be made by way of loan in such circumstances and on such terms as may be prescribed in, or determined in accordance with, the rules;
(f) for a grant to be made by way of making good a deficiency in monies held in trust by the Society under paragraph 6 or 6A of Schedule 1;
(g) as to the minimum and maximum grants payable in respect of a compensation claim (or a claim of a prescribed description);
(h) for the Society to be subrogated, to such extent as may be prescribed, to any rights and remedies of a person to whom a grant is made in relation to the loss in respect of which the grant is made.

(3) The circumstances which may be prescribed by virtue of subsection (2)(a) include in particular—

(a) the nature of the loss;
(b) in a case within subsection (1)(a) or (b), the nature of the act or omission.

(4) For the purposes of subsection (2)(f), there is a deficiency if the monies mentioned in that subsection are insufficient to satisfy the claims of all persons with a beneficial interest in the monies.

(5) The Society may prepare and publish guidance as to the criteria it will apply in deciding whether to make a grant in respect of a compensation claim, or any part of a compensation claim.

(6) Where the Society decides—

(a) not to make a grant in respect of a compensation claim or any part of a compensation claim, or
(b) to make a grant of less than the amount claimed,

it must give reasons for its decision.

(7) Rules under subsection (1) which are not regulatory arrangements within the meaning of the Legal Services Act 2007 are to be treated as such arrangements for the purposes of that Act.

(8) In this section—

"compensation claim" means a claim for the Society to make a grant of the kind mentioned in subsection (1);
"prescribed" means prescribed in rules under subsection (1).

36A Compensation funds

(1) Compensation rules may require or authorise the Society to establish or maintain a fund or funds ("compensation funds") for the purpose of making grants in respect of compensation claims.

(2) Compensation rules may require solicitors, or solicitors of a description prescribed in the rules, to make contributions to compensation funds of such amounts, at such times and in such circumstances, as may be prescribed in or determined in accordance with the rules.

(3) Any amount payable by virtue of such a requirement may be recovered as a debt due to the Society.

(4) Subsection (2) does not apply to a solicitor who is a Crown Prosecutor.

(5) The Society may invest any money which forms part of a compensation fund in any investments in which trustees may invest under the general power of investment in section 3 of the Trustee Act 2000 (as restricted by sections 4 and 5 of that Act).

(6) The Society may insure with authorised insurers, in relation to compensation funds, for such purposes and on such terms as it considers appropriate.

(7) The Society may, in such circumstances and subject to such conditions as may be prescribed in or determined in accordance with compensation rules—

(a) borrow for the purposes of a compensation fund;
(b) charge investments which form part of a compensation fund as security for borrowing by the Society for the purposes of that fund.

(8) A compensation fund may be applied by the Society for the purposes mentioned in subsection (9) (in addition to the making of grants in respect of compensation claims).

(9) The purposes are—

(a) payment of premiums on insurance policies effected under subsection (6);
(b) repayment of money borrowed by the Society for the purposes of the fund and payment of interest on any money so borrowed;
(c) payment of any other costs, charges or expenses incurred by the Society in establishing, maintaining, protecting administering or applying the fund;
(d) payment of any costs, charges or expenses incurred by the Society in exercising its powers under Part 2 of Schedule 1;
(e) payment of any costs or damages incurred by the Society, its employees or agents as a result of proceedings against it or them for any act or omission of its or theirs in good faith and in the exercise or purported exercise of such powers.

(10) In this section—

"compensation claim" has the same meaning as in section 36;

"compensation fund" has the meaning given by subsection (1);
"compensation rules" means rules under section 36(1)."

38 In section 37 (professional indemnity)—

(a) in subsection (1) for "Council, with the concurrence of the Master of the Rolls," substitute "Society", and
(b) in subsection (3)(h)—
 (i) for "Council" substitute "Society",
 (ii) for "they consider" substitute "it considers", and
 (iii) after "being" insert ", or have been,".

39 Omit section 37A (redress for inadequate professional services).

40 Omit section 40 (solicitor not to commence or defend actions while in prison).

41 (1) Section 41 (employment by solicitor of person struck off or suspended) is amended as follows.

(2) After subsection (1A) insert—

"(1B) Where—

(a) a solicitor ("the employed solicitor") is employed by another solicitor in accordance with a written permission granted under this section, and
(b) the employed solicitor is disqualified from practising as a solicitor by reason of a fact mentioned in subsection (1)(b) or (c),

section 20(1) does not apply in relation to anything done by the employed solicitor in the course of that employment."

(3) In subsection (3)—

(a) for "Master of the Rolls who" substitute "High Court which", and
(b) in paragraph (b) for "he" substitute "it".

(4) In subsection (4) for "shall" to the end substitute

"may—

(a) order that his name be struck off the roll,
(b) order that he be suspended from practice for such period as the Tribunal or court thinks fit, or
(c) make such other order in the matter as it thinks fit."

(5) After that subsection insert—

"(4A) In relation to an appeal under subsection (3) the High Court may make such order as it thinks fit as to payment of costs.

(4B) The decision of the High Court on an appeal under subsection (3) shall be final."

(6) Omit subsection (5).

42 (1) Section 43 (control of solicitors' employees and consultants) is amended as follows.

(2) For subsections (1), (1A) and (2) substitute—

"(1) Where a person who is or was involved in a legal practice but is not a solicitor—

(a) has been convicted of a criminal offence which is such that in the opinion of the Society it would be undesirable for the person to be involved in a legal practice in one or more of the ways mentioned in subsection (1A), or
(b) has, in the opinion of the Society, occasioned or been a party to, with or without the connivance of a solicitor, an act or default in relation to a legal practice which involved conduct on his part of such a nature that in the opinion of the Society it would be undesirable for him to be involved in a legal practice in one or more of the ways mentioned in subsection (1A),

the Society may either make, or make an application to the Tribunal for it to make, an order under subsection (2) with respect to that person.

(1A) A person is involved in a legal practice for the purposes of this section if the person—

(a) is employed or remunerated by a solicitor in connection with the solicitor's practice;
(b) is undertaking work in the name of, or under the direction or supervision of, a solicitor;
(c) is employed or remunerated by a recognised body;
(d) is employed or remunerated by a manager or employee of a recognised body in connection with that body's business;
(e) is a manager of a recognised body;
(f) has or intends to acquire an interest in such a body.

(2) An order made by the Society or the Tribunal under this subsection is an order which states one or more of the following—

(a) that as from the specified date—
 (i) no solicitor shall employ or remunerate, in connection with his practice as a solicitor, the person with respect to whom the order is made,
 (ii) no employee of a solicitor shall employ or remunerate, in connection with the solicitor's practice, the person with respect to whom the order is made,
 (iii) no recognised body shall employ or remunerate that person, and
 (iv) no manager or employee of a recognised body shall employ or remunerate that person in connection with the business of that body,

except in accordance with a Society permission;
(b) that as from the specified date no recognised body or manager or employee of such a body shall, except in accordance with a Society permission, permit the person with respect to whom the order is made to be a manager of the body;
(c) that as from the specified date no recognised body or manager or employee of such a body shall, except in accordance with a Society permission, permit the person with respect to whom the order is made to have an interest in the body.

(2A) The Society may make regulations prescribing charges to be paid to the Society by persons who are the subject of an investigation by the Society as to whether there are grounds for the Society—

(a) to make an order under subsection (2), or
(b) to make an application to the Tribunal for it to make such an order.

(2B) Regulations under subsection (2A) may—

(a) make different provision for different cases or purposes;
(b) provide for the whole or part of a charge payable under the regulations to be repaid in such circumstances as may be prescribed by the regulations.

(2C) Any charge which a person is required to pay under regulations under subsection (2A) is recoverable by the Society as a debt due to the Society from the person."

(3) In subsection (5) omit—

(a) "by any solicitor", and
(b) the words from "but" to the end.

(4) After that subsection insert—

"(5A) In this section—

"manager", in relation to a recognised body, has the same meaning as it has in relation to a body in the Legal Services Act 2007 (see section 207 of that Act);
"recognised body" means a body recognised under section 9 of the Administration of Justice Act 1985;
"specified date" means such date as may be specified in the order;
"Society permission" means permission in writing granted by the Society for such period and subject to such conditions as the Society may think fit to specify in the permission.

(5B) A person has an interest in a recognised body for the purposes of this section if the person has an interest in that body within the meaning of Part 5 of the Legal Services Act 2007 (see sections 72 and 109 of that Act)."

43 In section 44 (offences in connection with orders under section 43(2))—

(a) for subsection (1) substitute—

"(1) It is an offence for a person in respect of whom there is in force an order under section 43(2) which contains provision within section 43(2)(a)—

(a) to seek or accept any employment or remuneration from a solicitor, or an employee of a solicitor, in connection with the practice carried on by that solicitor without previously informing the solicitor or employee of the order;
(b) to seek or accept any employment or remuneration from a recognised body, or a manager or employee of a recognised body, in connection with that body's business, without previously informing the body, or manager or employee, of the order.

(1A) It is an offence for a person in respect of whom there is in force an order under section 43(2) which contains provision within section 43(2)(b) to seek or accept a position as a manager of a recognised body, without previously informing that body of the order.

(1B) It is an offence for a person in respect of whom there is in force an order under section 43(2) which contains provision within section 43(2)(c) to seek or accept an interest in a recognised body from any person, without previously informing that person and (if different) the recognised body of the order.

(1C) A person guilty of an offence under subsection (1), (1A) or (1B) is liable on summary conviction to a fine not exceeding level 3 on the standard scale.",

(b) in subsection (2) for "the employment of that person" substitute "the taking of any action", and
(c) after subsection (4) insert—

"(5) In this section—

"manager" has the same meaning as in section 43;
"recognised body" means a body recognised under section 9 of the Administration of Justice Act 1985;

and for the purposes of subsection (1B) a person seeks or accepts an interest in a recognised body if the person seeks or accepts an interest which if it were obtained by the person would result in the person having an interest in that body within the meaning of Part 5 of the Legal Services Act 2007 (see sections 72 and 109 of that Act)."

44 For section 44B (examination of files) substitute—

"44B Provision of information and documents by solicitors etc

(1) The Society may by notice require a person to whom this section applies—

(a) to provide information, or information of a description, specified in the notice, or
(b) produce documents, or documents of a description, specified in the notice.

(2) This section applies to—

(a) a solicitor;
(b) an employee of a solicitor;
(c) a recognised body;
(d) an employee or manager of, or a person with an interest in, a recognised body.

(3) The Society may give a notice under this section only if it is satisfied that it is necessary to do so for the purpose of investigating—

(a) whether there has been professional misconduct by a solicitor;
(b) whether a solicitor, or an employee of a solicitor, has failed to comply with any requirements imposed by or by virtue of this Act or any rules made by the Society;
(c) whether a recognised body, or any of its managers or employees has failed to comply with any requirement imposed by or by virtue of the Administration of Justice Act 1985 or any rules made by the Society and applicable to the body, manager or employee by virtue of section 9 of that Act;
(d) whether there are grounds for making, or making an application to the Tribunal for it to make, an order under section 43(2) with respect to a person who is or was involved in a legal practice (within the meaning of section 43(1A)).

(4) A notice under this section—

(a) may specify the time and place at which, and manner and form in which, the information is to be provided or document is to be produced;
(b) must specify the period within which the information is to be provided or the document produced;

(c) may require the information to be provided or document to be produced to the Society or to a person specified in the notice.

(5) The Society may pay to any person such reasonable costs as may be incurred by that person in connection with the provision of any information, or production of any document, by that person pursuant to a notice under this section.

(6) Paragraphs 9(3) and (4) and 13, 15 and 16 of Schedule 1 apply in relation to the powers to obtain information conferred by this section, but for this purpose—

(a) paragraph 9 of that Schedule has effect as if—
(i) in sub-paragraph (3) for "such documents" there were substituted "information to which a notice given to him under section 44B applies",
(ii) in that sub-paragraph for "sub-paragraph (1)" there were substituted "the notice", and
(iii) in sub-paragraph (4) for "produce" (in the first place) to the end there were substituted "provide information pursuant to a notice under section 44B to provide the information to any person appointed by the Society at such time and place as may be specified in the order.", and

(b) the reference to the solicitor or his personal representative in paragraph 13 of that Schedule is to be construed as a reference to the person to whom the notice was given under this section.

(7) Paragraphs 9 (other than sub-paragraphs (1) and (3)), 12, 13, 15 and 16 of Schedule 1 apply in relation to the powers to obtain documents conferred by this section as they apply in relation to the powers conferred by paragraph 9(1) of that Schedule, except that for this purpose—

(a) any reference in paragraph 9 of that Schedule to a person appointed, or to a requirement, under sub-paragraph (1) of that paragraph is to be construed as a reference to a person appointed, or to a requirement to produce documents, under this section,
(b) any reference in that paragraph to any such documents as are mentioned in paragraph 9(1) of that Schedule is to be construed as a reference to any documents to which a notice under this section applies,
(c) the references to the solicitor or his firm in paragraph 9(5) and (6) of that Schedule, and the reference to the solicitor or personal representative in paragraph 9(7) of that Schedule, are to be construed as references to the person to whom the notice was given under this section, and
(d) the reference in paragraph 9(12) of that Schedule to the Society is to be construed as including a reference to a person specified under subsection (4)(c).

(8) Where powers conferred by Part 2 of Schedule 1 to the 1974 Act are exercisable in relation to a person within paragraph (a), (b), (c) or (d) of subsection (2), they continue to be so exercisable after the person has ceased to be a person within the paragraph in question.

(9) In this section—

"manager" has the same meaning as in the Legal Services Act 2007 (see section 207 of that Act);
"recognised body" means a body recognised under section 9 of the Administration of Justice Act 1985;

and the reference to a person who has an interest in a recognised body is to be construed in accordance with sections 72 and 109 of the Legal Services Act 2007.

44BA Power to require explanation of document or information

(1) The Society may, by notice, require a person to whom a notice is given under section 44B (or a representative of the person) to attend at a time and place specified in the notice to provide an explanation of any information provided or document produced pursuant to the notice.

(2) The Society may pay to any person such reasonable costs as may be incurred by that person in connection with that person's compliance with a requirement imposed under subsection (1).

(3) Paragraphs 9(3) and (4) and 13, 15 and 16 of Schedule 1 apply in relation to a notice under this section, except that for this purpose—

(a) paragraph 9 of that Schedule has effect as if—

(i) in sub-paragraph (3) for "having" to "sub-paragraph (1)" there were substituted "refuses, neglects or otherwise fails to comply with a requirement under section 44BA(1)", and

(ii) in sub-paragraph (4) for "produce" (in the first place) to the end there were substituted "provide an explanation of any information provided or document produced pursuant to a notice under section 44B (or a representative of such a person) to attend at a time and place specified in the order to provide an explanation of any information so provided or document so produced.", and

(b) the reference to the solicitor or his personal representative in paragraph 13 of that Schedule is to be construed as a reference to the person to whom the notice was given under this section.

44BB Provision of information and documents by other persons

(1) The High Court, on the application of the Society, may order a person to whom section 44B does not apply—

(a) to provide information, or information of a description, specified in the notice, or
(b) to produce documents, or documents of a description, specified in the notice.

(2) The High Court may make an order under this section only if it is satisfied—

(a) that it is likely that the information or document is in the possession or custody of, or under the control of, the person, and
(b) that there is reasonable cause to believe that the information or document is likely to be of material significance to an investigation into any of the matters mentioned in section 44B(3)(a) to (d).

(3) An order under this section may direct the Society to pay to a person specified in the order such reasonable costs as may be incurred by that person in connection with the provision of any information, or production of any document, by that person pursuant to the order.

(4) Section 44B(4) applies in relation to an order under this section as it applies in relation to a notice under section 44B.

(5) Paragraphs 9(5A) and (7) to (12), 12, 13, 15 and 16 of Schedule 1 apply in relation to an order under this section as they apply in relation to an order under paragraph 9(4) of that Schedule, except that for this purpose—

(a) the reference to the solicitor or personal representative in paragraph 9(7) of that Schedule is to be construed as a reference to the person in respect of whom the order under this section is made,
(b) the reference in paragraph 9(12) of that Schedule to the Society is to be read as including a reference to a person specified under section 44B(4)(c) (as applied by subsection (4) of this section), and
(c) the reference to the solicitor or his personal representative in paragraph 13 of that Schedule is to be construed as a reference to the person to whom the notice was given under this section.

44BC Information offences

(1) It is an offence for a person who knows or suspects an investigation into any of the matters mentioned in section 44B(3)(a) to (d) is being or is likely to be conducted—

(a) to falsify, conceal, destroy or otherwise dispose of a document which the person knows or suspects is or would be relevant to the investigation, or
(b) to cause or permit the falsification, concealment, destruction or disposal of such a document.

(2) In proceedings for an offence under subsection (1) it is a defence for the accused to show that the accused had no intention of concealing facts disclosed by the documents from the person conducting the investigation.

(3) It is an offence for a person, in purported compliance with a requirement imposed on the person under section 44B, 44BA or 44BB—

(a) to provide information which the person knows to be false or misleading in a material particular, or

(b) recklessly to provide information which is false or misleading in a material particular.

(4) A person who is guilty of an offence under subsection (1) or (3) is liable—

(a) on summary conviction, to imprisonment for a term not exceeding 12 months or a fine not exceeding the statutory maximum, or both;
(b) on conviction on indictment, to imprisonment for a term not exceeding 2 years or a fine, or both.

(5) In relation to an offence under subsection (1) or (3) committed before the commencement of section 154(1) of the Criminal Justice Act 2003 the reference in subsection (4)(a) to 12 months is to be read as a reference to 6 months."

45 For section 44C (payment of costs of investigations) substitute—

"44C Power to charge for costs of investigations

(1) The Society may make regulations prescribing charges to be paid to the Society by solicitors who are the subject of a discipline investigation.

(2) A "discipline investigation" is an investigation carried out by the Society into—

(a) possible professional misconduct by a solicitor, or
(b) a failure or apprehended failure by a solicitor to comply with any requirement imposed by or by virtue of this Act or any rules made by the Society.

(3) Regulations under this section may—

(a) make different provision for different cases or purposes;
(b) provide for the whole or part of a charge payable under the regulations to be repaid in such circumstances as may be prescribed by the regulations.

(4) Any charge which a solicitor is required to pay under regulations under this section is recoverable by the Society as a debt due to the Society from the solicitor.

(5) This section (other than subsection (2)(a)) applies in relation to an employee of a solicitor as it applies in relation to a solicitor."

46 After that section insert—

"Disciplinary powers of the Society

44D Disciplinary powers of the Society

(1) This section applies where the Society is satisfied—

(a) that a solicitor or an employee of a solicitor has failed to comply with a requirement imposed by or by virtue of this Act or any rules made by the Society, or
(b) that there has been professional misconduct by a solicitor.

(2) The Society may do one or both of the following—

(a) give the person a written rebuke;
(b) direct the person to pay a penalty not exceeding £2,000.

(3) The Society may publish details of any action it has taken under subsection (2)(a) or (b), if it considers it to be in the public interest to do so.

(4) Where the Society takes action against a person under subsection (2)(b), or decides to publish under subsection (3) details of any action taken under subsection (2)(a) or (b), it must notify the person in writing that it has done so.

(5) A penalty imposed under subsection (2)(b) does not become payable until—

(a) the end of the period during which an appeal against the decision to impose the penalty, or the amount of the penalty, may be made under section 44E, or
(b) if such an appeal is made, such time as it is determined or withdrawn.

(6) The Society may not publish under subsection (3) details of any action under subsection (2)(a) or (b)—

(a) during the period within which an appeal against—

(i) the decision to take the action,
(ii) in the case of action under subsection (2)(b), the amount of the penalty, or
(iii) the decision to publish the details,

may be made under section 44E, or

(b) if such an appeal has been made, until such time as it is determined or withdrawn.

(7) The Society must make rules—

(a) prescribing the circumstances in which the Society may decide to take action under subsection (2)(a) or (b);
(b) about the practice and procedure to be followed by the Society in relation to such action;
(c) governing the publication under subsection (3) of details of action taken under subsection (2)(a) or (b);

and the Society may make such other rules in connection with the exercise of its powers under this section as it considers appropriate.

(8) Before making rules under subsection (7), the Society must consult the Tribunal.

(9) A penalty payable under this section may be recovered as a debt due to the Society, and is to be forfeited to Her Majesty.

(10) The Lord Chancellor may, by order, amend paragraph (b) of subsection (2) so as to substitute for the amount for the time being specified in that paragraph such other amount as may be specified in the order.

(11) Before making an order under subsection (10), the Lord Chancellor must consult the Society.

(12) An order under subsection (10) is to be made by statutory instrument subject to annulment in pursuance of a resolution of either House of Parliament.

(13) This section is without prejudice to any power conferred on the Society or any other person to make an application or complaint to the Tribunal.

44E Appeals against disciplinary action under section 44D

(1) A person may appeal against—

(a) a decision by the Society to rebuke that person under section 44D(2)(a) if a decision is also made to publish details of the rebuke;
(b) a decision by the Society to impose a penalty on that person under section 44D(2)(b) or the amount of that penalty;
(c) a decision by the Society to publish under section 44D(3) details of any action taken against that person under section 44D(2)(a) or (b).

(2) Subsections (9)(b), (10)(a) and (b), (11) and (12) of section 46 (Tribunal rules about procedure for hearings etc) apply in relation to appeals under this section as they apply in relation to applications or complaints, except that subsection (11) of that section is to be read as if for "the applicant" to "application)" there were substituted "any party to the appeal".

(3) Rules under section 46(9)(b) may, in particular, make provision about the period during which an appeal under this section may be made.

(4) On an appeal under this section, the Tribunal has power to make such order as it thinks fit, and such an order may in particular—

(a) affirm the decision of the Society;
(b) revoke the decision of the Society;
(c) in the case of a penalty imposed under section 44D(2)(b), vary the amount of the penalty;
(d) in the case of a solicitor, contain provision for any of the matters mentioned in paragraphs (a) to (d) of section 47(2);
(e) in the case of an employee of a solicitor, contain provision for any of the matters mentioned in section 47(2E);
(f) make such provision as the Tribunal thinks fit as to payment of costs.

(5) Where by virtue of subsection (4)(e) an order contains provision for any of the matters mentioned in section 47(2E)(c), section 47(2F) and (2G) apply as if the order had been made under section 47(2E)(c).

(6) An appeal from the Tribunal shall lie to the High Court, at the instance of the Society or the person in respect of whom the order of the Tribunal was made.

(7) The High Court shall have power to make such order on an appeal under this section as it may think fit.

(8) Any decision of the High Court on an appeal under this section shall be final.

(9) This section is without prejudice to any power conferred on the Tribunal in connection with an application or complaint made to it."

47 (1) Section 46 (solicitors disciplinary tribunal) is amended as follows.

(2) For subsection (5) substitute—

"(5) The Tribunal may pay its members such remuneration, fees or allowances as it may determine with the approval of the Legal Services Board."

(3) After that subsection insert—

"(5A) The Tribunal may do anything calculated to facilitate, or incidental or conducive to, the carrying out of any of its functions."

(4) Omit subsections (6) to (8).

(5) In subsection (9)—

- (a) for "Subject to subsections (6) to (8), the" substitute "The",
- (b) omit ", with the concurrence of the Master of the Rolls,", and
- (c) in paragraph (b) after "complaints" insert "(including provision about the composition of the Tribunal)".

48 After that section insert—

"46A Funding of the Tribunal

(1) The Tribunal must submit to the Society in respect of each year a budget for the year approved by the Legal Services Board.

(2) A budget for a year is a statement of the amount of money which the Tribunal estimates is required to enable it to meet all of its expenditure in that year (having regard to any amounts received but not spent in previous years).

(3) Before approving a statement for the purposes of subsection (1) the Legal Services Board must consult the Society.

(4) The budget for a year must be submitted to the Society under subsection (1) no later than the date in the preceding year specified by the Society for the purposes of this subsection.

(5) Before specifying a date for this purpose the Society must consult the Tribunal.

(6) The amount specified in a budget submitted under subsection (1) must be paid by the Society to the Tribunal—

- (a) in such instalments and at such times as may be agreed between the Society and the Tribunal, or
- (b) in the absence of such agreement, before the beginning of the year to which the budget relates.

(7) The Society may pay the Tribunal such other amounts as the Society considers appropriate.

(8) In this section "year" means a calendar year."

49 In section 47 (jurisdiction and powers of Tribunal)—

- (a) in subsection (1), after paragraph (e) insert—
- "(ea) by a solicitor who has been suspended from practice as a sole solicitor for an unspecified period, by order of the Tribunal, for the termination of that suspension;",
- (b) in subsection (2) for "subsection" (where it first occurs) substitute "subsections (2E) and",

(c) after subsection (2)(b) insert—

"(ba) the revocation of that solicitor's sole solicitor endorsement (if any);

(bb) the suspension of that solicitor from practice as a sole solicitor indefinitely or for a specified period;",

(d) in subsection (2)(c) omit "not exceeding £5,000",

(e) after subsection (2)(e) insert—

"(ea) the termination of that solicitor's unspecified period of suspension from practice as a sole solicitor;",

(f) after subsection (2D) insert—

"(2E) On the hearing of any complaint made to the Tribunal by virtue of section 34A(2) or (3), the Tribunal shall have power to make one or more of the following—

(a) an order directing the payment by the employee to whom the complaint relates of a penalty to be forfeited to Her Majesty;

(b) an order requiring the Society to consider taking such steps as the Tribunal may specify in relation to that employee;

(c) if that employee is not a solicitor, an order which states one or more of the matters mentioned in paragraphs (a) to (c) of section 43(2);

(d) an order requiring the Society to refer to an appropriate regulator any matter relating to the conduct of that employee.

(2F) Subsections (1) to (1C), (3) and (4) of section 44 apply in relation to an order under subsection (2E)(c) as they apply in relation to an order under section 43(2).

(2G) Section 44(2), paragraph 16(1)(d) and (1A)(d) of Schedule 2 to the Administration of Justice Act 1985 and paragraph 15(3A) of Schedule 14 to the Courts and Legal Services Act 1990 apply in relation to an order under subsection (2E)(c) as they apply in relation to an order under section 43(2).

(2H) For the purposes of subsection (2E)(d) an "appropriate regulator" in relation to an employee means—

(a) if the employee is an authorised person in relation to a reserved legal activity (within the meaning of the Legal Services Act 2007), any relevant approved regulator (within the meaning of that Act) in relation to that employee, and

(b) if the employee carries on activities which are not reserved legal activities (within the meaning of that Act), any body which regulates the carrying on of such activities by the employee.",

(g) after subsection (3A) insert—

"(3B) For the avoidance of doubt, nothing in this section permits the Tribunal to make an order requiring redress to be made in respect of any act or omission of any person.", and

(h) omit subsections (4) and (5).

50 In section 48 (orders of Tribunal)—

(a) in subsection (2)(b)—
  (i) after "(e)," insert "(ea),", and
  (ii) omit "in the London Gazette",

(b) in subsection (3) for "Subject to section 43(5), any" substitute "Any", and

(c) after subsection (4) insert—

"(5) In the case of orders of the Tribunal under section 44E, the reference in subsection (2)(a) to the application or complaint is to be read as a reference to the Tribunal's order."

51 (1) Section 49 (appeals from Tribunal) is amended as follows.

(2) In subsection (1) for "lie—" to the end substitute "lie to the High Court".

(3) In subsection (2), after "(3)" insert "and to section 43(5) of the Administration of Justice Act 1985".

(4) In subsection (3) for "legal aid work (within the meaning of that section)" substitute "providing representation funded by the Legal Services Commission as part of the Criminal Defence Service".

(5) In subsection (4)—

(a) omit “and the Master of the Rolls”, and
(b) for “they” substitute “it”.

(6) For subsection (6) substitute—

“(6) Any decision of the High Court—

(a) on an application under section 43(3) or 47(1)(d), (e), (ea) or (f), or
(b) against an order under section 43(3A),

shall be final.”

(7) Omit subsection (7).

52 After that section insert—

“49A Appeals to the Tribunal instead of the High Court

(1) The Society may, with the approval of the Tribunal, make rules which provide that in such circumstances as may be prescribed by the rules an appeal under any of the provisions listed in subsection (2) lies to the Tribunal and not to the High Court.

(2) Those provisions are—

(a) section 8(4);
(b) section 13A(6);
(c) section 16(5);
(d) section 28(3D);
(e) section 41(3);
(f) paragraph 14 of Schedule 14 to the Courts and Legal Services Act 1990 (foreign lawyers: appeals against conditions or refusals).

(3) Any decision of the Tribunal on an appeal by virtue of rules made under this section shall be final.”

53 In section 54 (restrictions on powers to strike names off roll)—

(a) in subsection (1) for “service under articles” substitute “persons seeking admission as solicitors”, and
(b) in subsection (2) for paragraphs (a) and (b) substitute—
“(a) that a solicitor who undertook a training responsibility for him under training regulations neglected or omitted to take out a practising certificate; or
(b) that the name of a solicitor who undertook such a responsibility for a period has been removed from or struck off the roll after the end of that period.”

54 (1) Section 56 (orders as to remuneration for non-contentious business) is amended as follows.

(2) In subsection (1)—

(a) in paragraph (a) for “Secretary of State” substitute “Lord Chancellor”,
(b) after paragraph (d) insert—
“(da) a member of the Legal Services Board nominated by that Board;”, and
(c) in paragraph (e) for “Secretary of State” substitute “Lord Chancellor”.

(3) In subsection (2) for “(the Secretary of State” to “think fit” substitute “(the Lord Chancellor being one), may make general orders prescribing the general principles to be applied when determining”.

(4) In subsection (3)—

(a) for “Secretary of State” substitute “Lord Chancellor”, and
(b) for “Council” (in both places) substitute “Society”.

(5) In subsection (4) for “An order” to the end of paragraph (a) substitute—

“The principles prescribed by an order under this section may provide that solicitors should be remunerated—”.

(6) In subsection (5)—

(a) for “An order” to “reference” substitute—

"The general principles prescribed by an order under this section may provide that the amount of such remuneration is to be determined by having regard", and

(b) in paragraph (d) after "solicitor" insert ", or any employee of his who is an authorised person,".

(7) After that subsection insert—

"(5A) In subsection (5) "authorised person" means a person who is an authorised person in relation to an activity which is a reserved legal activity, within the meaning of the Legal Services Act 2007 (see section 18 of that Act)."

(8) In subsection (6)(a) for "taxation" substitute "assessment".

(9) In subsection (7)—

(a) for "taxation" substitute "assessment", and
(b) for "regulated by" substitute "subject to".

55 In section 57 (non-contentious business agreements)—

(a) in subsection (2) for "stamps" substitute "taxes",
(b) in subsection (5)—
  (i) for "taxation" substitute "assessment", and
  (ii) for "taxing officer" substitute "costs officer", and
(c) in subsection (7)—
  (i) for "taxation" substitute "assessment", and
  (ii) for "taxing officer" substitute "costs officer".

56 In section 60 (effect of contentious business agreements)—

(a) in subsection (1) for "taxation" substitute "assessment",
(b) in subsection (2)—
  (i) for "taxed" substitute "assessed", and
  (ii) for "taxation" substitute "assessment", and
(c) for subsection (5) substitute—

"(5) A provision in a contentious business agreement that the solicitor shall not be liable for his negligence, or that of any employee of his, shall be void if the client is a natural person who, in entering that agreement, is acting for purposes which are outside his trade, business or profession.

(6) A provision in a contentious business agreement that the solicitor shall be relieved from any responsibility to which he would otherwise be subject as a solicitor shall be void."

57 In section 61 (enforcement of contentious business agreements)—

(a) in subsection (2)(b) for "taxed" substitute "assessed",
(b) in subsection (3) for "taxing officer" substitute "costs officer",
(c) in subsection (4)—
  (i) for "taxing officer" substitute "costs officer", and
  (ii) for "taxed" substitute "assessed",
(d) in subsection (4B)—
  (i) for "taxation" substitute "assessment", and
  (ii) for "taxing officer" substitute "costs officer", and
(e) in subsection (5) for "taxed" substitute "assessed".

58 In section 62 (contentious business agreements by certain representatives)—

(a) in subsection (1) for "taxing officer" substitute "costs officer", and
(b) in subsection (2)—
  (i) for "taxing officer" substitute "costs officer", and
  (ii) for "taxed" substitute "assessed".

59 In section 63 (effect on contentious business agreement of death etc)—

(a) in subsection (2)—
  (i) for "taxation" substitute "assessment", and
  (ii) for "taxing officer" substitute "costs officer", and
(b) in subsection (3)—
  (i) for "taxation" substitute "assessment",
  (ii) for "taxing officer" (in both places) substitute "costs officer", and

(iii) after "solicitor" (in the third place) insert ", or any of his employees,".

60 In section 64 (form of bill of costs for contentious business)—

(a) in subsection (3) for "taxed" substitute "assessed", and
(b) in subsection (4)—
(i) for "taxed" substitute "assessed",
(ii) for "taxation" substitute "assessment", and
(iii) for "taxing officer" (in both places) substitute "costs officer".

61 In section 65 (security for costs and termination of retainer), in subsection (1) for "taxation" substitute "assessment".

62 In section 66 (taxations with respect to contentious business)—

(a) in the section heading for "Taxations" substitute "Assessments",
(b) for "taxation" substitute "assessment",
(c) for "taxing officer" substitute "costs officer",
(d) in paragraph (a), after "solicitor" (in the second place) insert "or an employee of the solicitor", and
(e) in paragraph (b), after "him" insert "or by any employee of his who is an authorised person (within the meaning of section 56(5A))".

63 In section 67 (inclusion of disbursements in bill of costs), in paragraph (b)—

(a) for "taxed" substitute "assessed",
(b) for "taxing officer" substitute "costs officer", and
(c) for "taxation" substitute "assessment".

64 (1) Section 69 (action to recover solicitor's costs) is amended as follows.

(2) In subsection (1) for "taxed" substitute "assessed".

(3) For subsection (2) substitute—

"(2) The requirements referred to in subsection (1) are that the bill must be—

(a) signed in accordance with subsection (2A), and
(b) delivered in accordance with subsection (2C).

(2A) A bill is signed in accordance with this subsection if it is—

(a) signed by the solicitor or on his behalf by an employee of the solicitor authorised by him to sign, or
(b) enclosed in, or accompanied by, a letter which is signed as mentioned in paragraph (a) and refers to the bill.

(2B) For the purposes of subsection (2A) the signature may be an electronic signature.

(2C) A bill is delivered in accordance with this subsection if—

(a) it is delivered to the party to be charged with the bill personally,
(b) it is delivered to that party by being sent to him by post to, or left for him at, his place of business, dwelling-house or last known place of abode, or
(c) it is delivered to that party—
(i) by means of an electronic communications network, or
(ii) by other means but in a form that nevertheless requires the use of apparatus by the recipient to render it intelligible,

and that party has indicated to the person making the delivery his willingness to accept delivery of a bill sent in the form and manner used.

(2D) An indication to any person for the purposes of subsection (2C)(c)—

(a) must state the address to be used and must be accompanied by such other information as that person requires for the making of the delivery;
(b) may be modified or withdrawn at any time by a notice given to that person.

(2E) Where a bill is proved to have been delivered in compliance with the requirements of subsections (2A) and (2C), it is not necessary in the first instance for the solicitor to prove the contents of the bill and it is to be presumed, until the contrary is shown, to be a bill bona fide complying with this Act.

(2F) A bill which is delivered as mentioned in subsection (2C)(c) is to be treated as having been delivered on the first working day after the day on which it was sent (unless the contrary is proved)."

(4) At the end insert—

"(5) In this section references to an electronic signature are to be read in accordance with section 7(2) of the Electronic Communications Act 2000 (c 7).

(6) In this section—

"electronic communications network" has the same meaning as in the Communications Act 2003 (c 21);

"working day" means a day other than a Saturday, a Sunday, Christmas Day, Good Friday or a bank holiday in England and Wales under the Banking and Financial Dealings Act 1971 (c 80)."

65 In section 70 (taxation on application of party chargeable or solicitor)—

(a) in the section heading for "Taxation" substitute "Assessment",
(b) in subsection (1)—
 (i) for "taxed" substitute "assessed", and
 (ii) for "taxation" substitute "assessment",
(c) in subsection (2)—
 (i) for "taxation" (in both places) substitute "assessment", and
 (ii) for "taxed" substitute "assessed",
(d) in subsections (3) to (5) for "taxation" (in each place) substitute "assessment",
(e) in subsection (6)—
 (i) for "taxation" substitute "assessment", and
 (ii) for "taxed" substitute "assessed",
(f) in subsection (7)—
 (i) for "taxation" (in each place) substitute "assessment",
 (ii) for "taxing officer" substitute "costs officer", and
 (iii) for "tax" substitute "assess",
(g) in subsection (8) for "taxation" (in each place) substitute "assessment",
(h) in subsection (9)—
 (i) for "for taxation" (in both places) substitute "for assessment",
 (ii) for "the taxation" (in both places) substitute "the assessment",
 (iii) for "a taxation" substitute "an assessment", and
 (iv) for "one fifth of the amount of the bill is taxed off" substitute "the amount of the bill is reduced by one fifth",
(i) in subsection (10)—
 (i) for "taxing officer" substitute "costs officer", and
 (ii) for "taxation" (in both places) substitute "assessment",
(j) omit subsection (11), and
(k) in subsection (12)—
 (i) for "of the bill taxed off" substitute "of the reduction in the bill",
 (ii) for "taxation" substitute "assessment", and
 (iii) for "taxed" (in the second place) substitute "assessed".

66 In section 71 (taxation on application of third parties)—

(a) in the section heading for "Taxation" substitute "Assessment",
(b) in subsection (1) for "taxation" substitute "assessment",
(c) in subsection (3)—
 (i) for "taxed" substitute "assessed", and
 (ii) for "taxation" substitute "assessment",
(d) in subsection (4) for "taxation" substitute "assessment",
(e) in subsection (6)—
 (i) for "taxation" substitute "assessment", and
 (ii) for "taxed" substitute "assessed", and
(f) in subsection (7) for "taxed" substitute "assessed".

67 In section 72 (supplementary provisions as to taxations)—

(a) in the section heading for "taxations" substitute "assessments",
(b) in subsection (1) for "taxation" substitute "assessment",

(c) in subsection (2)—
   (i) for "taxing officer" (in each place) substitute "costs officer",
   (ii) for second and fourth "taxing" substitute "assessing", and
   (iii) for "tax" substitute "assess",
(d) in subsection (3)—
   (i) for "taxing officer" (in both places) substitute "costs officer",
   (ii) for "tax" substitute "assess", and
   (iii) for "taxing" (in second place) substitute "assessing", and
(e) in subsection (4)—
   (i) for "taxing officer" substitute "costs officer", and
   (ii) for "taxed" substitute "assessed".

68 In section 73 (charging orders), in subsection (1)—

(a) for "taxed" substitute "assessed", and
(b) for "taxation" substitute "assessment".

69 In section 74 (special provisions as to contentious business done in county courts)—

(a) in subsection (2)—
   (i) for "registrar" substitute "district judge",
   (ii) for "taxing officer" substitute "costs officer", and
   (iii) for "taxation" (in both places) substitute "assessment", and
(b) in subsection (3) for "taxation" substitute "assessment".

70 Omit the following provisions—

section 76 (non-practising solicitors eligible for membership of Society),
section 77 (annual subscription to Society), and
section 78 (cessation and suspension of membership of Society).

71 For section 79 (committees and sub-committees of the Council) substitute—

"79 Discharge of the Council's functions

(1) The Council may arrange for any function of the Council (including any function exercisable by the Council by virtue of section 80) to be exercised by—

(a) a committee of the Council,
(b) a sub-committee of such a committee,
(c) a body corporate which is established for the purpose of providing services to the Council (or any committee of the Council) and is a wholly-owned subsidiary of the Society, or
(d) an individual (whether or not a member of the Society's staff).

(2) Where by virtue of subsection (1) any function may be discharged by a committee, the committee may arrange for the discharge of the function by—

(a) a sub-committee of that committee,
(b) a body corporate which is established for the purpose of providing services to the Council (or any committee of the Council) and is a wholly-owned subsidiary of the Society, or
(c) an individual (whether or not a member of the Society's staff).

(3) Where, by virtue of subsection (1) or (2), any function may be discharged by a sub-committee, that sub-committee may arrange for the discharge of the function by an individual (whether or not a member of the Society's staff).

(4) Arrangements made under this section in respect of a function may provide that the function is to be exercised in accordance with the arrangements only (and not by the delegating body).

(5) In subsection (4) "the delegating body" means—

(a) in the case of arrangements under subsection (1), the Council;
(b) in the case of arrangements under subsection (2), the committee;
(c) in the case of arrangements under subsection (3), the sub-committee.

(6) Subsections (2) and (3) have effect subject to any contrary direction given by the Council.

(7) Where arrangements under subsection (3) relate to a function delegated by a committee under subsection (2), subsection (3) also has effect subject to any contrary direction given by that committee.

(8) Any power given by subsection (1), (2) or (3) may be exercised so as to impose restrictions or conditions on the body or individual by whom the function is to be discharged.

(9) A committee or sub-committee may include or consist of individuals other than—

(a) members of the Council;
(b) members of the Society;
(c) solicitors.

(10) A sub-committee of a committee may also include or consist of individuals other than members of the committee.

(11) The Council may make arrangements for the appointment and removal of members of any committee to be made other than by the Council.

(12) A committee or sub-committee may regulate its own procedure, including quorum.

(13) The validity of any proceedings of a committee or sub-committee is not affected by any vacancy among its members.

(14) In this section "wholly-owned subsidiary" has the meaning given by section 1159 of the Companies Act 2006.

(15) This section is subject to any provision to the contrary made by or under any enactment."

72 In section 80 (powers to act on behalf of Society)—

(a) in subsection (1) for "of any instrument made under it" substitute "any other enactment (or of any instrument made under this Act or any other enactment)", and
(b) omit subsection (2).

73 Omit sections 81 and 81A (administration of oaths and taking of affidavits).

74 Before section 87 (interpretation) insert—

"86A Rules

(1) Rules made by the Society under this Act may—

(a) make provision generally or subject to exceptions or only in relation to specified cases;
(b) make different provision for different cases or circumstances or for different purposes.

(2) Without prejudice to the generality of subsection (1), any rules prescribing a fee may provide for that fee to be reduced or waived in such circumstances as may be specified in the rules."

75 In section 87(1) (interpretation)—

(a) in the definition of "client account", for "in" to the end substitute "subject to rules under section 32(1)(a)",
(b) after the definition of "sole solicitor" insert—
""sole solicitor endorsement" has the same meaning as in section 1B;", and
(c) omit the following definitions—
"articles"
"controlled trust"
"duly certificated notary public"
"employee"
"indemnity conditions"
"replacement date"
"training conditions".

76 In section 89 (consequential amendments etc), omit subsection (7).

77 (1) Schedule 1 (intervention in solicitor's practice) is amended as follows.

(2) In paragraph 1 (grounds for intervention)—

(a) in sub-paragraph (1)(a)—
(i) for "Council have" substitute "Society has",
(ii) after "solicitor's practice" insert "or former practice", and

(iii) after "trustee" insert "or that employee is or was a trustee in his capacity as such an employee",

(b) after that sub-paragraph insert—

"(aa) the Society has reason to suspect dishonesty on the part of a solicitor ("S") in connection with—

(i) the business of any person of whom S is or was an employee, or of any body of which S is or was a manager, or

(ii) any business which is or was carried on by S as a sole trader;",

(c) in sub-paragraph (1)(b)—

(i) for "Council consider" substitute "Society considers", and

(ii) for "controlled trust" substitute "trust",

(d) in sub-paragraph (1)(c) for "Council are" substitute "Society is",

(e) in sub-paragraph (1)(ee)—

(i) for "Council are" substitute "Society is", and

(ii) after "illness" insert ", injury",

(f) in sub-paragraph (1)(h)—

(i) for "Council are" substitute "Society is", and

(ii) omit "sole",

(g) in sub-paragraph (1)(i) and (k) for "Council are" substitute "Society is",

(h) in sub-paragraph (1)(l)—

(i) for "Council are" substitute "Society is",

(ii) in sub-paragraph (iii) for "an officer" substitute "a manager", and

(iii) in that sub-paragraph for "Council of the Law Society" substitute "Society",

(i) after sub-paragraph (1)(l) insert—

"(m) the Society is satisfied that it is necessary to exercise the powers conferred by Part 2 of this Schedule (or any of them) in relation to a solicitor to protect—

(i) the interests of clients (or former or potential clients) of the solicitor or his firm, or

(ii) the interests of the beneficiaries of any trust of which the solicitor is or was a trustee.",

(j) after sub-paragraph (1) insert—

"(1A) In sub-paragraph (1) "manager" has the same meaning as in the Legal Services Act 2007 (see section 207 of that Act).", and

(k) omit sub-paragraph (2).

(3) In paragraph 3 (intervention following an undue delay)—

(a) for "10(3)" substitute "10(9)",

(b) for paragraph (a) substitute—

"(a) the Society is satisfied that there has been undue delay—

(i) on the part of a solicitor in connection with any matter in which the solicitor or his firm is or was acting on behalf of a client or with any trust, or

(ii) on the part of an employee of a solicitor in connection with any trust of which the employee is or was a trustee in his capacity as such an employee; and",

(c) in paragraph (c) for "Council regard" substitute "Society regards".

(4) In paragraph 4(2) (continuation of powers after death etc of solicitor)—

(a) after "6(2) and (3)" insert ", 6A",

(b) for "and (5)" substitute ", (5) and (6)", and

(c) for "10(1)" substitute "10(2) and (7)".

(5) In paragraph 6 (vesting of sums in Society)—

(a) in sub-paragraph (1)—

(i) for "Council pass" substitute "Society passes",

(ii) for "Council's" substitute "Society's", and

(iii) after "thereto" insert "and to rules under paragraph 6B",

(b) in sub-paragraph (2)(a) for "his practice" to the end substitute—

"(i) his practice or former practice,

(ii) any trust of which he is or formerly was a trustee, or

(iii) any trust of which a person who is or was an employee of the solicitor is or was a trustee in the person's capacity as such an employee;", and

(c) in sub-paragraph (2)(c) for "to which the complaint relates" substitute "in connection with which the Society is satisfied there has been undue delay as mentioned in sub-paragraph (a) of that paragraph".

(6) After paragraph 6 insert—

"**6A** (1) Without prejudice to paragraph 5, if the Society passes a resolution to the effect that any rights to which this paragraph applies shall vest in the Society, those rights shall vest accordingly.

(2) This paragraph applies to any right to recover or receive debts due to the solicitor or his firm in connection with his practice or former practice.

(3) Any sums recovered by the Society by virtue of the exercise of rights vested under sub-paragraph (1) shall vest in the Society and shall be held by it on trust to exercise in relation to them the powers conferred by this Part of this Schedule and, subject to those powers and to rules under paragraph 6B, upon trust for the persons beneficially entitled to them.

(4) The Society shall serve on the solicitor or his firm, and any person who owes a debt to which the order applies, a certified copy of the Society's resolution.

6B (1) The Society may make rules governing its treatment of sums vested in it under paragraph 6 or 6A(3).

(2) The rules may in particular make provision in respect of cases where the Society, having taken such steps to do so as are reasonable in all the circumstances of the case, is unable to trace the person or persons beneficially entitled to any sum vested in the Society under paragraph 6 or 6A(3) (including provision which requires amounts to be paid into or out of compensation funds (within the meaning of section 36A))."

(7) In paragraph 7(1) (holding of sums vested in Society)—

(a) after "paragraph 6" insert "or 6A(3)", and
(b) after "thereto" insert "and to rules under paragraph 6B".

(8) In paragraph 8 (information as to money held) for "holds money" to the end substitute—

"(a) holds money on behalf of the solicitor or his firm, or
(b) has information which is relevant to identifying any money held by or on behalf of the solicitor or his firm,

the court may require that person to give the Society information as to any such money and the accounts in which it is held."

(9) In paragraph 9 (documents)—

(a) in sub-paragraph (1)(a)—
 (i) after "possession" insert "or under the control", and
 (ii) for "or with any controlled trust" substitute "or former practice or with any trust of which the solicitor is or was a trustee",
(b) in sub-paragraph (1)(b)—
 (i) after "possession" insert "or under the control", and
 (ii) for "to which the complaint relates" substitute "of which the Society is satisfied",
(c) in sub-paragraph (3) after "possession" insert "or control",
(d) in sub-paragraph (5) after "the possession" insert "or under the control",
(e) after sub-paragraph (5) insert—

"(5A) In the case of a document which consists of information which is stored in electronic form, a requirement imposed by a notice under sub-paragraph (1) or an order under sub-paragraph (4) or (5), is a requirement to produce or deliver the information in a form in which it is legible or from which it can readily be produced in a legible form.",

(f) in sub-paragraph (6) after "possession of" insert "(a)",
(g) at the end of that sub-paragraph insert—
"(b) any property—
 (i) in the possession of or under the control of the solicitor or his firm, or
 (ii) in the case of an order under sub-paragraph (5), which was in the possession or under the control of such a person and has come into the possession or under the control of the person in respect of whom the order is made,

which the Society reasonably requires for the purpose of accessing information contained in such documents, and to use property obtained under paragraph (b) for that purpose.",

(h) in sub-paragraph (7) after "documents" insert "or other property",

(i) in sub-paragraph (8) after "documents" insert "or other property", and

(j) in sub-paragraph (10) after "documents" insert "or other property".

(10) For paragraph 10 (mail) substitute—

"Mail and other forms of communication

10 (1) The High Court, on the application of the Society, may from time to time make a communications redirection order.

(2) A communications redirection order is an order that specified communications to the solicitor or his firm are to be directed, in accordance with the order, to the Society or any person appointed by the Society.

(3) For the purposes of this paragraph—

(a) "specified communications" means communications of such description as are specified in the order;

(b) the descriptions of communications which may be so specified include—

(i) communications in the form of a postal packet;

(ii) electronic communications;

(iii) communications by telephone.

(4) A communications redirection order has effect for such time not exceeding 18 months as is specified in the order.

(5) Where a communications redirection order has effect, the Society or the person appointed by the Society may take possession or receipt of the communications redirected in accordance with the order.

(6) Where a communications redirection order is made, the Society must pay to—

(a) in the case of an order relating to postal packets, the postal operator concerned, and

(b) in any other case, the person specified in the order,

the like charges (if any) as would have been payable for the redirection of the communications to which the order relates if the addressee had permanently ceased to occupy or use the premises or other destination of the communications and had applied to the postal operator or the specified person (as the case may be) to redirect the communications to him as mentioned in the order.

(7) The High Court may, on the application of the Society, authorise the Society, or a person appointed by it, to take such steps as may be specified in the order in relation to any website purporting to be or have been maintained by or on behalf of the solicitor or his firm if the High Court is satisfied that the taking of those steps is necessary to protect the public interest or the interests of clients (or potential or former clients) of the solicitor or his firm.

(8) In this paragraph "postal operator" and "postal packet" have the meaning given by section 125(1) of the Postal Services Act 2000.

(9) This paragraph does not apply where the powers conferred by this Part of this Schedule are exercisable by virtue of paragraph 3."

(11) In paragraph 11(1) (trusts) for "controlled trust" substitute "trust".

(12) In paragraph 12 (liens) for "and documents" substitute ", documents and other property".

(13) After paragraph 13 (costs) insert—

"**13A** (1) The High Court, on the application of the Society, may order a former partner of the solicitor to pay a specified proportion of the costs mentioned in paragraph 13.

(2) The High Court may make an order under this paragraph only if it is satisfied that the conduct (or any part of the conduct) by reason of which the powers conferred by this Part were exercisable in relation to the solicitor was conduct carried on with the consent or connivance of, or was attributable to any neglect on the part of, the former partner.

(3) In this paragraph "specified" means specified in the order made by the High Court."

78 Omit Schedule 1A (inadequate professional services).

79 Omit Schedule 2 (the compensation fund).

Initial Commencement
To be appointed: see s 211(2).
Appointment
Paras 1, 2(b), 4(b), 7(b), 8(1), (2), 21, 31(1), (2)(a), (d), 34(1), (2)(a), (3), 38(a) (in part), 38(b)(i), (ii), 50(a)(ii), 53, 54(1), (4)(b), 64(1), (3), (4), 71, 72(a), 75(c) (in part): Appointment: 7 March 2008: see SI 2008/222, art 2(j)(i); for transitional provisions see art 7(2) thereof.
Paras 38(b)(iii), 47, 48, 54(2)(a), (c), (3), (4)(a), (5), (6)(a), (9)(b), 56(c): Appointment: 30 June 2008: see SI 2008/1436, art 2(d)(i); for transitional provisions see art 4 thereof.

PART 2
THE ADMINISTRATION OF JUSTICE ACT 1985 (C 61)

80 The Administration of Justice Act 1985 is amended in accordance with this Part of this Schedule.

81 (1) Section 9 (incorporated practices) is amended as follows.

(2) In subsection (1)—

(a) for "Council" (in both places) substitute "Society",
(b) in paragraph (a) for "by solicitors" to the end substitute "of legal services bodies;",
(c) in paragraph (b) for "any such services" substitute "any solicitor services or other relevant legal services", and
(d) in paragraph (c)—
(i) for "conditions" substitute "requirements", and
(ii) omit "corporate".

(3) After that subsection insert—

"(1A) Where the Society makes rules under subsection (1), it must by rules under subsection (1)(c) prescribe the requirement that (subject to any exceptions provided by the rules) recognised bodies must not provide services other than—

(a) solicitor services, or
(b) solicitor services and other relevant legal services.

(1B) "Relevant legal services" means—

(a) solicitor services, and
(b) where authorised persons other than solicitors or registered European lawyers are managers or employees of, or have an interest in, a recognised body, services of the kind provided by individuals practising as such authorised persons (whether or not those services involve the carrying on of reserved legal activities within the meaning of the Legal Services Act 2007).

(1C) The Society may by rules under this section provide that services specified, or of a description specified, in the rules are not to be treated as solicitor services or other relevant legal services."

(4) In subsection (2)—

(a) for "Council" (in both places) substitute "Society",
(b) in paragraph (a) for "are to be" to the end substitute ", or for the renewal of such recognition, are to be made, and requiring such applications to be accompanied by a fee of such amount as the Society may from time to time determine;",
(c) after that paragraph insert—
"(aa) for the manner and form in which other applications under the rules are to be made, and requiring such applications to be accompanied by a fee of such amount as the Society may from time to time determine;",
(d) for paragraphs (c) to (e) substitute—

"(c) about the time when any recognition, or renewal of recognition, takes effect and the period for which it is (subject to the provisions made by or under this Part) to remain in force;

(d) for the suspension or revocation of any such recognition, on such grounds and in such circumstances as may be prescribed by the rules;

(e) about the effect on the recognition of a partnership or other unincorporated body ("the existing body") of any change in the membership of the existing body, including provision for the existing body's recognition to be transferred where the existing body ceases to exist and another body succeeds to the whole or substantially the whole of its business;

(ea) for the keeping by the Society of a register containing the names and places of business of all bodies which are for the time being recognised under this section, and such other information relating to those bodies as may be specified in the rules;

(eb) for information (or information of a specified description) on such a register to be made available to the public, including provision about the manner in which, and times at which, information is to be made so available;", and

(e) after paragraph (f) insert—

"(fa) about the education and training requirements to be met by managers and employees of recognised bodies;

(fb) for rules made under any provision of the 1974 Act to have effect in relation to managers and employees of recognised bodies with such additions, omissions or other modifications as appear to the Society to be necessary or expedient;

(fc) requiring recognised bodies to appoint a person or persons to monitor compliance, by the recognised body, its managers and its employees, with requirements imposed on them by or by virtue of this Act or any rules applicable to them by virtue of this section;".

(5) After subsection (2) insert—

"(2A) If rules under this section provide for the recognition of legal services bodies which have one or more managers who are not legally qualified, the rules must make provision—

(a) for the recognition of such bodies to be suspended or revoked, on such grounds and in such circumstances as may be prescribed by the rules;

(b) as to the criteria and procedure for the Society's approving, as suitable to be a manager of a recognised body, an individual who is not legally qualified (and for the Society's withdrawing such approval).

(2B) Rules under this section may make provision for appeals to the High Court against decisions made by the Society under the rules—

(a) to suspend or revoke the recognition of any body;

(b) not to approve, as suitable to be the manager of a recognised body, an individual who is not legally qualified (or to withdraw such approval).

(2C) The rules may provide for appeals against decisions within subsection (2B)(b) to be brought by the individual to whom the decision relates (as well as the body).

(2D) In relation to an appeal under rules made by virtue of subsection (2B), the High Court may make such order as it thinks fit as to payment of costs.

(2E) The decision of the High Court on such an appeal shall be final.

(2F) Where the Society decides to recognise a body under this section it must grant that recognition subject to one or more conditions if—

(a) the case is of a kind prescribed for the purposes of this section by rules made by the Society, and

(b) the Society considers that it is in the public interest to do so.

(2G) While a body is recognised under this section, the Society—

(a) must direct that the body's recognition is to have effect subject to one or more conditions if—

  (i) the case is of a prescribed kind, and

  (ii) the Society considers that it is in the public interest to do so;

(b) may, in such circumstances as may be prescribed, direct that the body's recognition is to have effect subject to such conditions as the Society may think fit.

"Prescribed" means prescribed by rules made by the Society.

(2H) The conditions which may be imposed under subsection (2F) or (2G) include—

(a) conditions requiring the body to take specified steps that will, in the opinion of the Society, be conducive to the carrying on by the body of an efficient business;
(b) conditions which prohibit the body from taking any specified steps except with the approval of the Society;
(c) if rules under this section provide for the recognition of legal services bodies which have one or more managers who are not legally qualified, a condition that all the managers of the body must be legally qualified.

"Specified" means specified in the condition.

(2I) Rules made by the Society may make provision about when conditions imposed under this section take effect (including provision conferring power on the Society to direct that a condition is not to have effect until the conclusion of any appeal in relation to it).

(2J) Section 86A of the 1974 Act applies to rules under this section as it applies to rules under that Act.

(2K) Rules under this section may contain such incidental, supplemental, transitional or transitory provisions or savings as the Society considers necessary or expedient."

(6) For subsection (3) substitute—

"(3) Despite section 24(2) of the 1974 Act, section 20 of that Act (prohibition on unqualified person acting as solicitor) does not apply to a recognised body; and nothing in section 24(1) of that Act applies in relation to such a body."

(7) Omit subsection (4).

(8) In subsection (5) omit "corporate".

(9) In subsection (7)—

(a) for "Secretary of State" (in both places) substitute "Lord Chancellor", and
(b) for "the commencement of this section" substitute "or in the same session as the Legal Services Act 2007 was passed".

(10) In subsection (8)—

(a) after the definition of "the 1974 Act" insert—

""authorised person" means an authorised person in relation to an activity which is a reserved legal activity (within the meaning of the Legal Services Act 2007);",

(b) for ""the Council" and "the Society" have" substitute ""the Society" has",
(c) after the definition of "the Society" insert—

""legally qualified" and "legal services body" have the meaning given by section 9A;

"manager", in relation to a body, has the same meaning as in the Legal Services Act 2007 (see section 207 of that Act);",

(d) omit the definition of "officer",
(e) in the definition of "recognised body" omit "corporate", and
(f) after the definition of "registered European lawyer" insert—

""solicitor services" means professional services such as are provided by individuals practising as solicitors or lawyers of other jurisdictions;

and a person has an interest in a body if the person has an interest in the body within the meaning of Part 5 of the Legal Services Act 2007 (see sections 72 and 109 of that Act)."

(11) Omit subsection (9).

82 After that section insert—

"9A Legal services bodies

(1) For the purposes of section 9, a "legal services body" means a body (corporate or unincorporate) in respect of which—

(a) the management and control condition, and
(b) the relevant lawyer condition,

are satisfied.

(2) The management and control condition is satisfied if—

- (a) at least 75% of the body's managers are legally qualified,
- (b) the proportion of shares in the body held by persons who are legally qualified is at least 75%,
- (c) the proportion of voting rights in the body which persons who are legally qualified are entitled to exercise, or control the exercise of, is at least 75%,
- (d) all the persons with an interest in the body who are not legally qualified are managers of the body, and
- (e) all the managers of the body who are not legally qualified are individuals approved by the Society as suitable to be managers of a recognised body.

(3) The Society may by rules under section 9 provide that, in relation to specified kinds of bodies, subsection (2) applies as if the references to 75% were to such greater percentage as may be specified (and different percentages may be specified for different kinds of bodies).

(4) The relevant lawyer condition is satisfied in relation to a body if at least one manager of the body is—

- (a) a solicitor,
- (b) a registered European lawyer, or
- (c) a qualifying body.

(5) For that purpose a qualifying body is a body in respect of which—

- (a) the management and control condition [is] satisfied ...,
- (b) the relevant lawyer condition is satisfied by virtue of subsection (4)(a) or (b), and
- (c) the services condition is satisfied.

(6) For the purposes of this section the following are legally qualified—

- (a) an authorised person who is an individual;
- (b) a registered foreign lawyer (within the meaning of section 89 of the Courts and Legal Services Act 1990 (c 41));
- (c) a person entitled to pursue professional activities under a professional title to which the Directive applies in a state to which the Directive applies (other than the title of barrister or solicitor in England and Wales);
- (d) an authorised person which is a body in respect of which—
  - (i) the services condition is satisfied, and
  - (ii) the management and control condition would be satisfied if the references in subsection (2) to persons who are legally qualified were to persons who are legally qualified by virtue of paragraphs (a) to (c);
- (e) a body which provides professional services such as are provided by individuals who are authorised persons or lawyers of other jurisdictions, and in respect of which the management and control condition would be satisfied if the references in subsection (2) to persons who are legally qualified were to persons who are legally qualified by virtue of paragraphs (a) to (c).
- [(f) a legal partnership which—
  - (i) was in existence immediately before the commencement of this paragraph,
  - (ii) since that time has continued to be a partnership of the kind mentioned in rule 12.01(1)(b), 12.02(1)(b) or 12.04(1)(c)(i) of the pre-commencement conduct rules (framework of practice), and
  - (iii) has not, since that time, had a body corporate (other than a body within paragraph (g)) as a member;
- (g) a body corporate which—
  - (i) was recognised under section 9 immediately before the commencement of this paragraph, and
  - (ii) has since that time continued to satisfy the requirements of rule 14.03(1) and 14.04(1) to (3) or the requirements of rule 14.05(1) to (3) of the pre-commencement conduct rules (restrictions on directors, owners etc of incorporated practices);
- (h) a body which—
  - (i) is an authorised person and satisfies the services condition, or
  - (ii) provides professional services such as are provided by individuals who are authorised persons or lawyers of other jurisdictions,

and which satisfies the requirements of rules under subsection (6C).

(6A) For the purposes of subsection (6)(f), a partnership is to be treated as the same partnership despite a change in membership, if any person who was a member before the change remains a member.

(6B) For the purposes of subsection (6)(f) and (g), the references in the pre-commencement conduct rules to a recognised body are to be construed as references to a body which was recognised under section 9 immediately before the commencement of subsection (6)(f) and (g).

(6C) The Society must make rules for the purposes of paragraph (h) of subsection (6) prescribing the requirements relating to management and control which must be satisfied by or in relation to a body for it to fall within that paragraph.]

(7) For the purposes of this section, the services condition is satisfied in relation to a body if the body provides only services which may be provided by a recognised body (having regard to rules under section 9(1A) and (1C)).

(8) For the purposes of this section—

"authorised person" has the same meaning as in section 9;
"the Directive" means Directive 98/5/EC of the European Parliament and the Council, to facilitate practice of the profession of lawyer on a permanent basis in a Member State other than that in which the qualification was obtained;
["legal partnership" means a partnership in which a solicitor, a registered European lawyer or a recognised body is permitted to practise by virtue of rules made under section 31 of the Solicitors Act 1974 (c 47), as those rules had effect immediately before the commencement of subsection (6)(f);]
"manager", in relation to a body, has the meaning given by section 9;
["pre-commencement conduct rules" means rules under Part 2 of the Solicitors Act 1974 or section 9 of this Act, known as the Solicitors' Code of Conduct 2007, as those rules had effect immediately before the commencement of subsection (6)(f) and (g);]
"recognised body" has the same meaning as in section 9 [(subject to subsection (6B) above)];
"registered European lawyer" has the same meaning as in section 9;
"shares" has the same meaning as for the purposes of Part 5 of the Legal Services Act 2007 (see sections 72 and 109 of that Act);
["the Society" has the meaning given by section 87(1) of the Solicitors Act 1974;]
"specified" means specified in rules made by the Society;

and a person has an interest in a body if the person has an interest in the body for the purposes of section 9."

83 (1) Section 10 (penalty for pretending to be a body recognised under section 9) is amended as follows.

(2) In subsection (1) omit "corporate" (in both places).

(3) In subsection (2) omit "corporate".

(4) For subsection (3) substitute—

"(3) Where an offence under this section committed by a body corporate is proved to have been committed with the consent or connivance of or to be attributable to any neglect on the part of an officer of the body corporate, that officer (as well as the body corporate) is guilty of the offence and is liable to be proceeded against and punished accordingly.

(4) Where the affairs of a body corporate are managed by its members, subsection (3) applies in relation to the acts and defaults of a member in connection with the member's functions of management as it applies to an officer of the body corporate.

(5) Proceedings for an offence under this section alleged to have been committed by an unincorporated body are to be brought in the name of that body (and not in that of any of its members) and, for the purposes of any such proceedings, any rules of court relating to the service of documents have effect as if that body were a corporation.

(6) A fine imposed on an unincorporated body on its conviction of an offence under this section is to be paid out of the funds of that body.

(7) If an unincorporated body is charged with an offence under this section, section 33 of the Criminal Justice Act 1925 (c 86) and Schedule 3 to the Magistrates' Courts Act 1980 (c 43) (procedure on charge of an offence against a corporation) have effect in like manner as in the case of a corporation so charged.

(8) Where an offence under this section committed by an unincorporated body (other than a partnership) is proved to have been committed with the consent or connivance of, or to be attributable to any neglect on the part of, any officer of the body or any member of its governing body, that officer or member as well as the unincorporated body is guilty of the offence and liable to be proceeded against and punished accordingly.

(9) Where an offence under this section committed by a partnership is proved to have been committed with the consent or connivance of, or to be attributable to any neglect on the part of, a partner, that partner as well as the partnership is guilty of the offence and liable to be proceeded against and punished accordingly.

(10) In this section "officer", in relation to a body corporate, means—

- (a) any director, secretary or other similar officer of the body corporate, or
- (b) any person who was purporting to act in any such capacity."

84 (1) Section 43 (jurisdiction and powers of Solicitors Disciplinary Tribunal in relation to complaints against solicitors) is amended as follows.

(2) In subsection (2)(a) for "(7) to" substitute "(9) to".

(3) After subsection (3) insert—

"(3A) Nothing in section 157 of the Legal Services Act 2007 (approved regulators not to make provision for redress) prevents an order being made under subsection (3)."

(4) For subsection (5) substitute—

"(5) An appeal under section 49 of the Solicitors Act 1974 against an order of the Tribunal under subsection (3) lies only at the instance of the solicitor with respect to whom the legal aid complaint was made."

85 In the title of Schedule 2, for "Incorporated practices" substitute "Legal services practices".

86 In paragraph 1 of that Schedule (interpretation)—

- (a) in sub-paragraph (1) omit "corporate",
- (b) in sub-paragraph (2) omit—
  - (i) paragraph (b) and the "or" immediately preceding it,
  - (ii) "corporate", and
  - (iii) "or application",
- (c) after that sub-paragraph insert—

"(2A) References in this Schedule to a manager or employee of a recognised body, in relation to a complaint (other than such a complaint as is mentioned in paragraph 16(1A)(a)), include references to a person who was such a manager or employee at the time when the conduct to which the complaint relates took place.",

- (d) omit sub-paragraph (3),
- (e) in sub-paragraph (4) omit from "; and for those purposes" to the end,
- (f) in sub-paragraph (5) for "sub-paragraphs (3) and (4)" substitute "sub-paragraphs (4) and (6)", and
- (g) for sub-paragraph (6) substitute—

"(6) In this Schedule—

"manager", in relation to a body, has the same meaning as in the Legal Services Act 2007 (see section 207 of that Act);
"registered European lawyer" has the same meaning as in section 9A;
"the 1974 Act" means the Solicitors Act 1974."

87 For paragraph 2 of that Schedule (appeal against refusal of Council to grant recognition) substitute—

"Appeal against refusal of Society to grant recognition etc

2 (1) A body may appeal to the High Court against—

(a) a decision to refuse an application by the body for recognition under section 9;
(b) a decision to impose a condition under subsection (2F) of that section on the body's recognition under that section;
(c) a decision to impose a condition under subsection (2G) of that section on the body's recognition under that section.

(2) A recognised body whose recognition is subject to a condition within section 9(2H)(b) may appeal to the High Court against any decision by the Society to refuse to approve the taking of any step for the purposes of that condition.

(3) Rules made by the Society may make provision, as respects any application for recognition that is neither granted nor refused by the Society within such period as may be specified in the rules, for enabling an appeal to be brought under this paragraph in relation to the application as if it had been refused by the Society.

(4) On an appeal under sub-paragraph (1)(a) or (b), the High Court may—

(a) affirm the decision of the Society,
(b) direct the Society to grant the body recognition under section 9 free from conditions or subject to such conditions as the High Court may think fit,
(c) direct the Society not to recognise the body,
(d) if the Society has recognised the body, by order suspend the recognition, or
(e) make such other order as the High Court thinks fit.

(5) On an appeal under sub-paragraph (1)(c), the High Court may—

(a) affirm the decision of the Society,
(b) direct that the body's recognition under section 9 is to have effect subject to such conditions as the High Court may think fit,
(c) by order revoke the direction given by the Society under section 9(2G), or
(d) make such other order as the High Court thinks fit.

(6) On an appeal under sub-paragraph (2), the High Court may—

(a) affirm the decision of the Society,
(b) direct the Society to approve the taking of one or more steps for the purposes of a condition within section 9(2H)(b), or
(c) make such other order as the High Court thinks fit.

(7) In relation to an appeal under this paragraph, the High Court may make such order as it thinks fit as to payment of costs.

(8) The decision of the High Court on an appeal under this paragraph is final."

88 For paragraph 3 of that Schedule (accounts rules) substitute—

"3 (1) This paragraph applies where rules made under section 32(1) of the 1974 Act are applied—

(a) to recognised bodies in accordance with section 9(2)(f) of this Act, or
(b) to managers or employees of such bodies in accordance with section 9(2)(fb) of this Act.

(2) The Society may disclose a report on or information about the accounts of a recognised body, or a manager or employee of a recognised body, obtained in pursuance of such rules for use—

(a) in investigating the possible commission of an offence by the body or any of its managers or employees, and
(b) in connection with any prosecution of the body or any of its managers or employees consequent on the investigation."

89 In paragraph 4 of that Schedule (interest on clients' money)—

(a) in sub-paragraph (1)—
  (i) for "section 33(1)(a)" substitute "section 33(1)", and
  (ii) for the words from "and subject to" to the end substitute

", a recognised body is not liable to account to any client, other person or trust for interest received by the recognised body on money held at a bank or building society in an account which is for money received or held for, or on account of—

(a) clients of the recognised body, other persons or trusts, generally, or
(b) that client, person or trust separately.", and
(b) omit sub-paragraph (2).

90 After that paragraph insert—

"**4ZA** Where rules made under section 32 of the 1974 Act and containing any such provision as is referred to in section 33(1) of that Act are applied to managers or employees of recognised bodies in accordance with section 9(2)(fb), then, except as provided by the rules, a manager or employee to whom the rules are applied is not liable to account to any client, other person or trust for interest received by the manager or employee on money held at a bank or building society in an account which is for money received or held for, or on account of—

(a) clients of the recognised body, other persons or trusts, generally, or
(b) that client, person or trust, separately."

91 For paragraph 4A of that Schedule (inspection of bank accounts) substitute—

"**4A** (1) This paragraph applies where rules made under section 33A(1) of the 1974 Act are applied—

(a) to recognised bodies in accordance with section 9(2)(f) of this Act, or
(b) to managers or employees of such bodies in accordance with section 9(2)(fb) of this Act.

(2) The Society may disclose information about the accounts of a recognised body, or a manager or employee of a recognised body, obtained in pursuance of such rules for use—

(a) in investigating the possible commission of an offence by the body or any of its managers or employees, and
(b) in connection with any prosecution of the body or any of its managers or employees consequent on the investigation."

92 For paragraph 5 of that Schedule (accountants' reports) substitute—

"5 Where rules made under section 34 of the 1974 Act are applied to recognised bodies in accordance with section 9(2)(f), section 34(9) and (10) of that Act apply in relation to a recognised body as they apply in relation to a solicitor."

93 After that paragraph insert—

"**5A** Where rules made under section 34 of the 1974 Act are applied to managers or employees of recognised bodies in accordance with section 9(2)(fb), section 34(9) and (10) of that Act apply in relation to a manager or employee to which the rules are applied as they apply in relation to a solicitor."

94 For paragraph 6 of that Schedule (compensation fund) substitute—

"6 (1) Section 36 of the 1974 Act applies in relation to recognised bodies as if for paragraphs (a) and (b) of subsection (1) there were substituted—

"(a) an act or omission of a recognised body or former recognised body;
(b) an act or omission of a manager or employee, or former manager or employee, of a recognised body or former recognised body;

(2) Section 36A(2) and (3) of the 1974 Act applies in relation to recognised bodies as it applies in relation to solicitors."

95 In paragraph 7 of that Schedule (solicitor who is justice of the peace not to act in certain proceedings) for "an officer" (in both places) substitute "a manager".

96 In paragraph 9 of that Schedule (restriction on employment of person struck off roll or suspended)—

(a) the existing provision becomes sub-paragraph (1) and in that sub-paragraph after "recognised body" insert "(and any manager or employee of it)", and
(b) after that sub-paragraph insert—

"(2) No recognised body (or manager or employee of such a body) may, except in accordance with a written permission granted by the Society under this paragraph, permit a person to whom sub-paragraph (3) applies to—

(a) be a manager of the body, or
(b) have an interest in the body;

and for this purpose a person has an interest in the body if he has an interest in the body within the meaning of Part 5 of the Legal Services Act 2007 (see sections 72 and 109 of that Act).

(3) This sub-paragraph applies to a person who to the knowledge of the recognised body (or, as the case may be, the manager or employee) is a person—

(a) who is disqualified from practising as a solicitor by reason of one of the facts mentioned in section 41(1)(a), (b) or (c) of the 1974 Act (name struck off the roll, suspension etc), or
(b) in respect of whom there is a direction in force under section 47(2)(g) of that Act (prohibition on restoration to roll).

(4) Permission granted for the purposes of sub-paragraph (2) may be granted for such period and subject to such conditions as the Society thinks fit.

(5) A person aggrieved by the refusal of the Society to grant permission under sub-paragraph (4), or by any conditions attached by the Society to the grant of any such permission may appeal to the High Court which may—

(a) confirm the refusal or the conditions, as the case may be, or
(b) grant a permission under this paragraph for such period and subject to such conditions as it thinks fit.

(6) In relation to an appeal under sub-paragraph (5) the High Court may make such order as it thinks fit as to payment of costs.

(7) The decision of the High Court on an appeal under sub-paragraph (5) is final."

97 In paragraph 10 of that Schedule (failure to disclose striking off or suspension)—

(a) the existing paragraph becomes sub-paragraph (1) of that paragraph,
(b) in that sub-paragraph after "recognised body" insert "(or any manager or employee of such a body)", and
(c) after that sub-paragraph insert—

"(2) It is an offence for a person ("P") to whom sub-paragraph (3) applies—

(a) to seek or accept from any person an interest in a recognised body, without previously informing that person (and, if different, the recognised body) that P is a person to whom that sub-paragraph applies, or
(b) to seek or accept a position as a manager of a recognised body, without previously informing that body that P is such a person.

(3) This sub-paragraph applies to a person—

(a) who is disqualified from practising as a solicitor by reason of one of the facts mentioned in section 41(1)(a), (b) or (c) of the 1974 Act (name struck off the roll, suspension etc), or
(b) in respect of whom there is a direction in force under section 47(2)(g) of that Act (prohibition on restoration to roll).

(4) A person guilty of an offence under sub-paragraph (2) is liable on summary conviction to a fine not exceeding level 3 on the standard scale.

(5) Subsection (2) of section 42 of the 1974 Act applies in relation to an offence under sub-paragraph (2) as it applies in relation to an offence under that section.

(6) For the purposes of sub-paragraph (2)(a) a person seeks or accepts an interest in a recognised body if the person seeks or accepts an interest which if it were obtained by the person would result in the person having an interest in that body within the meaning of Part 5 of the Legal Services Act 2007 (see sections 72 and 109 of that Act)."

98 Omit paragraph 11 of that Schedule (control of employment of persons convicted of offences of dishonesty and certain other persons).

99 Omit paragraph 12 of that Schedule (offences in connection with orders under section 43(2) of the 1974 Act).

100 Omit paragraph 13 of that Schedule (redress for inadequate professional services).

101 For paragraph 14 of that Schedule (examination of files) substitute—

"Information about suitability for recognition

14 (1) The Society may give a notice under this paragraph if it is satisfied that it is necessary to do so for the purpose of investigating whether—

(a) a recognised body continues to be suitable to be recognised under section 9, or
(b) a manager of a recognised body who is not legally qualified (within the meaning of section 9A) continues to be suitable to be a manager of a recognised body.

(2) A notice under this paragraph is a notice which requires a person within sub-paragraph (3)—

(a) to provide information, or information of a description, specified in the notice, or
(b) to produce documents, or documents of a description, specified in the notice.

(3) The persons are—

(a) the recognised body;
(b) an employee or manager of the recognised body;
(c) a person who has an interest in the recognised body (within the meaning of the Legal Services Act 2007 (see sections 72 and 109 of that Act)).

(4) For the purposes of this paragraph, section 44B(4) to (7) of the 1974 Act applies—

(a) in relation to a notice under this paragraph as if it were a notice under section 44B of that Act, and
(b) in relation to a person given a notice under this paragraph as if that person were a person given a notice under that section,

and references in subsections (6) and (7) of that section to powers conferred by that section are to be read as references to powers conferred by this paragraph.

(5) Where powers conferred by Part 2 of Schedule 1 to the 1974 Act are exercisable in relation to a person within paragraph (a), (b) or (c) of sub-paragraph (3), they continue to be so exercisable after the person has ceased to be a person within the paragraph in question.

(6) Section 44BA of the 1974 Act (power to require explanation of document or information) applies in relation to a notice under this paragraph and the person to whom such a notice is given as it applies in relation to a notice under section 44B of the 1974 Act and the person to whom such a notice is given.

(7) Subsection (1) of section 44BC of that Act (falsification of documents etc) applies in relation to an investigation of the kind mentioned in sub-paragraph (1) as it applies in relation to the investigations mentioned in that subsection, and subsections (2), (4) and (5) of that section apply accordingly.

(8) Subsection (3) of that section (provision of false information etc) applies in relation to a requirement imposed under this paragraph as it applies in relation to a requirement imposed by section 44B of that Act, and subsections (4) and (5) of that section apply accordingly."

102 For paragraph 14A of that Schedule (payment of costs of investigations) substitute—

"Power to charge for costs of investigation

14A

(1) The Society may make regulations prescribing charges to be paid to the Society by recognised bodies who are the subject of a discipline investigation.

(2) A discipline investigation is an investigation carried out by the Society into a failure or apprehended failure by a recognised body to comply with any requirement imposed by or by virtue of this Act or any rules applicable to it by virtue of section 9.

(3) Regulations under this paragraph may—

(a) make different provision for different cases or purposes;
(b) provide for the whole or part of a charge payable under the regulations to be repaid in such circumstances as may be prescribed by the regulations.

(4) Any charge which a recognised body is required to pay under regulations under this paragraph is recoverable by the Society as a debt due to the Society from the recognised body.

(5) This paragraph applies in relation to a manager or employee of a recognised body as it applies in relation to a recognised body."

103 After that paragraph insert—

"Disciplinary powers of the Society

14B (1) This paragraph applies where the Society is satisfied that a recognised body, or a manager or employee of a recognised body, has failed to comply with a requirement imposed by or by virtue of this Act or any rules applicable to that person by virtue of section 9 of this Act.

(2) The Society may do one or both of the following—

(a) give the person a written rebuke;
(b) direct the person to pay a penalty not exceeding £2,000.

(3) The Society may publish details of any action it has taken under sub-paragraph (2)(a) or (b), if it considers it to be in the public interest to do so.

(4) Where the Society takes action against a person under sub-paragraph (2)(b), or decides to publish under sub-paragraph (3) details of such action under sub-paragraph (2)(a) or (b), it must notify the person in writing that it has done so.

(5) A penalty imposed under sub-paragraph (2)(b) does not become payable until—

(a) the end of the period during which an appeal against the decision to impose the penalty, or the amount of the penalty, may be made under paragraph 14C, or
(b) if such an appeal is made, such time as it is determined or withdrawn.

(6) The Society may not publish under sub-paragraph (3) details of any action under sub-paragraph (2)(a) or (b)—

(a) during the period within which an appeal against—
 (i) the decision to take the action,
 (ii) in the case of action under sub-paragraph (2)(b), the amount of the penalty, or
 (iii) the decision to publish the details,
may be made under paragraph 14C, or
(b) if such an appeal has been made, until such time as it is determined or withdrawn.

(7) The Society must make rules—

(a) prescribing the circumstances in which the Society may decide to take action under sub-paragraph (2)(a) or (b);
(b) about the practice and procedure to be followed by the Society in relation to such action;
(c) governing the publication under sub-paragraph (3) of details of action taken under sub-paragraph (2)(a) or (b);

and the Society may make such other rules in connection with the exercise of its powers under this paragraph as it considers appropriate.

(8) Before making rules under sub-paragraph (7), the Society must consult the Tribunal.

(9) A penalty under this paragraph may be recovered as a debt due to the Society, and is to be forfeited to Her Majesty.

(10) The Lord Chancellor may, by order, amend paragraph (b) of sub-paragraph (2) so as to substitute for the amount for the time being specified in that paragraph such other amount as may be specified in the order.

(11) Before making an order under sub-paragraph (10), the Lord Chancellor must consult the Society.

(12) An order under sub-paragraph (10) is to be made by statutory instrument subject to annulment in pursuance of a resolution of either House of Parliament.

(13) This paragraph is without prejudice to any power conferred on the Society, or any other person, to make an application or complaint to the Tribunal.

14C (1) A person may appeal against—

(a) a decision by the Society to rebuke that person under paragraph 14B(2)(a) if a decision is also made to publish details of the rebuke;
(b) a decision by the Society to impose a penalty on that person under paragraph 14B(2)(b) or the amount of that penalty;
(c) a decision by the Society to publish under paragraph 14B(3) details of any action taken against that person under paragraph 14B(2)(a) or (b).

(2) Subsections (9)(b), (10)(a) and (b), (11) and (12) of section 46 of the 1974 Act (Tribunal rules about procedure for hearings etc) apply in relation to appeals under this paragraph as they apply in relation to applications or complaints, except that subsection (11) of that section is to be read as if for "the applicant" to "application)" there were substituted "any party to the appeal".

(3) Rules under section 46(9)(b) of the 1974 Act may, in particular, make provision about the period during which an appeal under this paragraph may be made.

(4) On an appeal under this paragraph, the Tribunal has power to make an order which—

(a) affirms the decision of the Society;
(b) revokes the decision of the Society;
(c) in the case of a penalty imposed under paragraph 14B(2)(b), varies the amount of the penalty;
(d) in the case of a recognised body, contains provision for any of the matters mentioned in paragraph 18(2);
(e) in the case of a manager or employee of a recognised body, contains provision for any of the matters mentioned in paragraph 18A(2);
(f) makes such provision as the Tribunal thinks fit as to payment of costs.

(5) Where, by virtue of sub-paragraph (4)(e), an order contains provision for any of the matters mentioned in sub-paragraph (2)(c) of paragraph 18A, sub-paragraphs (5) and (6) of that paragraph apply as if the order had been made under sub-paragraph (2)(c) of that paragraph.

(6) An appeal from the Tribunal shall lie to the High Court, at the instance of the Society or the person in respect of whom the order of the Tribunal was made.

(7) The High Court shall have power to make such order on an appeal under this paragraph as it may think fit.

(8) Any decision of the High Court on an appeal under this section shall be final.

(9) This paragraph is without prejudice to any power conferred on the Tribunal in connection with an application or complaint made to it."

104 In paragraph 16 of that Schedule (complaints to Tribunal with respect to recognised bodies)—

(a) in sub-paragraph (1), in paragraph (a) omit "in the United Kingdom",
(b) in paragraph (b) of that sub-paragraph for "section 34 of the 1974 Act" substitute "any requirement imposed by or by virtue of this Act",
(c) for paragraph (c) of that sub-paragraph substitute—
"(c) a complaint that the body has acted in contravention of section 41 of the 1974 Act or paragraph 9(2) of this Schedule or of any conditions subject to which a permission has been granted under section 41 of that Act or that paragraph of this Schedule; or", and
(d) after that sub-paragraph insert—

"(1A) The Tribunal shall have jurisdiction to hear and determine any of the following complaints made to it under this paragraph with respect to a manager or employee of a recognised body ("the relevant person")—

(a) a complaint that the relevant person has been convicted by any court of a criminal offence which renders that person unsuitable to be a manager or employee (or both) of a recognised body;

(b) a complaint that the relevant person has failed to comply with any requirement imposed by or by virtue of this Act or any rules applicable to the relevant person by virtue of section 9 of this Act;

(c) a complaint that the relevant person has acted in contravention of section 41 of the 1974 Act or paragraph 9(2) of this Schedule or of any conditions subject to which a permission has been granted under that section or for the purposes of paragraph 9(2) of this Schedule;

(d) a complaint that the relevant person has knowingly acted in contravention of an order under section 43(2) of the 1974 Act or of any conditions subject to which a permission has been granted under such an order."

105 In paragraph 17 of that Schedule (procedure on applications and complaints)—

(a) for "(7)" substitute "(9)",

(b) in paragraph (a)—

(i) omit "11(1), 15(2) or",

(ii) omit "13(3) or", and

(iii) after "16(1)" insert "or (1A)", and

(c) in paragraph (c) after "body" insert "or, in the case of such a complaint as is mentioned in paragraph 16(1A), to a manager or employee of such a body".

106 In paragraph 18 of that Schedule (powers of Tribunal with respect to recognised bodies)—

(a) in sub-paragraph (1) after "this Schedule" insert "(other than paragraph 16(1A)",

(b) in paragraph (b) of that sub-paragraph for "section 34 of the 1974 Act" substitute "any requirement imposed by or by virtue of this Act",

(c) omit paragraph (d) of that sub-paragraph and the "or" immediately preceding it,

(d) in sub-paragraph (2) omit "not exceeding £3,000", and

(e) omit sub-paragraphs (3) and (4).

107 After that paragraph insert—

"18A (1) Where, on the hearing of any complaint made to it under paragraph 16(1A) of this Schedule, the Tribunal is satisfied that a manager or employee of a recognised body—

(a) has been convicted as mentioned in paragraph (a) of paragraph 16(1A),

(b) has failed to comply with any requirement imposed by or by virtue of this Act or any rules applicable to the relevant person by virtue of section 9 of this Act, or

(c) has acted as mentioned in paragraph (c) or (d) of paragraph 16(1A),

the Tribunal may, if it thinks fit, make one or more of the orders referred to in sub-paragraph (2).

(2) Those orders are—

(a) an order directing the payment by the relevant person of a penalty to be forfeited to Her Majesty;

(b) an order requiring the Society to consider taking such steps as the Tribunal may specify in relation to the relevant person;

(c) if the person is not a solicitor, an order which states one or more of the matters mentioned in sub-paragraph (3);

(d) an order requiring the Society to refer to an appropriate regulator any matter relating to the conduct of the relevant person.

(3) The matters referred to in sub-paragraph (2)(c) are—

(a) that as from the specified date—

(i) no solicitor or employee of a solicitor shall employ or remunerate, in connection with the practice carried on by that solicitor, the person with respect to whom the order is made, and

(ii) no recognised body, or manager or employee of such a body, shall employ or remunerate that person, in connection with the business of the recognised body,

except in accordance with a Society permission;

(b) that as from the specified date no recognised body or manager or employee of such a body shall, except in accordance with a Society permission, permit the person with respect to whom the order is made to be a manager of the body;

(c) that as from the specified date no recognised body or manager or employee of such a body shall, except in accordance with a Society permission, permit the person with respect to whom the order is made to have an interest in the body.

(4) For this purpose a person has an interest in a body if the person has an interest in the body within the meaning of Part 5 the Legal Services Act 2007 (see sections 72 and 109 of that Act).

(5) Subsections (1) to (1C), (3) and (4) of section 44 of the 1974 Act (offences in connection with orders under section 43(2) of that Act) apply in relation to an order under sub-paragraph (2)(c) as they apply in relation to an order under section 43(2) of that Act, except that references in those subsections to provision within section 43(2)(a), (b) or (c) of that Act are to be read as references to provision within sub-paragraph (3)(a), (b) or (c).

(6) Section 44(2) of the 1974 Act, paragraph 16(1)(d) and (1A)(d) of this Schedule and paragraph 15(3A) of Schedule 14 to the Courts and Legal Services Act 1990 apply in relation to an order under sub-paragraph (2)(c) as they apply in relation to an order under section 43(2) of the 1974 Act.

(7) For the purposes of sub-paragraph (2)(d) an "appropriate regulator" in relation to the relevant person means—

(a) if the person is an authorised person in relation to a reserved legal activity for the purposes of the Legal Services Act 2007, any relevant approved regulator (within the meaning of that Act) in relation to that person, and
(b) if the person carries on activities which are not reserved legal activities, any body which regulates the carrying on of such activities by the person."

108 In paragraph 20 of that Schedule (powers of Tribunal in respect of legal aid complaints), in sub-paragraph (1)—

(a) for "an officer" substitute "a manager",
(b) for "director" substitute "manager", and
(c) for "legal aid work" substitute "providing representation funded by the Legal Services Commission as part of the Criminal Defence Service",

and omit sub-paragraph (2).

109 In paragraph 21 of that Schedule (revocation of recognition by reason of default by director)—

(a) in sub-paragraph (1), in paragraph (a) for "director" substitute "manager",
(b) in paragraph (b) of that sub-paragraph for "director" (in both places) substitute "manager",
(c) in paragraph (c) of that sub-paragraph for "director" (in both places) substitute "manager",
(d) in sub-paragraph (3) for "director" (in both places) substitute "manager", and
(e) after that sub-paragraph insert—

"(4) The reference in paragraph (c) of sub-paragraph (1) to a person employed by a recognised body includes a reference to a person who was so employed at the time of the conduct leading to the making of the order referred to in that paragraph."

110 In paragraph 23 (orders as to remuneration for non-contentious business)—

(a) the existing provision becomes sub-paragraph (1) of that paragraph,
(b) in that sub-paragraph for "regulating (in accordance with paragraph 22)" substitute "prescribing (by virtue of paragraph 22) general principles to be applied when determining",
(c) in that sub-paragraph for paragraph (b) substitute—
"(b) in paragraph (d), the reference to the solicitor or any employee of the solicitor who is an authorised person were a reference to any manager or employee of the recognised body who is an authorised person.", and
(d) after that sub-paragraph insert—

"(2) In this paragraph "authorised person" means a person who is an authorised person in relation to an activity which is a reserved legal activity, within the meaning of the Legal Services Act 2007 (see section 18 of that Act)."

111 For paragraph 24 of that Schedule (effect of contentious business agreements) substitute—

"**24** (1) This paragraph applies in relation to a contentious business agreement made between a recognised body and a client.

(2) A provision in the agreement that the body shall not be liable for the negligence of any of its managers or employees shall be void if the client is a natural person who, in entering that agreement, is acting for purposes which are outside his trade, business or profession.

(3) A provision in the agreement that the body shall be relieved from any responsibility to which it would otherwise be subject in the course of carrying on its business as a recognised body shall be void.

(4) A provision in the agreement that any manager of the body shall be relieved from any responsibility to which the manager would otherwise be subject in the course of the carrying on by the body of its business as a recognised body shall be void."

112 In paragraph 25 of that Schedule (effect of supervening incapacity on contentious business agreements)—

(a) for sub-paragraph (1)(b) substitute—
"(b) a relevant insolvency event occurs in relation to the body;",
(b) in sub-paragraphs (2) and (3)—
  (i) for "taxation" (in each place) substitute "assessment", and
  (ii) for "taxing officer" (in each place) substitute "costs officer",
(c) in sub-paragraph (3) for "any officer" substitute "any manager", and
(d) after that sub-paragraph insert—

"(4) For the purposes of this paragraph a relevant insolvency event occurs in relation to a recognised body if—

(a) a resolution for a voluntary winding-up of the body is passed without a declaration of solvency under section 89 of the Insolvency Act 1986;
(b) the body enters administration within the meaning of paragraph 1(2)(b) of Schedule B1 to that Act;
(c) an administrative receiver within the meaning of section 251 of that Act is appointed;
(d) a meeting of creditors is held in relation to the body under section 95 of that Act (creditors' meeting which has the effect of converting a members' voluntary winding up into a creditors' voluntary winding up);
(e) an order for the winding up of the body is made."

113 In paragraph 26 of that Schedule (taxations with respect to contentious business)—

(a) in the paragraph heading for "Taxations" substitute "Assessments",
(b) the existing paragraph becomes sub-paragraph (1) and in that sub-paragraph—
  (i) for "taxation" substitute "assessment",
  (ii) for "taxing officer" substitute "costs officer",
  (iii) after "the body" (in the second place) insert "or any manager or employee of the body", and
  (iv) for "any solicitor, being an officer" substitute "any authorised person, being a manager", and
(c) after that sub-paragraph insert—

"(2) In this paragraph "authorised person" means an authorised person, in relation to an activity which is a reserved legal activity, within the meaning of the Legal Services Act 2007."

114 In paragraph 28 (power of court to order recognised body to pay over clients' money) after "client" (in the third place) insert "or any manager or employee of such a body".

115 For paragraph 29 of that Schedule (actions to recover costs) substitute—

"**29** (1) Subsection (2A) of section 69 of the 1974 Act shall have effect in relation to a bill of costs delivered by a recognised body as if for paragraphs (a) and (b) there were substituted—

"(a) signed on behalf of the recognised body by any manager or employee of the body authorised by it to do so, or
(b) enclosed in, or accompanied by, a letter which is so signed and refers to the bill.

(2) Subsection (2E) of that section shall have effect in relation to such a bill as if for "the solicitor" there were substituted "the recognised body"."

116 In paragraph 30 (power of Society to inspect files relating to certain proceedings), for paragraph (b) substitute—

"(b) for the appointment of an administrative receiver within the meaning of section 251 of the Insolvency Act 1986; or".

117 In paragraph 31 of that Schedule (bank accounts)—

(a) omit "or (2)", and
(b) after "bank" insert "or building society".

118 After that paragraph insert—

"**31A** Where rules made under section 32(1) of the 1974 Act are applied to managers or employees in accordance with section 9(2)(fb) of this Act, section 85 of the 1974 Act shall apply in relation to a manager or employee to whom the rules are applied who keeps an account with a bank or building society in pursuance of any such rules as it applies in relation to a solicitor who keeps such an account in pursuance of rules under section 32."

119 (1) Paragraph 32 of that Schedule (intervention by Society) is amended as follows.

(2) In sub-paragraph (1)(a)—

(a) for "Council are" substitute "Society is",
(b) after "recognised body" insert "or a manager of such a body", and
(c) for "it" substitute "the body or manager".

(3) For sub-paragraph (1)(c) substitute—

"(c) a relevant insolvency event occurs in relation to a recognised body; or".

(4) In sub-paragraph (1)(d)—

(a) for "Council have" substitute "Society has",
(b) for "officer" substitute "manager", and
(c) for "that body's" to the end substitute—
"(i) that body's business,
(ii) any trust of which that body is or was a trustee,
(iii) any trust of which the manager or employee is or was a trustee in his capacity as such a manager or employee, or
(iv) the business of another body in which the manager or employee is or was a manager or employee or the practice (or former practice) of the manager or employee; or".

(5) After sub-paragraph (1)(d) insert—

"(e) the Society is satisfied that it is necessary to exercise the powers conferred by Part 2 of Schedule 1 to the 1974 Act (or any of them) in relation to a recognised body to protect—
(i) the interests of clients (or former or potential clients) of the recognised body,
(ii) the interests of the beneficiaries of any trust of which the recognised body is or was a trustee, or
(iii) the interests of the beneficiaries of any trust of which a person who is or was a manager or employee of the recognised body is or was a trustee in that person's capacity as such a manager or employee;".

(6) After sub-paragraph (1) insert—

"(1A) For the purposes of this paragraph a relevant insolvency event occurs in relation to a recognised body if—

(a) a resolution for a voluntary winding-up of the body is passed without a declaration of solvency under section 89 of the Insolvency Act 1986;
(b) the body enters administration within the meaning of paragraph 1(2)(b) of Schedule B1 to that Act;
(c) an administrative receiver within the meaning of section 251 of that Act is appointed;
(d) a meeting of creditors is held in relation to the body under section 95 of that Act (creditors' meeting which has the effect of converting a members' voluntary winding up into a creditors' voluntary winding up);
(e) an order for the winding up of the body is made."

(7) Omit sub-paragraph (2).

120 For paragraph 33 of that Schedule (further grounds for intervention)—

(a) for paragraph (a) substitute—
"(a) the Society is satisfied that there has been undue delay—
(i) on the part of a recognised body in connection with any matter in which it is or was acting on behalf of a client or with any trust of which it is or was a trustee, or
(ii) on the part of a person who is or was a manager or employee of a recognised body in connection with any trust of which the manager or employee is or was a trustee in his capacity as such a manager or employee;", and
(b) in paragraph (c) for "Council regard" substitute "Society regards".

121 In paragraph 34 of that Schedule (powers of intervention on revocation of recognition etc), in sub-paragraph (1)—

(a) omit "corporate" (in both places), and
(b) in paragraph (a), after "revoked" insert "in accordance with rules under that section or".

122 In paragraph 35 of that Schedule (provision relating to the application of Part 2 of Schedule 1 to the Solicitors Act 1974)—

(a) in paragraph (a) omit "corporate", and
(b) omit "and" at the end of paragraph (b) and after paragraph (c) insert—
"(d) paragraph 6(2)(a) of that Schedule is to be construed as including a reference to sums of money held by or on behalf of the recognised body in connection with any trust of which a person who is or was a manager of the recognised body is or was a trustee in his capacity as such a manager;
(e) paragraph 9 of that Schedule is to be construed—
(i) as if sub-paragraph (1) included a reference to documents in the possession or under the control of the recognised body in connection with any trust of which a person who is or was a manager or employee of the recognised body is or was a trustee in his capacity as such a manager or employee, and
(ii) as applying to such a manager or employee and documents and property in his possession or under his control in connection with such a trust as it applies to a solicitor and documents and property in the possession or under the control of the solicitor;
(f) paragraph 11(1) of that Schedule is to be construed as including a power for the Society to apply to the High Court for an order for the appointment of a new trustee to a trust in substitution for a person who is a trustee, in his capacity as a manager or employee of the recognised body; and
(g) paragraph 13A of that Schedule is to be read as if the references to a former partner were references—
(i) in the case of a recognised body which is a partnership, to a former partner in the partnership, and
(ii) in any other case to a manager or former manager of the recognised body."

123 In paragraph 36 of that Schedule (privilege from disclosure etc)—

(a) for sub-paragraph (1) substitute—

"(1) Where a recognised body acts as such for a client, any communication, document, material or information is privileged from disclosure in like manner as if the recognised body had at all material times been a solicitor acting for the client.",

(b) in sub-paragraph (3) for "an officer" substitute "a manager", and
(c) after that sub-paragraph insert—

"(4) This paragraph does not apply to a recognised body which holds a licence under Part 5 of the Legal Services Act 2007 (alternative business structures)."

Initial Commencement

To be appointed: see s 211(2).

Appointment

Paras 80, 115: Appointment: 7 March 2008: see SI 2008/222, art 2(j)(ii).

Paras 81(1), (9), 86(g) (in part), 111, 112(a), (c), (d), 113(b)(iii): Appointment: 30 June 2008: see SI 2008/1436, art 2(d)(ii) (as amended by SI 2008/1591, art 2).

Amendment

Para 82: in the Administration of Justice Act 1985, s 9A(5)(a) (as set out) word "is" in square brackets substituted by SI 2008/3074, art 2(1), (2)(a).

Date in force: 27 November 2008: see SI 2008/3074, art 1.

Para 82: in the Administration of Justice Act 1985, s 9A(5)(a) (as set out) words omitted repealed by SI 2008/3074, art 2(1), (2)(b).

Date in force: 27 November 2008: see SI 2008/3074, art 1.

Para 82: in the Administration of Justice Act 1985, s 9A (as set out) sub-s (6)(f)–(h) and sub-ss (6A)–(6C) inserted by SI 2008/3074, art 2(1), (3).

Date in force: 27 November 2008: see SI 2008/3074, art 1.

Para 82: in the Administration of Justice Act 1985, s 9A(8) (as set out) definition "legal partnership" inserted by SI 2008/3074, art 2(1), (4)(a).

Date in force: 27 November 2008: see SI 2008/3074, art 1.

Para 82: in the Administration of Justice Act 1985, s 9A(8) (as set out) definition "pre-commencement conduct rules" inserted by SI 2008/3074, art 2(1), (4)(b).

Date in force: 27 November 2008: see SI 2008/3074, art 1.

Para 82: in the Administration of Justice Act 1985, s 9A(8) (as set out) in definition "recognised body" words "(subject to subsection (6B) above)" in square brackets inserted by SI 2008/3074, art 2(1), (4)(c).

Date in force: 27 November 2008: see SI 2008/3074, art 1.

Para 82: in the Administration of Justice Act 1985, s 9A(8) (as set out) definition "the Society" inserted by SI 2008/3074, art 2(1), (4)(d).

Date in force: 27 November 2008: see SI 2008/3074, art 1.

PART 3
THE COURTS AND LEGAL SERVICES ACT 1990 (C 41)

124 The Courts and Legal Services Act 1990 is amended in accordance with this Part of this Schedule.

125 In section 89 (foreign lawyers: recognised bodies and partnerships with solicitors)—

(a) for subsection (3)(a)(iv) substitute—
"(iv) sections 36 and 36A (compensation grants); and",
(b) in subsection (4), for paragraphs (a) to (d) substitute "to make different provision with respect to registered foreign lawyers to the provision made with respect to solicitors.",
(c) in subsection (5) for "Secretary of State" substitute "Lord Chancellor",
(d) in paragraph (a) of that subsection for "the commencement of this section" substitute "or in the same Session as the Legal Services Act 2007 was passed",
(e) in subsection (6) for "Secretary of State" substitute "Lord Chancellor",
(f) in subsection (7) for "Secretary of State" (in both places) substitute "Lord Chancellor",
(g) in paragraph (a) of that subsection for "the commencement of this section" substitute "or in the same Session as the Legal Services Act 2007 was passed",
(h) in that subsection for "officers" substitute "managers",
(i) after subsection (8) insert—

"(8A) Rules and regulations made by the Law Society under, or by virtue of, this section or Schedule 14 which are not regulatory arrangements within the meaning of the Legal Services Act 2007 are to be treated as such arrangements for the purposes of that Act.", and

(j) in subsection (9), after the definition of "foreign lawyer" insert—
""manager", in relation to a body, has the same meaning as in the Legal Services Act 2007 (see section 207 of that Act);".

126 Schedule 14 to that Act (foreign lawyers: partnerships and recognised bodies) is amended as follows.

127 In paragraph 1 (interpretation) omit the definitions of "the Council" and "controlled trust".

128 In paragraph 2 (application for registration)—

(a) for "Council" in each place substitute "Society",

(b) in sub-paragraph (1)(b) for "the Master of the Rolls" substitute "the Legal Services Board",
(c) in sub-paragraph (2)—
  (i) for "Law Society" substitute "Society", and
  (ii) for paragraphs (a) and (b) substitute "for members of that profession to be managers of recognised bodies.",
(d) omit sub-paragraph (3),
(e) in sub-paragraph (4)—
  (i) for "Master of the Rolls" substitute "Legal Services Board", and
  (ii) in paragraph (a) after "including" insert "the form of the register and",
(f) in that sub-paragraph, after paragraph (b) insert

"and

(c) the making available to the public of the information contained in the register (including the manner in which, and hours during which, the information is to be made so available and whether the information is to be made available free of charge).", and
(g) omit sub-paragraph (5).

129 After paragraph 2 insert—

"**2A** (1) The Society may direct that a foreign lawyer's registration is to have effect subject to such conditions as the Society thinks fit to impose.

(2) A direction under sub-paragraph (1) may be given in respect of a foreign lawyer

(a) at the time he is first registered, or
(b) at any time when the registration has effect."

130 In paragraph 3 (duration of registration) in sub-paragraphs (2) and (3)(c) for "Council" substitute "Society".

131 In paragraph 5 (intervention in practices)—

(a) in sub-paragraph (3)(a) and (b)—
  (i) for "Council have" substitute "Society has", and
  (ii) omit "by virtue of his being a member of that partnership",
(b) after sub-paragraph (3)(b) insert—
"(ba) the Society has reason to suspect dishonesty on the part of the registered foreign lawyer ("L") in connection with—
  (i) the business of any person of whom L is or was an employee, or of any body of which L is or was a manager, or
  (ii) any business which is or was carried on by L as a sole trader;",
(c) in sub-paragraph (3)(c) for "Council are" substitute "Society is",
(d) after sub-paragraph (3)(e) insert—
"(ea) the Society is satisfied that he has abandoned his practice;",
(e) in sub-paragraph (3)(i)—
  (i) for "Council are" substitute "Society is", and
  (ii) for "an officer" (in both places) substitute "a manager",
(f) after that sub-paragraph insert—
"(j) the Society is satisfied that it is necessary to exercise the intervention powers (or any of them) in relation to the registered foreign lawyer to protect—
  (i) the interests of clients (or former or potential clients) of the registered foreign lawyer or the multi-national partnership, or
  (ii) the interests of the beneficiaries of any trust of which the registered foreign lawyer is or was a trustee.",
(g) omit sub-paragraph (4),
(h) in sub-paragraph (5)(a) for "a complaint is made to the Society" substitute "the Society is satisfied",
(i) in sub-paragraph (5)(a)(ii) for "controlled trust" substitute "trust",
(j) in sub-paragraph (5)(c) for "Council regard" substitute "Society regards", and
(k) after sub-paragraph (9) insert—

"(10) In this paragraph "manager", in relation to a recognised body, has the same meaning as in the Legal Services Act 2007 (see section 207 of that Act)."

132 For paragraph 6 (compensation fund) substitute—

"6 Section 36 of the 1974 Act applies in relation to registered foreign lawyers as if for paragraphs (a) and (b) of subsection (1) there were substituted—

"(a) an act or omission of a registered foreign lawyer or former registered foreign lawyer;
(b) an act or omission of an employee or former employee of a registered foreign lawyer or former registered foreign lawyer;

133 For paragraph 7 (contributions to fund) substitute—

"7 Section 36A(2) and (3) of the 1974 Act applies in relation to registered foreign lawyers as it applies in relation to solicitors."

134 For paragraph 8 (accountants' reports) substitute—

"8 Section 34 of the Act of 1974 applies in relation to registered foreign lawyers as it applies in relation to solicitors."

135 In paragraph 14 (appeal against conditions or refusals)—

(a) in sub-paragraph (1)—
  (i) for "Master of the Rolls" substitute "High Court", and
  (ii) for "2(3)" substitute "2A",
(b) omit sub-paragraph (2),
(c) in sub-paragraph (3)—
  (i) omit "to him",
  (ii) for "Master of the Rolls" substitute "High Court", and
  (iii) for "he" substitute "it", and
(d) after that sub-paragraph insert—

"(4) In relation to an appeal under this paragraph the High Court may make such order as it thinks fit as to payment of costs.

(5) The decision of the High Court on an appeal under this paragraph shall be final."

136 In paragraph 15 (jurisdiction and powers of disciplinary tribunal)—

(a) after sub-paragraph (3) insert—

"(3A) Any person who alleges that a registered foreign lawyer has knowingly acted in contravention of any order under section 43(2) of the Act of 1974 or of any conditions subject to which a permission has been granted under such an order may make a complaint to the Tribunal.",

(b) in sub-paragraph (4)(c), omit "not exceeding £5,000", and
(c) omit sub-paragraph (5).

137 In paragraph 16(2) (foreign lawyers assisting Tribunal) for "Master of the Rolls" substitute "Legal Services Board".

138 In paragraph 17 (appeals from Tribunal)—

(a) in sub-paragraph (1) for "lie—" to the end substitute "lie to the High Court",
(b) in sub-paragraph (2)—
  (i) omit "and the Master of the Rolls", and
  (ii) for "they" substitute "it",
(c) in sub-paragraph (3) for "of the Master of the Rolls on an appeal under this paragraph" substitute "of the High Court on an appeal in the case of an order on an application under paragraph 15(2)(d) or (e), or the refusal of any such application,", and
(d) omit sub-paragraph (4).

Initial Commencement

To be appointed: see s 211(2).

Appointment

Paras 124, 126, 128(a), (c)(i), 130: Appointment: 7 March 2008: see SI 2008/222, art 2(j)(iii).

Paras 125(c)–(g), 128(c)(ii): Appointment: 30 June 2008: see SI 2008/1591, art 2(d)(iii) (as amended by SI 2008/1436, art 2).

SCHEDULE 17
LICENSED CONVEYANCING

Section 182

PART 1
ADMINISTRATION OF JUSTICE ACT 1985 (C 61)

1 Part 2 of the Administration of Justice Act 1985 (licensed conveyancing) is amended in accordance with this Part.

2 In section 11 (provision of conveyancing services by licensed conveyancers)—

(a) in subsection (1) for "by persons" to the end substitute "and other services by persons who hold licences in force under this Part or who are recognised bodies.",
(b) for subsection (3) substitute—

"(3) References in this Part to conveyancing services are references to—

(a) the preparation of transfers, conveyances, contracts and other documents in connection with, and other services ancillary to, the disposition or acquisition of estates or interests in land, and
(b) any other activities which are reserved instrument activities for the purposes of the Legal Services Act 2007 (see section 12 of and Schedule 2 to that Act).

(3A) For the purposes of subsection (3)—

(a) "disposition"
(i) does not include a testamentary disposition or any disposition in the case of such a lease as is referred to in section 54(2) of the Law of Property Act 1925 (short leases), but
(ii) subject to that, includes in the case of leases both their grant and their assignment, and
(b) "acquisition" has a corresponding meaning.", and
(c) omit subsection (4).

3 In section 12 (establishment of the Council), omit subsection (2).

4 (1) Section 15 (issue of licences by Council) is amended as follows.

(2) In subsection (3)(b), for "21" substitute "42".

(3) In subsection (4), for "the period of" to the end substitute "such period, beginning with the date of issue of the licence, as may be specified in the licence."

(4) Omit subsections (7) and (8).

5 (1) Section 16 (conditional licences) is amended as follows.

(2) In subsection (1)—

(a) after paragraph (c) insert—
"(ca) after the Investigating Committee established under section 24 has made any order in his case under section 24A;", and
(b) after paragraph (e) insert—
"(ea) when, having been required by rules made under section 22 to deliver to the Council a report by an accountant, he has not delivered such a report within the period required by the rules;
(eb) after having been disqualified under section 99 of the Legal Services Act 2007 (disqualification from being manager or employee of a licensed body etc);
(ec) after his holding of a restricted interest in a licensed body has been approved subject to conditions under paragraph 17, 28 or 33 of Schedule 13 to that Act (ownership of licensed bodies) or objected to under paragraph 19, 31 or 36 of that Schedule;".

(3) In subsection (4)—

(a) after "paragraph" insert "(ca),", and
(b) after "(e)," insert "(ea), (eb), (ec),".

(4) In subsection (5) for "or" at the end of paragraph (a) substitute—

"(aa) pending the hearing and determination of any appeal brought by the applicant under paragraph 18, 20, 29, 32, 34 or 37 of Schedule 13 to the Legal Services Act 2007;

(ab) pending the review by a licensing authority, in accordance with its licensing rules, of a determination that the applicant should be disqualified under section 99 of the Legal Services Act 2007; or".

(5) After that subsection insert—

"(6) In this section—

"licensed body", "licensing authority" and "licensing rules" have the same meaning as in the Legal Services Act 2007 (see sections 71, 73 and 83 of that Act);

"restricted interest", in relation to a body, has the same meaning as in Schedule 13 to that Act (ownership of licensed bodies)."

6 After section 16 insert—

"16A Additional fee payable by certain persons when applying for licences

(1) This section applies where a person applies for a licence at a time when section 16 has effect in relation to him by reason of the circumstances mentioned in section 16(1)(ea).

(2) The application must be accompanied by an additional fee of an amount prescribed by rules made by the Council for the purposes of this section."

7 (1) Section 17 (imposition of conditions during currency of licence) is amended as follows.

(2) In subsection (2)(a)—

(a) after "paragraph" insert "(ca),", and
(b) after "(e)," insert "(ea), (eb), (ec),".

(3) In subsection (4), for "or" at the end of paragraph (a) substitute—

"(aa) pending the hearing and determination of any appeal brought by the licensed conveyancer under paragraph 18, 20, 29, 32, 34 or 37 of Schedule 13 to the Legal Services Act 2007;

(ab) pending the review by a licensing authority, in accordance with its licensing rules, of a determination that the licensed conveyancer should be disqualified under section 99 of the Legal Services Act 2007; or".

(4) After subsection (5) insert—

"(6) In this section "licensing authority" and "licensing rules" have the same meaning as in the Legal Services Act 2007 (see sections 73 and 83 of that Act)."

8 After section 17 insert—

"17A Variation of conditions

(1) This section applies where a licensed conveyancer's licence has effect subject to conditions.

(2) On an application made by the licensed conveyancer, the Council may in prescribed circumstances direct—

(a) the removal of a condition;
(b) the variation of a condition in the manner described in the application.

(3) "Prescribed" means prescribed by rules made by the Council.

(4) Section 14 (applications for licences) applies in relation to an application under this section as it applies in relation to applications for a licence under this Part."

9 In section 18 (suspension or termination of licences), after subsection (2) insert—

"(2A) Where the power conferred by paragraph 6(1) or 9(1) of Schedule 5 has been exercised in relation to a licensed conveyancer by virtue of paragraph 1(1)(a)(i), (aa), (c) or (e) of that Schedule, the exercise of that power shall operate immediately to suspend any licence held by that person under this Part.

(2B) Subsection (2A) does not apply if, at the time when the power referred to there is exercised, the Council directs that subsection (2A) is not to apply in relation to the licensed conveyancer concerned.

(2C) If, at the time when the power referred to in subsection (2A) is exercised, the Council gives a direction to that effect, the licensed conveyancer concerned may continue to act in relation to any matter specified in the direction as if the licence had not been suspended by virtue of subsection (2A), but subject to such conditions (if any) as the Council sees fit to impose.

(2D) Subject to subsection (2E), where a licence is suspended by virtue of subsection (2A) the suspension of the licence shall continue until the licence expires.

(2E) The licensed conveyancer may, at any time before the licence expires, apply to the Council to terminate the suspension.

(2F) On an application under subsection (2E), the Council may in its discretion—

(a) by order terminate the suspension either unconditionally or subject to such conditions as the Council may think fit, or
(b) refuse the application.

(2G) If on an application by a licensed conveyancer under subsection (2E) the Council refuses the application or terminates the suspension subject to conditions, the licensed conveyancer may appeal against the decision of the Council to the High Court which may—

(a) affirm the decision, or
(b) terminate the suspension either unconditionally or subject to such conditions as it may think fit.

(2H) In relation to an appeal under subsection (2G) the High Court may make such order as it thinks fit as to payment of costs."

10 In section 20 (rules as to professional practice, conduct and discipline), in subsection (1) omit ", in pursuance of its general duty referred to in section 12(2),".

11 In section 22 (keeping of accounts and establishment of client accounts)—

(a) in subsection (3)(a) omit "qualified", and
(b) for subsections (4) and (5) substitute—

"(4) Provision made in rules by virtue of subsection (3)(a) may provide that the reports delivered to the Council must be reports given by accountants in respect of whom requirements prescribed by the rules are met."

12 (1) Section 24 (preliminary investigation of disciplinary cases) is amended as follows.

(2) In subsection (1)—

(a) for "preliminary investigation" substitute "consideration",
(b) omit paragraph (b), and
(c) omit from "with a view" to the end.

(3) After subsection (1) insert—

"(1A) The Investigating Committee shall make a preliminary investigation of such an allegation and—

(a) hear and determine the allegation, or
(b) refer the allegation to the Discipline and Appeals Committee established under section 25 for hearing and determination by that Committee under section 26."

(4) Omit subsection (2).

(5) In subsection (3) omit—

(a) "or (2)",
(b) "or complaint" (in both places), and
(c) "or paragraph (b)".

(6) After subsection (4) insert—

"(4A) The Council shall make rules as to the cases in which the Investigating Committee may hear and determine an allegation, and the cases in which they must refer an allegation to the Discipline and Appeals Committee."

(7) In subsection (5) omit "or complaint" (in both places).

(8) After that subsection insert—

"(6) Before making a direction under subsection (5), the Investigating Committee must give the licensed conveyancer an opportunity to make representations against the making of the proposed direction.

(7) In relation to proceedings under subsection (6), the Investigating Committee may make such order as they think fit as to the payment of costs by—

(a) the Council, or
(b) the licensed conveyancer.

(8) Where a direction under subsection (5) has been made, the licensed conveyancer may appeal to the Discipline and Appeals Committee, and on any such appeal the Committee may make such order as they think fit.

(9) Where an order has been made under subsection (7) the Council or the licensed conveyancer may appeal to the Discipline and Appeals Committee, and on any such appeal the Committee may make such order as they think fit.

(10) Where an order is made by the Discipline and Appeals Committee under subsections (8) or (9)—

(a) the person against whom the order is made, and
(b) if not within paragraph (a), the Council,

may appeal against the order to the High Court.

(11) On an appeal under subsection (10) the High Court may make such order as it thinks fit.

(12) The decision of the High Court on an appeal under subsection (10) shall be final."

13 After section 24 insert—

"24A Determination of allegations by Investigating Committee

(1) Where, on hearing an allegation by virtue of section 24(1A)(a), the Investigating Committee are satisfied that a licensed conveyancer—

(a) has, while holding a licence in force under this Part, failed to comply with any condition to which that licence was subject, or
(b) has failed to comply with any rules made by the Council under this Part,

the Committee may, if they think fit, make an order directing the payment by the licensed conveyancer of a penalty to be forfeited to Her Majesty.

(2) In relation to proceedings before the Investigating Committee by virtue of section 24(1A)(a), the Committee may make such order as they consider fit as to the payment of costs by—

(a) the Council,
(b) the licensed conveyancer against whom the proceedings were brought, or
(c) if the person on whose allegation the proceedings were brought was heard (in person, or through a representative) by the Committee in the course of the proceedings, that person.

(3) In subsection (2), for the purposes of paragraph (a) or (b) of that subsection, the reference to costs includes costs incurred in connection with a preliminary investigation of the allegation under section 24(1A).

(4) The amount of any penalty required to be paid under subsection (1) may not exceed such amount as may be prescribed by rules made by the Council for the purposes of this subsection.

(5) Paragraphs 1, 2(1) and (3) and 4 of Schedule 4 have effect in relation to—

(a) proceedings for the hearing and determination of an allegation by the Investigating Committee, as they have effect in relation to proceedings before the Discipline and Appeals Committee under section 26, and
(b) orders of the Investigating Committee, as they have effect in relation to orders of the Discipline and Appeals Committee.

(6) A person against whom an order is made by the Investigating Committee by virtue of subsection (1) may appeal to the Discipline and Appeals Committee, and on any such appeal the Discipline and Appeals Committee may make such order as they think fit.

(7) Where an order is made by the Investigating Committee by virtue of subsection (2), a person listed in paragraphs (a) to (c) of that subsection may appeal to the Discipline and Appeals Committee, and on any such appeal the Discipline and Appeals Committee may make such order as they think fit.

(8) Where an order is made by the Discipline and Appeals Committee under subsection (6) or (7)—

(a) a party to the appeal, or
(b) if not within paragraph (a), the Council,

may appeal against the order to the High Court.

(9) On an appeal under subsection (8) the High Court may make such order as it thinks fit.

(10) The decision of the High Court on an appeal under subsection (8) shall be final."

14 In section 25 (the Discipline and Appeals Committee), in subsection (1)(b) for "sections 27 to" substitute "section 24A, 27, 28 or".

15 (1) Section 26 (proceedings in disciplinary cases) is amended as follows.

(2) In subsection (1) after "allegation" insert "referred to them under section 24(1A)(b)".

(3) In subsection (2)—

(a) in paragraph (e), for "£3,000" substitute "such amount as may be prescribed by rules made by the Council for the purposes of this paragraph",
(b) for paragraph (f) substitute—
"(f) an order reprimanding the licensed conveyancer.", and
(c) omit paragraph (g).

(4) After subsection (2) insert—

"(2A) In relation to proceedings before the Discipline and Appeals Committee under this section, the Committee may make such order as they consider fit as to the payment of costs by—

(a) the Council;
(b) the licensed conveyancer against whom the proceedings were brought;
(c) if the person on whose allegation the proceedings were brought was heard (in person, or through a representative) by the Committee in the course of the proceedings, that person.

(2B) In subsection (2A), for the purposes of paragraph (a) or (b) of that subsection, the reference to costs includes costs incurred in connection with a preliminary investigation of the allegation under section 24(1A)."

(5) Omit subsections (5) and (6).

(6) After subsection (7) insert—

"(7A) Where the Discipline and Appeals Committee make an order under subsection (2A), a person listed in paragraphs (a) to (c) of that subsection may appeal to the High Court, and on any such appeal the High Court may make such order as it thinks fit."

(7) In subsection (8), after "(7)" insert "or (7A)".

16 In section 27 (removal of disqualification from holding a licence), after subsection (2) insert—

"(3) In relation to proceedings on an application under subsection (1), the Discipline and Appeals Committee may make such order as they consider fit as to the payment of costs by—

(a) the Council;
(b) the applicant."

17 In section 28 (revocation of licence on grounds of fraud or error), after subsection (4) insert—

"(5) In relation to proceedings for the revocation of a licence under subsection (1), the Discipline and Appeals Committee may make such order as they consider fit as to the payment of costs by—

(a) the Council;
(b) the licensed conveyancer to whose licence the proceedings relate.

(6) In relation to proceedings on an application under subsection (2), the Discipline and Appeals Committee may make such order as they consider fit as to the payment of costs by—

(a) the Council;
(b) the applicant."

18 In section 29 (appeals from decisions of Council in relation to licences)—

(a) in subsection (1), omit "or" at the end of paragraph (b),
(b) in that subsection, at the end of paragraph (c) insert
"or
(d) refuses an application made by that person under section 17A,", and
(c) in subsection (2), after paragraph (b) insert—
"(ba) in the case of an appeal under subsection (1)(d), by order direct the Council to grant the application;".

19 (1) Section 31 (application of Schedule 5) is amended as follows.

(2) In subsection (2) omit—

(a) "or complaint" (in each place), and
(b) "or paragraph (b)".

(3) In subsection (3), for "and 12" substitute "to 12A".

(4) In subsection (4) omit "or complaint".

20 (1) Section 32 (provision of conveyancing services by recognised bodies) is amended as follows.

(2) In subsection (1)(a) for "by licensed" (in the first place) to the end substitute "of conveyancing services bodies;".

(3) In subsection (1)(b) for "such services" substitute "conveyancing services or other relevant legal services".

(4) After subsection (1)(b) insert—

"(ba) prescribing the Council's arrangements for authorising recognised bodies, for the purposes of the Legal Services Act 2007, to carry on reserved instrument activities, or the administration of oaths, within the meaning of that Act;".

(5) In subsection (1)(c) for "conditions" substitute "requirements".

(6) In subsection (2) omit "corporate".

(7) In subsection (3)—

(a) in paragraph (a) after "section" insert ", or for the renewal of such recognition,",
(b) after that paragraph insert—
"(aa) for the payment of fees in connection with other applications under the rules;",
(c) for paragraph (c) substitute—
"(c) about the time when any recognition granted under this section, or renewal of such recognition, takes effect and the period for which it is (subject to the provisions of this Part) to remain in force;
(ca) for the suspension or revocation of any such recognition, on such grounds and in such circumstances as may be prescribed in the rules;
(cb) about the effect on the recognition of a partnership or other unincorporated body ("the existing body") of any change in its membership, including provision for the existing body's recognition to be transferred where the existing body ceases to exist and another body succeeds to the whole or substantially the whole of its business;",
(d) omit paragraph (d),
(e) in paragraph (e)—
  (i) for "a list" substitute "a register",
  (ii) omit "corporate", and
  (iii) for ", and for the" to the end substitute "and such other information relating to those bodies as may be specified in the rules;",
(f) after that paragraph insert—

"(ea) for information (or information of a specified description) on such a register to be made available to the public, and about the manner in which and times at which, information is to be made so available;",

(g) after paragraph (f) insert—

"(fa) about the education and training requirements to be met by managers and employees of recognised bodies;

(fb) for rules made under any other provision of this Part to have effect in relation to managers and employees of recognised bodies with such additions, omissions or other modifications as appear to the Council to be necessary or expedient;", and

(h) in paragraph (g) after "recognised bodies" insert "or managers or employees of such bodies".

(8) After subsection (3) insert—

"(3A) Rules made by the Council may provide for the Council to grant a body recognition under this section subject to one or more conditions.

(3B) At any time while a body is recognised under this section, the Council may, in such circumstances as may be prescribed, direct that the body's recognition is to have effect subject to such conditions as the Council may think fit.

"Prescribed" means prescribed by rules made by the Council.

(3C) The conditions which may be imposed under subsection (3A) or (3B) include—

(a) conditions restricting the kinds of conveyancing services that may be provided by the body;

(b) conditions imposed by reference to criteria of general application;

(c) conditions requiring the body to take any specified steps that will, in the opinion of the Council, be conducive to the body carrying on an efficient business;

and conditions may be imposed despite the fact that they may result in expenditure being incurred by the body.

(3D) On an application made by a recognised body, the Council may, in such circumstances as may be prescribed, direct—

(a) the removal of a condition subject to which the body's recognition has effect;

(b) the variation of such a condition in the manner described in the application.

(3E) For the purposes of subsection (3D)—

(a) section 14 applies in relation to an application under that subsection as it applies in relation to an application for a licence under this Part of this Act, and

(b) "prescribed" means prescribed by rules made by the Council.

(3F) Rules under subsection (3A) or (3B) may make provision about when conditions imposed take effect (including provision conferring power on the Council to direct that a condition is not to have effect until the conclusion of any appeal in relation to it).

(3G) Rules under this section may contain such incidental, supplemental, transitional or transitory provisions or savings as the Council considers necessary or expedient."

(9) Omit subsections (4) and (5).

(10) In subsection (6)—

(a) in paragraph (a) omit "corporate", and

(b) for paragraph (b) substitute—

"(b) that a body's recognition under this section does not have effect subject to any conditions or has effect subject to any particular conditions,".

(11) After subsection (7) insert—

"(8) In this section "conveyancing services body" and "relevant legal services" have the meaning given by section 32A.

(9) The Council is capable of being designated as a licensing authority for the purposes of, and subject to, Part 5 of the Legal Services Act 2007 (alternative business structures)."

21 After section 32 (provision of conveyancing by recognised bodies) insert—

"32A Conveyancing services bodies

(1) For the purposes of section 32 a "conveyancing services body" means a body (corporate or unincorporate) in respect of which—

(a) the management and control condition, and
(b) the services condition,

are satisfied.

(2) The management and control condition is satisfied in the case of a partnership if at least one of the partners is a licensed conveyancer.

(3) The management and control condition is satisfied in the case of an unincorporated body (other than a partnership), or a body corporate which is managed by its members, if at least one of those members is a licensed conveyancer.

(4) The management and control condition is satisfied in the case of any other body corporate if at least one director of the body is a licensed conveyancer.

(5) The services condition is satisfied in respect of a body if the body is carrying on a business consisting of the provision of—

(a) conveyancing services, or
(b) conveyancing services and other relevant legal services.

(6) For the purposes of this section—

"authorised person" means an authorised person in relation to an activity which is a reserved legal activity (within the meaning of the Legal Services Act 2007);

"relevant legal services", in relation to a body, means—

(a) conveyancing services, and
(b) where authorised persons are managers or employees of, or have an interest in, the body, services such as are provided by individuals practising as such authorised persons (whether or not those services involve the carrying on of reserved legal activities within the meaning of the Legal Services Act 2007);

and a person has an interest in a body if the person has an interest in the body within the meaning of Part 5 of the Legal Services Act 2007 (see sections 72 and 109 of that Act)."

22 For section 33 (legal professional privilege), substitute—

"33 Legal professional privilege

(1) Subsection (2) applies where a licensed conveyancer or recognised body acts as such for a client.

(2) Any communication, document, material or information is privileged from disclosure in like manner as if the licensed conveyancer or body had at all material times been acting as the client's solicitor.

(3) This section does not apply to a recognised body which holds a licence under Part 5 of the Legal Services Act 2007 (alternative business structures)."

23 After that section insert—

"33A Administration of oaths by licensed conveyancers

The Council may make rules prescribing its arrangements for authorising licensed conveyancers, for the purposes of the Legal Services Act 2007, to carry on activities which consist of the administration of oaths."

24 In section 34 (modification of existing enactments relating to conveyancing etc), omit subsection (2)(c) to (e).

25 In section 35 (penalty for pretending to be a licensed conveyancer or recognised body), in subsection (2) omit "corporate".

26 In section 36 (offences by bodies corporate)—

(a) the existing section becomes subsection (1) of that section and in that subsection for "director" to "capacity" substitute "officer of the body corporate", and

(b) after that subsection insert—

"(2) Where the affairs of a body corporate are managed by its members, subsection (1) applies in relation to the acts and defaults of a member in connection with the member's functions of management as it applies to an officer of the body corporate.

(3) Proceedings for an offence under this section alleged to have been committed by an unincorporated body are to be brought in the name of that body (and not in that of any of its members) and, for the purposes of any such proceedings, any rules of court relating to the service of documents have effect as if that body were a corporation.

(4) A fine imposed on an unincorporated body on its conviction of an offence under this section is to be paid out of the funds of that body.

(5) If an unincorporated body is charged with an offence under this section, section 33 of the Criminal Justice Act 1925 and Schedule 3 to the Magistrates' Courts Act 1980 (procedure on charge of an offence against a corporation) have effect in like manner as in the case of a corporation so charged.

(6) Where an offence under this section committed by an unincorporated body (other than a partnership) is proved to have been committed with the consent or connivance of, or to be attributable to any neglect on the part of, any officer of the body or any member of its governing body, that officer or member as well as the unincorporated body is guilty of the offence and liable to be proceeded against and punished accordingly.

(7) Where an offence under this section committed by a partnership is proved to have been committed with the consent or connivance of, or to be attributable to any neglect on the part of, a partner, that partner as well as the partnership is guilty of the offence and liable to be proceeded against and punished accordingly.

(8) In this section "officer", in relation to a body corporate, means—

(a) any director, secretary or other similar officer of the body corporate, or
(b) any person who was purporting to act in any such capacity."

27 In section 38 (rules)—

(a) omit subsection (1), and
(b) in subsection (2) for "such rules" substitute "rules made by the Council under this Part".

28 In section 39(1) (interpretation of Part 2)—

(a) in the definition of "client", in paragraph (a) omit "or his firm",
(b) omit the definitions of "director" and "officer",
(c) at the appropriate place insert—
""manager", in relation to a body, has the same meaning as in the Legal Services Act 2007 (see section 207 of that Act);", and
(d) in the definition of "recognised body" omit "corporate".

29 (1) Schedule 3 (Council for Licensed Conveyancers: supplementary provisions) is amended as follows.

(2) In paragraph 2(1), for "elected or nominated" substitute "appointed".

(3) In paragraph 2(2), for "elect" substitute "appoint".

(4) Omit paragraph 2(3).

(5) Omit paragraph 3.

(6) In paragraph 4(1)—

(a) for "election or nomination" (in both places) substitute "appointment",
(b) for "election of" substitute "appointment of", and
(c) for "elected or nominated" substitute "appointed".

(7) In paragraph 4(2), for "elected or nominated" (in each place) substitute "appointed".

(8) In paragraph 4(3), for the words from "Secretary of State" (in the first place) to the end substitute "Legal Services Board."

(9) In paragraph 4(4)—

(a) for "Secretary of State" (in both places) substitute "Legal Services Board",
(b) for "him" substitute "it", and
(c) for "he" (in both places) substitute "it".

(10) In paragraph 9, for "election or nomination" substitute "appointment".

(11) In paragraph 10 for "Secretary of State" (in both places) substitute "Lord Chancellor".

(12) In paragraph 11(3) for "Secretary of State" substitute "Lord Chancellor".

30 (1) Schedule 4 (the Discipline and Appeals Committee: supplementary provisions) is amended as follows.

(2) In paragraph 1 (rules of procedure)—

(a) omit sub-paragraphs (3) and (4), and
(b) in sub-paragraph (5), for "paragraphs 2 and 3" substitute "paragraph 2".

(3) Omit paragraph 3.

31 (1) Schedule 5 (intervention in licensed conveyancer's practice) is amended as follows.

(2) In paragraph 1 (grounds for intervention)—

(a) in sub-paragraph (1)(a) after "practice" insert "or former practice or in connection with any trust of which that licensed conveyancer is or was a trustee",
(b) after that sub-paragraph insert—
"(aa) the Council has reason to suspect dishonesty on the part of a licensed conveyancer ("L") in connection with—
(i) the business of any person of whom L is or was an employee, or of any body of which L is or was a manager, or
(ii) any business which is or was carried on by L as a sole trader;",
(c) in sub-paragraph (1)(b) after "practice" insert "or in connection with any trust",
(d) in sub-paragraph (1)(c), after "section" insert "20, 21(3)(c),",
(e) after sub-paragraph (1)(e) insert—
"(ea) the Council is satisfied that a licensed conveyancer has abandoned his practice;
(eb) the Council is satisfied that a licensed conveyancer has been practising in breach of any conditions subject to which his licence has effect;",
(f) in sub-paragraph (1)(f), after "illness" insert ", injury",
(g) for sub-paragraph (1)(g) substitute—
"(g) a licensed conveyancer lacks capacity (within the meaning of the Mental Capacity Act 2005) to act as a licensed conveyancer and powers under section 15 to 20 or section 48 of that Act are exercisable in relation to the licensed conveyancer;",
(h) after sub-paragraph (1)(h) insert—
"(i) the Council is satisfied that it is necessary to exercise the powers conferred by Part 2 of this Schedule (or any of them) in relation to a licensed conveyancer to protect—
(i) the interests of clients (or former or potential clients) of the licensed conveyancer or his firm, or
(ii) the interests of the beneficiaries of any trust of which the licensed conveyancer is or was a trustee.", and
(i) omit sub-paragraph (2).

(3) In paragraph 3 (intervention following an undue delay)—

(a) for "10(3)" substitute "10(9)",
(b) in paragraph (a) for "a complaint is made to the Council" substitute "the Council is satisfied",
(c) in that paragraph for "was instructed" substitute "is or was acting", and
(d) in that paragraph after "client" insert "or in connection with any trust".

(4) In paragraph 4(2) (continuation of powers after death etc of licensed conveyancer)—

(a) after "and (3)" insert ", 6A",
(b) for "and (5)" substitute ", (5) and (6)", and
(c) for "10(1)" substitute "10(2) and (7)".

(5) In paragraph 6 (vesting of sums in Council)—

(a) in sub-paragraph (1) after "thereto" insert "and to rules under paragraph 6B", and

(b) in sub-paragraph (2)(a) after "practice" insert "or former practice or with any trust of which he is or was a trustee".

(6) After paragraph 6 insert—

"**6A** (1) Without prejudice to paragraph 5, if the Council passes a resolution to the effect that any rights to which this paragraph applies shall vest in the Council, those rights shall vest accordingly.

(2) This paragraph applies to any right to recover or receive debts due to the licensed conveyancer or his firm in connection with his practice or former practice.

(3) Any sums recovered by the Council by virtue of the exercise of rights vested under sub-paragraph (1) shall vest in the Council and shall be held by it on trust to exercise in relation to them the powers conferred by this Part of this Schedule and, subject to those powers and to rules under paragraph 6B, upon trust for the persons beneficially entitled to them.

(4) The Council shall serve on the licensed conveyancer or his firm, and any person who owes a debt to which the order applies a certified copy of the Council's resolution.

6B (1) The Council may make rules governing its treatment of sums vested in it under paragraph 6 or 6A(3).

(2) The rules may, in particular, make provision in respect of cases where the Council, having taken such steps to do so as are reasonable in all the circumstances of the case, is unable to trace the person or persons beneficially entitled to any sum vested in the Council under paragraph 6 or 6A(3) (including provision which requires amounts to be paid into or out of a fund maintained under section 21)."

(7) In paragraph 7(1) (holding of sums vested in Council) after "thereto" insert "and to rules under paragraph 6B".

(8) In paragraph 8 for "holds money" to the end substitute—

"(a) holds money on behalf of the licensed conveyancer or his firm, or
(b) has information which is relevant to identifying any money held by or on behalf of the licensed conveyancer or his firm,

the court may require that person to give the Council information as to any such money and the accounts in which it is held."

(9) In paragraph 9 (documents)—

(a) in sub-paragraph (1)(a)—
 (i) after "possession" insert "or under the control", and
 (ii) after "practice" insert "or former practice or with any trust of which the licensed conveyancer is or was a trustee",
(b) in sub-paragraph (1)(b)—
 (i) after "possession" insert "or under the control", and
 (ii) for "to which the complaint relates" substitute "of which the Council is satisfied",
(c) in sub-paragraph (3) after "possession" insert "or control",
(d) in sub-paragraph (5) after "possession" insert "or are under the control",
(e) after that sub-paragraph insert—

"(5A) In the case of a document which consists of information which is stored in electronic form, the requirement imposed by a notice under sub-paragraph (1) or an order under sub-paragraph (4) or (5), is a requirement to produce or deliver the information in a form in which it is legible or from which it can readily be produced in a legible form.",

(f) in sub-paragraph (6) after "possession of" insert "(a)",
(g) at the end of that sub-paragraph insert—
"(b) any property—
 (i) in the possession or under the control of the licensed conveyancer or his firm, or
 (ii) in the case of an order under sub-paragraph (5), which was in the possession or under the control of such a person and has come into the possession or under the control of the person in respect of whom the order is made,
which the Council reasonably requires for the purpose of accessing information contained in such documents,

and to use property obtained under paragraph (b) for that purpose.",

(h) in sub-paragraph (7) after "documents" insert "or other property",
(i) in sub-paragraph (8) after "documents" insert "or other property", and
(j) in sub-paragraph (10) after "documents" insert "or other property".

(10) For paragraph 10 (mail) substitute—

"Redirection of communications

10 (1) The High Court, on the application of the Council, may from time to time make a communications redirection order.

(2) A communications redirection order is an order that specified communications to the licensed conveyancer or his firm are to be directed, in accordance with the order, to the Council, or any person appointed by the Council.

(3) For the purposes of this paragraph—

(a) "specified communications" means communications of such description as are specified in the order;
(b) the descriptions of communications which may be so specified include—
  (i) communications in the form of a postal packet;
  (ii) electronic communications;
  (iii) communications by telephone.

(4) A communications redirection order has effect for such time not exceeding 18 months as is specified in the order.

(5) Where a communications redirection order has effect, the Council or the person appointed by the Council may take possession or receipt of the communications redirected in accordance with the order.

(6) Where a communications redirection order is made the Council must pay to—

(a) in the case of an order relating to postal packets, the postal operator concerned, and
(b) in any other case, the person specified in the order,

the like charges (if any) as would have been payable for the redirection of the communications to which the order relates if the addressee had permanently ceased to occupy or use the premises or other destination of the communications and had applied to the postal operator or the specified person (as the case may be) to redirect the communications to him as mentioned in the order.

(7) The High Court may, on the application of the Council, authorise the Council, or a person appointed by it, to take such steps as may be specified in the order in relation to any website purporting to be or have been maintained by or on behalf of the licensed conveyancer or his firm if the High Court is satisfied that the taking of those steps is necessary to protect the public interest or the interests of clients (or potential or former clients) of the licensed conveyancer or his firm.

(8) In this paragraph "postal operator" and "postal packet" have the meaning given by section 125(1) of the Postal Services Act 2000.

(9) This paragraph does not apply where the powers conferred by this Part of this Schedule are exercisable by virtue of paragraph 3."

(11) After paragraph 10 insert—

"Trusts

10A (1) If the licensed conveyancer or his personal representative is a trustee of a trust, the Council may apply to the High Court for an order for the appointment of a new trustee in substitution for him.

(2) The Trustee Act 1925 has effect in relation to an appointment of a new trustee under this paragraph as it has effect in relation to an appointment under section 41 of that Act."

(12) In paragraph 11 (liens) for "and documents" substitute ", documents and other property".

(13) After paragraph 12 (costs) insert—

"**12A** (1) The High Court, on the application of the Council, may order a former partner of the licensed conveyancer to pay a specified proportion of the costs mentioned in paragraph 12.

(2) The High Court may make an order under this paragraph only if it is satisfied that the conduct (or any part of the conduct) by reason of which the powers conferred by this Part were exercisable in relation to the licensed conveyancer was conduct carried on with the consent or connivance of, or was attributable to any neglect on the part of, the former partner.

(3) In this paragraph "specified" means specified in the order made by the High Court."

32 (1) Schedule 6 (bodies recognised under section 32: supplementary provisions) is amended as follows.

(2) In paragraph 1—

(a) omit "corporate" (in both places), and
(b) in sub-paragraph (2) omit—
(i) "or complaint" (in both places), and
(ii) "or (b)".

(3) In paragraph 2 (disciplinary control of recognised bodies) after "24" insert ", 24A".

(4) In paragraph 3—

(a) in sub-paragraph (1), in paragraph (a)(i) omit "by any court in the United Kingdom",
(b) after paragraph (a) of that sub-paragraph insert—
"(aa) it is alleged that a manager or employee of a recognised body who is not a licensed conveyancer has failed to comply with any rules applicable to him by virtue of section 32;
(ab) it is alleged that a recognised body (while a recognised body) has failed to comply with a condition subject to which its recognition has effect.",
(c) in that sub-paragraph omit—
(i) paragraph (b), and
(ii) from "with a view" to the end, and
(d) after sub-paragraph (1) insert—

"(1A) After making such an investigation, the Investigating Committee may—

(a) hear and determine the allegation, or
(b) refer the allegation to the Discipline and Appeals Committee for hearing and determination by that Committee under paragraph 4.

(1B) The Council shall make rules as to the cases in which the Investigating Committee may hear and determine an allegation, and the cases in which they must refer an allegation to the Discipline and Appeals Committee."

(5) After paragraph 3 insert—

"**3A** (1) Where, on hearing an allegation by virtue of paragraph 3(1A)(a), the Investigating Committee are satisfied—

(a) in a case within paragraph 3(1)(a), that a recognised body has failed to comply with any such rules as are mentioned in sub-paragraph (ii) of that paragraph, or
(b) in a case within paragraph 3(1)(aa), that a manager or employee has failed to comply with any such rules as are mentioned in that paragraph, or
(c) in a case within paragraph 3(1)(ab), that a recognised body has failed to comply with any condition mentioned in that paragraph,

the Committee may make an order directing the payment by the recognised body, manager or employee of a penalty to be forfeited to Her Majesty.

(2) In relation to proceedings before the Investigating Committee by virtue of paragraph 3(1A)(a), the Committee may make such order as they consider fit as to the payment of costs by—

(a) the Council;
(b) the recognised body, manager or employee against whom the proceedings were brought;
(c) if the person on whose allegation the proceedings were brought was heard (in person, or through a representative) by the Committee in the course of the proceedings, that person.

(3) In sub-paragraph (2), for the purposes of paragraph (a) or (b) of that sub-paragraph, the reference to costs includes costs incurred in connection with a preliminary investigation of the allegation under paragraph 3.

(4) The amount of any penalty required to be paid under sub-paragraph (1) may not exceed such amount as is prescribed by rules made by the Council for the purposes of this sub-paragraph.

(5) Paragraphs 1, 2(1) and (3) and 4 of Schedule 4 have effect in relation to—

(a) proceedings for the hearing and determination of an allegation by the Investigating Committee, as they have effect in relation to proceedings before the Discipline and Appeals Committee under section 26, and
(b) orders of the Investigating Committee, as they have effect in relation to orders of the Discipline and Appeals Committee.

(6) A person against whom an order is made by the Investigating Committee by virtue of sub-paragraph (1) may appeal to the Discipline and Appeals Committee, and on any such appeal the Discipline and Appeals Committee may make such order as they think fit.

(7) If an order is made by the Investigating Committee by virtue of sub-paragraph (2), a person listed in paragraphs (a) to (c) of that sub-paragraph may appeal to the Discipline and Appeals Committee, and on any such appeal the Discipline and Appeals Committee may make such order as they think fit.

(8) Where an order is made by the Discipline and Appeals Committee under sub-paragraph (6) or (7)—

(a) a party to the appeal, or
(b) if not within paragraph (a), the Council,

may appeal against the order to the High Court.

(9) On an appeal under sub-paragraph (8) the High Court may make such order as it thinks fit.

(10) The decision of the High Court on an appeal under sub-paragraph (8) shall be final."

(6) In paragraph 4—

(a) in sub-paragraph (1) after "allegation" insert "within paragraph 3(1)(a) or (ab)",
(b) in that sub-paragraph, after paragraph (b) insert
", or
(c) has failed to comply with any such condition as is mentioned in paragraph 3(1)(ab),",
(c) in sub-paragraph (2), in paragraph (b), for "£3,000" substitute "such amount as may be prescribed by rules made by the Council for the purposes of this sub-paragraph",
(d) after paragraph (b) of that sub-paragraph insert—
"(ba) an order reprimanding that body;
(bb) an order that the recognition of that body under section 32 is to have effect subject to such conditions as may be specified in the order;",
(e) omit paragraph (c) of that sub-paragraph,
(f) after that sub-paragraph insert—

"(2A) Where on the hearing of any allegation within paragraph 3(1)(aa) the Discipline and Appeals Committee are satisfied that a manager or employee has failed to comply with any such rules as are mentioned in sub-paragraph (ii) of that paragraph, the Committee may, if they think fit, make one or more of the orders referred to in sub-paragraph (2B).

(2B) Those orders are—

(a) an order directing the payment by the manager or employee of a penalty not exceeding such amount as may be prescribed by rules made by the Council for the purposes of this sub-paragraph;
(b) an order requiring the Council to consider taking such steps as the Committee may specify in relation to the manager or employee;
(c) an order requiring the Council to refer to an appropriate regulator any matter relating to the conduct of the manager or employee.

(2C) For the purposes of sub-paragraph (2B)(c) an "appropriate regulator" in relation to a manager or employee means—

(a) if the person is an authorised person in relation to a reserved legal activity for the purposes of the Legal Services Act 2007, any relevant approved regulator (within the meaning of that Act) in relation to that person, and
(b) if the person carries on activities which are not reserved legal activities, any person who exercises regulatory functions in relation to the carrying on of such activities by the person.

(2D) In relation to proceedings under this paragraph, the Committee may make such order as they consider fit as to the payment of costs by—

(a) the Council;
(b) the recognised body or manager or employee against whom the proceedings were brought;
(c) if the person on whose allegation the proceedings were brought was heard (in person, or through a representative) by the Committee in the course of the proceedings, that person.

(2E) In sub-paragraph (2D), for the purposes of paragraph (a) or (b) of that sub-paragraph, the reference to costs includes costs incurred in connection with a preliminary investigation of the allegation under paragraph 3.", and

(g) omit sub-paragraphs (3), (3A) and (4).

(7) In paragraph 5—

(a) in sub-paragraph (1)—
  (i) after "26" insert "or paragraph 4", and
  (ii) for "director" (in each place) substitute "manager",
(b) in sub-paragraph (3) for "director" (in both places) substitute "manager", and
(c) after sub-paragraph (3) insert—

"(4) In relation to proceedings for the revocation of a recognition under sub-paragraph (1), the Discipline and Appeals Committee may make such order as they consider fit as to the payment of costs by—

(a) the Council;
(b) the body to whose recognition the proceedings relate.".

(8) In paragraph 6 (appeals against orders of the Committee)—

(a) in sub-paragraph (1)—
  (i) for "body corporate" substitute "person",
  (ii) after "4(1)" insert "or (2A)", and
  (iii) for "5" substitute "5(1)", and
(b) after that sub-paragraph insert—

"(1A) Where an order is made by the Committee under paragraph 4(2D) or 5(4) a person listed in that paragraph may appeal to the High Court, and on any such appeal the High Court may make such order as it thinks fit."

(9) After paragraph 7 (revocation of recognition on grounds of fraud or error)—

(a) in sub-paragraph (1) and (2) omit "corporate", and
(b) after sub-paragraph (2) insert—

"(3) In relation to proceedings for the revocation of a recognition under sub-paragraph (1), the Discipline and Appeals Committee may make such order as they consider fit as to the payment of costs by—

(a) the Council;
(b) the body to whose recognition the proceedings relate.

(4) In relation to proceedings on an application under sub-paragraph (2), the Discipline and Appeals Committee may make such order as they consider fit as to the payment of costs by—

(a) the Council;
(b) the applicant."

(10) In paragraph 8 (appeal against decision of Council in relation to grant of recognition)—

(a) in sub-paragraph (1) omit "corporate",

(b) in paragraph (b) of that sub-paragraph for "restrictions" substitute "conditions",
(c) after that paragraph insert
", or
(c) decides to give a direction in relation to that body under section 32(3B), or
(d) refuses an application by that body under section 32(3D),",
(d) in sub-paragraph (2) for "this paragraph" substitute "sub-paragraph (1)(a) or (b)",
(e) in paragraph (a) of that sub-paragraph—
 (i) for "restrictions" (in the first place) substitute "conditions", and
 (ii) for "restrictions falling within subsection (3)(d) of that section" substitute "conditions", and
(f) after that sub-paragraph insert—

"(2A) On an appeal under sub-paragraph (1)(c), the Discipline and Appeals Committee may—

(a) revoke the direction of the Council under section 32(3B),
(b) direct that the body's recognition is to have effect subject to such conditions as may be specified by the Council in the direction, or
(c) affirm the decision of the Council,

and the Committee may make such order as to the payment of costs by the Council or by that body as they think fit.

(2B) On an appeal under sub-paragraph (1)(d), the Discipline and Appeals Committee may—

(a) direct the Council to grant the application, or
(b) affirm the decision of the Council,

and the Committee may make such order as to the payment of costs by the Council or by that body as they think fit."

(11) In paragraph 9 (rules of procedure etc) in sub-paragraph (1)—

(a) for ", 2 and 3" substitute "and 2", and
(b) for "paragraph 4 or 5" substitute "paragraph 3A, 4 or 5".

(12) In paragraph 10 (intervention by Council)—

(a) in sub-paragraph (1), in paragraph (a) after "recognised body" insert "or a manager of such a body",
(b) after that paragraph insert—
"(aa) the Council is satisfied that a recognised body has been carrying on business in breach of any condition subject to which the body's recognition under section 32 of this Act has effect; or",
(c) for paragraph (c) of that sub-paragraph substitute—
"(c) a relevant insolvency event occurs in relation to a recognised body; or",
(d) in paragraph (d) of that sub-paragraph for "officer" substitute "manager",
(e) in that paragraph for "that body's" to the end of the paragraph substitute—
 "(i) that body's business,
 (ii) any trust of which that body is or was a trustee,
 (iii) any trust of which the manager or employee is or was a trustee in his capacity as such a manager or employee, or
 (iv) the business of another body in which the manager or employee is or was a manager or employee or the practice (or former practice) of the manager or employee;",
(f) after that paragraph insert
"or
(e) the Council is satisfied that it is necessary to exercise the powers conferred by Part 2 of Schedule 5 (or any of them) in relation to a recognised body to protect—
 (i) the interests of clients (or former or potential clients) of the recognised body,
 (ii) the interests of the beneficiaries of any trust of which the recognised body is or was a trustee, or
 (iii) the interests of the beneficiaries of any trust of which a person who is or was a manager or employee of the recognised body is or was a trustee in that person's capacity as such a manager or employee,",
(g) after sub-paragraph (1) insert—

"(1A) For the purposes of this paragraph a relevant insolvency event occurs in relation to a recognised body if—

(a) a resolution for a voluntary winding-up of the body is passed without a declaration of solvency under section 89 of the Insolvency Act 1986;
(b) the body enters administration within the meaning of paragraph 1(2)(b) of Schedule B1 to that Act;
(c) an administrative receiver within the meaning of section 251 of that Act is appointed;
(d) a meeting of creditors is held in relation to the body under section 95 of that Act (creditors' meeting which has the effect of converting a members' voluntary winding up into a creditors' voluntary winding up);
(e) an order for the winding up of the body is made.", and
(h) omit sub-paragraph (2).

(13) For paragraph 11(a) substitute—

"(a) the Council is satisfied that there has been undue delay on the part of—
(i) a recognised body in connection with any matter in which it is or was acting on behalf of a client or with any trust of which it is or was a trustee, or
(ii) a person who is or was a manager or employee of a recognised body in connection with any trust of which he is or was a trustee in his capacity as such a manager or employee; and".

(14) In paragraph 12(1) omit "corporate" (in both places).

(15) In paragraph 13—

(a) in paragraph (a) omit "corporate", and
(b) omit "and" at the end of paragraph (b) and after paragraph (c) insert—
"(d) paragraph 6(2)(a) of that Schedule is to be construed as including a reference to sums of money held by or on behalf of the recognised body in connection with any trust of which a person who is or was manager or employee of that body is or was a trustee in his capacity as such a manager or employee;
(e) paragraph 9 of that Schedule is to be construed—
(i) as if sub-paragraph (1) included a reference to documents in the possession or under the control of the recognised body in connection with any trust of which a person who is or was a manager or employee of that body is or was a trustee in his capacity as such a manager or employee, and
(ii) as applying to a person who is or was a manager or employee of the recognised body and documents and property in his possession or under his control in connection with such a trust as it applies to a recognised body and documents and property in the possession or under the control of that body;
(f) paragraph 10A(1) of that Schedule is to be construed as including power for the Council to apply to the High Court for an order for the appointment of a new trustee to a trust in substitution for a person who is a trustee in his capacity as a manager or employee of the recognised body; and
(g) paragraph 12A of that Schedule is to be read as if the references to a former partner were references—
(i) in the case of a recognised body which is a partnership, to a former partner in the partnership, and
(ii) in any other case to a manager or former manager of the recognised body."

(16) In paragraph 14 (examination of files)—

(a) for sub-paragraph (1) substitute—

"(1) Where the Investigating Committee are satisfied that it is necessary to do so for the purpose of investigating any such allegation as is mentioned in paragraph 3(1)(a)(ii), (aa) or (ab), the Committee may give an information notice to a relevant person.

(1A) An information notice is a notice requiring the production or delivery to any person appointed by the Committee, at a time and a place to be fixed by the Committee, of all documents in the possession or under the control of the relevant person in connection with the matters to which the allegation relates (whether or not they relate also to other matters).

(1B) In this section "relevant person" means—

(a) in the case of an allegation against a recognised body, the recognised body or any of its managers or employees, and
(b) in the case of an allegation against a manager or employee of a recognised body, the manager or employee, the recognised body or any other manager or employee of the recognised body.", and

(b) in sub-paragraph (2)—
 (i) for "and 12" substitute "to 12A",
 (ii) for "sub-paragraph (1) of this paragraph" (except where it appears in paragraph (d)) substitute "sub-paragraphs (1) and (1A) of this paragraph",
 (iii) in paragraph (b) after "body" insert ", manager or employee", and
 (iv) in paragraph (d) for "sub-paragraph (1)" substitute "sub-paragraph (1A)".

(17) Omit paragraph 15 (application of rules relating to accounts etc).

(18) In paragraph 16 (interest on client's money)—

(a) in sub-paragraph (1)—
 (i) after "recognised bodies" insert "or managers or employees of such bodies,",
 (ii) after "recognised body" insert ", manager or employee",
 (iii) for "it keeps" substitute "it or he keeps",
 (iv) for "its clients" substitute "clients of the recognised body", and
 (v) after "received by it" insert "or him", and
(b) in sub-paragraph (2), for "and any of its clients" substitute ", or any manager or employee of such a body, and any of the clients of the recognised body".

Initial Commencement
To be appointed: see s 211(2).
Appointment
Paras 1, 11: Appointment: 7 March 2008: see SI 2008/222, art 2(k).

PART 2
COURTS AND LEGAL SERVICES ACT 1990 (C 41)

33 The Courts and Legal Services Act 1990 is amended in accordance with this Part.

34 (1) Section 53 (the Council for Licensed Conveyancers) is amended as follows.

(2) For subsections (1) to (3) substitute—

"(1) The Council for Licensed Conveyancers has the powers necessary to enable it to become designated as an approved regulator in relation to one or more of the reserved legal activities within subsection (1A).

(1A) The reserved legal activities to which this subsection applies are—

(a) the exercise of a right of audience;
(b) the conduct of litigation;
(c) probate activities.

(2) If the Council becomes an approved regulator in relation to one or more of those activities, it may, in that capacity, authorise a person to carry on a relevant activity only if the person is a licensed conveyancer.

(3) Where the Council authorises a licensed conveyancer to carry on a relevant activity, it is to do so by issuing a licence to the licensed conveyancer."

(3) Omit subsection (5).

(4) For subsection (6) substitute—

"(6) Where the Council exercises any of its powers in connection with—

(a) an application for designation as an approved regulator in relation to a reserved legal activity within subsection (1A), or
(b) the authorising of a person to carry on a relevant activity,

it is to do so subject to any requirements to which it is subject in accordance with the provisions of the Legal Services Act 2007."

(5) In subsection (8), for "Secretary of State" substitute "Lord Chancellor".

(6) In subsection (9)—

(a) for "Secretary of State" substitute "Lord Chancellor", and
(b) omit paragraph (e).

(7) After that subsection insert—

"(10) For the purposes of this section—

(a) "right of audience", "conduct of litigation", "probate activities" and "reserved legal activity" have the same meaning as in the Legal Services Act 2007;
(b) references to designation as an approved regulator are to designation as an approved regulator—
 (i) by Part 1 of Schedule 4 to the Legal Services Act 2007, by virtue of an order under paragraph 5 of Schedule 22 to that Act, or
 (ii) under Part 2 of Schedule 4 to that Act;
(c) "relevant activity" means an activity which is a reserved legal activity—
 (i) which is within subsection (1A), and
 (ii) in relation to which the Council is designated as an approved regulator by Part 1 of Schedule 4 to that Act (by virtue of an order under paragraph 5 of Schedule 22 to that Act) or under Part 2 of that Schedule."

35 (1) Schedule 8 (licensed conveyancers) is amended as follows.

(2) In paragraph 1 (definitions)—

(a) in the definition of "advocacy licence" for "and constituting" to the end substitute "by which the Council authorises the licensed conveyancer concerned to exercise a right of audience;",
(b) in the definition of "litigation licence" for "and constituting" to the end substitute "by which the Council authorises the licensed conveyancer concerned to carry on activities which constitute the conduct of litigation;",
(c) in the definition of "probate licence" for "and constituting" to the end substitute "by which the Council authorises the licensed conveyancer concerned to carry on activities which constitute probate activities;", and
(d) at the end insert—

""reserved legal activity" has the same meaning as in the Legal Services Act 2007 (see section 12 of and Schedule 2 to that Act)."

(3) In paragraph 2 (qualification regulations and rules of conduct), in sub-paragraph (1)—

(a) for "rules of conduct" substitute "conduct rules", and
(b) for "granting of the rights or exemption" substitute "carrying on of the reserved legal activities".

(4) In paragraph 4 (issue of licences), in sub-paragraph (1)—

(a) in paragraph (a) for "rules of conduct" substitute "conduct rules", and
(b) in paragraph (c) for "provide the advocacy, litigation or probate services" substitute "carry on the reserved legal activities".

(5) In paragraph 5 (conditional licences)—

(a) for sub-paragraph (1)(d) substitute—
"(d) after the Investigating Committee have made any order in his case under section 24A(1) of the Act of 1985 or the Discipline and Appeals Committee have made any order in his case under section 26(1) of that Act.",
(b) in sub-paragraph (6)—
 (i) in paragraph (a) for "service that may be provided" substitute "activities that may be carried on", and
 (ii) in paragraph (b) for "provides the additional services" substitute "carries on the additional activities", and
(c) after sub-paragraph (7) insert—

"(8) Where a person applies for an advocacy, litigation or probate licence at a time when this paragraph has effect in relation to that person by reason of the circumstances mentioned in section 16(1)(ea) of the Act of 1985, section 16A(2) of that Act has effect as it has effect in relation to an application for a licence under Part 2 of that Act."

(6) Omit paragraph 7 (code of conduct).

(7) In paragraph 9 (removal of disqualification from holding a licence) after sub-paragraph (2) insert—

"(3) In relation to proceedings on an application under sub-paragraph (1), the Discipline and Appeals Committee may make such order as they consider fit as to the payment of costs by—

(a) the Council;
(b) the applicant."

(8) In paragraph 10 (revocation on grounds of error or fraud), after sub-paragraph (4) insert—

"(5) In relation to proceedings for the revocation of a licence under sub-paragraph (1), the Discipline and Appeals Committee may make such order as they consider fit as to the payment of costs by—

(a) the Council;
(b) the licensed conveyancer to whose licence the proceedings relate.

(6) In relation to proceedings on an application under sub-paragraph (2), the Discipline and Appeals Committee may make such order as they consider fit as to the payment of costs by—

(a) the Council;
(b) the applicant."

(9) Omit paragraph 11.

(10) In paragraph 12 (delegation of powers etc)—

(a) in sub-paragraph (1) for "Subject" to "enactment, the" substitute "The",
(b) in that sub-paragraph, for paragraph (b) substitute—
"(b) by a sub-committee of such a committee; or
(c) by an individual (whether or not a member of the Council's staff).",
(c) after that sub-paragraph insert—

"(1A) Where by virtue of sub-paragraph (1) any function may be discharged by a committee, the committee may arrange for the discharge of that function by—

(a) a sub-committee of that committee; or
(b) an individual, whether or not a member of the Council's staff.

(1B) Sub-paragraph (1A) is subject to any contrary direction given by the Council.

(1C) Arrangements made under sub-paragraph (1) or (1A) in respect of a function may provide that the function is to be exercised in accordance with the arrangements only (and not by the delegating body).

(1D) For this purpose "the delegating body" means—

(a) in the case of arrangements under sub-paragraph (1), the Council, and
(b) in the case of arrangements under sub-paragraph (1A), the committee.",
(d) for sub-paragraph (3) substitute—

"(3) Any power conferred by sub-paragraph (1), (1A) or (2) may be exercised so as to impose restrictions or conditions on the body or individual by whom the function is to be discharged.",

(e) for sub-paragraphs (6) and (7) substitute—

"(6) A committee or sub-committee established under this paragraph may include or consist of individuals other than—

(a) members of the Council;
(b) licensed conveyancers.

(7) A sub-committee of a committee established under this paragraph may also include or consist of individuals other than members of the committee.

(7A) The Council may make arrangements for the appointment and removal of members of any committee to be made other than by the Council.

(7B) A committee or sub-committee may regulate its own procedure, including quorum.", and

(f) after sub-paragraph (9) insert—

"(10) This paragraph is subject to any provision to the contrary made by or under any enactment."

(11) Omit paragraph 13 (Council's intervention powers).

Initial Commencement
To be appointed: see s 211(2).

SCHEDULE 18
IMMIGRATION ADVICE AND IMMIGRATION SERVICES

Section 186

PART 1
QUALIFYING REGULATORS

Designation orders

1 In this Part of this Schedule "designation order" means an order made under section 86A(6) of the Immigration and Asylum Act 1999 (c 33) (designated qualifying regulators entitled to authorise persons to provide immigration advice and immigration services).

Continuity of existing rights

2 Each of the following bodies is a qualifying regulator for the purposes of Part 5 of the Immigration and Asylum Act 1999—

(a) the Law Society;
(b) the Institute of Legal Executives;
(c) the General Council of the Bar.

Application to become a qualifying regulator

3 (1) This paragraph applies where a body wishes to become a qualifying regulator for the purposes of Part 5 of the Immigration and Asylum Act 1999.

(2) A body may apply to the Board for the Board—

(a) to designate the body as a qualifying regulator for those purposes, and
(b) to approve what the applicant proposes as its regulatory arrangements if a designation order is made ("the proposed regulatory arrangements").

(3) But a body may make an application under this paragraph only if—

(a) it is an approved regulator (other than the Board), or
(b) it has made an application under Part 2 of Schedule 4 (designation of approved regulators).

(4) An application under this paragraph must be made in such form and manner as the Board may specify in rules and must be accompanied by—

(a) details of the applicant's proposed regulatory arrangements,
(b) such explanatory material as the applicant considers is likely to be needed for the purposes of this Part of this Schedule, and
(c) the prescribed fee.

(5) The prescribed fee is the fee prescribed in, or determined in accordance with, rules made by the Board with the consent of the Lord Chancellor.

(6) An applicant may, at any time, withdraw the application by giving notice to that effect to the Board.

Consultation and representations

4 Paragraphs 4 to 12 of Schedule 4 (consultation requirements etc in relation to applications for designation as approved regulator) apply in relation to an application under paragraph 3 as they apply in relation to an application under paragraph 3 of that Schedule, but as if—

- (a) in paragraphs 6(2), 7(2), and 9(3) of that Schedule the references to making an order under paragraph 17 in accordance with the recommendation were references to making a designation order in respect of the applicant, and
- (b) in paragraph 6(2) of that Schedule the reference to the market for reserved legal services were a reference to the market for immigration advice and immigration services.

Determination of application

5 (1) The Board must make rules specifying how it will determine applications under paragraph 3.

(2) Rules under sub-paragraph (1) must, in particular, provide that the Board may grant an application only if it is satisfied—

- (a) that, if a designation order were to be made in relation to the applicant, the applicant would have appropriate internal governance arrangements in place at the time the order takes effect,
- (b) that, if such an order were made, the applicant would be competent to perform the role of designated qualifying regulator (within the meaning of section 86A of the Immigration and Asylum Act 1999 (c 33)) at that time,
- (c) that the arrangements made by the applicant for authorising persons to provide immigration advice or immigration services provide that persons may not be so authorised unless they are persons who are also authorised by the applicant to carry on activities which are reserved legal activities,
- (d) that the applicant's proposed regulatory arrangements make appropriate provision, and
- (e) that the applicant's proposed regulatory arrangements comply with the requirements imposed by sections 112 and 145 (requirements imposed in relation to the handling of complaints).

(3) The rules made for the purposes of sub-paragraph (2)(a) must in particular require the Board to be satisfied—

- (a) that the exercise of the applicant's regulatory functions would not be prejudiced by any of its representative functions, and
- (b) that decisions relating to the exercise of its regulatory functions would so far as reasonably practicable be taken independently from decisions relating to the exercise of its representative functions.

(4) In subsection (2)(c) the reference to persons who are also authorised by the applicant to carry on activities which are reserved legal activities includes, in relation to any application by the Law Society, registered foreign lawyers (within the meaning of section 89 of the Courts and Legal Services Act 1990).

6 (1) After considering—

- (a) the application and accompanying material,
- (b) any other information provided by the applicant,
- (c) any advice duly given and representations duly made by virtue of paragraph 4, and
- (d) any other information which the Board considers relevant to the application,

the Board must decide whether to grant the application.

(2) The Board must give notice of its decision to the applicant ("the decision notice").

(3) Where the Board decides to refuse the application, the decision notice must specify the reasons for that decision.

(4) The Board must publish the decision notice.

(5) Paragraph 15 of Schedule 4 (period within which decision must be made) applies in relation to a decision notice under this paragraph as it applies in relation to a decision notice under paragraph 14 of that Schedule.

Effect of application

7 (1) Where an application is granted under paragraph 6, the decision notice must specify that the applicant is a qualifying regulator for the purposes of Part 5 of the Immigration and Asylum Act 1999 (c 33).

(2) Where an application is granted under paragraph 6, the proposed regulatory arrangements are at the same time treated as having been approved by the Board.

(3) But if the application was made in reliance upon paragraph 3(3)(b), the applicant's status as such a qualifying regulator and the approval of its proposed regulatory arrangements under sub-paragraph (2) are conditional upon the Lord Chancellor making an order under Part 2 of Schedule 4 designating the body as an approved regulator in relation to one or more reserved legal activities.

Loss of qualifying regulator status

8 (1) Where a qualifying regulator—

(a) ceases to be an approved regulator, or
(b) ceases to be a designated qualifying regulator within the meaning of section 86A of the Immigration and Asylum Act 1999 by virtue of an order under subsection (3) or (4) of that section,

it also ceases to be a qualifying regulator.

(2) But sub-paragraph (1) is without prejudice to a body's ability to make a further application under paragraph 3.

(3) If a body in the list in paragraph 2 ceases to be a qualifying regulator by virtue of sub-paragraph (1), the Lord Chancellor must, by order, remove it from that list.

Initial Commencement
To be appointed: see s 211(2).

PART 2
AMENDMENTS OF THE IMMIGRATION AND ASYLUM ACT 1999 (C 33)

9 The Immigration and Asylum Act 1999 is amended in accordance with this Part of this Schedule.

10 In section 82(1) (interpretation of Part 5), after the definition of "designated professional body" insert—

""designated qualifying regulator" has the meaning given by section 86A;".

11 In section 83 (the Immigration Services Commissioner), after subsection (6) insert—

"(6A) The duties imposed on the Commissioner by subsections (3) and (5) apply in relation to persons within section 84(2)(ba) only to the extent that those duties have effect in relation to the Commissioner's functions under section 92 or 92A."

12 (1) Section 84 (provision of immigration services) is amended as follows.

(2) In subsection (2)—

(a) after paragraph (b) insert—
"(ba) a person authorised to provide immigration advice or immigration services by a designated qualifying regulator,", and
(b) in paragraph (c)(ii) after "(b)" insert "or (ba)".

(3) After subsection (3) insert—

"(3A) A person's entitlement to provide immigration advice or immigration services by virtue of subsection (2)(ba)—

(a) is subject to any limitation on that person's authorisation imposed by the regulatory arrangements of the designated qualifying regulator in question, and

(b) does not extend to the provision of such advice or services by the person other than in England and Wales (regardless of whether the persons to whom they are provided are in England and Wales or elsewhere).

(3B) In subsection (3A) "regulatory arrangements" has the same meaning as in the Legal Services Act 2007 (see section 21 of that Act)."

13 (1) Section 86 (designated professional bodies) is amended as follows.

(2) Omit subsections (1)(a), (d) and (e) and (4)(b).

(3) In subsection (5)(a) omit "England and Wales or".

(4) In subsection (6)—

(a) omit paragraph (a), and
(b) in paragraph (b) for "it" substitute "the order".

(5) In subsection (8) after "that a body" insert "(other than a body in England and Wales)".

14 After section 86 insert—

"86A Designated qualifying regulators

(1) "Designated qualifying regulator" means a body which is a qualifying regulator and is listed in subsection (2).

(2) The listed bodies are—

(a) the Law Society;
(b) the Institute of Legal Executives;
(c) the General Council of the Bar.

(3) The Secretary of State may by order remove a body from the list in subsection (2) if the Secretary of State considers that the body has failed to provide effective regulation of relevant authorised persons in their provision of immigration advice or immigration services.

(4) If a designated qualifying regulator asks the Secretary of State to amend subsection (2) so as to remove its name, the Secretary of State may by order do so.

(5) Where, at a time when a body is listed in subsection (2), the body ceases to be a qualifying regulator by virtue of paragraph 8(1)(a) of Schedule 18 to the Legal Services Act 2007 (loss of approved regulator status), the Secretary of State must, by order, remove it from the list.

(6) If the Secretary of State considers that a body which—

(a) is a qualifying regulator,
(b) is not a designated qualifying regulator, and
(c) is capable of providing effective regulation of relevant authorised persons in their provision of immigration advice or immigration services,

ought to be designated, the Secretary of State may, by order, amend the list in subsection (2) to include the name of that body.

(7) If the Secretary of State is proposing to act under subsection (3) or (6), the Secretary of State must, before doing so, consult the Commissioner.

(8) If the Secretary of State is proposing to act under subsection (3), the Secretary of State must, before doing so, also—

(a) notify the body concerned of the proposal and give it a reasonable period within which to make representations, and
(b) consider any representations duly made.

(9) An order under subsection (3) or (6) requires the approval of the Lord Chancellor.

(10) If the Legal Services Board considers that a designated qualifying regulator is failing to provide effective regulation of relevant authorised persons in their provision of immigration advice or immigration services, the Legal Services Board must make a report to this effect to—

(a) the Secretary of State, and
(b) the Lord Chancellor.

(11) In this section—

"qualifying regulator" means a body which is a qualifying regulator for the purposes of this Part of this Act by virtue of Part 1 of Schedule 18 to the Legal Services Act 2007 (approved regulators approved by the Legal Services Board in relation to immigration matters);

"relevant authorised persons", in relation to a designated qualifying regulator, means persons who are authorised by the designated qualifying regulator to provide immigration advice or immigration services."

15 (1) Section 90 (orders by disciplinary bodies) is amended as follows.

(2) In subsection (2), for paragraph (a) substitute—

"(a) appearing to the Secretary of State to be established for the purpose of hearing disciplinary charges against—
(i) members of a designated professional body, or
(ii) persons regulated by designated qualifying regulators; and".

(3) In subsection (3) after "body" insert "or designated qualifying regulator".

(4) In subsection (5)—

(a) after "means" insert

"—

(a) ", and
(b) after "that body" insert
", or
(b) a person who is authorised by the designated qualifying regulator concerned to provide immigration advice or immigration services."

16 In section 166(4) (orders requiring approval by Parliament), after paragraph (d) insert—

"(da) section 86A(3),".

17 (1) Schedule 5 (the Immigration Services Commissioner) is amended as follows.

(2) In paragraph 3 (code of standards)—

(a) after sub-paragraph (3)(a) insert—
"(aa) a person who is authorised by a designated qualifying regulator to provide immigration advice or immigration services;",
(b) in sub-paragraph (3)(b) after "paragraph (a)" insert "or (aa)",
(c) after sub-paragraph (6)(a) insert—
"(aa) each of the designated qualifying regulators;", and
(d) omit sub-paragraph (6)(b).

(3) In paragraph 4 (extension of scope of the code)—

(a) omit sub-paragraph (2)(b),
(b) in sub-paragraph (3)(a) omit "England and Wales or", and
(c) omit sub-paragraph (4)(a).

(4) In paragraph 5 (investigation of complaints)—

(a) in sub-paragraph (3), for the words from "but" to the end substitute—
"but not if the complaint is excluded by sub-paragraph (3A).",
(b) after that sub-paragraph insert—

"(3A) A complaint is excluded if—

(a) it relates to a person who is excluded from the application of subsection (1) of section 84 by subsection (6) of that section, or
(b) it relates to a person within section 84(2)(ba)."

Initial Commencement
To be appointed: see s 211(2).

Part 3
Transitional Provision

The transitional period

18 (1) In this Part of this Schedule references to "the transitional period" are to the period which—

(a) begins with the day appointed for the coming into force of section 13 (entitlement to carry on reserved legal activities), and
(b) ends with the day appointed by the Lord Chancellor by order for the purposes of this paragraph.

(2) Different days may be appointed under sub-paragraph (1)(b) for different purposes.

(3) An order may be made under sub-paragraph (1)(b) only on the recommendation of the Board.

Barristers etc

19 (1) During the transitional period, every barrister is deemed to be authorised by the General Council of the Bar to provide immigration advice and immigration services.

(2) That authority is exercisable in accordance with, and subject to, the regulatory arrangements of the General Council of the Bar.

(3) A person is not authorised under sub-paragraph (1) unless the person has in force a certificate issued by the General Council of the Bar authorising the person to practise as a barrister.

20 (1) During the transitional period, every registered European lawyer registered with the Inns of Court and the General Council of the Bar is deemed to be authorised by the General Council of the Bar to provide immigration advice and immigration services if the registered European lawyer is entitled to provide immigration advice and immigration services under his home professional title by virtue of the European regulations.

(2) That authority is exercisable in accordance with, and subject to, the regulatory arrangements of the General Council of the Bar (as they apply to the registered European lawyer by virtue of the European regulations).

(3) In this paragraph—

"European regulations" means the European Communities (Lawyer's Practice) Regulations 2000 (SI 2000/1119);
"home professional title" and "registered European lawyer" have the same meaning as in the European regulations.

Solicitors etc

21 (1) During the transitional period, each of the following is deemed to be authorised by the Law Society to provide immigration advice and immigration services—

(a) every qualified solicitor;
(b) every registered foreign lawyer (within the meaning of section 89 of the Courts and Legal Services Act 1990 (c 41));
(c) every legal partnership (within the meaning of paragraph 7(4) of Schedule 5);
(d) every body recognised under section 9 of the Administration of Justice Act 1985 (c 61).

(2) That authority is exercisable in accordance with, and subject to, the regulatory arrangements of the Law Society.

(3) "Qualified solicitor" means a person who is qualified under section 1 of the Solicitors Act 1974 (c 47) to act as a solicitor.

22 (1) During the transitional period, every registered European lawyer registered with the Law Society is deemed to be authorised by the Law Society to provide immigration advice and immigration services if the registered European lawyer is entitled to provide immigration advice and immigration services under his home professional title by virtue of the European regulations.

(2) That authority is exercisable in accordance with, and subject to, the regulatory arrangements of the Law Society (as they apply to the registered European lawyer by virtue of the European regulations).

(3) In this paragraph—

"European regulations" means the European Communities (Lawyer's Practice) Regulations 2000 (SI 2000/1119);

"home professional title" and "registered European lawyer" have the same meaning as in the European regulations.

Legal Executives

23 (1) During the transitional period, a person who is authorised by the Institute of Legal Executives to practise as a member of the profession of legal executives is deemed to be authorised by that Institute to provide immigration advice and immigration services.

(2) That authority is exercisable in accordance with and subject to the regulatory arrangements of the Institute of Legal Executives.

(3) A person is not authorised under sub-paragraph (1) unless the person has in force a certificate issued by the Institute of Legal Executives authorising the person to practise as a legal executive.

Initial Commencement
To be appointed: see s 211(2).

SCHEDULE 19
CLAIMS MANAGEMENT SERVICES

Section 187

1 The Compensation Act 2006 (c 29) is amended in accordance with this Schedule.

2 (1) Section 4 (provision of regulated claims management services) is amended as follows.

(2) After subsection (2) insert—

"(2A) The Secretary of State may not make an order under subsection (2)(e) unless—

(a) it is made in accordance with a recommendation made by the Legal Services Board, or
(b) the Secretary of State has consulted the Legal Services Board about the making of the order."

3 (1) Section 5 (the Regulator) is amended as follows.

(2) After subsection (1) insert—

"(1A) The Secretary of State may designate a person only on the recommendation of the Legal Services Board."

(3) In subsection (2) for "The Secretary of State may designate a person" substitute "The Legal Services Board may recommend a person for designation".

(4) Omit subsection (3).

(5) In subsection (4)—

(a) in paragraphs (a), (b), (d) and (e) for "Secretary of State" substitute "Legal Services Board", and
(b) omit paragraph (c).

(6) In subsection (8) after "may" insert ", on the recommendation of the Legal Services Board,".

(7) In subsection (9) for "Secretary of State" substitute "Legal Services Board".

(8) In subsection (10)—

(a) after "may" insert ", on the recommendation of the Legal Services Board,", and
(b) for "Secretary of State" (in the second place) substitute "Legal Services Board".

(9) After that subsection insert—

"(11) In discharging any function by virtue of subsection (9) or (10), the Legal Services Board must take such steps as are necessary to ensure an appropriate financial and organisational separation between the activities of the Board that relate to the carrying out of those functions and the other activities of the Board."

4 In section 6 (exemptions) after subsection (3) insert—

"(3A) The Secretary of State may not make an order under subsection (1) or (2) unless—

(a) it is made in accordance with a recommendation made by the Legal Services Board, or
(b) the Secretary of State has consulted the Legal Services Board about the making of the order."

5 (1) Section 7 (enforcement: offence) is amended as follows.

(2) In subsection (2)(b)—

(a) in sub-paragraph (i) for "51 weeks" substitute "12 months", and
(b) in sub-paragraph (ii) for "level 5 on the standard scale" substitute "the statutory maximum".

(3) For subsection (3) substitute—

"(3) In relation to an offence committed before the commencement of section 154(1) of the Criminal Justice Act 2003 the reference in subsection (2)(b)(i) to 12 months is to be read as a reference to 6 months."

6 (1) Section 8 (enforcement: the Regulator) is amended as follows.

(2) In subsection (5)—

(a) after "the Regulator" (in the second place) insert

"—

(a) ", and
(b) after "Part" insert
", and
(b) to take possession of any written or electronic records found on the search for the purposes of subsection (6)."

(3) After subsection (8) insert—

"(9) The Secretary of State may not make regulations under subsection (8) unless—

(a) they are made in accordance with a recommendation made by the Legal Services Board, or
(b) the Secretary of State has consulted the Legal Services Board about the making of the regulations."

7 In section 9 (regulations), after subsection (2) insert—

"(2A) The Secretary of State may not make regulations under this section unless—

(a) they are made in accordance with a recommendation made by the Legal Services Board, or
(b) the Secretary of State has consulted the Legal Services Board about the making of the regulations."

8 (1) Section 11 (pretending to be authorised etc) is amended as follows.

(2) In subsection (4)(b)—

(a) in sub-paragraph (i) for "51 weeks" substitute "12 months", and
(b) in sub-paragraph (ii) for "level 5 on the standard scale" substitute "the statutory maximum".

(3) For subsection (6) substitute—

"(6) In relation to an offence committed before the commencement of section 154(1) of the Criminal Justice Act 2003 the reference in subsection (4)(b)(i) to 12 months is to be read as a reference to 6 months."

9 In section 13 (appeals and references to Claims Management Services Tribunal), in subsection (4) for "against" substitute "on a point of law arising from".

10 In section 14 (interpretation), in the definition of "the Regulator" for "Secretary of State" substitute "Legal Services Board".

11 (1) The Schedule (claims management regulations) is amended as follows.

(2) In paragraph 5(3)(a) for ", guidance or a code given or issued" substitute "or guidance given".

(3) In paragraph 7—

- (a) in paragraph (e) for "Secretary of State" substitute "Legal Services Board",
- (b) in paragraph (g)—
  - (i) for "Secretary of State" substitute "Legal Services Board", and
  - (ii) after "Fund" insert "after consultation with the Secretary of State".

(4) In paragraph 8(2)(a)(ii) for "Secretary of State" substitute "Legal Services Board".

(5) In paragraph 9(2)(a)(ii) for "Secretary of State" substitute "Legal Services Board".

(6) In paragraph 14, in sub-paragraph (2) for "to enter" to the end substitute—

"(a) to enter and search premises on which a person conducts or is alleged to conduct regulated claims management business, for the purposes of—
  - (i) investigating a complaint about the activities of an authorised person, or
  - (ii) assessing compliance with terms and conditions of an authorisation, and

(b) to take possession of written or electronic records found on the search for the purposes of taking copies in accordance with regulations under sub-paragraph (3)."

Initial Commencement
To be appointed: see s 211(2).
Appointment
Paras 1, 5, 8, 9: Appointment: 7 March 2008: see SI 2008/222, art 2(l).
Paras 6(1), (2), 11(1), (6): Appointment: 30 June 2008: see SI 2008/1436, art 2(e).

SCHEDULE 20
AMENDMENTS IN RELATION TO THE LEGAL PROFESSION AND LEGAL AID (SCOTLAND) ACT 2007 (ASP 5)

Section 195

Solicitors (Scotland) Act 1980 (c 46)

1 (1) The Solicitors (Scotland) Act 1980 is amended as follows.

(2) In section 3A(5), omit paragraphs (a) and (ad).

(3) In section 15(2)—

- (a) in paragraph (e), for "38" substitute "62A", and
- (b) omit paragraph (j).

(4) In section 20(2), omit ", 53A(2)(ba)".

(5) In section 24C(2)—

- (a) in paragraph (d), for "38" substitute "62A", and
- (b) omit paragraph (i).

(6) In section 34, omit subsections (4), (4C) and (4D).

(7) Omit sections 38, 39, 42A and 42B.

(8) In section 42C—

- (a) in subsection (1)—
  - (i) omit paragraphs (a) and (c),
  - (ii) omit "to the solicitor or his firm or", and

(iii) omit "or, where" to the end,
(b) in subsection (2), in paragraphs (a) and (b) omit (in each place) "solicitor, firm or",
(c) in subsection (3)—
(i) in paragraph (a), omit "the solicitor or his firm or, as the case may be,",
(ii) in paragraph (b), omit "of which the solicitor" to "be,",
(d) in subsection (4), omit (in each place) "38,", and
(e) omit subsection (5).

(9) In section 51—

(a) in subsection (2)—
(i) omit "a solicitor may have been guilty" to "Fund) or", and
(ii) omit "or a solicitor" to "services", and
(b) omit subsection (2A).

(10) In section 52, in subsection (2)(aa) omit "42A(7) or".

(11) In section 53, omit subsections (3), (10) and (11).

(12) Omit sections 53A, 53B and 53C

(13) In section 54, omit subsections (1), (2B) and (2C).

(14) In section 55, omit subsection (8).

(15) Omit section 56A.

(16) In section 62A, in subsections (1) and (2) omit (in each place) "38,".

(17) In section 65—

(a) in subsection (1), omit the definition of "inadequate professional services", and
(b) omit subsection (5).

(18) In Part 2 of Schedule 3, in paragraph 5(1), (2) and (3) omit (in each place) "38,".

(19) In Part 2 of Schedule 4—

(a) in paragraph 9(a) and (b), omit (in each place) "or, as the case may be, of provision of inadequate professional services",
(b) in paragraph 16, omit sub-paragraphs (f) and (g), and
(c) in paragraph 23, omit ", 42A(7)".

(20) In the side-note to section 62A, omit "38,".

Law Reform (Miscellaneous Provisions) (Scotland) Act 1990 (c 40)

2 In the Law Reform (Miscellaneous Provisions) (Scotland) Act 1990, omit section 33.

Initial Commencement
To be appointed: see s 211(2).
Appointment
Appointment: 1 October 2008: see SI 2008/1436, art 3(b).
Extent
This Schedule applies to Scotland only: see s 212(2).

SCHEDULE 21
MINOR AND CONSEQUENTIAL AMENDMENTS

Section 208

Public Notaries Act 1801 (c 79)

1 The Public Notaries Act 1801 is amended in accordance with paragraphs 2 and 3.

2 In section 1 (no person to be created to act as public notary, to do any notarial act etc unless duly admitted), omit ", or use and exercise the office of a notary, or do any notarial act,".

3 In section 14 (Act not to extend to certain persons), omit from "proctor" to "any other".

Public Notaries Act 1843 (c 90)

4 The Public Notaries Act 1843 is amended in accordance with paragraphs 5 to 7.

5 After section 7 insert—

"7A Effect of admission or grant of faculty

(1) Despite any provision made by the Public Notaries Acts, a person's entitlement to carry on an activity which is a notarial activity is to be determined in accordance with the Legal Services Act 2007.

(2) Nothing in the Public Notaries Acts is to be regarded, for the purposes of paragraph 5(2) of Schedule 3 to the Legal Services Act 2007 (exempt persons in relation to notarial activities) as authorising a person to carry on such an activity.

(3) For this purpose—

"the Public Notaries Acts" means this Act and the Public Notaries Act 1801;
"exempt person" and "notarial activity" have the same meaning as in the Legal Services Act 2007."

6 In section 8 (Master of Faculties may issue commissions to take oaths)—

(a) the existing provision becomes subsection (1), and
(b) after that subsection insert—

"(2) For the purposes of the Legal Services Act 2007, the issue of a commission under subsection (1) is to be treated as an authorisation to carry on the relevant activities by virtue of another enactment (see paragraph 6(2) of Schedule 3 to that Act).

(3) In subsection (2), "relevant activities" means the activities authorised by the commission."

7 Omit section 10 (offence of practising as notary without authorisation).

Bills of Exchange Act 1882 (c 61)

8 The Bills of Exchange Act 1882 is amended in accordance with paragraphs 9 and 10.

9 In section 51 (noting or protest of bill), after subsection (7) insert—

"(7A) In subsection (7) "notary" includes a person who, for the purposes of the Legal Services Act 2007, is an authorised person in relation to any activity which constitutes a notarial activity (within the meaning of that Act)."

10 In section 94 (protest when notary not accessible)—

(a) the existing provision becomes subsection (1), and
(b) after that subsection insert—

"(2) In subsection (1), "notary" includes a person who, for the purposes of the Legal Services Act 2007, is an authorised person in relation to any activity which constitutes a notarial activity (within the meaning of that Act)."

Commissioners for Oaths Act 1889 (c 10)

11 The Commissioners for Oaths Act 1889 is amended in accordance with paragraphs 12 and 13.

12 In section 1(3) (powers of commissioners for oaths) omit from "in which" (in the first place) to "solicitor, or".

13 In section 6 (powers as to oaths and notarial acts abroad), after subsection (1) insert—

"(1A) In subsection (1), "notary public" includes a person who, for the purposes of the Legal Services Act 2007, is an authorised person in relation to any activity which constitutes a notarial activity (within the meaning of that Act)."

Benefices Act 1898 (c 48)

14 In section 3 of the Benefices Act 1898 (appeal against refusal of benefice)—

(a) in subsection (2) for "counsel or a solicitor" substitute "an authorised person", and
(b) after that subsection insert—

"(2A) In subsection (2) "authorised person" means a person who, for the purposes of the Legal Services Act 2007, is an authorised person in relation to an activity which constitutes the exercise a right of audience (within the meaning of that Act)."

Children and Young Persons Act 1933 (c 12)

15 The Children and Young Persons Act 1933 is amended in accordance with paragraphs 16 to 20.

16 In section 37(1) (power to clear court while child or young person giving evidence), for "counsel or solicitors" substitute "legal representatives".

17 In section 43 (admission of deposition in evidence), for "counsel or solicitor" substitute "legal representative".

18 In section 47(2)(b) (procedure in youth courts), for "solicitors and counsel" substitute "legal representatives".

19 In section 49(11) (restrictions on reports of proceedings), omit the definition of "legal representative".

20 In section 107 (interpretation), after the definition of "legal guardian" insert—

""legal representative" means a person who, for the purposes of the Legal Services Act 2007, is an authorised person in relation to an activity which constitutes the exercise of a right of audience or the conduct of litigation (within the meaning of that Act);".

London Building Acts (Amendment) Act 1939 (c xcvii)

21 In section 115 of the London Building Acts (Amendment) Act 1939 (jurisdiction of tribunal of appeal)—

(a) in subsection (2), for "counsel solicitor" substitute "an authorised person", and
(b) after that subsection insert—

"(2A) In subsection (2) "authorised person" means a person who, for the purposes of the Legal Services Act 2007, is an authorised person in relation to an activity which constitutes the exercise of a right of audience (within the meaning of that Act)."

Accommodation Agencies Act 1953 (c 23)

22 In section 1 of the Accommodation Agencies Act 1953 (illegal commissions and advertisements)—

(a) in subsection (3), after "solicitor" insert "or an authorised person", and
(b) in subsection (6), after "say:—" insert—
""authorised person" means a person (other than a solicitor) who, for the purposes of the Legal Services Act 2007, is an authorised person in relation to an activity which is a reserved legal activity (within the meaning of that Act);".

Geneva Conventions Act 1957 (c 52)

23 In section 3 of the Geneva Conventions Act 1957 (legal representation of certain persons), after subsection (5) insert—

"(6) In this section—

"counsel" includes any person who, for the purposes of the Legal Services Act 2007, is an authorised person in relation to an activity which constitutes the exercise of a right of audience (within the meaning of that Act);
"solicitor" includes any person who, for the purposes of that Act, is an authorised person in relation to an activity which constitutes the conduct of litigation (within the meaning of that Act)."

Horserace Betting Levy Act 1969 (c 14)

24 In section 4 of the Horserace Betting Levy Act 1969 (non-renewal of bookmaker's permit)—

(a) in subsection (2), for "or a solicitor" substitute ", a solicitor or an authorised person", and
(b) after that subsection insert—

"(2A) In subsection (2), "authorised person" means a person (other than counsel or a solicitor) who, for the purposes of the Legal Services Act 2007, is an authorised person in relation to an activity which constitutes the exercise of a right of audience or the conduct of litigation (within the meaning of that Act)."

Taxes Management Act 1970 (c 9)

25 In section 20B of the Taxes Management Act 1970 (restrictions on power to require documents)—

(a) in subsection (3), for "barrister, advocate or solicitor" (in both places) substitute "relevant lawyer",
(b) in subsection (8), for "barrister, advocate or a solicitor" substitute "relevant lawyer", and
(c) after subsection (14) insert—

"(15) In this section "relevant lawyer" means a barrister, advocate, solicitor or other legal representative communications with whom may be the subject of a claim to professional privilege."

Powers of Attorney Act 1971 (c 27)

26 In section 3 of the Powers of Attorney Act 1971 (proof of instruments creating powers of attorney)—

(a) in subsection (1)(b) for "duly certificated notary public" substitute ", authorised person", and
(b) in subsection (3) for from ""duly" to "Act and" substitute ""authorised person" means a person (other than a solicitor) who, for the purposes of the Legal Services Act 2007, is an authorised person in relation to any activity which constitutes a notarial activity (within the meaning of that Act) and".

Poisons Act 1972 (c 66)

27 In section 9(7) of the Poisons Act 1972 (right to conduct proceedings), omit "notwithstanding that he is not of counsel or a solicitor".

Local Government Act 1972 (c 70)

28 In section 223 of the Local Government Act 1972 (appearance of local authorities in legal proceedings), in subsection (1) for ", notwithstanding" to the end substitute "to conduct any such proceedings."

Matrimonial Causes Act 1973 (c 18)

29 In section 6 of the Matrimonial Causes Act 1973 (attempts at reconciliation of parties to marriage) in subsection (1) for "solicitor" substitute "legal representative".

Fair Trading Act 1973 (c 41)

30 In section 29 of the Fair Trading Act 1973 (powers of entry and seizure)—

(a) in subsection (5), for "barrister, advocate or solicitor" substitute "relevant lawyer", and
(b) after subsection (5) insert—

"(6) "Relevant lawyer" means a barrister, advocate, solicitor, or other legal representative communications with whom may be the subject of a claim to privilege."

Consumer Credit Act 1974 (c 39)

31 In section 146 of the Consumer Credit Act 1974 (exceptions from section 145), after subsection (2) insert—

"(2A) An authorised person (other than a barrister or solicitor) engaging in contentious business is not to be treated as doing so in the course of any ancillary credit business.

(2B) In subsection (2A)—

"authorised person" means a person who, for the purposes of the Legal Services Act 2007, is an authorised person in relation to an activity which constitutes the exercise of a right of audience or the conduct of litigation (within the meaning of that Act);
"contentious business" means business done in or for the purposes of proceedings begun before a court or before an arbitrator, not being non-contentious or common form probate business (within the meaning of section 128 of the Supreme Court Act 1981)."

Sex Discrimination Act 1975 (c 65)

32 In section 77 of the Sex Discrimination Act 1975 (validity and revision of contracts), in subsection (4BB)(a) for "a barrister" (in the first place) to the end substitute "a person who, for the purposes of the Legal Services Act 2007, is an authorised person in relation to an activity which constitutes the exercise of a right of audience or the conduct of litigation (within the meaning of that Act), and".

Bail Act 1976 (c 63)

33 The Bail Act 1976 is amended in accordance with paragraphs 34 and 35.

34 In section 3 (general provisions), in subsection (6)(e) for "an authorised advocate" to the end substitute "a person who, for the purposes of the Legal Services Act 2007, is an authorised person in relation to an activity which constitutes the exercise of a right of audience or the conduct of litigation (within the meaning of that Act);".

35 In section 5 (supplementary provisions about decisions on bail)—

(a) in subsection (5), for "is represented by counsel or a solicitor unless his counsel or solicitor" substitute "has legal representation unless his legal representative", and
(b) in subsection (6), for "is not represented by counsel or a solicitor" substitute "does not have legal representation".

Race Relations Act 1976 (c 74)

36 The Race Relations Act 1976 is amended in accordance with paragraphs 37 to 39.

37 In section 67A (national security: procedure), in subsection (3)(a) for "have a general" to the end substitute "be a person who, for the purposes of the Legal Services Act 2007, is an authorised person in relation to an activity which constitutes the exercise of a right of audience or the conduct of litigation (within the meaning of that Act), and".

38 In section 72 (validity and revision of contracts), in subsection (4BB)(a) for "a barrister" (in the first place) to the end substitute "a person who, for the purposes of the Legal Services Act 2007, is an authorised person in relation to an activity which constitutes the exercise of a right of audience or the conduct of litigation (within the meaning of that Act), and".

39 In Schedule 1A (bodies and other persons subject to general statutory duty), in Part 2, in the entry for the Chartered Institute of Patent Agents, for "Agents" substitute "Attorneys".

Patents Act 1977 (c 37)

40 In section 102 of the Patents Act 1977 (rights of audience etc in proceedings before the comptroller)—

(a) after subsection (2) insert—

"(2A) For the purposes of subsection (2), as it has effect in relation to England and Wales, "the enactment relating to the preparation of documents by persons not qualified" means section 14 of the Legal Services Act 2007 (offence to carry on a reserved legal activity if not entitled) as it applies in relation to an activity which amounts to the carrying on of reserved instrument activities within the meaning of that Act.", and

(b) for subsection (5) substitute—

"(5) Nothing in this section is to be taken to limit any entitlement to prepare deeds conferred on a registered patent attorney by virtue of the Legal Services Act 2007."

Estate Agents Act 1979 (c 38)

41 In section 11 of the Estate Agents Act 1979 (powers of entry and inspection)—

(a) in subsection (8), for "counsel or solicitor" substitute "a relevant lawyer", and
(b) after that subsection insert—

"(9) For the purposes of subsection (8) "relevant lawyer" means counsel, a solicitor or other legal representative communications with whom may be the subject of a claim to privilege."

Magistrates' Courts Act 1980 (c 43)

42 The Magistrates' Courts Act 1980 is amended in accordance with paragraphs 43 and 44.

43 In section 144 (rule committee and rules of procedure)—

(a) in subsection (3)(c), for from "granted" to "right" substitute "authorised by a relevant approved regulator", and
(b) after subsection (3) insert—

"(3A) In this section "relevant approved regulator" is to be construed in accordance with section 20(3) of the Legal Services Act 2007."

44 In section 150 (interpretation), in subsection (1), in the definition of "legal representative" for "an authorised advocate" to the end substitute "a person who, for the purposes of the Legal Services Act 2007, is an authorised person in relation to an activity which constitutes the exercise of a right of audience or the conduct of litigation (within the meaning of that Act);".

Supreme Court Act 1981 (c 54)

45 The Supreme Court Act 1981 is amended in accordance with paragraphs 46 and 47.

46 In section 86 (Crown Court Rule Committee)—

(a) in subsection (1)(g), for from "granted" to "right" substitute "authorised by a relevant approved regulator", and
(b) after subsection (6) insert—

"(7) In this section "relevant approved regulator" is to be construed in accordance with section 20(3) of the Legal Services Act 2007."

47 In section 90(3B) (conduct of proceedings by Official Solicitor) for "section 28(2)(a) of the Courts and Legal Services Act 1990" substitute "the fact that he is a person who, for the purposes of the Legal Services Act 2007, is an authorised person in relation to an activity which constitutes the conduct of litigation (within the meaning of that Act)".

Representation of the People Act 1983 (c 2)

48 The Representation of the People Act 1983 is amended in accordance with paragraphs 49 to 52.

49 In section 86 (authorised excuses for failures as to return and declarations)—

(a) in subsection (1A), for "or solicitor" substitute ", solicitor or authorised person", and
(b) after that subsection insert—

"(1B) In subsection (1A) "authorised person" means a person (other than a barrister or solicitor) who, for the purposes of the Legal Services Act 2007, is an authorised person in relation to an activity which constitutes the exercise of a right of audience (within the meaning of that Act)."

50 In section 156 (costs of trying election petition)—

(a) in subsection (5), for "or solicitor" substitute ", a solicitor or an authorised person", and
(b) after that subsection insert—

"(5A) In subsection (5) "authorised person" means a person (other than counsel or a solicitor) who, for the purposes of the Legal Services Act 2007, is an authorised person in relation to an activity which constitutes the exercise of a right of audience (within the meaning of that Act)."

51 In section 162 (member of legal and certain other professions)—

(a) the existing provision becomes subsection (1),
(b) in that subsection—
  (i) after "solicitor" insert ", authorised person", and
  (ii) for "or tribunal" (in both places) substitute ", tribunal or other body", and
(c) after that subsection insert—

"(2) In subsection (1) "authorised person" means a person (other than a barrister or solicitor) who, for the purposes of the Legal Services Act 2007, is an authorised person in relation to an activity which constitutes a reserved legal activity (within the meaning of that Act)."

52 In section 181 (Director of Public Prosecutions)—

(a) in subsection (3), for "or solicitor" substitute ", solicitor or authorised person", and
(b) after that subsection insert—

"(3A) In subsection (3) "authorised person" means a person (other than a barrister or solicitor) who, for the purposes of the Legal Services Act 2007, is an authorised person in relation to an activity which constitutes the exercise of a right of audience (within the meaning of that Act)."

Mental Health Act 1983 (c 20)

53 The Mental Health Act 1983 is amended in accordance with paragraphs 54 to 60.

54 In section 35 (remand to hospital for report on accused's mental condition), in subsection (6) for "counsel or a solicitor and his counsel or solicitor" substitute "an authorised person who".

55 In section 36 (removal of accused person to hospital for treatment), in subsection (5) for "counsel or a solicitor and his counsel or solicitor" substitute "an authorised person who".

56 In section 38 (interim hospital orders), in subsection (2) for "counsel or a solicitor and his counsel or solicitor" substitute "an authorised person who".

57 In section 52 (further provisions as to persons remanded by magistrates' courts), in subsection (7)(b) for "counsel or a solicitor" substitute "an authorised person".

58 In section 54 (requirements as to medical evidence), in subsection (3)(a)—

(a) for "counsel or a solicitor" substitute "an authorised person", and
(b) for "his counsel or solicitor" substitute "that authorised person".

59 In section 55 (interpretation of Part 3), in subsection (1) before the definitions of "child" and "young person" insert—

""authorised person" means a person who, for the purposes of the Legal Services Act 2007, is an authorised person in relation to an activity which constitutes the exercise of a right of audience (within the meaning of that Act);".

60 In section 78 (procedure of Mental Health Review Tribunals), in subsection (7) for "counsel or a solicitor" substitute "an authorised person (within the meaning of Part 3)".

County Courts Act 1984 (c 28)

61 In section 147 of the County Courts Act 1984 (interpretation), in subsection (1), in the definition of "legal representative" for "an authorised advocate" to the end substitute "a person who, for the purposes of the Legal Services Act 2007, is an authorised person in relation to an activity which constitutes the exercise of a right of audience or the conduct of litigation (within the meaning of that Act);".

Inheritance Tax Act 1984 (c 51)

62 In section 219 of the Inheritance Tax Act 1984 (power to require information)—

(a) in subsection (3) for "barrister or solicitor" substitute "relevant lawyer",
(b) in subsection (4) for "solicitor" (in both places) substitute "relevant lawyer", and
(c) after that subsection insert—

"(5) In this section "relevant lawyer" means a barrister, advocate, solicitor or other legal representative communications with whom may be the subject of a claim to professional privilege."

Companies Act 1985 (c 6)

63 In Schedule 15D of the Companies Act 1985 (disclosures)—

(a) the existing paragraph 46 becomes sub-paragraph (1) of that paragraph,
(b) in that sub-paragraph for "solicitor, barrister" substitute "relevant lawyer", and
(c) after that sub-paragraph insert—

"(2) "Relevant lawyer" means—

(a) a person who, for the purposes of the Legal Services Act 2007, is an authorised person in relation to an activity which constitutes a reserved legal activity (within the meaning of that Act),
(b) a solicitor or barrister in Northern Ireland, or
(c) a solicitor or advocate in Scotland."

Prosecution of Offences Act 1985 (c 23)

64 In section 15 of the Prosecution of Offences Act 1985 (interpretation), in subsection (1), in the definition of "legal representative" for "an authorised advocate" to the end substitute "a person who, for the purposes of the Legal Services Act 2007, is an authorised person in relation to an activity which constitutes the exercise of a right of audience or the conduct of litigation (within the meaning of that Act);".

Administration of Justice Act 1985 (c 61)

65 The Administration of Justice Act 1985 is amended in accordance with paragraphs 66 and 67.

66 In section 41 (application of disciplinary provisions to legal aid complaints against barristers), in subsection (2) after "those provisions" insert "and despite section 157 of the Legal Services Act 2007 (approved regulators not to make provision for redress)".

67 In section 69(2) (commencement) for "Secretary of State" substitute "Lord Chancellor".

Social Security Act 1986 (c 50)

68 In section 56 of the Social Security Act 1986 (legal proceedings), in subsection (1) omit "although not a barrister or solicitor".

Building Societies Act 1986 (c 53)

69 The Building Societies Act 1986 is amended in accordance with paragraphs 70 to 72.

70 In section 52 (powers to obtain information and documents etc)—

(a) in subsection (8) for "barrister, solicitor or advocate" substitute "relevant lawyer", and
(b) in subsection (13) after the definition of "approved" insert—
""relevant lawyer" means a barrister, advocate, solicitor or other legal representative communications with whom may be the subject of a claim to professional privilege;".

71 In section 67 (directors, etc, not to accept commission in connection with loans), in subsection (7), in the definition of "solicitor" for "licensed conveyancer" substitute "any person who, for the purposes of the Legal Services Act 2007, is an authorised person in relation to an activity which constitutes a reserved instrument activity (within the meaning of that Act)".

72 In section 69 (disclosure and record of income of related businesses), in subsection (17), in the definition of "solicitor" for "licensed conveyancer" to the end substitute "any person who, for the purposes of the Legal Services Act 2007, is an authorised person in relation to an activity which constitutes a reserved instrument activity (within the meaning of that Act)."

Ministry of Defence Police Act 1987 (c 4)

73 *In section 4 of the Ministry of Defence Police Act 1987 (representation at disciplinary proceedings)—*

(*a*) *in subsection (2) for "either by counsel or by a solicitor" substitute "by a relevant lawyer",*
(*b*) *in subsection (7) for "counsel or a solicitor" substitute "a relevant lawyer", and*
(*c*) *after that subsection insert—*

"(*8*) *In this section "relevant lawyer" means—*

(*a*) *in relation to Scotland or Northern Ireland, counsel or a solicitor, and*
(*b*) *in relation to England and Wales, a person who, for the purposes of the Legal Services Act 2007, is an authorised person in relation to an activity which constitutes the exercise of a right of audience (within the meaning of that Act)."*

Income and Corporation Taxes Act 1988 (c 1)

74 In the Income and Corporation Taxes Act 1988, in section 778 (power to obtain information)—

(a) in subsection (3) for "solicitor" substitute "relevant lawyer", and
(b) after that subsection insert—

"(4) In subsection (3) "relevant lawyer" means a barrister, advocate, solicitor or other legal representative communications with whom may be the subject of a claim to professional privilege or, in Scotland, protected from disclosure in legal proceedings on the grounds of confidentiality of communication."

Copyright, Designs and Patents Act 1988 (c 48)

75 The Copyright, Designs and Patents Act 1988 is amended in accordance with paragraphs 76 to 80.

76 In section 276 (persons entitled to describe themselves as patent agents)—

(a) in subsection (1) for "registered patent agent" substitute "registered patent attorney", and
(b) in subsection (4) for "agent" (in the second place) substitute "attorney".

77 In section 280 (privilege for communications with patent agents)—

(a) in subsection (1), after "to" (in the first place) insert

"—

(a) "
(b) at the end of that subsection insert

", and

(b) documents, material or information relating to any matter mentioned in paragraph (a).",
(c) for subsection (2) substitute—

"(2) Where a patent attorney acts for a client in relation to a matter mentioned in subsection (1), any communication, document, material or information to which this section applies is privileged from disclosure in like manner as if the patent attorney had at all material times been acting as the client's solicitor.",

(d) in subsection (3)—
  (i) for "agent" (in each place) substitute "attorney", and
  (ii) for "agents" substitute "attorneys", and
(e) omit subsection (4).

78 In section 281 (power of comptroller to refuse to deal with certain agents) in subsection (2) for "agents" (in both places) substitute "attorneys".

79 In section 286 (interpretation)—

(a) for "agent"" substitute "attorney"", and
(b) for "(1)" substitute "(2)".

80 Omit section 292 (rights and duties of registered patent agents in relation to proceedings in patent county courts).

Law of Property (Miscellaneous Provisions) Act 1989 (c 34)

81 In section 1 of the Law of Property (Miscellaneous Provisions) Act 1989 (deeds and their execution)—

(a) in subsection (5) for "a solicitor" (in the first place) to "conveyancer" (in the second place) substitute "a relevant lawyer, or an agent or employee of a relevant lawyer", and
(b) in subsection (6) for the definition of "duly certificated notary public" substitute—

""relevant lawyer" means a person who, for the purposes of the Legal Services Act 2007, is an authorised person in relation to an activity which constitutes a reserved instrument activity (within the meaning of that Act)."

Companies Act 1989 (c 40)

82 In section 87 of the Companies Act 1989 (exceptions from restrictions on disclosure)—

(a) in subsection (2), in paragraph (c)(i), for "solicitor" substitute "relevant lawyer", and
(b) after that subsection insert—

"(2A) In subsection (2)(c)(i) "relevant lawyer" means—

(a) a person who, for the purposes of the Legal Services Act 2007, is an authorised person in relation to an activity which constitutes a reserved legal activity (within the meaning of that Act),
(b) a solicitor or barrister in Northern Ireland, or
(c) a solicitor or advocate in Scotland."

Courts and Legal Services Act 1990 (c 41)

83 The Courts and Legal Services Act 1990 is amended in accordance with paragraphs 84 to 101.

84 Omit the following provisions—

(a) section 17 (the statutory objective and the general principle);
(b) section 18 (the statutory duty);
(c) section 18A (the Consultative Panel);
(d) section 27 (rights of audience);
(e) section 28 (rights to conduct litigation);
(f) section 29 (authorised bodies);
(g) section 31 (barristers and solicitors: rights of audience and rights to conduct litigation);
(h) section 31A (employed advocates).

85 In section 31B (advocates and litigators employed by Legal Services Commission)—

(a) for subsection (1) substitute—

"(1) This section applies where a person—

(a) is authorised by a relevant approved regulator ("the regulator") to carry on an activity which constitutes the exercise of a right of audience or the conduct of litigation, and
(b) is employed by the Legal Services Commission, or by any body established and maintained by that Commission.

(1A) Any rules of the regulator which fall within subsection (2) shall not have effect in relation to that person.",

(b) in subsection (2)—
    (i) for "body" (in each place) substitute "regulator", and

(ii) for "rules of conduct" substitute "conduct rules",

(c) in subsection (3) for "body" substitute "regulator", and

(d) after subsection (3) insert—

"(4) For the purposes of this section "relevant approved regulator" is to be construed in accordance with section 20(3) of the Legal Services Act 2007."

86 In section 31C (change of authorised body)—

(a) for subsection (1) substitute—

"(1) Where a person—

(a) has at any time been authorised by a relevant approved regulator to exercise a right of audience before a court in relation to proceedings of a particular description, and

(b) becomes authorised by another relevant approved regulator to exercise a right of audience before that court in relation to that description of proceedings,

any qualification regulations of the relevant approved regulator mentioned in paragraph (b) which relate to that right are not to have effect in relation to the person.",

(b) in subsection (2) for "the body" substitute "the relevant approved regulator",

(c) in subsection (3) for "body" (in each place) substitute "relevant approved regulator", and

(d) after that subsection insert—

"(4) In this section "relevant approved regulator" is to be construed in accordance with section 20(3) of the Legal Services Act 2007."

87 Omit sections 34 to 52 (extension of conveyancing services).

88 Omit sections 54 and 55 (preparation of probate papers etc).

89 In section 60 (regulation of right of Scottish and Northern Ireland lawyers to practise in England and Wales)—

(a) in subsection (1) for "Secretary of State" substitute "Lord Chancellor",

(b) in subsection (2) for "Secretary of State" substitute "Lord Chancellor",

(c) after subsection (2) insert—

"(2A) Regulations may be made under this section only if—

(a) the Legal Services Board has made a recommendation under section 60A,

(b) draft regulations were annexed to the recommendation, and

(c) the regulations are in the same form as, or a form not materially different from, the draft regulations.", and

(d) in subsection (4) for "Secretary of State" substitute "Lord Chancellor".

90 After that section insert—

"60A Procedural requirements relating to recommendations for the purposes of section 60

(1) Before making a recommendation under this section, the Legal Services Board must publish a draft of—

(a) the proposed recommendation, and

(b) the proposed draft regulations.

(2) The draft must be accompanied by a notice which states that representations about the proposals may be made to the Board within a specified period.

(3) Before making the recommendation, the Board must have regard to any representations duly made.

(4) If the draft regulations to be annexed to the recommendation differ from the draft regulations published under subsection (1)(b) in a way which is, in the opinion of the Board, material, the Board must, before making the recommendation, publish the draft recommendations along with a statement detailing the changes made and the reasons for the changes."

91 Omit section 63 (legal professional privilege).

92 Omit section 69 (exemption from liability for damages etc).

93 Omit section 70 (offences).

94 In section 71 (qualification for judicial and certain other appointments)—

(a) in subsection (4) for "granted by an authorised body" substitute "exercisable by virtue of an authorisation given by a relevant approved regulator",
(b) in subsection (6) for "the authorised body concerned" substitute "the relevant approved regulator", and
(c) after that subsection insert—

"(6A) In this section "relevant approved regulator" is to be construed in accordance with section 20(3) of the Legal Services Act 2007."

95 In section 75 (judges etc barred from legal practice), after paragraph (b) insert—

"(ba) carry on any notarial activities (within the meaning of the Legal Services Act 2007);".

96 Omit section 113 (administration of oaths and taking of affidavits).

97 (1) Section 119 (interpretation) is amended as follows.

(2) In subsection (1) omit the following definitions—

"authorised advocate"
"authorised body" and "appropriate authorised body"
"authorised litigator"
"authorised practitioner"
"Consultative Panel"
"duly certificated notary public"
"the general principle"
"qualified person"
"the statutory objective".

(3) In that subsection, for the definition of "court" substitute—

""court" has the same meaning as in the Legal Services Act 2007 (see section 207 of that Act);".

(4) In that subsection, for the definition of "qualification regulations" and "rules of conduct" substitute—

""qualification regulations" and "conduct rules", in relation to a body, have the same meaning as in the Legal Services Act 2007 (see section 21 of that Act);".

(5) In that subsection, in the definition of "right to conduct litigation"—

(a) in paragraph (a) after "court" insert "in England and Wales",
(b) for "and" at the end of that paragraph substitute—
"(aa) to commence, prosecute and defend such proceedings; and".

(6) In subsection (3) for from "(including" to the end substitute "to conduct rules includes a reference to practice rules (within the meaning of the Legal Services Act 2007 (see section 21 of that Act))."

98 In section 120 (regulations and orders) omit—

(a) in subsection (4)—
  (i) "26(1), 37(10), 40(1)", and
  (ii) from "paragraph 24" to "Schedule 9", and
(b) subsection (5).

99 In section 125 (power to make provision consequential on provision made by Part 2 of Administration of Justice Act 1985 etc)—

(a) in subsection (4) for "Secretary of State" substitute "Lord Chancellor", and
(b) for subsection (5) substitute—

"(5) In subsection (4)—

(a) "relevant enactments" means such enactments or instruments passed or made before or in the same Session as the Legal Services Act 2007 was passed as may be specified in the order, and

(b) the reference to Part 2 is a reference to that Part as amended by that Act or any enactment or instruments passed or made before or in the same Session as that Act was passed."

100 Omit the following provisions—

(a) Schedule 4 (authorised bodies);
(b) Schedule 5 (the Authorised Conveyancing Practitioners Board);
(c) Schedule 6 (the Conveyancing Appeals Tribunals);
(d) Schedule 7 (the Conveyancing Ombudsman Scheme);
(e) in Part 2 of Schedule 8 (amendments of provisions relating to powers of Conveyancing Licensing Council etc), paragraphs 14 to 20 and 21(1)(b);
(f) Schedule 9 (probate).

101 In paragraph 17 of Schedule 19 (revocation of appointment under section 1(1) of the Commissioners for Oaths Act 1889) for "Secretary of State" substitute "Lord Chancellor".

Environmental Protection Act 1990 (c 43)

102 In section 114 (appointment etc of inspectors), in subsection (4) omit ", although not of counsel or a solicitor,".

Friendly Societies Act 1992 (c 40)

103 In section 62 of the Friendly Societies Act 1992 (powers to obtain information and documents etc)—

(a) in subsection (7), for paragraphs (a) and (b) substitute—
"(a) by a relevant lawyer of a document or material contained in a privileged communication or, in Scotland, a communication which is protected from disclosure on the ground of confidentiality, made by or to the relevant lawyer in that capacity or the furnishing of information contained in such communication so made;", and
(b) in subsection (12), at the end insert

"; and

"relevant lawyer" means a barrister, advocate, solicitor or other legal representative communications with whom may be the subject of a claim to professional privilege or, in Scotland, be protected from disclosure in legal proceedings on grounds of confidentiality of communication."

Trade Union and Labour Relations Consolidation Act 1992 (c 52)

104 The Trade Union and Labour Relations Consolidation Act 1992 is amended in accordance with paragraphs 105 to 107.

105 In section 194 (offence of failure to notify), in subsection (2) omit ", although not of counsel or a solicitor,".

106 In section 216 (constitution and proceedings of court of inquiry)—

(a) in subsection (6) for "counsel or solicitor" (in both places) substitute "a relevant lawyer", and
(b) after subsection (6) insert—

"(7) In subsection (6) "relevant lawyer" means—

(a) a person who, for the purposes of the Legal Services Act 2007, is an authorised person in relation to an activity which constitutes the exercise of a right of audience or the conduct of litigation within the meaning of that Act, or
(b) an advocate or solicitor in Scotland."

107 In section 288 (restriction on contracting out), in subsection (4B)(a) for "a barrister" (in the first place) to the end substitute "a person who, for the purposes of the Legal Services Act 2007, is an authorised person in relation to an activity which constitutes the exercise of a right of audience or the conduct of litigation (within the meaning of that Act), and".

Finance Act 1993 (c 34)

108 In Schedule 21 of the Finance Act 1993 (oil taxation)—

(a) the existing paragraph 7 becomes sub-paragraph (1) of that paragraph,
(b) in that sub-paragraph for "barrister, advocate or a solicitor" substitute "relevant lawyer", and
(c) after that sub-paragraph insert—

"(2) "Relevant lawyer" means a barrister, advocate, solicitor or other legal representative communications with whom may be the subject of a claim to professional privilege."

Trade Marks Act 1994 (c 26)

109 The Trade Marks Act 1994 is amended in accordance with paragraphs 110 to 115.

110 In section 52 (power to make provision in connection with Community trade mark regulation), in subsection (3)(b) for "trade mark agents and registered trade mark agents" substitute "trade mark attorneys and registered trade mark attorneys".

111 In section 84 (unregistered persons not to be described as registered trade mark agents)—

(a) in subsection (1)—
  (i) for "agent" (in the first place) substitute "attorney",
  (ii) in paragraph (a) after "agent"" insert "or registered trade mark attorney", and
  (iii) in paragraph (b) after "agent" insert "or a registered trade mark attorney",
(b) in subsection (2)—
  (i) in paragraph (a) after "agent"" insert "or registered trade mark attorney", and
  (ii) in paragraph (b) after "agents"" insert "or registered trade mark attorneys", and
(c) in subsection (3)—
  (i) in paragraph (a) after "agent"" insert "or registered trade mark attorney", and
  (ii) in paragraph (b) after "agent" insert "or a registered trade mark attorney".

112 In section 86 (use of the term "trade mark attorney") in subsection (1) for "agent" substitute "attorney".

113 In section 87 (privilege for communications with registered trade mark agents)—

(a) in subsection (1), after "to" (in the first place) insert

"—

(a) ",
(b) at the end of that subsection insert
", and
(b) documents, material or information relating to any matter mentioned in paragraph (a).",
(c) for subsection (2) substitute—

"(2) Where a trade mark attorney acts for a client in relation to a matter mentioned in subsection (1), any communication, document, material or information to which this section applies is privileged from disclosure in like manner as if the trade mark attorney had at all material times been acting as the client's solicitor.", and

(d) in subsection (3)—
  (i) for "agent" (in each place) substitute "attorney", and
  (ii) for "agents" substitute "attorneys".

114 In section 88 (power of registrar to refuse to deal with certain agents)—

(a) in paragraph (b) for "agents" substitute "attorneys", and
(b) in paragraph (c) for "agents" substitute "attorneys".

115 In section 104 (index of defined expressions, in the entry for "registered trade mark agent"—

(a) for "agent" substitute "attorney", and
(b) for "(1)" substitute "(2)".

Criminal Justice and Public Order Act 1994 (c 33)

116 In section 38 of the Criminal Justice and Public Order Act 1994 (interpretation and savings for sections 34 to 37 of that Act) in subsection (1), in the definition of "legal representative" for "an authorised advocate" to the end substitute "a person who, for the purposes of the Legal Services Act 2007, is an authorised person in relation to an activity which constitutes the exercise of a right of audience or the conduct of litigation (within the meaning of that Act); and".

Environment Act 1995 (c 25)

117 In section 54 of the Environment Act 1995 (appearance in legal proceedings), omit "although not of counsel or a solicitor".

Disability Discrimination Act 1995 (c 50)

118 In Part 1 of Schedule 3A to the Disability Discrimination Act 1995 (validity and revision of contracts), in paragraph 2(5)(a) for "a barrister" (in the first place) to the end substitute "a person who, for the purposes of the Legal Services Act 2007, is an authorised person in relation to an activity which constitutes the exercise of a right of audience or the conduct of litigation (within the meaning of that Act); and".

...

119 ...

Employment Rights Act 1996 (c 18)

120 In section 203 of the Employment Rights Act 1996 (restrictions on contracting out), in subsection (4)(a) for "a barrister" (in the first place) to the end substitute "a person who, for the purposes of the Legal Services Act 2007, is an authorised person in relation to an activity which constitutes the exercise of a right of audience or the conduct of litigation (within the meaning of that Act), and".

Family Law Act 1996 (c 27)

121 In Schedule 4 of the Family Law Act 1996—

(a) for paragraph 1 substitute—

"1 In this Schedule "legal representative" means a person who, for the purposes of the Legal Services Act 2007, is an authorised person in relation to an activity which constitutes a reserved instrument activity (within the meaning of that Act).",

(b) in paragraph 3(3) for "solicitor" substitute "legal representative", and
(c) in paragraph 5(2)(a) for "solicitor" substitute "legal representative".

Civil Procedure Act 1997 (c 12)

122 In section 2 of the Civil Procedure Act 1997 (Civil Procedure Rule Committee)—

(a) in subsection (2), in paragraph (f) for from "granted" to "right" substitute "authorised by a relevant approved regulator", and
(b) after that subsection insert—

"(2A) In subsection (2)(f) "relevant approved regulator" is to be construed in accordance with section 20(3) of the Legal Services Act 2007."

Sexual Offences (Protected Material) Act 1997 (c 39)

123 In section 2 of the Sexual Offences (Protected Material) Act 1997 (meaning of other expressions), in subsection (1) in the definition of "legal representative" for "any authorised advocate" to "Act 1990)" substitute "a person who, for the purposes of the Legal Services Act 2007, is an authorised person in relation to an activity which constitutes the exercise of a right of audience or the conduct of litigation (within the meaning of that Act) and who is".

National Minimum Wage Act 1998 (c 39)

124 The National Minimum Wage Act 1998 is amended in accordance with paragraphs 125 and 126.

125 In section 33 (proceedings for offences)—

(a) in subsection (1) omit paragraph (a), and
(b) after that subsection insert—

"(1A) The persons who may conduct proceedings for an offence under this Act in England and Wales, before a magistrates' court, shall include any person authorised for the purpose by the Secretary of State."

126 In section 49 (restrictions on contracting out) for subsection (7)(a) substitute—

"(a) as regards England and Wales, a person who, for the purposes of the Legal Services Act 2007, is an authorised person in relation to an activity which constitutes the exercise of a right of audience or the conduct of litigation (within the meaning of that Act);".

Access to Justice Act 1999 (c 22)

127 The Access to Justice Act 1999 is amended in accordance with paragraphs 128 to 131.

128 In section 16(4) (code of conduct) after "consult" insert "the Legal Services Board,".

129 In section 44 (barristers employed by solicitors)—

(a) in subsection (1)—
  (i) omit "is employed by",
  (ii) for paragraphs (a) and (b) substitute—
"(a) is employed by an authorised person, or
(b) is a manager of such a person,", and
  (iii) for "his employer" substitute "the authorised person of which the barrister is an employee or a manager",
(b) in subsection (2) after "employees" insert "or managers of an authorised person", and
(c) after that subsection insert—

"(3) In this section—

"authorised person" means a person who, for the purposes of the Legal Services Act 2007, is an authorised person in relation to an activity which is a reserved legal activity (within the meaning of that Act), and
"manager" has the same meaning as in that Act (see section 207 of that Act)."

130 In section 45 (fees on application for appointment as Queen's Counsel), in subsections (1) and (2) for "Secretary of State" (in each place) substitute "Lord Chancellor".

131 In section 46 (Bar practising certificates)—

(a) omit subsection (2)(b) and the "but" immediately preceding it, and
(b) omit subsections (3) to (6).

Youth Justice and Criminal Evidence Act 1999 (c 23)

132 In section 63 of the Youth Justice and Criminal Evidence Act 1999 (general interpretation etc of Part 2), in subsection (1), in the definition of "legal representative" for "any authorised advocate" to the end substitute "a person who, for the purposes of the Legal Services Act 2007, is an authorised person in relation to an activity which constitutes the exercise of a right of audience or the conduct of litigation (within the meaning of that Act);".

Criminal Justice and Court Services Act 2000 (c 43)

133 In section 15 of the Criminal Justice and Court Services Act 2000 (right to conduct litigation and right of audience)—

(a) in subsection (2) for "section 28(2)(a) of the Courts and Legal Services Act 1990" substitute "the fact that he is a person who, for the purposes of the Legal Services Act 2007, is an authorised person in relation to that activity", and

(b) in subsection (3) for "section 27(2)(a) of the Courts and Legal Services Act 1990" substitute "the fact that he is a person who, for the purposes of the Legal Services Act 2007, is an authorised person in relation to that activity".

Finance Act 2002 (c 23)

134 The Finance Act 2002 is amended in accordance with paragraphs 135 and 136.

135 In Schedule 34 (stamp duty: withdrawal of group relief: supplementary provisions), in paragraph 10—

(a) in sub-paragraph (2) for "A barrister or solicitor" substitute "A relevant lawyer", and
(b) after that sub-paragraph insert—

"(2A) "Relevant lawyer" means a barrister, advocate, solicitor or other legal representative communications with whom may be the subject of a claim to professional privilege."

136 In Schedule 35 (stamp duty: withdrawal of relief for company acquisitions: supplementary provisions), in paragraph 11—

(a) in sub-paragraph (2) for "A barrister or solicitor" substitute "A relevant lawyer", and
(b) after that sub-paragraph insert—

"(2A) "Relevant lawyer" means a barrister, advocate, solicitor or other legal representative communications with whom may be the subject of a claim to professional privilege."

Income Tax (Earnings and Pensions) Act 2003 (c 1)

137 In section 343 of the Income Tax (Earnings and Pensions) Act 2003 (deduction for professional membership fees), in the table in subsection (2)—

(a) for "patent agent" and "patent agents" (in each place) substitute "patent attorney" and "patent attorneys" respectively, and
(b) for "trade mark agent" and "trade mark agents" (in each place) substitute "trade mark attorney" and "trade mark attorneys" respectively.

Finance Act 2003 (c 14)

138 In Schedule 13 to the Finance Act 2003 (stamp duty land tax: information powers)—

(a) in paragraph 22, in sub-paragraphs (1) and (2), for "barrister, advocate or solicitor" substitute "relevant lawyer",
(b) after sub-paragraph (2) of that paragraph insert—

"(3) "Relevant lawyer" means a barrister, advocate, solicitor or other professional legal adviser communications with whom may be the subject of a claim to legal privilege.

(4) "Legal privilege" here has the same meaning as in paragraph 35 of this Schedule.", and

(c) in paragraph 25 for "barrister, advocate or solicitor" substitute "relevant lawyer (within the meaning of paragraph 22(3))".

Licensing Act 2003 (c 17)

139 The Licensing Act 2003 is amended in accordance with paragraphs 140 and 141.

140 In section 58 (meaning of "certified copy" in section 57 of that Act), after subsection (3) insert—

"(4) In this section "notary" means a person (other than a solicitor) who, for the purposes of the Legal Services Act 2007, is an authorised person in relation to any activity which constitutes a notarial activity (within the meaning of that Act)."

141 In section 95 (meaning of "certified copy" in section 94 of that Act), after subsection (3) insert—

"(4) In this section "notary" means a person (other than a solicitor) who, for the purposes of the Legal Services Act 2007, is an authorised person in relation to any activity which constitutes a notarial activity (within the meaning of that Act)."

Courts Act 2003 (c 39)

142 The Courts Act 2003 is amended in accordance with paragraphs 143 and 144.

143 In section 70 (Criminal Procedure Rule Committee)—

(a) in subsection (2), in paragraph (i)(i) for from "granted" to "right" substitute "authorised by a relevant approved regulator", and
(b) after that subsection insert—

"(2A) In subsection (2)(i)(i) "relevant approved regulator" is to be construed in accordance with section 20(3) of the Legal Services Act 2007."

144 (1) Section 77 (Family Procedure Rule Committee) is amended as follows.

(2) In subsection (2)—

(a) in paragraph (k) for from "granted" to "right" substitute "authorised by a relevant approved regulator",
(b) in paragraph (l) for "granted that right" substitute "authorised", and
(c) in paragraph (m) for "granted that right" substitute "authorised".

(3) For subsection (5)(b) substitute—

"(b) is a relevant approved regulator in relation to the exercise of a right of audience or the conduct of litigation (or both)."

(4) After subsection (7) insert—

"(8) In this section "relevant approved regulator" is to be construed in accordance with section 20(3) of the Legal Services Act 2007."

Criminal Justice Act 2003 (c 44)

145 The Criminal Justice Act 2003 is amended in accordance with paragraphs 146 to 148.

146 In section 56 (interpretation of Part 8), in subsection (1), in the definition of "legal representative", for "an authorised advocate" to the end substitute "a person who, for the purposes of the Legal Services Act 2007, is an authorised person in relation to an activity which constitutes the exercise of a right of audience or the conduct of litigation (within the meaning of that Act),".

147 In section 159 (disclosure of pre-sentence reports etc), in subsection (2)(a) for "counsel or solicitor" substitute "legal representative".

148 In section 160 (other reports of local probation boards and members of youth offending teams) in subsection (2)(a) for "counsel or solicitor" substitute "legal representative".

Children Act 2004 (c 31)

149 In section 37 of the Children Act 2004 (Welsh family proceedings officers)—

(a) in subsection (2) for "section 28(2)(a) of the Courts and Legal Services Act 1990 (c 41)" substitute "the fact that he is a person who, for the purposes of the Legal Services Act 2007, is an authorised person in relation to that activity", and
(b) in subsection (3) for "section 27(2)(a) of the Courts and Legal Services Act 1990" substitute "the fact that he is a person who, for the purposes of the Legal Services Act 2007, is an authorised person in relation to that activity".

Civil Partnership Act 2004 (c 33)

150 In section 42 of the Civil Partnership Act 2004 (attempts at reconciliation of civil partners) in subsection (2) for "solicitor" substitute "legal representative".

Public Services Ombudsman (Wales) Act 2005 (c 10)

151 In section 13 of the Public Services Ombudsman (Wales) Act 2005 (investigations by Ombudsman)—

(a) in subsection (4)(b), for "counsel, solicitor" substitute "an authorised person", and
(b) after subsection (4) insert—

"(4A) In subsection (4) "authorised person" means a person who, for the purposes of the Legal Services Act 2007, is an authorised person in relation to an activity which constitutes the exercise of a right of audience or the conduct of litigation (within the meaning of that Act)."

Equality Act 2006 (c 3)

152 In Schedule 2 to the Equality Act 2006 (representations to Commission in relation to inquiry etc), in paragraph 8—

(a) in sub-paragraph (2)(b), for "a barrister, an advocate or a solicitor" substitute "a relevant lawyer", and
(b) after sub-paragraph (2) insert—

"(2A) "Relevant lawyer" means—

(a) an advocate or solicitor in Scotland, or
(b) a person who, for the purposes of the Legal Services Act 2007, is an authorised person in relation to an activity which constitutes the exercise of a right of audience or the conduct of litigation (within the meaning of that Act)."

Natural Environment and Rural Communities Act 2006 (c 16)

153 In section 12(2) of the Natural Environment and Rural Communities Act 2006 (power to bring criminal proceedings) omit "even though he is not a barrister or solicitor".

National Health Service Act 2006 (c 41)

154 In section 194(4) of the National Health Service Act 2006 (conduct of proceedings under section 194) omit ", although he is not a barrister or solicitor,".

National Health Service (Wales) Act 2006 (c 42)

155 In section 142(4) of the National Health Service (Wales) Act 2006 (conduct of proceedings under section 142) omit ", although he is not a barrister or solicitor,"."

Companies Act 2006 (c 46)

156 In Schedule 2 to the Companies Act 2006 (exceptions from restrictions on disclosure), in paragraph 67—

(a) for "solicitor, barrister, advocate" substitute "relevant lawyer", and
(b) for ""Foreign lawyer"" to the end substitute—

"In this paragraph—

"foreign lawyer" means a person (other than a relevant lawyer) who is a foreign lawyer within the meaning of section 89(9) of the Courts and Legal Services Act 1990;
"relevant lawyer" means—
(a) a person who, for the purposes of the Legal Services Act 2007, is an authorised person in relation to an activity which constitutes a reserved legal activity (within the meaning of that Act),
(b) a solicitor or barrister in Northern Ireland, or
(c) a solicitor or advocate in Scotland."

Income Tax Act 2007 (c 3)

157 The Income Tax Act 2007 is amended in accordance with paragraphs 158 to 161.

158 In section 748 (power to obtain information)—

(a) in subsection (4) for "solicitor" substitute "relevant lawyer",
(b) after that subsection insert—

"(4A) In this section "relevant lawyer" means a barrister, advocate, solicitor or other legal representative communications with whom may be the subject of a claim to professional privilege or, in Scotland, protected from disclosure in legal proceedings on grounds of confidentiality of communication.", and

(c) in subsection (5) for "solicitors" substitute "relevant lawyers".

159 In section 749 (restrictions on particulars to be provided by solicitors)—

(a) in the heading for "solicitors" substitute "relevant lawyers",
(b) for "solicitor" (in each place) substitute "relevant lawyer", and
(c) for subsection (7) substitute—

"(7) In this section—

"relevant lawyer" means a barrister, advocate, solicitor or other legal representative communications with whom may be the subject of a claim to professional privilege or, in Scotland, protected from disclosure in legal proceedings on grounds of confidentiality of communication;
"settlement" and "settlor" have the meanings given by section 620 of ITTOIA 2005."

160 In section 771 (power to obtain information)—

(a) in subsections (5) and (6) for "solicitor" (in each place) substitute "relevant lawyer", and
(b) after subsection (6) insert—

"(7) In this section "relevant lawyer" means a barrister, advocate, solicitor or other legal representative communications with whom may be the subject of a claim to professional privilege or, in Scotland, protected from disclosure in legal proceedings on grounds of confidentiality of communication."

161 In section 788 (power to obtain information)—

(a) in subsections (5) and (6) for "solicitor" (in each place) substitute "relevant lawyer", and
(b) after subsection (6) insert—

"(7) In this section "relevant lawyer" means a barrister, advocate, solicitor or other legal representative communications with whom may be the subject of a claim to professional privilege or, in Scotland, protected from disclosure in legal proceedings on grounds of confidentiality of communication."

Tribunals, Courts and Enforcement Act 2007 (c 15)

162 (1) Section 51 of the Tribunals, Courts and Enforcement Act 2007 (meaning of "relevant qualification") is amended as follows.

(2) In subsection (2), for from "awarded" to the end substitute "awarded by a body which, for the purposes of the Legal Services Act 2007, is an approved regulator in relation to the exercise of a right of audience or the conduct of litigation (within the meaning of that Act)."

(3) In subsection (4)—

(a) in paragraph (b), for "(2)(b)" substitute "(2)",
(b) in paragraph (c), for from "the body" to "of that Act" substitute
", for the purposes of the Legal Services Act 2007, the body—
  (i) is not an approved regulator in relation to the exercise of a right of audience (within the meaning of that Act), and
  (ii) is not an approved regulator in relation to the conduct of litigation (within the meaning of that Act),", and
(c) for from "paragraph 33(1)" to the end substitute "section 46 of the Legal Services Act 2007 (transitional etc provision in consequence of cancellation of designation as approved regulator)."

Initial Commencement
To be appointed: see s 211(2).
Amendment
Para 73: repealed by the Criminal Justice and Immigration Act 2008, s 149, Sch 28, Pt 8.
Date in force: to be appointed: see the Criminal Justice and Immigration Act 2008, s 153(7).
Para 119: repealed by the Criminal Justice and Immigration Act 2008, s 149, Sch 28, Pt 8.
Date in force: 1 December 2008: see SI 2008/2993, art 2(1)(f), (k)(iii).

SCHEDULE 22
TRANSITIONAL AND TRANSITORY PROVISION

Section 209

Transitory power to modify the functions of bodies

1 (1) Paragraphs 2 to 4 have effect until such time as the Board is first constituted in accordance with paragraph 1 of Schedule 1.

(2) Where an order under paragraph 2 has effect immediately before that time, it is to be treated from that time as if it were an order made by the Lord Chancellor under section 69 (and in accordance with that section and section 70).

(3) Where that order is made by virtue of paragraph 4, the reference in sub-paragraph (2) to section 69 is a reference to that section as modified by section 180.

2 (1) The Lord Chancellor may by order modify, or make any other provision relating to, the functions of a designated regulator or any other body.

(2) For this purpose "designated regulator" means—

(a) The Law Society;
(b) The General Council of the Bar;
(c) The Master of the Faculties;
(d) The Institute of Legal Executives;
(e) The Council for Licensed Conveyancers;
(f) The Chartered Institute of Patent Attorneys;
(g) The Institute of Trade Mark Attorneys;
(h) The Association of Law Costs Draftsmen;
(i) any other body which is a body to which sub-paragraph (3) applies.

(3) This sub-paragraph applies to—

(a) a body designated as an authorised body for the purposes of section 27 or 28 of the Courts and Legal Services Act 1990 (c 41) (rights of audience and rights to conduct litigation);
(b) a body approved under Schedule 9 to that Act (approval of body to grant exemption from prohibition on preparation of probate papers etc);
(c) a body prescribed by regulations under section 113 of that Act (administration of oaths and taking of affidavits).

(4) The Lord Chancellor may make an order under sub-paragraph (1) only if—

(a) the body to which the order relates has made a recommendation under this paragraph to which was annexed a draft order, and
(b) the body to which the order relates consents to the order which is made.

(5) The Lord Chancellor may make an order under this paragraph only for the purpose of enabling the body to which it relates to do one or more of the following—

(a) to become a body within sub-paragraph (3);
(b) to grant its members rights for the purposes of section 27 or 28 of the Courts and Legal Services Act 1990, to exempt its members for the purposes of section 55 of that Act or to authorise its members for the purposes of section 113 of that Act;
(c) if it is or becomes a designated regulator, to regulate its members more effectively or efficiently;
(d) if it is or becomes a designated regulator, to expand the categories of persons who are eligible to be members of the body;
(e) to do any of the things mentioned in paragraphs (a) to (e) of section 69(3) at a time after paragraph 1 of Schedule 4 comes into force.

(6) An order under this paragraph may make provision in relation to the body to which the order relates, and members of that body, corresponding to the provision which by virtue of subsection (4) or (5) of section 69 may be made by an order under that section in relation to an approved regulator and persons authorised by that regulator to carry on reserved legal activities or to provide immigration advice or immigration services.

(7) Any provision made by an order under this paragraph may be expressed to be conditional upon—

(a) the coming into force of paragraph 1 of Schedule 4;
(b) the body to which the order relates being designated by an order under Part 2 of that Schedule as an approved regulator, or by an order under Part 1 of Schedule 10 as a licensing authority, in relation to one or more reserved legal activities specified in the order;
(c) the body to which the order relates becoming a designated qualifying regulator under section 86A of the Immigration and Asylum Act 1999 (c 33).

(8) An order under this paragraph may modify provisions made by or under any enactment (including this Act or any Act passed after this Act), prerogative instrument or other instrument or document.

(9) The powers to make an order conferred by this paragraph are without prejudice to any powers (statutory or non-statutory) which a designated regulator or other body may have apart from this section.

(10) In this paragraph "member" in relation to a body includes any person who is not a member of the body but who may be subject to disciplinary sanctions for failure to comply with any of its rules.

3 (1) This paragraph applies where a body makes a recommendation under paragraph 2.

(2) The Lord Chancellor must publish a document containing—

(a) the recommendation, and
(b) the draft order annexed to it.

(3) The document must be accompanied by a notice which states that representations about it may be made to the Lord Chancellor within a specified period.

(4) The Lord Chancellor must give a copy of the document to the Office of Fair Trading and the Lord Chief Justice, and invite each of them to provide advice on it within that period.

(5) The Lord Chancellor may give a copy of the document to the Legal Services Consultative Panel or any other person, and invite them to provide advice on it within that period.

(6) The Lord Chancellor must have regard to any representations and advice duly given.

(7) If the order which the Lord Chancellor proposes to make differs from the draft order published under sub-paragraph (2), the Lord Chancellor must, before making the order, publish the revised draft order along with a statement detailing the changes made and the reasons for those changes.

4 Paragraphs 2 and 3 apply in relation to the Solicitors Disciplinary Tribunal as they apply in relation to a designated regulator, but as if in paragraph 2—

(a) in sub-paragraph (4)(a) the reference to the body to which the order relates were a reference to the Solicitors Disciplinary Tribunal or the Law Society, and
(b) for sub-paragraph (5) of that paragraph there were substituted—

"(5) The Lord Chancellor may make an order under this paragraph only for the purpose of enabling the Solicitors Disciplinary Tribunal to carry out its role more effectively or efficiently.", and

(c) sub-paragraphs (6) and (7) of that paragraph were omitted.

Approved regulators

5 (1) Sub-paragraph (2) applies where during the pre-commencement period—

(a) an Order in Council is made designating a body as an authorised body for the purposes of section 27 of the Courts and Legal Services Act 1990 (c 41) (rights of audience) and that body's qualification regulations and rules of conduct (within the meaning of that section) have been approved for the purposes of that section,

(b) an Order in Council is made designating a body as an authorised body for the purposes of section 28 of that Act (right to conduct litigation) and that body's qualification regulations and rules of conduct (within the meaning of that section) have been approved for the purposes of that section,

(c) an order is made under paragraph 4 of Schedule 9 to that Act (approval of body to grant exemption from prohibition on preparation of probate papers etc), or

(d) regulations are made prescribing a body for the purposes of section 113 of that Act (administration of oaths and taking of affidavits).

(2) The Lord Chancellor may by order modify the Table in paragraph 1 of Schedule 4 (existing regulators) so as—

(a) to insert, in the first column, a reference to the body and, in the second column, a reference to the relevant activities, or

(b) if the body is already listed in the first column, to add a reference to the relevant activities to the corresponding entry in the second column.

(3) Sub-paragraph (4) applies where during the pre-commencement period—

(a) an Order in Council is made revoking the designation of a body as an authorised body for the purposes of section 27 of the Courts and Legal Services Act 1990,

(b) an Order in Council is made revoking the designation of a body as an authorised body for the purposes of section 28 of that Act,

(c) an order is made under paragraph 6 of Schedule 9 to that Act revoking a body's approval, or

(d) regulations prescribing a body for the purposes of section 113 of that Act are revoked.

(4) The Lord Chancellor may by order modify the Table in paragraph 1 of Schedule 4 so as to—

(a) remove any reference to the relevant activities from the entry in the second column of that Table corresponding to the entry for the body in the first column, and

(b) if there are no other activities in that entry in the second column, remove the reference to the body from the first column of that Table.

(5) An order under sub-paragraph (2) in relation to a body may—

(a) in a case within sub-paragraph (1)(a) or (b), modify Part 1 of Schedule 5 (authorised persons: continuity of rights) so as to ensure the continuity of any authority given by the body to a person to exercise rights of audience or, as the case may be, to conduct litigation;

(b) in a case within sub-paragraph (1)(c), modify Part 1 of that Schedule (authorised persons: continuity of rights) to provide for exemptions granted by a body by virtue of section 55 of the Courts and Legal Services Act 1990 (c 41) (persons exempt from prohibition on preparation of probate papers etc) which have effect immediately before paragraph 1 of Schedule 4 comes into force to be deemed to be authorisations to carry on probate activities granted by that body at the time that paragraph comes into force;

(c) in a case within sub-paragraph (1)(d), modify Part 2 of Schedule 5, to provide during the transitional period for members of the body to be deemed to be authorised by the body to carry on the administration of oaths.

(6) An order under sub-paragraph (4) in relation to a body may—

(a) in a case within sub-paragraph (3)(a) or (b), modify Part 1 of Schedule 5 (authorised persons: continuity of rights) so as to remove provision made to ensure the continuity of any authority given by the body to a person to exercise rights of audience or, as the case may be, to conduct litigation;

(b) in a case within sub-paragraph (3)(c), modify Part 1 of that Schedule so as to remove any provision deeming persons to have been authorised by the body to carry on probate activities;

(c) in a case within sub-paragraph (3)(d), modify Part 2 of that Schedule so as to remove any provision deeming persons to have been authorised by the body to carry on the administration of oaths.

(7) No order under this paragraph may be made after the end of the pre-commencement period.

(8) In this paragraph—

"pre-commencement period" means the period before the coming into force of paragraph 1 of Schedule 4 (including any period before the passing of this Act);

"relevant activities" means—

(a) in a case within sub-paragraph (1)(a) or (3)(a), the exercise of a right of audience;
(b) in a case within sub-paragraph (1)(b) or (3)(b), the conduct of litigation;
(c) in a case within sub-paragraph (1)(c) or (3)(c), probate activities;
(d) in a case within sub-paragraph (1)(d) or (3)(d), the administration of oaths;

"the transitional period" has the meaning given by paragraph 3 of Schedule 5.

Licensed Conveyancers

6 (1) In this paragraph the transitional period means the period which—

(a) begins with the day on which paragraph 29 of Schedule 17 (which amends Schedule 3 to the Administration of Justice Act 1985 (c 61)) comes into force, and
(b) ends with the day on which members of the new Council are first appointed in accordance with a scheme approved by the Legal Services Board under Schedule 3 to that Act (as amended by that paragraph).

(2) During the transitional period, the Council for Licensed Conveyancers is to be constituted in accordance with Schedule 3 to that Act as it had effect immediately before paragraph 29 of Schedule 17 came into force.

(3) The term of office of persons who are members of the Council for Licensed Conveyancers by virtue of sub-paragraph (2) immediately before the end of the transitional period ends at the same time as the transitional period.

7 (1) This paragraph applies to any licence issued by the Council for Licensed Conveyancers under section 15 of the Administration of Justice Act 1985 (c 61) which—

(a) is endorsed under section 15(7) of that Act, and
(b) is in force when paragraph 4(4) of Schedule 17 (which repeals subsections (7) and (8) of section 15 of that Act (endorsement of licences)) comes into force.

(2) Notwithstanding the repeal of those subsections, until the licence expires—

(a) the licence continues to have effect in accordance with the endorsement, and
(b) rules made under section 15(8) of that Act continue to have effect in relation to the licence.

8 Until the repeal of paragraphs 17 and 19 of Schedule 8 to the Courts and Legal Services Act 1990 (c 41) by Schedule 23 to this Act comes into force, those paragraphs have effect as if—

(a) in paragraph 17 (inadequate professional services: failure to comply with direction), after sub-paragraph (2) there were inserted—

"(3) In relation to proceedings before the Discipline and Appeals Committee in respect of such a complaint, the Committee may make such order as they consider fit as to the payment of costs by—

(a) the Council;
(b) the licensed conveyancer against whom the complaint was made;
(c) if the person on whose complaint the proceedings were brought was heard (in person, or through a representative) by the Committee in the course of the proceedings, that person.", and

(b) paragraph 19(b) (inadequate professional services: costs) were omitted.

Exercise of Board's functions pending appointment of Chief Executive

9 (1) Until the first Chief Executive of the Board is appointed under paragraph 13 of Schedule 1, the Board's functions under—

(a) Schedule 1,
(b) Schedule 15, and
(c) paragraph 10(8) of this Schedule,

may be exercised by the ordinary members of the Board.

(2) For that purpose "ordinary member" has the same meaning as in Schedule 1.

Interim Chief Executive of the OLC

10 (1) The Lord Chancellor may appoint a person as the Interim Chief Executive of the OLC

(2) The Interim Chief Executive is to be—

(a) appointed on terms and conditions determined by the Lord Chancellor, and
(b) paid by the Lord Chancellor in accordance with provision made by or under the terms of appointment.

(3) Appointment as the Interim Chief Executive does not confer the status of Crown servant.

(4) In this paragraph—

"the first interim period" means the period which—
(a) begins when sub-paragraph (5) comes into force, and
(b) ends when the chairman of the Board, and at least 7 other ordinary members of the Board (within the meaning of Schedule 1), have been appointed in accordance with paragraph 1 of Schedule 1;

"the second interim period" means the period which—
(a) begins when the chairman of the Board, and at least 7 other ordinary members of the Board (within the meaning of Schedule 1), have been appointed in accordance with paragraph 1 of Schedule 1, and
(b) ends when the membership of the OLC is first constituted in accordance with paragraph 1 of Schedule 15.

(5) The Interim Chief Executive may incur expenditure and do other things in the name of and on behalf of the OLC—

(a) from the beginning of the first interim period, and
(b) after that time until the OLC determines otherwise.

(6) The things which may be done under sub-paragraph (5)—

(a) include the appointment of staff under paragraph 13 of Schedule 15 and making arrangements for assistance under paragraph 18 of that Schedule, but
(b) do not include the appointment of an ombudsman under section 122 or the making of scheme rules.

(7) During the first interim period, the Interim Chief Executive must comply with any supervisory directions given by the Lord Chancellor.

(8) During the second interim period, the Interim Chief Executive must comply with any supervisory directions given by the Board.

(9) The supervisory directions are—

(a) a direction requiring the Interim Chief Executive to provide the person giving the direction with a report on, or information relating to, such matters as are specified in the direction;
(b) a direction requiring the Interim Chief Executive to obtain the approval of the person giving the direction before incurring expenditure in such circumstances as are specified in the direction;
(c) any other direction relating to the exercise of the Interim Chief Executive's functions which the person giving the direction considers appropriate.

(10) Paragraph 34 of Schedule 15 (exemption from liability in damages) applies to the Interim Chief Executive as it applies to a member of the OLC

Solicitors

11 (1) Until such time as section 59(1) of the Constitutional Reform Act 2005 (c 4) comes into force, the reference in section 207(1), in the definition of "solicitor", to the Senior Courts is to be read as a reference to the Supreme Court.

(2) Until such time as section 59(2) of that Act (renaming of Supreme Court of Judicature of Northern Ireland as Court of Judicature of Northern Ireland) comes into force, the references in sections 8(5) and 190(5)(e), paragraph 2(4)(f) of Schedule 1, paragraphs 1(9) and 2(5) of Schedule 3 and paragraph 2(3)(e) of Schedule 15 to the Court of Judicature of Northern Ireland are to be read as references to the Supreme Court of Judicature of Northern Ireland.

Solicitors Act 1974 (c 47)

12 (1) During the transitional period, the reference to an authorised person in section 1A(d) of the Solicitors Act 1974 (practising certificates: employed solicitors) is to be read as a reference to a person listed in paragraph 15(1), other than a person listed in paragraph (b) or (c) of that paragraph.

(2) For this purpose "the transitional period" means the period which—

(a) begins with the day on which section 1A(d) of the Solicitors Act 1974 (as inserted by Schedule 16) comes into force, and
(b) ends with the day appointed for the coming into force of section 13 (entitlement to carry on a reserved legal activity).

13 (1) During the transitional period, section 44B of the Solicitors Act 1974 (provision of information and documents by solicitors etc) has effect as if the list of persons in subsection (2) of that section included a legal partnership (within the meaning of paragraph 7 of Schedule 5).

(2) For this purpose "the transitional period" means the period which—

(a) begins with the day on which section 44B of the Solicitors Act 1974 (as substituted by Schedule 16) comes into force, and
(b) ends with the day appointed for the coming into force of section 13 (entitlement to carry on a reserved legal activity).

14 (1) During the transitional period, section 69 of the Solicitors Act 1974 (action to recover solicitor's costs) has effect as if—

(a) after subsection (2A)(a) of that section there were inserted—
"(aa) in a case where the costs are due to a firm, signed by a partner of the firm, either in his own name or in the name of the firm, or on his behalf by any employee of the firm authorised by him to sign, or", and
(b) in subsection (2A)(b), after "paragraph (a)" there were inserted "or (aa)".

(2) For this purpose "the transitional period" means the period which—

(a) begins with the day on which subsections (2) to (2F) of that section (as substituted by Schedule 16) come into force, and
(b) ends with the day appointed for the coming into force of section 13 (entitlement to carry on a reserved legal activity).

(3) This paragraph does not apply in relation to section 69 of the Solicitors Act 1974 as it has effect by virtue of paragraph 29 of Schedule 2 to the Administration of Justice Act 1985.

Recognised bodies

15 (1) During the transitional period, any reference in sections 9, 9A or 32A of, or Schedule 2 or 6 to, the Administration of Justice Act 1985 (c 61) (recognition of legal services bodies and conveyancing services bodies) to an authorised person is to be read as a reference to—

(a) a person who has in force a certificate issued by the General Council of the Bar authorising the person to practise as a barrister,
(b) a person who is qualified under section 1 of the Solicitors Act 1974 (c 47) to act as a solicitor,
(c) a recognised body under section 9 of the Administration of Justice Act 1985,
(d) a registered European lawyer (within the meaning of the European Communities (Lawyer's Practice) Regulations 2000 (SI 2000/1119)),
(e) a person who has in force a certificate issued by the Institute of Legal Executives authorising the person to practise as a legal executive,
(f) licensed conveyancers (within the meaning of section 11(2) of the Administration of Justice Act 1985),
(g) a recognised body under section 32 of that Act,
(h) a duly certificated notary (within the meaning of paragraph 12(4) of Schedule 5),
(i) a person who (having regard to section 15) carries on notarial activities through an employee or manager of the person who is within paragraph (h),
(j) a registered patent attorney within the meaning given by section 275(1) of the Copyright, Designs and Patents Act 1988 (c 48),
(k) a patent attorney body (within the meaning of paragraph 14(7) of Schedule 5),

(l) a registered trade mark attorney within the meaning of the Trade Marks Act 1994 (c 26),
(m) a trade mark attorney body (within the meaning of paragraph 16(7) of Schedule 5),
(n) an authorised member of the Association of Law Costs Draftsmen (within the meaning of paragraph 17(2) of Schedule 5), or
(o) a person who (having regard to section 15) carries on an activity which is a reserved legal activity within paragraph 18(2) of Schedule 5 through an employee or manager of the person who is within paragraph (n).

(2) After the end of the transitional period, any reference in section 9, 9A or 32A of, or Schedule 2 or 6 to, the Administration of Justice Act 1985 (c 61) to an authorised person includes a person who is an exempt person—

(a) by virtue of paragraph 13 of Schedule 5, in relation to the carrying on of an activity which is a notarial activity, or
(b) by virtue of paragraph 18 of that Schedule, in relation to the carrying on of an activity which is a reserved legal activity within sub-paragraph (2) of that paragraph.

(3) For this purpose "the transitional period" means the period which—

(a) begins with the day on which sections 9, 9A, 32 and 32A of the Administration of Justice Act 1985 (as amended and substituted by Schedules 16 and 17) come into force, and
(b) ends with the day appointed for the coming into force of section 13 (entitlement to carry on a reserved legal activity).

16 (1) During the transitional period (within the meaning of paragraph 15), the Law Society may make rules to which this sub-paragraph applies only with the concurrence of the Lord Chancellor (as well as the Master of the Rolls).

(2) Sub-paragraph (1) applies to—

(a) rules made under section 9 of the Administration of Justice Act 1985 by virtue of subsections (1A), (1C), (2F), (2G) or (2I) of that section or section 9A of that Act, and
(b) any other rules made under section 9 of that Act, in so far as they apply in relation to bodies which have one or more managers who are not legally qualified (within the meaning of section 9A of that Act), or managers or employees of such bodies.

17 (1) During the relevant period, the legal professional privilege provisions apply to a body which—

(a) is recognised under section 9 of the 1985 Act, and
(b) has one or more managers who are not legally qualified (within the meaning of section 9A of that Act),

as if the body were a licensed body.

(2) Sub-paragraph (1) applies whether or not the legal professional privilege provisions have been brought into force for other purposes.

(3) The relevant period is the period which—

(a) begins when section 9A of the 1985 Act comes into force, and
(b) ends when paragraph 7 of Schedule 5 ceases to apply in relation to the body.

(4) The legal professional privilege provisions are—

(a) paragraph 36(4) of Schedule 2 to the 1985 Act (as inserted by Schedule 16 to this Act), and
(b) section 190(3) to (7) of this Act.

(5) During the transitional period (within the meaning of paragraph 15), section 190(5)(h) (as it applies by virtue of this paragraph) applies as if for "an authorised person in relation to an activity which is a reserved legal activity" there were substituted "within paragraph 15(1) of Schedule 22".

(6) "The 1985 Act" means the Administration of Justice Act 1985.

Functions transferred to the Lord Chancellor

18 (1) This paragraph applies where, by virtue of an amendment made to an enactment by this Act, a function of the Secretary of State is transferred to the Lord Chancellor.

(2) In this paragraph such a function is referred to as a "transferred function".

(3) Any subordinate legislation made by the Secretary of State in exercise of a transferred function is to have effect as if made or done by the Lord Chancellor.

(4) So far as is appropriate in consequence of the transfer, anything else done by the Secretary of State in exercise of a transferred function is to be treated as if done by the Lord Chancellor.

Initial Commencement
To be appointed: see s 211(2).
Appointment
Paras 1–5: Appointment: 7 March 2008: see SI 2008/222, art 2(m)(i).
Para 9: Appointment (for certain purposes): 7 March 2008: see SI 2008/222, art 2(m)(ii).
Para 18: Appointment: 30 June 2008: see SI 2008/1436, art 2(f).
Extent
This Schedule does not extend to Scotland: see s 212(1).
Subordinate Legislation
Legal Services Act 2007 (Functions of a Designated Regulator) Order 2008, SI 2008/3074 (made under para 22).

SCHEDULE 23
REPEALS

Section 210

Short title and chapter	*Extent of repeal*
Public Notaries Act 1801 (c 79)	In section 1, ", or use and exercise the office of a notary, or do any notarial act,". In section 14, from "proctor" to "any other".
Public Notaries Act 1843 (c 90)	Section 10.
Commissioners for Oaths Act 1889 (c 10)	In section 1(3), from "in which" (in the first place) to "solicitor, or".
Children and Young Persons Act 1933 (c 12)	In section 49(11), the definition of "legal representative".
Public Records Act 1958 (c 51)	In Schedule 1, "The Legal Services Ombudsman."
Parliamentary Commissioner Act 1967 (c 13)	In Schedule 2, "Authorised Conveyancing Practitioners Board." and "The Legal Services Complaints Commissioner."
Superannuation Act 1972 (c 11)	In Schedule 1, "Employment by the Legal Services Ombudsman" and "The office of the Legal Services Ombudsman".
Poisons Act 1972 (c 66)	In section 9(7), "notwithstanding that he is not of counsel or a solicitor".
Solicitors Act 1974 (c 47)	In section 1A— (a)"or" at the end of paragraph (b), and (b)in paragraph (c) "by the Council of the Law Society". In section 2—

Short title and chapter	*Extent of repeal*
	(a)in subsection (1), ", with the concurrence of the Secretary of State, the Lord Chief Justice and the Master of the Rolls,",
	(b)in subsection (3)(a)(i), ", whether by service under articles or otherwise,",
	(c)in subsection (3)(a)(v), "articles may be discharged or", and
	(d)subsections (4) and (5).
	Section 6(2) to (4).
	Section 8(5).
	Section 12.
	Section 12A.
	Section 14.
	In section 17(1) and (2), "in the London Gazette".
	Section 19.
	Sections 22 to 23.
	In section 26, ", 22 or 23".
	Section 27.
	In section 28—
	(a)in subsection (1), ", with the concurrence of the Secretary of State and the Lord Chief Justice,",
	(b)in subsection (1)(c), "and applications for them",
	(c)subsections (2) and (3),
	(d)in subsection (3A), the "and" at the end of paragraph (b), and
	(e)subsections (4) and (5).
	In section 31—
	(a)in subsection (1) ", with the concurrence of the Master of the Rolls,", and
	(b)subsections (3) and (4).
	In section 32(1)—
	(a)", with the concurrence of the Master of the Rolls,", and
	(b)from "and the rules" to the end.
	Section 32(2).
	In section 32(4) "or (2)".
	Section 32(6).
	In section 33(2), "and the rules" to the end.
	In section 33A(1) ", with the concurrence of the Master of the Rolls,".
	Section 34(7) and (8).
	Section 37A.
	Section 40.
	Section 41(5).
	In section 43(5)—
	(a)"by any solicitor", and
	(b)from "but" to the end.

Short title and chapter	*Extent of repeal*
	Section 46(6) to (8).
	In section 46(9) ", with the concurrence of the Master of the Rolls,".
	In section 47—
	(a)in subsection (2)(c), "not exceeding £5,000", and
	(b)subsections (4) and (5).
	In section 48(2)(b) "in the London Gazette".
	In section 49(4) "and the Master of the Rolls".
	Section 49(7).
	Section 70(11).
	Sections 76 to 78.
	Section 80(2).
	Sections 81 and 81A.
	In section 87(1) the definitions of—
	(a)"articles",
	(b)"controlled trust",
	(c)"duly certificated notary public",
	(d)"employee",
	(e)"indemnity conditions",
	(f)"replacement date", and
	(g)"training conditions".
	Section 89(7).
	In Schedule 1—
	(a)in paragraph 1(1)(h), "sole", and
	(b)paragraph 1(2).
	Schedule 1A.
	Schedule 2.
	In Schedule 3, paragraph 9.
House of Commons Disqualification Act 1975 (c 24)	In Part 2 of Schedule 1, "The Authorised Conveyancing Practitioners Board."
	In Part 3 of Schedule 1, "The Legal Services Complaints Commissioner." and "The Legal Services Ombudsman."
Northern Ireland Assembly Disqualification Act 1975 (c 25)	In Part 2 of Schedule 1, "The Authorised Conveyancing Practitioners Board."
	In Part 3 of Schedule 1, "The Legal Services Complaints Commissioner." and "The Legal Services Ombudsman."
Race Relations Act 1976 (c 74)	In Schedule 1A, in Part 2, "The Legal Services Consultative Panel."
Patents Act 1977 (c 37)	Section 102A.
Solicitors (Scotland) Act 1980 (c 46)	Section 3A(5)(a) and (ad).
	Section 15(2)(j).
	In section 20(2) ", 53A(2)(ba)".
	Section 24C(2)(i).
	Section 34(4), (4C) and (4D).
	Sections 38, 39, 42A and 42B.
	In section 42C(1)—

Short title and chapter	*Extent of repeal*
	(a)paragraphs (a) and (c), (b)"to the solicitor or his firm or", and (c)"or, where" to the end. In section 42C(2)(a) and (b) "solicitor, firm or" (in each place). In section 42C(3)— (a)in paragraph (a) "the solicitor or his firm or, as the case may be,", and (b)in paragraph (b) from "of which the solicitor" to "be,". In section 42C(4) "38," (in each place). Section 42C(5). In section 51(2)— (a)"a solicitor may have been guilty" to "Fund) or", and (b)"or a solicitor" to "services". Section 51(2A). In section 52(2)(aa) "42A(7) or". Section 53(3), (10) and (11). Sections 53A, 53B and 53C Section 54(1), (2B) and (2C). Section 55(8). Section 56A. In section 62A(1) and (2) "38," (in each place). In section 65— (a)in subsection (1), the definition of "inadequate professional services", and (b)subsection (5). In Schedule 3, in Part 2, in paragraph 5(1), (2) and (3) "38," (in each place). In Schedule 4, in Part 2— (a)in paragraph 9(a) and (b) "or, as the case may be, of provision of inadequate professional services" (in each place), (b)paragraph 16(f) and (g), and (c)in paragraph 23 ", 42A(7)". In the side-note to section 62A "38,".
Mental Health Act 1983 (c 20)	In Schedule 4, paragraph 38(a).
County Courts Act 1984 (c 28)	In Schedule 2, paragraph 49.
Prosecution of Offences Act 1985 (c 23)	Section 4(6).
Administration of Justice Act 1985 (c 61)	Section 2. Section 4. Sections 6 and 7. In section 9— (a)in subsection (1)(c) "corporate",

Short title and chapter	*Extent of repeal*
	(b)subsection (4), (c)in subsection (5) "corporate", (d)in subsection (8) the definition of "officer", and in the definition of "recognised body", "corporate", and (e)subsection (9). In section 10— (a)in subsection (1) "corporate" (in both places), and (b)in subsection (2) "corporate". Section 11(4). Section 12(2). Section 15(7) and (8). In section 20(1) ", in pursuance of its general duty referred to in section 12(2),". In section 22(3)(a) "qualified". In section 24— (a)in subsection (1), paragraph (b) and the "or" immediately preceding it, (b)in that subsection the words from "with a view" to the end, (c)subsection (2), (d)in subsection (3), "or (2)", "or complaint" (in both places) and "or paragraph (b)", and (e)in subsection (5), "or complaint" (in both places). Section 26(2)(g), (5) and (6). In section 29(1), "or" at the end of paragraph (b). In section 31— (a)in subsection (2), "or complaint" (in each place) and "or paragraph (b)", and (b)in subsection (4), "or complaint". In section 32— (a)in subsection (2) "corporate", (b)subsection (3)(d), (c)in subsection (3)(e) "corporate", (d)subsections (4) and (5), and (e)in subsection (6)(a) "corporate". Section 34(2)(c) to (e). In section 35(2), "corporate". Section 38(1). In section 39(1)— (a)in the definition of "client", in paragraph (a) "or his firm", (b)the definitions of "director" and "officer", and (c)in the definition of "recognised body", "corporate". In Schedule 1 paragraphs 5, 8(3), 9 and 14. In Schedule 2— (a)in paragraph 1(1) "corporate", (b)in paragraph 1(2)—

Short title and chapter	*Extent of repeal*
	(i)paragraph (b) and the "or" immediately preceding it, (ii)"corporate", and (iii)"or application", (d)paragraph 1(3), (e)in paragraph 1(4) from ", and for those purposes" to the end, (f)paragraph 4(2), (g)paragraphs 11, 12 and 13, (h)in paragraph 16(1), in paragraph (a) "in the United Kingdom", (i)in paragraph 17(a) "11(1), 15(2) or" and "13(3) or", (j)paragraph 18(1)(d) and the "or" immediately preceding it, (k)in paragraph 18(2) "not exceeding £3,000", (l)paragraph 18(3) and (4), (m)paragraph 20(2), (n)in paragraph 31 "or (2)", (o)paragraph 32(2), (p)in paragraph 34(1), "corporate" (in both places), and (q)in paragraph 35, in paragraph (a) "corporate" and the "and" at the end of paragraph (b). In Schedule 3, paragraphs 2(3) and 3. In Schedule 4, paragraphs 1(3) and (4) and 3. In Schedule 5, paragraph 1(2). In Schedule 6— (a)in paragraph 1 "corporate" (in both places), and in sub-paragraph (2) "or complaint" (in both places) and "or (b)", (b)in paragraph 3(1), in paragraph (a)(i) "by any court in the United Kingdom", paragraph (b), and from "with a view" to the end, (c)paragraph 3(2), (d)paragraph 4(2)(c), (e)paragraph 4(3), (3A) and (4), (f)in paragraph 7(1) and (2) "corporate", (g)in paragraph 8(1), "corporate", (h)paragraph 9(2), (i)paragraph 10(2), (j)in paragraph 12(1), "corporate" (in both places), (k)in paragraph 13, in paragraph (a) "corporate", and the "and" at the end of paragraph (b), (l)paragraph 15. In Schedule 9, paragraphs 2, 4 and 6.
Insolvency Act 1985 (c 65)	In Schedule 8, paragraph 25.
Social Security Act 1986 (c 50)	In section 56(1), "although not a barrister or solicitor".
Building Societies Act 1986 (c 53)	In Schedule 18, paragraph 11(2) and (3).

Short title and chapter	*Extent of repeal*
Copyright, Designs and Patents Act 1988 (c 48)	Section 279.
	In section 280—
	(a)in subsection (3) "or" at the end of paragraph (b), and
	(b)subsection (4).
	Section 292.
Law of Property (Miscellaneous Provisions) Act 1989 (c 34)	In Schedule 1, paragraph 8.
Law Reform (Miscellaneous Provisions) (Scotland) Act 1990 (c 40)	Section 33.
Courts and Legal Services Act 1990 (c 41)	Sections 17, 18 and 18A.
	Sections 21 to 29.
	Sections 31 and 31A.
	Sections 34 to 52.
	In section 53—
	(a)subsection (5), and
	(b)subsection (9)(e).
	Sections 54 and 55.
	Section 63.
	Sections 68 to 70.
	Section 73(5)(d).
	Section 86 to 88.
	Section 90.
	Section 93.
	Section 94(1) and (2).
	Section 96.
	Section 113.
	In section 119(1), the definitions of—
	(a)"authorised advocate",
	(b)"authorised body" and "appropriate authorised body",
	(c)"authorised litigator",
	(d)"authorised practitioner",
	(e)"Consultative Panel",
	(f)"duly certificated notary public",
	(g)"the general principle",
	(h)"qualified person", and
	(i)"the statutory objective".
	In section 120—
	(a)in subsection (4), "26(1), 37(10), 40(1)", and from "paragraph 24" to "Schedule 9", and
	(b)subsection (5).
	Schedules 3 to 7.

Short title and chapter	*Extent of repeal*
	In Schedule 8, paragraphs 7, 11, 13 to 20, 21(1)(b) and 23.
	Schedule 9.
	In Schedule 10, paragraph 64.
	In Schedule 14—
	(a)in paragraph 1, the definitions of "controlled trust" and "the Council",
	(b)paragraph 2(3) and (5),
	(c)in paragraph 5—
	(i)in sub-paragraph (3)(a) and (b), "by virtue of his being a member of that partnership", and
	(ii)sub-paragraph (4),
	(c)paragraph 14(2),
	(d)in paragraph 14(3) "to him",
	(e)in paragraph 15, in sub-paragraph (4)(c) "not exceeding £5,000", and sub-paragraph (5),
	(f)in paragraph 17(2), "and the Master of the Rolls", and
	(g)paragraph 17(4).
	Schedule 15.
	In Schedule 17, paragraphs 4, 8, 10 and 20.
	In Schedule 18—
	(a)in paragraph 1(1), ""The Authorised Conveyancing Practitioners Board"" and ""The Conveyancing Ombudsman"",
	(b)paragraph 1(2), and
	(c)paragraphs 9 to 12, 18, 20 and 56.
Environmental Protection Act 1990 (c 43)	In section 114(4), ", although not of counsel or a solicitor,".
Friendly Societies Act 1992 (c 40)	In Schedule 21, paragraph 5.
Trade Union and Labour Relations (Consolidation) Act 1992 (c 52)	In section 194(2), ", although not of counsel or a solicitor,".
Statute Law (Repeals) Act 1993 (c 50)	In Schedule 2, paragraph 3.
Trade Marks Act 1994 (c 26)	Section 85.
	In Schedule 4, paragraph 5.
Agricultural Tenancies Act 1995 (c 8)	Section 35.
Environment Act 1995 (c 25)	In section 54, "although not of counsel or a solicitor".
Bank of England Act 1998 (c 11)	Section 41(4).
	In Schedule 5, paragraph 67.
National Minimum Wage Act 1998 (c 39)	Section 33(1)(a).
Access to Justice Act 1999 (c 22)	Sections 35(2) to (4), 36, 37 and 40 to 42.
	In section 44(1), "is employed by".
	In section 46—
	(a)subsection (2)(b) and the word "but" immediately preceding it, and

Short title and chapter	*Extent of repeal*
	(b)subsections (3) to (6).
	Section 47.
	Sections 49 to 52.
	In Schedule 4, paragraph 46.
	Schedule 5.
	In Schedule 6, paragraphs 1 to 3, 5 to 8 and 11.
	In Schedule 7, paragraphs 7(2)(a) and 10 to 12.
	Schedule 8.
	In Schedule 14, paragraph 14.
Immigraion and Asylum Act 1999 (c 33)	In section 86—
	(a)subsections (1)(a), (d) and (e),
	(b)subsection (4)(b),
	(c)in subsection 5(a), "England and Wales or", and
	(d)subsection (6)(a).
	In Schedule 5—
	(a)paragraph 3(6)(b),
	(b)paragraph 4(2)(b),
	(c)in paragraph 4(3)(a) "England and Wales or", and
	(d)paragraph 4(4)(a).
Trustee Act 2000 (c 29)	In Schedule 2, paragraph 37.
Freedom of Information Act 2000 (c 36)	In Part 6 of Schedule 1—
	(a)"The Authorised Conveyancing Practitioners Board.",
	(b)"The Legal Services Complaints Commissioner.",
	(c)"The Legal Services Consultative Panel.", and
	(d)"The Legal Services Ombudsman."
Enterprise Act 2002 (c 40)	In Schedule 25, paragraph 23(2) to (6) and (10).
Pensions Act 2004 (c 35)	In Schedule 4, paragraph 21.
Constitutional Reform Act 2005 (c 4)	In Schedule 4, paragraphs 92 and 202.
	In Schedule 11, paragraphs 1(2), 21(3) and 23(2) and (3).
Mental Capacity Act 2005 (c 9)	In Schedule 6, paragraph 22(2).
Serious Organised Crime and Police Act 2005 (c 15)	In Part 3 of Schedule 7, paragraph 42(2).
Natural Environment and Rural Communities Act 2006 (c 16)	In section 12(2) "even though he is not a barrister or solicitor".
Compensation Act 2006 (c 29)	Section 5(3), (4)(c) and (5).
	Section 15(6).
National Health Service Act 2006 (c 41)	In section 194(4), ", although he is not a barrister or solicitor,".
National Health Service (Wales) Act 2006 (c 42)	In section 142(4), ", although he is not a barrister or solicitor,".
Legal Profession and Legal Aid (Scotland) Act 2007 (asp 5)	Section 77.

Initial Commencement
To be appointed: see s 211(2).
Appointment
Appointment (in part): 7 March 2008: see SI 2008/222, art 2(n).
Appointment (in part): 30 June 2008: see SI 2008/1436, art 2(g).
Appointment (in part): 1 October 2008: see SI 2008/1436, art 3(c).

SCHEDULE 24
INDEX OF DEFINED EXPRESSIONS

Section 213

Expression	*Interpretation provisions*
administration of oaths	Schedule 2
approved regulator	section 20
authorised person, in relation to an activity	section 18
barrister	section 207
the Board	section 2
compensation arrangements	section 21
complainant (in Part 6)	section 160
conduct of litigation	Schedule 2
conduct rules	section 21
consumers	section 207
conveyancing services	section 207
court	section 207
discipline rules	section 21
document	section 201
exempt person	section 19 and Schedules 3 and 5
functions	section 207
"immigration advice" and "immigration services"	section 207
indemnification arrangements	section 21
independent trade union	section 207
indirect interest (of a non-authorised person in a licensable body)	section 72
interest, in a body	section 72
intervention direction	section 41
legal activity	section 12
licensable body	section 72
licensed activity (in Part 5)	section 111
licensed body	section 71
licensing authority	section 73
licensing rules	section 83
manager, in relation to a body	section 207
material interest, in a body (in Part 5)	Schedule 13
modify	section 207
non-authorised person (in Part 5)	section 111

Expression	*Interpretation provisions*
non-commercial legal services	section 207
non-reserved activity (in Part 5)	section 111
not for profit body	section 207
notarial activities	Schedule 2
the OFT	section 207
the OLC	section 114
ombudsman	section 122
the ombudsman scheme	section 115
person	section 207
practice rules	section 21
probate activities	Schedule 2
qualification regulations	section 21
regulatory arrangements	section 21
regulatory functions	section 27
regulatory objectives	section 1
relevant appellate body (in Part 5)	section 111
relevant approved regulator, in relation to an activity	section 20
relevant approved regulator, in relation to a person	section 20
relevant authorising body (in Part 6)	section 160
relevant licensing authority, in relation to a licensed body (in Part 5)	section 73
relevant licensing authority, in relation to an applicant for a licence (in Part 5)	section 73
representative functions	section 27
reserved instrument activities	Schedule 2
reserved legal activity	section 12 and Schedule 2
reserved legal services	section 207
respondent (in Part 6)	section 160
right of audience	Schedule 2
scheme rules (in Part 6)	section 115
shares	section 72
solicitor	section 207
terms of a licence (in Part 5)	section 85

Initial Commencement
To be appointed: see s 211(2).

Legal Services Act 2007

EXPLANATORY NOTES

These notes refer to the Legal Services Act 2007 (c.29) which received Royal Assent on 30th October 2007.

INTRODUCTION

1. These explanatory notes relate to the Legal Services Act which received Royal Assent on 30th October 2007. They have been prepared by the Ministry of Justice in order to assist the reader in understanding the Act. They do not form part of the Act and have not been endorsed by Parliament.

2. The notes need to be read in conjunction with the Act. They are not, and are not meant to be, a comprehensive description of the Act. So where a section or part of a section does not seem to require any explanation or comment, none is given.

OVERVIEW OF THE ACT

3. This Act has 214 sections and 24 Schedules. The explanatory notes are divided into nine Parts, reflecting the structure of the Act.

4. An overview of the Act is set out below. A detailed description of each Part is contained in the commentary. Terms used are defined in the text where they first appear, and Schedule 24 contains an index of defined expressions. An explanation to accompany each Schedule is contained within the section that introduces the Schedule.

TERRITORIAL EXTENT

5. This Act extends only to England and Wales, except for the provisions of sections 195 and 196(1) and Schedule 20 which extend to Scotland, and any amendments or repeals of legislation which extends to Scotland or Northern Ireland, which have the same extent as the enactment (or relevant part of the enactment) to which the amendment or repeal relates.

6. There is no effect on the National Assembly and no other effect specifically in relation to Wales.

SUMMARY

7. Part 1: The Regulatory Objectives sets out the eight regulatory objectives, which guide the Legal Services Board (the Board), the approved regulators, and the Office for Legal Complaints (OLC) in exercising their functions.

8. Part 2: The Legal Services Board sets out the structure and functions of the Board, including its duty to act compatibly with the regulatory objectives, to assist in the maintenance and development of standards in regulation, education and training and to establish a Consumer Panel. It also sets out the requirements for both appointment to, and membership of, the Board and the powers that the Lord Chancellor has in relation to these processes.

9. Part 3: Reserved Legal Activities lists and defines the reserved legal activities. It explains who is entitled to carry out these activities, and the penalties for those who carry out, or pretend to be entitled to carry out, these activities where they are not entitled. It provides for transitional arrangements for those currently allowed to carry on reserved legal activities. It also explains the process for altering the scope of the reserved legal activities. Approved regulators are the bodies that authorise and regulate persons to carry on reserved legal activities. This Part of the Act explains what an approved regulator is, lists those bodies designated by the Act as approved regulators, and explains how other bodies can become an approved regulator in the future.

10. Part 4: Regulation of Approved Regulators prescribes the general duties of approved regulators, and the powers that the Board has to ensure that these are being properly carried out. It details how the Board can intervene when there is a problem, the procedures that it must follow, and the persons that it must consult. The Board's powers include target-setting, censure, financial penalties, direct intervention in the approved regulator's regulation of its members, and, ultimately, the power to recommend to the Lord Chancellor that an order be made cancelling the approved regulator's designation.

11. Part 5: Alternative Business Structures (ABS) makes provision for the licensing of new business structures in legal services. These will allow lawyers and non-lawyers to work together to deliver legal and other services. This Part of the Act sets out the arrangements for authorisation, by the Board, of licensing authorities and how, in the absence of an appropriate licensing authority, the Board can license ABS firms directly. It makes provision for the regulation of ABS.

12. Part 6: Legal Complaints establishes an independent OLC, which is responsible for administering an ombudsman scheme, under which all complaints will be dealt with by a Chief Ombudsman, assistant ombudsmen, and staff appointed by the OLC. Part 6 removes the ability of approved regulators to provide redress to complainants, and grants this power to the ombudsman scheme. The OLC will draw up scheme rules setting out the detail of the ombudsman scheme. This Part makes provision for the appointment process and terms of office for members of the OLC Board and the Chief Ombudsman and the assistant ombudsmen. It also makes provision for the accountability of the OLC to the Board, the framework of rules by which the OLC will establish its operating procedures, and changes to the regulatory arrangements of approved regulators.

13. Part 7: Further Provisions Relating to the Board and the OLC makes provision as to the guidance that the Board may give. It also requires the Board to make rules providing for the payment by approved regulators of a levy, to recoup the expenditure of the Board and OLC. The rules may include provision as to the rate and times at which the levy is payable, and circumstances in which the levy may be waived. This section also makes provision for the Board to enter into voluntary arrangements with any person, for example to promote best regulatory practice.

14. Part 8: Miscellaneous Provisions about Lawyers makes provision for the following matters:

- the requirement for alteration of the rules of the Solicitors Disciplinary Tribunal to be approved by the Board, and empowering the Board to give a limited range of directions to the Tribunal;
- the maintenance of the register of trade mark attorneys and the register of patent attorneys;
- the application of legal professional privilege in relation to authorised persons who are not barristers or solicitors;
- amendment of the Immigration and Asylum Act 1999 (which regulates the provision of immigration advice services) and the Compensation Act 2006 (which makes provision in relation to claims management services), in consequence of the new regime established by the Act;
- the making of costs orders in relation to *pro bono* legal representation; and
- conferring competence on the Scottish Legal Complaints Commission in respect of certain reserved matters.

15. Part 9: General makes provision regarding offences committed by bodies corporate and unincorporated bodies. It provides that certain functions conferred on the Lord Chancellor by the Act may not be transferred to another Minister by a transfer of functions order. It states how notices issued pursuant to provision made in the Act are to be given and makes provision governing the procedure for making orders and regulations under powers in the Act. It allows for minor and consequential amendments to be made by order, and makes provision regarding the extent, commencement and short title of the Act.

16. The Legal Services Act establishes a new framework for the regulation of legal services in England and Wales.

17. The Act makes provision for:

- A new regulatory framework that replaces the existing framework which comprises a number of oversight regulators with overlapping responsibilities.
- The establishment of the Legal Services Board: a single oversight body, independent both from Government and from the "front-line" approved regulators such as the Law Society and Bar Council. The Board has a duty to promote the regulatory objectives set out in Part 1.
- The establishment of an independent Office for Legal Complaints: a body with statutory power to establish a scheme for handling complaints about services provided by persons subject to oversight regulation by the Board, and to award redress in appropriate circumstances.

Alternative Business Structures to enable lawyers and non-lawyers to work together to deliver legal and other services. New business structures are expected to give legal providers greater flexibility to respond to market demands, within the UK and overseas. Licences will be conferred by licensing authorities, with various safeguards in place.

It is for the Board to advise the Government on any areas where it identifies problems within the legal services market, or "regulatory gaps".

BACKGROUND

18. In 2001 the Office of Fair Trading (OFT)[1] published a report recommending that rules governing the legal professions should be subject to competition law and that unjustified restrictions on competition be removed. Following this, the Government carried out a consultation, and published a report into competition and regulation in the legal services market.[2]

[1] Office of Fair Trading, 2001, Competition in the Professions – A Report by the Director General of Fair Trading

[2] Department for Constitutional Affairs, 2003, Competition and Regulation in the Legal Services Market – A Report Following the Consultation "In the Public Interest?"

19. In 2003 Sir David Clementi was appointed by the Government to conduct an independent review of the regulation of legal services. He found that many areas were in need of restructuring and development, and agreed with the Government's earlier conclusion that the current regulatory framework was "inflexible, outdated and over-complex".[3] Sir David highlighted concerns about the current:

regulatory framework,

complaints handling systems, and

restrictive nature of business structures.

[3] Clementi, Sir David, 2004, Review of the Regulatory Framework for Legal Services in England and Wales – Final Report

20. In October 2005 the Government published a White Paper, *The Future of Legal Services: Putting Consumers First.*[4] The White Paper set an agenda for reforming the delivery of legal services. It proposed a new regulatory framework that would direct regulation to those areas where it is needed: "We will create a Legal Services Board, an Office for Legal Complaints and we will take steps to enable firms to provide services under alternative business structures to those presently available."

[4] Department for Constitutional Affairs, 2005, The Future of Legal Services: Putting Consumers First

21. The draft Legal Services Bill was published in May 2006 and was subject to pre-legislative scrutiny by a Joint Committee of both Houses of Parliament. The Joint Committee reported in July 2006, and the Government published its response to this in September of the same year.

The legal services sector prior to the Act

22. Six pre-existing forms of legal service or activity are covered by the Act. These are:

the right of audience in the courts,
the right to conduct litigation,
reserved instrument activities,
probate activities,
notarial activities,
the administration of oaths.

23. Prior to the commencement of this Act, these services were regulated by legal professional bodies such as the Law Society or the Bar Council, as well as – to varying degrees – higher level regulators such as the Secretary of State, the Master of the Rolls and the OFT. In addition to these different regulators, there were also a range of major purchasers in the market who acted as quasi-regulators, by setting their own contract terms and prices – for example, the Legal Services Commission, and commercial organisations who operate "panel" systems. This Act does not directly affect these quasi-regulators.

24. Prior to commencement, there were a number of restrictions on the type of business structures through which legal services could be provided, mainly in regulators' professional rules. Some existing regulators prohibited lawyers from entering into partnership with non-lawyers. They also placed restrictions on unregulated persons being formally involved in the management of these businesses, and unregulated persons having any stake in the ownership of such businesses. In many cases, these restrictions were at least partly due to the fact that legal regulators did not have the powers they needed to effectively regulate practices in which non-lawyers exercised some form of control. This generally meant that lawyers were limited in the extent to which they could form businesses with non-lawyers or with different types of lawyer. The Act seeks to facilitate a regulatory framework in which different types of lawyer and non-lawyer are able to form businesses together, and in which regulators can be given effective powers to regulate such businesses.

25. Previously, if consumers wished to complain about any of the legal services listed above, they needed to take that complaint up, in the first instance, with the person they were complaining about. If the complaint was not resolved in-house, consumers could then make a complaint to the regulatory body responsible for regulating the person providing the service (for example, the Law Society, the Bar Council). In the event that a complainant was not satisfied with the way in which a complaint has been handled by a regulatory body, the complainant was then able to refer the complaint to the Legal Services Ombudsman. The Ombudsman investigated the way in which the complaint was handled and the response from the professional body. If the Ombudsman believed that a complaint had not been investigated properly, they could require that the professional body look at the matter again. The Ombudsman also had powers to investigate individual complaints. In 2004, the Ombudsman exercised this power in less than 1% of cases.[5]

[5] Legal Services Ombudsman, 2005, *Annual Report of the Legal Services Ombudsman for England and Wales 2004/2005*

SCHEDULES

26. Explanatory notes to accompany each Schedule are contained within the notes for the section introducing the Schedule.

COMMENTARY ON SECTIONS

PART 1: THE REGULATORY OBJECTIVES

Section 1: The Regulatory Objectives

27. This section sets out the eight regulatory objectives that the Board, the approved regulators and the OLC will be under a duty to observe when exercising their functions. These include promoting and maintaining adherence to the professional principles by those authorised to carry on reserved legal activities.

28. The Act does not rank these objectives and principles in order of importance. The Legal Services Board, the Office for Legal Complaints and the approved regulators will be best placed to consider how competing objectives are to be balanced in a particular instance. Section 3 sets out the Board's responsibilities in relation to the regulatory objectives. Sections 28 and 116 do the same in respect of the approved regulators and the Office for Legal Complaints.

PART 2: THE LEGAL SERVICES BOARD

29. This Part of the Act makes provision regarding the Board's constitution and its functions.

Background

30. Part 3 of the Act identifies the "reserved legal activities", that is the forms of legal activities or services the provision of which is subject to the new regulatory regime.

31. Prior to commencement of the Act, regulators, such as the Law Society and the Bar Council, regulated the practitioners providing these services. In addition to these regulators, the system involved a number of other bodies acting in a regulatory capacity, including:

the Secretary of State,
the Master of the Rolls,

the higher judiciary,
the Legal Services Ombudsman,
the Legal Services Complaints Commissioner,
the Immigration Services Commissioner,
the Home Secretary,
the Department for Trade and Industry,
the Office of Fair Trading,
the Financial Services Authority, and
the Archbishop of Canterbury.

32. In his 2004 independent review of legal services,[6] Sir David Clementi referred to observations that the current regulatory arrangements resembled a "maze" and stated that he agreed with the Government's earlier statement[7] that the existing regulatory system for legal services was "outdated, inflexible, over-complex and not accountable or transparent enough". In 2005, following Sir David's report, the Department for Constitutional Affairs published a White Paper, *The Future of Legal Services: Putting Consumers First.*[8] The White Paper detailed proposals to reform the current system by implementing a new regulatory framework that would remove the "regulatory maze" of oversight regulators.

[6] Clementi, 2004
[7] Department for Constitutional Affairs, 2003
[8] Department for Constitutional Affairs, 2005

33. This Part of the Act establishes the Legal Services Board which acts as an independent oversight regulator. It sits at the head of the new regulatory framework. The Board oversees the new approved regulators, and seeks to ensure that they carry out their regulatory functions to the required standards. Both the Board and the approved regulators must have regard to the regulatory objectives when exercising their functions.

34. This Part of the Act sets out the structure and functions of the Board. It outlines the functions that the Board has in relation to the regulatory objectives, and the ways that it will maintain these objectives. It also sets out the requirements for both appointment to and dismissal from the Board and the powers that the Lord Chancellor will have in relation to these processes.

Section 2: The Legal Services Board

35. This section establishes a corporate body called the Legal Services Board to act as an independent oversight regulator.

36. Schedule 1 is about the Board and includes:

the membership of the Board,
the terms of appointment and tenure of members,
staffing,
committees,
the Board's powers of delegation, and
borrowing and accounts rules in relation to the Board.

37. Sub-paragraph (1) of paragraph 1 provides that the Board is to be constituted by a chairman, a Chief Executive and between seven and ten other persons. The Lord Chancellor will appoint all Board members other than the Chief Executive, following consultation with the Lord Chief Justice. The Board will appoint the Chief Executive.

38. The chairman and the majority of the Board must be a lay as defined by sub-paragraph (4) of paragraph 2 of Schedule 1. "Lay persons" are persons who have never been authorised to conduct activities that are reserved legal activities under the Act. Claims managers and Scottish and Northern Irish lawyers also fall outside the definition of "lay person".

39. Paragraph 3 makes provision regarding criteria the Lord Chancellor must have regard to when appointing "ordinary" Board members. "Ordinary members" are members of the Board other than the Chief Executive.

40. As required by the Commissioner for Public Appointments, all Ministerial appointments to the Board must be made in accordance with the Commissioner's Code of Practice. As part of the planning of the appointments process, the Lord Chancellor will seek the views of interested parties on issues such as selection criteria and the diversity of skills and experience needed on the

Board. The Lord Chief Justice will also be consulted on the appointments process (sub-paragraph (3) of paragraph 1). In accordance with the Commissioner's Code of Practice, a selection panel, including, amongst others, a representative from the public body itself and an independent assessor will conduct the key stages of the appointments process. The outcome of the Panel's deliberations will form a recommendation to be made to the Lord Chancellor, who will then consult the Lord Chief Justice.

41. Terms of appointment are set out in paragraphs 4 to 9 of the Schedule. An ordinary member must be appointed for a fixed period, which must not exceed five years. A person may only be re-appointed once for a further period not exceeding five years.

42. Paragraph 7 of Schedule 1 sets out the circumstances in which the Lord Chancellor may remove ordinary Board members. Where the Lord Chancellor wishes to remove an ordinary Board member, the Lord Chancellor must first consult with the Lord Chief Justice. Where the member is not the chairman, the Lord Chancellor must also consult the chairman.

43. The chairman or other members may also resign by giving notice to the Lord Chancellor. These provisions do not apply to the Chief Executive who is appointed by the Board.

44. Paragraphs 10 to 12 set out the terms of remuneration of members. The Board is able, if it is considered necessary, to pay pensions, allowances or gratuities to the chairman and other ordinary members of the Board. The Board may also pay compensation to the chairman or other ordinary members in certain circumstances.

45. Paragraphs 13 to 18 make provision regarding the appointment of staff members by the Board. The Board must appoint a Chief Executive, and may appoint any other staff that it considers appropriate to assist in the performance of its functions. Paragraph 17 allows the Board to pay compensation to its staff or former staff for loss of employment. Paragraph 18 provides that a member of staff may also be a member of the Board, but may not be the chairman.

46. Paragraph 20 sets out the Board's powers to form committees which may in turn form sub-committees. Paragraphs 21 and 22 enable the Board to regulate its own proceedings and those of its committees.

47.Paragraph 23 allows the Board to authorise individual Board members, committees and sub-committees of the Board and members of the Board's staff to carry out the Board's functions on its behalf. The Board may not delegate its rule-making functions under the Act, save for any rule-making functions it has in respect of its own procedures, the procedures of its committees and sub-committees and in its capacity as an approved regulator or a licensing authority.

48. Paragraph 24 allows the Board to borrow money, subject to the authorisation of the Lord Chancellor.

49. Paragraph 25 requires the Board to keep proper financial accounts. Requirements to produce an annual report are set out in section 6. At the end of each financial year the Lord Chancellor must lay before Parliament a copy of the statement of accounts for that year and a copy of the Comptroller and Auditor General's report on that statement.

50. Paragraph 26 states that the Board is not to be regarded as having the same status as the Crown. Accordingly, the Board's property is not to be regarded as property held on behalf of the Crown and staff are not to be regarded as servants or agents of the Crown or as enjoying the same status.

51. Paragraphs 30 to 32 make provision for amendments to the House of Commons Disqualification Act 1975, the Northern Ireland Assembly Disqualification Act 1975, the Freedom of Information Act 2000 and the Public Records Act 1958. These are standard provisions which apply to many public bodies.

52.Paragraph 33 provides that the Board, its members and its staff will not be held liable for any damages resulting from the exercise of the Board's functions, except in the cases where an act or omission is carried out in bad faith or was unlawful in accordance with section 6(1) of the Human Rights Act 1998.

Section 3: Board's duty to promote regulatory objectives etc

53. This section states that the Board must, so far as reasonably practicable, act in a way that is compatible with the regulatory objectives. It also requires the Board to have regard to the

principles of best regulatory practice. Specifically, the section refers to the importance of regulatory activities being transparent, accountable, proportionate, consistent and targeted only at cases in which action is needed.

Section 4: Standards of regulation, education and training

54. This section imposes a duty on the Board to assist in the maintenance and development of standards of regulation by approved regulators of regulated persons and also the education and training of those persons. For example, the Board may issue guidance on, or disseminate examples of, good education and training practices or principles of professional conduct that have been developed for a reserved legal activity by one approved regulator to all approved regulators.

Section 5: Corporate governance

55. This section requires that the Board have regard to generally accepted principles of good corporate governance in managing its affairs.

Section 6: Annual report

56. This section states that the Board must prepare an annual report on the discharge of its functions. This will be laid before Parliament. It will include the extent to which, in the Board's opinion, the Board has met the regulatory objectives.

57. Paragraph 25 of Schedule 1 sets out the nature of financial accountability in relation to the Board's accounts.

Section 8: The Consumer Panel

Section 9: Committees and the procedure of the Consumer Panel

Section 10: Representations by the Consumer Panel

Section 11: Advice and research functions of the Consumer Panel

58. Section 8 requires the Board to set up and maintain a Consumer Panel – a Panel of persons whose task will be to represent the interests of consumers (as defined in section 207). Appointments to the Panel will be made by the Board with the approval of the Lord Chancellor, and one of the Panel members will be appointed as chairman of the Panel by the Board. Section 8 also sets out the categories of person who may not sit on the Panel.

59. Section 9 enables the Panel to make arrangements for committees established by it to provide advice to it. Section 10 provides that the Board must consider representations made to it by the Consumer Panel and must publish a notice where it disagrees with the Panel's advice. Under section 11, at the Board's request, the Panel may also carry out research for the Board and provide the Board with advice.

PART 3: RESERVED LEGAL ACTIVITIES

60. This Part of the Act lists and defines the reserved legal activities. It explains who is entitled to carry on these activities, and sets out the criminal penalties for those who pretend to be entitled, or offer or carry out these activities when not entitled to do so. It sets out transitional arrangements for those currently allowed to carry on reserved legal activities. It also explains the process for altering the scope of the reserved legal services, and the roles of the different bodies involved in this.

61. This Part also defines what an approved regulator is, designates certain bodies as approved regulators, and makes provision allowing for other bodies to achieve this status in the future.

Background

62. The Act identifies six forms of legal activity which are reserved. These are:

the exercise of a right of audience in the courts,
the conduct of litigation,
reserved instrument activities,

probate activities,
notarial services, and
the administration of oaths.

63. The existing regulators, which the Act recognises as approved regulators, are:

the Law Society,
the General Council of the Bar,
the Master of the Court of Faculties,
the Institute of Legal Executives,
the Council for Licensed Conveyancers,
the Chartered Institute of Patent Attorneys,
the Institute of Trade Mark Attorneys, and
the Association of Law Costs Draftsmen.

Section 12: Meaning of "reserved legal activities" and "legal activity"

64. This section lists the legal activities that are to be regulated under the Act (the "reserved legal activities"). Schedule 2 sets out the meaning of each activity. The definition of "legal activity" is set out at *section 12(3)*, though not every legal activity is necessarily regulated under the Act. However, under section 24 the Lord Chancellor may, by order, amend section 12 and Schedule 2 so as to add any legal activity to the list of reserved legal activities for the purposes of the Act.

65. The "reserved legal activities" defined by section 12 are all activities that were regulated under previously enacted legislation.

Section 13: Entitlement to carry on a reserved legal activity

66. This section provides that a person (including a body corporate or an unincorporated body) is entitled to carry on a reserved legal activity only if the person is:

an authorised person (see section 18), or
an exempt person (see section 19).

67. This is subject to transitional protection for non-commercial bodies, which is provided for in section 23.

Section 14: Offence to carry on a reserved legal activity if not entitled

68. This section makes it an offence for a person who is not entitled to carry on a reserved legal activity to carry out that activity. Persons guilty of the offence may be liable to a term of imprisonment of up to two years and/or a fine.

69. A person who commits an offence in relation to rights of audience or rights to conduct litigation in relation to any proceedings (or contemplated proceedings) is also guilty of contempt of the court involved, and may be punished accordingly.

Section 15: Carrying on of a reserved legal activity: employers and employees etc

70. This section concerns the carrying on of reserved legal activities by employers and employees. *Section 15(2) to 15(3)*, together with *section 15(11)*, make it clear that where a person carries on an activity through an employee or manager both that person and the employee or manager are regarded as carrying on the activity and so both must be entitled to carry on the activity under the Act.

71. *Section 15(4)*, together with *section 15(5)*, provides that where an individual employee carries out a service for an employer which would ordinarily be a reserved legal activity (for example, litigation services), the employer will not be treated as carrying out a reserved legal activity if the service is not provided to the public or a section of the public in the course of or as an aspect of the employer's business. The effect of this is, for example, that where a body employs lawyers to provide in-house legal services to that body or to certain persons connected to the body, but not to the public or a section of the public, the body in question will not need to be an authorised person. This does not alter the fact that any individual lawyers which the body employs to provide reserved activities will need to be authorised persons.

72. *Sections 15(6) to 15(8)* deal with trade unions. People who are provided with relevant services by virtue of membership (including the membership of another person, and former membership) do not constitute the public or a section of the public where legal services that the union is providing are excepted membership services. These are defined in section 15(7) as services related to a member's relevant activities, other activities arising from them, events that have occurred in the course of them, and activities that are connected with a person's union membership. The Lord Chancellor may specify other services by order and, under section 15(8), may make orders about the circumstances in which services are connected with these matters. *Section 15(12)* defines relevant activities for trade union purposes as any employment, trade, occupation, or other activity to which union membership relates.

73. Under *section 15(9)* the Lord Chancellor may also by order make provision about what constitutes a "section of the public", and the circumstances in which the provision of services does or does not form "part of the employer's business". These orders can only be made on the Board's recommendation (*section 15(10)*).

Section 16: Offence to carry on a reserved legal activity through person not entitled

74. This section provides that if an employer carries on a reserved legal activity through a manager or employee who is not entitled to carry on that activity, the employer will commit an offence, even if the employer is so entitled, unless the employer has taken all reasonable precautions and exercised all due diligence to avoid committing the offence. This offence carries a maximum penalty of an unlimited fine and/or two years' imprisonment.

Section 17: Offence to pretend to be entitled

75. This section makes it an offence for a person who is not entitled to carry on a reserved legal activity, to pretend to be entitled to carry on that activity, or to use a name, title or description which implies that that person is so entitled. The penalties for committing this offence are the same as those for carrying on a reserved legal activity when not entitled.

Section 18: Authorised persons

76. A person is an "authorised person" in relation to a particular reserved legal activity if the person is authorised to carry on that activity by a relevant approved regulator (other than by virtue of a licence under Part 5) or the person is a licensable body and holds a licence under Part 5 which authorises the carrying on of the activity.

77. *Sections 18(3) and (4)* (together with Schedule 5 and Schedule 22) provide that certain existing bodies which would otherwise be required to obtain a licence under Part 5, are either deemed to be authorised or treated as exempt persons during a transitional period, after which point such bodies will need to become licensed.

Section 19: Exempt persons

78. Section 19 introduces Schedule 3 which makes provision exempting certain persons from the requirement to be authorised to conduct particular reserved legal activities. For example, an individual who carries on probate activities other than for fee, gain or reward is exempt. The Lord Chancellor may, by order, add or remove exempt persons from the Schedule. This may only be done on the recommendation of the Board.

Section 20: Approved regulators and relevant approved regulators

79. This section defines "approved regulator" and "relevant approved regulator", and introduces Schedule 4, which concerns the designation of bodies as approved regulators.

80. Part 1 of Schedule 4 lists the bodies which automatically became approved regulators when the Act came into force. The regulatory arrangements for these bodies are to be treated as having been approved by the Board at the time paragraph 1 comes into force. Sub-paragraph (3) of paragraph 2 makes it clear that the Board may exercise its power to direct a regulator to alter its regulatory arrangements even where the regulator and its regulatory arrangements are approved under this paragraph.

81. Part 2 of the Schedule makes provision regarding the procedure to be followed by bodies applying for designation as an approved regulator in respect of a reserved legal activity.

82. The Schedule details the material that must accompany an application and provides that the application must be accompanied by a prescribed fee, set by the Board with the consent of the Lord Chancellor.

83. The Board is required to make rules setting out the criteria by which it may refuse to consider an application. Where the Board decides to refuse to consider the application further, it must give notice to the applicant of its decision and the reasons behind it.

84. Where the Board proceeds to consider the application, it has a duty to seek advice before granting the application. Paragraph 5 requires that the Board must give a copy of the application and accompanying material to:

the Office of Fair Trading (OFT),
the Consumer Panel,
the Lord Chief Justice, and
such other persons as the Board considers it reasonable to consult regarding the application.

85. Paragraphs 6 to 9 set out the duties of the consultees:

The OFT and the Consumer Panel must give advice to the Board in respect of the application, as they think fit.

The OFT must, in particular, consider whether granting an application would, or would be likely to, restrict, distort or prevent competition within the market for reserved legal services. The Consumer Panel must have regard to the likely impact that granting an application would have on consumers.

Those other persons whom the Board considers it reasonable to consult may give advice in respect of the application.

The Lord Chief Justice must then consider this advice, and give advice to the Board regarding whether the application should be granted. The Lord Chief Justice must, in particular, have regard to the likely impact of granting an application on the courts in England and Wales.

86. Paragraph 10 allows the consultees, for the purpose of giving advice, to ask that the applicant, or any other person, provide additional specified information.

87. The Board (which must make rules governing the making of representations) must give the applicant copies of any of the advice given by consultees. The applicant may make representations to the Board within the time period specified in paragraph 11.

88. Paragraph 12 of the Schedule explains that once the period for representations has passed, the Board must publish any advice provided by the consultees and any representations made. This does not prevent anyone who has given advice under paragraphs 6 to 9, or made a representation under paragraph 11, from publishing that material. Any publisher must, so far as practicable, exclude any matter which relates to the private affairs of a particular individual whose interests might be affected, seriously and prejudicially, by publication.

89. The Board must make rules specifying how it will determine applications. Paragraph 13 sets out the criteria that the Board must apply when determining an application.

90. Paragraph 14 sets out the procedure that the Board must follow in considering its decision. It must consider the advice and representations referred to in paragraph 85 of these Explanatory Notes, above, as well as any other information that it considers relevant, and then decide whether to grant the application. The Board may grant the application in whole or in part, and must give notice in writing of its decision to the applicant, and publish this notice.

91. Paragraph 15 states that the Board must give its decision within twelve months, beginning with the day on which the application is made to the Board. The Board may extend this decision period by issuing and publishing a notice, only after consultation with the OFT, the Consumer Panel, and the Lord Chief Justice.

92. Under paragraph 16, where an application is granted, the Board must recommend to the Lord Chancellor that an order be made designating the body as an approved regulator in relation to the appropriate reserved legal activity or activities. Where the application relates to more than one reserved legal activity, the Board may grant it in relation to all or some of those activities. The Board must publish its recommendation.

93. The Lord Chancellor may then make an order in accordance with the recommendation (or a part of it), or refuse to make such an order. Paragraph 17 sets out the procedure for doing this. If

the Lord Chancellor decides not to make an order, the Lord Chancellor must give the applicant and the Board notice of that decision and of the reasons for it, and publish this notice.

94. Part 3 of the Schedule sets out how alterations to the regulatory arrangements of an approved regulator must be approved. If an approved regulator alters its regulatory arrangements, the alteration will not have effect until it is approved for the purposes of this Act. An alteration can include an addition to the arrangements, or a revocation of any part. Paragraph 19 sets out the circumstances in which an alteration will be approved.

95. Paragraph 20 provides that the Board may make rules specifying the way in which an application by an approved regulator to alter its regulatory arrangements must be made, and makes certain requirements as to the material that must accompany the application. Paragraph 21 sets out what the Board must do on receipt of an application. It may grant the application, or it may issue and publish a notice stating that it is considering whether to refuse the application.

96. Under paragraph 22, where the Board has given the approved regulator a notice, it may invite such persons as it considers appropriate to give it advice regarding whether the application should be granted. The consultees may, for the purpose of giving advice, ask that the approved regulator, or any other person, to provide additional information.

97. The Board must give the approved regulator copies of any of the advice given above. The approved regulator may make representations to the Board within 28 days, or such longer period as the Board allows, as specified in paragraph 23 of the Schedule. The Board must make rules governing the making of representations.

98. Paragraph 24 of the Schedule requires that once the period for representations has passed, the Board must publish the advice and representations. This does not prevent anyone who has given advice under paragraph 22, or made a representation under paragraph 23, from publishing that material. Any publisher must, so far as practicable, exclude any matter which relates to the private affairs of a particular individual whose interests might be seriously and prejudicially affected by publication.

99. Paragraph 25 sets out the material that the Board is required to consider before deciding whether to grant the application. The Board may grant the application in whole or in part, and must give notice in writing of its decision to the applicant, and publish this notice. The Board may refuse the application only if it is satisfied that one of the conditions set out in sub-paragraph (3) of paragraph 25 is met. If the Board decides to refuse the application, it must specify the reasons in its published notice.

100. Paragraph 26 provides that if the Board does not give the approved regulator notice of its decision within the decision period (twelve months), then the application is deemed to have been granted. The Board may extend the decision period with the consent of the Lord Chancellor. The total decision period must not exceed eighteen months.

Section 21: Regulatory arrangements

101. This section defines the "regulatory arrangements" of bodies. These include the arrangements made for the body to authorise persons to carry on reserved legal activities, the body's conduct rules, and disciplinary arrangements etc. The regulatory arrangements do not include arrangements which are made in connection with any role the body may have in representing or promoting the interests of persons regulated by it. This section also provides that regulatory arrangements include compensation and indemnification arrangements (and defines such arrangements).

Section 22: Continuity of existing rights to carry on reserved legal activities

102. Part 1 of Schedule 5, which is introduced by this section, provides that for the purposes of determining whether a person is an authorised person as defined in section 18, it is immaterial whether a person's authorisation to exercise a right of audience or conduct litigation was granted by an approved regulator before or after the day upon which it is designated. Part 2 of the Schedule makes provision deeming certain categories of person to be authorised by an approved regulator to conduct certain reserved legal activities for the duration of the transitional period, or to be exempt during that period. The duration of the transitional period is to be determined by the Lord Chancellor. At the conclusion of the transitional period, unless a person is authorised or exempt under the Act, under section 14 the person will commit an offence if the person carries out a reserved legal activity.

103. This provision ensures that rights people have under the existing arrangements will be protected during the transitional period. Every barrister, qualified solicitor, legal partnership, legal executive authorised by ILEX, licensed conveyancer, duly certified notary public, registered patent attorney, registered trade mark attorney and law costs draftsmen is deemed to have been authorised to carry on certain reserved legal activities by their professional body, as listed in Part 2 of the Schedule.

Section 23: Transitional protection for non-commercial bodies

104. Section 23 ensures that, during a transitional period, non-commercial bodies (as defined by *section 23(2)*) are entitled to carry on reserved activities without committing an offence. Without this, they would be unable to operate before the ABS licensing regime came into effect.

Section 24: Extension of the reserved legal activities

105. This section allows the Lord Chancellor, by order, to extend the activities within the scope of the definition of "relevant legal activities", by amending section 12 or Schedule 2. The Lord Chancellor can make this order only on the recommendation of the Board. This will enable any legal services to be regulated at a later date where it would be in consumers' interests to do so.

106. Schedule 6, introduced by this section, sets out the procedure for adding new activities to the list of reserved legal activities. It also sets out the procedure for determining whether a recommendation should be made under section 26 (recommendations that activities should cease to be reserved legal activities).

107. The following individuals/bodies may request that the Board investigate whether the reserved legal activities should be extended, or whether an activity should cease to be a reserved legal activity:

the Lord Chancellor,
the OFT,
the Consumer Panel, or
the Lord Chief Justice.

108. Where such a request is made, preliminary inquiries for an investigation by the Board may take up to three months, although this can be extended by agreement with the Lord Chancellor. Anybody else may make a request of this kind, although in such cases the Board will not be obliged to make preliminary enquiries. The Board can also instigate investigations even if no request has been made.

109. Paragraph 5 enables the Board to seek advice from the OFT and/or the Consumer Panel before determining whether it is appropriate to hold an investigation. If asked for advice, the OFT and the Consumer Panel must each give the Board such advice as it sees fit. The OFT must, in particular, consider whether making a change would, or would be likely to, restrict, distort or prevent competition in the market for reserved legal services. The Consumer Panel must have regard to the likely impact that making a change would have on consumers. Each may, for the purpose of giving advice, ask any person to provide additional specified information.

110. Paragraph 6 states that, if the Board seeks the advice of the Lord Chief Justice, the Lord Chief Justice must consider any advice provided to the Board by the OFT and/or the Consumer Panel, and then give such advice to the Board as the Lord Chief Justice sees fit. In deciding what advice to give, the Lord Chief Justice must, in particular, have regard to the likely impact of the proposed change on the courts in England and Wales. The Board must consider, and publish, any advice given by those persons.

111. Under paragraph 8, if the Board receives an application by the Lord Chancellor, OFT, the Consumer Panel or the Lord Chief Justice to investigate whether the reserved legal activities should be extended, or whether an activity should cease to be a reserved legal activity, it may only refuse to undertake the investigation where:

the Board has consulted, and received advice from, the OFT, the Consumer Panel or the Lord Chief Justice (sub-paragraph (3) of paragraph 8); and

either,

the Lord Chancellor consents to the Board's refusal (sub-paragraph (4) of paragraph 8, or
the original request for investigation was made by the Lord Chancellor.

112. If the request proceeds to a full investigation, the Board must give notice of this to the Lord Chancellor, the OFT, the Consumer Panel, and the Lord Chief Justice. The Board must publish this notice.

113. Within twelve months the Board must produce and publish a report with its provisional recommendation and reasons, as stated in paragraph 10. The Board may extend this investigation period by issuing and publishing a notice, only after consultation with the OFT, the Consumer Panel, and the Lord Chief Justice.

114. The Board may make rules governing the making of representations and the giving of evidence. Paragraphs 12 to 15 set out what the Board must consider in making these rules, and the process by which such rules may be made. Paragraph 18 permits the Board to pay such costs of a person as the Board considers reasonable, for the purpose of facilitating the giving of oral evidence or representations.

115. Paragraph 16 sets out the process that the Board must follow in making its final report. It must decide:

whether or not to make a recommendation to extend the reserved legal activities,
whether or not to make a recommendation that an activity should cease to be a reserved legal activity.

116. The Board must make its report within the "final reporting period", as set out in paragraph 17. Paragraph 16 requires the report to:

set out the Board's decision and reasons for it, and
where applicable, its recommendation, and any statement of further statutory changes that may be needed if an order is made in accordance with the recommendation.

117. The Board must give a copy of this report to the Lord Chancellor, and publish it.

118. Section 24 provides that the Lord Chancellor must consider the report and publish a decision. Where the Lord Chancellor decides not to make an order that the Board has recommended, the Lord Chancellor must state reasons for this. The Lord Chancellor will not be able to make an order otherwise than on the Board's recommendation, nor will the Lord Chancellor be able to amend an order that the Board has recommended. This Act does not give the Lord Chancellor the power to make changes on the Lord Chancellor's own initiative (including amending Board recommendations as they are implemented).

Section 25: Provisional designation as approved regulators and licensing authorities

119. This provision enables the Lord Chancellor to determine applications by bodies for designation as an approved regulator or a licensing authority in respect of an activity which is a "provisional reserved legal activity", that is, an activity which may become a reserved legal activity in the future.

Section 26: Recommendations that activities should cease to be reserved legal activities

120. This section enables the Board to recommend to the Lord Chancellor that an activity should cease to be a reserved legal activity. The applicable procedure is set out in Schedule 6. If the Lord Chancellor agrees with a recommendation by the Board that an activity should cease to be a reserved legal activity, there is no procedure under the Act to implement such a recommendation and it would be for the Lord Chancellor to pursue this by other means (for example, further primary legislation or, possibly, a regulatory reform order).

PART 4: REGULATION OF APPROVED REGULATORS

121. This Part of the Act sets out the duties of approved regulators, makes provision to ensure that approved regulators maintain an appropriate separation of their regulatory and representative functions, and confers powers on the Board to ensure that the approved regulators' duties are being carried out appropriately. It details how the Board can intervene when there is a problem, the procedures that it must follow, and the bodies that it must consult before exercising its powers. The Board's powers include target-setting, censure, financial penalties, a power of direction, direct intervention in the approved regulator's regulation of its members, and in extreme cases the removal of a body's authorisation.

Background

122. As already stated in the background section to the Legal Services Board,[9] Sir David Clementi's 2004 independent review of legal services referred to observations that the current regulatory arrangements resembled a "maze" and stated that he agreed with the Government's earlier statement[10] that the existing regulatory system for legal services was "outdated, inflexible, over-complex and not accountable or transparent enough". He proposed that an independent oversight regulator be established to simplify regulation and ensure that the system was clear to consumers. The Government's White Paper, The Future of Legal Services: Putting Consumers First,[11] set out how it was envisaged that this oversight regulator should operate: it should authorise approved regulators to carry out day-to-day regulation, and it would also need to be able to act if these approved regulators failed.

[9] Clementi, 2004
[10] Department for Constitutional Affairs 2003
[11] Department for Constitutional Affairs, 2005

123. The White Paper stated that in most cases, the Board would want to work alongside regulators to help them improve where areas of weakness have been identified. However, where a regulator continued to fail, the Board would be able to remove authorisation in a particular area or areas of regulation, and either identify an alternative regulator, or carry out the regulatory functions itself.

Section 27: Regulatory and representative functions of approved regulators

124. This section defines what is meant by the regulatory and representative functions of an approved regulator under the Act.

Section 28: Approved regulator's duty to promote the regulatory objectives etc

125. When discharging its regulatory functions, an approved regulator will be under a duty to act in a way that is compatible with the regulatory objectives so far as it is reasonably practicable to do so. In addition, the approved regulator must have regard to principles of best regulatory practice.

Section 29: Prohibition on the Board interfering with representative functions

126. This section provides that the Board is not authorised to exercise its functions in relation to any representative function of an approved regulator. However, the Board is authorised to take action for the purpose of ensuring that the exercise of an approved regulator's regulatory functions is not prejudiced by its representative functions, and that decisions are taken independently of each other in relation to the regulatory and the representative functions.

Section 30: Rules relating to the exercise of regulatory functions

127. This section requires the Board to make rules setting out requirements to be met by approved regulators for the purpose of ensuring that their regulatory and representative functions are appropriately separated ("internal governance rules"). The rules must include provision which ensures that persons exercising regulatory functions can, independently from any representative functions, make representations to the Board, the Consumer Panel, the OLC and other approved regulators (including notifying the Board if they feel that their independence or effectiveness is being compromised), and that they are appropriately resourced to carry out their functions.

Section 31: Performance targets and monitoring

128. The Board may set, or direct an approved regulator to set, performance targets relating to the performance of the approved regulator's regulatory functions, as defined in section 27. For example, where an approved regulator is failing to deal with misconduct cases quickly enough, the Board may set targets in relation to how long consideration of a misconduct case should take. *Section 31(2)* sets out the thresholds that must be met before the Board can exercise this power, and in considering whether it is appropriate to take action, the Board must consider the impact of taking action on the other regulatory objectives.

Section 32: Directions

Section 33: Directions: procedure

Section 34: Enforcement of directions

129. Under section 32 the Board may use its power of direction where any of the threshold conditions in *section 32(1)* is satisfied, including that the Board has considered the impact of taking action on the other regulatory objectives.

130. In such circumstances, the Board may direct the approved regulator in question to take steps to remedy any failure or counter any adverse impact, mitigate its effect, or prevent its recurrence. It must publish any direction that it issues to a regulator.

131. *Section 32(4)* sets out the scope of a direction. A direction may only require an approved regulator to take steps which it has power to take, and it may require the regulator to take steps with a view to the modification of any part of its regulatory arrangements in order to achieve the desired effect.

132. The Board can monitor compliance with a direction, and it may revoke a direction by giving notice to the regulator, and publishing the notice.

133. Under section 33, when the Board gives a direction to a regulator to take specific steps, the procedure set out in Schedule 7 will apply. Schedule 7 includes requirements for giving notice to the approved regulator, for consulting with the Lord Chancellor, the OFT, the Consumer Panel and the Lord Chief Justice, and for making representations.

134. Under section 34, where an approved regulator has failed to comply with a direction, the Board may make an application to the High Court. Upon such an application, if the High Court agrees that the approved regulator has failed to comply with the direction, it may make an order requiring the approved regulator to take such steps as it considers appropriate in order to ensure that direction is complied with.

Section 35: Public censure

Section 36: Public censure: procedure

135. Section 35 sets out the threshold conditions which must be met before the Board can exercise this power, including the requirement for the Board to consider the impact of taking action on the other regulatory objectives. Section 36 sets out the procedure that must be complied with before a statement of censure can be issued, and requires the Board to give prior notice of the terms of the proposed statement and other matters, and to consider any representations which are duly made before publishing the statement.

Section 37: Financial penalties

Section 38: Financial penalties: procedure

136. *Section 37(1)* sets out the threshold conditions that must be met before the Board can exercise its power to impose financial penalties. The Board is required to make rules by statutory instrument (subject to the negative resolution procedure – see section 206(6)), prescribing the maximum amount of the penalty that may be imposed and the Lord Chancellor's consent to these rules is required. Section 38 sets out the procedure that applies to the imposition of financial penalties.

Section 39: Appeals against financial penalties

137. This section makes provision for an approved regulator to appeal against a financial penalty on the grounds set out at *section 39(2)*.

138.The appeal is by way of application to the High Court (to be made within three months of notification of the decision appealed against). The High Court can quash the penalty, substitute a different amount or, where the penalty is payable by instalments, vary the time by which the penalty must be paid (*section 39(4)*), and may make an order as to interest on any substituted penalty (*sections 39(5) and 39(6)*).

Section 40: Recovery of financial penalties

139. Where an approved regulator has not paid a financial penalty, the Board has the power to recover the penalty, and any interest, as a debt payable to the Board (*sections 40(3) and 40(4)*). If all or part of a penalty is not paid by the time specified, the unpaid balance carries interest (*section 40(1)*). Where an appeal is made by an approved regulator against a financial penalty, the penalty does not have to be paid until the appeal has been determined or withdrawn.

Section 41: Intervention directions

140. This section defines an intervention direction, and provides for the scope of such directions and the conditions under which the Board can impose such directions on an approved regulator in relation to its regulatory functions. An intervention direction (*section 41(2)*) is a direction that the Board, or the Board's nominee, will exercise one or more of the approved regulator's regulatory functions. Where the Board exercises its powers under an intervention direction, it will be able to nominate a person or persons to carry out the regulatory function. The Board may also require the approved regulator to comply with any instructions set by the Board or the nominated person.

141. *Section 41(1)* sets out the threshold conditions which must be met before the Board can issue an intervention direction, which mirror those in section 31(2), including the requirement for the Board to consider the impact of taking action on the other regulatory objectives. *Section 41(3)* additionally provides that the Board must not give an intervention direction unless it is satisfied that the approved regulator's act or omission cannot be adequately addressed by the exercise of the powers available under sections 31 to 40.

142. *Section 41(4)* refers to part 1 of Schedule 8, which sets out the procedure for giving an intervention direction. This includes procedures for giving notice to the approved regulator, for consulting with the Lord Chancellor, the OFT, the Consumer Panel and the Lord Chief Justice, and for making representations.

Section 42: Intervention directions: further provision

143. Where an intervention direction has been made and is in effect in relation to a function of an approved regulator, the approved regulator must give the Board, or a person nominated by the Board, all such assistance as it is reasonably able to give, to allow the Board, or nominated person, to pursue the direction through the exercise of the function to which the direction relates. Under *section 42(3)*, the Board, a person nominated by the Board or any such person's appointee may apply for a warrant authorising them to enter and search the approved regulator's premises and to seize the records it finds. *Section 42(6)* requires the Lord Chancellor to make regulations prescribing the criteria that will apply when deciding whether to issue a warrant.

Section 43: Intervention directions: enforcement

144. This section makes provision for the enforcement of intervention directions by way of application to the High Court.

Section 44: Revocation of intervention directions

145. *Section 44(1)* provides that an intervention direction has effect until such time as it is revoked by the Board. *Section 44(2)* refers to Part 2 of Schedule 8, which contains the procedure for revocation of an intervention direction. This includes procedures for giving notice to the approved regulator, for consulting with the Lord Chancellor, the OFT, the Consumer Panel and the Lord Chief Justice, and for making representations.

146. Paragraph 13 of the Schedule provides that where an intervention direction has effect in respect of a regulatory function of an approved regulator, the regulator can apply to the Board for the Board to revoke the direction, or the Board can give notice to the regulator that it intends to revoke the direction.

Section 45: Cancellation of designation as approved regulator

147. The Lord Chancellor may, by making an order, cancel a body's designation as an approved regulator in relation to one or more of the reserved legal activities for which it is designated (*section 45(1)*). But the Lord Chancellor may act only on the recommendation of the Board (*section 45(2)*).

148. Under *section 45(3)*, if a body applies to the Board to have its designation as an approved regulator cancelled, and the Board is satisfied that the rules that it has set for this process have been met, then the Board must make such a recommendation to the Lord Chancellor.

149. The Board may also recommend that a cancellation order be made if it is satisfied that the conditions listed in *section 45(5)* (including the requirement for the Board to consider the impact of taking action on the other regulatory objectives) have been met and that the matter cannot be adequately addressed by the Board exercising its powers under sections 31 to 43. The Board must specify the reasons for suggesting cancellation when making its recommendation.

150. Schedule 9, introduced by this section, applies where the Board considers that it may be appropriate for it to make a recommendation under section 45(5). It requires the Board to notify the body of the proposed recommendation, and to seek advice in respect of the recommendation. This Schedule sets out the procedures for giving notice to the approved regulator, for consulting with the OFT, the Consumer Panel and the Lord Chief Justice, and for making representations.

Section 46: Cancellation of a designation: further provision

Section 47: The Board's power to recommend orders made under section 46

151. Section 46 allows the Lord Chancellor to make transfer arrangements by order when a body has its designation in relation to one or more reserved legal activities cancelled. The Lord Chancellor may make such an order only on the recommendation of the Board, and only in substantially the same form as recommended by the Board (*section 46(7)*). Section 47 sets out the procedure that the Board must follow when making a recommendation for the cancellation of an approved regulator's designation. This procedure requires the publication of a draft recommendation and order, and that the Board take account of any representations made. It also provides for re-publication of the recommendation and order, if the Board makes any amendments which it considers material after the initial publication.

152. The purpose of section 46 is to minimise disruption to the regulation of authorised persons following the cancellation of an approved regulator's designation. It allows for regulatory responsibility for the authorised persons concerned to be transferred to another approved regulator (assuming that the regulator in question consents to assuming such responsibility) or, where no suitable alternative approved regulator has been identified, to the Board, in its capacity as an approved regulator.

153. Where such a transfer takes place, the relevant regulated persons will be subject to the regulatory arrangements of the new regulator, or the Board, as appropriate.

154. Section 47 also allows money raised from practising fees and held by the old regulator (or a part of the money so held) to be paid to the new regulator and treated in the same way as if the money had been raised by the new regulator by way of practising fees.

Section 48: Cancellation of designation: powers of entry etc

155. This section applies where an approved regulator has had its designation removed. The old regulator must give reasonable assistance to the new regulator and Board for the continuation of regulation.

156. A person appointed by the Board to act on its behalf may apply to a judge of the High Court, a circuit judge or justice of the peace for a warrant authorising that person to enter and search the premises of the old regulator, and to take possession of written or electronic documents found there. The person may take copies of records found on a search, and the Board must make rules as to the persons it may appoint for these purposes.

157. A warrant may not be issued unless it is necessary or desirable for the purpose of continuing regulation. The Lord Chancellor must make regulations specifying any further matters that the judge or justice of the peace must be satisfied of or have regard to before issuing a warrant, and regulating the exercise of a power conferred by the warrant. The regulations must be made in accordance with a recommendation of, or following consultation with, the Board. The regulations must in particular make provision as to the circumstances in which documents may be copied or must be returned.

Section 49: The Board's policy statements

Section 50: Policy statements: procedure

158. Section 49 requires the Board to prepare and issue a policy statement concerning its functions under sections 31, 32, 35, 37, 41, 45 and 76. The Board may also issue a statement of policy with respect to any other matter, where it considers it appropriate. In preparing a statement, the Board must have regard to the principle that its principal role is the oversight of approved regulators, and that it should not exercise its powers unless the act or omission of an approved regulator was unreasonable. The statement must take account of the desirability of resolving informally matters between the Board and the approved regulators, and specify how the Board will comply with the requirements of section 3(3). Any policy statement may be amended or replaced from time to time, and the Board must publish the new or amended statement. The Board must have regard to any relevant policy statement in exercising, or deciding whether to exercise, any of its functions (see *section 49(8)*).

159. Before the Board issues a policy statement, it must publish the proposed statement in draft, and allow representations to be made about it. Section 50 outlines the procedure for making policy statements.

Section 51: Control of practising fees charged by approved regulators

160. This section requires the Board to make rules setting out the purposes for which practising fees payable under the regulatory arrangements of approved regulators may be applied. These rules must allow for practising fees to be applied for the purposes set out at *section 51(4)*. This provision further provides that a practising fee charged by an approved regulator to the persons it authorises will only be payable if the Board has approved the level of the fee. The Board must also make rules setting out how it will deal with applications for the approval of practising fees.

Section 52: Regulatory conflict with approved regulators

161. This section deals with the possibility that conflicts between regulatory arrangements may arise where an approved regulator regulates entities comprising persons authorised by different approved regulators – for example, solicitors and barristers. Regulators of such entities will be required to take steps to prevent conflicts of this type in their rules, as set out at *section 52(1)*. In the event that a conflict does arise between the regulator of the entity, and another approved regulator who authorises persons practising within the entity, the conflict is to be resolved as set out at *section 52(4)*.

Section 53: Modification of provision made about regulatory conflict

162. To counter any imbalance arising from the outcome of the provision in section 52(4), section 53 provides that approved regulators whose members are affected by the rules of another approved regulator may ask that the Board exercise its powers under section 32 to direct that the approved regulator take steps to address the offending provision in its regulatory arrangements. *Section 53(3)* requires approved regulators to consider any request from persons authorised by them or a manager or employee of such persons to make such an application to the Board. The Board must consider representations from both regulators, and may consult others as appropriate, before making a decision over whether or not to modify the rules (see *section 53(5)*).

Section 54: Regulatory conflict with other regulatory regimes

163. This section places approved regulators under an obligation to make provision in their regulatory arrangements to prevent and resolve regulatory conflicts with external regulators, as well as to avoid unnecessary duplication of regulation. This applies to approved regulators who regulate entities involving persons regulated by an external, non-legal services regulator, for example, the Financial Services Authority. The Board must provide guidance to approved regulators on dealing with external regulatory conflicts. With the Board's consent, the approved regulator's regulatory arrangements may provide for the Board to act in the resolution of conflicts between the approved regulator and relevant external regulators.

Section 55: Provision of information to the Board

Section 56: Enforcement of notices under section 55

164. Section 55 confers power on the Board to require an approved regulator, by notice, to provide such information or produce such documents in such form, within such period and to such person nominated by the Board, as the Board specifies in the notice. Section 56 provides for enforcement in the event of an approved regulator failing to comply with such a notice. Enforcement is by way of application to the High Court for an order requiring the approved regulator to comply with the original notice that was issued by the Board.

Section 57: Reports by the OFT

Section 58: The Board's response to OFT report

Section 59: Referral of report by the Lord Chancellor to the Competition Commission

Section 60: Duties of the Competition Commission

Section 61: Lord Chancellor's power to give directions

165. These sections make provision conferring investigation powers and duties on the OFT and the Competition Commission in respect of regulatory arrangements of approved regulators where they in effect prevent, restrict or distort competition within the market for reserved legal services. Under section 57, the OFT may prepare a report if it believes that an approved regulator's regulatory arrangements (or any part of them) have this effect, or are likely to do so. The section also sets out the matters which the OFT's report should cover. It further provides that such reports attract absolute privilege for the purposes of the law of defamation.

166. Section 58 details how the Board should respond to a report from the OFT. It provides that the Board must allow at least 28 days for the approved regulator to make representations to the Board regarding the OFT's report. Section 58 further allows for the Consumer Panel to give such advice to the Board as it considers appropriate and requires the Board to have regard to any such representations and advice before informing the OFT what action (if any) it proposes to take.

167. Section 59 and section 60 provide that, in the event that the OFT believes that the Board has not given the OFT's report full and proper consideration, the OFT may give a copy of the report to the Lord Chancellor, who must, in turn, give a copy of the report to the Competition Commission. The Competition Commission must then investigate the matter and make its own report (unless it judges that this would serve no useful purpose). Under *section* 61, the Lord Chancellor has the power to direct the Board to take action in connection with any matter raised in the OFT's report. Before giving a direction, the Lord Chancellor must consider any report given by the Competition Commission under *section* 60. Any direction given under *section* 61 must be published

Section 62: The Board as an approved regulator

Section 63: The Board's designation under section 62(1)(a)

Section 64: Modification of the Board's functions under section 62(1)(b)

Section 65: Cancellation of the Board's designation under section 62(1)(c)

Section 66: The Board's power to recommend orders made under section 62

168. This group of sections make provision for the Board to be able to act as an approved regulator in relation to any one or more of the reserved legal activities. Section 62 provides that the Lord Chancellor may, by order:

designate the Board as an approved regulator in relation to one or more reserved legal activities;

modify the functions of the Board, with a view to enabling the Board to discharge its functions as an approved regulator effectively and efficiently; and

cancel the Board's designation as an approved regulator in relation to one or more reserved legal activity.

169. Such an order may also modify other legislation as appears necessary or expedient to the Lord Chancellor (see *section 62(5)*). If the Board is designated by such an order, it must take the necessary action to ensure an appropriate financial and organisational separation between its functions as approved regulator and its other activities.

170. The Lord Chancellor's power to make such an order is exercisable only if the Board has made a recommendation for such an order; and it may not be used so as make an order which differs materially from that recommended (*section 62(2)*). Section 66 makes provision about the Board's recommendations for orders under section 62. The Lord Chancellor is not bound to accept a recommendation, but must provide the Board with a notice stating reasons for refusal and must publish that notice (*section 62(3)*).

171. Section 63 provides that the Board may be designated as an approved regulator only in instances where an approved regulator's designation has been cancelled, or where the activity in question is a new reserved legal activity. By virtue of *section 63(3)*, the Board may be designated as an approved regulator in advance of either of these eventualities. The order designating the Board must also ensure that the Board acting as approved regulator is separate from the Board acting in its "general" capacity so that the Board as approved regulator may only make or modify its regulatory arrangements with the approval of the Board in its general capacity.

172. Section 64 specifies some of the powers that may be conferred on the Board by an order made under section *62(1)(b)* modifying the Board's functions in order to enable it to fulfil its role as an approved regulator more effectively.

173. Section 65 makes provision regarding the cancellation of the Board's designation as an approved regulator. In such cases, sections 46 and 47 which provide for "transfer arrangements") will apply in relation to the Board and persons authorised by it as they apply to an approved regulator whose designation is cancelled under section 45, and to persons authorised by that regulator.

174. Section 66 sets out the procedure that the Board must follow before making a recommendation for an order under section 62.

Section 68: Regulatory conflict and the Board as approved regulator

175. This section sets out how regulatory conflict will be resolved in instances where the Board acts as an approved regulator. It provides for requests to be made to the Board (in its capacity as an approved regulator) for it to reconsider the provision made by its regulatory arrangements, so as to prevent a conflict with another approved regulator. Such a request may be made by an approved regulator (on its own initiative) or following a request by an affected person (as defined by *section 68(11)*). Such a request may also be made by a person authorised by the Board (in its capacity as an approved regulator) to carry on a reserved legal activity or a manager or employee of such a person. Such a person may also apply to the Board in its capacity as an oversight regulator, requesting that it exercise its powers under section 32 to direct the approved regulator to take the appropriate action in respect of regulatory arrangements to resolve a regulatory conflict.

Section 69: Modification of the functions of approved regulators etc

Section 70: Procedural requirements relating to recommendations under section 69

176. Section 69 confers the power on the Lord Chancellor to make an order modifying or making other provision in relation to the functions of an approved regulator or other body other than the Board. Such an order may only be made following a recommendation by the Board, and such orders may only be made to achieve the purposes specified in *section 69(3)*, namely:

to enable a body to become an approved regulator or licensing authority in relation to one or more reserved legal activities;

to enable a body to regulate different categories of legal persons;

- to enable a body to carry out its role as an approved regulator/licensing authority more effectively or efficiently;
- to enable a body to become a qualifying regulator for immigration services; or
- (where the body is already a qualifying regulator) to enable it to authorise persons to provide any additional advice or services which amount to immigration advice or services.

177. Furthermore, the Board may only make a recommendation that such an order be made with the consent of the approved regulator to which the recommendation relates. Section 70 sets out the procedural requirements relating to the making of such recommendations.

PART 5: ALTERNATIVE BUSINESS STRUCTURES

178. This Part of the Act makes provision for new alternative business structures as a vehicle for providing legal and other advice and services. It enables lawyers and non-lawyers to form legal partnerships and companies as vehicles for the provision of reserved legal services. Where non-lawyers are managers of, or have an interest in, such a body, the body must become a licensed body, licensed and regulated by a licensing authority, in accordance with the provisions of Part 5. Existing regulators of legal services may apply to the Board to become licensing authorities. If there are no other appropriate licensing authorities, the Board itself can act as a licensing authority.

179. Consumers can complain about matters relating to the services provided by ABS firms: first through in-house complaints arrangements, and if necessary, to the new ombudsman scheme that will be administered by the OLC.

Background

180. Historically, there have been a number of statutory restrictions on the type of business structures through which legal services may be provided. Some existing regulators have also prohibited lawyers from entering into partnership with non-lawyers. Certain regulators have also placed restrictions on the ways in which non-lawyers can participate in the management of firms. In other cases, regulators do not have the powers they need to regulate a more diverse range of business structures.

181. In March 2001, the OFT identified a number of rules of the legal profession that were potentially unduly restrictive, and that might have negative implications for consumers.[12] The OFT recommended that rules governing the legal professions should be fully subject to competition law and that unjustified restrictions on competition should be removed.

[12] OFT, 2001

182. Following the 2004 Clementi Review,[13] in 2005 the Government published a White Paper, *The Future of Legal Services: Putting Consumers First.*[14] It proposed ABS, which would allow different types of lawyers and non-lawyers to work together in an ABS firm or company, and/or the possibility of non-lawyer ownership and investment. It identified potential benefits for both consumers and legal services providers.

"Potential benefits for consumers:

- more choice: consumers will have greater flexibility in deciding from where to obtain legal and some non-legal services;
- reduced prices: consumers should be able to purchase some legal services more cheaply. This should arise where ABS firms realise savings through economies of scale and reduce transaction costs where different types of legal professionals are part of the same firm;
- better access to justice: ABS firms might find it easier to provide services in rural areas or to less mobile consumers;
- improved consumer service: consumers may benefit from a better service where ABS firms are able to access external finance and specialist non-legal expertise;
- greater convenience: ABS firms can provide one-stop-shopping for related services, for example car insurance and legal services for accident claims; and
- increased consumer confidence: higher consumer protection levels and an increase in the quality of legal services could flow from ABS firms which have a good reputation in providing non-legal services. These firms will have a strong incentive to keep that reputation when providing legal services.

"Potential benefits for legal service providers:

increased access to finance: at present, providers can face constraints on the amount of equity, mainly debt equity, they can raise. Allowing alternative business structures will facilitate expansion by firms (including into international markets) and investment in large-scale capital projects that increase efficiency;
better spread of risk: a firm could spread its risk more effectively among shareholders. This will lower the required rate of return on any investment, facilitate investment and could deliver lower prices;
increased flexibility: non-legal firms such as insurance companies, banks and estate agents will have the freedom to realise synergies with legal firms by forming ABS firms and offering integrated legal and associated services;
easier to hire and retain high-quality non-legal staff: ABS firms will be able to reward non-legal staff in the same way as lawyers; and
more choice for new legal professionals: ABS firms could contribute to greater diversity by offering those who are currently under-represented more opportunities to enter and remain within the profession."

[13] Clementi, 2004
[14] Department for Constitutional Affairs, 2005

Section 71: Carrying on activities by licensed bodies

183. This section introduces Part 5. *Section 71(2)* defines "licensed body" as a body holding a licence under Part 5.

Section 72: "Licensable body"

184. This section defines licensable bodies. They are bodies that have at least one manager who is not an authorised person (as defined in section 111) or at least one person who has an interest or an indirect interest in shares in the body who is not an authorised person. Section 207 defines a manager as: a member, in relation to a body corporate whose affairs are managed by its members; a director, in relation to a body corporate if its affairs are not managed by its members; a partner, if the body is a partnership; and a member of its governing body, if it is an unincorporated body other than a partnership.

185. By *section 72(3)*, a person holds an interest in a body if he owns shares in it or is entitled to exercise or control the exercise of voting rights in it. By section 72(6), "shares" means:

where the body has share capital, allotted shares as defined in the Companies Acts;
where it has capital but no share capital, the right to share in its capital; and
where it has no capital, an interest with the right to share in profits or the liability to contribute to losses, or giving rise to an obligation to contribute to the body's debts or expenses on winding up.

Section 73: Licensing authorities and relevant licensing authorities

186. This section provides that a licensing authority is either the Board or an approved regulator who is designated as a licensing authority under Part 1 of Schedule 10. Under *section 73(2)*, the Board is a licensing authority in relation to all reserved legal activities, but an approved regulator is only a licensing authority in relation to those reserved legal activities for which it has been designated under Schedule 10. By *section 73(3)* the Board may delegate its functions as licensing authority and must ensure that it appropriately separates its functions as licensing authority from its other functions.

Section 74: Designation of approved regulator as licensing authority

187. Part 1 of Schedule 10, introduced by this section, sets out the procedure to be followed when an approved regulator seeks designation as a licensing authority. It is similar to the procedure for a designation of a body as an approved regulator.

188. Paragraph 1 of the Schedule sets out certain requirements for applications for designation as a licensing authority.

189. Paragraph 11 obliges the Board to make rules governing the way it determines applications. Sub-paragraphs (2) and (3) of paragraph 11 sets out conditions that must be met (and must be reflected in the rules) before the Board can grant an application.

190. Paragraph 12 sets out the matters the Board must consider before deciding whether to grant the application in whole or (where it relates to more than one reserved legal activity) in respect of any of the activities in the application. The Board's decision notice must give reasons for any refusal and must be published.

191. Paragraph 13 provides that the deadline for deciding applications is 12 months from the day of the application. That period can be extended any number of times up to a maximum of 16 months, but only after consulting the OFT, the Consumer Panel and the Lord Chief Justice, and obtaining the Lord Chancellor's consent.

192. Paragraph 14 sets out the process by which the Board must make a recommendation to the Lord Chancellor to make an order designating the applicant as a licensing authority.

193. Paragraph 15 provides that when the Lord Chancellor receives a recommendation from the Board the Lord Chancellor may either make the recommended order or refuse to make it. If the applicant has also applied to be designated as an approved regulator, the Lord Chancellor must first make the appropriate order. If the Lord Chancellor makes a modified order, or declines to make an order, the reasons for that decision must be published. Paragraph 16 provides that the making of the order has the effect that the proposed licensing rules are treated as approved by the Board (but remain subject to the power of the Board to make directions under section 32).

Section 75: Automatic cancellation of designation as licensing authority

194. This section provides that if a licensing authority loses its status as an approved regulator, it automatically loses its status as a licensing authority.

Section 76: Cancellation of designation as licensing authority by order

195. This section sets out how the designation of a licensing authority may be cancelled in whole or in part. Cancellation is by the Lord Chancellor on the recommendation of the Board. The Board must recommend cancellation where the licensing authority requests it and adheres to the requirements under *section* 76(3). Under *section* 76(5) the Board may make a recommendation for cancellation where an act or omission of the licensing authority, or a series of such acts or omissions has had, or is likely to have, an adverse impact on the regulatory objectives, and in all the circumstances of the case it is appropriate to cancel the designation. In considering whether it is appropriate to cancel the designation, the Board must consider the impact of taking action on the other regulatory objectives. By *section* 76(6) the Board may not exercise this power unless it is satisfied that the use of any of the powers set out in sections 31 to 43 (performance targets, directions and public censure) would not adequately deal with the situation. *Section* 76(7) introduces Part 2 of Schedule 10, which makes provision about recommendations under section 76(5).

196. The Lord Chancellor may decide not to make the order recommended by the Board, but must give reasons and publish them.

197. Part 2 of Schedule 10 sets out the details of the procedure to be used when the Board is considering making a recommendation for cancellation under section 76(5). Paragraph 18 provides that the Board must give the licensing authority a warning notice, setting out its reasons for cancellation, which it must publish. The licensing authority may then make written representations (or oral representations, if authorised by the Board) within 28 days or a longer period specified by the Board. The Board must publish a report about those representations after having regard to the licensing authority's comments about the draft report.

198. Paragraphs 19 to 24 set out the process whereby the Board must consult the OFT, the Consumer Panel, the Lord Chief Justice and such other persons that the Board considers reasonable to consult.

199. Paragraph 25 requires the Board to provide to the licensing authority a copy of any advice from those persons, and to publish that advice together with any representations made by the licensing authority under paragraph 18. The licensing authority and any body licensed by that authority may then make written representations and, if authorised by the Board, oral representations. The Board may also allow others to make written or oral representations. The remainder of the paragraph sets out related procedures.

Section 77: Cancellation of designation: further provision

200. This section allows consequential provision to be made by the Lord Chancellor where the designation of a licensing authority is cancelled. Two types of order are possible. The first, under *section 77(2)*, enables legislation etc to be modified to take account of the cancellation. The second, under *section 77(3)*, allows arrangements to be made transferring licensed bodies from the regulation of the original licensing authority to another that consents to act as their licensing authority. Such arrangements must include provision for placing the transferred bodies under the "new" licensing authority's rules (*section 77(6)(a)*) and may include provisions for transferring licensing fees to the new authority (*section 77(6)(b)*). *Section 77(8)* provides that the Lord Chancellor may only make an order under this section on the recommendation of the Board, and only one that is materially the same as the order drafted by the Board.

Section 78: The Board's power to recommend orders made under section 77

201. This section provides for the process that must be followed by the Board if it wishes to make a recommendation that the Lord Chancellor exercise the powers conferred under section 77.

Section 79: Cancellation of designation: powers of entry etc

202. Where an approved regulator has its designation cancelled, this section provides for the Board to request assistance from the former licensing authority to enable regulation by the new licensing authority to continue. *Section 79(3) to 79(10)* make provision for the Board to obtain a warrant to enter and search the premises of the former licensing authority and to take possession of written or electronic records where necessary or desirable to enable regulation to continue. The Lord Chancellor must make regulations, either on the Board's recommendation or after consulting it, which specify further matters that the judge must take into account before issuing a warrant, which regulate the exercise of the warrant power and set out the circumstances in which records can be copied.

Section 80: Functions of appellate bodies

Section 81: Procedural requirements relating to recommendations under section 80

203. Section 80 allows the Lord Chancellor, on the Board's recommendation, to establish appellate bodies by order, or to modify the operation of the Solicitors Disciplinary Tribunal or the Discipline and Appeals Committee of the CLC, for the purposes of appeals under Part 5. The order may also make provision about fees and costs and may make modifications to any enactment. The order must be in a form that is not materially different from the draft attached to the recommendation by the Board under section 81.

204. Section 81 sets out procedural requirements about recommendations by the Board for an order under section 80.

Section 82: Licensing authority policy statement

205. Section 82 requires licensing authorities to issue and publish policy statements setting out how they will comply with the regulatory objectives when carrying out their functions under Part 5. These statements have to be approved by the Board, as do any amendments or replacement statements.

Section 83: Licensing rules

206. This section requires the Board, acting in its capacity as a licensing authority, to make suitable licensing rules (which mean suitable regulatory arrangements as defined in Schedule 12) within a period of 12 months from a decision of the Board under Schedule 12 that a licensable body is entitled to apply to it for a licence. Under Schedule 12, such a decision would be made because no other approved regulator has suitable regulatory arrangements in relation to the body in question, or in the case of certain non-commercial bodies (as listed in sub-paragraph (6) of paragraph 1 of Schedule 12), no other approved regulator is prepared to offer appropriate terms. Those rules must be made or modified by the Board acting as licensing authority, with the approval of the Board acting in its capacity as oversight regulator rather than licensing authority or approved regulator. *Section 83(3)* provides that licensing rules made by an approved regulator only have effect while that regulator is also a licensing authority. *Section 83(4)* defines licensing

rules. *Section 83(5)* details the provisions that must be contained in licensing rules, including conduct, discipline and practice rules; appropriate provision requiring the licensing authority to take account of the objective of improving access to justice of a proposed application for a licence; the regulatory conflict provisions of sections 52 and 54; and the complaint handling provisions of sections 112 and 145. *Section 83(7)* introduces Schedule 11, which makes further provision as to licensing rules. *Sections 83(8) and 83(9)* provide that the licensing rule requirements in section 83(5) and Schedule 11 are subject to sections 105 and 106, which make special provision in relation to trade unions and other special bodies.

207. Schedule 11 describes licensing rules in detail. It has four parts, dealing with licensing procedure, the structural requirements of licensed bodies, the practice requirements of those bodies, and their regulation. Decisions about individual licences are taken by licensing authorities without reference to the Board or the Lord Chancellor.

208. Part 1 of this Schedule outlines licensing procedures.

209. Section 84 (described below) sets out the basic conditions for the way licensing authorities must deal with applications for licences. Part 1 of the Schedule makes detailed provision about licensing decisions. Under paragraphs 1 to 6 licensing rules must include provision about how an application for a licence, or for the modification of a licence, should be made, and they may include provision as to the period for which a licence is to remain in force and the renewal of licences.

210. Paragraphs 7 and 8 make provision in similar terms to that described above in relation to applications under section 106, which deals with the power to modify the application of licensing rules to the special bodies detailed in section 106. In particular, licensing rules must make provision obliging a special body to notify the licensing authority where it becomes a different kind of special body or ceases to be a special body, within 30 days or a longer period provided for in the licensing rules.

211. Part 2 of the Schedule outlines the three basic structural requirements that must be covered in the licensing rules. Paragraphs 9 and 10 require all licensed bodies to have at least one manager who is an authorised person, who can be either an individual or an entity (which is not a licensed body); prohibit a licensed body having a manager who is disqualified (provision about disqualification can be found in section 99); permit licensing rules to be made about managers; and prohibit licensing rules from specifying that all the managers must be authorised persons.

212. Paragraphs 11 and 12 require licensing rules to provide that licensed bodies must also have a designated Head of Legal Practice (HoLP) who is approved by the licensing authority, is an authorised person and not disqualified. Under sub-paragraph (4) of paragraph 11, a HoLP may be approved only if the person is fit and proper to undertake the duties set out in section 91. Paragraph 12 requires provision in the rules about the procedures and criteria that the licensing authority will apply in determining whether a person is fit and proper, and in determining whether to withdraw its approval of the person as fit and proper. It also requires that licensing authorities make provision for review of these decisions. Paragraph 12 also allows the rules to suspend the requirement to have a HoLP for a specified period, so long as the licensed body complies with other requirements set out in the rules.

213. Paragraphs 13 and 14 make similar provision in relation to the requirement to have a designated Head of Finance & Administration ("HoFA") approved by the licensing authority.

214. Part 3 of the Schedule outlines practice requirements. Licensing rules must cover four basic practice requirements:

- under paragraph 15 a licensed body that is not a company or limited liability partnership with its registered office in England or Wales must have a practising address which is a place in England & Wales where the body carries out some or all of the reserved legal activities for which it is licensed;
- under paragraph 16 licensed activities may be carried on only by or under the supervision of entitled persons;
- under paragraph 18 disqualified persons may not work in licensed bodies as employees or officers; and
- under paragraph 20 clients' money must be accounted for.

215. Paragraph 17 requires licensing rules to require licensed bodies to have suitable arrangements in place to ensure that:

they, and their managers and employees, comply with the duties in section 176,
they, and such of their managers and employees as are authorised persons, maintain the professional principles set out in section 1; and
non-authorised persons subject to the duty in section 90 comply with it.

216. Paragraph 19 provides that for the purpose of giving effect to indemnity and compensation arrangements, licensing rules may make provision authorising or requiring funds to be maintained by the licensing authority, insurance to be taken out by the licensing authority, or insurance to be taken out by licensed bodies.

217. Under paragraph 21 of the Schedule, all licensed bodies must pay periodic licensing fees, although different fees can be set for different kinds of body.

218. Part 4 of the Schedule covers a number of areas of regulation of licensed bodies. Descriptions of the various paragraphs in this Part are included within the sections to which they relate.

Section 84: Application for licence

219. This section sets out the way licensing authorities must deal with applications for licences. Licensing authorities must determine applications that come from licensable bodies with the required fee and may not grant an application unless they are satisfied that the body will comply with licensing rules. Under *section 84(4)* licensing authorities must issue the licence as soon as reasonably practicable after the application has been granted and under *section 84(5)* the licence has effect from that date. Applications for licences may only be made to the Board (acting in its non- licensing authority capacity) under Schedule 12.

220. The Schedule deals with the limited circumstances in which licensable bodies can apply to the Board for a licence. That is when:

there is no competent licensing authority, and none that is potentially competent (sub-paragraph (3) of paragraph 1) – "competent" and "potentially competent" are defined in paragraphs 5 and 6 as an approved licensing authority that is designated or which the Board anticipates becoming designated in relation to the reserved legal activities that the body proposes to carry out;
no licensing authority or potential licensing authority has or plans to have suitable regulatory arrangements (sub-paragraph (4) of paragraph 1). Licensable bodies can apply to licensing authorities for determinations of this ground under paragraph 3, and paragraph 7 defines the factors to be taken into account in considering whether arrangements are suitable; or
if the body is of a kind listed in sub-paragraph (6) of paragraph 1 (not for profit bodies, community interest companies, trade unions and prescribed bodies), no licensing authority has terms that are appropriate to it (sub-paragraph (5) of paragraph 1).

221. Paragraph 2 then specifies that the Board must determine whether the licensable body is entitled to apply to it for a licence and give reasons for its decision. Different timescales for the determination apply to each of the grounds (sub-paragraph (2) of paragraph 2). The Board is obliged to make rules providing for a review of its decision, in particular for cases where the ground for its decision no longer applies (sub-paragraphs (4) and (5) of paragraph 2).

Section 85: Terms of licence

222. This section prescribes what terms licences must contain when they are granted. Every licence must specify the reserved legal activities that the licensed body is licensed to carry on, and any conditions attached to the licence (*section 85(1)*). Under *sections 85(4) and 85(5)* one condition is obligatory: that the licensed body or any employee, manager etc, must comply with obligations imposed on them by the licensing rules or in legislation. The licensing authority may impose such other conditions as it considers appropriate (*section 85(6)*), including conditions as to the non-reserved activities that a licensed body may carry out (*section 85(7)*). If the body is one for which an order has been made under section 106, *section 85(2)* requires the licence also to set out the terms of the order.

Section 86: Modification of licence

223. This section provides for modification of licences where an application is made in accordance with licensing rules or where licensing rules allow modifications to be made in other

circumstances (*section 86(1)*). Under *section 86(3)* modifications are made by notice in writing. Under *section 86(4)*, licensing authorities' powers are subject to the constraints as to conditions set out in section 85 and licensing rules about modification of licences.

Section 87: Registers of licensed bodies

224. This section sets out requirements for registers of licensed bodies. Each licensing authority must keep a register of the names and places of business of all the bodies that it licenses or has licensed (*section 87(1)*) and must make a note of any suspensions in that register (*section 87(2)*). The register must be available for inspection free of charge, during office hours (*section 87(3)*). The Board may make other rules about its own and licensing authorities' registers, in particular about other information that registers should contain (*sections 87(4) and 87(5)*).

Section 88: Evidence of status

225. Under this section a signed certificate of a licensing authority stating that a person does or does not, or did or did not, hold a licence granted by the licensing authority, is evidence of those facts unless proved otherwise.

Section 89: Ownership of licensed bodies

226. Schedule 13, introduced by this section, deals with the ownership of licensed bodies. Section 105 provides that this Schedule does not apply to trade unions.

227.Schedule 13 imposes restrictions on the holding of certain types of interests in licensed bodies (restricted interests) by non-authorised persons. Any non-authorised persons holding, or seeking to hold, restricted interests, must be approved by the licensing authority before the body can be licensed. Once the body is licensed any further acquisition or holding of restricted interests by non-authorised persons must also be approved.

228. The main type of restricted interest is a material interest (Schedule 13, paragraph 3), which arises when a person:

has an interest in at least 10% or more of the shares in it or in its parent company;

can exercise or control the exercise of 10% of the voting rights in (or, in some cases, has power to direct the policy of) it or its parent company; or

can exercise significant influence over the management of the company or its parent company by virtue of their shareholding or voting power in it.

229. If they wish, licensing authorities can make licensing rules specifying a lower proportion than 10% for defining material interest (sub-paragraph (2) of paragraph 3).

230. Licensing rules may provide for a second type of restricted interest, a "controlled interest". This is a shareholding in the licensed body or a parent undertaking of a percentage specified in licensing rules, or an entitlement to exercise or control the exercise of voting power in a licensed body or parent undertaking of a percentage specified in licensing rules. Licensing rules may only specify a percentage which exceeds the percentage which constitutes a material interest.

231. For the purposes of deciding whether a person has material interest or a controlled interest in a licensed body, account may be taken of interests held by a person's associates, who are defined in paragraph 5. The Lord Chancellor has power in paragraph 9 to change the definitions of "material interest" and "associate", on the Board's recommendation.

232. Paragraph 6 sets out the approval requirements. A non-authorised person's holding of a restricted interest will be approved if the licensing authority is satisfied that it would not compromise the regulatory objectives or compliance by the licensed body and such of its managers and employees who are authorised persons with the duties in section 176. The licensing authority must also be satisfied that the person is a fit and proper person to hold the interest. Licensing rules must include criteria and procedure for making this decision.

233. Paragraph 7 provides that if a person holds a restricted interest by virtue of holding a certain percentage of a body's shares or controlling a certain percentage of the voting power in a body, any restricted interest held by virtue of a lesser percentage of shares (where the approved interest is in the form of shares) or voting power (where the approved interest is in the form of voting power) is also treated as being approved by the licensing authority. For example, if the

material interest threshold is a 10% shareholding and the controlled interest threshold is a 20% shareholding, a person who is approved to hold a controlled interest will also be approved in relation to the material interest.

234. Part 2 covers the identification to licensing authorities of non-authorised persons, and the approval of those persons. At the initial licensing stage, a body seeking a licence must identify any person that it knows holds a restricted interest or expects to hold one when the licence is issued, (sub-paragraphs (1) and (2) of paragraph 10). This includes telling the licensing authority if the identities of such people change after the application has been made (sub-paragraph (2) of paragraph 10). Failing to do so is an offence, punishable on summary conviction by a fine up to level 5 on the standard scale.

235. Under paragraph 13, the applicant body must also notify the non-authorised persons whom it has identified to the licensing authority. Failure to do this is also an offence, punishable in the same way. The notification must explain the effect of paragraph 14, which enables the licensing authority to seek more information from non-authorised persons who have been identified. The deliberate provision of false or misleading information is an offence, punishable by a fine not exceeding the statutory maximum on summary conviction or by a fine and/or two years in prison on conviction on indictment.

236. If the licensing authority is satisfied that the non-authorised person meets the approval requirements in paragraph 6, and that the person has not been disqualified, it may grant the application for a licence. The licensing authority may also approve the holding of the interest subject to conditions (paragraphs 17 and 18), or it may object to the holding of the interest (paragraphs 19 and 20).

237. After a licence has been granted, the acquisition of interests by non-authorised persons is still regulated in the manner set out in part 3 of the Schedule. Under paragraph 21, if an investor intends to take steps to acquire an interest in a licensed body that would give the investor a restricted interest in it, the investor must notify both the licensed body and the licensing authority. Where the investor acquires an interest without taking steps to do so – for instance, by inheriting it – the investor must give the notifications within a time limit set by the Lord Chancellor on the Board's recommendation. Under paragraphs 22 and 23, failure to give notification is an offence, punishable on summary conviction by a fine of level 5 on the standard scale. Taking a proposed acquisition step without obtaining approval from a licensing authority is also an offence, punishable by a fine not exceeding the statutory maximum on summary conviction or by an unlimited fine and/or two years in prison on conviction on indictment (paragraph 24).

238. Again, the licensing authority may approve the holding of the interest, approve it subject to conditions, or object to it. The procedure and criteria for this are set out in paragraphs 25 to 32. Where the licensing authority approves a proposed interest (with or without conditions) it may specify a period within which the investor must acquire it. If it does not, the period is automatically one year from the date of the approval notice. If the investor does not acquire the interest by the deadline, the approval lapses (paragraph 30).

239. The licensing authority also has power to impose conditions on, or object to the holding of an interest after it has been acquired. The procedure and criteria for this are set out in paragraphs 33 to 37.

240. Conditions imposed under either paragraph 28 or paragraph 33 may be varied or waived on application by the investor, (sub-paragraph (1) of paragraph 35). In addition, the licensing authority may cancel a condition on its own initiative, (sub-paragraph (2) of paragraph 35).

241. Part 4 of the Schedule enables licensing rules to be made specifying an upper "ceiling" limit for the holders of shares in licensed bodies by a non-authorised person. If such a limit is imposed, no non-authorised person may exceed it, regardless of whether or not they meet the approval requirements at paragraph 6.

242. Part 5 of the Schedule deals with enforcement. The "divestiture" provisions enable the court, on application of a licensing authority, to order the sale of shares held by a person who holds an interest in a licensed body. This may be done in the following circumstances:

- where an investor has taken steps to obtain an interest without the licensing authority's approval – this can lead to divestiture even if the investor has not been charged with or convicted of the offence under paragraph 24;
- where an investor holds a restricted interest in breach of conditions imposed under paragraphs 17, 28 or 33; and

where an investor holds an interest to which the licensing authority has objected under paragraphs 31 or 36.

243. The court may also order the sale of shares where a non-authorised person's shareholding exceeds any ceiling imposed by licensing rules made under Part 4 of the Schedule.

244. Divestiture is limited by paragraph 41 to licensed bodies that are companies with shares. The number of shares the court may order to be sold is limited – essentially only as many as necessary to ensure that the person is no longer in breach of the requirements of the Schedule (sub-paragraphs (2) and (3) of paragraph 45). If the court orders shares to be sold, it may make whatever other orders it sees fit as to the sale or transfer of the shares (sub-paragraph (6) of paragraph 45). The proceeds of sale have to be paid into court for the benefit of whomever is beneficially interested in them – usually the investor – and any such person may apply for part or all of the proceeds. The cost of conducting the sale is first deducted from the proceeds (sub-paragraph (7) of paragraph 45).

245. Where the conditions for divestiture are satisfied, paragraph 44 allows the licensing authority to issue a restriction notice imposing certain restrictions on the shares. It is expected that a restriction notice will be issued when the licensing authority believes that it must act as a matter or urgency before an application for divestiture to the High Court. The restrictions which may be imposed are:

any transfer of the shares or agreement to transfer them is void (including transfer of the right to receive unissued shares),
the shares' voting rights cannot be exercised,
no further shares can be issued to the investor, or
the investor cannot be paid any sums due on the shares (dividends etc), unless the company goes into liquidation.

246. A restriction notice ceases to have effect after a High Court order (the court may make such an order on an application for sale of the shares); if no application has been made to the court for divestiture within a prescribed time limit on the expiry of that time limit, or when the licensed body ceases to be licensed.

247. The court may also remove any restrictions imposed under paragraph 45, set out in sub-paragraph (4) of paragraph 46.

248. Divestiture will not always be possible. Paragraph 46 provides an alternative mechanism for enforcement in a case where a person holds a restricted interest in breach of any conditions imposed on the holding of that interest. The licensing authority may apply to the High Court for an order enforcing the conditions.

249. Paragraphs 47 to 50 provide for the Board to be notified of decisions under this Schedule to object to a person holding an interest, or to impose conditions on their holding it. Paragraph 51 requires the Board to maintain lists of persons who have been subject to objections and conditions, which will be available to licensing authorities and, will enable them to make informed regulatory decisions.

Section 90: Duties of non-authorised persons

250. Section 90 imposes a duty on non-authorised persons who are employees or managers of, or have certain interests in, a licensed body, not to do anything that would cause or substantially contribute to a breach by the licensed body or an authorised person within it of the duties in section 176. Section 176 requires persons regulated by an approved regulator to comply with the regulatory arrangements of that regulator.

Section 91: Duties of Head of Legal Practice

Section 92: Duties of Head of Finance and Administration

251. Sections 91 and 92 describe the duties of the HoLP and HoFA respectively, further provision about these roles is made in Schedule 11. The HoLP must take all reasonable steps to ensure compliance with the terms of the licensed body's licence, and that the licensed body and employees or managers of the body who are subject to the duties under section 176 comply with

them, and to ensure that non-authorised persons comply with the duty under section 90. The HoLP must report any failures to do so to the licensing authority as soon as reasonably practicable.

252. The HoFA's duty under section 92 is to ensure that the licensed body complies with the accounts rules in the licensing rules; they must, like the HoLP, report failures to do as soon as practicable. *Section 91(2)* therefore excludes accounts rules from the HoLP's responsibilities.

Section 93: Information

Section 94: Enforcement of notices under section 93

253. These sections deal with the information that a licensing authority may require from a licensed body and others to determine whether the terms of its licence are being complied with. The licensing authority may require information or documents (*section 93(1)*) from the body itself and any manager, officer or employee, and from any non-authorised person who holds a material interest in the body, *section 93(2)*. Requests for information are made by notice, which can specify the form in which the information is to be provided and set a deadline for doing so, and also inform the provider of the information to whom it must be provided, as set out in *section 93(3)*.

254. The licensing authority can require those persons, or a representative, to give an explanation of that material (*section 93(4)*). It may pay reasonable expenses to cover the cost of providing information and of attending to provide an explanation (*section 93(5)*). It may also copy or take extracts from any documents it receives (*section 93(6)*).

255. If persons asked for information under section 93 cannot provide it, they must give the licensing authority an explanation (*section 94(1)*). If a person fails to comply with a request, the licensing authority may apply to the High Court for an order compelling that person to comply (*section 94(2)*).

Section 95: Financial penalties

256. This section allows licensing authorities to impose financial penalties for breaches of licences, up to a maximum set by the Board in rules made with the Lord Chancellor's consent. Penalties are payable to the licensing authority. Under paragraph 22 of Schedule 11, licensing rules must make provision as to the acts and omissions in respect of which the licensing authority may impose a penalty, and the criteria and procedure to be applied.

Section 96: Appeals against financial penalties

257. Licensed bodies may appeal to the relevant appellate body (defined in section 111) against financial penalties. Appeals have to be made within a deadline set by the Board in rules. There are limited grounds for appeal, (*section 96(2)*):

that the imposition of the penalty was unreasonable in all the circumstances,
that the amount of the penalty was unreasonable, and
that the payment timetable was unreasonable.

258. The appellate body can quash the penalty, reduce it, or change the payment timetable (*section 96(3)*). If it reduces the penalty or changes the timetable, it may add interest to the whole of the penalty or part of it (*sections 96(4) and 96(5)*). Further appeals to the High Court on a point of law are possible under *section 96(6)*, and the High Court can then make any order it thinks fit (*section 96(7)*). *Section 96(8)* prevents penalties being challenged by any other means.

Section 97: Recovery of financial penalties

259. This section describes the process for recovering financial penalties that have not been paid on time. In general, if a payment is late, and so long as no appeal is pending, it is recoverable as a civil debt under *section 97(2)*. Interest is added automatically under *section 97(1)* and can be recovered alongside the basic penalty. All recovered penalties have to be paid into the Consolidated Fund (*section 97(3)*).

Section 98: Referral of employees etc to appropriate regulator

260. This section allows licensing authorities to refer the conduct of licensed bodies' employees, managers, HoLPs and HOFAs to appropriate regulators – any relevant approved regulators for authorised persons, and any other regulator for persons who are not. The licensing authority may also refer such conduct matters to the Board.

Section 99: Disqualification

261. This section provides that people can be disqualified from being employees or managers of licensed bodies, or from holding the HoLP or HoFA posts, if they breach the duties that the Act places on them or cause or contribute to breaches of the body's licence.

262. Under paragraph 23 of Schedule 11, licensing authorities must have rules about the criteria and procedure to be used when considering whether to disqualify someone under this section. This includes rules for reviewing disqualifications and how to determine whether they should cease to have effect.

Section 100: Lists of disqualified persons

263. This section requires the Board to keep lists of persons who are disqualified under section 99 and whose disqualification remains in force. *Section 100*(3) provides that a disqualification will no longer be in force if the appropriate licensing authority determines that it should not be, whether after a review or otherwise. If a person was disqualified by a regulator that is no longer a licensing authority, a successor authority can decide that the disqualification is no longer in force (*section 100*(4)). Under *section 100*(5), the successor authority is either the licensing authority that currently licenses the body where the disqualified person was working, or (if that is impossible) another authority designated for the purpose by the Board on the disqualified person's application. *Section 100*(6) requires the Board to publish the lists.

Section 101: Suspension and revocation of licence

264. This section provides that a licensing authority can suspend or revoke any licensed body's licence. Paragraph 24 of Schedule 11 requires licensing rules to empower the licensing authority to do this in the following circumstances:

paragraph 24, sub-paragraph (3): if a body is no longer a licensable body;
paragraph 24, sub-paragraph (4): where the licensed body fails to comply with licensing rules, under paragraph 16 of Schedule 11 (reserved legal activities must be carried on through an entitled person);
paragraph 24, sub-paragraph (5): where non-authorised persons hold interest in licensed bodies in breach of Schedule 13,
paragraph 24, sub-paragraph (6): where a non-authorised person breaches the duties in section 90;
paragraph 24, sub-paragraph (7): where an employee or manager who is an authorised person fails to comply with the duties under section 176;
paragraph 24, sub-paragraph (8): where a licensed body has a manager or employee has been disqualified from acting as a manager or employee, on specified grounds; and
paragraph 24, sub-paragraph (9): where a licensed body is unable to comply with the licensing rules about the HoLP or HoFA.

265. A licensing authority must give at least 28 days notice of its intention to suspend or revoke a licence, in accordance with sub-paragraphs (10) and (11) of paragraph 24.

266. Paragraph 25 allows licensing authorities to make rules about other circumstances in which it may suspend or revoke a licence.

267. Under paragraph 26 licensing rules must also include provisions about the criteria and procedure to be used when deciding on any suspension or revocation under paragraphs 24 or 25, and must provide for a review of that decision.

Section 102: Intervention

268. This section introduces Schedule 14 which makes provision about the circumstances in which a licensing authority may intervene in the practice of a licensed body, and the powers exercisable upon intervention. The intervention grounds and powers are based on those available

to the Law Society and the Council for Licensed Conveyancers (CLC) under the Solicitors Act 1974 and Administration of Justice Act 1985 as amended by Schedules 16 and 17 of this Act.

269. Paragraph 1 of the Schedule provides that a licensing authority may intervene in a licensed body as set out in the Schedule where a licence granted to a body has expired or where one or more of the conditions set out at sub-paragraph (2) of paragraph 1 are satisfied.

270. Under sub-paragraphs (5) and (6) of paragraph 1, the powers in the Schedule are exercisable in relation to a body whose licence has been suspended or revoked, or whose license has expired or ceased to have effect.

271. Paragraph 2 provides that a licensing authority can apply to the High Court for an order to prohibit a person who is holding money on behalf of a licensed body from making any payment of that money, unless they have the leave of the High Court to do so.

272.Under paragraph 3, certain sums of money held by or on behalf of the licensed body, and the right to recover or receive them, can be vested in the licensing authority for people who are beneficially entitled to them. The sums of money are then held on trust by the licensing authority for persons that are beneficially entitled to them, and for use in exercising its intervention powers. Sub-paragraphs (5) to (9) of paragraph 3 set out procedure relating to such vesting, and procedure by which the licensing authority must give the licensed body, and anyone else who has money that is subject to the decision, a copy of the decision and a notice prohibiting any payments out of the money. Sub-paragraph (6) of paragraph 3 allows the body and anyone else who receives the notice to apply to the High Court to contest the licensing authority's decision. If the licensed body or other person breaches the notice, it commits an offence and is liable, on summary conviction, to a fine not exceeding level 3 on the standard scale.

273. Under paragraph 4, a licensing authority may decide that the right to recover debts of the licensed body should vest in it.

274. Paragraph 5 requires the licensing authority to put any money that it receives by virtue of these vesting powers into a special account in either its name or the name of a nominated person. The money is held on trust for persons beneficially entitled, and for use in exercising the intervention powers. Paragraph 6 enables the licensing authority to make rules governing the treatment of such money, particularly where, despite reasonable steps by the licensing authority, beneficiaries cannot be traced.

275. Paragraph 7 allows a licensing authority to apply to the High Court for an order requiring a person to give the licensing authority information about any money held by that person on behalf of a licensed body, and the accounts in which it is held. Licensing authorities may also require information that is relevant for tracing purposes.

276. A licensing authority may also give notice to a licensed body requiring it to produce all the documents in its possession or under its control relating to its activities as a licensed body, or to certain trusts. Paragraph 8 sets out what the notice may require. Sub-paragraph (4) of paragraph 8 makes it an offence to refuse, neglect or otherwise fail to comply with the notice. Under sub-paragraph (6) of paragraph 8, a person found guilty is liable, on summary conviction, to a fine not exceeding level 3 on the standard scale. However, it is not an offence if the licensing authority has made an application to the High Court for the production or delivery of the documents. Paragraph 9 sets out the procedure to be followed by the High Court in considering and implementing an order. Paragraph 10 sets out the procedure that a licensing authority must follow if it takes possession of documents under notice or order, as detailed in paragraph 8 and 9.

277. Under paragraph 11, a licensing authority may apply to the High Court for a Communications Redirection Order for a period not exceeding 18 months, which causes mail, telephone and electronic communications to be directed to the licensing authority, or to a person appointed by the licensing authority, who may take possession or receipt of the communications. Sub-paragraph (8) of paragraph 11 allows the licensing authority to apply to the High Court to take steps in relation to a licensed body's website, for the purpose of protecting the public interest and/or the interests of any current, former or potential clients of the body. Sub-paragraph (10) of paragraph 11 prevents licensing authorities from applying for these powers where they have intervened on the grounds of undue delay.

278. Paragraph 12 allows a licensing authority in possession of documents acquired through notices, orders, or communications redirection (paragraphs 8, 9 or 11) to apply to the High Court for an order to dispose of, or destroy, the documents. The High Court may make any order it

thinks fit. Under paragraph 13 a licensing authority may take copies of, or extracts from, documents acquired through notices, orders or communications redirection.

279. Where a licensed body, or one of its managers or employees, is the trustee of any trust, paragraph 14 allows the licensing authority to apply to the High Court to order the appointment of a new trustee in substitution for that person.

280. Paragraph 15 allows the powers conferred by this Schedule in relation to sums of money and documents to be exercised despite any lien on them or right to their possession. Paragraph 16 allows the licensing authority to do all things that are reasonably necessary to facilitate the exercise of its powers under this Schedule.

281. Paragraphs 17 and 18 set out how the licensing authority may recover its intervention costs from the licensed body. Under paragraph 18, the licensing authority can apply to the High Court to recover costs from certain persons where the Court is satisfied that the conduct that led to the intervention was carried on with the consent or connivance of, or was attributable to any neglect on the part of, those persons.

Section 103: Regulatory conflict and the Board as licensing authority

282. This section provides that the rules about regulatory conflict in sections 52, 54 and 68 apply to the Board in its capacity as a licensing authority.

Section 104: Prevention of regulatory conflict: accounts rules

283. This section ensures that a licensing authority's accounts rules (made under Schedule 11) apply to licensed bodies that are carrying on business through solicitors or licensed conveyancers. It does this by replacing the rules under the Solicitors Act 1974 or the Administration of Justice Act 1985 that would otherwise apply.

Section 105: Trade union exemptions

Section 106: Power to modify application of licensing rules etc to special bodies

Section 107: Modifications under section 106: supplementary

Section 108: "Low risk body"

284. These sections provide that certain types of body are eligible to apply for certain statutory requirements and/or licensing rules to be waived or otherwise modified in relation to them. Modifications are given effect by orders made by licensing authorities. The bodies in question are:

- trade unions – from which section 105 removes the HoLP and HoFA requirements and the ownership provisions in Schedule 13;
- not for profit bodies, defined in section 207 by reference to their charitable or public purpose and prohibitions on distributing income or assets to members;
- community interest companies;
- low-risk bodies – bodies in which levels of non-authorised control falls under a *de minimis* threshold, defined in section 108 as bodies where fewer than 10% of the managers are non-authorised persons, and the proportion of shares and voting rights held by non-authorised persons in less than 10%; and
- other bodies of types set out in an order made by the Lord Chancellor on the Board's recommendation.

285. In considering whether modifications are appropriate, the licensing authority must consider the legal activities the body aims to carry on, the people to whom it plans to offer services, any non-authorised persons who part-own or manage the body, and any other factors set out in the authority's licensing rules, as laid out in section 106(5). Some provisions cannot be modified at all; others cannot be waived but may otherwise be modified. Otherwise, licensing authorities have discretion to modify requirements in licensing rules and the application of Schedule 13 (*section 106(3)*), and can make whatever modifications are appropriate, whether or not they were what the body asked for (*section 106(4)*). Section 107 then sets out the circumstances in which a licensing authority can change modifications. Where the licensed body is no longer one to which

section 106 applies, the licensing authority must revoke the modification order. Otherwise, it may revoke or modify an order if the licensed body requests it or on its own motion.

Section 109: Foreign bodies

286. This section allows the Lord Chancellor to adapt provisions in this Part of the Act in their application to bodies formed under law outside of England and Wales. A company formed under the law of a foreign country might, for example, have different ownership structures for which the Part 5 provisions need to be adapted.

Section 110: Reporting requirements relating to Part 5

287. Section 110 obliges the Board to include in its annual report (section 6) an assessment of how the activities of licensing authorities and licensed bodies have affected the regulatory objectives. The requirement is not imposed from the first annual report but instead takes effect in the first financial year in which an ABS licence is issued.

Section 111: Interpretation of Part 5

288. This section defines some provisions for the purposes of Part 5.

PART 6: LEGAL COMPLAINTS

289. This Part of the Act establishes an independent Office for Legal Complaints (OLC), which administers an ombudsman scheme that is empowered to deal with all complaints about lawyers and where appropriate, provide redress to complainants of up to £30,000. The ombudsman scheme operates by reference to rules devised by the OLC and approved by the LSB – "scheme rules". Prior to commencement of the Act, approved regulators had the ability to provide redress to complainants. The Act removes this ability and confers it on ombudsmen. The ombudsman scheme is expressly prohibited from taking any disciplinary action against a lawyer, the power to do so remains solely with the approved regulators.

290. In this Part, provision is made for the appointment process and necessary qualifications of the members and staff of the OLC, and the Chief Ombudsman and assistant ombudsmen responsible for making determinations under the ombudsman scheme. Provision is also made for the accountability of the OLC through the Board, the framework of rules for the OLC's operating procedures and the changes to the regulatory arrangements of approved regulators necessary in consequence.

291. The OLC's membership must bring together a wide range of expertise and backgrounds. The OLC has a chairman and between six and eight members. The OLC is chaired by a lay person and the majority of its members are also lay persons. The OLC is responsible for administering the ombudsman scheme and it sets policy and rules in relation to complaints handling to ensure that best practice is promoted.

292. The OLC is accountable to the Board in respect of its targets and funding. OLC members are appointed by the Board (in the case of the chairman, with the Lord Chancellor's consent and, in the case of other members, after consultation with the chairman). In order to establish the ombudsman scheme the OLC must draw up draft scheme rules to be approved by the Board. The OLC itself appoints the Chief Ombudsman, and, with the consent of the Chief Ombudsman, may also appoint assistant ombudsmen as necessary.

Complaints Handling – the previous position

293. Prior to commencement of the Act, each of the approved regulators maintained its own complaints handling and disciplinary arrangements. A complainant who was dissatisfied with the way in which a complaint had been handled could refer the complaint to the Legal Services Ombudsman (LSO), who could ask an approved regulator to reconsider a complaint.

294. The following bodies were subject to the jurisdiction of the LSO:

the Law Society (also subject to the jurisdiction of Legal Services Complaints Commissioner),
the Bar Council,
the Council for Licensed Conveyancers,
the Institute of Legal Executives,
the Institute of Trade Mark Attorneys, and

the Chartered Institute of Patent Attorneys.

295. Under the previous complaints system, anyone who wished to complain about a person regulated by any of the organisations listed above would need to establish and make contact with the appropriate regulatory body. In the event that a complainant was not satisfied with the way in which a complaint had been handled by the appropriate regulatory body they could refer their complaint to the LSO. The LSO investigated the way in which the complaint was handled and the response from the professional body. If the LSO believed that a complaint had not been investigated properly, they could recommend that the professional body looked at the matter again. The LSO also had the power to re-investigate a complaint – in 2006 the LSO widened an investigation to look at the original complaint in less than 1% of cases.[15]

[15] Legal Services Ombudsman, 2005

296. Sir David Clementi's *Review of the Regulatory Framework for Legal Services in England and Wales*, published in 2004,[16] observed that there were a number of issues which arise from the manner in which complaints were dealt with under those previous arrangements:

the record of complaints handling by the approved bodies – substantial delays and questionable quality in terms of outcome,

the low level of consumer confidence in the independence of the system,

the inconsistency and lack of clarity for redress arrangements for consumers in respect of regulatory bodies with overlapping activities, and

the overlaps in the oversight regime.

[16] Clementi, 2004

297. Sir David concluded: "There is a considerable concern about how complaints are dealt with. The concern arises at a number of levels: at an operating level there is an issue about the efficiency with which the systems are run; at an oversight level there is a concern about the overlapping powers of the oversight bodies; and at a level of principle, there is an issue about whether systems for complaints against lawyers, run by lawyers themselves, can achieve consumer confidence." [17]

[17] Clementi, 2004

298. The Government's 2005 White Paper, *The Future of Legal Services: Putting Consumers First* [18] proposed the creation of an independent Office for Legal Complaints (OLC), which would be comprised of a management Board and a single complaints handling body that would provide redress for consumers, both of which would enhance consumer confidence in the complaints process.

[18] Department for Constitutional Affairs, 2005

Complaints Handling – the new system

299. The OLC and ombudsman scheme have clearly defined powers. The ombudsman scheme can deal with consumer complaints about any services provided by authorised persons – that is persons (including bodies) regulated (in relation to a reserved legal activity) by approved regulators. Ombudsman and/or OLC staff investigate complaints, and must refer any indication or allegation of misconduct to the relevant approved regulator (which retains power to take disciplinary action). The ombudsmen may monitor the decisions that are made in respect of the alleged misconduct, but are not able to take any disciplinary action themselves. If necessary, an ombudsman may report any concerns to the Board for its consideration.

300. All authorised persons are required to maintain in-house complaints handling arrangements. These are the first port of call for a consumer, and the ombudsman scheme does not consider complaints that have not been considered in-house in the first instance, except in very limited circumstances as may be set out in scheme rules. If the complaint is not resolved satisfactorily in-house, the consumer is able to bring complaints to the ombudsman scheme free of charge.

301. The handling of complaints is the responsibility of the ombudsmen (headed by the Chief Ombudsman), although the Act enables certain functions, for example, investigations, to be delegated to members of staff who are not ombudsmen. However, the determination of

complaints cannot be delegated. The OLC is responsible for making scheme rules by which the complaints handling scheme operates, but the Act generally envisages that, in the first instance, a complaint will be allocated to a case worker who will investigate and attempt to mediate the complaint.

302. The Chief Ombudsman and assistant ombudsmen become involved where mediation by a caseworker has not been successful, in which case, an ombudsman is responsible for making a final determination which, if accepted by the complainant, is final and becomes binding on all parties to the complaint.

303.When determining a complaint, the ombudsman may direct the respondent to do one or more of the following:

apologise to the complainant;
forego all or part of the respondent's fee;
pay the complainant a determined amount to compensate for any loss, inconvenience or distress;
correct or redo any work responsible for any error, omission or deficiency at their own expense (with no charge to the complainant); or
at their own expense, take such other action as is specified in the direction and in the interest of the complainant.

304. The "total value" of the orders together cannot exceed more than £30,000 (not including any amount by way of repayment of fees, or any interest, the rates for which will be set out in scheme rules).

305. The costs of the OLC and the ombudsman scheme are recouped from the legal professions by a combination of a general levy on approved regulators, and case fees payable in circumstances specified in scheme rules by individual respondents to complaints.

306. The detail of the way in which complaints will be dealt with under the ombudsman scheme is set out in scheme rules (the power to make those rules is set out at section 133).

Section 112: Complaints procedures of authorised persons

307. This section provides that each approved regulator must require each authorised person subject to its regulation to maintain in-house complaints procedures, and must make provision for the enforcement of this requirement. The provisions made by the approved regulator must satisfy any requirements specified by the Board.

Section 113: Overview of the scheme

308. *Section 113(1)* describes the purpose of the ombudsman scheme which is to be established; namely the resolution of complaints which relate to an act or omission of a person in carrying out an activity and which are within the jurisdiction of the scheme (as defined by section 125).

309. *Section 113(2) to 113(4)* define the boundary between the ombudsman scheme and the regulatory arrangements of an approved regulator or the Board (in its capacity as a licensing authority). Awarding redress to a complainant is reserved to the ombudsman scheme (section 157), and the taking of disciplinary action is reserved to the approved regulators (or the Board when acting in that capacity).

Section 114: The Office for Legal Complaints

310. This section provides for the establishment of the OLC.

311. Schedule 15 makes provision for such structural matters as the membership of the OLC, the terms of appointment and tenure of members, staffing, committees, the delegation of functions, the OLC's status, budget and accounting requirements, and the initial location of its principal office.

312. Sub-paragraph (1) of paragraph 1 of the Schedule provides for the OLC to consist of a chairman appointed by the Board with the approval of the Lord Chancellor, and between six and eight other persons appointed by the Board following consultation with the chairman.

313. Paragraph 2 provides for the OLC to have a lay chairman and a lay majority, a lay person being defined as someone who has never been an authorised person. An "authorised person" for

this purpose includes, by virtue of section 161, a person authorised by the claims management regulator under Part 2 of the Compensation Act 2006 to provide regulated claims management services. Under paragraph 3, an ombudsman may be a member (but not chairman) of the OLC, but ombudsmen must not make up the majority of the Board. In appointing members of the OLC, the Board must have regard to the desirability of securing that the OLC includes members who (between them) have experience in or knowledge of a range of the matters. Paragraph 4 lists these.

314. Terms of appointment for OLC members are set out in paragraphs 5 to 9, and are similar to those for members of the Board. Members must be appointed for a fixed period, which must not exceed five years. A person can be re-appointed once only. A lay member of the OLC who becomes an authorised person will for that reason cease to be a member of the OLC. The chairman may be removed from office by the Board, with the approval of the Lord Chancellor. The Board may also remove other OLC members, but only after consultation with the chairman. Sub-paragraph (2) of paragraph 8 limits the circumstances in which the Board can remove OLC members, essentially to those indicating unfitness or inability to discharge the functions of office.

315. Paragraphs 10 to 12 set out the terms of remuneration of members. The Board is able, if it is considered necessary, to pay pensions, allowances or gratuities to the chairman and other ordinary members of the Board. The Board may also pay compensation to the chairman or other members in certain circumstances.

316. Paragraphs 13 to 17 enable the OLC to appoint staff to assist in the performance of its functions, and makes provision for their terms and conditions.

317. Paragraph 18 allows the OLC to make arrangements with those it considers appropriate to provide assistance to it or to the ombudsman. Arrangements can be made with approved regulators and include arrangements for assistance to be provided to an ombudsman in relation to the investigation and consideration of a complaint. In making such arrangements the OLC may pay those persons providing assistance.

318. Paragraphs 19 to 21 allow the OLC to establish committees and sub-committees to carry out any of its functions, and provide that a vacancy in any office or a defect in the appointment, or disqualification, of the chairman or any member is not to affect the validity of any act of the OLC.

319. Under paragraph 22 the OLC may delegate specified functions to any member of the OLC, any staff member of the OLC or any committee or sub-committee. However, the OLC will retain accountability for the exercise of its statutory functions.

320. Paragraph 23 sets out the arrangements for the OLC's budget, which must be approved in advance by the Board. Paragraph 25 confers restricted borrowing powers on the OLC with the result that it can borrow money only with the consent of the Board or in accordance with general authorisation given by the Board. The Board can give the OLC consent, or a general authorisation, only with the consent of the Lord Chancellor.

321. By virtue of paragraph 24, the OLC must not acquire or dispose of an interest in land without the consent of the Lord Chancellor. Paragraph 24 applies for five years beginning with the day on which the first interim Chief Executive of the OLC is appointed under paragraph 10 of Schedule 22, or the first member of the OLC is appointed, whichever is first.

322. Paragraph 26 sets out the requirements for the OLC's accounts. The OLC must keep proper accounts and proper records, and prepare an annual financial statement of accounts, with oversight by the Comptroller and Auditor General and ultimately Parliament.

323. Paragraph 27 sets out the OLC's status. As an independent body it is not to be regarded as having the same status as the Crown. The staff appointed under paragraph 13 are not to be regarded as servants or agents of the Crown or as enjoying the same status.

324. Paragraphs 31 to 33 make provision for amendments to the House of Commons Disqualification Act 1975, the Northern Ireland Assembly Disqualification Act 1975, the Freedom of Information Act 2000 and the Public Records Act 1958. These are standard provisions which apply to many public bodies.

325. Paragraph 34 exempts the OLC, any member of the OLC, any ombudsman and any member of the OLC's staff from being liable for damages for anything done in the exercise of their functions. This exemption does not apply to anything done in bad faith or prevent an award of damages in respect of act which is unlawful as a result of section 6(1) of the Human Rights Act 1998.

Section 116: General obligations

326. The OLC, like the Board and the approved regulators, has a duty to act compatibly with the regulatory objectives in section 1, and to act in a way which it considers most appropriate to meet those objectives. It also has to have regard to the principles of best practice in relation to the administration of ombudsman schemes.

Section 117: Corporate governance

327. This section requires the OLC to have regard to generally accepted principles of good corporate governance in managing its affairs.

Section 118: Annual report

328. This section places a duty on the OLC to produce an annual report to be sent to the Board, reporting the extent to which, in the OLC's opinion, it has met the regulatory objectives. The report must include a copy of the annual report prepared by the Chief Ombudsman under section 123. This report will be laid before Parliament by the Lord Chancellor.

Section 119: Supplementary powers

329. This section makes standard provision empowering the OLC to do anything necessary for carrying out its functions.

Section 120: Reporting to the Board

330. This section empowers the Board to require a report from the OLC, separately from the annual report. This enables the Board to, for example, monitor the OLC's performance or to seek its views on a particular issue. The Board has a duty to publish any report made by the OLC under this section.

Section 121: Performance targets and monitoring

331. This section empowers the Board to set performance targets for the OLC in relation to any of its functions, or to direct it to set its own targets relating to its functions. *Sections 121(3) and 121(4)* state that any targets must be published. *Section 121(5)* allows the Board to monitor the extent to which the OLC has met these targets.

Section 122: Appointment of Chief Ombudsman and assistant ombudsmen

332. This section sets out the appointment process whereby the OLC must appoint a person (who must be a lay person, and who will cease to hold office if that person ceases to be a lay person) to act as Chief Ombudsman. The OLC may also appoint assistant ombudsmen with the consent of the Chief Ombudsman. Any person appointed must (by virtue of *section 122(4)*) have appropriate qualifications and experience. Although assistant ombudsmen, unlike the Chief Ombudsman, are not required to be lay persons, section 122(3) specifies that assistant ombudsmen must not carry out any reserved legal activity for reward during their period of appointment and *section 122(7)* requires the assistant ombudsman's terms and conditions to set out what consequences may ensue on breach of this condition. *Section 122(8)* makes provision for the terms and conditions of any ombudsman's appointment to be such as will ensure their independence, and *section 122(9)* (related to paragraph 27 of Schedule 15) makes it clear that an ombudsman is not a Crown servant.

Section 123: Annual report of Chief Ombudsman

333. Section 123 requires the Chief Ombudsman to prepare a report each financial year on the discharge of the functions of the ombudsmen. The report is to comply with any requirements specified by the OLC (which the OLC must publish), and is to be included in the annual report which the OLC is required to produce by virtue of section 118.

Section 124: Additional reports of Chief Ombudsman

334. Section 124 enables the OLC to require the Chief Ombudsman to prepare a report in respect of any other specified matter relating to the functions of the ombudsmen, as the OLC considers necessary.

Section 125: Jurisdiction of the ombudsman scheme

335. This section broadly defines what types of person are eligible to bring complaints to the OLC and who may be the subject of a complaint. A complaint will fall within the jurisdiction of the ombudsman scheme if:

- it is not excluded under sections 126 or 127 (because the respondent's "in-house" complaints procedures have not been used, or the complaint is otherwise excluded by provision made in the scheme rules);
- if the respondent falls within section 128 (i.e. the respondent was an authorised person at the relevant time); and
- the complainant falls within section 128 and wishes to have the complaint dealt with under the scheme.

336. *Section 125(3)* prevents an authorised or other person from restricting in any contract or notice the right of a person to bring a complaint.

Section 126: Complaints excluded because respondent's complaints procedures not used

337. *Section 126(1)* provides that a complaint does not fall within the jurisdiction of the ombudsman scheme unless the complainant has first used the respondent's in-house complaints procedure (defined in *section 126(2)*). *Section 126(3)* allows for the scheme rules to disapply section 126(1) in certain circumstances.

Section 127: Complaints excluded by scheme rules

338. *Section 127(1)* provides that the scheme rules may exclude certain described complaints from the jurisdiction of the scheme. *Section 127(2)* states that complaints cannot be excluded on the ground that they relate to any matter which could be dealt with under an authorised body's disciplinary arrangements.

Section 128: Parties

339. This section sets out further conditions as to the parties to a complaint to be handled by the ombudsman scheme. *Section 128(1)* defines the respondent as an authorised person in relation to a reserved legal activity; but it does not matter if the matter being complained about relates to a reserved legal activity or not. *Section 128(2) to 128(4)* set out the conditions for a complainant to be eligible. The first condition (section 128(3)) is that the complainant is not excluded (see *section 128(5)*) and is either:

- an individual, or
- a person (other than an individual) described in an order made by the Lord Chancellor, pursuant to a recommendation under section 130.

340. In addition to this, a complainant must also show that (section 128(4)):

- the respondent provided the services being complained about to the complainant directly;
- the respondent provided the services being complained about to an authorised person who procured them on the complainant's behalf (for example, where a solicitor instructs counsel);
- the respondent provided the services being complained about in their capacity as a personal representative or trustee and the complainant is the beneficiary of the property or trust;
- the respondent provided the services being complained about to a person acting on behalf of the complainant as their personal representative or trustee and the complainant is the beneficiary of the property or trust; or
- the complainant meets such other conditions as set out in an order made by the Lord Chancellor pursuant to a recommendation under section 130.

341. Under section 128(5), a complainant is excluded from the ombudsman scheme if:

the complainant is an authorised person in relation to a reserved legal activity, and procured the services to which the complaint relates on behalf of another person, (so that, for example, a solicitor who instructs counsel on behalf of a client may not complain about counsel),
the complainant is a public body (defined in section 128(7)), or
the complainant falls within an order made by the Lord Chancellor pursuant to a recommendation made under section 130.

Section 129: Pre-commencement acts and omissions

342. This section makes transitional provision to cover cases where the act or omission complained of took place before commencement of the ombudsman scheme, so that the respondent will not have been an authorised person within the terms of the Act. Its effect is that the complaint will be within the jurisdiction of the scheme as long as the respondent was at the time a person who, after commencement, comes within the definition of "authorised person".

Section 130: Orders under section 128

343. The Lord Chancellor is empowered to make an order under section 128(3)(b), (4)(d) or (5)(c) only on the recommendation of an interested body. The effect of these orders is for new categories of complainants or complaints to be included in or excluded from the scope of the ombudsman scheme's jurisdiction. For these purposes the "interested bodies" are the OLC, the Board and the Consumer Panel. The Lord Chancellor may require those bodies to consider making a recommendation under this section. If the Lord Chancellor declines to accept a recommendation, the Lord Chancellor must publish reasons for doing so.

Section 131: Acts and omissions by employees etc

344. This section establishes vicarious responsibility in respect of matters which are the subject of complaints. Any act or omission by an employee which is in the course of their employment will, for the purposes of the ombudsmen scheme, be treated as an act or omission on the part of the employer as well as the employee. Similarly, an act or omission by a partner in a partnership, in the course of carrying on the partnership's normal business in the usual way, will be treated as an act or omission of the partnership, unless the partner had no authority to act for the partnership and this was known to the person seeking to rely on the partnership's liability.

Section 132: Continuity of complaints

345. This section makes provision to ensure that a complaint does not fail simply because of a change in membership of the partnership or body against which the complaint is made. This section also requires the OLC to make rules setting out the circumstances in which complaints can be continued where a legal person ceases to exist (for example, where a partnership is dissolved) but another person succeeds to the business, and for the continuation of a complaint by persons specified in scheme rules where a complainant dies or becomes unable to act.

Section 133: Operation of the ombudsman scheme

346. This section provides for the detailed framework for the ombudsman scheme to be determined by the OLC in scheme rules. It allows the OLC the flexibility to adapt its procedures in line with changing notions of best practice. The rules made by the OLC under this section will determine how complaints are to be made and how they are investigated, considered and determined by the ombudsman. Procedures for making scheme rules, including requirements as to consent and prior consultation, are set out in sections 155 and 205.

347. *Section 133(1)* provides a broad duty to make scheme rules. *Section 133(2)* requires scheme rules to establish time limits for the making of complaints, and allows for the possibility of extension in circumstances specified in the rules. *Section 133(3)* lists areas in which the OLC may wish to make rules. This list is intended purely as an indicative one, and not to limit the breadth of the OLC's power to make rules in other areas or to require them to make rules in the areas specified. *Section 133(4)* provides further detail about the circumstances in which rules may provide for complaints to be summarily dismissed (one of the matters listed in section 133(3)). *Section 133(5)* prevents the power to make scheme rules from being used to compel disclosure where a person could not be so compelled in civil proceedings before the High Court.

Section 133(6) enables scheme rules to provide for awards of costs to bear interest at such rate as specified in or determined in accordance with the rules.

Section 134: Delegation of an ombudsman's functions

348. This section enables the delegation of the ombudsman's functions to a member of the OLC's staff, with two exceptions: staff to whom these functions are delegated may investigate or consider a complaint, but they may not make a determination, nor may they dismiss a complaint summarily in the terms prescribed by section 133(3)(a). This will enable OLC staff to carry out initial handling of complaints, and work directed to mediation, with the Chief Ombudsman and assistant ombudsmen becoming directly involved with a complaint if the parties do not accept the caseworker's solution. In this instance the caseworker would submit the complaint to an ombudsman for a binding determination under section 137. Similarly, if on initial investigation a complaint appears manifestly unfounded or frivolous, the caseworker would refer it to an ombudsman to consider dismissal (in accordance with section 133(3)(a)). The Chief Ombudsman's powers of delegation are further restricted, in that they may not delegate powers of consent to the appointment of an assistant ombudsman, or the duties imposed to produce an annual report.

Section 135: Notification requirements

349. This section makes provision to the effect that if a complaint is excluded, dismissed, referred to another scheme, settled, withdrawn or abandoned, then the ombudsman must inform the complainant, the respondent and any relevant authorising body in relation to the respondent. If a complaint is dismissed, referred to another body or excluded, the ombudsman must give reasons for doing so.

Section 136: Charges payable by respondents

350. The OLC will be partly funded through "case fees" payable, subject to the exceptions set out below, by respondents (i.e. those legal professionals who are the subject of complaints). By *section 136*(2), scheme rules must provide for fees to be waived or wholly refunded where:

the complaint is determined or otherwise resolved in favour of the respondent; and
where the ombudsman is satisfied that the respondent took all reasonable steps to try and resolve the complaint under the respondent's complaints procedures.

351. *Section 136(4)* defines the scope of the respondent's complaints procedures.

352. In accordance with *section 136*(*5*), scheme rules may also provide for case fees to be reduced, waived or refunded in other circumstances. This subsection also allows the rules to set different charges for different stages of a complaint.

353. Scheme rules can provide that unpaid case fees incur interest and, by virtue of *section 136*(6), unpaid case fees can be recovered by the OLC as a debt.

354. The OLC will, as is the procedure with all scheme rules, be obliged to consult and gain the Board's approval before making rules on case fees under this section and, in addition, (by virtue of section 155) must also obtain the consent of the Lord Chancellor.

Section 137: Determination of complaints

355. This section makes provision for the ombudsman's powers in making a determination. The governing principle, set out in *section 137*(*1*), is that the ombudsman must determine a complaint according to what is fair and reasonable in all the circumstances of the case. *Sections 137*(*2*) *and 137*(*3*) set out the directions which the ombudsman may make in a determination, namely:

that the respondent make an apology to the complainant;
that the respondent's fees for the services to which the complaint relates are limited to a specified amount (and any other action be taken, such as a refund, which may be necessary to give effect to this);
that the respondent pay compensation for loss, inconvenience or distress;
that the respondent at their own expense secure rectification of any specified error, omission or other deficiency in connection with the matter under complaint; or
that the respondent at their own expense take such other action in the interests of the complainant as the direction may specify.

356. *Section 137(4)* allows for any amount payable pursuant to a determination to bear interest. *Section 137(5)* provides that the powers of the ombudsman in making a determination are not confined to cases where the complainant may have a cause of action in negligence (and so may be available in cases of "simple" inadequate professional service).

Section 138: Limitation on value of directions under the ombudsman scheme

357. This section ensures the total value of the directions made under section 137(2)(c) to (e) on the determination of a complaint under the ombudsman scheme does not exceed £30,000 (excluding interest – see subsection (3)). Prior to the commencement of the Act, the highest level of compensation in the legal sector was £15,000.

358. *Section 138(2)* explains "total value" as the aggregate of the amount of any compensation payable, plus the amount of expenses reasonably incurred by the respondent in rectifying any specified error, omission or deficiency. It does not include any reduction in the level of fees payable, or associated refund etc, by virtue of a direction under section 137(2)(b).

Section 139: Alteration of limit

359. This section empowers the Lord Chancellor, by order, to amend the limit on the total value of directions imposed by section 138, on the recommendation of an "interested body" (the OLC, the Board or the Consumer Panel). The body recommending alteration of the limit must first publish its proposed recommendation and consider representations made in respect of it. If asked to do so by the Lord Chancellor, an interested body must consider whether it is appropriate to make a recommendation under this section.

Section 140: Acceptance or rejection of determination

360. In determining a complaint the ombudsman is required to prepare a written statement of the determination (*section 140(1)*). *Section 140(2)* sets out the detail of what should be included in this statement, and *section 140(3)* lists the people and bodies to whom the statement must be supplied. If the determination is accepted by the complainant, it is binding on both parties (*section 140(4)*), and no further legal proceedings can be instituted with regard to the matter that was the subject of the complaint (*section 140(11)*); but if the complainant does not notify acceptance within the time specified for this purpose, the complainant is to be taken as having rejected the determination (*section 140(5) and 140(8)*). However, there may be circumstances where a person is unable to reply to the determination within the time specified and *sections 140(6) and 140(7)* provide for this. On acceptance or rejection by the complainant, the ombudsman must give notice to those parties set out in section 140(7), and the ombudsman's certificate of determination is evidence that the determination was duly made under the scheme (*sections 140(9) and 140(10)*).

Section 141: Enforcement by complainant of directions under section 137

361. This section makes provision for enforcement of directions made by an ombudsman. The complainant or an ombudsman can apply to the High Court or a county court. The court may order that any amount due under a direction to refund fees or pay compensation, including interest, is recoverable as if the amount were payable under an order of the court. If the respondent fails to comply with any other direction pursuant to a determination, the court may, on the application of the complainant or an ombudsman, order the respondent to take such steps as the court directs to comply with it. An ombudsman may only make an application with the complainant's consent and only in circumstances specified by scheme rules (*section 141(5)*).

Section 142: Reporting court orders made against authorised persons

362. This section makes provision governing reporting of any order for enforcement of directions made by a court under section 141. The court must give the OLC notice of any order made against a person, and the OLC in turn must make arrangements to inform any relevant approved regulators, and may require the approved regulator to report on what action it has taken. If, in such a case, an ombudsman is not satisfied with the action taken, then it may inform the Board.

Section 143: Reporting possible misconduct to approved regulators

363. In the course of consideration of a complaint, it may become apparent that there is a possibility that a respondent, or other person in relation to the matter concerned, has breached their regulator's rules of conduct. Where the ombudsman is of such an opinion, this section allows the ombudsman to notify that person's regulator, and to notify the complainant that they have done this. The regulator can be required to report to the ombudsman on the actions it takes. If the ombudsman, on studying the report, is of the opinion that the approved regulator is seriously or persistently failing to enforce its rules of conduct, the ombudsman may report this to the Board.

Section 144: Duties to share information

364. *Section 144(1)* requires scheme rules to set out that the OLC, an ombudsman or a member of the OLC's staff must disclose information to an approved regulator. The information to be disclosed must be specified in the rules, as must the circumstances in which it must be disclosed. Each approved regulator must provide in its regulatory arrangements for the provision of information to the OLC, an ombudsman or members of the OLC's staff, of such description and in such circumstances as may be specified in the arrangements (*section 144(2)*). The Board may specify requirements which arrangements under section 144(2) or rules under section 144(1) must fulfil (and must publish any such requirements). In specifying those requirements, the Board must take into account the need, so far as is reasonably practicable, to avoid duplication of investigations and to ensure that the OLC assists approved regulators and vice versa (*section 144(4) to 144(6)*). *Sections 144(7) and 144(8)* impose a mutual obligation on the OLC and on approved regulators to consult one another in relation to draft rules/provisions of the kind described in sections 144(1) and 144(2), and, when seeking the Board's consent to those rules/provisions, to identify any ongoing objections on the part of the other party.

Section 145: Duties of authorised persons to co-operate with investigations

365. *Section 145(1)* requires each approved regulator to make provision in its regulatory arrangements that all authorised persons regulated by it must provide co-operation and assistance to the ombudsmen in relation to an investigation, consideration or determination of a complaint; and this must include provision for enforcing that requirement. The Board may specify requirements which such provision must satisfy (*subsection 145(2)*), and must publish any such requirements (*subsection 145(3)*).

Section 146: Reporting failures to co-operate with an investigation to approved regulators

366. Where an authorised person fails to co-operate with an ombudsman as stated in section 146 the ombudsman can notify that person's approved regulator. The regulator may be required to report to the ombudsman on the action it takes; and if the ombudsman is of the opinion that the approved regulator is seriously or persistently failing to enforce its rules of conduct, the ombudsman may report this to the Board (and may do so even if the complaint is subsequently withdrawn).

Section 147: Information and documents

367. This section empowers an ombudsman to require such information and/or documents from parties to a complaint as the ombudsman may specify, before the end of such period (which must be a reasonable period) as the ombudsman may specify, and in such manner or form as the ombudsman may specify (*sections 147(1) and 147(2)*); provided that the ombudsman considers that the information necessary to determine the complaint (*section 147(3)*). The ombudsman may take copies of or extracts from a document and, in the absence of a document may require the person asked to produce it to state to the best of that person's knowledge and belief where it is (*sections 147(4) and 147(5)*). None of these powers may be used to compel disclosure which could not be compelled in civil proceedings before the High Court (*section 147(6)*).

Section 148: Reporting failures to provide information or produce documents

368. This section follows the approach and structure of sections 142 and section 146. Where the ombudsman considers that an authorised person has failed to co-operate with an ombudsman as required by section 147, the ombudsman can notify that person's authorising body, which can be

required to report to the ombudsman on the actions it takes. If the ombudsman is of the opinion that the authorising body is seriously or persistently failing to enforce its rules of conduct, the ombudsman may report this to the Board (and may do so even if the complaint is subsequently withdrawn).

Section 149: Enforcement of requirements to provide information or produce documents

369. This section applies if a party, other than the authorised person (the defaulter), has failed to co-operate with an ombudsman as required by section 147. In such a case, the ombudsman may inform the court (which in this case means the High Court -*section 149(7)*) of the person's failure to comply with the request for information. However (by virtue of *sections 149(5) and 149(6)*), where the defaulter is an authorised person, the ombudsman must first be satisfied that each relevant authorising body to which a report was made under section 148 has been given a reasonable opportunity to take action, and that the defaulter has continued to be in default. The High Court may thereupon enquire into the case, and if satisfied that the defaulter has failed without reasonable excuse to comply with the requirement, it may deal with the defaulter (and, in the case of bodies corporate and other legal persons, any directors or similar persons) as if the defaulter were in contempt (*section 149(4)*).

Section 150: Reports of investigations

370. The OLC may publish a report about the investigation, consideration and determination of any particular case if it considers it appropriate. The report may not contain the complainant's name or any other identifying information, unless the complainant consents to the inclusion of that information.

Section 151: Restricted information

371. Under this section, "restricted information" is any information that has been collected during an investigation of a complaint. This section protects the complainant in that all such information is classed as confidential and, except as listed under section 152, must not be disclosed except to the extent that it is excluded information. Excluded information is information which was obtained more than 70 years before the date of disclosure, or which is already available to the public, or which is in an appropriately "anonymised" form so that information relating to a particular individual cannot be ascertained from it.

Section 152: Disclosure of restricted information

372. This section makes exceptions to section 151. First, one restricted person (i.e. the OLC, an ombudsman or a member of the OLC's staff – see section 151(2)) may disclose restricted information to another restricted person (*section 152(1)*). Second, restricted information may be disclosed for the purposes of the investigation in the course of which, or for the purposes of which, it was obtained (*section 152(2)*); and third, restricted information may be disclosed for a variety of specific and limited purposes listed in *section 152(3)*, with the possibility (section 152(3)(g)) of additional purposes being added by order made by the Lord Chancellor.

373. The section also confers on the Lord Chancellor a power to make an order preventing the disclosure of information in circumstances or for purposes prescribed in the order.

Section 153: Data protection

374. This section amends the Data Protection Act 1998 to ensure that Part 6 of the Legal Services Act is able to operate compatibly with it by exempting personal data processed by the OLC in complaints handling from the subject information provisions where application of those provisions would prejudice the proper discharge of the complaints handling functions. This will ensure that frivolous applications do not impact adversely on the ombudsman scheme. This amendment is similar to provision made in the 1998 Act for certain other regulators and ombudsmen and will ensure that privileged information may be disclosed in certain specific situations.

Section 154: Protection from defamation claims

375. This section makes provision placing OLC proceedings and publications on a par with court proceedings for the purposes of the law of defamation.

Section 155: Consent requirements for rules

376. This section requires the consent of the Board prior to any scheme rules being made or modified by the OLC. It also specifically requires the consent of the Lord Chancellor to rules under section 136 which impose charges on respondents to complaints. The OLC is required to consult on its proposed rules before seeking the necessary consent: the consultation requirements are in section 205.

Section 156: The Board's powers in respect of rules

377. Under this section the Board has the power to direct the OLC to amend any of its rules. The direction may be in general terms or it may require a specific modification. Before making a direction under *section 156(1)(b)* to make a specific modification, the Board must give the OLC a formal notice that gives details of the proposed modifications, and must publish that notice and take account of any representations made (*section 156(2)*). In such a case the consultation procedure under section 205 is disapplied, as is the requirement to obtain the Board's consent (*section 156(3)*).

Section 157: Approved regulators not to make provision for redress

378.The OLC is to be the single point of entry for all complaints. This is subject to the requirement, in section 126, that complaints (except in specified circumstances) must, in the first place, be considered under the respondent's internal complaints procedures.

379. The OLC will investigate complaints and provide redress, but it will report any possible misconduct to the relevant approved regulator, which will take any necessary disciplinary action. There is therefore a clear split between the power to consider redress (OLC), and consideration of disciplinary action (approved regulators). As part of the provision for this split, this section prohibits approved regulators from including in their regulatory arrangements any provision relating to redress (defined in *section 157(4)*).

380. In accordance with *section 157(5)* the prohibition on provision relating to redress does not prevent provision for certain types of arrangements: compensation arrangements, indemnification arrangements and certain regulatory arrangements (as specified in section 158).

381. Transitional arrangements cover proceedings in respect of complaints under way at the date of commencement of the OLC's operations, which are made by order under section 211 (*sections 157(2) and 157(3)*).

Section 158: Regulatory arrangements not prohibited by section 157

382. Section 158 makes clear that section 157 does not prohibit approved regulators from making provision in their regulatory arrangements requiring, or authorising the approved regulator to require, an authorised person to take certain action of a type described in *sections 158(1)(a) to (f)*. That action is to investigate whether there are any persons who may have a claim for redress against the relevant authorised person (section 158(1)(a)), to report back to the approved regulator on the outcome (section 158(1)(b)), to identify any affected persons who may have a claim and notify them that they may have a claim (sections 158(1)(c) and (d)), and to provide any affected persons with information about the authorised person's complaints procedures and the ombudsman scheme and ensure that the complaints procedures operate as if the affected person had made a formal complaint (sections 158(1)(e) and (f)). The intention behind the section is to ensure that approved regulators are not prevented by section 157 from making provisions – subject to the Board's approval – requiring authorised persons to take proactive steps in cases where a number of clients may have been affected by the relevant authorised persons' acts or omissions and may have a claim for redress against them.

Section 159: Legal Services Complaints Commissioner and Legal Services Ombudsman

383. This section abolishes the offices of Legal Services Complaints Commissioner and Legal Services Ombudsman. Until this section is commenced, the Legal Services Ombudsman will examine the handling of individual complaints by legal professional bodies on behalf of members of the public, and the Legal Services Complaints Commissioner will examine the Law Society's capability to handle complaints made about its members efficiently and effectively. The complaints handling scheme which this Act establishes replaces these offices.

Section 161: Extension of Part 6 to claims management services

384. This section extends Part 6 of the Act to bring claims management services within the ombudsman scheme complaints handling jurisdiction. Although the provision of regulated claims management services is not designated as a reserved legal activity, this section brings those persons authorised under Part 2 of the Compensation Act 2006 within the ombudsman scheme's jurisdiction on the same basis as authorised persons in relation to an activity which is a reserved legal activity.

385. For the purposes of Part 6, the claims management regulator is treated as an approved regulator, and regulated claims management services are treated as a reserved legal activity. This affects, among other things, the definition of a lay person in Schedule 15, which is to be read as excluding a person authorised under Part 2 of the 2006 Act (so that a person who is or has been authorised under Part 2 of the 2006 Act may not be appointed as Chief Ombudsman).

PART 7: FURTHER PROVISIONS RELATING TO THE BOARD AND THE OLC

386. This Part of the Act makes provision for the funding of the Board and OLC by way of levy on the approved regulators, including requirements for rules to be made by the Board clarifying when the levy is to be made payable, and the amount payable as well as the circumstances in which the levy may be waived.

387. It also defines the type of guidance that the Board may give. It makes provision allowing the Board to enter into voluntary arrangements for the purpose of improving standards in the provision of legal services, and provision for extending the jurisdiction of the OLC to a further range of complaints. This Part also provides that information obtained by the Board (whether in its capacity as an approved regulator or licensing authority or otherwise) may be used by the Board for any purpose connected to the exercise of its functions.

Section 162: Guidance

388. *Section 162(1)* sets out a non-exhaustive list of matters about which the Board may give guidance. This guidance may include information or advice, and *section 162(3)* allows the Board to give financial or other assistance to persons who provide that information or advice. The Board will be able to publish its guidance and offer copies for sale. Following any guidance being issued, the Board may consider the extent to which an approved regulator has complied with such guidance when exercising its regulatory functions. *Section 162(6)* requires that, when the Board acts as approved regulator or a licensing authority under Part 5 of the Act, it must have regard to any guidance it has issued under this section.

Section 163: Voluntary arrangements

389. This section allows the Board to enter into voluntary arrangements with any person for the purposes of improving standards and promoting best practice in the legal services sector.

Section 164: Power to establish voluntary scheme for resolving complaints

390. This section gives the OLC a power, subject to an order made by the Lord Chancellor, to establish a complaints scheme which is separate from the ombudsman scheme under Part 6. A scheme set up under this section can make provision in relation to complaints about acts or omissions of persons providing legal services who are not authorised persons. Such a scheme is referred to as a "voluntary scheme" and the rules under this section are referred to as "voluntary scheme rules". The Lord Chancellor's order can limit the kinds of complaint that come within the scheme by reference to the description of the complainant, the respondent, or the legal services to

which the complaint relates. The voluntary scheme can provide redress to consumers but cannot be used to discipline respondents. *Section 164(9)* makes clear that the consent requirements and the Board's powers in respect of rules (in sections 155 and 156 respectively) apply to voluntary scheme rules in the same way as they apply to scheme rules. *Section 164(8)* makes clear that section 131, which establishes vicarious responsibility in respect of matters which are the subject of complaints, applies for the purposes of the voluntary scheme as it applies for the purposes of the ombudsman scheme.

Section 165: Procedure for making orders under section 164

391. This section sets out the procedure for making an order under *section 164(2)*. The Lord Chancellor can only make such an order upon recommendation by one of the interested bodies (the OLC, the Board or the Consumer Panel). Following a request from the Lord Chancellor an interested body must consider whether it is appropriate to make a recommendation. Before making a recommendation, an interested body must publish the draft recommendation and invite and consider representations from the public. Upon receipt of a recommendation the Lord Chancellor must consider whether to follow it. If the Lord Chancellor decides not to follow a recommendation the Lord Chancellor must publish reasons for this.

Section 166: Operation of voluntary scheme

392. This section sets out the circumstances in which complaints may be determined and provides for a way in which further detail of the voluntary scheme is provided. A complaint may be determined under the voluntary jurisdiction scheme only if the complainant falls within a class of persons specified in voluntary scheme rules, if the complainant wants the voluntary scheme to deal with their complaint, if (at the time of the act or omission complained of) the respondent was participating in the scheme and if (when the complaint is made) the respondent has not withdrawn from the scheme.

393. Further, complaints received and determined under the auspices of the voluntary jurisdiction scheme will be dealt with in accordance with standard terms fixed by the OLC with the Board's consent. In particular, standard terms may provide for the payment of a fee to the OLC by persons participating in the scheme and/or awards of costs on the determination of a complaint (including awards in favour of the OLC to provide a contribution to its costs in dealing with the complaint).

Section 167: Restricted Information

394. Under this section, "restricted information" is any information obtained by the Board in the exercise of its functions. A restricted person is the Board (including in its capacity as approved regulator or licensing authority) or a person authorised by the Board to carry out its functions. Restricted information must not be disclosed by a restricted person or by any person who has received the information from a restricted person. Section 168 provides an exception to this rule. Restricted information does not include "excluded information", namely information which was obtained more than 70 years before the date of disclosure, or which is already available to the public, or which is in an appropriately "anonymised" form so that information relating to a particular individual cannot be ascertained from it.

Section 168: Disclosure of restricted information

395. This section makes exceptions to section 167. The first is that a restricted person may disclose restricted information to another restricted person. The second is that restricted information may be disclosed for the purposes of enabling the Board to exercise its functions. *Section 168(3)* sets out a list of further specific and limited circumstances in which restricted information may be disclosed, with the possibility (section 168(3)(g)) of additional purposes being added by order made by the Lord Chancellor. Such orders may only be made in order to allow disclosure to persons (other than approved regulators) who exercise regulatory functions. The section also allows the Lord Chancellor to prevent the disclosure of restricted information under section 167 by order for the purposes prescribed in that order.

Section 169: Disclosure of information to the Board

396. This section sets out a list of permitted persons and allows for the disclosure of information by them to the Board to enable or assist it in exercising its functions. The section prohibits the

disclosure of information where it contravenes the Data Protection Act 1988, where it is prohibited by Part 1 of the Regulation of Investigatory Powers Act 2000 or, if it is being disclosed on behalf of the Commissioners for Her Majesty's Revenue and Customs, where it has not been authorised by the Commissioners. The section allows the Lord Chancellor to designate other persons as persons who can disclose information to the Board, where their functions are of a public nature.

Section 170: Data protection

397. This section amends the Data Protection Act 1998 to ensure that the Legal Services Act 2007 is able to operate compatibly with it by exempting personal data processed by the Legal Services Board from the subject information provisions, where application of those provisions would prejudice the proper discharge of the functions. This will ensure that the Board is able to use its information powers to the benefit of the public by highlighting areas of concern. This amendment is similar to provision made in the 1998 Act for certain other regulators and ombudsmen, for example the Financial Services Authority.

Section 172: Funding

398. This section sets out the mechanism by which the Board and the OLC receive funding to meet their expenditure in carrying out their functions. The Lord Chancellor may pay sums to the Board or the OLC to cover their expenditure under or for the purposes of the Act. The Lord Chancellor may also pay sums to the Board to cover expenditure for the purposes of its functions under any other enactment. This is to ensure that the Board can, via the levy, recover amounts in respect of expenditure resulting from functions which it has under other Acts by virtue of amendments made by this Act. The Lord Chancellor may determine the manner in which, and times at which, sums are to be paid and may impose conditions on the payments.

Section 173: The levy

399. This section makes provision for a levy. The purpose of the levy is to cover:

expenditure by the Board under or for the purposes of the Act or any other enactment;
expenditure by the OLC under or for the purposes of the Act; and
expenditure of the Lord Chancellor on the establishment of the Board and the OLC.

400. This expenditure is met in the first instance by sums paid by the Lord Chancellor's grant under section 172. The levy, which is paid into the Consolidated Fund, recoups this expenditure from the "leviable bodies". The leviable bodies are the approved regulators, the person designated as the regulator in relation to claims management services under the Compensation Act 2006, and such other persons as the Lord Chancellor may prescribe by order (*section 173(5)*). The Board must be satisfied that the rules concerning the apportionment of the levy are fair and proportionate. To ensure that expenditure is not recovered twice, the expenditure to which the levy relates is the difference between the total of the expenditure of the Board and OLC and the expenditure of the Lord Chancellor (for the establishment of the Board and OLC) and the total of any sums received by the Board and OLC as:

application fees;
charges for providing statements, guidance, rules;
sums received in the Board's capacity as approved regulator;
sums received in the Board's capacity as licensing authority;
amounts received by the OLC by way of charges paid by respondents;
costs paid to the OLC in relation to complaints;
amounts paid to the Board in respect of voluntary arrangements; and
amounts paid to the Board under paragraph 7(g) of the Schedule to the Compensation Act 2006.

401. The OLC's leviable expenditure excludes any cost incurred that may reasonably be attributed to the exercise of its functions under sections 164, 165 and 166.

Section 174: The levy: supplementary provisions

402. In addition, the levy rules require the Board to calculate the apportionment of the levy among the bodies which are required to pay it, and to notify those bodies of their liability to pay the levy and of the times it is payable.

403. In addition, the levy rules require the Board to calculate the apportionment of the levy among approved regulators and to notify approved regulators of their liability to pay the levy and the times at which it is to be paid.

Section 175: Amounts payable into the Consolidated Fund

404.All monies received by the Board or the OLC must be paid into the Consolidated Fund. This section lists the different sources of income of the Board and OLC that must be paid into the Consolidated Fund.

PART 8: MISCELLANEOUS AND GENERAL PROVISIONS ABOUT LAWYERS

405. This Part makes provision regarding the Board's relationship with the Solicitors Disciplinary Tribunal. This Part also makes provision regarding the register of trade mark attorneys and the register of patent attorneys. It makes provision about legal professional privilege and amendments to the Immigration and Asylum Act 1999. It furthermore provides for the amendment of legislation relating to the Law Society and the Council for Licensed Conveyancers.

Section 176: Duties of regulated persons

406. Under this section all authorised persons, and all managers and employees of authorised persons, have a statutory duty to comply with the regulatory arrangements applicable to them. *Section 176(3)* confirms that regulatory arrangements include those that the Board makes in its capacity as licensing authority.

Section 177: The Law Society, solicitors, recognised bodies and foreign lawyers

407. This section introduces Schedule 16 which amends the Solicitors Act 1974, the Administration of Justice Act 1985 and the Courts and Legal Services Act 1990 to update the Law Society's regulatory framework and powers. Part 1 of Schedule 16 amends the 1974 Act; Part 2 amends the 1985 Act; and Part 3 amends the 1990 Act. A large number of the amendments are minor and consequential changes so that the terminology of the three Acts being amended is consistent with the Legal Services Act 2007, along with changes of references to the Council of the Law Society so that they refer to the Law Society, as the approved regulator, which follows on from the requirement in section 30 to maintain arrangements providing for an appropriate separation between the representative and regulatory roles. The notes below do not deal in detail with the paragraphs which solely or mainly make such amendments, but concentrate on those paragraphs making more substantive changes.

408. As part of the change to a new structure with the Board as oversight regulator, the functions of the Master of the Rolls in respect of the approval of rules and regulations made by the Law Society, and as an appellate authority in relation to certain Law Society decisions, are removed (provision for the necessary amendments to the 1974 Act, among other things, is made by paragraphs 4, 5, 8, 16, 17, 20, 30, 31, 32, 34, 38, 41, 47 and 51). As the relevant rules fall within the definition of regulatory arrangements, as set out at section 21 of the Legal Services Act 2007, they must be approved by the Board under the provision made in Schedule 4; and the route of appeal for decisions previously appealed to the Master of the Rolls is instead to the High Court.

409. Paragraph 3, along with paragraphs 15, 22 and 36 expand the regulatory remit of the Law Society to enhance its powers over Sole Practitioners and give it new powers over employees of solicitors or recognised bodies. They require a Sole Practitioner to be approved for status as such by virtue of an application for an endorsement on their practising certificate to that effect. They also make related regulatory provisions which allow the Law Society to place conditions on a Sole Practitioners practising rights and to suspend recognition as a sole practitioner. This will allow the Society to specify, for example, that a Sole Practitioner is not allowed to provide a specific type of legal service or to suspend their Sole Practitioner status if the Society considers it is no longer appropriate for him to be recognised as such. Various other minor amendments related to these substantive changes have been included in Schedule 16 in recognition of these enhanced powers (for example, new section 10A(2)(b) of the 1974 Act (contained in paragraph 10)).

410. Employees of solicitors are covered in paragraph 36. This allows the Law Society regulatory control over employees of solicitors in respect of professional practice, conduct and discipline. For example, if an employee breaches the rules under section 34 of the 1974 Act (as

amended) in relation to accountants' reports, the Law Society can make a complaint to the Solicitor's Disciplinary Tribunal in respect of that employee. Under paragraph 46 of Schedule 16 (new section 44D of the 1974 Act or paragraph 103 of Schedule 16 (new section 14B) to the 1985 Act), action can be taken against an employee of a solicitor.

411. Paragraph 4 removes the requirement in section 2 of the 1974 Act that the Lord Chancellor and the Master of the Rolls must approve the training regulations made by the Law Society. It also removes references to training "articles" from section 2.

412. Paragraph 5 amends section 3 of the 1974 Act so as to transfer the Master of the Rolls' functions in respect of the admission of solicitors to the Law Society. Paragraph 8 amends section 8 of the 1974 Act so as to transfer to the High Court the Master of the Rolls' appellate functions in respect of Law Society decisions concerning the restoration of a solicitor's name to the roll.

413. Paragraphs 9 and 10 substitute new provisions for the existing sections 9 and 10 of the 1974 Act, which deal with applications for and the issuing of practising certificates. The new provisions provide that certificates will only be issued in accordance with regulations made by the Law Society under section 28 of the 1974 Act. A new section 10A requires the Law Society to keep a register of all solicitors holding practising certificates.

414. Paragraph 14 replaces section 13 of the 1974 Act with a new provision that provides that the High Court will have jurisdiction in respect of appeals in connection with the issue of practising certificates. Paragraphs 16 and 17 amend sections 13A and 13B of the 1974 Act so as to transfer from the Master of the Rolls to the High Court responsibility for handling appeals against the imposition of conditions on practising certificates and the suspension of practising certificates.

415. Paragraph 21 amends section 17 of the 1974 Act so as to remove the requirement that the Law Society publish details of the termination of the suspension of a solicitor's practising certificate in the London Gazette on the application of the solicitor in question. Paragraph 30 amends section 28 of the 1974 Act so as to allow the Law Society to make regulations covering a broad range of matters relating to the right to practise as a solicitor.

416. Paragraph 31 amends section 31 of the 1974 Act so as to allow the Law Society to make rules regarding the fitness to practise of solicitors, and to remove the requirement that rules made regarding the professional practice, conduct and discipline of solicitors be approved by the Master of the Rolls in order to have effect. The Board takes over the Master of the Rolls' function in this regard.

417. Paragraphs 33 to 35 cover sections 33, 33A and 34 of the 1974 Act, which deal with matters relating to solicitors' accounts. These provisions have been amended in order to transfer certain rule-making powers from the Law Society Council to the Law Society itself, and to broaden the scope of these powers.

418. Paragraph 37 makes provision to allow the Law Society to make rules about how its compensation arrangements (including but not limited to the compensation fund) will operate. This removes the previous restrictions in the Solicitors Act 1974 so that there is greater flexibility about the circumstances in which grants of compensation may be made, what payments may be used for, and how monies may be collected.

419. Paragraph 41 amends section 41 of the 1974 Act so as to transfer to the High Court the Master of the Rolls' functions in respect of appeals against decisions of the Law Society prohibiting a solicitor from employing certain persons. Paragraph 41 also widens the range of sanctions that can be imposed where a solicitor acts in contravention of section 41 of the 1974 Act.

420. Paragraph 43 extends the order-making powers of the Law Society and the Solicitors Disciplinary Tribunal under section 44 of the 1974 Act. The new order-making powers are consequent on the new forms of bodies that the Law Society may recognise and regulate under amendments to section 9 of the Administration of Justice Act 1985, found at paragraph 81 of this Schedule. The Law Society can now decide whether or not to order that non-solicitors are prohibited from being employed or remunerated by solicitors, registered European lawyers and recognised bodies, and also that they are prohibited from being managers of or from having an interest in recognised bodies. This flexibility will also ensure that, during the interim period before Part 5 of the Act (Alternative Business Structures) is fully commenced, the Law Society has the

appropriate regulatory control over the up-to-25% non-lawyer managed legal disciplinary partnerships that are permitted by Schedule 16 amendments to previous legislation (see paragraph 430 of these Explanatory Notes, below).

421. Section 44(1) of the 1974 Act makes it an offence for any person in respect of whom a section 43 order is made, to seek employment or remuneration from a solicitor or recognised body, or to seek or acquire an interest in a recognised body. Section 44(2) of the 1974 Act, together with sub-paragraph (1)(d) of paragraph 16 and new sub-paragraph (1A)(d) of paragraph 16 (see amendment below) of Schedule 2 to the Administration of Justice Act 1985, and together with new sub-paragraph (3A) of paragraph 15 of the Courts and Legal Services Act 1990, allow complaints to be made to the Solicitors Disciplinary Tribunal where a solicitor, registered foreign lawyer, registered European lawyer, recognised body, or manager or employee or interest-holder in a recognised body breaches the section 43(2) order.

422. Paragraph 44 sets out a new section 44B of the 1974 Act which provides for new powers for the Society to require information and documents for the purpose of investigating whether there has been misconduct by a solicitor, employee of a solicitor, recognised body or employee of a recognised body, or where that person or body has failed to comply with requirements under statute or rules made by the Society. A new paragraph 44BA of the 1974 Act provides the Society with the power to require an explanation of the information provided under 44B, and a new paragraph 44BB provides that the High Court may, on an application by the Law Society, order other persons to provide information and documents relating to an investigation under 44B. A new paragraph 44BC makes it an offence for persons to falsify, conceal or destroy information that may be relevant to an investigation under 44B, and if found guilty, that person is liable to imprisonment or a fine or both. Paragraph 45 sets out a new section 44C which provides that the Law Society may charge for the costs of disciplinary investigations.

423. Paragraph 46 sets out a new section 44D of the 1974 Act which provides the Law Society with the power to rebuke and/or impose a limited fine on a solicitor or an employee of a solicitor where that person has failed to comply with requirements or rules, or there has been misconduct by a solicitor. It also provides for an appeal route for those persons to the Solicitors Disciplinary Tribunal, and an appeal route from the Tribunal to the High Court under the new section 44E.

424. Paragraph 54 amends section 56 of the 1974 Act so as to require that the committee established under section 56(1) of that provision include members of the Board. Paragraph 54 also makes provision amending the purposes for which orders may be made under section 56.

425. Section 60(5) of the 1974 Act provides that a provision of a contentious business agreement is void if it provides that the solicitor is not liable for negligence. Paragraph 56 amends that section so as to disapply this provision if the client entering into the agreement does so for purposes of the client's trade, business or profession. In relation to other clients such provision continues to be void.

426. Paragraph 64 amends section 69 of the 1974 Act so that solicitors may bill their clients electronically. Previously, solicitors could bill clients only in hard copy form.

427. Paragraph 71 replaces the previous section 79 of the 1974 Act with a new provision regarding the ability of the Council of the Law Society to delegate its functions, and for persons whom to the Council has delegated such functions to further delegate to other persons, providing such delegation is in accordance with the provision made in that section. Under the previous section 80, functions could only be delegated in respect of the 1974 Act or any instrument made under it. The new provision extends this to other enactments.

428. Paragraphs 77 and 119 to 122 amend Schedule 1 to the 1974 Act and paragraphs 32 to 35 of Schedule 2 to the 1985 Act, in order to modify certain intervention powers of the Law Society. These amendments add to the grounds upon which the Law Society may intervene in solicitors' and recognised bodies' practices: where it is necessary to protect the interests of current, former or potential clients or the beneficiaries of trusts of which the solicitor, the recognised body or one of its managers or employees is or was a trustee. The Law Society's intervention powers have also been extended in certain respects. For example, the Law Society can decide not only to have sums of money vest in it, but also the right to recover the solicitor's or the recognised body's debts. It can also now make rules about what to do with any money received under these powers when beneficiaries cannot be traced, after reasonable steps have been taken. The Law Society's power to compel production and take possession of documents, upon High Court authorisation in certain circumstances, has been extended to include electronic documents and to allow it to take possession of property, including computers, in order to access information. The Law Society's

power, also upon High Court authorisation, to have mail redirected has also been extended to include electronic documents and other communications. The Law Society can also apply to the High Court in order to take steps with respect to solicitors' and recognised bodies' websites. The amendments also enable the Law Society to recover their costs of intervention from certain persons where the conduct that led to the intervention was carried on with the consent or connivance of, or was attributable to the neglect of those persons. These amendments also allow for the exercise of certain powers against the managers and employees of recognised bodies, to reflect the fact that these individuals sometimes hold client money, or are trustees in their capacity of managers and employees of recognised bodies. The amendments made to the Council for Licensed Conveyancers' intervention powers (see paragraphs 1 to 6 of Schedule 17) are consistent with these changes; and the intervention powers given to licensing authorities in Schedule 14 are also consistent with these updated powers.

429. Paragraphs 80 to 123 amend the 1985 Act and in doing so extend the Law Society's power to regulate entities. Under the previous section 9 of the 1985 Act, the Law Society already had the power to regulate bodies corporate, including LLPs, that it "recognises" as suitable to carry on certain services. This power has now been extended to include other entities through which solicitors practice, such as partnerships and unincorporated bodies, and to allow legal disciplinary practices (LDPs). The rule-making powers under section 9 of the 1985 Act have also been enhanced to enable the Society to impose conditions upon a recognition granted to a body. A new section 9A has also been added to the 1985 Act, to set certain requirements for legal disciplinary practices i.e. firms or companies that include solicitors and other legal practitioners or bodies that are "authorised persons" under the provisions of the 2007 Act.

430. The amendments to section 9 and the new section 9A also allow limited forms of ABS. These bodies will be LDPs and they will be restricted to the provision of legal services, but permitted to have up to 25% non-lawyer managers before the full ABS regime is available. These amendments allow the Law Society to regulate LDPs and various regulatory powers over LDPs, for example, the Society is able to make rules which can require a body to have less than 25% non-lawyer involvement or to appoint a person similar to a Head of Legal Practice in Part 5 of the Act.

431. These bodies will be licensable bodies and as such, will have to apply for a licence to practice as an ABS after Part 5 has become fully operational and the entire range of ABS is available as an option for legal professionals. These amendments also allow the Law Society to apply rules to managers (as defined in the 2007 Act) and employees within them. Amendments are also made to Schedule 2 to the 1985 Act, and to sections 43 to 44 of the 1974 Act (as described above) to reflect the fact that individuals within recognised bodies – whether solicitors or not – are subject to rules and to sanctions for breach of rules. The changes include new order-making powers for the Solicitors Disciplinary Tribunal, new powers to require information from recognised bodies and their managers and employees in order to investigate a body's suitability to remain recognised, and consequential amendments as a result of changes made to the 1974 Act (for example in relation to intervention powers and compensation).

432. Paragraph 83 amends section 10 of the 1985 Act, which relates to the offence of pretending to be a recognised body, to cover the different forms of entity which may now be recognised bodies. Paragraph 103 provides the Society with powers to rebuke and/or impose a limited fine on recognised bodies, or a manager or employee of a recognised body where they have failed to comply with requirements or rules applicable to them. It also provides for an appeal route for those persons to the Tribunal, and an appeal from the Tribunal to the High Court.

433. Paragraphs 124 to 138 make amendments to provisions in section 89 and Schedule 14 to the 1990 Act related to registered foreign lawyers, in order to achieve consistency with provision made elsewhere (for example, reading across, in relation to compensation arrangements, to the new provision introduced into the 1974 Act by paragraph 37).

434. Paragraph 111 amends paragraph 24 of Schedule 2 to the 1985 Act to remove the automatic void of any provision within a contentious business agreement that a body shall not be liable for negligence, so long as a person entering into the agreement does so for purposes of their trade, business or profession. Any such provision relating to persons not acting under this capacity will still be automatically void.

Section 178: The Solicitors Disciplinary Tribunal: approval of rules

435. This section is the first of three which make provision in respect of the Solicitors Disciplinary Tribunal, so that the Tribunal's position, as a body statutorily separate from the Law

Society but performing functions which are part of the Law Society's regulatory structure, may be properly reflected. The approach is in essence to apply to the Tribunal certain provisions which apply to approved regulators, with modifications and/or exclusions to reflect the Tribunal's particular role and position. This section makes provision bringing the Tribunal's rules within the structure of consent requirements for regulatory arrangements, so that there is a degree of monitoring by the Board, but this is kept to the minimum necessary. Accordingly, subsection (1) provides for any alteration of the Tribunal's rules under section 46(9)(b) of the Solicitors Act 1974 to require approval by the Board, unless it is exempt; and *section 178(2) to 178(6)* set out the procedures for approval, should an alteration be made.

Section 179: Board's power to give directions to the Tribunal

436. This section applies the Board's power to give directions to an approved regulator under sections 32 to 34 to the Tribunal. The power is considerably restricted, however, to reflect the fact that the Tribunal is not itself an approved regulator, but is a statutorily independent body which performs functions which form a part of the regulatory structure of the Law Society. The circumstances in which the Board can direct the Tribunal are limited to those in which the Tribunal has failed to perform any of its functions to an adequate standard (or at all). As is the case for directions to approved regulators, under section 32(4) the Board will not have the power to direct the Tribunal in respect of specific disciplinary cases or proceedings.

Section 180: Functions of the Tribunal

437. This section applies sections 69 and 70 to the Tribunal with limitations to reflect the Tribunal's particular position and so enables the Lord Chancellor to modify the functions of the Tribunal for certain limited purposes on the recommendation of the Board and with the consent of the Tribunal (and in particular enables amendment of the statutory provisions governing the Tribunal at the Tribunal's request).

Section 181: Unqualified person not to pretend to be a barrister

438. This section makes it an offence for any person who is not a barrister (as defined in section 207) to pretend to be a barrister, and sets out the penalties that may be imposed on such persons for doing so.

Section 182: Licensed conveyancers

439.This section introduces Schedule 17 which makes a number of amendments to provisions relating to licensed conveyancers, conveyancing services, and the CLC, which is an approved regulator and is listed in Part 1 of Schedule 4. Schedule 17 amends the Administration of Justice Act 1985 and the Courts and Legal Services Act 1990.

440. Paragraphs 1 to 7 deal with the issuing of conveyancing licences. Paragraph 2 amends the definition of conveyancing services to ensure that it includes all the activities contained in the definition of "reserved instrument activities" in the Legal Services Act 2007. The CLC is an approved regulator under the 2007 Act in relation to reserved instrument activities. Paragraph 4 amends section 15 of the 1985 Act so as to allow the CLC discretion as to the duration of a conveyancing licence. Paragraph 4 further amends section 15 of the 1985 Act so as to allow the CLC 42 days in which to determine applications for licences (prior to the 2007 Act, the period was 21 days).

441. Paragraphs 5 to 8 deal with the imposition of conditions on a licence. Conditions can, for example, be imposed where the Council has required an accountants report to be delivered within a specified time-frame and this has not been done. Provision is made enabling the CLC to impose an additional fee in certain cases to recover the additional costs in dealing with certain applications. In addition amendments made here allow for a condition to be put on a licence as a result of an order made by the Investigating Committee under their new powers. Paragraph 7 amends section 17 of the 1985 Act by prescribing additional circumstances in which the Council may direct that a licensed conveyancer's licence shall have effect subject to conditions.

442. Paragraph 8 inserts a new section into the 1985 Act to allow the CLC to remove or vary conditions on a licensed conveyancer's licence.

443. Paragraph 9 amends section 18 of the 1985 Act, in order to provide for the immediate suspension of a licensed conveyancer's licence in instances where the Council exercises certain powers of intervention in respect of a licensed conveyancer's practice in certain defined circumstances.

444. Paragraphs 12 and 13 operate to amend the provisions that provide for the CLC's current disciplinary arrangements. The effect of these paragraphs is to allow the Investigating Committee, which previously had only an investigative role, to make a determination on minor infractions of the Council's rules and to fine a licensed conveyancer an amount to be specified in the Council's rules (not to exceed the sum of £1,000). Paragraph 32 makes similar amendments to the equivalent provisions relating to recognised bodies.

445. Paragraph 12 (sub-paragraph (8)), paragraph 13 paragraph 15 (sub-paragraph (4)), paragraph 16, paragraph 17, paragraph 32 (sub-paragraphs (5), (6), (7), (9) and (10)) and paragraph 35 (sub-paragraph (7)) amend the 1985 Act and the 1990 Act, in order to enable the Investigating Committee and the Discipline and Appeals Committee to make orders for the payment of costs. The order may relate to all or part of the costs. A successful party would not be entitled to costs as of right: the award will be at the discretion of the committees.

446. Sub-paragraph (3) of paragraph 15 amends section 26 of the 1985 Act, which makes provision regarding the fining power of the CLC. Previously, the CLC could fine a licensed conveyancer no more than £3,000. The amendment to section 26 allows the CLC to make rules setting its own limit (subject to the approval of the Board). At sub-paragraph 6 of paragraph 32 of Schedule 17 to the 2007 Act, an amendment is made to the equivalent provision relating to recognised bodies (paragraph 4 of Schedule 6 to the 1985 Act). Paragraphs 13 and 15 of Schedule 17 to the 2007 Act allow the Investigating Committee and the Discipline and Appeals Committee respectively to make orders for costs in relation to proceedings before them.

447. Paragraphs 20 to 21 make amendments to the CLC's powers that are similar to the amendments to the Law Society's powers under section 9 and new section 9A of the 1985 Act. These paragraphs amend section 32 of the 1985 Act and add new section 32A to allow that the CLC may "recognise" and regulate new forms of bodies, including partnerships and unincorporated bodies, and including bodies that carry out not just conveyancing services but also other legal services carried out by "authorised persons" under the 2007 Act. These amendments also allow the CLC to make rules applicable to managers and employees of the bodies that it recognises, and make consequential changes to a number of related provisions in Schedule 6 (see paragraph 32 of the Schedule). Amendments to Schedule 6 also give the Discipline and Appeals Committee additional order-making powers to reflect the fact that managers and employees may be found in breach of rules applicable to them.

448. Paragraph 22 amends section 33 of the 1985 Act to ensure that the legal professional privilege of clients of recognised bodies that are actually "licensable bodies" (and that will therefore need to be licensed under Part 5 of the 2007 Act), is governed by the same provision as that for other licensed bodies: section 190 of the 2007 Act.

449. Paragraph 23 inserts a new section 33A into the Administration of Justice Act 1985 to confer on the CLC the power to make arrangements for authorising licensed conveyancers to administer oaths. Under the 2007 Act, the CLC is an approved regulator in relation to authorising persons to administer oaths (see part 1 of Schedule 4).

450.Paragraph 25 amends section 35 of the 1985 Act, which relates to the offence of pretending to be a recognised body, to cover the different forms of entity which may now be recognised bodies.

451. Paragraph 29 amends Schedule 3 to the 1985 Act to allow CLC members to be appointed as opposed to "elected or nominated". Paragraph 30 amends paragraph 1 of Schedule 4 to the 1985 Act so as to remove the requirement that the rules made by the CLC regarding the procedure and practice of the Discipline and Appeals Committee shall not come into force until approved by the Lord Chancellor.

452. Paragraph 31 amends Schedule 5 to the 1985 Act, which provides the CLC with intervention powers, to achieve similar outcomes for the CLC as those made to the Law Society's intervention powers by virtue of amendments to Schedule 1 to the 1974 Act and Schedule 2 to the 1985 Act.

453. Paragraph 32, amongst other things, amends paragraph 14 of Schedule 6 to the 1985 Act to allow the CLC to require the production of information to a person appointed by the Investigating Committee for the purpose of investigating an allegation of failing to comply with rules a licensed conveyancer must adhere to.

454. Part 2 of Schedule 17 amends the 1990 Act to allow the CLC to apply to become an approved regulator of reserved legal activities such as probate activities or the exercise of a right of audience.

455. It also brings the 1990 Act into line with the 1985 Act as amended and the 2007 Act by updating the Council's powers in respect of, for example, the new disciplinary powers conferred on the Investigating Committee and the Discipline and Appeals Committee under sections 24A and 26 of the 1985 Act.

Section 183: Commissioners for oaths

456. This section provides that legislative references to "commissioners for oaths" include persons authorised under the Act to conduct the reserved legal activity of administering oaths. It also confers upon such persons the right to use the title "Commissioner for Oaths."

457. It further sets out the circumstances in which an authorised person's right to administer oaths is proscribed, makes certain requirements relating to the way in which the oath or affidavit is taken and proved. The section also sets out the mechanism by which the fees charged by authorised persons for the administration of oaths and taking of affidavits may be determined by the Lord Chancellor.

Section 184: Trade mark attorneys

Section 185: Patent attorneys

458. These sections provide for amendments to the Trade Marks Act 1994 and the Copyright, Designs and Patents Act 1998. These amendments transfer the Secretary of State's functions in respect of the registers of trade mark attorneys and patent attorneys to the Institute of Trade Mark Attorneys (ITMA) and the Chartered Institute of Patent Agents (CIPA) respectively, and allow for both bodies to make regulations in respect of the registration of trade mark attorneys and patent agents. These regulations may provide for the payment of registration fees and the removal of names from the register. The Secretary of State may make an order, subject to the affirmative resolution procedure, transferring responsibility for the register to a new person. For example, should ITMA and CIPA merge, their responsibilities in respect of the registers could be transferred to the merged body.

459. These amendments confer statutory powers on ITMA and CIPA. They allow ITMA to make regulations governing the carrying on of trade mark attorney work by registered trade mark attorneys and CIPA to make regulations governing the carrying on of registered patent attorney work by registered patent attorneys. This represents a significant expansion of CIPA and ITMA's powers. All regulations made under these provisions are subject to the Board's oversight whether or not they are "regulatory arrangements" as defined by section 21.

Section 186: Immigration advisers and immigration service providers

460. This section introduces Schedule 18, which amends the Immigration and Asylum Act 1999. Under the 1999 Act, two categories of person may provide immigration services: persons registered with Immigration Services Commissioner, and persons authorised by a designated professional body. The amendments to the 1999 Act effected by Schedule 18 introduce a third category of person who may provide immigration services: persons authorised by a designated qualifying regulator. The Law Society, the Institute of Legal Executives and the General Council of the Bar are all designated qualifying regulators by virtue of Schedule 18. Prior to commencement of the Schedule, these bodies were designated professional bodies. For other bodies, becoming a designated qualifying regulator is a two-step process: first the Board must grant the body's application to become a "qualifying regulator" under part 1 of Schedule 18, then the Secretary of State must make an order under section 86A(6) of the 1999 Act making it a "designated qualifying regulator". Designated professional bodies are subject to the oversight of the Immigration Services Commissioner, whereas designated qualifying regulators will be subject to the oversight of the Board. Where the Board is of the view that a designated qualifying regulator is failing to regulate the provision of immigration services effectively, the Board may report its view

to the Lord Chancellor and to the Secretary of State. The Secretary of State has the power to remove a body's status as a designated qualifying regulator, and a body will also cease to have that status if it ceases to be an approved regulator under the Legal Services Act 2007. The intention of the provision under sub-paragraph (4)(c) of paragraph 3 for fees to cover the reasonable costs associated with the application, etc, to which they relate.

461. Part 1 of Schedule 18 sets out the procedure by which a body may apply to the Board to become a "qualifying regulator". Only "qualifying regulators" may become designated qualifying regulators. Part 2 of the Schedule sets out the amendments to Part 5 of the 1999 Act that are required in order to establish the new framework. Part 3 of the Schedule makes transitional provision protecting persons presently authorised to provide immigration services by those designated professional bodies that will become designated qualifying regulators under the new framework.

Section 187: Claims management services

462. Schedule 19 makes amendment to Part 2 of the Compensation Act 2006. The amendments provide for regulatory oversight functions of the Claims Management regulator to transfer from the Secretary of State to the Board. This includes ensuring that a regulator can only be designated by the Secretary of State on the recommendation of the Board, and that any regulations made by the Secretary of State are on the recommendation, or in consultation with, the Board. Section 161 provides for complaints handling to come under the jurisdiction of the Office for Legal Complaints.

Section 188: Duties of advocates and litigators

463. This section reproduces the effect of sections 27(2A) and 28(2A) of the Courts and Legal Services Act 1990, which are repealed by the Legal Services Act 2007. Authorised persons who exercise rights of audience or rights to conduct litigation have a duty to the court to act with independence in the interests of justice, and a duty to comply with conduct rules applicable to them. These duties override any other obligations that the persons may have (otherwise than under the criminal law) if they are inconsistent with them.

Section 189: Employed advocates

464. This section replicates section 31A of the Courts and Legal Services Act 1990 which is repealed by the Legal Services Act 2007. It ensures that qualification regulations and conduct rules which apply to the exercise of a right of audience by a person employed as a Crown Prosecutor or in any other employment are not more restrictive than the regulations and rules applying to other persons exercising that right.

Section 190: Legal professional privilege

465. This section states that legal professional privilege ("LPP") applies to any communication, document, material or information relating to a service provided by an individual who is not a barrister or solicitor at any time when the individual is providing advocacy services, litigation services, conveyancing services or probate services in the individual's capacity as an authorised person. Such a communication is to be treated as if it were a communication made by a solicitor for the purposes of disclosure. This section reproduces the effect of section 63 of the Courts and Legal Services Act 1990.

466. *Section 190(3) to 190(5)* provide that communications made by a licensed body in legal proceedings will be privileged to the same extent that they would be privileged had they been made by a "relevant lawyer", provided that the communications in question are made through, or under the supervision of, a "relevant lawyer". "Relevant lawyer" means a barrister, solicitor, or person otherwise entitled to conduct reserved legal activities. These provisions ensure that the clients of certain legal services providers (such as authorised litigators and advocates, recognised bodies, licensed conveyancers, trade mark and patent firms and Alternative Business Structures) have similar LPP protection to clients of solicitors under the common law.

Section 191: Rights of audience etc of employees of housing management bodies

467. This section amends the County Courts Act 1984 by inserting a new section 60A. Section 60A now gives a right of audience in certain county court proceedings, and a right to

conduct litigation in relation to those proceedings, to employees of a housing management body who have written authorisation from that body. Section 60A applies to proceedings that are within *sub section (3)* of the new *section* 60A – for example proceedings for demotion, possession and injunctions on grounds of anti-social behaviour – brought by a housing management body on behalf of the local housing authority by virtue of a housing management agreement under section 27 of the Housing Act 1985.

Section 192: Powers of court in respect of rights of audience and conduct litigation

468. This section preserves the rights of courts to refuse to hear persons who would otherwise have a right of audience before them. It replicates provision to the same effect in sections 27 and 28 of the Courts and Legal Services Act 1990. Those sections are repealed by the Legal Services Act 2007.

Section 193: Solicitors to public departments and the City of London

469. This section provides that nothing in the Act shall prejudice or affect the rights or privileges of the Treasury Solicitor and certain other office holders. It also provides that such clerks and officers are not required to be admitted or enrolled, or to hold a practising certificate under the Solicitors Act 1974 in order to conduct a reserved legal activity, if they would have been able to conduct that activity without a practising certificate by virtue of section 88 of the Solicitors Act 1974, had the provision in the Legal Services Act 2007 not been made. *Section 193(4)* preserves the rights and privileges enjoyed by the Solicitor of the City of London.

470. This section also imposes a duty on persons exercising rights of audience or the right to conduct litigation by virtue of this section to act with independence in the interests of justice. This duty overrides any obligations which such a person may have (otherwise than under the criminal law) if it is inconsistent with them.

Section 194: Payments in respect of pro bono representation

471. This section enables a court to make an order in civil cases requiring a person to make a payment where a party to the proceedings was represented by a legal representative whose services were provided *pro bono* (i.e. free of charge). Under the previous costs law, an unsuccessful party would not have been required to pay any amount in respect of that representation because the services were provided free of charge and so there were no costs. Under this section, awards will be at the discretion of the court and will be paid directly to a designated charitable body, established to administer and distribute the monies to organisations who conduct *pro bono* work.

Section 195: Application of the Legal Profession and Legal Aid (Scotland) Act 2007

472. The Legal Profession and Legal Aid (Scotland) Act 2007 establishes a Scottish Legal Complaints Commission, and provides for the Commission's main functions to be to handle consumer complaints about the service provided by legal practitioners and to oversee the handling of conduct complaints by the legal professional bodies in Scotland. This section extends the remit of that body to areas which are reserved to the UK Parliament.

473. Regulation of the legal profession in Scotland is devolved by the Scotland Act 1998 (Schedule 5, head C3), but there are a few areas where the Scottish legal professional bodies are the regulatory body or co-regulatory body in terms of a UK statute, the subject matter of which is reserved. The areas in question are consumer credit, insolvency, immigration and financial services.

474. To ensure that the Legal Profession and Legal Aid (Scotland) Act 2007 fell within devolved competence, it was necessary to exclude these reserved areas from the remit of that Act, which is achieved by section 47 of that Act.

475. *Section 195(1)* applies the provisions of the Legal Profession and Legal Aid (Scotland) Act 2007 to:

- any element of a complaint relating to advice, services or activities in the reserved areas specified in *section 195(2)*, and
- the provision by a practitioner of such advice, services or activities.

476. The advice, services or activities in question fall within areas reserved to the UK Parliament and also the competence of the Scottish Parliament.

477. *Section 195(2)* defines such advice, services and activities to be:

Consumer credit services: activities carried out by virtue of a group licence under section 22(1)(b) of the Consumer Credit Act 1974. The Law Society of Scotland holds such a licence which is granted by the Office of Fair Trading (OFT). The licence enables members of the Society to provide services in the areas of consumer credit, credit brokerage, debt-adjusting and debt-counselling and debt-collecting.

Insolvency services: activities of an insolvency practitioner within the meaning of Part 13 of the Insolvency Act 1986. The Law Society of Scotland is a recognised professional body under the 1986 Act and issues licences to Scottish solicitors who wish to be appointed as insolvency practitioners.

Immigration advice or immigration services: the Law Society of Scotland and the Faculty of Advocates are designated professional bodies under the Immigration and Asylum Act 1999. Designation under the Act removes the need for Scottish solicitors and advocates to be individually registered with the Immigration Services Commissioner. The Commissioner has the power to receive complaints against Scottish solicitors giving immigration advice and is required to monitor how any complaints which are passed to the Law Society of Scotland or the Faculty of Advocates are handled (Schedule 5, paragraph 10 of the 1999 Act). The Commissioner is required to review the list of designated professional bodies and report to Scottish Ministers if a designated professional body in Scotland is failing to provide effective regulation of its members.

Financial services:

Activities mentioned in sub-paragraph (1)(a) of paragraph 5 of Schedule 3 to the Financial Services Act 1986. The Law Society of Scotland was a recognised professional body under the 1986 Act and still retains the function of dealing with complaints against Scottish solicitors in relation to investment business carried on under the 1986 Act. This function of recognised professional bodies was saved, on the repeal of the 1986 Act.

Regulated activity within the meaning of section 22 of the Financial Services and Markets Act 2000, other than activities falling within paragraph (f) of subsection (2), in respect of which the Financial Services Authority has by virtue of Part 20 of that Act arranged for its regulatory role to be carried out by the Law Society of Scotland.

Exempt regulated activities within the meaning of section 325(2) of the Financial Services and Markets Act 2000. Since 30th November 2001 the Law Society of Scotland has been a designated professional body under the Financial Services and Markets Act 2000 and responsible for the licensing and regulating of solicitor firms which conduct incidental investment business (i.e. investment work which is incidental and complementary to the provision of legal services). The Financial Services Authority has been responsible since that date for the authorisation and direct regulation of solicitor firms in Scotland which wish to conduct mainstream investment business under the 2000 Act.

478. *Section 195(3)* provides for references to "complaint" and "practitioner" to have the same meaning as in Part 1 of the Legal Profession and Legal Aid (Scotland) Act 2007. "Complaint" is defined by that Act to include any expression of dissatisfaction. "Practitioner" is defined to cover:

an advocate,
a conveyancing practitioner
an executry practitioner
a firm of solicitors
an incorporated practice
a person exercising a right to conduct litigation or a right of audience acquired by virtue of section 27 of the Law Reform (Miscellaneous Provisions) (Scotland) Act 1990, and
a solicitor.

479. *Section 195(4)* repeals section 77 of the Legal Profession and Legal Aid (Scotland) Act 2007, which is no longer required as the Legal Services Act 2007 provides full competence for the Scottish Legal Complaints Commission in relation to both reserved and devolved areas.

480. *Section 195(5)* introduces Schedule 20 to the Legal Services Act 2007 which sets out minor and consequential amendments in relation to the Legal Profession and Legal Aid (Scotland) Act 2007.

Section 196: Scottish legal services ombudsman: functions

481. *Section 196(1)* disapplies the functions of the Scottish Legal Services Ombudsman in relation to advice, services and activities mentioned in *section 195(2)*. The Legal Profession and Legal Aid (Scotland) Act 2007 effects the repeal of those functions of the Ombudsman which fall within devolved competence. It provides a power for Scottish Ministers to modify the functions of the Scottish Legal Services Ombudsman by order; and to abolish that office by order when the Ombudsman has no remaining functions.

482. Section 196(2) makes consequential amendments to the Immigration and Asylum Act 1999. The Office of the Immigration Services Commissioner retains its oversight function in relation to the Law Society of Scotland and the Faculty of Advocates which are "designated professional bodies" in terms of section 86(1)(c) of the Immigration and Asylum Act 1999.

483. Where the Lord Chancellor is proposing to de-designate a professional body in terms of section 86(2) of the 1999 Act, the Lord Chancellor must consult the Scottish Legal Services Ombudsman, if the proposed order would affect a designated professional body in Scotland. Section 196(2) amends the reference in section 86(4)(c) of the Immigration and Asylum Act 1999 to require that consultation to be with the Scottish Legal Complaints Commission instead of the Scottish Legal Services Ombudsman.

484. Where the Lord Chancellor proposes to apply the code of conduct for immigration advisers to members of a designated professional body in Scotland, the Lord Chancellor is required by sub-paragraph (2)(c) of paragraph 4 of Schedule 5 to the 1999 Act to consult the Scottish Legal Services Ombudsman. Section 196(2) substitutes a reference to the Scottish Legal Complaints Commission for the existing reference to the Scottish Legal Services Ombudsman.

PART 9: GENERAL

485. This Part makes provision regarding offences committed by bodies corporate and unincorporated bodies. It makes provision setting out how notices issued pursuant to provision in the Act are to be given. It sets out the procedure for making orders under the Act. It specifies the extent of the Act and makes provision regarding the interpretation of terms used in the Act.

Section 197: Offences committed by bodies corporate and unincorporated bodies

486. This section provides that where an offence is committed by a body corporate or an unincorporated body, it will be possible, in certain circumstances, to prosecute both the body and the relevant officers.

Section 198: Local weights and measures authorities

487. This section replicates the provision made in section 22A of the Solicitors Act 1974. It provides local weights and measures authorities with powers to investigate and prosecute persons who carry on reserved instrument activities when not entitled to do so or through an employee or manager who is not entitled to do so.

Section 199: Protected functions of the Lord Chancellor

488. This section protects the functions of the Lord Chancellor set out in the Act and in the other Acts specified, so that those functions may only be carried out by the Lord Chancellor and cannot be transferred to another minister by means of an order under the Ministers of the Crown Act 1975.

Section 200: Notices and directions

489. This section makes provision requiring notices and directions given under provision made in the Act to be given in writing.

Section 201: Documents

490. This section defines the term "document" for the purposes of the Act. By virtue of this provision, "document" includes information recorded in any form. If the information is not in a legible form, references to the production of the information are to the production of it in a legible form or a form from which it can readily be produced in a legible form.

Section 202: The giving of notices, directions and other documents

491. This section makes provision about how notices, directions and other documents required to be given to a person under the Act may be given. Where the notice, direction or document is to be given to a body corporate, a partnership, or some other form of unincorporated body, the section provides that it may be given to certain individuals connected with the body.

Section 203: The giving of notices, directions and other documents in electronic form

492. This section provides that where a notice, direction or other document is to be given pursuant to provision made in the Act, it may be given in an electronic format providing that certain conditions are met.

493. *Section 203(3)* provides that where the Board, the OLC or an ombudsman is the recipient of a notice, direction or other document, they must agree to the manner of its transmission and the form the document will take if it is to be sent electronically. The combined effect of *section 203(4)* and *section 203(5)* is that where the Board, the OLC or an ombudsman proposes to transmit a notice, direction or other document to another person electronically, the recipient must agree to the manner of transmission and the form the document will take. *Section 203(7)* provides that where the Board, the OLC or an ombudsman imposes any requirement regarding the electronic transmission of documents, it must publish that requirement.

Section 204: Orders, regulations and rules

494. This section sets out that any order or regulations made by the Lord Chancellor, must be done by statutory instrument. Any rules made by the Board must also be made by statutory instrument as if the Board were a Minister of the Crown, in accordance with the Statutory Instruments Act 1946. It also sets out further information as to what may be contained in the instrument.

Section 205: Consultation requirements for rules

495. This section requires the Board and the OLC to comply with certain consultation requirements before making rules under the Act. The rule-making body must publish a draft of any rules it proposes. The rule-making body must then consider any representations made. If, following representations, the rules differ from the original draft, it must publish the details of the difference. It must publish any rules it makes and can charge a fee to provide either the draft or final rules.

Section 206: Parliamentary control of orders and regulations

496. This section lists the orders which must be made under the negative Parliamentary procedure, those which require no Parliamentary procedure, and those which must be made under the affirmative procedure.

Section 207: Interpretation

497. This section defines the meaning of various words and phrases used in the Act.

Section 208: Minor and consequential provision etc

498. This section states that the Lord Chancellor may by order make supplementary, incidental or consequential provision and any transitory, transitional or saving provision.

499. Schedule 21 contains minor and consequential amendments to other legislation.

Section 209: Transitional and transitory provision

500. This section introduces Schedule 22, which sets out provision made to avoid regulatory gaps during the transitional period between the current and new regulatory systems.

501. Paragraphs 1 to 4 create a transitory power, similar to the power at section 69, for the Lord Chancellor to modify the functions of "designated regulators", such as the Law Society and Bar Council, and other relevant bodies, such as the Solicitors Disciplinary Tribunal. This power will apply before the Board is established and therefore able to make recommendations under

section 69. These provisions therefore set out different procedures for the making of an order, including the requirement at paragraph 3 that the Lord Chancellor invite the Lord Chief Justice and the Office of Fair Trading to provide advice on the draft provisions. Sub-paragraph (5) of paragraph 2 sets out the purposes for which orders may be made. These are similar to the purposes for which orders may be made under section 69 of the Act. Any orders made will be subject to the affirmative resolution procedure by virtue of section 206(4)(u).

502. Paragraph 5 makes provision for the possibility that, before the principal provisions of the Act come into force, additional bodies will be designated as "authorised bodies" under section 27 or 28 of the Courts and Legal Services Act 1990 (bodies which can grant persons rights of audience or rights to conduct litigation), approved under paragraph 4 of Schedule 9 to that Act (bodies that can grant exemptions from prohibition on preparation of probate papers etc) or prescribed for the purposes of section 113 of that Act (bodies whose members are entitled to administer oaths etc). Paragraph 5 ensures that provision can be made in relation to these bodies, by order, which is equivalent to that already made by the Legal Services Act 2007 for bodies designated, approved or prescribed under these statutory provision before the beginning of the pre-commencement period.

503. Under the provision made in Schedule 17, the membership of the Conveyancing Licensing Council is to be appointed, where at present it is "elected or nominated". Paragraph 6 makes transitional provision to ensure that the Council's membership as "elected or nominated" under the present arrangements will continue to exercise the Council's functions until such time as a new Council is appointed under the new arrangements. Schedule 17 to the Act repeals the provision in the Administration of Justice Act 1985 that provides for the endorsement of conveyancing licences. Paragraph 7 provides that endorsements of licences made under that provision will continue to have force until the expiry of the licences in question, notwithstanding the repeal of the enabling provision.

504. Paragraph 9 makes provision for the ordinary members of the Board to exercise the Board's functions under Schedule 1 and Schedule 15 in advance of the Board's Chief Executive being appointed. For example, the ordinary members of the Board are able to appoint the OLC without waiting until the Board's Chief Executive has been appointed.

505. Paragraph 10 makes provision for the appointment of an Interim Chief Executive of the OLC by the Lord Chancellor. Sub-paragraph (2) states that the Lord Chancellor will determine the terms and conditions of the appointment. Sub-paragraphs (5) and (6) provide for the Interim Chief Executive to incur expenditure and do other things in the name of and on behalf of the OLC, including appointing staff and making arrangements for assistance. Sub-paragraphs (7) and (8) require the Interim Chief Executive to comply with supervisory directions made by the Lord Chancellor and subsequently by the Board. Sub-paragraphs (7) and (8) ensure appropriate lines of accountability between the Interim Chief Executive and the Lord Chancellor in the first instance and then, once appointed, the Board.

Section 212: Extent

506. *Section 212(2)* provides for sections 195 and section 196(1) and Schedule 20 to extend to Scotland only. *Section 212(3)* provides that an amendment or repeal has the same extent as the enactment to which the amendment or repeal relates.

507. Schedule 4 to the Legal Profession and Legal Aid (Scotland) Act 2007 makes a number of minor amendments and repeals, consequential on its provisions to the Solicitors (Scotland) Act 1980 and the Law Reform (Miscellaneous Provisions) (Scotland) Act 1990. These are mainly concerned with the adjustment of statutory references, and the removal of unnecessary references, as a result of the introduction of the new arrangements for the handling of complaints against lawyers in Scotland following the creation of a Scottish Legal Complaints Commission.

508. Modifications made to the 1980 and 1990 Acts by Schedule 4 to the Legal Profession and Legal Aid (Scotland) Act 2007 apply only to the devolved aspects of such provisions and it has been necessary to preserve certain provisions to deal with reserved activities. Schedule 20 repeals such provisions and ensures that these modifications are comprehensive in nature, and extend to reserved aspects of both service and conduct complaints.

Commencement

509. Section 211 specifies that certain sections in the Act will come in to force on the day that the Act is passed. The remaining sections will come into force on such day as the Lord Chancellor appoints by order.

Hansard References

510. The following table sets out the dates and Hansard references for each stage of this Act's passage through Parliament.

Stage	Date	Hansard reference
House of Lords		
Introduction	23rd November 2006	Vol. 687, Col. 430
Second Reading	6th December 2006	Vol. 687, Cols. 1161–1213
Committee	9th January 2007 22nd January 2007 23rd January 6th February 2007 21st February 2007 6th March 2007	Vol. 688, Cols. 116–179 Vol. 688, Cols. 896–961, 972–994 Vol. 688, Cols. 1004–1066, 1077–1094 Vol. 689, Cols. 616–665, 682–700 Vol. 689, Cols. 1088–1136, 1148–1168 Vol. 690, Cols. 147–218
Report	16th April 2007 18th April 2007 8th May 2007	Vol. 691, Cols. 11–25, 39–73, 91–110 Vol. 691, Cols. 223–280, 297–320 Vol. 691, Cols. 1272–1296, 1310–1337, 1355–1438
Third Reading	15th May 2007	Vol. 692, Cols. 219–157
House of Commons		
Introduction	16th May 2007	No debate
Second Reading	4th June 2007	Vol. 461, Cols. 24–106
Committee	12th to 26th June 2007	Hansard Public Bill Committee (Bill 108)
Report and Third Reading	15th October 2007	Vol. 464, Cols. 571–668
Ping pong		
Lords Consideration of Commons Amendments	17th October 2007	Vol. 695, Cols. 713–761
Commons Consideration of Lords Message	24th October 2007	Vol. 465, Cols. 295–312
Lords Consideration of Commons Amendments	25th October 2007	Vol. 695, Cols. 1142–1153

Royal Assent – 30th October 2007	House of Lords Hansard: Vol.695, Col.1293
	House of Commons Hansard: Vol.465, Col.629

Index

[*all references are to paragraph number*]